Wheelock's Latin Grammar

The Lord is my shepard,
I shall fear no Latin

HARPERCOLLINS COLLEGE OUTLINE

Wheelock's Latin Grammar

4th Edition Revised

Frederic M. Wheelock

HarperPerennial
A Division of HarperCollins*Publishers*

An American BookWorks Corporation Production
Project Manager: William R. Hamill
Contributing Editor: Effie Coughanowr, Villanova University

ISBN: 0-06-467177-1

92 93 94 95 96 ABW/RRD 10 9 8 7 6 5 4 3

Contents

Preface

Why a new beginners' Latin book when so many are already available? The question may rightly be asked, and a justification is in order.

It is notorious that every year increasing numbers of students enter college without Latin; and consequently they have to begin Latin in college, usually as an elective, if they are to have any Latin at all. Though some college beginners do manage to continue their study of Latin for two or three years, a surprising number have to be satisfied with only one year of the subject. Among these, three groups predominate: Romance language majors, English majors, and students who have been convinced of the cultural and the practical value of even a little Latin.[1] Into the hands of such mature students (and many of them are actually Juniors and Seniors!) it is a pity and a lost opportunity to put textbooks which in pace and in thought are graded to high-school beginners. On the other hand, in the classical spirit of moderation, we should avoid the opposite extreme of a beginners' book so advanced and so severe that it is likely to break the spirit of even mature students in its attempt to cover practically everything in Latin, including supines and the historical infinitive.

Accordingly, the writer has striven to produce a beginners' book which is mature, humanistic, challenging, and instructive, and which, at the same time, is reasonable in its demands. Certainly it is not claimed that Latin can be made easy and effortless. However, the writer's experience with these chapters in mimeographed form over a number of years shows that Latin can be made interesting despite its difficulty; it can give pleasure and profit even to the first-year student and to the student who takes only one year; it can be so presented as to afford a sense of progress and literary accomplishment more nearly commensurate with that achieved, for instance, by the student of Romance languages. The goal, then, has been a book which provides both the roots and at least some literary fruits of a sound Latin experience for those who will have only one year of Latin in their entire educational career, and a book which at the same time provides adequate introduction and encouragement for those who plan to continue their studies in the field. The distinctive methods and devices used to attain this goal are here listed with commentary.

1. SENTENTIAE ANTĪQUAE AND LOCĪ ANTĪQUĪ

It can hardly be disputed that the most profitable and the most inspiring approach to ancient Latin is through original Latin sentences and passages derived from the ancient authors themselves. With this conviction the writer perused a number of likely ancient works,[2] excerpting sentences and passages which could constitute material for the envisioned beginners' book. A prime desideratum was that the material be interesting per se and be not chosen merely because it illustrated forms and syntax. These extensive excerpts provided a good cross section of Latin literature on which to base the choice of the forms, the syntax, and the vocabulary to be presented in the book.[3] All the sentences which constitute the regular reading exercise in each chapter under the heading of *Sententiae Antīquae* are derived from this body of original Latin, as is demonstrated by the citing of the ancient author's name after each sentence. The same holds for the connected passages which appear in many of the chapters and in the section entitled *Locī Antīquī*. Experience has shown that the work of the formal chapters can be covered in about three-quarters of an academic year, and that the remaining quarter can be had free and clear for the crowning experience of the year — the literary experience of reading real Latin passages from ancient authors,[4] passages which cover a wide range of interesting topics such as love, anecdotes, wit, biography, philosophy, religion, morality, friendship, philanthropy, games, laws of war, satirical comment. These basic exercises, then, are derived from Latin literature[5]; they are not "made" or "synthetic" Latin. In fact, by the nature of their content they constitute something of an introduction to Roman experience and thought; they are not mere inane collections of words put together simply to illustrate vocabulary, forms, and rules — though they contrive to do this too.

2. VOCABULARIES AND VOCABULARY DEVICES

Each chapter has a regular vocabulary of words to be memorized thoroughly in all their parts. These are basic words for general reading; there is no pervasive clutter of military verbiage. In addition, many chapters have lists of words under the title of *Recognition Vocabulary*. It is generally acknowledged that there is in any foreign language a class of words which the ordinary student of the language can recognize and translate with some degree of accuracy from the foreign language into English, but which he cannot use with equal facility in the reverse procedure. Such is the category of words in the recognition vocabularies. Although they are definitely valuable for general knowledge and for translating from Latin, they do not normally constitute material for translating from English to Latin in the present book. This is a device for easing the burden of the regular vocabularies, but the instructor may require that these words, too, be learned as regular vocabulary, especially by students who plan to continue their study of Latin beyond the first year.

Related to the preceding is the problem of the *hapax legomena*, which inescapably occur if we are to use original Latin material as indicated. Better than (1) overloading the lesson vocabularies with these words, or (2) supplying merely the English meaning in notes, or (3) requiring the student to thumb the general vocabulary at the end of the book, is the device here used of providing the full vocabulary entry of these words in the notes at the end of a Latin sentence.[6] This device saves time and eyestrain for the student while nonetheless insuring the desirable discipline of determining the specific form of the verb, the noun, and so on in a given sentence. In fact, the meanings of many of these words are so obvious from English derivatives that they could easily be made part of the recognition vocabulary.

Finally, in view of the proverb "Repetitio mater memoriae," when once a word has been listed in a regular vocabulary, great effort has been made to secure its repetition in the *Sententiae Antīquae* or in the *Practice and Review* of a number of the immediately following chapters, as well as elsewhere in the rest of the book. This practice holds, though sometimes to a less degree, for the words of the recognition vocabularies.

3. SYNTAX

Although the above-mentioned corpus of excerpts constituted the logical guide to the syntactical categories which should be introduced into the book, common sense dictated the mean between too little and too much, as stated above. The categories which have been introduced prove adequate for the reading of the mature passages of *Locī Antīquī* and also provide a firm foundation for those who wish to continue their study of Latin beyond the first year. In fact, with the skill acquired in handling this mature Latin and with a knowledge of the supplementary syntax given in the Appendix, a student can skip the traditional second-year course in Caesar and proceed directly to the third-year course in Cicero and other authors. The syntax has been explained in as simple and unpedantic a manner as possible, and each category has been made concrete by an unusually large number of examples, which provide both the desirable element of repetition and also self-tutorial passages for students. Finally, in the light of the sad experience that even English majors in college may have no real knowledge of grammar, explanations of the grammatical terms have been added, usually with benefit of etymology; and these explanations have not been relegated to some general summarizing section (students usually avoid such) but have been worked in naturally as the terms first appear in the text.

4. FORMS AND THEIR PRESENTATION

The varieties of inflected and uninflected forms presented here are normal for a beginners' book. However, the general practice in this book has been to alternate lessons containing substantive forms with lessons containing verbal forms. This should help reduce the ennui which results from too much of one thing at a time. The same consideration prompted the postponement of the locative case, adverbs, most irregular verbs, and numerals to the latter part of the book where they could provide temporary respite from subjunctives and other heavy syntax.

Considerable effort has been made to place paradigms of more or less similar forms side by side for easy ocular cross reference in the same lesson[7] and also, as a rule, to have new forms follow familiar related ones in natural sequence (as when adjectives of the third declension follow the i-stem nouns). On the other hand, the introduction of the imperfect indicative has been deliberately postponed until after the perfect tense has been mastered, a sequence which in actual practice has achieved the goal of a clearer understanding of the peculiar force of the imperfect.

The rate at which the syntax and the forms can be absorbed will obviously depend on the nature and the caliber of the class; the instructor will have to adjust the assignments to the situation. Though each chapter forms a logical unit, it has been found that two assignments have to be allotted to many of the longer chapters: the first covers the English text, the paradigms, the vocabularies, and some of the *Sententiae Antīquae* (or the *Practice and Review*); the second one requires review, the completion of the *Sententiae*, the reading passage (if any), and the section on etymology. Both these assignments are in themselves natural units, and this double approach contains the obvious gain of repetition. Other chapters can be completed in one assignment. In any event, there will never be found too little material for one assignment in a chapter, as is sometimes the case when a high-school textbook is used in a college class.

5. PRACTICE AND REVIEW

The *Practice and Review* sentences were introduced as additional insurance of repetition of forms, syntax, and vocabulary, which is so essential in learning a language. If a modern author of a textbook can start with a predetermined sequence of vocabulary and syntax, for example, and is himself free to compose sentences based thereon, he should find it a fairly simple matter to make the sentences of succeeding lessons repeat the items of the previous few lessons, especially if the intellectual content of the sentences is not a prime concern. On the other hand, such repetition is obviously much more difficult to achieve when one works under the exacting restrictions outlined above in Section I. Actually, most of the items introduced in a given chapter do re-appear in the *Sententiae Antīquae* of the immediately following chapters as well as *passim* thereafter; but the author frankly concocted the *Practice and Review* sentences[8] to fill in the lacunae, to guarantee further repetition than could otherwise have been secured, and to provide exercises of continuous review. The English sentences, though few in number on the grounds that the prime emphasis rests on learning to read Latin, should, however, be done regularly, but the others need not be assigned as part of the ordinary outside preparation. They are easy enough to be done at sight in class as time permits; and, in any event, they can be used as a basis for review after every fourth or fifth chapter in lieu of formal review lessons.

VI. ETYMOLOGIES

Unusually full lists of English derivatives are provided in parentheses after the words in the vocabularies to help impress the Latin words on the student, to demonstrate the direct or indirect indebtedness of English to Latin, and to enlarge the student's own vocabulary. Occasionally, English cognates have been added. At the end of each chapter a section entitled *Etymology* covers the *hapax legomena* of the sentences and interesting points which could not be easily indicated in the vocabulary. From the beginning, the student should be urged to help himself by consulting the lists of prefixes and suffixes given in the Appendix under the heading of *Some Etymological Aids*. To interest students of Romance languages and to suggest the importance of Latin to the subject, optional Romance derivatives have been listed from time to time.

The Introduction sketches the linguistic, literary, and palaeographical background of Latin. This background and the actual Latin of the *Sententiae Antīquae* and the *Locī Antīquī* give the student considerable insight into Roman literature, thought, expression, and experience, and evince the continuity of the Roman tradition down to our own times. In fine, it is hoped that the Introduction and the nature of the lessons will establish this book as not just another Latin grammar but rather as a humanistic introduction to the reading of genuine Latin.

The book had its inception in a group of mimeographed lessons put together rather hurriedly and tried out in class as a result of the dissatisfaction expressed above at the beginning of this Preface. The lessons worked well, despite immediately obvious imperfections traceable to their hasty composition. To Professor Lillian B. Lawler of Hunter College I am grateful for her perusal of the mimeographed material and for her suggestions. I also wish to acknowledge the patience of my students and colleagues at Brooklyn College who worked with the mimeographed material, and their helpfulness and encouragement in stating their reactions to the text. Subsequently these trial lessons were completely revised and rewritten in the light of experience. I am indebted to Professor Joseph Pearl of Brooklyn College for his kindness in scrutinizing the forty chapters of the manuscript in their present revised form and for many helpful suggestions. To the Reverend Joseph M.-F. Marique, S.J., of Boston College I herewith convey my appreciation for his encouraging and helpful review of the revised manuscript. Thomas S. Lester of Northeastern University, a man of parts and my *alter idem amicissimus* since classical undergraduate years, has my heartfelt thanks for so often and so patiently lending to my problems a sympathetic ear, a sound mind, and a sanguine spirit. To my dear wife, Dorothy, who so faithfully devoted herself to the typing of a very difficult manuscript, who was often asked for a judgment, and who, in the process, uttered many a salutary plea for clarity and for compassion toward the students, I dedicate my affectionate and abiding gratitude. My final thanks go to Dr. Gladys Walterhouse and her colleagues in the editorial department of Barnes & Noble for their friendly, efficient, and often crucial help in many matters. It need hardly be added that no one but the author is responsible for any infelicities which may remain.

THE SECOND AND THIRD EDITIONS

Because of the requests of those who found that they needed more reading material than that provided by the *Locī Antīquī*, the author prepared a second edition which enriched the book by a new section entitled *Locī Immūtātī*. In these passages the original ancient Latin texts have been left unchanged except for omissions at certain points. The footnotes are of the general character of those in the *Locī Antīquī*. It is hoped that these readings will prove sufficiently extensive to keep an introductory class well supplied for the entire course, will give an interesting additonal challenge to the person who is tutoring himself, and will provide a very direct approach to the use of the regular annotated texts of classical authors.

Because of the indisputable value of repetition for establishing linguistic reflexes, the third edition includes a new section of self-tutorial exercises. These consist of questions on grammar and syntax, and sentences for translation. A key provides answers to all the questions and translations of all the sentences.

The second and third editons would be incomplete without a word of deep gratitude to the many who in one way or another have given kind encouragement, who have made suggestions, who have indicated emendanda. I find myself particularly indebted to Professors Josephine Bree of Albertus Magnus College, Ben L. Charney of Oakland City College, Louis H.

Feldman of Yeshiva College, Robert J. Leslie of Indiana University, Mr. Thomas S. Lester of Northeastern University, the Reverend James R. Murdock of Glenmary Home Missioners, Professors Paul Pascal of the University of Washington, Robert Renehan of Harvard University, John E. Rexine of Colgate University, George Tyler of Moravian College, Ralph L. Ward of Hunter College, Dr. Gladys Walterhouse of the Editorial Staff of Barnes & Noble, and my wife.

ADDENDUM 1991—LOCATION OF THE SENTENTIAE ANTIQUAE

Though all the *Sententiae Antiquae* are clear and substantial in themselves, some can be even further enriched by some knowledge of their source and setting. Consequently, to satisfy frequently expressed interest in specific information of this sort, a catalog of the location of the *Sententiae Antiquae* has been added on pages 416–418. The abbreviations used in this catalog arc chiefly drawn from the list of abbreviations of Harper & Row's *Latin Dictionary*, and they are summarized on pages 402–403. Occasionally the vocabulary or thought of a *sententiae antiquae* will be found embedded in a number of lines in the original text. All the *Sententiae* of Publilius Syrus (which are cited as in the Bipontine edition of Phaedrus) are actually isolated and independent sentences and thus have no informative context.

Footnotes

[1] I have even had inquiries about my lessons from graduate students who suddenly discovered that they needed some Latin and wanted to study it by themselves — much as I taught myself Spanish from E. V. Greenfield's *Spanish Grammar* (College Outline Series of Barnes & Noble) when I decided to make a trip to Mexico. Such instances really constitute a fourth group, adults who wish to learn some Latin independently of a formal academic course.

[2] Caesar's works were studiously avoided because there is a growing opinion that Caesar's military tyranny over the first two years is infelicitous, intolerable, and deleterious to the cause, and that more desirable reading matter can be found.

[3] At the same time these items were constantly checked against numerous studies in the field.

[4] A half-dozen passages from late Latin and medieval authors are included to illustrate, among other things, the continuance of Latin through the Middle Ages.

[5] To be sure, at times the Latin has had to be somewhat edited in order to bring an otherwise too difficult word or form or piece of syntax within the limits of the student's experience. Such editing most commonly involves unimportant omissions, a slight simplification of the word order, or the substitution of an easier word, form, or syntactical usage. However, the thought and the fundamental expression still remain those of the ancient author.

[6] Occasionally one will here find a basic word which appears as an entry in the main vocabulary of some later lesson. This practice helps meet some immediate exigencies and should cause no confusion.

[7] The same device has been carefully employed in the Appendix.

[8] Ancient Latin sentences suggested some of them.

Introduction

Wer fremde Sprachen nicht kennt, weiss nichts von seiner eigenen.
Apprendre une langue, c'est vivre de nouveau.

Interest in learning Latin can be considerably increased by even a limited knowledge of some background details such as are sketched in this introduction. The paragraphs on the position of the Latin language in linguistic history provide one with some linguistic perspective not only for Latin but also for English. The brief survey of Latin literature introduces the authors from whose works have come the *Sententiae Antīquae* and the *Locī Antīquī* of this book; and even this abbreviated survey develops literary perspective which the student may never otherwise experience. The same holds for the account of the alphabet; and, of course, no introduction would be complete without a statement about the sounds which the letters represent.

THE POSITION OF THE LATIN LANGUAGE IN LINGUISTIC HISTORY

Say the words *I, me, is, mother, brother, ten,* and you are speaking words which, in one form or another, men of Europe and Asia have used for thousands of years. In fact, we cannot tell how old these words actually are. If their spelling and pronunciation have changed somewhat from period to period and from place to place, little wonder; what does pique the imagination is the fact that the basic elements of these symbols of human thought have had the vitality to traverse such spans of time and space down to this very moment on this new continent. The point is demonstrated in the considerably abbreviated and simplified table on the next page.[1]

English	I	me	is	mother	brother	ten
Sanskrit[2]	aham	ma	asti	matar	bhratar	daca
Iranian[3]	azem	ma	asti	matar	bratar	dasa
Greek	ego	me	esti	meter	phrater	deka
Latin	ego	me	est	mater	frater	decem
Anglo-Saxon[4]	ic	me	is	moder	brothor	tien
Old Irish[5]		me	is	mathir	brathir	deich
Lithuanian[6]	asz	mi	esti	mote	broterelis	deszimtis
Russian[7]	ia	menya	jest'	mat'	brat'	desiat'

You can see from these columns of words that the listed languages are related.[8] And yet, with the exception of the ultimate derivation of English from Anglo-Saxon,[9] none of these languages stems directly from another in the list. Rather, they all go back through intermediate stages to a common ancestor, which is now lost but which can be predicated on the evidence of the languages which do survive. Such languages the philologist calls "cognate" (Latin for "related"). The name most commonly given to the now lost ancestor of all these "relatives," or cognate languages, is *Indo-European* because its descendants are found both in or near India (Sanskrit, Iranian) and also in Europe (Greek and Latin and the Germanic, the Celtic, the Slavic, and the Baltic languages).[10] The oldest of these languages on the basis of documents written in them are Sanskrit, Iranian, Greek, and Latin, and these documents go back centuries before the time of Christ.

The difference between derived and cognate languages can be demonstrated even more clearly by the relationship of the Romance languages to Latin and to each other. For here we are in the realm of recorded history and can see that with the Roman political conquest of such districts as Gaul (France), Spain, and Dacia (Roumania) there occurred also a Roman linguistic conquest. Out of this victorious ancient Latin as spoken by the common people (*vulgus*, hence "vulgar" Latin) grew the Romance languages, such as French, Spanish, Portuguese, Roumanian, and, of course, Italian. Consequently, we can say of Italian, French, and Spanish, for instance, that they are derived from Latin and that they are *cognate* with each other.

Parent	Cognate Romance Derivatives			
Latin	Italian	Spanish	French	English Meaning
amīcus	amico	amigo	ami	friend
liber	libro	libro	livre	book
tempus	tempo	tiempo	temps	time
manus	mano	mano	main	hand
bucca	bocca	boca	bouche	mouth (cheek *in cl. Lat.*)[11]
caballus[12]	cavallo	caballo	cheval	horse
filius	figlio	hìjo	fils	son
ille	il	el	(le)[13]	the (that *in cl. Lat.*)
illa	la	la	la	the (that *in cl. Lat.*)

Parent	Cognate Romance Derivatives			
Latin	Italian	Spanish	French	English Meaning
quattuor	quattro	cuatro	quatre	four
bonus	buono	bueno	bon	good
bene	bene	bien	bien	well (*adv.*)
facere	fare	hacer	faire	make, do
dīcere	dire	decir	dire	say
legere	leggere	leer	lire	read

Although it was noted above that English ultimately stems from Anglo-Saxon, which is cognate with Latin, there is much more than that to the story of our own language. Anglo-Saxon itself had early borrowed a few words from Latin; and then in the 7th century more Latin words[14] came in as a result of the work of St. Augustine (the Lesser), who was sent by Pope Gregory to Christianize the Angles. After the victory of William the Conqueror in 1066, Norman French became the polite language and Anglo-Saxon was held in low esteem as the tongue of vanquished men and serfs. Thus Anglo-Saxon, no longer the language of literature, became simply the speech of humble daily life. Some two centuries later, however, as the descendants of the Normans finally amalgamated with the English natives, the Anglo-Saxon language reasserted itself; but in its poverty it had to borrow hundreds of French words (literary, intellectual, cultural) before it could become the language of literature. Borrow it did abundantly, and in the 13th and 14th centuries this development produced what is called Middle English.[15] Along with the adoption of these Latin-rooted French words there was also some borrowing directly from Latin itself, and the renewed interest in the classics which characterized the Renaissance naturally intensified this procedure during the 16th and the 17th centuries.[16] From that time to the present Latin has continued to be a source of new words, particularly for the scientist.[17]

Consequently, since English through Anglo-Saxon is cognate with Latin and since English directly or indirectly has borrowed so many words from Latin, we can easily demonstrate both cognation and derivation by our own vocabulary. For instance, our word "brother" is *cognate* with Latin **frāter** but "fraternal" clearly is *derived* from **frāter**. Other instances are:

English	Latin Cognate[18]	English Derivative
mother	māter	maternal
two	duo	dual, duet
tooth	dēns, stem dent-	dental
foot	pēs, *stem* ped-	pedal
heart	cor, *stem* cord-	cordial
bear	ferō	fertile

In fact, here you see one of the reasons for the richness of our vocabulary, and the longer you study Latin the more keenly you will realize what a limited language ours would be without the Latin element.

Despite the brevity of this survey you can comprehend the general position of Latin in European linguistic history and something of its continuing importance to us of the 20th century. It is the cognate[19] of many languages and the parent of many; it can even be called the adoptive parent of our own. In summary is offered the much abbreviated diagram on page xviii.[20]

A BRIEF SURVEY OF LATIN LITERATURE

Since throughout the entire book you will be reading sentences and longer passages taken from Latin literature, a brief outline is here sketched to show both the nature and the extent of this great literature. You will find the following main divisions reasonable and easy to keep in mind, though the trite warning against dogmatism in regard to the names and the dates of periods can still be sounded.

- I. Early Period (down to ca. 80 B.C.)
- II. Golden Age (80 B.C.-14 A.D.)
    - A. Ciceronian Period (80-43 B.C.)
    - B. Augustan Period (43 B.C.-14 A.D.)
- III. Silver Age (14 A.D.-ca. 138)
- IV. Patristic Period (late 2nd-5th cens. of our era)
- V. Medieval Period (6th-14th cens. of our era)
- VI. Period from the Renaissance (ca. 15th cen.) to the Present

THE EARLY PERIOD (DOWN TO CA. 80 B.C.)

The apogee of Greek civilization, including the highest development of its magnificent literature and art, was reached during the 5th and the 4th centuries before Christ. In comparison, Rome during those centuries had nothing to offer. Our fragmentary evidence shows only a rough, accentual native meter called Saturnian, some native comic skits, and a rough, practical prose for records and speeches.

In the 3d century B.C., however, the expansion of the Roman power brought the Romans into contact with the Greek civilization. Somehow the hard-headed, politically and legally minded Romans were fascinated by what they found, and the writers among them went to school to Greek literature. From this time on, Greek literary forms, meters, rhetorical devices, subjects, and ideas had a tremendous and continuing influence on Roman literature.[22]

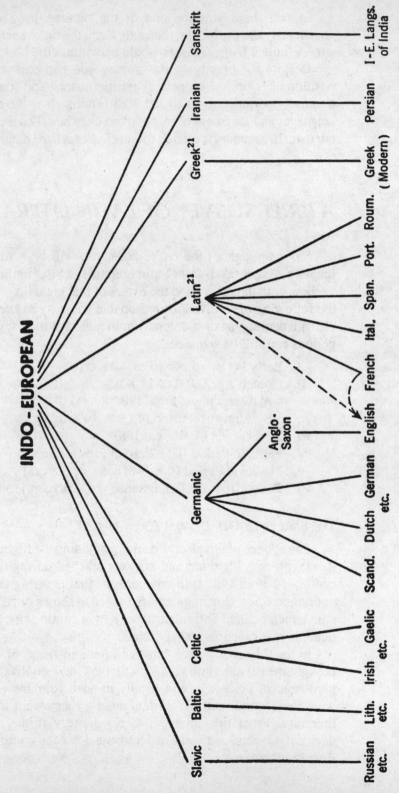

²¹ Actually, Latin was only one of a number of Italic dialects (among which were Oscan and Umbrian), and some time passed before Latin won out over the other dialects in Italy. Similarly, among the Greeks there were a number of dialects: (Aeolic, Ionic, Doric).

In fact, the Romans themselves did not hesitate to admit as much. Although the Romans now composed epics, tragedies, satires, and speeches, the greatest extant accomplishments of this period of apprenticeship to Greek models are the comedies of Plautus (ca. 254-184 B.C.) and Terence (185-159 B.C.). These were based on Greek plays of the type known as New Comedy, the comedy of manners, and they make excellent reading today. Indeed, a number of these plays have influenced modern playwrights; Plautus' *Menaechmi*, for instance, inspired Shakespeare's *Comedy of Errors*.

THE GOLDEN AGE (80 B.C.–14 A.D.)

During the first century before Christ the Roman writers perfected their literary media and made Latin literature one of the world's greatest. It is particularly famous for its beautiful, disciplined form, which we know as classic, and for its real substance as well. If Lucretius complained about the poverty of the Latin vocabulary, Cicero so molded the vocabulary and the general usage that Latin remained a supple and a subtle linguistic tool for thirteen centuries and more.[23]

The Ciceronian Period (80-43 B.C.). The literary work of the Ciceronian Period was produced during the last years of the Roman Republic. This was a period of civil wars and dictators, of military might against constitutional right, of selfish interest, of brilliant pomp and power, of moral and religious laxity. Outstanding authors important for the book which you have in hand are:

Lucretius (Titus Lūcrētius Cārus, ca 96?-55 B.C.): author of *Dē Rērum Nātūrā*, a powerful didactic poem on happiness achieved through the Epicurean philosophy. This philosophy was based on pleasure[24] and was buttressed by an atomic theory which made the universe a realm of natural, not divine, law and thus eliminated the fear of the gods and the tyranny of religion, which Lucretius believed had shattered men's happiness.

Catullus (Gāius Valerius Catullus, ca 84-54 B.C.): lyric poet, the Robert Burns of Roman literature, an intense and impressionable young provincial from northern Italy who fell totally under the spell of an urban sophisticate, Lesbia (Clodia), but finally escaped bitterly disillusioned.

Cicero (Mārcus Tullius Cicerō, 106-43 B.C.): the greatest Roman orator, whose eloquence thwarted the conspiracy of the bankrupt aristocrat Catiline[25] in 63 B.C. and twenty years later cost Cicero his own life in his patriotic opposition to Anthony's high-handed policies; great also as an authority on Roman rhetoric, as an interpreter of Greek philosophy to his countrymen, as an essayist on friendship (*De Amīcitiā*) and on old age (*Dē Senectūte*), an,d in a less formal style, as a writer of self-revealing letters. What Cicero did for the Latin language has already been mentioned.

Caesar (Gāius Iūlius Caesar, 102 or 100-44 B.C.): orator, politician, general, statesman, dictator, author; to past generations of students best known for his military memoirs, *Bellum Gallicum* and *Bellum Cīvīle*.

Nepos (Cornēlius Nepōs, 99-24 B.C.): friend of Catullus and Caesar and a writer of biographies noted rather for their relatively easy and popular style than for greatness as biographies.

Pūblilius Syrus (X. ca. 45 B.C.): a slave who was taken to Rome and who there became famous for his mimes, which today are represented only by a collection of epigrammatic sayings.

THE AUGUSTAN PERIOD (43 B.C.–14 A.D.).

The first Roman Emperor gave his name to this period. Augustus wished to correct the evils of the times, to establish civil peace by stable government, and to win the Romans' support for his new regime. With this in mind he and Maecenas, his unofficial prime minister, sought to enlist literature in the service of the state. Under their patronage Virgil and Horace became what we should call poets laureate. Some modern critics feel that this fact vitiates the noble sentiments of these poets; others see in Horace a spirit of independence and of genuine moral concern, and maintain that Virgil, through the character of his epic hero Aeneas, is not simply glorifying Augustus but is actually telling the emperor what is expected of him as head of the state.[26]

Virgil (Pūblius Vergilius Marō, 70-19 B.C.): peasant's son from northern Italy; lover of nature; profoundly sympathetic student of humankind; Epicurean and mystic; severe and exacting self-critic, master craftsman, linguistic and literary architect, "lord of language"; famous as a writer of pastoral verse and of a beautiful didactic poem on farm life; greatest as the author of one of the world's great epics,[27] the *Aeneid*, a national epic with ulterior purposes, to be sure, but one also with ample universal and human appeal to make it powerful 20th-century reading.

Horace (Quīntus Horātius Flaccus, 65-8 B.C.): freedman's son who, thanks to his father's vision and his own qualities, rose to the height of poet laureate; writer of genial and self-revealing satires; author of superb lyrics both light and serious; meticulous composer famed for the happy effects of his linguistic craftsmanship (*cūriōsa fēlīcitās*, "painstaking felicity"); synthesist of Epicurean *carpe diem* ("enjoy today") and Stoic *virtūs* ("virtue"); preacher and practicer of *aurea mediocritās* ("the golden mean").

Livy (Titus Līvius, 59 B.C.-17 A.D.): friend of Augustus but an admirer of the Republic and of olden virtues; author of a monumental, epic-spirited history of Rome, and portrayer of Roman character at its best as he judged it.

Ovid (Pūblius Ovidius Nāsō, 43 B.C.-17 A.D.): author of much love poetry which was hardly consonant with Augustus' plans; most famous today as the writer of the long and clever hexameter work on mythology entitled *Metamorphōsēs*, which has proved a thesaurus for subsequent poets. Ovid, like Pope, "lisped in numbers, for the numbers came"; he lacked the will to prune.

THE SILVER AGE (14– ca. 138 A.D.).

In the Silver Age there is excellent writing; but often there are also artificialities and conceits, a striving for effects and a passion for epigrams, characteristics which indicate a less sure literary sense and power. Hence the distinction between "Golden" and "Silver." The temperaments of not a few emperors also had a limiting or blighting effect on the literature of this period.

Seneca (Lūcius Annaeus Seneca , 4 B.C.-65 A.D.): Stoic philosopher from Spain; tutor of Nero; author of noble moral essays of the Stoic spirit; author also of tragedies, which are marred by too much rhetoric and too many conceits but which had considerable influence on the early modern drama of Europe.

Quintilian (Mārcus Fabius Quīntiliānus, ca. 35-95 A.D.): teacher and author of the *Institūtiō Ōrātōria*, a famous pedagogical work which discusses the entire education of a person who is to become an orator; a great admirer of Cicero's style and a critic of the rhetorical excesses of his own age.

Martial (Mārcus Valerius Mārtiālis, 45-104 A.D.): famed for his witty epigrams and for the satirical twist which he so often gave to them. As he himself says, his work may not be great literature but people do enjoy it.

Pliny (Gāius Plīnius Caecilius Secundus, ca. 62-113 A.D.): a conscientious public figure, who is now best known for his *Epistulae,* letters which reveal the finer side of Roman life during this imperial period.

Tacitus (Pūblius Cornēlius Tacitus, 55-117 A.D.): most famous as a satirical, pro-senatorial historian of the period from the death of Augustus to the death of Domitian.

Juvenal (Decimus Iūnius Iuvenālis, ca. 55-post 127 A.D.): a relentless satirist of the evils of his times, who concludes that the only thing for which one can pray is a *mēns sāna in corpore sānō* ("a sound mind in a sound body"). His satires inspired Dr. Samuel Johnson's *London* and *The Vanity of Human Wishes.*

THE ARCHAISING PERIOD.

(To fill out the 2nd century there may be distinguished an archaising period, in which it was considered clever to revert to the vocabulary and the style of early Latin and to incorporate items from vulgar Latin.)

THE PATRISTIC PERIOD (Late 2nd Cen.–5th Cen.).

The name of the Patristic Period comes from the fact that most of the vital literature was the work of the Christian leaders, or fathers (*patrēs*), among whom were Tertullian, Cyprian, Lactantius, Jerome, Ambrose, and Augustine. These men had been well educated; they were familiar with, and frequently fond of, the best classical authors; many of them had even been teachers or lawyers before going into service of the Church. At times the classical style was deliberately employed to impress the pagans, but more and more the concern was to reach the common people (*vulgus*) with the

Christian message. Consequently, it is not surprising to see vulgar Latin re-emerging[28] as an important influence in the literature of the period. St. Jerome in his letters is essentially Ciceronian, but in his Latin edition of the Bible, the Vulgate (383-405 A.D.), he uses the language of the people. Similarly St. Augustine, though formerly a teacher and a great lover of the Roman classics, was willing to use any idiom that would reach the people (*ad ūsum vulgī*) and said that it did not matter if the barbarians conquered Rome provided they were Christian.

THE MEDIEVAL PERIOD (6th–14th Cens.).

During the first three centuries of the Medieval Period vulgar Latin underwent rapid changes[29] and, reaching the point when it could no longer be called Latin, it became this or that Romance language according to the locality.

On the other hand, Latin, the literary idiom more or less modified by the *Vulgate* and other influences,[30] continued throughout the Middle Ages as the living language of the Church and of the intellectual world. It was an international language, and Medieval Latin literature is sometimes called "European" in contrast to the earlier "national Roman." In this Medieval Latin was written a varied and living literature (religious works, histories, anecdotes, romances, dramas, sacred and secular poetry). The long life of Latin is attested in the early 14th century by the facts that Dante composed in Latin the political treatise *Dē Monarchiā*, that he wrote in Latin his *Dē Vulgārī Ēloquentiā* to justify his use of the vernacular Italian for literature, and that in Latin pastoral verses he rejected the exhortation to give up the vernacular, in which he was writing the *Divine Comedy*, and compose something in Latin.[31]

THE PERIOD FROM THE RENAISSANCE (ca. 15th Cen.) TO THE PRESENT.

Because of Petrarch's new-found admiration of Cicero, the Renaissance scholars scorned Medieval Latin and turned to Cicero in particular as the canon of perfection. Although this return to the elegant Ciceronian idiom was prompted by great affection and produced brilliant effects, it was an artificial movement which made Latin somewhat imitative and static compared with the spontaneous, living language which it had been during the Middle Ages. However, Latin continued to be effectively used well into the modern period,[32] and the ecclesiastical strain is still very much alive as the language of the Roman Catholic Church and seminaries. Furthermore, the rediscovery of the true, humanistic spirit of the ancient Latin and Greek literatures and the fresh attention to literary discipline and form as found in the classics proved very beneficial to the native literature of the new era.

The purpose of this abbreviated outline has been to provide some sense of the unbroken sweep of Latin literature from the 3rd century B.C. down to our own times. Besides enjoying its own long and venerable history, Latin literature has also inspired, schooled, and enriched our own English and other occidental literatures to a degree beyond easy assessment. Add to this the wide influence of the Latin language as outlined above and you can hardly escape the conclusion that Latin is dead only in a technical sense of the word, and that even a limited knowledge of Latin is a great asset to anyone who works with or is interested in English and the Romance languages and literatures.

THE ALPHABET AND PRONUNCIATION

The forms of the letters which you see on this printed page are centuries old. They go back through the earliest Italian printed books of the 15th century[33] and through the finest manuscripts of the 12th and 11th centuries to the firm, clear Carolingian bookhand of the 9th century as perfected under the inspiration of the Carolingian Renaissance by the monks of St. Martin's at Tours in France. These monks developed the small letters from beautiful clear semi-uncials, which in turn lead us back to the uncials[34] and square capitals of the Roman Empire. Today we are in the habit of distinguishing the Roman alphabet from the Greek, but the fact is that the Romans learned to write from the Etruscans, who in turn had learned to write from Greek colonists who had settled in the vicinity of Naples during the 8th century B.C. Actually, therefore, the Roman alphabet is simply one form of the Greek alphabet. But the Greeks were themselves debtors in this matter, for, at an early but still undetermined date, they received their alphabet from a Semitic source, the Phoenicians.[35] And finally the early Semites appear to have been inspired by Egyptian hieroglyphs. This brief history of the forms of the letters which you see in our books today provides one more illustration of our indebtedness to antiquity.

The Roman alphabet was like ours except that it lacked the letters *j* and *w*. Furthermore, the letter *v* originally stood for both the sound of the vowel *u* and the sound of the consonant *w*.[36] Not till the second century of our era did the rounded *u*-form appear, but for convenience both *v* and *u* are employed in the Latin texts of most modern editions. The letter *k* was rarely used, and then only before *a*, in a very few words. The letters *y*[37] and *z* were introduced toward the end of the Republic to be used in spelling words of Greek origin.

The following tables indicate approximately the sounds of Latin and how the letters were used by the Romans to represent those sounds.

Vowels	Long[38]	Short[38]
	ā as in *father*: dās, cārā	ă as in *Dinah*: dăt, căsă
	ē as in *they*: mē sēdēs	ĕ as in *pet*: ĕt, sĕd
	ĭ as in *machine*: hĭc, sĭcă	ĭ as in *pin*: hĭc, s ĭccă
	ō as in *clover*: ōs, mōrēs	ŏ as in *orb, off*: ŏs mŏră
	ū as in *rude*: tū, sūmō	ŭ as in *put*: tŭm, sŭm
	y as in French *tu* or German *über*	

Diphthongs

ae as *ai* in *aisle*: cārae, saepe

au as *ou* in *house*: aut, laudō

ei as in *reign*: deinde

eu as Latin e + u, pronounced rapidly as a single syllable: seu.
The sound is not found in English and is rare in Latin.

oe as *oi* in *oil*: coepit, proelium

ui as in Latin u + i, spoken as a single syllable. This diphthong occurs only in huius, cuius, huic, cui, hui. Elsewhere the two letters are spoken separately as in fu-it, frūctu-ĭ.

Consonants

Latin consonants had the same sounds as the English consonants with the following exceptions:

bs and bt were pronounced *ps* and *pt* (e.g., urbs, obtineō); otherwise Latin b had the same sound as our letter (e.g., bibēbant).

c was always hard as in *can*, never soft as in *city*: cum, cĭvis, facilis.

g was always hard as in *get,* never soft as in *gem*: glōria, gerō.

i was usually a consonant with the sound of y as in *yes* when used before a vowel at the beginning of a word (iūstus = yustus); between two vowels within a word it served in double capacity: as the vowel *i* forming a diphthong with the preceding vowel, and as the consonant y (reiectus = rei-yectus, maior = maiyor, cuius = cui-yus); otherwise it was usually a vowel.

r was trilled: cūrāre, retrahere.

s was always voiceless as in *see*; never voiced as in our word *ease*: sed, posuissēs, mĭsistis.

t always had the sound of *t* as in *tired,* never of *sh* as in *nation*: taciturnitās, nātiōnem, mentiōnem.

v had the sound of our *w*: vivō = wĭwō, vĭnum = wĭnum.

x had the sound of *ks* as in *axle*; not of *gz* as in *exert*: mixtum, exerceō.

ch represented Greek *chi* and had the sound of *ckh* in *block head,* not of *ch* in *church*: chorus, Archilochus.

ph represented Greek *phi* and had the sound of *ph* in *up hill*, not of *ph* in our pronunciation of *philosophy*: philosophia.

th represented Greek *theta* and had the sound of *th* in *hot house,* not of *th* in *thin* or *the*: theātrum.

The Romans quite appropriately pronounced double consonants as two separate consonants; we in our haste or slovenliness usually render them as a single consonant. For instance, the **rr** in the Latin word **currant** sounded like the two *r*'s in *the cur ran*; and the tt in **admittent** sounded like the two *t*'s in *admit ten*.

Syllables

A Latin word has as many syllable as it has vowels or diphthongs.

In dividing a word into syllables:

1. Two contiguous vowels or a vowel and a diphthong are separated: **dea, de-a; deae, de-ae**.
2. A single consonant between two vowels goes with the second vowel: **amīcus, a-mi-cus**.
3. When two or more consonants stand between two vowels, the last consonant goes with the second vowel: **mittō, mit-tō; servāre, ser-vā-re; cōnsūmptus, cōn-sūmp-tus**. However, a stop (**p, b, t, d, c, g**) + a liquid (**l, r**) count as a single consonant and go with the following vowel:[39] **patrem, pa-trem; castra, cas-tra**. Also counted as single consonants are **ch, ph, th**, and **qu: architectus, ar-chi-tec-tus; loquācem, lo-quā-cem**.

A syllable is long *by nature* if it has a long vowel or a diphthong; a syllable is long *by position* if it has a short vowel followed by two or more consonants[40] or **x**, which is a double consonant (= *ks*). Otherwise a syllable is short.

Syllables long by nature: *lau-dō, cā-rae, a-mĭ-cus*.
Syllables long by position: **lau**-*dan*-**tem**, **mi**-*sis*-**se**, *ax*-**is** (= *ak-sis*).

Accent

In a word of two syllables the accent falls on the first syllable: **sér-vo, sa´e-pe, ní-hil**.

In a word of three or more syllables (1) the accent falls on the syllable which is second from the end if that syllable is long (**ser-vắ-re, cōn-sér-vat, for-tū́-na**); (2) otherwise, the accent falls on the syllable which is third from the end (**mó-ne-ō, pá-tri-a, pe-cū́-ni-a, vó-lu-cris**).

Footnotes

[1]Some refinements such as macrons have been omitted as not immediately necessary. The words in the table are only a few of the many which could be cited.

[2]The language of the sacred writings of ancient India, parent of the modern Indo-European dialects of India.

[3]Avestan and Old Persian, represented today by modern Persian.

[4]As an example of the Germanic languages; others are Gothic, German, Dutch, Danish, Norwegian, Swedish, Icelandic, English.

[5]As an example of the Celtic languages; others are Gallic, Breton, Scotch (Gaelic), Welsh.

[6]As an example of the Baltic group; others are Lettish and Old Prussian.

[7]As an example of the Slavic group; others are Polish, Bulgarian, Czech.

[8]This large family of languages shows relationship in the matter of inflections also, but no attempt is made here to demonstrate the point. An inflected language is one in which the nouns, pronouns, adjectives, and verbs have variable endings by which the relationship of the words to each other in a sentence can be indicated. In particular, note that Anglo-Saxon, like Latin, was an inflected language but that its descendant English has lost most of its inflections.

[9] The later connection between English and Latin will be pointed out below.

[10] Note that many languages (e.g., the Semitic languages, Egyptian, Basque, Chinese, the native languages of Africa and the Americas) lie outside the Indo-European family.

[11] The classical Latin word for *mouth* was **os, ōris.**

[12] The classical Latin word for *horse* was **equus.**

[13] Derived from **ille** but not actually cognate with *il* and *el.*

[14] Many of these were of Greek and Hebrew origin but had been Latinized. The Latin *Vulgate* played an important role.

[15] One thinks of Chaucer, who died in 1400.

[16] Thomas Wilson (16th century) says: "The unlearned or foolish fantastical, that smells but of learning (such fellows as have been learned men in their days), will so Latin their tongues, that the simple cannot but wonder at their talk, and think surely they speak by some revelation." Sir Thomas Browne (17th century) says: "If elegancy still proceedeth, and English pens maintain that stream we have of late observed to flow from many, we shall within a few years be fain to learn Latin to understand English, and a work will prove of equal facility in either." These statements are quoted by permission from the "Brief History of the English Language" by Hadley and Kittredge in Webster's *New International Dictionary,* Second Edition, copyright, 1934, 1939, 1945, 1950, 1953, 1954, by G. & C. Merriam Co.

[17] And apparently our 20th-century composers of advertisements would be reduced to near beggary if they could not draw on the Latin vocabulary and the classics in general.

[18] Grimm's law catalogues the Germanic shift in certain consonants (the stops). This shows how such apparently different words as English *heart* and Latin *cor, cord-,* are in origin the same word.

[19] Take particular care to note that Latin is simply cognate with Greek, not derived from it.

[20] In the interests of simplicity and clarity a number of languages and intermediate steps have been omitted. In particular be it noted that no attempt has been made to indicate the indebtedness of English to Greek.

[21] Actually, Latin was only one of a number of Italic dialects (among which were Oscan and Umbrian), and some time passed before Latin won out over the other dialects in Italy. Similarly, among the Greeks there were a number of dialects' (Aeolic, Ionic, Doric).

[22] This statement is not to be construed as meaning that the Romans had no originality. They did, but there is not space here to demonstrate the point.

[23] See below under Medieval and Renaissance Latin.

[24] However, that it meant simply "eat, drink, and be merry" is a vulgar misinterpretation.

[25] See introductory note to reading selection in Ch. 30.

[26] See, for instance, E. K. Rand, *The Builders of Eternal Rome* (Harvard Univ. Press, 1943).

[27] The *Aeneid* is always bracketed with Homer's *Iliad* and *Odyssey*, to which it owes a great deal, and with Dante's *Divine Comedy* and Milton's *Paradise Lost*, which owe a great deal to it.

[28] Vulgar Latin has already been mentioned as the language of the common people. Its roots are in the early period. In fact, the language of Plautus has much in common with this later vulgar Latin, and we know that throughout the Golden and the Silver Ages vulgar Latin lived on as the colloquial idiom of the people but was kept distinct from the literary idiom of the texts and the polished conversation of those periods.

[29] E.g., the loss of most declensional endings and the increased use of prepositions; extensive employment of auxiliary verbs; anarchy in the uses of the subjunctive and the indicative.

[30] The quality of Medieval Latin fluctuates considerably.

[31] At the same time, by token of Dante's success and that of others in the use of the vernacular languages, it must be admitted that Latin had begun to wage a losing battle.

[32] For instance, note its use by Erasmus and Sir Thomas More in the 16th century, by Milton, Bacon, and Newton in the 17th century, and by botanists, classical scholars, and poets of the later centuries.

[33] Called "incunabula" because they were made in the "cradle days" of printing. The type is called "Roman" to distinguish it from the "black-letter" type which was used in northern Europe (cp. the German type). The Italian printers based their Roman type on that of the finest manuscripts of the period, those written for the wealthy, artistic, exacting Renaissance patrons. The scribes of those manuscripts, seeking the most attractive kind of script with which to please such patrons, found it in manuscripts written in the best Carolingian book-hand.

[34] The uncial letters are similar to the square capitals except that the sharp corners of the angular letters have been rounded so that they can be written with greater rapidity. An illustration can be found Webster's *Collegiate Dictionary*, entry *uncial.*

[35] The twenty-two letters of the Phoenician alphabet represented only consonant sounds. The Greeks showed their originality in using some of these letters to designate vowel sounds.

[36] Note that our letter *w* is simply double *u* of the *v*-shaped variety.

[37] This was really Greek *u*, upsilon (Υ), a vowel with a sound intermediate between *u* and *i*, as in French *u*.

[38] Ordinarily only long vowels are marked; short ones are left unmarked.

[39] But in poetry the consonants may be separated according to the rule for two consonants.

[40] But remember that a stop + a liquid regularly count as a single consonant: e.g., **pa-trem.**

1

The First and the Second Conjugations: Present Infinitive, Indicative, and Imperative Active

If asked to conjugate the English verb *to praise* in the present tense and the active voice of the indicative mood,[1] you would say:

	Singular	Plural
1st person	I praise	we praise
2nd person	you praise	you praise
3rd person	he (she, it) praises	they praise

The person and the number of five of these six forms cannot be determined in English without the aid of pronouns *I, you, we, they*. Only in the third person singular can you omit the pronoun *he* (*she, it*) and still make clear by the special ending of the verb that *praises* is third person and singular.

PERSONAL ENDINGS

What the English can accomplish in only one of the six forms, Latin can do in each of the six forms by means of personal endings, which indicate distinctly the person, the number, and the voice. Since these personal endings will be encountered at every turn, the time taken to memorize[2] them at this point will prove an excellent investment. For the active voice they are:

Singular

1st person	**-ō** or **-m**, which corresponds to *I*.
2nd person	**-s**, which corresponds to *you* (*thou*).
3rd person	**-t,** which corresponds to *he, she, it*.

Plural

1st person	**-mus,** which corresponds to *we*.
2nd person	**-tis,** which corresponds to *you*.
3rd person	**-nt,** which corresponds to *they*.

The next step is to find a verbal stem to which these endings can be added.

PRESENT INFINITIVE[3] ACTIVE AND PRESENT STEM

The present active infinitives of the model verbs of the first and the second conjugations are respectively:

　　　laudāre, *to praise*　　　　　　monēre, *to advise*

You see that **-āre** characterizes the first conjugation and **-ēre** characterizes the second.

Now from the infinitives drop the **-re,** which is the actual infinitive ending, and you have the present stems:

　　　laudā-　　　　　　　　　monē-

To this present stem add the personal endings and you are ready to read or to say something in Latin about the present: e.g., **laudā-t,** *he praises*; **monē-mus,** *we advise*.

This leads to the first of many paradigms. "Paradigm" (pronounced páradim) derives from Greek paradeigma, which means *pattern, example*; and paradigms are used at numerous points throughout the chapters and in the Appendix to provide summaries of forms according to convenient patterns. Of course, the ancient Romans learned the many inflected forms from their parents and from daily contacts with other people by the direct method, as we ourselves learn English today. However, since we lack this natural Latin environment and since we usually begin the study of Latin at a relatively late age under the urgency of haste, the analytical approach through paradigms, though somewhat artifical and uninspiring, is generally found to be the most efficacious method. In the process of memorizing all paradigms, be sure to say them *aloud*, for this gives you the help of two senses, both sight and sound.

PRESENT INDICATIVE ACTIVE OF Laudō & Moneō[4]

Singular

1. la'udō,[5] *I praise, am praising, do praise*[6]   móneō,[5] *I advise*, etc.
2. la'udās, *you praise, are praising, do praise*   mónēs, *you advise*, etc.
3. la'udat, *he (she, it) praises*, is praising,   mónet, *he (she, it) advises*,etc.
   does praise

Plural

1. laudā́mus, *we praise, are praising, do praise*   monḗmus, *we advise*, etc.
2. laudā́tis, *you praise, are praising, do praise*   monḗtis, *you advise*, etc.
3. la'udant, *they praise, are praising,*   mónent, *they advise*, etc.
   do praising

PRESENT ACTIVE IMPERATIVE

By using the simple present stem without any ending you can express a command in the second person singular: **la'udā mē**, *praise me;* **mónē mē**, *advise me*. Add **-te** to the singular form and you have the second person plural, which in English cannot be distinguished from the singular: **laudā́-te mē**, *praise me;* **monḗ-te mē**, *advise me*.

2nd person singular	la'udā, *praise*	mónē, *advise*
2nd person plural	laudā́te, *praise*	monḗte, *advise*

VOCABULARY

(*Note:* In memorizing the vocabularies be sure always to say all the Latin words *aloud* as you learn the meanings.)

mē, me

níhil, nothing (*nihilism, annihilate*)

nōn, not

sa'epe, often

sī, if

ámō, amā́re, love (*amatory*)

cōgitō, cōgitā́re, think, ponder, consider, plan (*cogitate*)

débeō, dēbére, owe; ought, must (*debt, debit*)

dō', dáre, give, offer (*date*)

láudō, laudā́re, praise (*laud, laudable*)

móneō, monére, advise, warn (*admonish, admonition, monitor, monument, monster*)

sérvō, servā́re, preserve, save, keep (*reserve, reservoir*) cōnsérvō, -serváre (con-servō), a stronger form of servō, preserve, conserve (*conservative, conservation*)

váleō, valére, be strong, have power; be well; válē (valéte), good-bye, farewell (*valid, invalidate, prevail, prevalent, valedictory*)

vídeō, vidére, see; understand (*provide, evident, view, review*)

vócō, vocáre, call, summon (*vocation, advocate, vocabulary, convoke, evoke, invoke, provoke, revoke*)

RECOGNITION VOCABULARY[7]

quid, what

érrō, erráre, wander, err, go astray, be mistaken (*erratic, error*)

SENTENCES[8]

1. Labor mē vocat.[9]
2. Monē mē sī errō.
3. Festīnā lentē. (A saying of Augustus. — festīnāre, *to hasten, make haste*. — lentē, *slowly*.)
4. Laudās mē; culpant mē. (culpāre, *to blame, censure*.)
5. Saepe peccāmus. (peccāre, *to sin*.)
6. Quid dēbēmus cōgitāre?
7. Cōnservāte mē.
8. Rūmor volat. (volāre, *to fly*.)
9. Mē nōn amat.
10. Nihil mē terret. (terrēre, *to terrify*.)
11. Apollō mē servat.
12. Maecēnās et Vergilius mē laudant. (Maecenas, the patron, and Virgil, the poet, were both friends of Horace. — et, *and*.)
13. Quid vidētis? Nihil vidēmus.
14. Saepe nihil cōgitās.
15. Bis dās sī cito dās. (bis, *twice*. — cito, *quickly*. — A proverb which still holds good.)
16. Sī valēs, valeō. (A friendly sentiment with which Romans often commenced a letter.)
17. Salvē!...Valē! *or* Salvēte!...Valēte! (salvēre, *to be in good health*. "Salvē" was the word of greeting when friends met; "valē" was the word when they parted.)
18. What does he see?
19. They are giving nothing.
20. You ought not to praise me.
21. If I err, he often warns me.
22. If you love me, save me.

Footnotes

[1]A *verb* (derived from Latin **verbum,** *word*) is *the* word of a sentence: it asserts something about the subject of the sentence. *Tense* (Latin **tempus,** *time*) indicates the time of the verb as present, past, future, etc. *Voice* (**vōx, vōcis,** *voice*) is the way of speaking which shows whether the subject performs the action of the verb (active voice) or receives the action of the verb (passive voice). *Mood,* or *mode* (**modus,** *manner*), is the manner of expressing the action of the verb as a fact (indicative mood), a command (imperative mood), etc. To conjugate (**coniugāre,** *to join together*) a verb is to give together the inflected forms of the verb according to the requirements of person, number, tense, mood, and voice.

[2]Be sure *always* to say *all* paradigms *aloud* as you memorize them. In this way you can rely on two senses, both sight and hearing, to prompt your memory and to check it.

[3]The *infinitive* (**īnfīnītus, īnfīnītīvus,** *not limited*) simply gives the basic idea of the verb; its form is not limited by person and number, though it is limited by tense and voice.

[4]Note that the accent marks used in the paradigms and the vocabularies are simply a device to indicate the syllable on which the stress falls. They are not an integral part of the word indicating vowel quality as in French.

[5]For **laudā-ō;** the **ā** and the **ō** have contracted to **ō.** In **moneō** the long stem vowel, **-ē-,** has become short before another vowel. Also in both conjugations the long stem vowels have become short before **-t** and **-nt.**

[6]Note that Latin has only one form for the three English expressions; Latin lacks separate forms for *am praising* and *do praise.*

[7]For an explanation of the nature and use of "Recognition Vocabularies" in this book, see Preface, p. viii.

[8]All these sentences are based on ancient Roman originals but most of them had to be considerably adapted to meet the exigencies of this first chapter.

[9]The verb commonly comes at the end of a Latin sentence.

2

Cases; First Declension; Agreement of Adjectives

CASES

*A*s *a Latin verb has various terminations with which to accomplish its particular role in a given sentence, so a Latin noun has various terminations to show whether it is used as the subject or the object of a verb, whether it indicates the idea of possession, and so on. The various forms of a noun are called cases, the more common uses and meanings of which are catalogued below. For illustrative purposes it will be convenient to refer to the following English sentences,[1] which later in the chapter will be converted into Latin for further analysis.*

- A. The poet is giving the girl large roses (or is giving large roses to the girl).
- B. The girls are giving the poet's roses to the sailors.
- C. By (their) money they are saving the girls' country (*or* the country of the girls).

Nominative Case

The Romans used the nominative case most commonly to indicate the subject of a finite verb; e.g., *poet* in sentence A and *girls* in sentence B.

Genitive Case

When one noun was used to modify[2] another, the Romans put the modifying, or limiting, noun in the genitive case, as we do in such instances as *poet's* in sentence B and *girls'* in sentence C. One idea very commonly conveyed by the genitive is possession and, although other categories besides the genitive of possession are distinguished, the meaning of the genitive can generally be ascertained by translating it with the preposition *of*.

Dative Case   The Romans used the dative most commonly to mark the person or thing indirectly affected by the action of the verb, as *girl* (*to the girl*) in sentence A and *to the sailors* in B. In most instances the sense of the dative can be determined by using *to* or *for* with the noun.

Accusative Case   The Romans used the accusative case to indicate the *direct* object of the action of the verb, the person or thing directly affected by the action of the verb. It can also be used with certain prepositions; e.g., **ad,** *to;* **in,** *into;* **post,** *after, behind.* In sentences A and B, *roses* is the direct object of *is* (*are*) *giving;* in C, *country* is the object of *are saving.*

Ablative Case   The ablative case we sometimes call the adverbial[3] case because it was the case used by the Romans when they wished to modify, or limit, the verb by such ideas as *means* ("by what"), *agent* ("by whom"), *accompaniment* ("with whom"), *manner* ("how"), *place* ("where; from which"), *time* ("when or within which"). The Romans used the ablative sometimes with a preposition[4] and sometimes without one. There is no simple rule of thumb for translating this complex case. However, you will find little difficulty when a Latin preposition is used (**ab,** *by, from;* **cum,** *with;* **dē** and **ex,** *from;* **in,** *in, on*); and in general you can associate with the ablative such English prepositions as *by, with, from, in, on, at.*[5] The more troublesome of these uses will be taken up at convenient points in the following chapters.

Vocative Case   The Romans used the vocative case, sometimes with **Ō**, to address (**vocāre,** *to call*) a person or thing directly; e.g., (**Ō**) **Caesar,** (*O*) *Caesar;* **Ō fortūna,** *O fortune.* In modern punctuation the vocative is separated from the rest of the sentence by commas. With one major exception to be studied later, the vocative has the same form as that of the nominative, and so it is ordinarily not listed in the paradigms.

FIRST DECLENSION[6] — NOUN AND ADJECTIVE

porta, *gate* **Base: port-**	**magna,** *large* **Base: magn-**		**Endings**
Singular			
Nom. porta	magna	the (a)[7] large gate	**-a**
Gen. portae	magnae	of the large gate	**-ae**
Dat. portae	magnae	to/for the large gate	**-ae**
Acc. portam	magnam	the large gate	**-am**
Abl. portā	magnā	by/with/from, etc., the large gate	**-ā**
Voc. porta	magna	O large gate	**-a**

Plural

Nom.	portae	magnae	*the large gates* or *large gates*	**-ae**
Gen.	portārum	magnārum	*of the large gates*	**-ārum**
Dat.	portīs	magnīs	*to/for the large gates*	**-īs**
Acc.	portās	magnās	*the large gates*	**-ās**
Abl.	portīs	magnīs	*by/with/from*, etc.,	
			the large gates	**-īs**
Voc.	portae	magnae	*O large gates*	**-ae**

DECLENSION OF NOUN OR ADJECTIVE = BASE + ENDINGS

The simple rule for declining a noun or an adjective is to add the case endings to the base.

The base of a noun or an adjective is found by dropping the ending of the genitive singular, which for nouns is always given in the vocabulary. Therefore, it is of the utmost importance to know the genitive of a noun. Any special problems with adjectives will be explained as they come up.

GENDER OF FIRST DECLENSION = FEMININE

Like English, Latin distinguishes three genders: masculine, feminine, and neuter. Nouns indicating male beings are naturally masculine and those indicating female beings are feminine. Other nouns, however, the Romans classified *grammatically* as masculine or feminine or neuter, commonly on the basis of the nominative singular ending.

Nouns of the first declension are normally feminine; e.g., **puella,** *girl;* **rosa,** *rose;* **pecūnia,** *money;* **patria,** *country.* A few indicating males are masculine; e.g., **poēta,** *poet;* **nauta,** *sailor;* **agricola,** *farmer.*

In this book, as a practical procedure the gender of a noun will not be specifically labeled *m., f.,* or *n.* in the notes, if it follows the general rules.

ADJECTIVES

The normal role of adjectives is to accompany nouns and to modify, or limit, them in size, color, texture, character, and so on; and, like nouns, adjectives are declined. Naturally, therefore, an adjective agrees with its noun in gender, number, and case. An adjective (**adiectum,** *added*) is a word *added* to a noun.

SYNTAX

The Greek verb **syntattein** means to draw up an army in orderly array. Similarly, in grammatical terminology *syntax* is the orderly marshaling of words according to the service which they are to perform in a sentence. To explain the syntax of a given word you state its form, the word on which it depends, and the reason for the form.

Sentences A, B, and C, turned into Latin will provide some good examples of syntax.

A. Poēta puellae magnās rosās dat.
B. Puellae nautīs rosās poētae dant.[8]
C. Pecūniā patriam puellārum cōnservant.

The syntax of some of these words can be conveniently stated thus:

Word	Form	Dependence	Reason
Sentence A			
poēta	nom. sing.	dat	subject
puellae	dat. sing.	dat	indirect object
magnās	acc. plu.	rosās	agreement of adj.with its noun
Sentence B			
puellae	nom. plu.	dant	subject
nautīs	dat. plu.	dant	indirect object
rosās	acc. plu.	dant	direct object
poētae	gen. sing.	rosās	possession
Sentence C			
pecūniā	abl. sing.	cōnservant	means

Be ready to explain all the other forms in these sentences.

VOCABULARY

fáma, -ae, *f.,* rumor, report; fame (*defame, infamy*)

fortúna, -ae, *f.,* fortune, luck (*fortunate, unfortunate*)

pátria, -ae, *f.,* fatherland, native land, (one's) country (*expatriate, repatriate*)

pecúnia, -ae, *f.,* money (*pecuniary, impecunious;* cp. *peculation*)

puélla, -ae, *f.,* girl

víta, -ae, *f.,* life; mode of life (*vital, vitals, vitality, vitamin, vitalize, devitalize, revitalize*)

antíqua, -ae, *adj.,* ancient, old-time, of old (*antique, antiquities, antiquated, antiquarian*)

mágna, -ae, *adj.,* large, great (*magnify, magnificent, magnate, magnitude*)

méa, -ae, *adj.,* my

múlta, -ae, *adj.*, much, many (*multitude, multiply, multiple; multi-*, a prefix as in *multi-millionaire*)

túa, -ae, *adj.*, your (*singular number*)

et, *conjunction*, and

Ō, *interjection*, O!, Oh!, *commonly used with the vocative*

síne, *preposition* + *abl.*, without (*sinecure*)

est, is

RECOGNITION VOCABULARY

fórma, -ae, *f.*, form, shape; beauty (*formal, format, formula, formless, deform, inform*, etc.; but not *formic, formidable*)

íra, -ae, *f.*, ire, anger (*irate, irascible;* but not *irritate*)

philosóphia, -ae, *f.* (*Greek* philosophia, love of wisdom), philosophy

po'ena, -ae, *f.*, penalty, punishment (*penal, penalize, penalty, pain*)

SENTENTIAE ANTĪQUAE[9]

1. Salvē, Ō patria! (Plautus.)
2. Fāma volat. (Virgil.)
3. Dā veniam puellae. (Terence. — venia, -ae, *favor, pardon.*)
4. Clēmentia tua multās vītās cōnservat. (Cicero. — clēmentia, -ae, *clemency.*)
5. Multam pecūniam dēportat. (Cicero. — dēportāre, *to carry away.*)
6. Fortūnam et vītam antīquae patriae saepe laudās sed recūsās. (Horace. — sed, *but.* — recūsāre, *refuse, reject.*)
7. Mē vītāre turbam iubēs. (*Seneca. — vītāre, *avoid.* — turba, -ae, *crowd, multitude.* — iubēre, *to bid.*)
8. Mē philosophiae dō. (Seneca.)
9. Philosophia est ars vītae. (*Cicero. — ars, nom. sing., *art.*)
10. Sānam fōrmam vītae tenēte. (*Seneca. — sāna, -ae, *sound, sane.* — tenēre, *have, hold.*)
11. Immodica īra creat īnsāniam. (Seneca. — immodica, -ae, *immoderate, excessive.* — creāre, *create.* —īsānia, -ae, *unsoundness, insanity.*)
12. Dēbēmus īram vītāre. (Seneca.)
13. Nūlla avāritia sine poenā est. (*Seneca. — nūlla, *no.*— avāritia, -ae, *avarice.*)
14. Mē saevīs catēnīs onerat. (Horace. — saeva, -ae, *cruel.* — catēna, -ae, *chain;* the case is ablative. — onerāre, *to load, oppress.*)
15. Rotam fortūnae nōn timent. (Cicero. — rota, -ae, *wheel.* — timēre, *to fear.*)
16. Luck gives beauty to many girls.
17. Without philosophy fortune and money often go astray.
18. If your land is strong, you ought to praise your great fortune.
19. We often see the penalty of anger.

VALĒ, PUELLA!

Puella poētam nōn amat. Valē, puella! Catullus obdūrat; puellam invītam nōn rogat. (Catullus. On Catullus see Introduction. — obdūrāre, *be firm.* — invīta, -ae, *against her will.* — rogāre, *ask, seek.*)

ETYMOLOGY

(Note that "etymology" comes from the Greek **etymos,** *true, real,* and **logos,** *word, account.* Consequently, the etymology of a word traces the derivation of the word and shows its original meaning. Under this heading will be introduced various items not covered by the derivatives listed in the vocabularies. However, each chapter so abounds in such material that complete coverage cannot be attempted.)

Pecūnia is connected with **pecus,** *cattle,* just as English *fee* is related to German *Vieh, cattle.*

Fortūna derives from **fors,** *chance, accident.*

Explain the meanings of the following English words on the basis of the appropriate Latin words found in the sentences indicated. Further aid, if needed, can be obtained from a good dictionary.

volatile (2)	tenet (10)	onerous (14)
venial (3)	creature (11)	rotary, rotate (15)
turbulent (7)	nullify (13)	obdurate
insane (10)	concatenation (14)	*(Reading Passage)*

Footnotes

[1] These sentences have been limited to the material available in Chapters 1 and 2 so that they may readily be understood when turned into Latin.

[2] *Modify* derives its meaning from Latin **modus** in the sense of "limit"; it means to limit one word by means of another. For example, in sentence B *roses* by itself gives a general idea but the addition of *poet's* modifies, or limits, *roses* so that only a specific group is in mind. The addition of *red* would have modified, or limited, *roses* still further by excluding white and yellow ones.

[3] Latin **ad verbum** means *to* or *near the verb;* an adverb modifies a verb, an adjective, or another adverb.

[4] A preposition (**prae-positus,** *having been placed before*) is a word placed before a noun or a pronoun to make a phrase which modifies another word in the capacity of an adverb or an adjective. In Latin most prepositional phrases are adverbial.

[5] For instance: **pecūniā,** *by* or *with money;* **ab puellā,** *by* or *from the girl;* **cum puellā,** *with the girl;* **cum īrā,** *with anger, angrily;* **ab (dē, ex) patriā,** *from the*

fatherland; **in patriā,** *in the fatherland;* **in mēnsā,** *on the table;* **ūnā hōrā,** *in one hour.*

[6] The term *declension* is connected with the verb **dē-clīnāre,** *to lean away from.* The idea of the ancient grammarians was that the other cases "lean away from" the nominative; they deviate from the nominative.

[7] Since classical Latin had no words corresponding exactly to our definite article *the* or our indefinite article *a,* **porta** can mean *gate* or *the gate* or *a gate.*

[8] A verb naturally agrees with its subject in *person* and *number.*

[9] Sentences of ancient Roman origin. Henceforth, the author of every ancient Latin sentence will be named. An asterisk before an author's name means that the sentence is quoted verbatim. The lack of an asterisk means that the original sentence had to be somewhat altered to bring it into line with the student's limited experience, but the student may be assured that the thought and the expression are those of the author indicated.

3

Second Declension: Masculine Nouns and Adjectives; Word Order

*T*he second declension follows the rule already given for the first declension: base + endings. However, the endings differ from those of the first declension except in the dative and the ablative plural.

SECOND DECLENSION—MASCULINES IN -us

Base:	amícus, friend amíc-	magnus, great magn-		Endings
Singular				
Nom.	amícus	mágnus	*a great friend*	-us
Gen.	amícī	mágnī	*of a great friend*	-ī
Dat.	amícō	mágnō	*to/for a great friend*	-ō
Acc.	amícum	mágnum	*a great friend*	-um
Abl.	amícō	mágnō	*by/with/from[1] a great friend*	-ō
Voc.	amíce	mágne	*O great friend*	-e

				Endings
Plural				
Nom.	amícī	mágnī	*great friends*	-ī
Gen.	amīcṓrum	magnṓrum	*of great friends*	-ōrum
Dat.	amícīs	mágnīs	*to/for great friends*	-īs
Acc.	amícōs	mágnōs	*great friends*	-ōs
Abl.	amícīs	mágnīs	*by/with/from[1] great friends*	-īs
Voc.	amícī	mágnī	*O great friends*	-ī

SECOND DECLENSION—MASCULINES IN -er

	puer, *boy*	ager, *field*		
Base:	puer-	agr-		**Endings**
Singular				
Nom.	púer[2]	áger[2]	[mágnus[3]	(none)
Gen.	púerī	ágrī	mágnī	-ī
Dat.	púerō	ágrō	mágnō	-ō
Acc.	púerum	ágrum	mágnum	-um
Abl.	púerō	ágrō	mágnō	-ō
Voc.	púer	áger	mágne	(none)
Plural				
Nom.	púerī	ágrī	mágnī	-ī
Gen.	púerṓrum	agrṓrum	magnṓrum	-ōrum
Dat.	púerīs	ágrīs	mágnīs	-īs
Acc.	púerōs	ágrōs	mágnōs	-ōs
Abl.	púerīs	ágrīs	mágnīs	-īs
Voc.	púerī	ágrī	mágnī]	-ī

DECLENSION

What in the instance of **puer** and **ager** particularly proves the importance of knowing the genitive as well as the nominative? Most -**er** nouns of the second declension follow the pattern of **ager**.[4]

For what cases do **amícī, amícō,** and **amícīs** stand?

Only in the singular of -**us** nouns and adjectives of the second declension does the vocative differ in spelling from the nominative: singular **amícus, amíce;** but plural **amícī, amícī.** Nouns in -ius (e.g., **fílius,** *son,* **Vergílius,** *Virgil*) and **meus,** *my* have a single -ī in the vocative singular: **mī fílī,** *my son;* **Ō Vergílī,** *O Virgil.*

Given **vir, virī,** *man,* decline **vir** in full.

GENDER

The **-us** and the **-er** nouns of the second declension are regularly masculine.

APPOSITION

Gāium, fīlium meum, in agrō videō.
I see Gaius, my son, in the field.

In this sentence **fīlium** is in apposition with **Gāium**. An appositive is a noun which is "put beside"[5] another noun as the explanatory equivalent of the other noun, and it naturally stands in the same construction as that of the other noun. An appositive is commonly separated from the rest of the sentence by commas.

WORD ORDER

A typical order of words in a simplified Latin sentence or subordinate clause is this: (1) the subject and its modifiers, (2) the indirect object, (3) the direct object, (4) adverbial words or phrases, (5) the verb. In formal composition, the tendency to place the verb at the end of its clause is probably connected with the Romans' fondness for the periodic style, which seeks to keep the reader or listener in suspense until the last word of a sentence has been reached. However, although the pattern described above is a good one to follow in general, the Romans themselves made many exceptions to this rule for the purposes of variety and emphasis. In fact, in highly inflected languages like Latin, the order of the words is relatively unimportant to the sense, thanks to the inflectional endings, which tell so much about the interelationship of the words in a sentence, as was explained under Syntax in Ch. 2, p. 9. On the other hand, in English, where the inflections are relatively few, the sense commonly depends on certain conventions of word order.

For example, study the following idea as expressed in the one English sentence and the four Latin versions, which all mean the same despite the differences of word order.

(1) *The boy is giving the pretty girl a rose.*
(2) Puer puellae bellae rosam dat.
(3) Bellae puellae puer rosam dat.
(4) Bellae puellae rosam dat puer.
(5) Rosam puer puellae bellae dat.

(etc.)

Whatever the order of the words in the Latin sentence, the sense remains the same (though the emphasis does vary). Note also that according to its ending, **bellae** must modify **puellae** no matter where these words stand. But if you change the order of the words in the English sentence, you change the sense:

(1) *The boy is giving the pretty girl a rose.*
(2) *The pretty girl is giving the boy a rose.*
(3) *The girl is giving the boy a pretty rose.*
(4) *The girl is giving the pretty boy a rose.*
(5) *The rose is giving the boy a pretty girl.*

In all these sentences the same words are used with the same spellings, but the sense of each sentence is different in accordance with the conventions of English word order. Furthermore, where the fifth English sentence is senseless, the fifth Latin sentence, though in much the same order, makes perfectly good sense.

VOCABULARY

amícus, -ī, *m.,* friend (*amicable, amiable, amity;* cp. **amō**)

fílius, -iī, *m.,* son (*filial, affiliate*)

númerus, -ī, *m.,* number (*numeral, innumerable, enumerate*)

pópulus, -ī, *m.,* the people, a nation (*population, popularity, populous*)

púer, púerī, *m.,* boy; *plu.* boys, children (*puerile, puerility*)

sapiéntia, -ae, *f.,* wisdom (*sapient, savant*)

vir, vírī, *m.,* man (*virtue, virile;* not *virulent*)

pa′ucī (*m.*), **pa′ucae** (*f.*), *adj., usu. in plu.,* few, a few (*paucity*)

Rōmā́nus(*m.*), **Rōmā́na** (*f.*), *adj.,* Roman (*Romance, romance, romantic, romanticism, Romanesque, Roumania*)

dē, *prep. + abl.,* down from, from; concerning, about; *also as a prefix* **dē-** *with such meanings as* down, away, aside, out, off

in, *prep. + abl.,* in, on

sémper, *adv.,* always (*sempiternal*)

hábeō, -ére, have, hold, possess, consider (*in-habit, "hold in"; ex-hibit, "hold forth"; habit, habitat*)

PRACTICE AND REVIEW

1. Fīlium virī in agrīs vidēmus.
2. Puerī puellās vocant.
3. Fōrmam puellārum semper laudat.
4. Multī virī philosophiam antīquam laudant.
5. Sī īra valet, saepe errāmus et poenās damus. (poenās dare, *pay the penalty.*)
6. Fortūna virōs magnōs amat.
7. Without a few friends life is not strong.
8. O great Virgil, you have great fame in your country.
9. We do not see great fortune in your sons' lives.
10. He always gives my boy money.

SENTENTIAE ANTĪQUAE

1. Dēbētis, amīcī, dē populō Rōmānō cōgitāre. (Cicero.)
2. Maecēnās, amīcus Augustī, mē in numerō amīcōrum habet. (Horace. — Maecēnās, a name in nom. sing., v. Ch. 1, sent. 12. — Augustus, -ī.)
3. Libellus meus vītās virōrum monet. (Phaedrus. — libellus, -ī, *little book.*)
4. Paucī virī sapientiae student. (Cicero. — studēre + dat., *to be eager for.*)
5. Fortūna adversa virum magnae sapientiae nōn terret. (Horace. — adversus, adversa, adj. = English. — terreō, -ēre, *terrify.*)
6. Cimōn, vir magnae fāmae, magnam benevolentiam habet.(Nepos. — Cimōn, proper name nom. sing. — benevolentia, -ae = English.)
7. Semper avārus eget. (*Horace. — avārus, *avaricious*, = avārus vir. — egēre, *be in need.*)
8. Nūlla cōpia pecūniae avārum virum satiat. (Seneca. — cōpia, -ae, *abundance.* — satiāre, *satisfy, sate.*)
9. Pecūnia avārum irrītat, nōn satiat. (Publilius Syrus. — irrītō, -āre, *excite, exasperate.*)
10. Sēcrētē amīcōs admonē: laudā palam. (*Publilius Syrus. — sēcrētē, adv., *in secret.* — admonē = monē. — palam, adv., *openly.*)
11. Modum tenēre dēbēmus. (*Seneca. — modus, -ī, *moderation.* — tenēre, *have, observe.*)

ETYMOLOGY

The following are some of the Romance words which you can recognize on the basis of the vocabulary of this chapter.

Latin	Italian	Spanish	French
amīcus	amico	amigo	ami
fīlius	figlio	hijo	fils
numerus	numero	número	numéro
populus	popolo	pueblo	peuple
paucī	poco	poco	peu
semper	sempre	siempre	
habēre	avere	haber	avoir
dē	di	de	de

Footnotes

[1] Remember that this is only an imperfect, makeshift way of representing the ablative, and remember that prepositions are commonly used with the ablative, especially when the noun indicates a person.

[2] The underlined forms are the ones which call for special attention.

[3] Added for the sake of comparison and contrast. Note the combination of **puer magnus,** *a big boy,* and **Ō puer magne,** *O big boy.*

[4] Helpful also in remembering whether or not the **-e-** is dropped are English derivatives; e.g., puerile, agriculture, magistrate (**magister, -trī,** *master*), library (**liber, librī,** *book*).

[5] **ad** (*to, near*) + **pōnō, positus** (*put*).

4

Second Declension Neuters; Adjectives; Present Indicative of Sum; Predicate Nouns and Adjectives

*I*n the first declension there are no nouns of neuter gender but in the second declension there are many. They are declined as follows.

SECOND DECLENSION—NEUTERS

	dōnum, *gift*	cōnsilium, *plan*	magnum, *great*	Endings
Base:	dōn-	cōnsili-	magn-	
Singular				
Nom.	dṓnum	cōnsílium	mágnum	-um
Gen.	dṓnī	cōnsíliī[1]	mágnī	-ī
Dat.	dṓnō	cōnsíliō	mágnō	-ō
Acc.	dṓnum	cōnsílium	mágnum	-um
Abl.	dṓnō	cōnsíliō	mágnō	-ō

				Endings
Plural				
Nom.	dóna	cōnsília	mágna	-a
Gen.	dōnórum	cōnsiliórum	magnórum	-ōrum
Dat.	dōnĭs	cōnsíliīs	mágnīs	-ĭs
Acc.	dóna	cōnsília	mágna	-a
Abl.	dōnĭs	cōnsíliīs	mágnīs	-ĭs

DECLENSION

The forms of the neuters are the same as those of the masculines except in the nominative, the accusative, and the vocative. Note particularly that the form of the accusative is the same as that of the nominative. The vocative, likewise, has the same form as that of the nominative.

DECLENSION AND AGREEMENT OF ADJECTIVES

The recurrent **magnus** has illustrated the point that, while the base remains constant, the adjective has masculine, feminine, or neuter endings according to the gender of the noun with which it is used, and it likewise agrees with its noun in number and case. Although there is nothing new in **magnus**, the full declension of the adjective provides a good review of the first two declensions.

Masc.		**Fem.**	**Neut.**
Singular			
Nom.	mágnus	mágna	mágnum
Gen.	mágnī	mágnae	mágnī
Dat.	mágnō	mágnae	mágnō
Acc.	mágnum	mágnam	mágnum
Abl.	mágnō	mágnā	mágnō
Voc.	mágne	mágna	mágnum
Plural			
Nom.	mágnī	mágnae	mágna
Gen.	magnórum	magnárum	magnórum
Dat.	mágnīs	mágnīs	mágnīs
Acc.	mágnōs	mágnās	mágna
Abl.	mágnīs	mágnīs	mágnīs
Voc.	mágnī	mágnae	mágna

Henceforth, such first and second declension adjectives will appear thus in the vocabularies:

meus, -a, -um   multus, -a, -um   paucī, -ae, a (plu. only)

Sum: PRESENT INFINITIVE AND PRESENT INDICATIVE

As the English verb *to be* is irregular, so is the Latin **sum**. Although the personal endings can be distinguished, the stem varies so much that the best procedure is to memorize these very common forms as they are given. Notice that in the case of **sum** we do not refer to the voice as active or passive.

PRESENT INFINITIVE OF Sum: esse, *to be*

PRESENT INDICATIVE OF Sum

Singular	**Plural**
1. sum, *I am*	sumus, *we are*
2. es, *you are*	estis, *you are*
3. est, *he (she, it) is, there is*	sunt, *they are, there are*

PREDICATE NOUNS AND ADJECTIVES

Sum is an intransitive verb and cannot take a direct object. *Intransitive* in a verb implies action within, but the verb *does not take an object*: i.e., *run* or *walk* have action but not a direct object, therefore they are intransitive. **Sum** is a *link* verb, it nas *no* action, it is a shadow of a verb. Rather, like a coupling which connects two cars on a train, **sum** usually serves to connect its subject with a predicate noun or adjective.[2] Predicate nouns and adjectives are those which refer directly to the subject through **sum**,[3] and they naturally agree with the subject in case and number and, wherever possible, in gender. Examples follow.

Vergilius est amīcus Augustī, *Virgil is the friend of Augustus*.
Vergilius est poēta, *Virgil is a poet*.
Vergilius est magnus, *Virgil is great*.
Fāma Vergiliī est magna, *the fame of Virgil is great*.
Puellae sunt bellae, *the girls are pretty*.
Dōnum est magnum, *the gift is large*.
Dōna sunt magna, *the gifts are large*.
Sumus Rōmānī, *we are Romans* (*Roman men;* v. note 5).
Sumus Rōmānae, *we are Roman women*. (v. note 5).

VOCABULARY

béllum, -ī, *n.,* war (*bellicose, belligerent*)

cúra, -ae, *f.,* care, attention, caution, anxiety (*cure, curator, curious, curiosity, curio, curettage*)

móra, -ae, *f.,* delay (*moratorium*)

níhil, *indeclinable, n.,* nothing

óculus, -ī, *m.,* eye (*ocular, oculist*)

offícium, -iī, duty, service (*office, officer, official, officious*)

perículum, -ī, danger, risk (*peril, perilous*)

bónus, -a, -um, good, kind (*bonus, bonny, bounty*)

málus, -a, -um, bad, evil, wicked (*malice, malign, malaria, malady, malefactor, malfeasance, malevolent; mal-,* a prefix as in *maladjustment, maltreat, malapropos*)

párvus, -a, -um, small, little

stúltus, -a, -um, foolish; **stúltus, -ī,** *m.,* a fool

vérus, -a, -um, true, real (*verify, verisimilitude, very*)

sum, esse, be

RECOGNITION VOCABULARY

magíster, -trī, *m.,* schoolmaster, teacher, master (*magistrate, master, mister, mistress, miss*)

ōtium, -iī, *n.,* leisure, peace (*otiose*)

béllus, -a, -um, pretty, handsome, charming (*belle, beau, beauty, embellish, belladonna, belles-lettres*). *Do not confuse with* **bellum,** war.

PRACTICE AND REVIEW

1. Ōtium est bonum.
2. Bella sunt mala. (**Bella** from **bellum, -ī,** *n.*)
3. Officium mē dē ōtiō vocat.
4. Paucī virī multās fōrmās perīculī in pecūniā vident.
5. Etsī (*even if*) multam pecūniam habētis, nōn estis sine cūrīs.
6. Ōtium multōrum virōrum est parvum.
7. Sumus vērī amīcī.
8. Perīculum est in morā.
9. You (singular) are in great danger.
10. My son's cares are often foolish.
11. The sons of great men are not always great.
12. Without wisdom good fortune is nothing.

SENTENTIAE ANTĪQUAE

1. Fortūna est caeca. (*Cicero. — caecus, -a, -um, *blind*.)
2. Sī perīcula sunt vēra, īnfortūnātus es. (Terence. — infortūnātus, -a, -um, *unfortunate*.)
3. Ō amīce, vir bonus es. (Terence.)
4. Nōn bella est fāma tuī fīliī. (Horace.)
5. Errāre[4] est hūmānum. (Seneca. — hūmānus, -a, -um = English.)
6. Nihil est omnīnō beātum. (Horace. — omnīnō, adv., *wholly*. — beātus, -a, -um, *happy, fortunate*.)
7. Remedium īrae est mora. (Seneca. — remedium, -iī = Eng.)
8. Bonus Daphnis ōtium amat. (Virgil. — Daphnis is a pastoral character.)
9. Magistrī puerīs parvīs crustula saepe dant. (Horace. — crustulum, -ī, *cookie*.)
10. Puellam meam magis quam oculōs meōs amō. (Terence. — magis quam, *more than*.)
11. Dā mihi multa bāsia. (Catullus. — mihi, dat., *to me*. — bāsium, iī, *kiss*.)
12. Īnfīnītus est numerus stultōrum. (Ecclesiastes. — īnfīnītus, -a, -um = Eng.)
13. Praeclāra[5] sunt rāra. (Cicero. — praeclārus, -a, -um, *remarkable;* rārus, -a, -um = Eng.)
14. Officium vocat. (Persius.)
15. Malī[5] sunt in nostrō (*our*) numerō et dē exitiō bonōrum virōrum cōgitant. Bonōs adiuvāte; cōnservāte populum Rōmānum. (Cicero. — exitium, -iī, *destruction*. — adiuvō, -āre, *to help*.)

ETYMOLOGY

Some Romance derivatives:

Latin	Italian	Spanish	French
oculus	occhio	ojo	œil
ōtium	ozio	ocio	oisiveté
perīculum	pericolo	peligro	péril
officium	officio	oficio	office
bonus	buono	bueno	bon
vērus	vero	verdadero	vrai
magister	maestro	maestro	maître
bellus	bello	bello	belle
hūmānus	umano	humano	humain
beātus	beato	beato	béat
bāsium	bacio	beso	baiser
rārus	raro	raro	rare

Footnotes

[1] The genitive singular of second declension nouns ending in **-ius** or **-ium** was spelled with a single **-ī** (**fīlius**, gen. **fīlī**; **cōnsilium**, gen. **cōnsilī**) through the Ciceronian Period. However, since the genitive form **-iī** (**fīliī**, **cōnsiliī**) became established during the Augustan Period and since **-iī** was always the rule in adjectives (**eximius**, gen. **eximiī**), this is the form which will be used in the text.

[2] The two main divisions of a sentence are the subject and the predicate. The predicate is composed of the verb and all its dependent words and phrases.

[3] And similar verbs to be learned later.

[4] An infinitive may be used as the subject of a verb. As such, it is an indeclinable noun of neuter gender.

[5] The Romans often used an adjective by itself without a noun. Such an adjective is to be translated as a noun according to its gender and the context: **bonus,** *good man;* **bona** (fem. sing.), *good woman;* **bona** (neut. plu.), *good things, goods;* **bonōs,** *good men;* **bonārum,** *of good women;* etc.

5

First and Second Conjugations: Future; Adjectives in -er

The Romans indicated future time in the first two conjugations by inserting a future tense sign between the present stem and the personal endings. The final form of these future endings is seen in the following paradigm.

FUTURE INDICATIVE ACTIVE OF Laudō AND Moneō

Singular
1. laudá-bō,[1] *I shall praise*   monébō, *I shall advise*
2. laudá-bi-s, *you will praise*   monébis, *you will advise*
3. laudá-bi-t, he *will praise*   monébit, *he will advise*

Plural
1. laudá-bi-mus, *we shall praise*   monébimus, *we shall advise*
2. laudá-bi-tis, *you will praise*   monébitis, *you will advise*
3. laudá-bu-nt,[1] *they will praise*   monébunt, *they will advise*

Translating the form **laudā-bi-t** in the sequence of its component parts we get, in effect, *praise-will-he*, which can easily be arranged into our idiomatic *he will praise*.

ADJECTIVES OF THE FIRST AND SECOND DECLENSION IN -er.

The problem of **e** before **r** appears in adjectives as well as in nouns like **puer** and **ager** (v. Ch. 3). Actually, this problem is no great one if you memorize the forms of the adjectives as given in the vocabularies (nominative masculine, feminine, neuter); for the base, whether with or without the **-e-**, appears in the feminine and the neuter forms[2]:

līber	līber-a	līber-um	*free*
pulcher	pulchr-a	pulchr-um	*beautiful*

The rest of the paradigm continues the base thus established and the endings are regular.

	Masc.	Fem.	Neut.	Masc.	Fem.	Neut.
Nom.	líber	líbera	líberum	púlcher	púlchra	púlchrum
Gen.	líberī	líberae	líberī	púlchrī	púlchrae	púlchrī
Dat.	líberō	líberae	líberō	púlchrō	púlchrae	púlchrō
		(etc.)			(etc.)	

VOCABULARY

ánimus, -ī, *m.*, soul, spirit, mind; **ánimī, -ōrum,** high spirits, pride, courage (*animus, animosity, unanimous, pusillanimous*)

cúlpa, -ae, *f.*, fault, blame (*culpable, culprit, exculpate, inculpate*)

glória, -ae, *f.*, glory, fame (*glorify, glorious, inglorious*)

tē, *accusative sing.*, you; yourself; *cp.* **mē**

nóster, nóstra, nóstrum, our, ours, (*nostrum*)

ígitur, *conjunction, postpositive,*[3] therefore, consequently

-ne, *enclitic*[4] *added to the emphatic word placed at the beginning of a sentence to indicate a question the answer to which is uncertain.* (*For other types of direct questions see* **nōnne** *and* **num** *in the Appendix, p. 350.*)

própter, *prep. + acc.*, on account of, because of

sátis, *indecl. noun, adj., and adv.*, enough, sufficient (-ly) (*satisfy, satiate, insatiable, sate; assets, from* **ad,** up to + *satis*)

tum, *adv.*, then, at that time; thereupon, in the next place

remáneō, -ére, *or* **máneō, -ére,** remain, stay, stay behind, abide, continue (*permanent, remnant, mansion, manor*)

súperō, -áre, be above (*cp.* **super,** above), have the upper hand, surpass, overcome, conquer (*superable, insuperable*)

PRACTICE AND REVIEW

1. Officium līberōs virōs semper vocābit.
2. Habēbimusne multōs virōs magnōrum animōrum?
3. Perīcula bellī nōn sunt parva.
4. Propter culpās malōrum patria nostra nōn valēbit.
5. Mora animōs nostrōs superābit.
6. Culpae nostrae nōn sunt bellae.
7. Paucī virī dē cūrā animī cōgitant.
8. Propter īram in culpā estis et poenās dabitis.
9. Vērum ōtium nōn habētis.
10. Nihil est sine culpā.
11. Will war always remain in our land?
12. Does our friend see our fault?
13. Therefore, you (sing.) will save the reputation of our foolish boys.
14. Money and glory will not conquer the soul of a good man.

SENTENTIAE ANTĪQUAE

1. Invidiam populī Rōmānī nōn sustinēbis. (Cicero. — invidia, -ae, *dislike*. — sustinēre, *to endure, sustain*.)
2. Perīculumne igitur remanēbit? (Cicero.)
3. Angustus animus pecūniam amat. (Cicero. — angustus, -a, -um, *narrow*.)
4. Superā animōs et īram tuam. (Ovid.)
5. Culpa est mea. (Cicero.)
6. Dā veniam fīliō nostrō. (Terence.)
7. Propter adulēscentiam, fīliī meī, mala vītae nōn vidētis. (Terence. — adulēscentia, -ae, *youth;* cp. adolescence.)
8. Amābō tē, cūrā fīlium meum. (Cicero. — amābō tē: explain how this can be used as an emphatic expression for *please*. — cūrō, -āre, *take care of*.)
9. Vīta est supplicium. (Seneca. — supplicium, *punishment*.)
10. Satisne sānus es? (Terence. — sānus, -a, -um, *sound, sane*.)
11. Sī quandō satis pecūniae habēbō, tum mē philosophiae dabō. (Seneca. — quandō, adv., *ever;* pecūniae, gen. case.)
12. Semper glōria et fāma tua manēbunt. (Virgil.)
13. Vir bonus et perītus aspera verba poētārum culpābit. (Horace. — perītus, -a, -um, *skillful*. — verbum, -ī, *word*. — asper, aspera, asperum, *rough, harsh*. — culpō, -āre, the verb of culpa.)

AT THERMOPYLAE IN 480 B.C.

(Cicero reports the following conversation between a Persian and a Spartan just before the battle.)

Persian, boasting about the power of the Persian army: "Caelum propter numerum sagittārum nōn vidēbitis."

Spartan laconically: "In umbrā, igitur, pugnābimus."

Et Leōnidās exclāmat: "Pugnāte magnīs cum animīs, Lacedaemoniī: hodiē apud īnferōs fortasse cēnābimus."

(Cicero, *Tusc. Disp*. 1.42.101. — caelum, -ī, *sky*. — sagitta, -ae, *arrow*. — umbra, -ae, *shade*. — pugnāre, *to fight*. — Leōnidās, nom. case, Spartan king in command at Thermopylae. — cum magnīs animīs: cum + abl., *with*. — Lacedaemonius, -iī, *a Spartan*. — hodiē, adv., *today*. — apud + acc., *among*. — īnferī, -ōrum, *those below, the dead*. — fortasse, adv., *perhaps*. — cēnāre, *to dine*.)

ETYMOLOGY

Related to **animus** is **anima, -ae,** *the breath of life;* hence, *animal, animated, inanimate*.

Envy came to us from **invidia** (sent. 1) indirectly through French; *invidious* we borrowed directly from Latin.

Expert and *experience* are both related to **peritus** (13). The **ex** here is intensive (= *thoroughly*) and the stem **peri-** means *try, make trial of*. What, then, is an experiment? Apparently there is no experiment without some risk (**perī-culum**).

Also in sentence 13	*asperity and exasperate* (**ex** again intensive); *verb, adverb, verbatim, verbal*.
In the reading passage	*celestial; sagittate; umbrella* (through Italian, with diminutive ending), *umbrage, adumbrate; pugnacious, pugilist*.

Footnotes

[1] The tense sign is somewhat altered in the first person singular and the third person plural.

[2] English derivatives also indicate the base, as they do for the **-er** nouns in Ch. 3: liberal, miserable (**miser**); pulchritude, nostrum (**noster**).

[3] A postpositive word is one which does not appear as a first word of a sentence; it is put after (**post-pōnō**) the first word.

[4] An enclitic has no separate existence; it must always be attached to the end of a word and is said to "lean on" that word.

6

Sum: Future and Imperfect Indicative; Possum: Complementary Infinitive

A*s you return to the irregular verb* **sum**, *the best procedure once again is to dispense with rules[1] and simply memorize the paradigms. That done,* **possum** *will prove easy.*

SUM

Future Indicative	Imperfect Indicative[2]
1. érō, *I shall be*	éram, *I was*
2. éris, *you will be*	érās, *you were*
3. érit, *he (she, it) will be*	érat, *he (she, it) was*
1. érimus, *we shall be*	erā́mus, *we were*
2. éritis, *you will be*	erā́tis, *you were*
3. érunt, *they will be*	érant, *they were*

POSSUM, *BE ABLE, CAN*

Present Indicative	Future Indicative	Imperfect Indicative[2]
I am able, can	*I shall be able*	*I was able, could*
1. pós-sum	pót-erō	pót-eram
2. pót-es	pót-eris	pót-erās
3. pót-est	pót-erit	pót-erat
1. pós-sumus	pot-érimus	pot-erā́mus
2. pot-éstis	pot-éritis	pot-erā́tis
3. pós-sunt	pót-erunt	pót-erant

PRESENT INFINITIVE: POSSE, TO BE ABLE

Conjugation of Possum

The forms of **possum** in the paradigms represent a combination of **pot** (**potis,** *able*) + sum. Where *t* stood before *s*, the Romans changed the *t* to *s* (**pot-sum: pos-sum; pot-sunt: pos-sunt**). Otherwise the *t* remained unchanged (**pot-est,** etc.).

According to this rule, the infinitive should be **pot-esse,** a form which does appear in early Latin, but the shortened form **posse** came to be the accepted one.

COMPLEMENTARY INFINITIVE

Possum, exactly like the English *be able* or *can*, regularly requires an infinitive to complete its meaning. Hence we have the term "complementary" infinitive, which simply means "completing" infinitive, a point that is emphasized by the spelling: complementary in contrast to compl*i*mentary. You have already seen the complementary infinitive used with **dēbeō,** and you will find it used with other verbs.

Our friends were able to overcome (could overcome) many dangers.
Amīcī nostrī poterant superāre multa perīcula.

My friend is not able to stand (cannot stand).
Amīcus meus nōn potest stāre.

You ought to save my friend.
Dēbēs cōnservāre amīcum meum.

Note that a complementary infinitive has no separate subject of its own; its subject is the same as that of the verb on which it depends.

VOCABULARY

lǐber, lǐbrī, *m.*, book (*library, libretto*); *not to be confused with* **lǐber,** free
tyránnus, -ī, *m.*, absolute ruler, tyrant (*tyrannous, tyrannicide*)
vítium, -ǐī, *n.*, fault, crime, vice (*vitiate, vicious;* but not *vice* in *vice versa*)
Gra'ecus, -a, -um, Greek; **Gráecus, -i,** *m.*, a Greek
perpétuus, -a, -um, perpetual, uninterrupted, continuous (*perpetuate, perpetuity*)
véster, véstra, véstrum, your (*plu.*), yours
-que, *enclitic conjunction,* and. *It is appended to the second of two words to be joined:* **fāma glōriaque,** fame and glory.
sed, *conj.,* but
ubi: (1) *rel. adv. and conj.,* where, when; (2) *interrog. adv. and conj.,* where? (*ubiquitous*)
possum, posse, be able, can (*posse, possible, puissant*)

RECOGNITION VOCABULARY

īnsídiae, -árum, *f.*, ambush, plot, treachery (*insidious*)

ibi, *adv.*, there (*ib.* or *ibid.*)

tólerō, toleráre, bear, endure (*tolerate, toleration, tolerable, intolerable, intolerance*)

PRACTICE AND REVIEW

1. Oculī nostrī sine cūrā nōn valēbunt.
2. Sine pecūniā tyrannus superāre populum Rōmānum nōn poterit.
3. Nōn poterant tē dē poenā amīcōrum tuōrum monēre.
4. Parvus numerus Graecōrum ibi remanēre poterit.
5. Magister puerōs sine morā vocābit.
6. Glōria puellārum erat et est et semper erit fōrma.
7. Satisne sapientiae habēbimus?
8. Multī librī antīquī propter sapientiam erant magnī.
9. Glōria bonōrum librōrum semper manēbit.
10. Possuntne pecūnia ōtiumque cūrās vītae superāre?
11. Therefore, we cannot always see the real vices of a tyrant.
12. Few men will be able to tolerate an absolute ruler.
13. We shall always praise the great books of the Greeks.
14. Where can glory and (*use* -que) fame be perpetual?

SENTENTIAE ANTĪQUAE

1. Dionȳsius tum erat tyrannus Syrācūsānōrum. (Cicero. — Dionȳsius, -iī, a name. — Syrācūsānus, -ī, *a Syracusan.*)
2. Optāsne meam vītam fortūnamque gustāre? (Cicero. — optō, -āre, *wish.* — gustō, -āre, *taste.*)
3. Possumusne in malīs īnsidiīs esse salvī? (Cicero. — salvī is nom. plu. of salvus, -a, -um, *safe.* Can you explain why the nom. is used?)
4. Propter cūram meam in perpetuō perīculō nōn eritis. (Cicero.)
5. Propter vitia tua nihil tē in patriā tuā dēlectāre potest. (Cicero. — dēlectō, -āre, *delight.*)
6. Fortūna Pūnicī bellī secundī varia erat. (Livy. — Pūnicus, -a, -um, *Punic, Carthaginian.* — secundus, -a, -um, *second.* — varius, -a, -um, *varied.*)
7. Patria Rōmānōrum erat plēna Graecōrum librōrum statuārumque. (Cicero. — plēnus, -a, -um, *full.* — statua, -ae, *statue.*)
8. Sine deō animus nōn potest bonus esse. (Seneca. — deus, -ī, *god.*)
9. Vestra vīta mors est. (Cicero. — mors. nom. sing., *death.*)
10. Sī animus īnfīrmus est, nōn poterit bonam fortūnam tolerāre. (Publilius Syrus. — īnfīrmus, -a, -um, *not strong, weak.*)
11. Nec vitia nostra nec remedia tolerāre possumus. (Livy. — nec . . . nec, *neither . . . nor.* — remedium = English.)

12. Ubi lēgēs valent, ibi populus potest valēre. (Publilius Syrus. — lēgēs, nom. plu., *laws*.)

"I DO NOT LOVE THEE, DOCTOR FELL"

Nōn amo[3] tē, Sabidī, nec possum dīcere quārē.
Hoc Tantum possum dīcere: nōn amo tē.
(*Martial 1.32; meter: elegiac couplet — Sabidius, -iī, a name. — dīcere, *to say*. — quārē, *why*. — hoc tantum, *this only*, acc. case.)

ETYMOLOGY

English *library* is clearly connected with **liber**. Many European languages, however, derive their equivalent from **bibliothēca**, a Latin word of Greek origin meaning in essence the same thing as our word. What, then, do you suppose **biblos** meant in Greek? Cp. the Bible.

In the sentences[4]   2. option, adopt. — gusto, disgust. 5. delectable, delight. 7. plenary, plenipotentiary, plenty. 12. legal, legislative, legitimate, loyal.

French *y* in such a phrase as *il y a* ("there is") may prove more understandable when you know that *y* derives from **ibi**.

The following French words are derived from Latin as indicated: *êtes*, **estis**; *nôtre*, **noster**; *vôtre*, **vester**; *goûter*, **gustāre**. What, then, is one thing which the French circumflex accent indicates?

Footnotes

[1]It is easy, however, to pick out the personal endings.
[2]The imperfect of other verbs than **sum** and its compounds will be studied later.
[3]In a nom. sing. and in a polysyllabic 1st pers. sing. final -ō is often treated as short by poetic license.

[4]For the sake of brevity this phrase will henceforth be used to direct attention to words etymologically associated with words in the sentences indicated.

7

Third Declension: Nouns

*T*he general rule for the third declension, as for the first two declensions, is to add the case endings to the base.

NOUNS OF THE THIRD DECLENSION

	rēx, m. *king* rēg-	virtūs, f. *merit* virtūt-	homō, m. *man* homin-	corpus, n. *body* corpor-	Case Endings M. & F.	N.
Base						
Nom.	rēx(rēg-s)	vírtūs	hómō	córpus	-s —	—
Gen.	rḗg-is	virtū́tis	hóminis	córporis	-is	-is
Dat.	rḗg-ī	virtū́tī	hóminī	córporī	-ī	-ī
Acc.	rḗg-em	virtū́tem	hóminem	córpus	-em	—
Abl.	rḗg-e	virtū́te	hómine	córpore	-e	-e
Nom.	rḗg-ēs	virtū́tēs	hóminēs	córpora	-ēs	-a
Gen.	rḗg-um	virtū́tum	hóminum	córporum	-um	-um
Dat.	rḗg-ibus	virtū́tibus	homínibus	corpóribus	-ibus	-ibus
Acc.	rḗg-ēs	virtū́tēs	hóminēs	córpora	-ēs	-a
Abl.	rḗg-ibus	virtū́tibus	homínibus	corpóribus	-ibus	-ibus

DECLENSION

One of the greatest difficulties in this declension is the fact that the nominative singular frequently provides little clue about the form of the base[1] as it appears in the genitive. However, with a knowledge of the genitive and the endings, the rest of the declension is easy. The vocative has the same form as that of the nominative.

GENDER

The second great difficulty in this declension is gender. Rules have been concocted but, aside from the fact that nouns denoting human beings are masculine or feminine according to sense, the exceptions to most of the other rules are numerous.[2] The safest procedure is to learn the gender of each noun as it occurs.[3]

VOCABULARY

cívitās, -tátis, *f.,* state, citizenship (*city*)

hómō, hóminis, *m.,* human being, man; *cp.* **vir** (*homicide, homage;* but not the prefix *homo-*)

lábor, -ṓris, *m.,* labor, work, toil (*laboratory, belabor, collaborate, elaborate*)

líttera, -ae, *f.,* a letter of the alphabet; **lítterae, -ā́rum,** *plural,* a letter (epistle), literature (*literal, letters, belles-lettres, illiterate, alliteration*)

mōs, mṓris, *m.,* habit, custom, manner; **mṓrēs, mṓrum,** *plu.,* character (*mores, moral, immoral*)

pāx, pā́cis, *f.,* peace (*pacify, pacific, pacifist*)

térra, -ae, *f.,* earth, ground, land, country (*terrestrial, terrace, terrier, territory, inter* [verb], *subterranean, terra cotta*)

témpus, témporis, *n.,* time; occasion, opportunity (*temporary, contemporary, temporal, temporize, extempore, tense* of a verb)

vírtūs, virtū́tis, *f.,* manliness, courage, excellence, character, worth, virtue; *cp.* **vir** (*virtuoso, virtuosity, virtual*)

post, *prep.* + *acc.,* after, behind (*posterity, posterior, posthumous, P.M. = post meridiem, post-* as a prefix, *postgraduate, postlude,* etc.)

aúdeō, audḗre, dare (*audacious, audacity*)

RECOGNITION VOCABULARY

ámor, amṓris, *m.,* love (*amorous, enamored;* cp. **amō, amī́cus**)

vírgō, vírginis, *f.,* maiden, virgin (*Virginia*)

sub, *prep.* + *abl. with verbs of rest,* + *acc. with verbs of motion,* under, up under, close to (*sub-* or by assimilation *suc-, suf-, sug-, sup-, sus-,* in countless compounds: *suburb, succeed, suffix, suggest, support, sustain*)

PRACTICE AND REVIEW

1. Tum litterās magistrī vidḗbis.
2. Sine morā cīvitātem dē īnsidiīs monḗbit.
3. Nōn igitur audḗbunt ibi remanḗre.
4. Mṓrēs Graecōrum nōn erant sine culpīs vitiīsque.
5. Ubi hominēs satis virtūtis semper habent?
6. Tyrannus vester animōs sed malōs mōrēs habet.

7. Propter mōrēs hominum pācem vēram nōn habēbimus.
8. Poteritne cīvitās perīcula temporum nostrōrum superāre?
9. Post bellum multōs librōs dē pāce vidēbitis.
10. Officia sapeintiamque oculīs animī possumus vidēre. (**oculīs** = abl. of means.)
11. Without good character we cannot have peace.
12. Many human beings have small time for Greek literature.
13. After bad times true virtue and much labor will save the state.
14. The sons of your friends will have a small number of virtues.

SENTENTIAE ANTĪQUAE

1. Homō sum. (*Terence.)
2. Nihil sub sōle novum (*Ecclesiastes. — sōl, sōlis, m., *sun.* — (est) novum: novus, -a, -um, *new*.)
3. Carmina nova virginibus puerīsque cantō. (Horace. — carmen, -minis, n., *poem.* — cantō, -āre, *sing*.)
4. Laudās fortūnam et mōrēs antīquae plēbis. (*Horace. — plēbs, plēbis, f., *the common people*.)
5. Bonī propter amōrem virtūtis peccāre ōdērunt. (Horace. — peccō, -āre, *sin.* — ōdērunt, defective vb., 3d per. plu., *hate*.)
6. Sub principe dūrō temporibusque malīs audēs esse bonus. (Martial. — prīnceps, -cipis, *chief, prince;* dūrus, -a, -um, *hard, harsh*.)
7. Populus stultus virīs indignīs honōrēs saepe dat. (Horace. — honor, -ōris, *honor, office.* — indignus, -a, -um, *unworthy*.)
8. Nōmina stultōrum in parietibus vidēmus. (Cicero. — "Nihil novum"; the desire to scribble names and sentiments in public places is as old as antiquity! — nōmen, -inis, n., *name.* — pariēs, parietis, m., *wall of a building*.)
9. Ōtium sine litterīs mors est. (*Seneca. — mors, mortis, f., *death*.)
10. Dominus nōn potest timōrem pecūniā fugāre et post equitem sedet ātra cūra. (Horace. — dominus, -ī, *lord, master.* — timor, -ōris, *fear.* — fugō, -āre, *rout.* — eques, equitis, *horseman.* — sedeō, -ēre, *sit.* — āter, ātra, ātrum, *dark*.)
11. Multae nātiōnēs servitūtem tolerāre possunt; nostra cīvitās nōn potest. Praeclāra est recuperātiō lībertātis. (Cicero. — nātiō, -ōnis = Eng. — servitūs, -tūtis, *servitude.* — recuperātiō, -ōnis, *recovery.* — lībertās, -tātis = Eng.)
12. Nihil sine magnō labōre vīta mortālibus dat. (Horace. — mortālis, -is, *a mortal*.)
13. Quōmodo in perpetuā pāce esse poterimus? (Cicero. — quōmodo, *how*.)
14. Glōria in altissimīs Deō et in terrā pāx in hominibus bonae voluntātis. (*Luke. — altissimīs, abl. plu., *the highest.* — Deus, -ī, *God.* — voluntās, -tātis, *will*.)

ETYMOLOGY

From what Latin word do you suppose It. *uomo*, Sp. *hombre*, and Fr. *homme* and *on* are derived?

Tense meaning the "time" of a verb comes from **tempus** through old Fr. *tens;* but *tense* meaning "stretched tight" goes back to **tendō,...tēnsum**, *stretch.*

In late Latin **cīvitās** came to mean *city* rather than *state,* and thus it became the parent of the Romance words for city: It. *città*, Sp. *ciudad*, Fr. *cité*.

In the sentences   2. solar, solstice. — novel, novelty, novice, novitiate, innovate, renovate. 3. chant, enchant, incantation, cant, recant, canto, cantabile, precentor. 4. plebeian, plebe, plebiscite. 5. peccant, peccadillo. 6. dour, duration, endure, obdurate. 10. sediment, sedentary, dissident, reside, subside, subsidy, supersede. 14. volunteer, involuntary.

It may prove helpful to list the Romance and English equivalents of three suffixes given above in note 2.

Latin	Italian	Spanish	French	English
-tās, -tātis	-tà	-dad	-té	-ty
vēritās	verità	verdad	vérité	verity (truth)
antīquitās	antichità	antigüedad	antiquité	antiquity
-tiō, -tiōnis	-zione	-ción	-tion	-tion
nātiō	nazione	nación	nation	nation
ratiō	razione	ración	ration	ration
-tor, -tōris	-tore	-tor	-teur	-tor
inventor	inventore	inventor	inventeur	inventor
actor	attore	actor	acteur	actor

Footnotes

[1]As has been pointed out before, English derivatives are often helpful in this matter; e.g., **iter, itineris,** *journey:* itinerary; **cor, cordis,** *heart:* cordial; **custōs, custōdis,** *guard:* custodian.

[2]However, the following rules have few or no exceptions:

Masculine
-or, -ōris (amor, -ōris; labor, -ōris)
-tor, -tōris (victor, -tōris; scrīptor, -tōris, *writer*)
Feminine
-tās, -tātis (vēritās, -tātis, *truth;* lībertās, -tātis)
-tūs, -tūtis (virtūs, -tūtis; senectūs, -tūtis, *old age)*
-tūdō, -tūdinis (multitūdō, -tūdinis; pulchrūdō, -tūdinis)
-tiō, -tiōnis (nātiō, -tiōnis; ōrātiō, -tiōnis)

Neuter
-us (corpus, corporis; tempus, temporis; genus, generis)
-e, -al, -ar (mare, maris, *sea;* animal, animālis)
The gender of nouns under these rules will not be given in the notes.

[3]Actually, a very helpful device is to learn the proper form of some adjective like **magnus, -a, -um,** with the noun. This practice provides an easily remembered clue to the gender and is comparable to the learning of the definite article with nouns in Romance languages. For example: **magna virtūs, magnum corpus, magnus labor, magna arbor** *(tree),* **magnum marmor** *(marble).*

8

Third Conjugation: Present Infinitive, Present and Future Indicative, Imperative

*T*he present indicative and the future indicative of verbs of the third and the fourth conjugations, though not inherently difficult, cause students as much trouble as any other thing in the paradigms of conjugation; and yet these forms are among the most common. A little extra effort invested in mastering these forms promptly will pay rich dividends in every subsequent chapter.

PRESENT INFINITIVE ACTIVE: Dūcere, TO LEAD

PRESENT INDICATIVE ACTIVE

1. dū́c-ō   (*I lead*)
2. dū́c-is   (*you lead*)
3. dū́c-it   (*he leads*)

1. dū́c-imus   (*we lead*)
2. dū́c-itis   (*you lead*)
3. dū́c-unt   (*they lead*)

FUTURE INDICATIVE ACTIVE

1. dū́c-am   (*I shall lead*)
2. dū́c-ēs   (*you will lead*)
3. dū́c-et   (*he will lead*)

1. dūc-ḗmus   (*we shall lead*)
2. dūc-ḗtis   (*you will lead*)
3. dūc-ent   (*they will lead*)

PRESENT IMPERATIVE ACTIVE

2. **Sing.** (dū́c-e) dūc (*lead*)   2. **Plu.** dū́c-ite (*lead*)

PRESENT INFINITIVE

As **-āre** and **-ēre** by this time immediately indicate to you the first and the second conjugations respectively, so **-ĕre** will indicate the third. What, then, distinguishes the infinitive **dūcere** from the infinitive **monēre**?

PRESENT STEM AND PRESENT INDICATIVE

According to the rule for finding the present stem, you drop the infinitive ending **-re** and have **dūce-** as the present stem. To this you would naturally expect to add the personal endings to form the present indicative. The difficulty is that in this conjugation the stem vowel **-e-** has suffered so many changes that it is completely lost to view.[1] Consequently, the practical procedure is to memorize the endings.[2]

FUTURE INDICATIVE

The striking peculiarity of the future tense is the lack of the tense sign **-bi-**. Here **e** is the sign of the future in all the forms except the first.

PRESENT IMPERATIVE

In accordance with the rule already learned, the second person singular of the present imperative is simply the present stem; e.g., **mitte (mitte-re,** *send*), **pōne (pōne-re,** *put*). So **dūce** was the original form, and it appears in the early writer Plautus. Later, however, the **-e** was dropped from **dūce**, and it is wanting in three other forms: **dīc (dīce-re,** *say*), **fac (face-re,** *do*), and **fer (fer-re,** *bear*). The other verbs of this conjugation follow the rule as illustrated by **mitte** and **pōne**.

VOCABULARY

cópia, -ae, *f.,* abundance, supply; **cópiae, -árum,** *plu.,* supplies, troops, forces (*copious, copy*)

rátiō, -ōnis, *f.,* calculation; reason, judgment, consideration; system; manner, method (*ratio, ration, rational, irrational, ratiocination*)

ad, *prep. + acc.,* to, up to, near to, *in the sense of "place to which" with verbs of motion; contrast the dat. of indirect object. In compounds the* **d** *is sometimes assimilated to the following consonant so that* **ad** *may appear, for instance, as* **ac-** (**accipiō: ad-capiō**), **ap-** (**appellō: ad-pellō**), **a-** (**aspiciō: ad-spiciō**).

ex *or* **ē,** *prep. + abl.* out of, from; by reason of, on account of. (*The Romans used* **ex** *before consonants or vowels;* **ē** *before consonants only.*)

dum, *conj.,* while, as long as, at the same time that

ágō, ágere, drive, lead, do, act; pass, spend (*life or time*); **grātiās agere +** *dat.,* to thank someone (*agent, agenda, agile, agitate*)

dóceō, -ére, teach (*docile, document, doctor, doctrine, indoctrinate*) dúcō, -ere, lead; consider, regard (*ductile, abduct, adduce, deduce, educe, induce, produce, reduce, seduce*)

scríbō, -ere, write, compose (*ascribe, circumscribe, conscript, describe, inscribe, proscribe, postscript, rescript, subscribe, transcribe, scribble*)

PRACTICE AND REVIEW

1. Tempora nostra sunt mala; vitia nostra, magna.
2. Scrībit (scribet, scrībunt) igitur dē officiīs.
3. Tyrannus populum stultum ē terrā vestrā dūcet (dūcit).
4. Ubi satis ratiōnis animōrumque in hominibus erit?
5. Cōpia vērae virtūtis multās culpās superāre poterat.
6. In līberā cīvitāte vītam agimus.
7. Tyrannum tolerāre nōn dēbēmus.
8. Post parvam moram litterās dē īnsidiīs hominum stultōrum scrībēmus.
9. Your (plu.) money will remain there under the ground.
10. Write (sing. and plu.) many things about the glory of our state.
11. Does reason always lead men to virtuc?
12. Many books of the Greeks teach reason and wisdom.

SENTENTIAE ANTĪQUAE

1. Frāter meus vītam in ōtiō semper aget. (Terence. — frāter, -tris, *brother*.)
2. Age, age! Dūc mē ad fīlium meum. (Terence. — age, age = *come, come!*)
3. Ō amīcī, lībertātem perdimus. (Laberius. — lībertās, -tātis.[3] — perdō, -ere, *destroy*.)
4. Perīcula populō Rōmānō expōnam sine morā. (Cicero. — expōnō, -ere, *set forth*.)
5. Numquam perīculum sine perīculō vincēmus. (Publilius Syrus. — numquam, *never*. — vincō, -ere, *conquer*.)
6. Ex meīs errōribus hominibus rēctum iter dēmōnstrāre possum. (Seneca. — error, -ōris. — rēctus, -a, -um, *right*. — iter, itineris, *n., road, way*. — dēmōnstrō, -āre.)
7. Catullus Mārcō Tulliō Cicerōnī magnās grātiās agit. (Catullus. — Mārcus Tullius Cicerō.)
8. Eximia fōrma virginis oculōs hominum convertit. (Livy. — eximius, -a, -um, *extraordinary*.— convertō, -ere, *turn around, attract*.)
9. Agamemnon magnās cōpiās ē terrā Graecā ad Troiam dūcet. (Cicero. — Agamemnon, -onis.)
10. Amor laudis hominēs trahit. (Cicero. — laus, laudis, *f., praise*. — trahō, -ere, *draw, drag*.)
11. Auctōrēs pācis Caesar cōnservābit. (Cicero. — auctor, -ōris, *author*. — Caesar, -aris.)

12. Inter multās cūrās labōrēsque poēmata scrībere nōn possum. (Horace. — inter, prep. + acc., *among*. — poēma, poēmatis, n.)

13. Dum in magnā urbe dēclāmās, mī amīce, scrīptōrem Troiānī bellī in ōtiō relegō. (Horace. — urbs, urbis, f., *city*. — dēclāmō, -āre, *declaim*. — scrīptor, *writer*. — Troiānus, -a, -um. — re-legō, -ere, *re-read*.)

14. Nōn vītae, sed scholae, discimus. (*Seneca. — vitae and scholae, datives expressing purpose. — schola, -ae, *school*. — discō, -ere, *learn*) *See* Seneca, *Epistulae* 106.12.

15. Hominēs, dum docent, discunt. (*Seneca.)

16. Ratiō mē dūcet, nōn fortūna. (Livy.)

ETYMOLOGY

In the sentences   5. convince, evince, invincible, Vincent. 6. rectitude; cp. Eng. cognate *right*. — itinerary, itinerant. 11. kaiser, czar. 14. *School* comes through Lat. **schola** from Greek **scholē**, *leisure*. — disciple.

Footnotes

[1]It appears as -**i**- and -**u**-. Therefore, the present stem + the personal endings should actually be represented thus: **dūci-t, dūcu-nt**, etc.; but the division marked in the paradigm has been used deliberately to emphasize the variation of the vowel.

[2]This crude mnemonic device may help: (a) for the present use an IOU (**i** in 4 forms, **o** in the first, **u** in the last);

(b) for the future you have the remaining vowels, **a** and **e**.

[3]Hereafter in the notes, when a Latin word easily suggests an English derivative, the English meaning will be omitted.

9

Demonstrative Pronouns: Hic, Ille, Iste

$\mathbf{D}$*emonstrative pronouns are so called from the fact that the Romans used them when they pointed out*[1] *a person or thing as "this here" or "that there."*

ille, *that*				hic, *this*		
	M.	**F.**	**N.**	**M.**	**F.**	**N.**
Singular						
Nom.	ílle	ílla	íllud	hic[2]	haec	hoc
Gen.	illíus	illíus	illíus	huius[3]	huius	huius
Dat.	íllī	íllī	íllī	huic[4]	huic	huic
Acc.	íllum	íllam	íllud	hunc	hanc	hoc
Abl.	íllō	íllā	íllō	hōc	hāc	hōc
Plural						
Nom.	íllī	íllae	ílla	hī	hae	haec
Gen.	illórum	illárum	illórum	hórum	hárum	hórum
Dat.	íllīs	íllīs	íllīs	hīs	hīs	hīs
Acc.	íllōs	íllās	ílla	hōs	hās	haec
Abl.	íllīs	íllīs	íllīs	hīs	hīs	hīs

DECLENSION

In the paradigm the difficult forms have been underlined for special attention and memorization. Once past the irregular nominative forms and the characteristic - **īus** of the genitive singular and the **-ī** of the dative, you see that practically all the remaining forms follow the familiar pattern of **magnus**.

Iste, ista, istud, *that* (*near you*), *that of yours:* **Iste** follows the declension of **ille:** *Nom.* íste, ísta, ístud; *gen.* istíus, istíus, istíus; *Dat.* ístī, ístī, ístī; etc. Be ready to give all the forms orally.

DEMONSTRATIVES AS ADJECTIVES AND PRONOUNS

When demonstratives modify nouns, they play the role of adjectives. The following examples will provide practice with some of the more troublesome forms.

hic liber, *this book*
ille liber, *that book*
illīus librī, *of that book*
illī librī, *those books*
illī librō, *to that book*
illō librō, *by that book*
istīus amīcī, *of that friend (of yours)*
istī amīcī, *those friends (of yours)*
istī amīcō, *to that friend (of yours)*

hanc cīvitātem, *this state*
huic cīvitātī, *to this state*
illī cīvitātī, *to that state*
illae cīvitātēs, *those states*
haec cīvitās, *this state*
haec cōnsilia, *these plans*
hoc cōnsilium, *this plan*
hōc cōnsiliō, *by this plan*
huic cōnsiliō, *to this plan*

When used alone, demonstratives are pronouns[5] and can commonly be translated as "man," "woman," "thing," and the like, according to their gender and their context.

hic, *this man*
hanc, *this woman*
hunc, *this man*
haec, *this woman*
haec, *these things*
istum, *that man*
istārum, *of those women*

ille, *that man*
illa, *that woman*
illa, *those things*
huius, *of this man or woman*[6]
illī, *to that man or woman*[6]
illī, *those men*

ADJECTIVES WITH GENITIVE IN -īus AND DATIVE IN -ī.

The singular of nine adjectives of the first and the second declensions is irregular in that the genitive ends in -īus and the dative in -ī, following the pattern of illīus and illī above. Elsewhere in the singular and throughout the plural these are regular[7] adjectives of the first and the second declensions.

	sōlus, -a, -um, *alone, only*			**alius, alia, aliud,** *another, other*		
Singular						
Nom.	sólus	sóla	sólum	álius	ália	áliud
Gen.	solíus	solíus	solíus	alteríus[8]	alteríus	alteríus
Dat.	sólī	sólī	sólī	álī	álī	álī
Acc.	sólum	sólam	sólum	álium	áliam	áliud
Abl.	sólō	sólā	sólō	áliō	áliā	áliō
Plural						
Nom.	sólī	sólae etc.	sóla	álī	áliae etc.	ália

The other common adjectives in this group are:

ūnus, -a, -um (ūnĩus, etc.), *one*
alter, altera, alterum (alterĩus, etc.), *the other* (*of two*)
tōtus, -a, -um (tōtĩus, etc.), *whole*
ūllus, -a, -um (ūllĩus, etc.), *any*
nūllus, -a, -um (nūllĩus, etc.), *no, none*

VOCABULARY

lócus, -ī, *m.*, place; passage in literature; *plu.* **loca, -ōrum,** *n.*, places, region;
   loci, -ōrum, *m.*, passages (*allocate, dislocate, locality, locomotion*)
hic, haec, hoc, this; the latter; *at times weakened to* he, she, it, they
ílle, ílla, íllud, that; the former; the famous; he, she, it, they
íste, ísta, ístud, that of yours, that; such; *sometimes with contemptuous force*
álter, áltera, álterum, the other (of two), second; *cp.* **alius,** an-other
   (*alter, alteration, alternate, alternative, altercation, altruism*)
núllus, -a, -um, no, not any, none (*null, nullify, annul*)
sólus, -a, -um, alone, only, the only; **nōn sólum...sed etiam,** not only...but also (*sole, solitary, soliloquy, solo, desolate*)
tótus, -a, -um, whole, entire (*total, in toto*)
únus, -a, -um, one, single, alone (*unit, unite, union, onion, unanimous, unicorn, uniform, unique, unison, universal*)
énim, *postpositive conj.*, for, in fact, truly
in, *prep. + acc.*, into (also **in** + *abl.*, in, *v. Ch. 3*). *In composition* **in-** *may also appear as* **il-, ir-, im-;** *and it may have its literal meanings or have simply an intensive force. (Contrast the inseparable negative prefix* **in-,** *not, un-, in-.)*
nunc, *adv.*, now, at present

PRACTICE AND REVIEW

1. Tōtus liber litterās Rōmānās laudat.
2. Hī igitur illī grātiās agent.
3. Illud dē vitiīs huius scrībam.
4. Ille alterī magnam cōpiam pecūniae tum dabit.
5. Potestne bona fortūna huius terrae esse perpetua?
6. Labor ūnīus nōn poterit tōtam cīvitātem cōnservāre.
7. Mōrēs istīus tyrannī erant malī.
8. Nūllī magistrī sub istō audent vēra docēre.
9. Valēbitne pāx post hoc bellum?
10. Dum illī ibi remanent, hī nihil agunt.
11. This (man) is writing about the glory of the other man.
12. The whole state will thank this man alone.
13. On account of that courage of yours those (men) will lead no troops into these places.

14. Will one good book overcome the faults of our times?

SENTENTIAE ANTĪQUAE

1. Ubi illās nunc vidēre possum? (Terence.)
2. Hic illam in mātrimōnium dūcet. (Terence. — mātrimōnium, -iī.)
3. Huic cōnsiliō palmam dō. (Terence. — palma, -ae, *palm branch* of victory.)
4. Virtūtem enim illīus virī amāmus. (Cicero.)
5. Sōlus hunc servāre potes. (Terence.)
6. Poena istīus ūnīus hunc morbum cīvitātis relevābit sed perīculum remanēbit. (Cicero. — morbus, -ī, *disease*. — relevō, -āre, *relieve, diminish.*)
7. Hī enim dē exitiō huius cīvitātis et tōtīus orbis terrārum cōgitant. (Cicero. — exitium, -iī, *destruction*. — orbis, -is, m., *circle, orb;* orbis terrārum, *the world.*)
8. Nōn est locus istīs hominibus in hāc terrā. (Martial. — hominibus, dat. case.)
9. Nōn sōlum ēventus hoc docet (iste est magister stultōrum) sed etiam ratiō. (Livy. —ēventus, nom. sing. masc., *outcome.*)

"SATIS"

Habet Āfricānus mīliēns, tamen captat.
Fortūna multīs dat nimis, satis nūllī.

(*Martial 12.10; meter: choliambic. — Āfricānus, -ī, a proper name. — mīliēns, call it *millions*. — tamen, *nevertheless*. — captō, -āre, *hunt for legacies*. — nimis, *too much*. — nūllī, here dat. to nēmō, *no one.*)

"SATIS"

Sī vīs studēre philosophiae animōque, hoc studium nōn potest valēre sine frūgālitāte. Haec frūgālitās est paupertās voluntāria. Tolle, igitur, istās excūsātiōnēs: "Nōndum satis pecūniae habeō. Sī quandō illud 'satis' habēbō, tum mē tōtum philosophiae dabō." Incipe nunc philosophiae, nōn pecūniae, studēre.

(Seneca, *Epistulae* 17.5. — vīs, irreg. form, *you wish*. — studeō, -ēre, + dat., *be eager for, devote oneself to;* studium, -iī. — frūgālitās -tātis. — paupertās, -tātis, *small means, poverty*. — voluntārius, -a, -um. — tollō, -ere, *take away*. — excūsātiō, -ōnis. — nōndum, *not yet*. — quandō, *ever*. — incipe, imperative, *begin.*)

ETYMOLOGY

A few examples of **in-** as a prefix connected with the preposition: invoke, induce, induct, inscribe, inhibit, indebted.

Some examples of **in-** as an inseparable negative prefix: invalid, innumerable, insane, insuperable, intolerant, inanimate, infamous, inglorious, impecunious, illiberal, irrational.

Latin **ille** provided Italian, Spanish, and French with the definite article and with pronouns of the third person; and Latin **ūnus** provided these languages with the indefinite article. Some of these forms and a few other derivatives are shown in the following table:

Latin	Italian	Spanish	French
ille, illa	il, la	el, la	le, la
ille, illa	egli, ella	él, ella	il, elle
ūnus, ūna	un(o), una	un(o), una	un, une
tōtus	tutto	todo	tout
sōlus	solo	solo	seul
alter	altro	otro	autre

French *là* ("there") comes from **illắc** (**viā**), an adverbial form meaning *there* (*that way*); similarly, It. *là* and Sp. *allá*.

Footnotes

[1]**Dēmōnstrō, -āre,** *point out, show.*
[2]Where **-c** appears, it is an enclitic (originally **-ce**) and not part of the declensional ending.
[3]Pronounce as if spelled **húi-yus.**
[4]The **ui** in **huic** is a diphthong, not two separate vowels (Introd. p. xxvii).
[5]A pro-noun is a word used in place of a noun (**prō,** *for, in place of*).
[6]As a rule, only the nominative and the accusative of the neuter were used as pronouns. In the genitive, the dative, and the ablative cases the Romans preferred to use the demonstrative as an adjective in agreement with the noun for "thing"; e.g., **huius reī,** *of this thing.*
[7]Except for the neuter singular form **aliud** (cp. **illud**).
[8]This form, borrowed from **alter,** is more common than the regular one, **alius.**

10

Fourth Conjugation and -iō Verbs of the Third

*T*his chapter introduces the last of the regular conjugations: the fourth conjugation: **audiō, audīre**, hear; the **-iō** verbs of the third conjugation: **capiō, cápere**, take.

PRESENT INDICATIVE ACTIVE

1. dúcō[1]	aʹudi-ō	cápi-ō	(*I hear, take*)
2. dúcis	aʹudī-s	cápĭ-s	(*you hear, take*)
3. dúcit	aʹudi-t	cápi-t	(*he, she, it, hears, takes*)
1. dúcimus	aʹudĭ-mus	cápĭ-mus	(*we hear, take*)
2. dúcitis	aʹudī-tis	cápĭ-tis	(*you hear, take*)
3. dúcunt	aʹudi-unt	cápi-unt	(*they hear, take*)

FUTURE INDICATIVE ACTIVE

1. dúcam	aʹudi-am	cápi-am	(*I shall hear, take*)
2. dūcēs	aʹudi-ēs	cápi-ēs	(*you will hear, take*)
3. dúcet	aʹudi-et	cápi-et	(*he will hear, take*)
1. dūcémus	aʹudi-émus	capi-émus	(*we shall hear, take*)
2. dūcétis	aʹudi-étis	capi-étis	(*you will hear, take*)
3. dúcent	aʹudi-ent	cápi-ent	(*they will hear, take*)

PRESENT IMPERATIVE ACTIVE

2. dūc(e)	aʹudī	cápe	(*hear, take*)
2. dúcite	audī-te	cápĭ-te	(*hear, take*)

CONJUGATION OF Audiō

The -**īre** distinguishes the infinitive of the fourth conjugation from the infinitives of the other conjugations (**laud-áre, mon-ére, dúc-ĕre, aud-íre, cáp-ĕre**).

As in the case of the first two conjugations, the rule for the formation of the present indicative is to add the personal endings to the present stem (**audi-**). In the third person plural this rule would give us **audi-nt** but the actual form is **audi-unt**, reminiscent of **dūcunt**. Note that by a long **i** the Romans could in pronunciation distinguish three forms in the present of **audiō** from three otherwise identical forms of **dūcō**:

> aúdīs, audīmus, audītis
> dúcis, dúcimus, dúcitis

For the future of **audiō** a good rule of thumb is this: to the present stem, **audī-**, add the future endings of **dūcō**: -am, -ēs, -et, -ēmus, -ētis, -ent. Once again, as in the third conjugation, **-e-** is the characteristic vowel of the future.

In forming the present imperative of **audiō** did the Romans follow the rules for **laudō** and **moneō**?

CONJUGATION OF Capiō

The infinitive **capĕre** is clearly an infinitive of the third conjugation, not of the fourth. The imperative forms also show that this is a verb of the third conjugation.

The present and the future indicative of **capiō** follow the pattern of **audiō**, except that **capiō**, like **dūcō**, has a short **i** in **cápis, cápimus, cápitis**.

VOCABULARY

> **nātúra, -ae,** *f.*, nature (*natural, preternatural, supernatural*)
>
> **cum,** *prep.* + *abl.*, with. *As a prefix* **cum** *may appear as* **com-, con-, cor-, col-, co-,** *and means* with, together, completely, *or simply has an intensive force.*
>
> **cápiō, cápere,** take, capture, get. *In compounds the* ă *becomes* ĭ, **-cipiō:** **ac-cipiō, ex-cipiō, in-cipiō, re-cipiō,** *etc.* (*capable, capacious, capsule, captious, captive, captor*)
>
> **fáciō, fácere,** make, do. *In compounds the* ă *becomes* ĭ, **-ficiō:** **cōn-ficiō, per-ficiō,** *etc.* (*facile, fact, faction, factotum, facsimile, faculty, fashion, feasible, feat*)

fúgiō, fúgere, flee, hurry away, avoid, shun (*fugitive, fugue, refuge, subterfuge*)

véniō, veníre, come (*advent, adventure, avenue, convene, contravene, covenant, event, intervene, parvenu, prevent, provenience*)

invéniō, -íre, come upon, find (*invent, inventory*)

vívō, vívere, live (*convivial, revive, survive, vivacity, vivid, viviparous, vivisection*)

RECOGNITION VOCABULARY

fília, -ae, *f.*, daughter

hóra, -ae, *f.*, hour, time

senéctūs, -útis, *f.*, old age

vía, -ae, *f.*, way, road, street (*via, viaduct, deviate, devious, voyage, pervious, impervious, previous*)

PRACTICE AND REVIEW

1. Quid facere dēbēmus?
2. Nihil cum ratiōne agitis.
3. Ille virtūtem labōris docēre audet.
4. Hic dē senectūte scrībit; ille, dē amōre.
5. Ex librīs ūnīus virī nātūram hārum īnsidiārum vidēmus.
6. Istī sōlī bellum amant.
7. Ubi cīvitās virōs bonōrum mōrum inveniet?
8. Ex multīs terrīs in ūnum locum cum amīcīs venīte.
9. Post paucās hōrās viam invenīre poterāmus.
10. Cōpiae vestrae illum ibi nōn capient.
11. Alter Graecus hanc pecūniam sub hōc librō inveniet.
12. We shall come to your land with your friend.
13. While he lives, we can have no peace.
14. The whole state now shuns and will always shun these vices.
15. He will thank the whole people.

SENTENTIAE ANTĪQUAE

1. Cupiditātem pecūniae glōriaeque fugite. (Cicero. —cupiditās, -tātis, *desire.* — pecūniae, gen. case.)
2. Officium meum faciam. (*Terence.)
3. Fāma tua et vīta fīliae tuae in perīculum venient. (Terence.)
4. Vīta nōn est vīvere sed valēre. (Martial.)
5. Semper magnō cum timōre incipiō dīcere. (Cicero. — timor, -ōris, m., *fear.* — incipiō, -ere, *begin.* — dīcō, -ere, *speak.*)
6. Sī mē dūcēs, Mūsa, corōnam magnā cum laude capiam. (Lucretius — Mūsa, -ae, *Muse.* —corōna, -ae, *crown.* — laus, laudis, f., *praise.*)

7. Vīve memor mortis; fugit hōra. (Persius. — memor, adj. nom. sing. masc., *mindful*. — mors, mortis, f., *death*.)

8. Rapite, amīcī, occāsiōnem dē hōrā. (Horace. — rapiō, -ere, *snatch*. — occāsiō, -ōnis, f., *opportunity*.)

9. Paucī veniunt ad senectūtem. (*Cicero.)

10. Sed fugit, intereā, fugit tempus. (Virgil. — intereā, *meanwhile*.)

11. Fāta viam invenient. (*Virgil. — fātum, -ī, *fate*.)

12. Bonum virum nātūra, nōn ōrdō, facit. (*Publilius Syrus. — ōrdō, -inis, *rank*.)

13. Nihil cum amīcitiā illīus possum comparāre. (Cicero. — amīcitia, -ae, abstract noun of amīcus. — comparō, -āre.)

14. Obsequium parit amīcōs; vēritās parit odium. (Cicero. — obsequium, -iī, *compliance*. — pariō, -ere, *produce*. — vēritās, -tātis, *truth*. — odium, -iī, *hate*.)

ETYMOLOGY

In the sentences

5. timorous, timid, timidity, intimidate. — incipient, inception. 6. museum, music. — corona, coronation, coronary, coroner, corolla, corollary. 7. memory, memoir, commemorate. 8. rapid, rapture, rapacious. 14. obsequious. — verity. — odium, odious.

Footnote

[1]Dūcō is repeated here for comparison and review; see Ch. 8.

11

Personal Pronouns Ego and Tū; Demonstrative Pronouns Is and Īdem

*T*he Romans had distinct pronouns by which they could designate the first person (I, me, we, us) and the second person (you, singular and plural). However, to indicate the third person (he, him, she, her, it, they, them) they used a somewhat colorless demonstrative pronoun (**is, ea, id,** this, that, he, she, it), which is declined much as **ille** is.

Singular

1st Person — Ego, *I*			2nd Person — Tū, *You*	
Nom.	égo	(*I*)	tū	(*you*)
Gen.	méī	(*of me*)	túī	(*you*)
Dat,	míhi	(*to/for me*)	tíbi	(*to/for you*)
Acc.	mē	(*me*)	tē	(*you*)
Abl.	mē	(*by/with/from me*[1])	tē	(*by/with/from you*[1])

Plural

Nom.	nōs	(*we*)	vōs	(*you*)
Gen.	{ nóstrum (*of us*)		{ véstrum (*of you*)	
	{ nóstrī (*of us*)		{ véstrī (*of you*)	
Dat.	nóbīs	(*to/for us*)	vóbīs	(*to/for you*)
Acc.	nōs	(*us*)	vōs	(*you*)
Abl.	nóbīs	(*by/with.from us*)	vóbīs	(*by/with/from you*)

3RD PERSON = DEMONSTRATIVE Is, Ea, Id, He, She, It, This, That

	Masculine		Feminine		Neuter	
Singular						
N.	is	(*he*[2])	éa	(*she*[2])	id	(*it*[2])
G.	eius[3]	(*of him, his*)	eius	(*of her, her*)	eius	(*of it, its*)
D.	éī	(*to/for him*)	éī	(*to/for her*)	éī	(*to/for it*)
A.	éum	(*him*)	éam	(*her*)	id	(*it*)
A.	éō	(*by/w./fr. him*)	éā	(*by/w./fr. her*)	éō	(*by/w./fr. it*)
Plural						
N.	éī, íī	(*they,* masc.)	éae	(*they,* fem.)	éa	(*they,* neut.)
G.	eórum	(*of them, their*)	eárum	(*of them, their*)	eórum	(*of them, their*)
D.	éīs	(*to/for them*)	éīs	(*to/for them*)	éīs	(*to/for them*)
A.	éōs	(*them*)	éās	(*them*)	éa	(*them*)
A.	éīs	(*by/w./fr. them*)	éīs	(*by/w./fr. them*)	éīs	(by/w/fr. them)

USE OF PRONOUNS

Since these pronouns are employed as substitutes for nouns, they are naturally used as their corresponding nouns would be used: as subjects, direct objects, indirect objects, objects of prepositions, and the like.

Ego tibi (vōbīs) librōs dabō, *I shall give the books to you.*
Ego eī (eīs) librōs dabō, *I shall give the books to him* or *her* (*to them*).
Tū mē (nōs) nōn capiēs, *you will not capture me* (*us*).
Eī id ad nōs mittent, *they* (masc.) *will send it to us.*
Vōs eōs (eās, ea) nōn capiētis, *you will not capture them* (*them*).
Eae ea ad tē mittent, *they* (fem.) *will send them* (*those things*) *to you.*

Notice, however, that the Romans used the nominatives of the pronouns (**ego, tū,** etc.) only when they wished to stress the subject. Commonly, therefore, the pronominal subject of a Latin verb is not indicated except by the ending.

Dabō, *I shall give.*   Capiētis, *you will capture.*
Ego dabō, **I** *shall give.*   Vōs capiētis, **you** *will capture.*

Notice also that the genitives of **ego** and **tū** (namely **meī, nostrum, nostrī; tuī;, vestrum, vestrī**) were not used to indicate possession.[4] To convey this idea, the Romans preferred the possessive pronouns, which you have already learned:

meus, -a, -um, *my*   tuus, -a, -um, *your*
noster, -tra, -trum, *our*   vester, -tra, -trum, *your*

The genitives of **is, ea, id,** on the other hand, *were* used to indicate possession. For these genitives we have the following translations:

eius, *of him, his*   eōrum, *of them, their* (masc.)
eius, *of her, her*   eārum, *of them, their* (fem.)
eius, *of it, its*   eōrum, *of them, their* (neut.)

Study the possessives in the following examples, in which **mittam** governs all the nouns.

Mittam (I shall send)

pecūniam meam (*my money*).   amīcōs meōs (*my friends*).
pecūniam nostram (*our money*).   amīcōs nostrōs (*our friends*).
pecūniam tuam (*your money*).   amīcōs tuōs (*your friends*).
pecūniam vestram (*your money*).   amīcōs vestrōs (*your friends*).
pecūniam eius (*his, her, money*). amīcōs eius (*his, her friends*).
pecūniam eōrum (*their money*).   amīcōs eōrum (*their friends*).
pecūniam eārum (*their money*).   amīcōs eārum (*their friends*).

The possessive pronouns of the first and the second persons naturally agree with their noun in *gender*, *number*, and *case*, as all adjectives agree with their nouns. The possessive genitives **eius, eōrum,** and **eārum,** being genitives, remain unchanged regardless of the gender, number, and case of the noun on which they depend.[5]

DEMONSTRATIVE Īdem, Eadem, Idem, *the Same*

To the forms of **is, ea, id** add the indeclinable suffix **-dem** and you can say "the same" in Latin; e.g., **eius-dem, eō-dem, eae-dem, eōs-dem.** The only troublesome forms are these:

Singular

	M.	F.	N.
Nom.	īdem	éadem	ĭdem
Acc.	eúndem[6]	eándem	ĭdem

Plural

	M.	F.	N.
Gen.	eōrúndem[6]	eārúndem	eōrúndem

VOCABULARY

égo, méi, I, *etc.* (*ego, egoism, egotism, egotistical*)
tū, túī, you
is, ea, id, this, that; he, she, it (i.e. = id est, that is)
īdem, éadem, ĭdem, the same (*id., identical, identity, identify*)
némō, nūllíus,[7] néminī, néminem, núllō[7] *or* núllā, *m. or f.*, no one, nobody
cárus, -a, -um, dear (*caress, charity, cherish*)

a′utem, *postpositive adv.*, however; moreover

béne, *adv. of* **bonus,** well (*benefit, benefactor, beneficient*)

míttō, -ere, send (*admit, commit, emit, omit, permit, remit, submit, transmit*)

séntiō, -íre, feel, perceive, think, experience (*assent, consent, dissent, presentiment, resent*)

PRACTICE AND REVIEW

1. Eum ad eam mittunt.
2. Tū autem fīliam eius amās.
3. Ego hoc faciō. Quid tū faciēs?
4. Vōsne eāsdem litterās ad eum mittere audēbitis?
5. Dūc mē ad eius magistrum (ad tuum magistrum).
6. Post eius labōrem grātiās magnās eī agēmus.
7. Tūne dē senectūte eius scrībis?
8. Audē esse semper ídem.
9. Venitne nātūra mōrum nostrōrum ex nōbīs sōlīs?
10. Dum ratiō nōs dūcit, valēmus.
11. Hanc virtūtem in hōc virō ūnō invenīmus.
12. Sine autem labōre pāx in cīvitātem eōrum nōn veniet.
13. His life was dear to the whole people.
14. You will find them with me.
15. We, however, shall capture their forces on this road.
16. I shall write the same things to him about you.

SENTENTIAE ANTĪQUAE

1. Virtūs tua mē amīcum tibi facit. (Horace. — **amicum** here is an adjective agreeing with **mē** and meaning *friendly*.)
2. Id sōlum est cārum mihi. (Terence.)
3. Sī valēs, bene est; ego valeō. (Pliny. — bene est, *it is well*.)
4. Bene est mihi quod tibi bene est. (Pliny. — quod, *because*.)
5. "Valē." "Et tū bene valē." (Terence.)
6. Quid hī dē tē sentiunt? (Cicero.)
7. Omnēs ídem sentiunt. (*Cicero. — omnēs, *all men,* nom. plu.)
8. Videō nēminem[8] ex eīs esse amīcum tibi. (Cicero.)
9. Tū nōbīscum[9] vīvere nōn potes, quod tū et tuī dē exitiō tōtīus cīvitātis cōgitātis. (Cicero. — quod, *because*. — tuī, *your men*. — exitium, -iī, *destruction*.)
10. Ēdúc tēcum[9] tuōs ex hōc locō. (Cicero. — ē-dūcō.)
11. Hominēs vidēre caput eius in Rōstrīs poterant. (Livy. — caput, -itis, n., *head*. — eius: Antony proscribed Cicero and had the great orator's head displayed on the Rostra! — Rōstra, -ōrum; see Etymology below.)

12. Nōn omnēs eadem amant. (Horace.)

13. Nec tēcum possum vīvere nec sine tē (*Martial. — nec...nec, *neither...nor.*)

14. Vērus amīcus est alter īdem. (Cicero. — Explain how **alter īdem** can mean "a second self.")

ETYMOLOGY

Cārus was sometimes used in the sense of *expensive* just as English "dear" can be used.

In the sentences   10. educate (ē + stem **dūc-**). 11. capital, captain, capitulate, decapitate. — **Rōstra,** the ramming beaks of captured ships affixed to the speakers' platform in the Roman Forum to attest a victory won in 338 B.C. at Antium (Anzio). These beaks gave their name to the platform. Though the plural *rostra* is still the regular form, we sometimes use the singular *rostrum.*

Some Romance derivatives from the Latin personal pronouns follow.

Latin	Italian	Spanish	French
ego, tū	io, tu	yo, tu	je, tu
mihi, tibi	mi, ti		
mē, tē	me, te	me, te	me, moi, te, toi[10]
nōs, vōs (nom.)	noi, voi	nosotros, vosotros[11]	nous, vous
nōs, vōs (acc.)		nos, os	nous, vous

Footnotes

[1]You will find that a preposition is used in Latin with most ablatives when the noun or pronoun in the ablative indicates a person.

[2]Also *this/that man, woman, thing.*

[3]Pronounced e'i-yus.

[4]They were used as genitives of the whole (**magna pars meī,** *a large part of me;* **quis nostrum,** *who of us*) or as objective genitives (**timor tuī** or **nostrī,** *fear of you* or *of us*). **Nostrum** and **vestrum** were used as partitive genitives: **nostrī** and **vestrī** were used as objective genitives.

[5]Possessives were often omitted where easily supplied from the context.

[6]Try pronouncing **eumdem** or **eōrumdem** rapidly and you will probably end up changing the **m** to **n** before **d** as the Romans did.

[7]The genitive and ablative forms of **nūllus** are usually found in place of **nēminis** and **nēmine.**

[8]**Nēminem** is the subject of **esse.** Note that the subject of the infinitive is put in the accusative case.

[9]When used with a personal or a relative pronoun, **cum** is regularly appended to the pronoun as an enclitic: **nōbīscum** for **cum nōbīs,** **tēcum** for **cum tē,** etc.

[10]*moi, toi* came from accented **mē, tē,** and *me, te* came from unaccented **mē, tē.**

[11]*-otros* from **alterēs.**

12

Perfect Active System of All Verbs; Principal Parts

As *you turn to the perfect[1] system of Latin verbs (i.e., the perfect, the pluperfect, and the future perfect tenses), you will be pleased to learn that you no longer have to worry about four different conjugations. For in the perfect active system verbs of all conjugations follow the same rule: perfect stem + appropriate endings.*

PRINCIPAL PARTS

To ascertain the perfect stem of a Latin verb you must know the principal parts of the verb, just as you must similarly know the principal parts of an English verb[2] if you want to use English correctly. The normal principal parts of a normal Latin verb are four as illustrated by **laudō** in the following paradigm. The first two principal parts are already familiar to you.

1. Present Active Indicative: laúdō, *I praise*
2. Present Active Infinitive: laudā́re, *to praise*
3. Perfect Active Indicative: laudā́vī, *I praised, have praised*
4. Perfect Passive Participle: laudā́tum,[3] *praised, having been praised*

The principal parts of the verbs which have appeared in the paradigms are as follows:

Pres. Ind.	Pres. Inf.	Perf. Ind.	Perf. Pass. Partic.
la'udō	laudā́re	laudā́vī, *I praised*	laudā́tum, *having been praised*
móneō	monḗre	mónuī, *I advised*	mónitum, *having been advised*
dū́cō	dū́cere	dū́xī, *I led*	dúctum, *having been led*
cápiō	cápere	cḗpī, *I took*	cáptum, *having been taken*
a'udiō	audī́re	audī́vī, *I heard*	audítum, *having been heard*
sum	ésse	fúī, *I was*	futū́rus,[4] *about to be*
póssum	pósse	pótuī, *I was able*	———[4]

53

THE PERFECT ACTIVE SYSTEM

A glance at the verb forms in the column headed "Perfect Indicative" shows that no one rule can be formulated to cover all the changes from the present to the perfect tenses.[5] Those changes must be a matter of memory or reference.

A second glance at the column, however, shows that all perfects do have one thing in common, the final -ī. The dropping of this -ī gives the perfect stem, to which can be added endings to form the perfect, the pluperfect, and the future perfect indicative.

PERFECT INDICATIVE ACTIVE

I praised, have praised[6]	*I led, have led*	*I was, have been*	**Endings**
1. laudā́v-ī	dū́x-ī	fú-ī	-ī
2. laudāv-ístī	dūx-ístī	fu-ístī	-istī
3. laudā́v-it	dū́x-it	fú-it	-it
1. laudā́v-imus	dū́x-imus	fú-imus	-imus
2. laudāv-ístis	dūx-ístis	fu-ístis	-istis
3. laudāv-é̄runt[7]	dūx-é̄runt[7]	fu-é̄runt[7]	-ḗrunt[7]

Pluperfect Active Indicative		**Future Perfect Active Indicative**[8]	
I had praised	*I had been*	*I shall have praised*	*I shall have been*
1. laudā́v-eram	fú-eram	laudā́v-erō	fú-erō
2. laudā́v-erās	fú-erās	laudā́v-eris	fú-eris
3. laudā́v-erat	fú-erat	laudā́v-erit	fú-erit
1. laudāv-erā́mus	fu-erā́mus	laudāv-érimus	fu-érimus
2. laudāv-erā́tis	fu-erā́tis	laudāv-éritis	fu-éritis
3. laudā́v-erant	fú-erant	laudā́v-erint	fú-erint

The perfect endings are quite new and must be memorized.

The pluperfect, being "more (than) perfect,"[9] is in effect the perfect stem + **eram,** the imperfect of **sum.**

The future perfect is in effect the perfect stem + **erō,** the future of **sum.** Note, however, that the third person plural is -**erint,** not -**erunt.**

PRINCIPAL PARTS OF VERBS IN THE VOCABULARIES

The principal parts of the verbs in the previous vocabularies, as listed below, and of all verbs in subsequent vocabularies, *must be memorized*, and this can best be done by saying them aloud. Try to view this necessity with imagination not only as increasing your Latin power but also as increasing your knowledge of English. Many English words have the same stem as that of the second principal part of the Latin verb, and many others have the same stem as that of the fourth principal part. Consequently, English words can help you with Latin principal parts, and Latin principal parts can increase your understanding of English words; e.g., de-duce (**dūcere**), de-duct (**ductum**); re-mit (**mittere**); re-miss (**missum**); in-scribe (**scrībere**), con-script (**scrīptum**); future (**futūrus**); con-vince (**vincere**), con-vict (**victum**).[10]

amō, amāre, amāvī, amātum, *love*
cōgitō, -āre, -āvī, -ātum, *think, plan*
dō, dāre, -dedī, -datum, *give* (Note the irregularity short a's.)
(errō, -āre, -āvī, -ātum, *wander, err*)
servō, -āre, -āvī, -ātum, *save, keep*. Similarly, cōnservō (1).
superō (1), *surpass, conquer*
(tolerō (1), *bear, endure*)
vocō (1), *call*

audeō, audēre, ausus sum, *dare (ausus sum* will be explained later)
dēbeō, dēbēre, dēbuī, dēbitum, *owe, ought*
doceō, docēre, docuī, doctum, *teach*
habeō, habēre, habuī, habitum, *have, hold, possess*
valeō, valēre, valuī, valitūrus, *be strong or well, fare well*
videō, -ēre, vīdī, vīsum, *see*
remaneō, -ēre, -mānsī, -mānsum, *remain*

agō, agere, ēgī, actum, *drive, lead, do*
mittō, mittere, mīsī, missum, *send*
scrībō, -ere, scrīpsī, scrīptum, *write*
vīvō, -ere, vīxī, victum, *live*

sentiō, sentīre, sēnsī, sēnsum, *feel, perceive*
veniō, venīre, vēnī, ventum, *come*
inveniō, -īre, -vēnī, -ventum, *come upon, find*

faciō, facere, fēcī, factum, *make, do*
fugiō, -ere, fūgī, fugitum, *flee, avoid*

VOCABULARY

déus, déí, *m., nom. plu.* **dí,** *dat. and abl. plu.,* **dís**[11] , god (*adieu, deify, deity*)

líbértās, -tátis, *f.,* liberty (cp. **líber,** free; **líberáre,** to free)

rēx, régis, *m.,* king (*regal, regalia, royal, regicide;* cp. *rajah*)

díū, *adv.,* long, for a long time

díco, -ere, díxí, díctum, say, tell, speak; name, call (*dictate, dictum, diction, dictionary, dight, ditto, contradict, indict, edict, verdict*)

vínco, -ere, vící víctum, conquer, overcome (*convince, convict, evince, evict, invincible, Vincent, victor, vanquish*)

RECOGNITION VOCABULARY

Ásia, -ae, *f.,* Asia, *commonly referring to Asia Minor*

ca'elum, -í, *n.,* sky, heaven (*ceiling, celestial, Celeste*)

Ca'esar, -aris, *m.,* Caesar (*kaiser, czar*)

PRACTICE AND REVIEW

1. Vōs nōbis dē eius ratiōnibus scrīpsistis.
2. Ratiōnēs alterīus fīliae nōn fuērunt eaedem.
3. Nēmō in hanc viam ex alterā viā fūgerat.
4. Illī autem ad nōs cum eius amīcō vēnērunt.
5. Idem vitium in tē sēnsimus.
6. Sōlus enim vir bonus ista vitia vincet.
7. Post paucās hōrās Caesar Asiam cēpit.
8. Ūnus vir nātūram hōrum perīculōrum sēnsit.
9. Potuistisne bonam vītam sine lībertāte agere?
10. Pāx fuit tōtī populō cāra.
11. Caesar did not remain there a long time.
12. You had not seen the nature of that place.
13. We had found no fault in him.
14. They sent her to him with me.

SENTENTIAE ANTÍQUAE

1. In prīncipiō Deus creāvit caelum et terram; et Deus creāvit hominem. (Genesis. — prīncipium, -iī, *beginning.* — creō (1).)
2. In triumphō Caesar praetulit hunc titulum: "Vēnī, vīdī, vīcī." (Suetonius. — triumphus, -ī, *triumphal procession,* here celebrating his quick victory at Zela in Asia Minor in 47 B.C. — praeferō, -ferre, -tulī, -lātum, *display.* — titulus, -ī, *placard.*)
3. Vīxit, dum vīxit, bene. (*Terence.)
4. Adulēscēns vult diū vīvere; senex diū vīxit. (Cicero. — adulēscēns, -ntis, *young man.* — vult, irreg., *wishes.* — senex, senis, *old man.*)
5. Nōn ille diū vīxit sed diū fuit. (*Seneca.)
6. Hui, dīxistī pulchrē![12] (*Terence. — hui, an exclamatory sound.)

7. Sophoclēs ad summam senectūtem tragoediās fēcit. (*Cicero. — Sophoclēs, -is. — summam, *extreme*. — tragoedia, -ae, *tragedy*.)

8. Illī nōn sōlum pecūniam sed etiam vītam prō patriā prōfūdērunt. (Cicero. — prō + abl., *in behalf of*. — prōfundō, -ere, -fūdī, -fūsum, *pour forth*.)

LIBERTY

Rēgēs Rōmam ā prīncipiō habuērunt; lībertātem Lūcius Brūtus Rōmānīs dedit. (Tacitus. — ā + abl., *from*.)

Sub Caesare autem lībertātem perdidimus. (Laberius. — perdō, -ere, -didī, -ditum, *destroy, lose*.)

Ubi lībertās cecidit, nēmō līberē dīcere audet. (Publilius Syrus. — cadō, -ere, cecidī, cāsum, *fall*.)

AN UNTIMELY DEATH

Fundānus, amīcus noster, fīliam āmīsit, et haec tibi dē eius morte scrībō. Illa puella cāra nōn annōs trēdecim (= XIII) implēverat. Magnā cum patientiā valētūdinem tulit et vigor animī dūrāvit ad extrēmum. Ō acerba mors!

(Pliny. — Fundānus, -ī, a name. — ā-mittō, *lose*. — mors, mortis, f., *death*. — annus, -ī, *year*. — impleō, -plēre, -plēvī, -plētum, *complete*. — patientia, -ae. — valētūdō, -dinis. f., (*ill*) *health*. — ferō, ferre, tulī, lātum, *bear*. — vigor, -ōris, m. — dūrō (1), *last*. — extrēmum, *the last*. — acerbus, -a, -um, *bitter*.)

ETYMOLOGY

Further examples of the help of English words in learning principal parts of Latin verbs are:

Latin Verb	Pres. Stem in Eng. Word	Perf. Partic. Stem In Eng. Word
videō	pro-vide (vidēre)	pro-vision (vīsum)
maneō	per-manent (manēre)	mansion (mānsum)
agō	agent (agere)	act (āctum)
vīvō	re-vive (vīvere)	victuals (vīctum)
doceō	docile (docēre)	doctor (doctum)
sentiō	sentiment (sentīre)	sense (sēnsum)
veniō	inter-vene (venīre)	inter-vention (ventum)
faciō	facile (facere)	fact (factum)

In the sentences   2. prefer, prelate. — title, titular. 4. adolescent. — senile, senescent. 8. confound, confuse, effuse, effusive, fuse, fusion, refund, refuse, transfusion. *Liberty:* perdition. — cadence, case, casual, accident, incident, coincidence, decay, deciduous, occasion, occident. *Untimely Death:* mortify, mortal, immortal. — complete, deplete, replete. — valetudinarian. — acerbity, exacerbate.

Footnotes

[1]Per + factus, *thoroughly done*, therefore *past* relative to a present, a past, or a future time.

[2]In fact the principal parts of an English verb closely parallel those of a Latin verb:

(1) Present Tense:

praise	lead	take	see	sing	be/am

(2) Past Tense:

praised	led	took	saw	sang	was

(3) Past Participle:

praised	led	taken	seen	sung	been

Note that, since the pres. ind. and the pres. inf. are normally identical in English, only one form need be given. Note also that the past participle is really a past passive participle like the Latin **laudātum**

[3]It is convenient to use only the neuter form as the 4th principal part. However, in the case of transitive verbs this participle is a complete verbal adjective of the 1st and the 2nd declensions: **laudātus, -a, -um**. The use of this form will be explained later, in Ch. 19 and Ch. 23.

[4]Some verbs, like **sum**, lack a perfect passive participle but do have a future active participle, which can be used as a 4th principal part; some verbs, like **possum**, lack the 4th principal part entirely.

[5]However, verbs of the first conjugation usually have the characteristic sequence of **-āre, -āvī, -ātum**. Consequently, a vocabulary entry reading **vocō** (1) means that this is a verb of the first conjugation with principal parts like those of **laudō**.

[6]Note that the perfect serves both as a simple past tense, *I praised*, and as a present perfect, *I have praised*.

[7]The alternate ending, **-ēre** (**laudāvēre, dūxēre, fuēre**), appears only once or twice in this book.

[8]Actually the future perfect is not common except in conditions.

[9]*Plūs (quam) perfectum;* also called "past perfect" because it indicates time prior to a past time.

[10]Therefore, whenever a verb appears in a vocabulary, be sure to examine the English words associated with it for evidence of this sort.

[11]The plural forms **deī, deīs** became established during the Augustan Period.

[12]The Romans regularly made adverbs out of 1st and 2nd declension adjectives by adding **ē** to the base of the adjective; e.g., **vērus: vērē**, *truly;* **pulcher: pulchrē**, *beautifully;* **līber: līberē**, *freely.* **Bene** comes somewhat irregularly from **bonus**.

13

Reflexive Pronouns and Possessives; Intensive Pronoun

REFLEXIVE PRONOUNS

Reflexive pronouns differ from other pronouns in that they are used ordinarily only in the predicate and refer to the subject. "Reflexive," which derives from re-flexus, -a, -um (reflectō, -ere, -flexī, -flexum, bend back) means bent back; and so reflexive pronouns are in thought "bent back" through the verb to the subject, or, to put it another way, they "reflect" the subject. English examples are:

Reflexive Pronouns	Personal Pronouns
I praised *myself*.	You praised *me*.
Cicero praised *himself*.	Cicero praised *him* (Caesar).

DECLENSION OF REFLEXIVE PRONOUNS

Since reflexive pronouns by definition cannot serve as subjects of finite[1] verbs, they naturally have no nominative case. Otherwise, the declension of the reflexives of the first and the second persons is the same as that of the corresponding personal pronouns.

The reflexive pronoun of the third person, however, has its own peculiar forms.

REFLEXIVE PRONOUNS

	1st Person	**2nd Per.**	**3rd Person**
Singular			
Nom.	—	—	—
Gen.	méī (*of myself*)	túī	súī (*of himself, herself, itself*)
Dat.	míhi (*to/for myself*)	tíbi	síbi (*to/for himself, etc.*)
Acc.	mē (*myself*)	tē	sē (*himself, herself, itself*)
Abl.	mē (*by/w./fr. myself*[2])	tē	sē (*by/w./fr. himself, etc.*)
Plural			
Nom.	—	—	—
Gen.	nóstrī (*of ourselves*)	véstrī	súī (*of themselves*)
Dat.	nóbīs (*to/for ourselves*)	vóbīs	síbi (*to/for themselves*)
Acc.	nōs (*ourselves*)	vōs	sē (*themselves*)
Abl.	nóbīs (*by/w./fr. ourselves*)	vóbīs	sē (*by/w./fr. themselves*)

PARALLEL EXAMPLES OF REFLEXIVE AND PERSONAL PRONOUNS OF 1ST AND 2ND PERSONS.[3]

1. Tū laudāvistī **tē**, *you praised yourself.*
2. Cicerō laudāvit **tē**, *Cicero praised you.*

3. Nōs laudāvimus **nōs**, *we praised ourselves.*
4. Cicerō laudāvit **nōs**, *Cicero praised us.*

5. Egō scrīpsī litterās **mihi**, *I wrote a letter to myself.*
6. Cicerō scrīpsit litterās **mihi**, *Cicero wrote a letter to me.*

PARALLEL EXAMPLES OF REFLEXIVE AND PERSONAL PRONOUNS OF 3RD PERSON

1. Cicerō laudāvit **sē**, *Cicero praised himself.*
2. Cicerō laudāvit **eum**, *Cicero praised him* (e.g., Caesar).

3. Rōmānī laudāvērunt **sē**, *the Romans praised themselves.*
4. Rōmānī laudāvērunt **eōs**, *the Romans praised them* (e.g., the Greeks).

5. Cicerō scrīpsit litterās **sibi**, *Cicero wrote a letter to himself.*
6. Cicerō scrīpsit litterās **eī**, *Cicero wrote a letter to him* (Caesar).

REFLEXIVE POSSESSIVES

The reflexive possessives of the first and the second persons are identical with the regular possessives already familiar to you: **meus, tuus, noster, vester**. They will never cause you any difficulty.

The reflexive possessive of the third person, however, is the adjective **suus, sua, suum,** *his (own), her (own), its (own), their (own)*. This must be carefully distinguished from the nonreflexive possessive genitives **eius, eōrum, eārum** (v. Ch. 11), which do not refer to the subject.

1. Cicerō laudāvit amīcum **suum,** *Cicero praised his (own) friend.*
2. Cicerō laudāvit amīcum **eius,** *Cicero praised his* (Caesar's) *friend.*

3. Rōmānī laudāvērunt amīcum **suum,** *the Romans praised their (own) friend.*
4. Rōmānī laudāvērunt amīcum **eōrum,** *the Romans praised their* (the Greeks') *friend.*

5. Cicerō scrīpsit litterās amīcīs **suis,** *Cicero wrote a letter to his (own) friends.*
6. Cicerō scrīpsit litterās amīcīs **eius,** *Cicero wrote a letter to his* (Caesar's) *friends.*
7. Cicerō scrīpsit litterās amīcīs **eōrum,** *Cicero wrote a letter to their* (the Greeks') *friends.*

THE INTENSIVE PRONOUN Ipse

The intensive **ipse, ipsa, ipsum,** *myself, yourself, himself, herself, itself,* etc., follows the peculiar declensional pattern of the demonstratives in the genitive and the dative singular; otherwise, it is like **magnus, -a, -um.**[4] The Romans used the intensive pronoun to emphasize a noun or pronoun of any person in either the subject or the predicate of a sentence.

Cicerō **ipse** laudāvit mē, *Cicero himself praised me.*
Cicerō laudāvit mē **ipsum,** *Cicero himself praised me myself* (*actually*).
Ipse laudāvī eius amīcum, *I myself praised his friend.*
Cicerō scrīpsit litterās vōbīs **ipsīs,** *Cicero wrote a letter to you yourselves.*
Cicerō mīsit Caesaris litterās **ipsās,** *Cicero sent Caesar's letter itself* (*the actual letter*).

VOCABULARY

Cícerō, -ónis, *m.,* Cicero
córpus, córporis, *n.,* body (*corps, corpse, corpuscle, corpulent, corporal, corporeal, corporation, incorporate, corset*)
ípse, ípsa, ípsum, *intensive pronoun,* himself, herself, itself, *etc.*

nómen, nóminis, *n.*, name (*nomenclature, nominate, nominative, nominal, noun, pronoun, renown, denomination, ignominy*)

súi, *reflex. pron. of 3rd per.*, himself, herself, itself, themselves (*suicide, per se*)

súus, -a, -um, *reflex. poss. adj. of 3rd per.*, his own, her own, its own, their own

ánte, *prep. + acc.*, before (*in place or time*), in front of; *as adv.*, **ānte,** before, previously; *not to be confused with Greek "anti," against* (*antedate, ante-room, anterior, antediluvian, A.M. = ante meridiem*)

nam, *conjunction,* for

númquam, *adv.*, never

per, *prep. + acc.*, through; **per-,** *as a prefix,* through, thoroughly, completely, very (*perchance, perforce, perhaps, perceive, perfect, perspire, percolate, percussion, perchloride*)

iúngō, -ere, iúnxī, iúnctum, join (*join, joint, junction, juncture, adjunct, conjunction, enjoin, injunction, subjunctive*)

RECOGNITION VOCABULARY

díligō, -ere, dīléxī, dīléctum, esteem, love

PRACTICE AND REVIEW

1. Sē tēcum iūnxērunt.
2. Tōtus populus lībertātem amāvit.
3. Rēx enim mē ipsum capere numquam potuit.
4. Ad rēgem eōrum per illum locum fūgistis.
5. Dī animōs in corpora hominum ē caelō mittunt.
6. Ipsī per sē eum vīcērunt.
7. In viā Cicerō amīcum eius vīdit, nōn suum.
8. Nēmō fīliam Augustī ipsīus diū dīligere potuit.
9. Hī Cicerōnem ipsum sēcum iūnxērunt.
10. Ante illam hōram litterās suās mīserat.
11. Ille bonam senectūtem habuit, nam bene vīxerat.
12. Cicero came to Caesar himself.
13. Cicero will join his (Caesar's) name with his own.
14. Cicero esteemed himself and you esteem yourself.
15. Cicero praised his own books and I now praise my own books.
16. Cicero himself had not seen his (Caesar's) book.

SENTENTIAE ANTĪQUAE

1. Ipse ad eōs contendit equitēsque ante sē mīsit. (Caesar. — contendō, -ere, -tendī, -tentum, *hasten.* — eques, equitis, *horseman.*)
2. Ipsī nihil per sē sine eō facere potuērunt. (Cicero.)

3. Ipse signum suum et litterās suās recognōvit. (Cicero. —signum, -ī, *seal.* — recognōscō, -ere, -cognōvī, -cognitum, *recognize.*)

4. Quisque ipse sē dīligit, nam quisque per sē sibi cārus est. (Cicero. — quisque, quidque, *each one.*)

5. Ex vitiō alterīus sapiēns ēmendat suum. (*Publilius Syrus. — alterīus, v. Ch. 9, n. 8. — sapiēns, -ntis, *wise man, philosopher.* — ēmendō (1), *correct.*)

6. Recēde in tē ipsum. (*Seneca. — recēdō, -ere, -cessī, -cessum, *withdraw.*)

7. Animus sē ipse alit. (*Seneca. — alō, -ere, aluī, altum, *nourish.*)

8. Homō doctus in sē semper dīvitiās habet. (Phaedrus. — doctus, -a, -um, v. doceō. — dīvitiae, -ārum, *riches.*)

ALEXANDER AT THE TOMB OF ACHILLES or
THE PEN IS MIGHTIER THAN THE SWORD

Magnus ille Alexander multōs scrīptōrēs āctōrum suōrum sēcum habuit. Is enim ante tumulum Achillis ōlim stetit et dīxit: "Fortūnātus fuistī, Ō adulēscēns, quod Homērum laudātōrem tuae virtūtis invēnistī." Et vērē! Nam, sine *Īliade* illā, īdem tumulus et corpus eius et nōmen obruere potuit.

(Cicero, *Prō Archiā* 24. — ille, when placed after the word which it modifies, means *that famous.* — scrīp-tor, -ōris. — ācta, -ōrum. — tumulus, -ī, *mound, grave.* — Achillēs, -is. — ōlim, adv., *once.* — stō, stāre, stetī, statum, *stand.* — quod, *because.* — Īlias, -adis, f., *Iliad.* — obruō, -ere, -ruī, -rutum, *overwhelm, bury.* — potuit, *could have, might have.*)

AUTHORITARIANISM

Amīcī Pȳthagorae in disputātiōnibus saepe dīxērunt: "Ipse dīxit." 'Ipse' autem erat Pȳthagorās; nam huius auctōritās etiam sine ratiōne valuit.

(Cicero, *Dē Nātūrā Deōrum* 1.5.10. —Pȳthagorās, -ae. — disputātiō, -ōnis, *debate.* — auctōritās, -tātis, *authority.* — etiam, adv., *even.*)

ETYMOLOGY

In the sentences 1. contend, contention, contentious. — equestrian; cp. equus, *horse.* 3. signet, signal, sign, signify, design, ensign, insignia, resign. 5. emend, emendation, mend. 6. recede, recession. 7. alimentary, alimony. *Alexander:* stable, state, station, statue, stature, status, stanza, circumstance, constant, estate, extant, instance, obstacle, substance; cp. stand (= Eng. cognate).

Footnotes

[1]"Finite" verb forms are those which are limited (**fīnītus, -a, -um,** *having been limited, bounded*) by person and number.

[2]See Ch. 11, n. 1.

[3]The order of the words in these illustrations was determined by the desire to illustrate the nature of the reflexive graphically.

[4]*Gen.* ipsíus, ipsíus, ipsíus; *Dat.* ípsī, ípsī, ípsī; *Acc.* ípsum, ípsam, ípsum, etc. See Appendix for full paradigm.

14

I-Stem Nouns of the Third Declension; Ablatives of Means, Accompaniment, and Manner

*S*ome nouns of the third declension differ from those already learned in that they show a characteristic i at certain points. Because of this i these nouns are called i-stem nouns, and the rest are known as consonant-stem nouns.

Cons.-stem Reviewed	Parisyllabics[1]		Base In 2 Consonants	Neut. In -e, -al, -ar	Irregular
rēx, rēgis, m., *king*	cīvis, -is, m., *citizen*	nūbēs, -is, f., *cloud*	urbs, -is, f., *city*	mare, -is, n., *sea*	vīs, vīs, f., *force;* plu. *strength*
N. rḗx	cī́vis	nūbḗs	úrbs	máre	vīs
G. rḗgis	cī́vis	nū́bis	úrb-is	máris	(vīs)
D. rḗgī	cīvī́	nūbī́	úrbī́	márī	(vī)
A. rḗgem	cī́vem	nū́bem	úrbem	máre	vim
A. rḗge	cī́ve	nū́be	úrbe	márī	vī
N. rḗgēs	cī́vēs	nūbḗs	úrbēs	mária	vī́rēs
G. rḗgum	cī́vium	nū́bium	úrbium	márium[3]	vī́rium
D. rḗgibus	cī́vibus	nū́bibus	úrbibus	máribus	vī́ribus
A. rḗgēs	cī́vēs[2]	nūbḗs[2]	úrbēs[2]	mária	vī́rēs[2]
A. rḗgibus	cī́vibus	nū́bibus	úrbibus	máribus	vī́ribus

DECLENSION

Although the **i** in the **-ium** of the genitive plural marks the only consistent difference between most **i**-stem nouns and the consonant-stem nouns, the following summary of the chief categories of **i**-stem nouns will prove helpful.

Masculine and Feminine.[4]

A. Parisyllabic[5] nouns ending in **-is** (nom.), **-is** (gen.) or **-ēs** (nom.), **-is** (gen.).

> hostis, hostis, m.; hostium; *enemy*
> nāvis, nāvis, f.; nāvium; *ship*
> mōlēs, mōlis, f.; mōlium; *mass, structure*

B. Nouns in **-s** or **-x** which have a base ending in two consonants.

> ars, art-is, f.; artium; *art, skill*
> dēns, dent-is, m.; dentium; *tooth*
> nox, noct-is, f.; noctium; *night*
> arx, arc-is, f.; arcium; *citadel*

Neuters in -e, -al, -ar: mare, animal, exemplar.

Note that in this category the characterizing **i** appears not only in the genitive plural but in the ablative singular and the nominative and accusative plural as well. This category of nouns is relatively small in common usage; only **mare** is important for this book.

IRREGULAR VĪS

The common and irregular **vīs** must be thoroughly memorized and must be carefully distinguished from **vir**. Note that the characteristic **i** appears in most forms. Practice with the following forms: **virî, virēs, virîs, vîrium, vîribus, virōs, virum.**

ABLATIVE WITHOUT A PREPOSITION

So far the ablative has appeared in conjunction with prepositions and for that reason has occasioned little dfficulty. However, the Romans frequently used a simple ablative without a preposition to express ideas which in English are introduced by a preposition. The proper interpretation of such ablatives requires two things: (1) a knowledge of the prepositionless categories and (2) an analysis of the context to see which category is the most logical.

ABLATIVE OF MEANS OR INSTRUMENT

The ablative of means is one of the most important of the prepositionless categories. It answers the questions *by means of what?*, *by what?*, *with what?* and its English equivalent is a phrase introduced by the prepositions *by*, *by means of*, *with*.

Litterās stilō scrīpsit, *he wrote the letter with a pencil* (stilus, -ī).
Cīvēs pecūniā vīcit, *he conquered the citizens with/by money*.
Id meīs oculīs vīdī, *I saw it with my own eyes*.
Suīs labōribus urbem cōnservāvit, *by his own labors he saved the city*.

ABLATIVES OF ACCOMPANIMENT AND MANNER

You have already learned the use of **cum** + ablative to indicate (1) accompaniment, which answers the question *with whom?* and (2) manner, which answers the question *how?*

Cum amīcīs vēnērunt, *they came with friends* (= with whom?)
Cum celeritāte vēnērunt, *they came with speed* (= how?; *speedily*. — celeritās, -tātis).
Id cum eīs fēcit, *he did it with them* (= with whom?).
Id cum virtūte fēcit, *he did it with courage* (=how?; *courageously*).

Your only real difficulty will come in translating from English to Latin. If *with* tells *with whom* or *how*, use **cum** + ablative; if *with* tells *by means of what*, use the ablative without a preposition.

VOCABULARY

ars, ártis, *f.*, art, skill (*artifact, artifice, artificial, artless, artist, artisan, inert, inertia*)

cívis, cívis, *m. and f.*, citizen (*civil, civilian, civility, incivility, civilize, civic;* cp. **cívitās, cīvilis**)

iūs, iúris, *n.*, right, law (*jurisdiction, jurisprudence, juridical, jurist, jury, just, justice*)

máre, máris, *n.*, sea (*marine, mariner, marinate, maritime, submarine; mere* = Eng. cognate, archaic for "small lake.")

mors, mórtis, *f.*, death (*mortal, immortal, mortify, mortgage; murder* = Eng. cog.)

pars, pártis, *f.,* part, share; direction (*party, partial, partake, participate, participle, particle, particular, partisan, partition, apart, apartment, depart, impart, repartee*)

senténtia, -ae, feeling, thought, opinion (*sentence, sententious;* cp. **sentiō**)

urbs, úrbis, *f.,* city (*urban, urbane, suburban*)

vis, vis, *f.,* force, power, violence; **vírēs, vírium,** *plu.,* strength (*vim*)

gérō, -ere, géssī, géstum, carry, carry on, manage, conduct, accomplish (*gerund, gesture, gesticulate, jest, congest, digest, suggest, exaggerate*)

téneō, -ére, ténuī, téntum, hold, keep, possess; restrain; **-tineō, -ēre, -tinuī, -tentum** *in compounds, e.g.,* **contineō** (*tenable, tenacious, tenant, tenet, tenure, tentacle, tenor, continue, content, continent, pertinent, pertinacity, lieutenant, appertain, detain, retain, sustain*)

RECOGNITION VOCABULARY

trāns, *prep.* + *acc.,* across

cúrrō, -ere, cucúrrī, cúrsum, run (*current, cursive, cursory, course, coarse, discursive, incur, occur, recur*)

tráhō, -ere, tráxī, tráctum, draw, drag (*attract, contract, retract, subtract, tractor,* etc.; v. Etymology section below.)

PRACTICE AND REVIEW

1. Magnam partem illārum urbium capiet vī pecūniae; cum virtūte.
2. Ante Caesaris ipsīus oculōs trāns viam cucurrimus et fūgimus.
3. Nēmō vitia sua videt.
4. Monuitne eōs dē vīribus illārum urbium?
5. Ipsī lībertātem cīvium suōrum servāverant.
6. Nōmina multārum urbium Americānārum ab nōminibus urbium antīquārum trāximus.
7. Pars cīvium per urbem ad mare cucurrit.
8. That tyrant did not long preserve the rights of these citizens.
9. Great is the force of the arts.
10. The king will do that with care; with money; with his own friends.
11. Cicero felt and said the same thing concerning himself and the nature of death.

SENTENTIAE ANTĪQUAE

1. Et Deus aquās maria appellāvit. (Genesis. — aqua, -ae, *water;* **aquās** is direct object; **maria** is predicate accusative, or objective complement.[6] — appellō (1) *call, name.*)
2. Terra ipsa hominēs et animālia creāvit. (Lucretius. — creō (1).)

3. Pān servat ovēs et magistrōs ovium. (Virgil. — Pān, nom., the god Pan. — ovis, -is, f., *sheep*.)

4. Parva formīca onera magna ōre trahit. (Horace. — formīca, -ae, *ant*. — onus, oneris, n., *load*. — ōs, ōris, n., *mouth*.)

5. Auribus teneō lupum. (*Terence. — a picturesque, proverbial statement of a dilemma. — auris, -is, f., *ear*.— lupus, -ī, *wolf*.)

6. Ille magnam turbam clientium habet. (Horace. — turba, -ae, *throng*. — cliēns, -ntis, "*client*," *dependent*.)

7. Hunc nēmō vī neque pecūniā superāre potuit. (Ennius. — neque, *nor*.)

8. Animus eius erat ignārus artium malārum. (Sallust. — ignārus, -a, -um, *ignorant*.)

9. Magna pars meī mortem vītābit. (Horace. — vitō (1), *avoid*.)

10. Vōs exemplāria Graeca semper versāte. (Horace. — exemplar, -āris, n., *model, original*. — versō (1), *turn, study*.)

11. Nōn vīribus et celeritāte corporum magna gerimus, sed sapientiā et sententiā et arte. (Cicero. — celeritās, -tātis, *swiftness*.)

12. Istī caelum, nōn animum suum, mūtant sī trāns mare currunt. (Horace. — mūtō (1), *change*.)

13. Numquam in hāc urbe prōditōrēs patriae iūra cīvium tenuērunt. (Cicero. — prōditor, -ōris, *betrayer*.)

14. Saepe in hāc cīvitāte perniciōsōs cīvēs morte multāvērunt. (Cicero. — perniciōsus, -a, -um. — multō (1), *punish*.)

15. Cum perniciōsīs cīvibus aeternum bellum geram. (Cicero. — aeternus, -a, -um, *eternal*.)

STORE TEETH

Thāis habet nigrōs, niveōs Laecānia dentēs.
Quae ratiō est? Ēmptōs haec habet, illa suōs.
(*Martial 5.43; meter: elegiac couplet. — Thāis and Laecānia are names of women. — niger, -gra, -grum, *black*. — niveus, -a, -um, *snowy*. — quae (interrog. adj. modifying **ratiō**), *what*. — ēmptōs (dentēs), perf. pass. partic., *bought, purchased*.)

ETYMOLOGY

Also connected with **trahō** are: abstract, detract, detraction, distract, distraction, distraught, extract, protract, portray, portrait, retreat, trace, tract, tractable, intractable, traction, contraction, retraction, trait, treat, treaty.

In the Sentences 2. creator, creature, procreate, recreate, recreation. 4. formic, formaldehyde. — onus, onerous. — oral, orifice; cp. **ōrō**, Ch. 36. 6. turbid, turbulent, disturb, perturb, perturbation, imperturbable. 9. evitable, inevitable. 11. celerity, accelerate, accelerator. 12. mutable, immutable, mutual, commute, transmute, permutation. *Store Teeth*. Negro (Spanish from *niger*), Negroid; dental, dentist, dentifrice, dentil, indent, dandelion (Fr. *dent de lion*), tooth = Eng. cognate.

Pan (sent. 3), the Greek god of woods and countryside, was accredited with the power of engendering sudden fear in people. Hence from Greek comes our work *panic*. (However, *pan-*, as in *Pan-American*, comes from another Greek word meaning *all*.)

Study the following Romance derivatives:

Latin	Italian	Spanish	French
ars, artis; artem	arte	arte	art
mors, mortis; mortem	morte	muerte	mort
pars, partis; partem	parte	parte	parti
pēs, pedis; pedem	piede	pie	pied
dēns, dentis; dentem	dente	diente	dent
nāvis, nāvis; nāvem	nave	nave	navire
			nef (*nave*)
nox, noctis; noctem	notte	noche	nuit

Clearly these Romance derivatives do not come from the nominative of the Latin words.[7] The rule is that Romance nouns and adjectives of Latin origin generally derive from the accusative form, often with the loss of some sound or feature of the final syllable.

Footnotes

[1]See note 5 below.

[2]There is an alternate acc. plu. form in -īs (the regular form until the Augustan Period), which is not used in this book.

[3]This form is given arbitrarily even though it does not occur in extant Roman literature.

[4]The majority of these nouns are feminine, but the exceptions still make it necessary to learn the gender of each noun.

[5]I.e., having the same number of syllables in the nom. sing. and the gen. sing.; **pār** (*equal*) + **syllaba.**

Canis, canis, *dog*, and **iuvenis, -is,** *youth*, are exceptions, having **-um** in the gen. plu.

[6]Such verbs as *call* (**appellō, vocō**), *consider* (**dūcō, habeō**), *choose* (**legō**), *make* (**faciō, creō**) may be followed by two accusatives: one is the direct object; the other is a predicate noun or adjective, as can be seen by inserting "to be" between the two accusatives.

[7]The only exception thus far in this book has been Fr. fils, *son*, from Lat. **fīlius.** (Old Fr. fiz, whence Eng. Fitz-, *natural son*, e.g., Fitzgerald.)

15

Imperfect Indicative Active of the Four Conjugations; Ablative of Time

*A*s *in the perfect system, the endings of the imperfect tense are the same in all conjugations[1]: tense sign -bā- plus the personal endings of the present system as given in Chapter I. These endings (-bam, -bās, -bat, etc.) are added to the present stem as the paradigms below indicate. In early Latin audiō had an imperfect audī-bam, according to the rule, but it later acquired an -ē- from the third conjugation, which gives us the form audī-ēbam.*

IMPERFECT INDICATIVE ACTIVE

	(laudā-re)	(monē-re)	(dūce-re)	(audī-re)	(cape-re)
1.	laudā́-ba-m	monḗbam	dūcḗbam	audiḗbam	capiḗbam
2.	laudā-bā́-s	monḗbās	dūcḗbās	audiḗbās	capiḗbās
3.	laudā́-ba-t	monḗbat	dūcḗbat	audiḗbat	capiḗbat
1.	laudā-bā́-mus	monēbā́mus	dūcēbā́mus	audiēbā́mus	capiēbā́mus
2.	laudā-bā́-tis	monēbā́tis	dūcēbā́tis	audiēbā́tis	capiēbā́tis
3.	laudā́-ba-nt	monḗbant	dūcḗbant	audiḗbant	capiḗbant

MEANING OF THE IMPERFECT

What did the Romans accomplish by this imperfect tense? Whereas the perfect tense was used to indicate a *single* act in past time (i.e. our simple past tense) or an act which took place in the past but which has results in or relevance for the present (i.e., our present perfect tense), the imperfect portrayed an action as *going on, repeated,* or *habitual* in past time. If the perfect tense is a snapshot of the past, the imperfect is a moving picture of the past.

Eum monuī, { *I warned him* (simple past).
                    { *I have warned him* (present perfect).

Eum monēbam, { *I was warning him, kept warning him.*
                        { *I used to warn him, habitually warned him.*

Dabam, *I was giving, used to give.*

Ipse dīcēbat, *he himself was in the habit of saying, used to say.*
    (Ipse dīxit, *he himself said.*)
Rōmānī vincēbant, *the Romans used to conquer.*
Fugiēbāmus, *we were fleeing.*
Vocābat, *he kept calling.*
Veniēbātis saepe, *you came* (*used to come*) *often.*

Clearly the imperfect is more descriptive and alive than the perfect; and, if you keep this in mind, you will find the analysis of the imperfects very interesting.

ABLATIVE OF TIME WHEN OR WITHIN WHICH

The idea of *time when* or *within which* the Romans expressed by the ablative without a preposition. The English equivalent is usually a prepositional phrase introduced by *at, on, in,* or *within.*

Eō tempore nōn poteram id facere, *at that time I could not do it.*
Eōdem diē vēnērunt, *they came on the same day* (**diē,** abl. of **diēs,** *day*).
Aestāte lūdēbant, *in summer they used to play.*
Paucīs hōrīs id faciet, *in (within) a few hours he will do it.*

VOCABULARY

Itália, -ae, *f.*, Italy (*italics, italicize*)
páter, pátris, *m.*, father; *cp.* **patria** (*paternal, patrician, patrimony, patron*)

míser, mísera, míserum, wretched, miserable, unfortunate (*misery, Miserere*)

ínter, *prep.* + *acc.*, between, among (*common as Eng. prefix*)

ítaque, *adv.*, and so, therefore

quóniam, *conj.*, since

commíttō, -ere, -mísī, -míssum, entrust, commit (*committee, commission, commissary, commitment, noncommissioned, noncom*)

exspéctō, -áre, -ávī, -átum, look for, expect (*expectancy, expectation*)

iáciō, iácere, iḗcī, iáctum, throw, hurl. *This verb appears in compounds as* -iciō, -icere, -iēcī, iectum: *e.g.,* ēiciō, -ere, ēiēcī, ēiectum, throw out, drive out (*abject, adjective, conjecture, dejected, eject, inject, interject, object, project, subject, reject, trajectory*)

intéllegō, -ere, intellḗxī, intelléctum, understand (*intelligent, intelligible, intellect*)

mū́tō, -áre, -ávī, -átum, change, alter; exchange (*mutable, immutable, mutual, commute, permutation, transmutation, molt*)

tímeō, -ére, tímuī, fear, be afraid of, be afraid (*timid, timorous, intimidate*)

PRACTICE AND REVIEW

1. Inter ea perícula mortem timēbāmus.
2. Fīlius per agrōs cum patre currēbat.
3. Itaque rēx puerum miserum in mare iēcit, nam īram cīvium timuit.
4. Nēmō eandem partem Asiae ūnā hōrā vincet.
5. Illās urbēs ūnā viā iūnxērunt.
6. Itaque librōs eius trāns Italiam mīsistis.
7. Lībertātem et iūra hārum urbium artibus bellī cōnservāvimus.
8. Dī Graecī sē inter hominēs cum virtūte saepe nōn gerēbant.
9. Cicerō multōs Rōmānōs vī sententiārum suārum dūcēbat.
10. Sententiae eius eum cārum mihi fēcērunt.
11. The tyrant never used to entrust his life to his friends.
12. The king kept throwing money among them.
13. At that time we saved his life with that letter.
14. Through their friends they used to conquer the citizens of many cities.

SENTENTIAE ANTĪQUAE

1. Diū in istā nāve fuī et propter tempestātem semper mortem exspectābam. (Terence. — nāvis, -is, f., *ship.* — tempestās, -tātis.)
2. Paucīs hōrīs ad eam urbem vēnimus. (Cicero.)
3. Italia illīs temporibus erat plēna Graecārum artium et multī Rōmānī ipsī hās artēs colēbant. (Cicero. — plēnus, -a, -um, *full.* — artēs, in the sense of studies, literature, philosophy. — colō, -ere, -uī, cultum, *cultivate, pursue.*)

4. Inter bellum et pācem dubitābant. (Tacitus. — dubitō (1), *hesitate, waver.*)
5. Eō tempore istum ex urbe ēiciēbam. (Cicero.)
6. Dīcēbat ille miser: "Cīvis Rōmānus sum." (Cicero.)
7. Mea puella passerem suum amābat et passer ad eam sōlam semper pīpiābat. (Catullus. — passer, -eris, m., *sparrow*, a pet bird. — pīpiō (1), *chirp.*)
8. Fīliī meī frātrem meum dīligēbant, mē fugiēbant; meam mortem exaspectābant. Nunc autem mōrēs meōs mūtāvī et fīliōs ad mē traham. (Terence. — frāter, -tris, *brother.*)

CYRUS' DYING WORDS ON IMMORTALITY

Dum eram vōbīscum, animum meum nōn vidēbātis sed ex meīs factīs intellegēbātis eum esse in hōc corpore. Itaque crēdite animum esse eundem post mortem.

(Cicero, *Dē Senectūte* 22.79. — factum, -ī, *deed, act.* — crēdō, -ere, crēdidī, crēditum, *believe.*)

FABIAN TACTICS

(After the Romans had been defeated in a number of direct encounters with Hannibal, Fabius instituted the practice of harassing Hannibal but of refusing to meet him in the open field. Though this policy saved the day for the Romans, it became unpopular with them.)

Dē Quīntō Fabiō Maximō Ennius dīxit: "Ūnus homō cīvitātem nōbīs cūnctātiōne cōnservāvit. Rūmōrēs nōn pōnēbat ante salūtem."

(Ibid. 4.10. — Ennius, a Roman author. — cūnctātiō, -ōnis, *delay.* — rūmor, -ōris, *rumor, gossip.* — pōnō, -ere, posuī, positum, *put.* — salūs, -ūtis, f., *safety.*)

UNEASY LIES THE HEAD

Dionȳsius tyrannus, quoniam tōnsōrī collum committere timēbat, fīliās suās barbam et capillum tondēre docuit. Itaque virginēs tondēbant barbam et capillum patris.

(Cicero, *Tusc. Disp.* 5.20.58. — tōnsor, -ōris, *barber.* — collum, -ī, *neck.* — barba, -ae, *beard.* — capillus, -ī, *hair.* — tondeō, -ēre, totondī, tōnsum, *shave, cut.*)

ETYMOLOGY

The connection between Latin **pater** and **patria** (*father-land*) is obvious. However, although English *patriarch, patriot,* and *patronymic* have in them a stem, **patr-,** which is meaningful to one who knows the Latin words, nevertheless these English words are actually derived from Greek, in which the stem **patr-** is cognate with the same stem in Latin; cp. Greek **patér,** *father,* **pátrā** or **patrís,** *fatherland,* **patriá,** *lineage.*

From the intensive verb **iactō**, which derives from the **iactum** of **iaciō**, stems (through Vulg. Lat. **iectō**[2]) the French word *jeter* ("throw"), which in turn is the source of our *jet, jetsam, jettison, jut.*

In the sentences   1. tempestuous. 3. cult, culture, agriculture (**ager,** *field*), horticulture (**hortus,** *garden*), colony. 7. passerine. — pipe, both verb and noun, an onomatopoetic (imitative) word widely used; e.g., Gk. *pipos, a young bird,* and *pipizein* or *peppizein, to peep, chirp,* Ger. *piepen* and *pfeifen,* Eng. *peep,* Fr. *piper. Uneasy Lies:* tonsorial, tonsure. — collar, decollate, décolleté. — barber, barb, barbed, barbate. — capillary, capillaceous.

Footnotes

[1] The irregular imperfect of **sum** you have already learned (Ch. 6).

[2] Cf. Lat. **con-iectō, -āre.**

16

Adjectives of the Third Declension

*C*orresponding to adjectives of the first and the second declensions we find adjectives of the third. These belong to the i-stem declension, and so follow the pattern of *cīvis*[1] and **mare**. The majority of them are adjectives of two endings in the nominative singular; they have one set of endings for the masculine and the feminine (like those of *cīvis*, which is both masculine and feminine) and one set for the neuter (like those of **mare**). Even the relatively few which have three endings or only one ending in the nominative singular are throughout the rest of the paradigm just like the adjectives of two endings. *Cīvis* and **mare** are repeated in the paradigms to show that there is very little new to be learned in the adjectives of the third declension.

| | I-Stem Nouns Reviewed[2] | | Adj. of 2 Endings fortis, forte, *strong, brave* | |
	M. or F.	N.	M. & F.	N.
Nom.	cívis	máre	fórtis	fórte
Gen.	cívis	máris	fórtis	fórtis
Dat.	cívī	márī	fórtī	fórtī
Acc.	cívem	máre	fórtem	fórte
Abl.	cíve	márī	fórtī	fórtī
Nom.	cívēs	mária	fórtēs	fórtia
Gen.	cívium	márium	fórtium	fórtium
Dat.	cívibus	máribus	fórtibus	fórtibus
Acc.	cívēs[3]	mária	fórtēs[3]	fórtia
Abl.	cívibus	máribus	fórtibus	fórtibus

	Adj. of 3 Endings ācer, ācris, ācre, *keen, severe, fierce*		Adj. of 1 Ending potēns, potentis, *powerful*	
	M. & F.	N.	M. & F.	N.
Nom.	ácer, ácris	ácre	pótēns	pótēns
Gen.	ácris	ácris	poténtis	poténtis
Dat.	ácrī	ácrī	poténtī	poténtī
Acc.	ácrem	ácre	poténtem	pótēns
Abl.	ácrī	ácrī	poténtī	poténtī
Nom.	ácrēs	ácria	poténtēs	poténtia
Gen.	ácrium	ácrium	poténtium	poténtium
Dat.	ácribus	ácribus	poténtibus	poténtibus
Acc.	ácrēs	ácria	poténtēs	poténtia
Abl.	ácribus	ácribus	poténtibus	poténtibus

OBSERVATIONS

Note carefully the places in which the characteristic **i** appears,[4] as indicated in the paradigms:

(1) **-ī** in the ablative singular of all genders.
(2) **-ium** in the genitive plural of all genders.
(3) **-ia** in the nominative and accusative plural of the neuter.

Note also that an adjective of the third declension can be used with a noun of any declension just as an adjective of the first and the second declensions can. In the following illustrations **omnis, -e**, *every, all*, is used as the example of an adjective of two endings.

omnis amīcus *or* homō	ācer amīcus/homō	potēns amīcus/homō
omnis rēgina *or* māter[5]	ācris rēgina/māter	potēns rēgina/māter
omne bellum *or* animal	ācre bellum/animal	potēns bellum/animal

For the sake of practice, study and analyze the forms in the following phrases:

omnī prōvinciae[6]	in omnī prōvinciā	omnium prōvinciārum
omnī vīcō[6]	in omnī vīcō	omnium vīcōrum
omnī ōrdinī[6]	in omnī ōrdine	omnium ōrdinum
omnī urbī	in omnī urbe	omnium urbium
omnī marī	in omnī marī	omnium marium

VOCABULARY

a′etās, aetátis, *f.*, period of life, life, age, an age

memória, -ae, *f.*, memory, recollection (*memoir, memorial, memorize, memorandum, commemorate*)

beātus, -a, -um, happy, fortunate, blessed, (*beatific, beatify, beatitude, Beatrice*)

brévis, -e, short, small, brief (*brevity, breviary, abbreviate, abridge*)

céler, céleris, célere, swift, quick, rapid (*celerity, accelerate*)

difficilis, -e, hard, difficult, troublesome (*cp.* **facilis,** *vocab. Ch. 27.*)

dúlcis, -e, sweet; pleasant, agreeable (*dulcify, dulcet, dulcimer*)

fórtis, -e, strong, brave (*fort, forte, fortify, fortitude, force, comfort, effort*)

lóngus, -a, -um, long (*longitude, longevity, elongate, oblong, prolong;* Eng. *long* is cognate.)

ómnis, -e, all, every (*omnibus, bus, omnipresent, omnipotent, omniscient, omnivorous*)

iúvō (*or* ádiuvō), -áre, iúvī, iútum, help, aid, assist, please (*adjutant, coadjutant, aid*)

RECOGNITION VOCABULARY

fémina, -ae, *f.*, woman (*feminine, femininity, feminism, female, effeminate*)

máter, -tris, *f.*, mother (*maternal, matriarchy, matrimony, matricide, matriculate, matron*)

quam, *adv.*, how

PRACTICE AND REVIEW

1. Fortēs virī ante nostram aetātem vīvēbant.
2. Eōs miserōs trāns maria difficilia mittēbat.
3. Omnēs cupiditātēs (*desires*) ex sē ēiēcērunt, nam nātūram corporis timuērunt.
4. Ipse, quoniam sē dīlēxit, sē cum eīs numquam iūnxit.
5. Itaque tē inter eōs cum animō fortī exspectābam.
6. Celer rūmor per caelum currēbat.
7. Vīs bellī vītam eius paucīs hōrīs mūtāvit.
8. Sē ex marī trāxērunt sēque Caesarī potentī commīsērunt.
9. Caesar nōn poterat suās cōpiās cum celeribus cōpiīs rēgis iungere.
10. Themistoclēs nōmina omnium cīvium ācrī memoriā tenēbat.
11. The father and the mother used to come to the city with their sweet daughter.
12. The brave souls of brave men will never fear difficult times.
13. Does he understand all the rights of all these men (**homō**)?
14. They could not help the brave man, for death was swift.

SENTENTIAE ANTĪQUAE

1. Quam dulcis est lībertās! (Phaedrus.)
2. Labor omnia vincit. (*Virgil.)
3. Fortūna fortēs adiuvat. (Terence.)
4. Quam celeris est mēns! (Cicero. — mēns, mentis, f., *mind.*)

5. Polyphēmus erat mōnstrum horrendum, īnfōrme, ingēns. (Virgil. — mōnstrum, -ī. — horrendus, -a, -um, *horrible*. — infōrmis, -e, *formless, hideous*. — ingēns, -ntis, *huge*.)

6. Varium et mūtābile semper fēmina. (*Virgil. — Order: fēmina semper [est] varium et mūtābile. — varius, -a, -um, *varying, fickle*. — mūtābilis, -e, *changeable;* the neuters varium and mūtābile are used to mean "a fickle and changeable *thing*.")

7. Difficile est saturam nōn scrībere. (Juvenal. — satura, -ae, *satire*.)

8. Īra furor brevis est; animum rege. (*Horace. — furor, -ōris, m., *madness*. — regō, -ere, rēxī, rēctum, *rule;* cp. rēx.)

9. Ars poētica est nōn omnia dīcere. (*Servius. — poēticus, -a, -um.)

10. Nihil est ab omnī parte beātum. (*Horace. — ab + abl., *in*, lit. *from*.)

11. Liber meus hominēs prūdentī cōnsiliō adiuvat. (Phaedrus. — prūdēns, -ntis. — cōnsilium, -iī, *counsel*.)

12. Māter omnium bonārum artium sapientia est. (*Cicero.)

13. Clēmentia rēgem salvum facit; nam amor omnium cīvium est inexpugnābile mūnīmentum rēgis. (Seneca. — clēmentia, -ae. — salvus, -a, -um, *safe*. — inexpugnābilis, -e, *impregnable*. — mūnīmentum, -ī, *fortification, defense*.)

14. Vīta est brevis; ars, longa. (Hippocrates.)

15. Breve autem tempus aetātis satis longum est ad bene vīvendum. (Cicero. — vivendum, *living*, verbal noun obj. of ad.)

16. Vīvit et vīvet per omnium saeculōrum memoriam. (*Velleius Paterculus. — saeculum, -ī, *century, age*.)

ETYMOLOGY

In the sentences   4. mental, mention. 5. monstrous. — horrendous. — informal, inform (adj. with neg. prefix in-), inform (verb with prep. prefix in-). 6. variety, variegated, vary, unvaried, invariable. 8. furor. — regent, regular, regiment, correct, direct; cp. right. 11. **prūdēns**, syncopated form of **prōvidēns** as seen in providence, providential. 13. clement, Clement, Clementine, clemency, inclement.

Footnotes

[1] Except in the ablative singular.
[2] See Ch. 14.
[3] I-stem nouns and adjectives have an alternate -īs ending in the acc. plu. (the regular ending until the Augustan Period), but it will not be used in this book.
[4] A few third-declension adjectives of one ending are declined without this characteristic i in one or more of the three places; e.g., **vetus, veteris**, *old:* **vetere** (abl. sing.), **veterum** (gen. plu.), **vetera** (neut. nom. and acc. plu.). The problem of comparatives and present participles will be **taken up later.**
[5] **rēgīna, -ae**, *queen;* **māter, mātris**, *mother*.
[6] **prōvincia, -ae**, *province;* **vīcus, -ī**, *village;* **ōrdō, ōrdinis**, m., *rank*.

17

The Relative Pronoun

The forms of the relative pronoun are so diverse that the only practical procedure is to memorize them forthwith. However, it is easy to see that the endings of genitive cuius and dative cui are related to those of illius and illi; and it is easy to identify the case, the number, and often the gender of many of the remaining forms.

THE RELATIVE PRONOUN

QUI, QUAE, QUOD, *WHO, WHICH*

Singular			**Plural**		
M.	**F.**	**N.**	**M.**	**F.**	**N.**
quī	quae	quod	quī	quae	quae
cuius[1]	cuius	cuius	quōrum	quārum	quōrum
cui[1]	cui	cui	quibus	quibus	quibus
quem	quam	quod	quōs	quās	quae
quō	quā	quō	quibus	quibus	quibus

USE AND AGREEMENT OF THE RELATIVE

A relative[2] pronoun introduces a subordinate clause[3] which it joins to a preceding noun or pronoun.

The logic which determines what specific form of the relative is to be used in a given instance can be demonstrated by analyzing and translating the following sentence:

The girl whom you love is pretty.

1. The main clause of the sentence reads:
     The girl...is pretty,   puella...est bella.
2. *Whom* introduces a subordinate, relative clause modifying *girl*.
3. *Girl* (**puella**) stands before the relative *whom* and so is called the
    antecedent of *whom* (**ante,** *before,* + **cēdere,** *to go*).
4. *Whom* has a double loyalty: (1) to its antecedent, **puella,** and (2) to
    the subordinate clause in which it stands.
       a. Since the antecedent, **puella,** is feminine and singular, *whom*
    in   Latin will have to be feminine and singular.
       b. Since in the subordinate clause *whom* depends on (*you*)
    love,   **amās,** as the direct object, it must be in the accusative case.
       c. Therefore, the Latin form must be *feminine* and *singular*
    and   *accusative:* **quam.**

The complete sentence in Latin appears thus:

     Puella quam amās est bella.

Succinctly, the rule is this: the *gender* and the *number* of a relative are
determined by the antecedent; the *case* of a relative is determined by the
use of the relative in its own clause.

Analyze the gender, the number, and the case of each of the relatives in
the following sentences[4]:

1. Amō puellam **quae** ex Italiā vēnit, *I love the girl who came from Italy.*
2. Homō dē **quō** dīcēbās est stultus, *the man about whom you were
   speaking is stupid.*
3. Puella **cui** librum dat est bella, *the girl to whom he is giving the
   book is pretty.*
4. Puer **cuius** patrem iuvābāmus est miser, *the boy whose father we
   used to help is unfortunate.*
5. Vītam meam committam eīs virīs **quōrum** virtūtēs laudābās, *I shall
   entrust my life to those men whose virtues you used to praise.*
6. Timeō perīculum **quod** timētis, *I fear the danger which you fear.*

VOCABULARY

amicítia, -ae, *f.,* friendship (*cp.* amō, amícus)

vḗritās, -tā́tis, *f.,* truth (*verify; cp.* vḗrus)

qui, quae, quod, *rel. pron.,* who, which, what, that (*quorum*)

aut, *conj.,* or; aut...aut, either...or

nímis *or* nímium, *adv.,* too, too much, excessively

co'epī, coepísse, co'eptum, began, *defective verb used in the perfect
   system only; the present system is supplied by* incipiō.

incípiō, -ere, -cḗpī, -céptum, begin (*incipient, inception;* cp. *capiō*)

déleō, -ére, dēlḗvī, dēlḗtum, destroy, wipe out, erase (*delete*)

néglegō, -ere, neglḗxī, neglḗctum, neglect, disregard (negligent, negligee)

RECOGNITION VOCABULARY

fáctum, -i, *n.*, deed, act, achievement (*fact, feat*)

PRACTICE AND REVIEW

1. Magna est vīs artium.
2. Miserōs hominēs sēcum iungere coeperant.
3. Nam illā aetāte pars populī iūra cīvium numquam tenuit.
4. Incipimus vēritātem intellegere, quae hominēs adiuvat.
5. Quam difficile est bona aut dulcia ex bellō trahere!
6. Mortem patris exspectābant, cuius mōrēs numquam dīlēxerant.
7. Puer mātrem timēbat, quae eum in viam ēiciēbat.
8. Inter omnia perīcula illa fēmina sē cum sapientiā gessit.
9. Itaque celer rūmor et mors per urbēs cucurrērunt.
10. Quoniam memoria factōrum nostrōrum dulcis est, beātī sumus.
11. They feared the king whose city they were holding by force.
12. We began to help those to whom we had given our friendship.
13. We fear that book with which he is beginning to destroy our liberty.

SENTENTIAE ANTĪQUAE

1. Salvē, bone amīce, cui fīlium meum commīsī. (Terence.)
2. Dionȳsius, dē quō ante dīxī, ad Siciliam nāvigābat. (Cicero. — Sicilia, -ae, *Sicily.* — nāvigō (1), *sail.*)
3. Multī cīvēs aut ea perīcula quae imminent nōn vident aut ea quae vident neglegunt. (Cicero. — immineō, -ēre, *impend, threaten.*)
4. Bis dat quī cito dat. (Publilius Syrus. — bis. *twice.* — cito, *quickly.*)
5. Quī coepit, dīmidium factī habet. Incipe! (Horace. — dīmidium, -iī, *half.*)
6. Nōn caret is quī nōn dēsīderat. (*Cicero. — careō, -ēre, -uī, -itūrus, *lack, want.* — dēsīderō (1), *desire.*)
7. Levis est fortūna: id cito reposcit quod dedit. (Publilius Syrus. — levis, -e, *light, fickle.* — reposcō, -ere, *demand back.*)
8. Fortūna eum stultum facit quem nimium amat. (Publilius Syrus.)
9. Nōn sōlum fortūna ipsa est caeca sed etiam eōs caecōs facit quōs semper adiuvat. (Cicero. — caecus, -a, -um, *blind.*)
10. Bis vincit quī sē vincit in victōriā. (*Publilius Syrus. — victōria, -ae.)
11. Simulātiō dēlet vēritātem sine quā nōmen amīcitiae valēre nōn potest. (Cicero. — simulātiō, -ōnis, *pretense, insincerity.*)
12. Virtūtem enim illīus virī amāvī, quae cum corpore nōn periit. (Cicero. — pereō, -īre, periī, -itum, *perish.*)
13. Turbam vītā. Cum hīs vīve quī tē meliōrem facere possunt; illōs admitte quōs tū potes facere meliōrēs. (Seneca. — turba, -ae, *crowd.* — vītō (1), *avoid.* — melior, -ius, *better.* — admittō, -ere, -mīsī, -missum, *admit, receive.*)

14. Liber quem recitās meus est; sed cum male eum recitās, incipit esse tuus. (Martial. — recitō (1). — cum, *when.* — male, adv. of **malus.**)

ETYMOLOGY

The Latin relative pronoun was the parent of the following Romance forms: It. *chi, che;* Sp. *que;* Fr. *qui, que.*

If the suffix **-scō** shows a Latin verb to be an inceptive verb, what force or meaning does this ending impart to the verb? — **tremō,** *tremble;* **tremēscō** = ?

In medieval manuscripts many texts begin with an "incipit"; e.g., Liber prîmus Epistolārum Plînii incipit.

To Latin **aut** can be traced It. *o,* Sp. *o,* Fr. *ou.*

In the French expression *fait accompli,* from what Latin word should you suppose *fait* to be derived?

In the sentences   2. navigation, navigator. 3. imminent. 6. desideratum, desire. 7. levity, alleviate. 11. simulation, simulator, dissimulation. 12. **perîre:** Fr. *périr, périssant:* Eng. *perish.* 13. ameliorate.

Footnotes

[1] For the pronunciation of the **ui** in **cuius** (as if spelled *cui-yus*) and in **cui** see Ch. 9, n. 3 and 4, and Introd. p. xxiv.

[2] "Relative" is connected with the verb **referō, -ferre, rettulî, relātum,** *bear back, refer.*

[3] A clause is a group of words containing a subject and a predicate.

[4] For pedagogical reasons the Latin word order is not always followed.

18

Present, Imperfect, and Future Indicative Passive of Laudō and Moneō; Ablative of Agent

*T*he rule for the formation of the present, the imperfect, and the future indicative passive of the first and the second conjugations is an easy one with few exceptions: simply substitute the passive endings for the active ones.

PRESENT INDICATIVE PASSIVE OF Laudō and Moneō

PASSIVE ENDINGS

1.	-r	la'ud-or[1]	móneor[1]	*I am (am being) praised, warned*
2.	-ris[2]	laudá-ris[2]	monéris[2]	*you are (are being) praised, warned*
3.	-tur	laudá-tur	monétur	*he is (is being) praised, warned*
1.	-mur	laudá-mur	monému	*we are (are being) praised, warned*
2.	-minī	laudá-minī	monémin	*you are (are being) praised, warned*
3.	-ntur	laudá-ntur	monéntur	*they are (are being) praised, warned*

IMPERFECT INDICATIVE PASSIVE

I was being praised[3]	*I was being warned*[3]
1. laudā-ba-r	monḗbar
2. laudā-bā́-ris	monēbā́ris
3. laudā-bā́-tur	monēbā́tur
1. laudā-bā́-mur	monēbā́mur
2. laudā-bā́-minī	monēbā́minī
3. laudā-bā́-ntur	monēbántur

FUTURE INDICATIVE PASSIVE

I shall be praised	*I shall be warned*
1. laudā́-*b-or*[1]	monḗbor[1]
2. laudā́-be-ris[4]	monḗberis[4]
3. laudā́-bi-tur	monḗbitur
1. laudā́-bi-mur	monḗbimur
2. laudā-bí-minī	monēbíminī
3. laudā-bú-ntur	monēbúntur

THE PRESENT PASSIVE INFINITIVE

The present passive infinitive of the first and the second conjugations is formed by changing the final **e** of the active to **ī**.

laudā́r-ī, *to be praised*   monḗr-ī, *to be warned*

THE PASSIVE VOICE

When the verb is in the active voice, the subject acts: it performs the action of the verb. When the verb is in the passive voice, the subject is acted upon: it suffers or passively permits[5] the action of the verb. As a rule, only transitive verbs can be used in the passive; and what had been the object of the transitive verb (receiving the action of the verb) now becomes the subject of the passive verb (still receiving the action of the verb).

Caesarem admonet, *he is warning Caesar.*
Caesar admonētur, *Caesar is being warned.*

Urbem dēlēbant, *they were destroying the city.*
Urbs dēlēbātur, *the city was being destroyed.*

Patriam cōnservābit, *he will save the country.*
Patria cōnservābitur, *the country will be saved.*

ABLATIVE OF PERSONAL AGENT

(AB + ABLATIVE)

The personal *agent by whom* the action of a passive verb is performed is indicated by **ab** and the ablative. (The *means by which* the action is accomplished is indicated by the ablative of means without a preposition, as you have already learned.)

Dī Caesarem admonent, *the gods are warning Caesar.*

Caesar ā dīs admonētur, *Caesar is warned by the gods.* (Agent)

Caesar hīs prōdigiīs admonētur, *Caesar is warned by these omens.* (Means); prōdigium, -iī, *omen.*

Malī virī urbem dēlēbant, *evil men were destroying the city.*

Urbs ab malīs virīs dēlēbātur, *the city was being destroyed by evil men.* (Agent)

Urbs flammīs dēlēbātur, *the city was being destroyed by flames.* (Means); flamma, -ae.

Hī cīvēs patriam cōnservābunt, *these citizens will save the country.*

Patria ab hīs cīvibus cōnservābitur, *the country will be saved by these citizens.* (Agent)

Patria armis et vēritāte cōnservābitur, *the country will be saved by arms and truth.* (Means)

VOCABULARY

cōnsílium, -iī, plan, purpose, advice, judgment (*counsel, counselor*)

génus, géneris, *n.*, origin, kind, sort, class (*genus, generic, genitive, gender, general, generous, genuine, degenerate*)

álius, ália, áliud (*for declension v. Ch. 9*), other, another; *cp.* **alter** (*alias, alibi, alien*)

ā (*before consonants*), **ab** (*before vowels or consonants*), *prep. + abl.*, from; by (*personal agent*); *frequent in compounds*

étiam, *adv.*, even

légō, -ere, légi, léctum, pick out, choose; read (*elect, elegant, eligible, lecture, legend, legible, intellect*)

móveō, -ére, móvī, mótum, move; arouse, affect (*mobile, motion, motive, motor, commotion, emotion, remote*)

térreō, -ére, térruī, térritum, frighten, terrify; *also* **terreō** (*terrible, terrific, terror, deter*)

vídeor, -érī, vísus sum, *pass. of* **videō,** be seen, seem, appear

RECOGNITION VOCABULARY

lúdus, -ī, *m.*, game, sport; school (*ludicrous, delude, elude, illusion, interlude, prelude, postlude*)

PRACTICE AND REVIEW

1. Multī morte nimis terrentur.
2. Beāta memoria amīcitiārum dulcium numquam dēlēbitur.
3. Illa fēmina omnia genera artium intellēxit.
4. Pater vester, ā quō iuvābāmur, multa dē celeribus perīculīs maris dīcere coepit.
5. Memoriā illōrum factōrum movēmur.
6. Cōnsilia rēgis bellō longō et difficilī dēlēbantur.
7. Itaque māter mortem fīliī exspectābat, cuius aetās erat brevis.
8. Bella difficilia sine eius cōnsiliō numquam gerēbam.
9. Tē cum aliīs miserīs ad Caesarem trahent.
10. Rēgem, quī officia neglēxerat, ex urbe ēiēcērunt.
11. Rights will be given by them even to the citizens of other cities.
12. Many are moved by money but not by truth.
13. The state will be destroyed by the king, whom they are beginning to fear.
14. We are not frightened by plans of that sort.

SENTENTIAE ANTĪQUAE

1. Possunt quia posse videntur. (*Virgil. — quia, *because*.)
2. Etiam fortēs virī subitīs perīculīs terrentur. (Tacitus. — subitus, -a, -um, *sudden*.)
3. Tua cōnsilia sunt clāra nōbīs; tenēris scientiā hōrum cīvium omnium. (Cicero. — clārus, -a, -um; scientia, -ae, *knowledge*.)
4. Malum est cōnsilium quod mūtārī nōn potest. (*Publilius Syrus.)
5. Fās est ab hoste docērī. (Ovid. — fās e*st, it is right.* — hostis, -is, *enemy*.)
6. Eō tempore erant[6] circēnsēs lūdī, quō genere spectāculī numquam teneor. (Pliny. — circēnsēs lūdī, contests in the Circus. — spectāculum, -ī.)
7. Haec est nunc vīta mea: salūtō bonōs virōs quī ad mē veniunt; deinde aut scrībō aut legō; post haec omne tempus corporī datur. (Cicero. — salūtō (1), *greet* at the early morning reception. — deinde, *then*.)
8. Nihil igitur mors est quoniam nātūra animī habētur mortālis. (Lucretius. — mortālis, -e.)
9. Omnia mūtantur; omnia fluunt; quod fuimus aut sumus, crās nōn erimus. (Ovid. — fluō, -ere, flūxī, flūxum, *flow.* — crās, adv., *tomorrow*.)
10. Amor miscērī cum timōre nōn potest. (*Publilius Syrus. — misceō, -ēre, miscuī, mixtum, *mix.* — timor, -ōris, *fear*.)
11. Numquam enim temeritās cum sapientiā commiscētur. (*Cicero. — temeritās, -tātis, *rashness*.)
12. Dīligēmus eum quī pecūniā nōn movētur. (Cicero.)

13. Laudātur ab hīs; culpātur ab illīs. (*Horace. — culpō (1), *blame*.)
14. Probitās laudātur — et alget. (*Juvenal. — probitās, -tātis = virtūs. — algeō, -ēre, alsī, *be cold, be neglected*.)

ETYMOLOGY

In the sentences   3. clarity, clarify, clarion, declare. — science. 5. hostile. 6. circus. — spectator, spectacle, specter, spectacular. 9. fluent, fluid, flux, affluence, confluence (cp. Coblenz), influence, influenza, "flu," influx, refluent, superfluous. 10. miscible, miscellaneous, admixture. — timorous. 11. temerity (contrast timidity).

Footnotes

[1]This form is exceptional in that the passive ending, -r, is added directly to the full active form: **laudo-r, moneo-r; laudābo-r, monēbo-r.**

[2]There is an alternate ending -re in the 2nd per. sing.; e.g., **laudā-ris** or **laudā-re, laudābāris** or **laudābāre, laudāberis** or **laudābere.** This you will have to be able to recognize when you come to more advanced reading in Latin authors, but for the sake of simplicity only the **-ris** ending is used in this book.

[3]Or *used to be praised* or *warned*, etc.

[4]Note that here the tense sign -bi- becomes -be-.

[5]"Passive" is derived from **patior, patī, passus sum,** *suffer, permit.* V. Ch. 1, n. 1.

[6]**Est, sunt,** etc., often mean *there is, there are,* etc.

19

Perfect Passive System of All Verbs; Interrogative Pronouns and Adjectives

*The Romans combined the perfect passive participle[1] with **sum, eram,** and **erō** to form the perfect, the pluperfect, and the future perfect passive, respectively. This rule holds regardless of the conjugation to which a verb belongs,[2] just as in the perfect active system all conjugations are treated alike.*

PERFECT INDICATIVE PASSIVE

1. laudā́tus, -a, -um sum, *I was praised, have been praised*
2. laudā́tus, -a, -um es, *you were praised, have been praised*
3. laudā́tus, -a, -um est, *he, she, it was praised, have been praised*

1. laudā́tī, -ae, -a súmus, *we were praised, have been praised*
2. laudā́tī, -ae, -a éstis, *you were praised, have been praised*
3. laudā́tī, -ae, -a sunt, *they were praised, have been praised*

PLUPERFECT INDICATIVE PASSIVE

I had been praised, etc.

1. laudā́tus, -a, -um éram
2. laudā́tus, -a, -um érās
3. laudā́tus, -a, -um érat

1. laudā́tī, -ae, -a erā́mus
2. laudā́tī, -ae, -a erā́tis
3. laudā́tī, -ae, -a érant

FUTURE PERFECT PASSIVE

I shall have been praised, etc.

1. laudā́tus, -a, -um érō
2. laudā́tus, -a, -um éris
3. laudā́tus, -a, -um érit

1. laudā́tī, -ae, -a érimus
2. laudā́tī, -ae, -a éritis
3. laudā́tī, -ae, -a érunt

Observations (1) The perfect passive participle is treated as a predicate adjective, and consequently it agrees with the subject of the verb in gender, number, and case. (2) Note carefully the regular translation of the perfect and the pluperfect passive: **laudātus sum,** *I was* (not *I am*) *praised;* **laudātus eram,** *I had been* (not *I was*) *praised.*

Puella est laudāta, *the girl was praised.*
Puellae erant laudātae, *the girls had been praised.*
Puerī sunt monitī, *the boys were warned.*
Perīculum nōn erat vīsum, *the danger had not been seen.*
Perīcula nōn sunt vīsa, *the dangers were not seen.*
Litterae sunt scrīptae, *the letter was written.*

THE INTERROGATIVE PRONOUN

The interrogative pronoun **quis? quid?** is declined in the plural exactly as the relative pronoun is. In the singular, also, it follows the pattern of the relative with two exceptions: (1) the masculine and the feminine have the same forms; (2) the nominative forms have their distinctive spelling **quis, quid.**

| | Singular | | Plural | | |
	M. & F.	N.	M.	F.	N.
Nom.	quis	quid	quī	quae	quae
Gen.	cuius	cuius	quōrum	quārum	quōrum
Dat.	cui	cui	quíbus	quíbus	quíbus
Acc.	quem	quid	quōs	quās	quae
Abl.	quō	quō	quíbus	quíbus	quíbus

INTERROGATIVE *Quis* AND
RELATIVE *Quī* DISTINGUISHED

The forms **quis** and **quid** can be spotted at once as not being relatives. The other forms, which are spelled alike, can be distinguished by the following questions:

1. Does the form introduce a question as shown by the sense and punctuation?

2. Does the form have an antecedent? (The relative does have an antecedent, expressed or implied; the interrogative does not.)

These criteria will prove especially helpful in translating *who* and *what* from English to Latin.

Quis librum tibi dedit? *Who gave the book to you?*
Vir **quī** librum tibi dedit tē laudāvit, *the man who gave the book to you praised you.*

Cuius librum Cicerō tibi dedit? *Whose book did Cicero give to you?*
Vir **cuius** librum Cicerō tibi dedit tē laudāvit, *the man whose book Cicero gave to you praised you.*

Cui librum Cicerō dedit? *To whom did Cicero give the book?*
Vir **cui** Cicerō librum dedit tē laudāvit, *the man to whom Cicero gave the book praised you.*

Quid dedit? *What did he give?*
Praemium **quod** dedit erat magnum, *the reward which he gave was large* (**praemium, -iī,** *n.*).

Ā quō praemium datum est? *By whom was the reward given?*
Vir **ā quō** praemium datum est tē laudāvit, *the man by whom the reward was given praised you.*

THE INTERROGATIVE ADJECTIVE

The interrogative adjective **quī? quae? quod?** is identical with the relative pronoun in its forms but (1) it modifies a noun interrogatively; and (2) it has no antecedent.

Quem librum tibi dedit?   *What book did he give you?*
Quod praemium tibi dedit?   *What reward did he give you?*
Ex quā urbe vēnit?   *From what city did he come?*

VOCABULARY

sénex, *gen.* sénis, *adj. and noun,* old, aged; old man (*senate, senator, senescent, senile, senior, seniority, sir, sire*)

stúdium, -iī, *n.,* eagerness, zeal, pursuit, study (*studio, studious*)

quis? quid?, *interrog. prn.,* who? what? which? (*quiddity, quidnunc, cui bono*)

quī? quae?, quod? *interrog. adj.,* what? which? what kind of?

cértus, -a, -um, definite, sure, certain, reliable (*ascertain, certify, certificate*)

nóvus, -a, -um, new; strange

at, *conj.* but; but, mind you; but, you say; *a more emotional adversative than* **sed**

líberō (1), free, liberate (*deliver;* cp. **lībertās**)

párō (1), prepare, provide, get, obtain (*apparatus, compare, parachute, parapet, parasol, pare, parry, repair, separate*)

RECOGNITION VOCABULARY

iūdícium, -iī, *n.,* judgment, decision, opinion (*adjudge, adjudicate, judicial, judicious, prejudge, prejudice*)

PRACTICE AND REVIEW

1. Quis lībertātem eōrum dēlēre coepit?
2. Cuius lībertās dēlēta est?
3. Quōs librōs lēgistī?
4. Fēminae librōs difficilēs lēgērunt quōs mīserās.
5. Quid omnī aetāte nimis laudātur? Pecūnia!
6. Itaque id genus lūdōrum, quod laudābātur, nōs nōn movet.
7. Puerī miserīs factīs patrum aut mātrum saepe terrentur.
8. Illī vēritātem timēbant, quā multī adiūtī erant.
9. Vēritās etiam ab rēgibus saepe nōn intellegitur.
10. Quī vir fortis, dē quō lēgistī, aetātem brevem mortemque celerem exspectābat?
11. Who saw the man who had prepared this?
12. What was neglected by him?
13. We were helped by the study which had been neglected by him.
14. Whose plans did the old men of all cities fear?

SENTENTIAE ANTĪQUAE

1. Cui hunc novum librum dabō? (Catullus.)
2. Quae est nātūra animī? (Lucretius.)
3. Illa argūmenta vīsa sunt certa. (Cicero. — argūmentum, -ī, *proof.*)
4. Quid nōs facere dēbēmus? (Cicero.)
5. Quid ego ēgī? In quod perīculum iactus sum? (Terence.)
6. Ō dī immortālēs! In quā urbe vīvimus? Quam cīvitātem habēmus? (Cicero. — immortālis, -e.)
7. Quī sunt bonī cīvēs nisi eī quī beneficia patriae memoriā tenent? (Cicero. — nisi, *if not, except.* — beneficium, -iī, *kindness, benefit.*)
8. Alia, quae pecūniā parantur, ab eō stultō parāta sunt; at mōrēs eius vērōs amīcōs parāre nōn potuērunt. (Cicero.)

DISILLUSIONED CATULLUS BIDS A BITTER FAREWELL TO LESBIA

Valē, puella, iam Catallus obdūrat.
Scelesta, vae tē! Quae tibi manet vīta?
Quis nunc tē adībit? Cui vidēberis bella?
Quem nunc amābis? Cuius esse dīcēris?
At tū, Catulle, dēstinātus obdūrā.

(*Catullus 8, verses 12, 15-17, 19; meter, choliambic. — iam, *now, already.* — obdūrō (1), *be hard.* — scelestus, -a, -um, *wicked, accursed.* — vae tē, *woe to you.* — adībit, *will visit.* — dīcē-ris, fut. indic. passive. — dēstinātus, -a, -um, *resolved, firm.*)

THE AGED PLAYWRIGHT SOPHOCLES HOLDS HIS OWN

Sophoclēs ad summam senectūtem tragoediās fēcit; sed propter hoc studium familiam neglegere vidēbātur et ā fīliīs in iūdicium vocātus est. Tum eam tragoediam quam proximē scrīpserat, "Oedipum Colōnēum," iūdicibus recitāvit. Ubi haec tragoedia recitāta est, senex sententiīs iūdicum est līberātus.

(Cicero. *De Sen.* 7.22. — summam, *extreme.* — tragoedia, -ae; the diphthong *oe* has become *e* in the English word. — familia, -ae, *household.* — proximē, *shortly before.* — "Oedipus at Colonus." — iūdex, -icis, *juryman.* — recitō (1).)

ETYMOLOGY

In the sentences   3. argument (lit. "a making clear"). 7. beneficent, beneficial, beneficiary, benefactor. *Catallus:* obdurate. *Aged Playwright:* sum, summary, consummate. — family, familiar, familiarity. — judiciary, judicious, judge, adjudicate, adjudge. — recital, recitative.

Footnotes

[1] See Ch. 12, n. 3.
[2] Thus in the paradigms **monitus, ductus, audītus, captus** or any similar participle could be substituted for **laudātus.**

20

Fourth Declension; Ablatives of Place from Which and Separation

*T*he letter *u* is the characterizing letter in all but two of the endings of the fourth declension. Note also that of all the -us endings only the nominative singular has a short *u*.

FOURTH DECLENSION

	frūctus, -ūs, m. *fruit*	cornū, -ūs, n. *horn*	Endings M. & F.	N.
Nom.	frúctus	córnū	-us	-ū
Gen.	frúctūs	córnūs	-ūs	-ūs
Dat.	frúctuī	córnū	-uī	-ū
Acc.	frúctum	córnū	-um	-ū
Abl.	frúctū	córnū	-ū	-ū
Nom.	frúctūs	córnua	-ūs	-ua
Gen.	frúctuum	córnuum	-uum	-uum
Dat.	frúctibus	córnibus	-ibus	-ibus
Acc.	frúctūs	córnua	-ūs	-ua
Abl.	frúctibus	córnibus	-ibus	-ibus

GENDER IN THE FOURTH DECLENSION

Most nouns of the fourth declension are masculine; they end in **-us.**

Of the few feminines, which also end in **-us, manus** is the only one that you will meet with any frequency.[1] The feminines have the same declension as the masculines.

The neuters end in **-ū,** and they are rare.

ABLATIVES OF PLACE FROM WHICH AND SEPARATION

The ablative of *place from which* (**ab, dē, ex** + abl.) has been familiar to you in practice ever since the introduction of the prepositions **ab, dē, ex.** It emphasizes *motion* from, say, point A to point B (A–> B) and is regularly accompanied by a preposition.

Mīsērunt nūntium ab exercitū (A) ad senātum (B), *they sent a messenger from the army to the senate* (A–> B). (nūntius, -iī, *messenger.* — exercitus, -ūs, *army.* — senatus, -ūs.)

Nūntius cucurrit ab exercitū (A) ad senātum (B), *the messenger ran from the army to the senate* (A–> B).

The ablative of *separation* emphasizes *being apart* — the fact that A and B are separated, are kept from meeting.

Prohibuērunt nūntium (A) ab senātū (B), *they kept the messenger from the senate* (A///B).

Multī puerī (A) carent frūctū (B), *many children are without fruit* (A///B).

After verbs meaning *to free, to lack,* and *to deprive*, the ablative of separation is used without a preposition; after other similar verbs, a preposition (**ab, dē, ex**) may or may not be used, though it is regularly used with a person.

VOCABULARY

frū́ctus, -ūs, *m.*, fruit, profit, enjoyment (*fructify, frugal*)

Gra'ecia, -ae, *f.*, Greece

má̄nus, -ūs, *f.*, hand, band; handwriting (*manual, manufacture, manuscript; emancipate, manacle, manage*)

métus, -ūs, *m.*, fear, dread, anxiety

scélus, scéleris, *n.*, evil deed, crime, sin, wickedness

senátus, -ūs, *m.*, senate (*cp.* **senex**)

sérvitūs, -útis, *f.*, servitude, slavery

vérsus, -ūs, *m.*, line of verse (*versify*)

commūnis, -e, common, general (*communal, commune, communicate, communion*)

gravis, -e, heavy, weighty, serious, important, severe, grievous (*aggravate, grieve, grave, gravity*)

cóntrā, *prep.* + *acc.,* against (*contra-* in compounds such as *contradict, contrast, contravene, contrapuntal; contrary, counter, encounter, pro and con*)

néque *or* **nec,** *conj.* and not, nor; **neque...neque,** neither...nor

cáreō, -ēre, cáruī, caritū́rus, + *abl. of separation,* be without, be deprived of, want, lack; be free from (*caret*)

PRACTICE AND REVIEW

1. Etiam senēs cōnsiliīs certīs saepe carent.
2. Quam memoriā mātris dulcis adiūtus est!
3. Quoniam nimis fortia facta faciēbat, aetās eius erat brevis.
4. Nostrā aetāte pauca manū parantur.
5. Vēritās nōs metū longō līberābit quō territī sumus.
6. Quibus generibus scelerum illae cīvitātēs dēlētae sunt?
7. Quis sine amīcitiā potest esse beātus?
8. Pecūniam ex Graeciā in suam patriam movēre coeperat.
9. Ā quibus studium difficilium artium neglēctum est?
10. Ubi versūs lēctī sunt, poēta laudātus est.
11. We cannot have the fruits of peace unless (**nisi**) we ourselves free men from heavy dread.
12. Those bands of unfortunate men will come to us from other countries in which they are deprived of the rights of citizens.
13. The old men lacked neither games nor serious pursuits.
14. Who began to perceive our common fears of the fruits of crime?

SENTENTIAE ANTĪQUAE

1. Cornua cervum ā perīculīs dēfendunt. (Martial. — cervus, -ī, *stag.* — dēfendō, -ere, dēfendī, dēfēnsum.)
2. Oedipūs oculīs sē prīvāvit. (Cicero. — prīvō (1), *deprive.*)
3. Themistoclēs bellō Persicō Graeciam servitūte līberāvit. (Cicero. — Persicus, -a, -um, *Persian.*)
4. Dēmosthenēs multōs versūs ūnō spīritū prōnūntiābat. (Cicero. — spīritus, -ūs, *breath.* — prōnūntiō (1).)
5. Persicōs apparātūs ōdī, (Horace. — apparātus, -ūs, *equipment, display.* — ōdī, defective vb., *I hate.*)
6. Iste commūnī sēnsū caret. (Horace. — sēnsus, -ūs, *feeling, discretion, tact.*)

7. Senectūs nōs prīvat omnibus voluptātibus neque longē abest ā morte. (Cicero. — voluptās, -tātis, *pleasure*. — longē, adv. of longus. — absum, *be away*.)

8. Nēmō accūsātor caret culpā; omnēs peccāvimus. (Seneca. — accūsātor, -ōris. — peccō (1), *sin*.)

9. Nūlla pars vītae vacāre officiō potest. (Cicero. — vacō (1), *be free from*.)

10. Prīma virtūs est vitiō carēre. (Quintilian.)

11. Vir scelere vacuus nōn eget iaculīs neque arcū. (Horace. — vacuus, -a, -um, *free from*. — egeō, -ēre, -uī, *need*. — iaculum, -ī, *javelin*. — arcus, -ūs, *bow*.)

12. Magnī tumultūs eō tempore in urbe erant. (Cicero. — tumultus, -ūs.)

13. Litterae senātuī populōque Allobrogum manū coniūrātī ipsīus erant scrīptae. (Cicero. — Allobrogēs, -um, a Gallic tribe whom the Catilinarian conspirators tried to arouse against Rome. — coniūrātus, -ī, *conspirator*.)

14. Habēmus senātūs cōnsultum vehemēns et grave contrā tē. (Cicero. — cōnsultum, -ī, *decree*. — vehemēns, -ntis, *powerful*.)

15. Discēde ex urbe cum malā manū scelerātōrum. (Cicero. — discēdō, -ere, -cessī, -cessum, *depart*. — scelerātus, -a, -um, cp. scelus.)

16. Magnō metū mē līberābis sī ex urbe manum tuam tēcum ēdūcēs. (Cicero.)

ETYMOLOGY

If one knows the derivation of *caret*, one is not likely to confuse this word with *carat*.

Other derivatives of **manus** are: amanuensis, manipulate, manumit, maneuver.

In the sentences   1. defend (lit. "strike" or "ward off"), defense, fence, fender, offend. 4. spirit, spirited, inspiration, sprite. — pronounce, enunciate. 5. peach (Persian apple). 7. voluptuous. — absent. 9. vacant, vacuous, vacate, vacation, vacuity, evacuate. 11. arc, arcade. 12. tumult, tumultuous. 14. vehement, vehemence.

Footnote

[1]**Domus, -ūs** is also a feminine of the fourth declension except that **domō** (abl. sing.) is more common than **domū and domōs (acc. plu.)** is more common than **domūs**. However, **domus** is most common in certain special forms which will be taken up later under place constructions (Ch. 37).

21

Third and Fourth Conjugations: Passive Voice

*R*eview the passive endings of the present system as given in Ch. 18.

The rule of substituting these passive endings for the active ones holds in general for the third and the fourth conjugations, but careful attention should be given to the bold forms.

PRESENT INDICATIVE PASSIVE

1. dū́cor	a'udior	cápior
2. dū́cĕris	audíris	cápĕris
3. dū́citur	audítur	cápitur
1. dū́cimur	audímur	cápimur
2. dūcíminī	audíminī	capíminī
3. dūcúntur	audiúntur	capiúntur

FUTURE INDICATIVE PASSIVE

dū́car	audiar	cápiar
dūcḗris	audiḗris	capiḗris
dūcḗtur	audiḗtur	capiḗtur
dūcḗmur	audiḗmur	capiḗmur
dūcḗminī	audiḗminī	capiḗminī
dūcḗntur	audiéntur	capiéntur

IMPERFECT INDICATIVE PASSIVE

1. dūcḗbar	audiḗbar	capiḗbar
2. dūcēbáris	audiēbáris	capiēbáris
3. dūcēbátur	audiēbátur	capiēbátur

1. dūcēbā́mur	audiēbā́mur	capiēbā́mur
2. dūcēbā́minī	audiēbā́minī	capiēbā́minī
3. dūcēbántur	audiēbántur	capiēbántur

PERFECT PASSIVE SYSTEM

The perfect passive system of all verbs has been explained in Ch. 19.

PRESENT INFINITIVE PASSIVE

The present infinitive passive of the fourth conjugation is formed by changing the final **-e** to **-ī**, as in the first two conjugations; but in the third conjugation, including **-iō** verbs, the whole **-ere** is changed to **-ī**.

(audīre)	audī́rī, *to be heard* (cp. laudā́rī, monḗrī)
(dū́cere)	dū́cī, *to be led*
(cápere)	cápī, *to be taken*

Capiō REVIEWED

Note that **capiō** is like **audiō** in spelling[1] throughout the present, the future, and the imperfect indicative active and passive, except in the second person singular of the present indicative passive: **capĕris, audīris.**

In the present infinitives and the imperative **capiō** follows the pattern of the third conjugation:

Infinitives: capere, capī   **Imperative:** cape, capite

VOCABULARY

ca'usa, -ae, *f*., cause, reason; **causā,** *abl. with a preceding genitive,* for the sake of, on account of (*accuse, because, excuse*)

fínis, -is, *m*., end, limit, boundary, purpose; **fī́nēs, -ium,** boundaries, territory (*affinity, confine, define, final, finale, finance, fine, finial, finicky, finish, finite, infinite, refine*)

gēns, géntis, *f*., clan, race, nation, people; *cp*. **genus** (*gentile, gentle, genteel, gentry*)

laus, la'udis, *f*., praise, glory, fame (*laud, laudable, laudatory, magna cum laude*)

átque *or* ac (*only bef. cons.*), *conj.*, and, and also, and even

quod, *conj.*, because

contíneō, -ḗre, -tínuī, -téntum, hold together, contain, keep, enclose, restrain (*content, discontent, malcontent, continual, continuous, incontinent*)

iúbeō, -ḗre, iússī, iússum, bid, order, command (*jussive*)

rápiō, rápere, rápuī, ráptum, seize, snatch, carry away (*rapacious, rapid, rapine, rapture, ravage, ravine, ravish*)

scíō, -íre, scívī, scítum, know (*science, scientific, conscience, conscious, prescience, scilicet*)

RECOGNITION VOCABULARY

múndus, -ī, *m.*, world, universe (*mundane, demimonde*)

tángō, -ere, tétigī, táctum, touch (*tangent, tangible, tact, tactile, contact, contagious, contiguous, contingent, integer*)

PRACTICE AND REVIEW

1. Laus nimis saepe est neque certa neque magna.
2. Senēs ab fīliīs numquam neglegēbantur.
3. Quis iussus erat Graeciam metū līberāre?
4. Salūtis commūnis causā eōs ex urbe ēdūcī iussit. (salūs, -ūtis, *f.*, *safety*.)
5. Aliī coepērunt īram nostram contrā senātum movēre quod omnēs metū novō territī erant.
6. Omnia genera servitūtis videntur gravia.
7. Rapiēturne Cicerō ex manibus istōrum?
8. Quī fīnis metūs atque servitūtis in eā cīvitāte potest vidērī?
9. At senectūtis bonae causā iam bene vīvere dēbēmus.
10. The truth will not be found without great labor.
11. Many nations are being destroyed by crimes or wars; they lack true peace.
12. Their fears can now be conquered because our deeds are understood by all.
13. Those serious pursuits are neglected for the sake of money or praise.

SENTENTIAE ANTĪQUAE

1. Numquam perīculum sine perīculō vincitur. (Publilius Syrus.)
2. Novius est vīcīnus meus et manū tangī dē fenestrīs meīs potest. (Martial. — Novius, -iī, a name. — vīcīnus, -ī, *neighbor.* — fenestra, -ae, *window*.)
3. Nōnne iubēbis hunc in vincula dūcī et ad mortem rapī? (Cicero. — nōnne introduces a question which anticipates the answer "yes." — vinculum, -ī, *chain*.)
4. Erunt etiam altera bella atque iterum ad Troiam magnus mittētur Achillēs. (*Virgil. — altera bella, *the old wars over again.* — iterum, *again*.)
5. Altera aetās bellīs cīvīlibus teritur et Rōma ipsa suīs vīribus dēlētur. (Horace. — cīvīlis, -e. — terō, -ere, trīvī, trītum, *wear out*.)
6. At amīcitia nūllō locō exclūditur; numquam intempestīva est. (Cicero. — exclūdō, -ere, -clūsī, -clūsum, *shut out*. — intempestīvus, -a, -um, *untimely*.)

7. Futūra scīrī nōn possunt. (Cicero. — futūrus, -a, -um.)
8. Prīncipiō ipse mundus deōrum hominumque causā factus est, et quae in eō sunt, ea parāta sunt ad frūctum hominum. (Cicero. — principium, -iī, *beginning*.)
9. Quam cōpiōsē ā Xenophonte agrīcultūra laudātur in eō librō quī "Oeconomicus" inscrībitur. (Cicero. — cōpiōsē, adv., cp. cōpia. — Xenophōn, -ntis. — agrīcultūra, -ae, — inscrībō, *entitle*.)
10. Vulgus vult dēcipī. (*Phaedrus. — vulgus, -ī, n., *the common people*. — vult, *want* (irreg. form). — dēcipiō, *deceive*.)
11. Ubi sapientia invenītur? (Job.)
12. Vēritās nimis saepe labōrat; exstinguitur numquam. (Livy. — labōrō (1), *labor, be hard pressed*. — exstinguō, -ere, -stinxī, -stinctum.)

THE UNIVERSALITY OF ANCIENT GREEK

Trahimur omnēs studiō laudis et multī glōriā dūcuntur. Quī autem putat minōrem frūctum glōriae ex Graecīs versibus capī quam ex Latīnīs, errat, quod Graecae litterae leguntur in omnibus ferē gentibus sed Latīnae litterae suīs fīnibus continentur. (Cicero. — putō (1), *think*. — minōrem, *smaller*. — quam, *than*. — errō (1). — ferē, adv. modifying omnibus, *almost*.)

ETYMOLOGY

Exemplī causā was Cicero's equivalent of the somewhat later **exemplī grātiā**, whence obviously our abbreviation *e.g.*

Romance derivatives from some of the words in the vocabulary:

Latin	Italian	Spanish	French
causa	cosa	cosa	chose
fīnis	fine	fin	fin
gēns	gente	gente	gent; gens (plu.)
continēre	continere	contener	contenir
mundus	mondo	mundo	monde

In the sentences   2. vicinity. — **fenestra:** It. *finestra,* Fr. *fenêtre*. Again a common use of the French circumflex is illustrated. 3. vinculum (in mathematics). 4. iterate, iterative, reiterate. 5. civil; cp. **cīvis, cīvitās.** — trite, contrite, contrition, attrition, detriment. 6. **ex + claudō** (-ere, -clausī, -clausum, *shut, close*): conclude, include, preclude, seclude, recluse, clause, close, closet, cloister.

Footnote

[1]There are differences in the quantity of the stem vowel.

22

Fifth Declension; Summary of Ablatives

The fifth declension is the last of the declensions. Fortunately, the general pattern of this declension has little about it which is strikingly novel. In the endings of the fifth declension, e is definitely the characteristic vowel.

FIFTH DECLENSION

	rēs, reī, f. thing	diēs, diēī, m. day	Case Endings
Nom.	rēs	dīēs	-ēs
Gen.	réī	diéī	-ĕ̄ī[1]
Dat.	réī	diéī	-ĕ̄ī[1]
Acc.	rem	dīem	-em
Abl.	rē	dīē	-ē
Nom.	rēs	dīēs	-ēs
Gen.	rérum	diérum	-ērum
Dat.	rébus	diébus	-ēbus
Acc.	rēs	dīēs	-ēs
Abl.	rébus	diébus	-ēbus

GENDER

Nouns of the fifth declension, like those of the first, are feminine, with the exception of **diēs,** which is regularly masculine.

ABLATIVE OF MANNER WITH AND WITHOUT Cum

You have already learned in Ch. 14 that the Romans expressed the idea of manner by **cum** with the ablative. However, when the noun is modified by an adjective, **cum** may be omitted.

Id cum cūrā fēcit, *he did it with care.* (**Cum** is necessary.)
Id magnā cum cūrā fēcit, *he did it with great care.* (**Cum** is optional.)
Id magna cūrā fēcit, *he did it with great care.* (**Cum** is optional.)

TABULAR REVIEW OF SPECIAL ABLATIVE CATEGORIES

I. THE ABLATIVE WITH A PREPOSITION

The ablative is used with:
1. **cum** to indicate *accompaniment* (Ch. 14).
   Cum amīcō id scrīpsit, *he wrote it with his friend.*
2. **cum** to indicate *manner* (Ch. 14).
   Cum cūrā id scrīpsit, *he wrote it with care.*
3. **in** to indicate *place where* (catalogued here for the first time).
   In urbe id scrīpsit, *he wrote it in the city.*
4. **ab, dē, ex** to indicate *place from which* (Ch. 20).
   Ex urbe id mīsit, *he sent it from the city.*
5. **ab, dē, ex** to indicate *separation* (Ch. 20); cp. II. 4 below.
   Ab urbe eōs prohibuit, *he kept them from the city.*
6. **ab** to indicate *personal agent* (Ch .18).
   Ab amīcō id scrīptum est, *it was written by his friend.*

II. THE ABLATIVE WITHOUT A PREPOSITION

The ablative is used without a preposition to indicate:
1. *means* (Ch . 14).
   Suā manū id scrīpsit, *he wrote it with his own hand.*
2. *manner*, when an adjective is used (Ch. 15).
   Magnā cūrā id scrīpsit, *he wrote it with great care.*
3. *time when or within which* (Ch.15).
   Eō tempore *or* ūnā hōrā id scrīpsit, *at that time* or *in one hour he wrote it.*
4. *separation,*especially with ideas of freeing, lacking, depriving (Ch. 20).
   Metū eōs līberāvit, *he freed them from fear.*

VOCABULARY

díēs, diḗi, *m.*, day (*diary, dial, diurnal, journal, adjourn, journey, sojourn*)

fídēs, fídeī, *f.*, faith, trust, trustworthiness, fidelity, protection (*confide, diffident, infidel, perfidy*)

ígnis, -is, *m.*, fire (*igneous, ignite, ignition*)

módus, -i, *m.*, measure, bound, limit; manner, method, mode (*model, moderate, modern, modest, modicum, modify, mood*)

rēs, réī, *f.*, thing, matter, business, affair (*real, realistic, realize, reality, real estate*)

rēs pūblica, réī pūblicae, *f.*, state, commonwealth, republic

spēs, spéī, *f.*, hope

incértus, -a, -um (in-certus), uncertain, doubtful

ērípiō, -ere, -rípuī, -réptum (ē-rapiō), snatch away, take away; rescue

inquit, *defective verb*, he says *or* said, *placed after one or more words of a direct quotation*

tóllō, -ere, sústulī, sublátum, raise, lift up; take away, remove, destroy (*extol*)

RECOGNITION VOCABULARY

médius, -a, -um, middle; *used partitively*, the middle of: **media urbs,** the middle of the city (*mediocre, mediterranean, medium, median, mediate, mean, medieval, immediate*)

quóndam, *adv.*, formerly, once (*quondam*)

álō, -ere, álui, áltum, nourish, support, sustain, increase, cherish (*alible, aliment, alimentary, alimony*)

PRACTICE AND REVIEW

1. Mundus multōs frūctūs continet.
2. Gentēs Graeciae parvīs fīnibus continēbantur.
3. Quis iussit illam rem pūblicam servitūte līberārī?
4. "Iste," inquit, "sceleribus suīs tollētur."
5. Contrā aliās manūs malōrum cīvium eaedem rēs parābuntur.
6. Senectūs senēs ā mediīs rēbus āmovet.
7. At rēs gravēs neque vī neque spē geruntur sed cōnsiliō.
8. Sī versūs poētārum neglegētis, magnā parte litterārum carēbitis.
9. Eōdem tempore nostrae spēs vestrā fidē altae sunt.
10. Nova genera scelerum parantur quod multī etiam nunc bonīs mōribus carent.
11. Great fidelity will be found in many citizens of this commonwealth.
12. His new hope had been destroyed by the common fear of uncertain things.
13. On that day the courage and the faith of brave men were seen by all.
14. With great hope the tyrant ordered that state to be destroyed.

SENTENTIAE ANTĪQUAE

1. Dum vīta est, spēs est. (Cicero.)
2. Aequum animum in rēbus difficilibus servā. (Horace. — aequus, -a, -um, *level, calm.*)
3. Ubi tyrannus est, ibi plānē est nūlla rēs pūblica. (*Cicero. — plānē, *clearly.*)
4. Fuērunt quondam in hāc rē pūblicā virī magnae virtūtis et antīquae fideī. (Cicero.)
5. Hanc rem pūblicam salvam esse volumus. (*Cicero. — salvus, -a, -um, *safe.* — volumus, *we wish.*)
6. Spēs coniūrātōrum mollibus sententiīs multōrum cīvium alitur. (Cicero. — coniūrātus, -ī, *conspirator.* — mollis, -e, *soft, mild.*)
7. Rēs pūblica cōnsiliīs meīs eō diē ex igne atque ferrō ērepta est. (Cicero. — ferrum -ī, *iron, the sword.*)
8. Dē pāce cum fidē agēbant. (Livy. — agō, *negotiate.*)
9. Dīc mihi bonā fidē: tū eam pecūniam ex eius manibus nōn ēripuisti? (Plautus.)
10. Amīcus certus in rē incertā cernitur. (Ennius. — cernō, -ere, crēvī, crētum, *discern.*)
11. Homērus audītōrem in mediās rēs rapit. (Horace. — audītor, -ōris, *listener.*)
12. Fēlīx est quī potest causās rērum intellegere; et fortūnātus ille quī deōs antīquōs dīligit. (Virgil. — fēlīx, -īcis, *happy.* — fortūnātus, -a, -um.)
13. Stōicus noster, "Vitium," inquit, "nōn est in rēbus sed in animō ipsō." (Seneca. — Stōicus, -ī, *a Stoic.*)
14. Et mihi rēs subiungam, nōn mē rēbus. (Horace. — subiungō, -ere, -iūnxī, -iūnctum, *subject.*)
15. Est modus in rēbus; sunt certī fīnēs ultrā quōs virtūs invenīrī nōn potest. (Horace. — **ultrā** + acc., *beyond.*)

ETYMOLOGY

Connected with **diēs** is the adjective **diurnus**, *daily*, whence come the words for *day* in Italian and French: It. *giorno*, Fr. *jour*, *journée*; cp. Sp. *día*. In late Latin there was a form **diurnālis**, from which derive It. *giornale*, Fr. *journal*, Eng. *journal*; cp. Sp. *diario*.

English *dismal* stems ultimately from **diēs malus**.

The stem of **fidēs** can be found in the following words even though it may not be immediately obvious: affidavit, defy, affiance, fiancé. Eng. *faith* is from early Old French *feit, feid*, from Latin **fidem**.

Other words connected with **modus** are: modulate, accommodate, commodious, discommode, incommode, à la mode.

The adjective **altus, -a, -um,** *high,* literally means *having been nourished,* and so, *grown large;* hence altitude, alto, contralto, exalt, hautboy, oboe.

In the sentences 2. equal, equanimity, equator. 6. mollify, emollient, mollusk. 7. ferric, ferro-, ferriferous. 10. discreet. 12. Felix, felicity, felicitous. 13. The Stoic philosophy was so called because Zeno, its founder, used to teach in a certain stoa (portico) at Athens. 14. subjunctive. 15. ultra-, ne plus ultra.

Footnote

[1]The e is short when preceded by a consonant (**rĕī**); it is long when preceded by a vowel (**dĭēī**).

23

Participles

*N*ormal transitive verbs have four participles: two active, the present and the future; two passive, the perfect and the future. These are formed as follows.

	Active	Passive
Pres.	present stem + -ns (gen. -ntis)	————
Perf.	————	partic. stem[1] + -us, -a, -um
Fut.	participial stem[1]+ -ūrus, -ūra, -ūrum[2]	pres. stem + -ndus, -nda, -ndum

It is important to know the proper stem for each participle as well as the proper ending. Note that two are made on the present stem (the present active and the future passive) and that two are made on the participial stem (the future active and the perfect passive). This situation can perhaps best be mastered by memorizing the participles of **agō,** in which the difference between the present stem and the participial stem is sufficient to eliminate any confusion.

agō, agere, ēgi, āctum, do[3]

	Active	Passive
Pres.	ágēns, agéntis,[4] *doing*	————
Perf.	————	áctus, -a, -um,[4] *done, having been done*
Fut.	āctū́rus, -a, -um, *about to do, going to do*	agéndus, -a, -um,[4] *to be done,* *deserving* or *fit to be done*

The participles of three of the model verbs follow.

	Act.	Pass.	Act.	Pass.	Act.	Pass.
Pres.	dū́cēns	————	a′udiēns[5]	————	cápiēns[5]	————
Perf.		dúctus		audítus		cáptus
Fut.	ductū́rus	dūcéndus	audītū́rus	audiéndus	captū́rus	capiéndus

DECLENSION OF PARTICIPLES

The present participle is declined like **potēns** (Ch. 16) except that it has -e in the ablative singular.[6] All other participles are declined like **magnus, -a, -um.**

PARTICIPLES AS VERBAL ADJECTIVES[7]

Participles are verbal adjectives. As *adjectives*, participles naturally agree in gender, number, and case with the nouns which they modify. Sometimes also, like adjectives, they depend on no expressed noun but are themselves used as nouns: **amāns,** *a lover;* **sapiēns,** *a wise man, philosopher;* **venientēs,** *those coming.*

As *verbs*, participles have tense and voice; they may take direct objects or other constructions used with the particular verb; and they may be modified by an adverb or an adverbial phrase.

The tense of a participle, however, is not absolute but is relative to that of the main verb. For example, the action of a present participle is contemporaneous with the action of the verb of its clause, no matter whether that verb is in a present, a past, or a future tense. A similar situation obtains for the other participles, as can be seen in the following table.

1. Present participle = action *contemporaneous* with that of the verb (the same time).

2. Perfect participle = action *prior* to that of the verb (time before).

3. Future participle = action *subsequent* to that of the verb (time after).

Graecī nautae, videntēs Polyphēmum, tremunt; tremuērunt; trement.
Greek sailors, seeing Polyphemus, tremble; trembled; will tremble.

Graecī nautae, vīsī ā Polyphēmō, tremunt; tremuērunt; trement.
Greek sailors, (having been) seen by P., tremble; trembled; will tremble.

Graecī nautae, vīsūrī Polyphēmum, tremunt; tremuērunt; trement.
Greek sailors, about to see Polyphemus, tremble; trembled; will tremble.

The voice of a participle, like that of a verb, is active or passive according to the form, as you have already seen. However, note very carefully the lack of a present passive participle and a perfect active participle. Especially, be on your guard not to translate such forms as **laudātus** or **ductus** by *having praised* or *having led.* What is wrong with this translation and how should these forms be rendered literally?

THE TRANSLATION OF A PARTICIPLE

A participle can often be more effectively translated by a clause or by some phrase other than the simple participial expressions used above. The specific translation has to be chosen according to the context.

Vidéntēs: *on seeing P.* they tremble, trembled, will tremble; *when, since, if, as,* etc., *they see P.,* they tremble, will tremble; *when, since, if, as,* etc., *they saw P.,* they trembled.

Vīsī: *when, since,* etc., *they have been seen by P.,* they tremble, will tremble; *when, since,* etc., *they had been seen by P.,* they trembled.

Vīsūrī: *when, since,* etc., *they are going to see P.,* they tremble, will tremble; *when, since,* etc., *they were going to see P.,* they trembled.

VOCABULARY

áliquis, áliquid (*gen.* **alicu′ius,** *dat.* **álicui;** *cp. decl. of* **quis, quid,** *Ch. 19; nom. and acc. neut. plu. are* **áliqua**), *indef. pron.,* someone, somebody, something

iūcúndus, -a, -um, pleasant, delightful, agreeable, pleasing (*jocund*)

líber, líbera, líberum, free (*liberal, liberality, libertine;* cp. **lībertās, líberō**)

úmquam, *adv., in questions or neg. clauses,* ever, at any time

a′udiō, -íre, -ívī, -ítum, hear, listen to (*audible, audience, audit, audition*)

cúpiō, -ere, -ívī, -ítum, desire, wish, long for (*cupid, cupidity, covet*)

osténdō, -ere, osténdī, osténtum, exhibit, show, display (*ostentation, ostentatious, ostensible, ostensive*)

pétō, -ere, petívī, petítum, seek, aim at, beg, beseech (*appetite, compete, competent, impetuous, petition, petulant, repeat*)

prémō, -ere, préssi, préssum, press, press hard; **-primō** *in compounds as seen in* **opprimō** *below* (*compress, depress, express, impress, imprint, print, repress, reprimand, suppress*)

ópprimō, -ere, -préssī, -préssum, suppress, overwhelm, overpower, check (*oppress*)

vértō, -ere, vértī, vérsum, turn; change; so **ā-vértō,** turn away, avert (*adverse, advertise, avert, averse, convert, controversy, divers, diverse, divorce, invert, obverse, pervert, revert, subvert, subversive, transverse, verse, version, animadvert*)

RECOGNITION VOCABULARY

dónum, -í, *n.,* gift, present (*donation, condone;* cp. **dō**)

ōrátor, -óris, *m.,* orator, speaker (*oratory, oratorio*)

sígnum, -í, *n.,* sign, signal, indication, seal (*assign, consign, countersign, design, ensign, insignia, resign, seal, signet*)

PRACTICE AND REVIEW

1. Aliquid nōn ante audítum sciō.
2. Illum ōrātōrem petentem fīnem bellōrum scelerumque nōn adiūvistis.
3. Certī frūctūs pācis ab territō senātū cupiēbantur.
4. Quis aliās gentēs gravī metū servitūtis līberābit?
5. Nēmō fidem neglegēns metū umquam carēbit.

6. Patriae causā haec cōnsilia contrā eōs malōs aluit.
7. Oppressūrī illam gentem līberam virōs magnae sapientiae dēlēre coepērunt.
8. Tollēturne fāma eius istīs versibus novīs?
9. At vīta illīus modī aliquid iūcundum continet.
10. Quō diē ex igne atque morte certā ēreptus es?
11. We gave many things to nations lacking hope.
12. That man, (when) called, will come with great eagerness.
13. They saw the old man running from the city.
14. He himself was overpowered by uncertain fear because he desired neither truth nor liberty.

SENTENTIAE ANTĪQUAE

1. Timeō Danaōs et dōna ferentēs. (*Virgil. — Danaōs = Graecōs — et = etiam. — ferō, ferre, tulī, lātum, *bear*.)
2. Vīvēs meīs praesidiīs oppressus. (Cicero. — praesidium, -iī, *guard*.)
3. Illī autem, tendentēs manūs, vītam petēbant. (Livy. — tendō, -ere, tetendī, tentum and tēnsum, *stretch*.)
4. Tantalus sitiēns, flūmina ā labrīs fugientia tangere cupiēbat. (Horace. — sitiō, -īre, -īvī, *be thirsty*. — flūmen, -minis, n., *river*. — labrum, -ī, *lip*.)
5. Signa rērum futūrārum ā dīs ostenduntur. (Cicero.)
6. Graecia capta ferum victōrem cēpit. (*Horace. — ferus, -a, -um, *wild, uncultured*. — victor, -ōris, here = Rome.)
7. Atticus Cicerōnī ex patriā fugientī multam pecūniam dedit. (Nepos. — Atticus, a friend of Cicero.)
8. Sī mihi eum ēducandum committēs, studia eius fōrmāre ab īnfantiā incipiam. (Quintilian. — ēducō (1). — fōrmō (1). — īnfantia, -ae.)
9. Saepe stilum verte, bonum librum scrīptūrus. (Horace. — stilum vertere, *to invert the stilus* = to use the eraser.)
10. Cūra ōrātōris dictūrī eōs audītūrōs dēlectat. (Quintilian — dēlectō (1), *delight*.) *See Institutiones Oratoriae* XI.3.157.
11. Mortī Sōcratis semper illacrimō legēns Platōnem. (Cicero. — Sōcratēs, -tis. — illacrimō (1) + dat., *weep over*. — Platō, -ōnis.)
12. Memoria vītae bene āctae multōrumque bene factōrum iūcunda est. (Cicero.)
13. Quī timēns vīvet, līber nōn erit umquam. (Horace. — quī = is quī.)
14. Nōn is est miser quī iussus aliquid facit, sed is quī invītus facit. (Seneca. — invītus, -a, -um, *unwilling*.)
15. Verbum semel ēmissum volat irrevocābile. (Horace. — verbum, -ī, *word*. — semel, *once*. — ē-mittō. — volō (1), *fly*. — irrevocābilis, -e.)

ETYMOLOGY

Audiō is the ultimate ancestor of these surprising descendants: "obey" through Fr. *obéir* from Lat. **obēdire** (**ob** + **audīre**); "obedient" (**ob** + **audiēns**); "oyez, oyez" from Fr. *ouir,* Lat. **audire.**

In the sentences   3. tend, tent, tense, attend, contend, distend, extend, extent, extensive, intend, intent, intense, portend, pretend, subtend, superintendent; cp. **ostendō** in the vocabulary. 4. tantalize, Greek derivative from Tantalus. — flume. 9. stilus, style. 11. lachrymose. 15. verb, verbal, verbatim, verbose. — volatile, volley.

Footnotes

[1]The stem of the perfect passive participle as seen in the fourth principal part minus its ending: **laudāt-um.** In fact, the fourth principal part of most verbs is nothing but the perfect passive participle itself; see Ch. 29 and Ch. 12 n. 3.

[2]The ending of the future active participle is very easy to remember if you keep in mind the fact that our word *future* comes from **futūrus, -a, -um,** the future (and, incidentally, the only) participle of **sum.**

[3]This is, of course, only one of the numerous meanings of **agō.**

[4]The English derivatives from these participles are instructive: *agent* (**agēns**), "a person *doing* some-thing"; *act* (**āctum**), "something *done*"; *agenda* (**agenda**), "things *to be done*."

[5]Note that in the fourth conjugation the ending of the present participle is actually **-ēns,** not simple **-ns,** and that similarly the ending of the future passive is **-endus,** not **-ndus. Capiō** follows the pattern of **audiō.**

[6]The present participle has **-ī** in the ablative singular when used strictly as an attributive adjective: **ab amantī patre,** *by the loving father;* but **ab amante,** *by a lover,* or **patre amante fīlium,** *with the father loving the son.*

[7]"Participle" is derived from *participiō, to share in,* because it "partakes" of both a verb and an adjective.

24

Ablative Absolute; Passive Periphrastic; Dative of Agent

---

*T*he participles which you have just learned can be put to work in two idiomatic and very common Latin constructions: the ablative absolute and the passive periphrastic conjugation.

ABLATIVE ABSOLUTE

In Latin a noun (or a pronoun) and a participle agreeing with it are often put in the ablative case to indicate the circumstances under which the action of the main verb occurs.[1]

Hīs rēbus audītīs, coepit timēre.
These things having been heard, he began to be afraid.

Or in much better English[2]:

When (since, after, etc.) these things had been heard, he began...
When (since, after, etc.) he had heard these things, he began...

Eō imperium tenente, ēventum timeō.
With him holding the power,
Since he holds the power,
When he holds the power, → *I fear the outcome.*
If he holds the power,
Although he holds the power.

111

Caesare duce,[3] nihil timēbimus.
Caesar being the commander,
Under Caesar's command,
With Caesar in command,
Since (when, if, etc.) Caesar is the commander,

→ *we shall fear nothing.*

The Romans used this construction only *when the noun or the pronoun of the ablative absolute phrase was not referred to elsewhere in the clause as subject or object.* For instance, in the following sentence the ablative absolute cannot be used because **eum** is the object of **timeō**:

Eum imperium tenentem timeō, *I fear him when he holds the power.*

THE PASSIVE PERIPHRASTIC CONJUGATION: GERUNDIVE[4] + Sum

Despite its horrendous name, the passive periphrastic conjugation is simply the gerundive[4] with **sum** in any form required by the sentence. The gerundive, as a predicate adjective, agrees with the subject of **sum** in gender, number, and case.

The passive periphrastic expresses *obligation* or *necessity.*

Hoc est faciendum mihi, *this is to be done by me.*
  This ought to be (has to be, must be) done by me.
  I ought to do this, must do this.

Haec Caesarī facienda erant, *these things were to be done by Caesar.*
  These things had to be done by Caesar.
  Caesar had to do these things.

THE DATIVE OF AGENT

Instead of the ablative of agent, the dative of agent is used with the passive periphrastic. This is illustrated by **mihi** and **Caesarī** above.

VOCABULARY

  dux, dúcis, *m.,* leader, guide; commander, general (*duke, ducal, ducat, duchess, duchy, doge*)

  impérium, -iī, *n.,* power to command, supreme power, authority, command, control (*imperial, imperialism, imperious, empire*) sérvus, -ī, *m.*, slave (*serf, servile, service*)

quísque, quídque (*gen.* cuiūsque; *dat.* cu'íque), *indef. pron.*, each one, each person

re- *or* red-, *prefix*, again, back *(re-)*

cūr, *adv.*, why

accípiō, -ere, -cḗpī, -céptum, take (*to one's self*), get, receive, accept (*cp.* capiō, *Ch. 10*)

recípiō, -ere, -cḗpī, -céptum, take back, regain, admit, receive (*recipe, R$_x$, receipt, recipient, receptacle, reception*)

péllō, -ere, pépulī, púlsum, strike, push, drive out, banish (*compel, compulsion, compulsory, dispel, expel, impel, propel, repel, pelt, pulsate, pulse*)

expéllō, -ere, éxpulī, expúlsum, drive out, expel, banish

qua'erō, qua'erere, quaesḗvī, quaesḗtum, seek, look for, strive for; ask, inquire (*acquire, conquer, exquisite, inquire, inquest, inquisition, perquisite, query, quest, question, request, require*)

relínquō, -ere, lḗquī, -líctum, leave behind, leave, abandon, desert (*relinquish, reliquary, relict, relic, delinquent, dereliction*)

RECOGNITION VOCABULARY

cupíditās, -tátis, *f.*, desire, longing, passion, cupidity, avarice

nárrō (1), tell, report, narrate

rídeō, -ḗre, rḗsī, rḗsum, laugh, laugh at (*deride, derisive, ridicule, ridiculous, risibilities*)

PRACTICE AND REVIEW

1. Igne vīsō, omnēs fēminae territae sunt.
2. Populō diū metū oppressō, tyrannus ex urbe ēiciendus est.
3. Ōrātor, signō ab senātū datō, eō diē revēnit.
4. Gēns Rōmāna versūs eius magnā laude quondam recēpit.
5. Laudēs atque dōna ab ōrātōribus cupiēbantur.
6. Imperiō acceptō, dux fidem suam reī pūblicae ostendit.
7. Aliquis eōs servōs ex igne ēripī iusserat.
8. Scīsne omnia quae tibi scienda sunt?
9. Ille, ā marī reveniēns, ab istīs hominibus premī coepit.
10. Cupiō tangere manum illīus virī quī metū caruit atque gravia scelera contrā rem pūblicam oppressit.
11. When the common danger had been averted, our sons came back from Asia.
12. The hopes of our state must not be destroyed by evil men.
13. Since the people of all nations are seeking peace, all leaders must conquer the passion for (= of) power. (For "since" do not use a subordinating conjunction. For "must" do not use dēbeō.)

14. The leader, having been driven out by free men, could not regain his command.

SENTENTIAE ANTĪQUAE

1. Carthāgō dēlenda est. (Cato. — Carthāgō, -inis, f.)
2. Asiā victā, dux Rōmānus servōs multōs in Italiam mīsit. (Pliny the Elder.)
3. Omnibus perterritīs, quisque sē servāre cupiēbat. (Caesar. — perterreō.)
4. Cūr fābulam meam rīdēs? Nōmine mūtātō, dē tē fābula narrātur. (Horace. — fābula, -ae, *story*.)
5. Omnia quae dīcenda sunt, līberē dīcam. (Cicero. — līberē, adv. of līber.)
6. Haec omnia vulnera bellī tibi nunc sānanda sunt. (Cicero. — vulnus, -eris, n., *wound*. — sānō (1), *heal*.)
7. Nec tumultum nec mortem violentam timēbō Augustō terrās tenente. (Horace. — tumultus -ūs, *disturbance, civil war*. — violentus, -a, -um. — Augustus, -ī.)
8. Tarquiniō expulsō, nōmen rēgis audīre nōn poterat populus Rōmānus. (Cicero. — Tarquinius, -iī, an Etruscan, the last king of Rome.)
9. Ad ūtilitātem vītae omnia cōnsilia factaque nōbīs dīrigenda sunt. (Tacitus. —ūtilitās, -tātis, *benefit, advantage*. — dīrigō, -ere, dīrēxī, dīrēctum, *direct*.)

DĒ CUPIDITĀTE

Homō stultus, "Ō cīvēs, cīvēs," inquit, "pecūnia ante omnia quaerenda est; virtūs post pecūniam."

Pecūniae autem cupiditās fugienda est. Fugienda etiam est cupiditās glōriae; ēripit enim lībertātem. Neque imperia semper petenda sunt neque semper accipienda sunt. (Adapted from Horace, *Epistulae* 1.1.53 and Cicero, *Dē Officiīs* 1.20.68.)

Herculēs, in caelum propter virtūtem receptus, deōs salūtāvit; sed Plūtō veniente, quī est fīlius Fortūnae, Herculēs oculōs āvertit. Tum, causā quaesītā, "Iste," inquit, "spernendus est quod lucrī causā omnia corrumpit." (Adapted from Phaedrus 4.12.)

(Herculēs, -is. — salūtō (1), *greet*. — Plūtus, -ī, god of wealth. — spernō, -ere, sprēvī, sprētum, *scorn*.— lucrum, -ī, *gain*. — corrumpō, -ere, -rūpī, -ruptum.)

ETYMOLOGY

In the sentences   4. fable, fabled, fabulous, confab, ineffable. 6. vulnerable, invulnerable. — sanatorium. 7. tumultuous. — Violent is clearly based on **vîs**. — Originally the Romans, counting March as the first month of the year, named the fifth month **Quintîlis** (**quintus,** *fifth*), but Julius Caesar renamed it **Jūlius** (July) because he was born in July. Subsequently, when the Roman Senate gave Octavian, Caesar's heir, the title of Augustus (the august, the revered one), the Senate also changed the name of the sixth month (**Sextîlis**) to **Augustus** (August). 9. direction, director, directory, indirect, redirect. *Dē Cupiditāte:* Herculean — salute. — plutocrat, a work of Greek origin. — English *spurn* is cognate with Latin **spernō**. — lucre, lucrative. — corrupt, incorruptible.

Footnotes

[1]In origin this was probably an *ablative of attendant circumstance,* which is closely related to the *with*-idea in the ablatives of accompaniment and means. Though the ablative absolute came to be regarded as somewhat loosely connected with the rest of the sentence, it is not quite so "absolute" as the term suggests.

[2]Note the variety of forces which this ablative acquired (cause, time, concession, etc.), and in your finished translation always try to use some such clause intead of the more clumsy literal rendering.

[3]Notice that even two nouns in the ablative or a noun and an adjective in the ablative without a participle can constitute an ablative absolute for the simple reason that **sum** has no present participle, which is the form that would be required in such circumstances: *Caesar (being) the commander;* **Caesare invîtō,** *Caesar (being) unwilling.*

[4]"Gerundive" is another name for the future passive participle.

25

All Infinitives Active and Passive; Indirect Statement

*O*f the five infinitive forms in common use you already know two: the present active and the present passive. These vary according to the conjugation which they represent. The rest are easily formed according to rule; and in them there is no problem of different conjugations because the rule given for each infinitive holds for all conjugations.

	Active	Passive
Pres.	-āre, -ēre, -ĕre, -īre[1]	-ārī, -ērī, -ī, īrī
Perf.	perfect stem + **isse**	perf. pass. participle (in acc.) + **esse**
Fut.	fut. act. participle (in acc.) + **esse**	[supine in **-um** + **īrī**][2]

INFINITIVES OF agō, agere, ēgī, āctum, do

	Active	Passive
Pres.	ágere, *to do*	ágī, *to be done*
Perf.	ēgísse, *to have done*	áctus, -a, -um[3] esse, *to have been done*
Fut.	āctúrum, -am, -um[3] esse, *to be about to do, to be going to do*	[áctum īrī, *to be about to be done, to be going to be done*]

The infinitives of the model verbs are as follows.

Active

Pres.	laudáre	monére	dúcere	audíre	cápere
Perf.	laudávísse	monuísse	dūxísse	audīvísse	cēpísse
Fut.	laudātúrum, -am, -um, esse	monitúrum -am, -um, esse	ductúrum, -am, -um, esse	audītúrum, -am, -um, esse	captúrum -am, -um, esse

Passive

Pres.	laudā́rī	monḗrī	dū́cī	audī́rī	cápī
Perf.	laudā́tum,	mónitum,	dúctum,	audī́tum	cáptum
	-am, -um,	-am, -um,	-am,-um,	-am,-um,	-am,-um,
	esse	esse	esse	esse	esse
[*Fut.*	laudā́tum	mónitum	dúctum	audī́tum	cáptum
	īrī	īrī	īrī	īrī	īrī]

INFINITIVE IN INDIRECT STATEMENT WITH SUBJECT ACCUSATIVE

The following sentences are *direct* statements:

He is helping her.   Is iuvat eam.
He helped her.   Is iūvit (iuvābat) eam.

In English, when we report direct statements indirectly[4] after verbs of *saying* and the like, we regularly put these statements into subordinate clauses introduced by *that*.

They say *that* he is helping her.
They will say *that* he helped her.

In Latin, however, to report statements indirectly after verbs of *saying, knowing, thinking, perceiving,* and the like,[5] the Romans used the infinitive of indirect statement with subject accusative. (Cf. Eng. I consider *him to be* the best candidate. I saw *him run* past.) In classical Latin there was no word corresponding to our *that*.

The subject of an infinitive is put in the accusative case. Therefore, the original subject nominative of the direct statement becomes subject accusative of the infinitive of indirect statement. This subject is always expressed, even when it is the same as the subject of the verb of *saying*, etc. (See also p. 118 under use of the reflexive in indirect statement.)

(Is) iūvit eam, *he helped her.*

Dīcunt eum iūvisse eam, *they say that he helped her.*

(Ea) est iūta ab eō, *she was helped by him.*

Dīcunt eam esse iūtam[6] ab eō, *they say that she was helped by him.*

TENSES OF THE INFINITIVE

Study the *tenses* in the following groups of sentences.

Dīcunt -They say

A. eum **iuvāre** eam.   *that he is helping her.*
B. eum **iūvisse** eam.   *that he helped her.*
C. eum **iūtūrum esse** eam.   *that he will help her.*

Dīxērunt - They said

A. eum **iuvāre** eam.   *that he was helping her.*
B. eum **iūvisse** eam.   *that he had helped her.*
C. eum **iūtūrum esse** eam.   *that he would help her.*

Dīcent - They will say

A. eum **iuvāre** eam.   *that he is helping her.*
B. eum **iūvisse** eam.   *that he helped her.*
C. eum **iūtūrum esse** eam.   *that he will help her.*

You probably noticed that after any tense of the main verb (*dīcunt, dīxērunt, dīcent*) the present, the perfect, or the future tense of the infinitive may be used. This fact shows that the tenses of the infinitive are not absolute but are relative.

To put it another way, *regardless of the tense of the main verb:*

1. the *present infinitive* indicates *time before* that of the main verb (= contemporaneous infinitive).
2. the *perfect infinitive* indicates *time after* that of the main verb (= prior infinitive).
3. the *future infinitive* indicates *time after* that of the main verb (= subsequent infinitive).

USE OF THE REFLEXIVE IN AN INDIRECT STATEMENT

When a pronoun or a possessive adjective in an indirect statement refers to the subject of the verb of *saying,* etc., the Romans used the reflexive forms.

Gāius dīxit **sē** iūvisse eam,
    Gaius said that he (Gaius) had helped her.
Gāius dīxit **eum** iūvisse eam,
    Gaius said that he (e.g., Marcus) had helped her.
Gāius dīcit litterās scrīptās esse ā **sē,**
    G. says that the letter was written by him (Gaius).
Gāius dīcit litterās scrīptās esse ab **eō,**
    G. says that the letter was written by him (Marcus).

Rōmānī dīxērunt fīliōs **suōs** missōs esse,
   the Romans said that their own sons had been sent.
Rōmānī dīxērunt fīliōs **eōrum** missōs esse,
   the Romans said that their (e.g., the Greeks') sons had been sent.

VOCABULARY

hóstis, -is, *m.,* an enemy (*of the state*); **hóstēs, -ium,** the enemy (*hostile, host*)

hūmā́nus, -a, -um, pertaining to man (**homō**), human; humane, kind, refined, cultivated (*humanity, humanism, the humanities, humanist, inhuman, superhuman*)

immortā́lis, -e, not subject to death, immortal (*cp.* **mors**)

áit, áiunt, he says, they say, assert, *commonly used in connection with proverbs and anecdotes*

crḗdō, -ere, crḗdidī, crḗditum, believe, trust (*credence, credentials, 4credible, incredible, credulity, credulous, creed, credo, credit, creditable*)

négō (1), deny, say that...not (*negate, negative, abnegate, renegade, renege*)

nū́ntiō (1), announce, report, relate (*denounce, enunciate, pronounce, renounce*)

pútō (1), reckon, suppose, judge, think, imagine (*compute, count, depute, dispute, impute, putative, repute*)

spḗrō (1), hope for, hope, *regularly + fut. inf. in ind. statement* (*despair, desperado, desperate, prosper*)

victū́rus, -a, -um, *from* **vincō;** **vīctū́rus, -a, -um,** *from* **vīvō**

RECOGNITION VOCABULARY

adulḗscēns, -ntis, *m.,* young man (*adolescent*)
fidḗlis, -e, faithful, loyal (*infidel;* cp. **fidēs**)
hĭc, *adv.,* here
nésciō, -íre, -ívī, ítum, not to know

LIST OF VERBS CAPABLE OF INTRODUCING INDIRECT STATEMENT[7]

1. *saying:* dī́cō, négō, áit, nū́ntiō, nárrō, scrī́bō, dóceō, osténdō
2. *knowing:* scíō, nésciō, intéllegō, memóriā téneō
3. *thinking:* crḗdō, pútō, spḗrō
4. *perceiving:* aúdiō, vídeō, séntiō

PRACTICE AND REVIEW

1. "Quisque," inquit, "putat suās rēs esse magnās."
2. Audīvimus servōs dōnōrum causā pācem petīvisse.

3. Vim ignis magnā virtūte āvertērunt quod laudem atque dōna cupīvērunt.

4. Hoc signum perīculī tōtam gentem tanget.

5. Tyrannō expulsō, spēs fidēsque virōrum līberōrum rem pūblicam continēbunt.

6. Cūr iūcundus Horātius culpās hūmānās rīdēbat?

7. Crēdimus fidem antīquam omnibus gentibus alendam esse.

8. Dux ad senātum missus imperium accēpit.

9. Rēs pūblica librīs huius modī tollī potest.

10. Aliquī negant hostēs victōs servitūte opprimendōs esse.

11. We thought that you were writing the letter.

12. They will show that the letter was written by him.

13. He said that the letter had not been written.

14. We hope that she will write the letter.

SENTENTIAE ANTĪQUAE

1. Id factum esse nōn negāvit. (Terence.)

2. Hīs rēbus nūntiātīs, eum esse hostem scīvistī. (Cicero.)

3. Eum ab hostibus exspectārī sentīs. (Cicero.)

4. Vīdī eōs in urbe remānsisse et nōbīscum esse. (Cicero.)

5. Itaque aeternum bellum cum malīs cīvibus ā mē susceptum esse videō. (Cicero. — sus-cipiō, *undertake*.)

6. Idem crēdō tibi faciendum esse. (Cicero.)

7. Tē enim esse fidēlem mihi sciēbam. (Terence.)

8. Hostibus appropinquantibus, senātus Cincinnātō nūntiāvit eum factum esse dictātōrem. (Cicero. — appropinquō (1), *approach*. — Cincinnātus, -ī. — dictātor, -ōris.)

9. Dīcō tē, Pyrrhe, Rōmānōs posse vincere. (Ennius. — Pyrrhus, -ī.)

10. Dīc, hospes, Spartae tē nōs hīc iacentēs vīdisse, patriae fidēlēs. (Cicero; epigram on the Spartans who died at Thermopylae. — hospes, -itis, *stranger*. — Sparta, -ae. — iaceō, -ēre, iacuī, *lie*.)

11. Sōcratēs putābat sē esse cīvem tōtīus mundī. (Cicero.)

12. Negant quemquam virum esse bonum nisi sapientem. (Cicero. — quisquam, quidquam, *anyone, anything*. — nisi, *except*. — sapiēns, -ntis, *philosopher*.)

13. Negāvī mortem timendam esse. (Cicero.)

14. Crēdō deōs immortālēs sparsisse animōs in corpora hūmāna. (Cicero. — spargō, -ere, sparsī, sparsum, *scatter, sow*.)

15. Adulēscēns spērat sē diū vīctūrum esse; senex potest dīcere sē diū vīxisse. (Cicero.)

16. Aiunt enim multum legendum esse, nōn multa. (*Pliny.)

ETYMOLOGY

Hostis meant originally *stranger* and then *enemy*, since any stranger in early times was a possible enemy. From **hostis**, *enemy*, stems our *host* in the sense of *army*. **Hospes, hospitis,** which is an ancient compound of **hostis**, *stranger*, and **potis**, *having power over, lord of* (cf. Russian gospodin, *lord, gentleman*), means *host* (one who receives strangers or guests) and also *guest;* cp. hospital, hospitality, hostel, hotel (Fr. *hôtel*), and Eng. cognate *guest*.

In the sentences   5. susceptible; and note that *under-take* is a very literal translation of **sub-capiō**. 8. propinquity. — Cincinnati, both the organization composed originally of the officers who served under George Washington and also the city named after the organization. 9. Pyrrhus, the Greek general, defeated the Romans twice, but the victories cost him almost as many men as they cost the Romans; hence the term "Pyrrhic victory." 10. adjacent, interjacent, subjacent; "Hic Iacet" on tombstones. 14. aspersion, disperse, intersperse, sparse.

Footnotes

[1] Actually, the ending of the present active infinitive is -re, which is added to the present stem; but for purposes of distinction it is convenient to use the forms given in the paradigm.

[2] The future passive infinitive is given in brackets because it is not a common form and does not occur in this book. The Romans preferred a substitute expression like fore ut + subjunctive (result clause). The supine in -um has the same spelling as that of the perf. pass. part. in the nom. neut. sing.

[3] The participles are regarded as predicate adjectives and so are made to agree with the subject of esse.

[4] That is, not directly in quotation marks.

[5] For such Latin verbs see the list following the Recognition Vocabulary below.

[6] Note carefully the agreement of the participle with the subject of the infinitive.

[7] Others to be introduced later are respondeō, answer; dēmōnstrō, point out; cognōscō, learn, know; arbitror, think.

26

Comparison of Adjectives; Declension of Comparatives

The forms of the adjective which you have learned so far indicate a basic quality or quantity associated with the modified noun: a happy man, *beātus vir. This is called the positive degree of the adjective.*

However, in comparison with the first man, another may have more of this quality. The greater amount of the quality is indicated by the comparative degree of the adjective: a happier (more happy) man, *beātior vir.*

Finally, if a third man has even more of the quality than the other two, he has it in the superlative degree: the happiest (most happy) man, *beātissimus vir.*

FORMATION OF THE COMPARATIVE AND THE SUPERLATIVE

The form of the positive degree is learned from the vocabulary.

The forms of the comparative and the superlative of regular adjectives are made on the *base* of the positive as follows[1]:

Comparative: base[2] of positive + -ior (m. & f.), -ius (n.)
Superlative: base of positive + issimus, - issima, -issimum

Positive	Comparative	Superlative
cārus, -a, -um (*dear*)	cárior, -ius (*dearer*)	cāríssimus, -a, -um (*dearest*)
lóngus, -a, -um (*long*)	lóngior, -ius (*longer*)	longíssimus, -a, -um (*longest*)
fórtis, -e (*brave*)	fórtior, -ius (*braver*)	fortíssimus, -a, -um (*bravest*)
félix, *gen.* fēlícis (*happy*)	fēlícior, -ius (*happier*)	fēlīcíssimus, -a, -um (*happiest*)
pótēns, *gen.* poténtis (*powerful*)	poténtior, -ius (*more powerful*)	potentíssimus, -a, -um (*most powerful*)
sápiēns, *gen.* sapiéntis (*wise*)	sapiéntior, -ius (*wiser*)	sapientíssimus, -a, -um (*wisest*)

DECLENSION OF COMPARATIVES

Comparatives are two-ending adjectives of the third declension, but they follow the *consonant declension;* and so they constitute the chief exception to the rule that adjectives of the third declension belong to the i-stem declension.[3]

	Singular M. & F.	N.	Plural M. & F.	N.
Nom.	fórtior	fórtius	fortiórēs	fortióra
Gen.	fortióris	fortiórīs	fortiórum	fortiórum
Dat.	fortiórī	fortiórī	fortióribus	fortióribus
Acc.	fortiórem	fórtius	fortiórēs	fortióra
Abl.	fortiórē	fortiórē	fortióribus	fortióribus

SPECIAL MEANINGS OF THE COMPARATIVE AND THE SUPERLATIVE

The comparative sometimes has the force of *too* or *rather:*
Vīta eius erat brevior, *his life was too short, rather short.*

The superlative sometimes has the force of *very:*
Vīta eius erat brevissima, *his life was very short.*

CONJUNCTION Quam, *than.*

After a comparative the second of the compared words or ideas can be connected with the first by **quam,** *than.* The word or idea after **quam** has the same construction as the corresponding member before **quam.**

Hī librī sunt clāriōrēs quam illī.
These books are more famous than those.
Dīcit hōs librōs esse clāriōrēs quam illōs.
He says that these books are more famous than those.

VOCABULARY

a'uctor, -ŏris, *m.,* increaser, author, originator (*authority*)

lūx, lúcis, *f.,* light (*lucid, elucidate, translucent, lucubration, illustrate, illuminate*)

quĭdam, qua'edam, quíddam (*pron.*) or **quóddam** (*adj.*), *indef. pron. and adj.; as pron.,* a certain one or thing, someone, something; *as adj.,* a certain, some (*gen.* **cuiúsdam,** *dat.* **cui'dam,** *etc.*)

acérbus, -a, -um, harsh, bitter, grievous (*acerbity, exacerbate*)

clárus, -a, -um, clear, bright; renowned, famous, illustrious (*clarify, clarity, claret, clarinet, clarion, declare, Clara, Clarissa, Claribel*)

pótēns, *gen.* **poténtis,** *pres. part. of* **possum** *as an adj.,* able, powerful, mighty, strong.(*potent, impotent, omnipotent, potentate, potential*)

túrpis, -e, ugly, shameful, base, disgraceful (*turpitude*)

prō, *prep.* + *abl.,* in front of, before, on behalf of, for the sake of, in return for, instead of, for, as; *also as prefix* (*pros and cons, pro-* as a prefix)

quam, *adv. and conj. after comparatives,* than; *with superlatives, as...as possible:* **quam fortissimus,** as brave as possible (*cp.* **quam,** how, *Ch. 16*)

vītō (1), avoid, shun; *not to be confused with* **vīvō** (*inevitable*)

RECOGNITION VOCABULARY

remédium, -iī, *n.,* cure, remedy (*remedial, irremediable*)

PRACTICE AND REVIEW

1. Nescīvit sē imperium acceptūrum esse.
2. "Quĭdam," inquit, "imperium quondam petēbant et līberōs virōs opprimere cupiēbant."
3. Eōdem diē hostēs ab duce fidēlī āversī sunt.
4. Morte tyrannī nūntiātā, quisque sē ad ōrātōrem magnā spē vertit.
5. Rīdēns, ōrātor aliquid iūcundius nārrāvit.
6. Hīs rēbus audītīs, adulēscēns propter pecūniae cupiditātem studium litterārum relinquet.
7. Adulēscēns ostendit fidem esse cāriōrem sibi quam pecūniam.
8. Negāvit sē umquam vīdisse servum fidēliōrem quam hunc.
9. Iūcundior modus vītae hominibus quaerendus est.
10. Crēdimus līberōs virōs vītam iūcundissimam agere.
11. What is sweeter than a very pleasant life?

12. Certain men, however, say that death is sweeter than life.
13. When these very sure signs had been reported, we sought advice from the most powerful leader.
14. Our author says that all men seek as happy lives as possible.

SENTENTIAE ANTĪQUAE

1. Senectūs est loquācior. (Cicero. — loquāx, loquācis, *garrulous*.)
2. Tua cōnsilia omnia nōbis clāriōra sunt quam lūx. (Cicero.)
3. Quaedam remedia graviōra sunt quam ipsa perīcula. (Seneca.)
4. Eō diē virōs fortissimōs atque amantissimōs reī pūblicae ad mē vocāvī. (Cicero. — amāns r.p., *patriotic*.)
5. Quī imperia libēns accēpit, partem acerbissimam servitūtis vītat. (Seneca. — libēns, gen. -ntis, *willing*.)
6. Mēns quiēta, vīrēs, prūdēns simplicitās, amīcī — haec vītam beātiōrem faciunt, iūcundissime amīce. (Martial. — quiētus, -a, -um. — prūdēns, gen. prūdentis. — simplicitās, -tātis.)
7. Iūcundissima dōna semper sunt ea quae auctor ipse cāra facit. (Ovid.)
8. Beātus vir forum vītat et superba līmina potentiōrum cīvium. (Horace. — forum, -ī. — superbus, -a, -um, *haughty*. — līmen, -inis, n., *threshold*.)
9. Quid est turpius quam ab aliquō illūdī? (Cicero. — illūdō, -ere, illūsī, illūsum, *deceive*.)
10. Quid enim stultius quam incerta prō certīs habēre, falsa prō vērīs? (*Cicero. — falsus, -a, -um.)
11. Saepe mihi dīcis, cārissime amīce: "Scrībe aliquid magnum; dēsidiōsissimus homō es." (Martial. — dēsidiōsus, -a, -um, *lazy*.)
12. Verba currunt; at manus notāriī est vēlōcior quam verba. (Martial. — verbum, -ī, *word*. — notārius, -iī, *stenographer*. — vēlōx, gen. vēlōcis, *swift*.)
13. Multī putant rēs bellicās graviōrēs esse quam rēs urbānās; sed haec sententia mūtanda est, nam multae rēs urbānae sunt graviōrēs clāriōrēsque quam bellicae. (Cicero. — bellicus, -a, -um, adj. of bellum. — urbānus, -a, -um, adj. of urbs.)
14. Invītātus ad cēnam, fūrtificā manū lintea neglegentiōrum sustulistī. Hoc salsum esse putās? Rēs sordidissima est! Itaque mihi linteum remitte. (Catullus. — invītō (1), *invite*. — cēna, -ae, *dinner*. — fūrtificus, -a, -um, *thievish*. — linteum, -ī, *linen, napkin*. — neglegēns, -ntis, *careless*. — salsus, -a, -um, *salty, witty*. — sordidus, -a, -um, *dirty, mean*.)

ETYMOLOGY

In Spanish the comparative degree of an adjective is regularly formed by putting *más* (*more*) before the adjective: *más caro, más alto*. This *más* comes from the **magis** mentioned in footnote 1 below. Spanish and Italian both retain some vestiges of the Latin superlative ending **-issimus**. Forms with this ending, however, are not the normal superlative forms, but they are used to convey the intensive idea of *very, exceedingly*.

Latin	Italian	Spanish	
cārissimus	carissimo	carisimo	*very dear*
clārissimus	chiarissimo	clarisimo	*very clear*
altissimus	altissimo	altisimo	*very high*

In the sentences   1. loquacious, loquacity. 8. forum, forensic. 9. illusion, illusive, illusory. 12. notary, note. 13. urban, urbane, urbanity, suburb. 14. lint. — From **salsus** through French come sauce, saucer, saucy, sausage.

Footnotes

[1]Occasionally an adjective is compared by adding **magis** (*more*) and **maximē** (*most*) to the positive. This is regular in adjectives like **idōne-us, -a, -um** (*suitable*) where a vowel precedes the endings: **magis idōneus, maximē idōneus.**

[2]Remember that to find the base you drop the ending of the genitive singular: **cārus, cār-(ī); fort-(is); fēlīx, fēlīc-(is); potēns, potent-(is).**

[3]I.e., comparatives do *not* have the **-ī** in the abl. sing., the **-ium** in the gen. plu., and the **-ia** in the nom. and the acc. neut. plu. which characterize other adjs. of the 3d declension. See Ch. 16

27

Special and Irregular Comparison of Adjectives

ADJECTIVES HAVING PECULIAR FORMS IN THE SUPERLATIVE

Two groups of adjectives, which are otherwise regular, have peculiar forms in the superlative:

I. Six adjectives ending in **-lis**[1] form the superlative by adding **-limus, -lima, -limum** to the *base*.

Positive	Comparative	Superlative
fácilis, -e (*easy*)	facílior, -ius (*easier*)	facíl-limus, -a, -um (*easiest*)
diffícilis, -e (*difficult*)	difficílior, -ius (*more d.*)	difficíllimus, -a, -um (*most d.*)
símilis, -e (*like*)	simílior, -ius (*more l.*)	simíllimus, -a, -um (*most l.*)

II. Any adjective which has a masculine in **-er**, regardless of the declension, forms the superlative by adding **-rimus** to this masculine **-er**.

Positive	Comparative	Superlative
līber, -era, -erum (*free*)	lībérior, -ius (*freer*)	lībér-rimus, -a, -um (*freest*)
púlcher, -chra, -chrum (*beautiful*)	púlchrior, -ius (*more b.*)	pulchérrimus, -a, -um (*most b.*)
ácer, ácris, ácre (*keen*)	ácrior, ácrius (*keener*)	ācérrimus, -a, -um (*keenest*)

ADJECTIVES OF IRREGULAR COMPARISON

More important from the consideration of frequency of appearance are a few adjectives which are so irregular in their comparison that the only solution to the difficulty is memorization. However, English derivatives from the irregular forms greatly aid the memorization (see p. 130–131). A list of the most useful of these adjectives follows.[2]

Positive	Comparative	Superlative
bónus, -a, -um (*good*)	mélior, -ius (*better*)	óptimus, -a, -um (*best*)
mágnus, -a, -um (*great*)	ma'ior, -ius (*greater*)	máximus, -a, -um (*greatest*)
málus, -a, -um (*bad*)	pe'ior, -ius (*worse*)	péssimus, -a, -um (*worst*)
múltus, -a, -um (*much*)	—, plūs (*more*)	plúrimus, -a, -um (*most*)
párvus, -a, -um (*small*)	mínor, mínus (*smaller*)	mínimus, -a, -um (*smallest*)
(prae, prō)	príor, -ius (*former*)	prímus, -a, -um (*first*)
súperus, -a, -um (*that above*)	supérior, -ius (*higher*)	súmmus, -a, -um (*highest*) suprēmus, -a, -um (*last*)

DECLENSION OF Plūs

None of the irregular forms offers any declensional difficulty except **plūs**.

	Singular		Plural	
	M. & F.	N.	M. & F.	N.
Nom.	——	plūs	plúrēs	plúra
Gen.	——	plúris	plúrium	plúrium
Dat.	——	——	plúribus	plúribus
Acc.	——	plūs	plúrēs	plúra
Abl.	——	plúre	plúribus	plúribus

In the singular **plūs** is used only as a noun, and it is commonly followed by a genitive: **plūs pecūniae,** *more money*.

VOCABULARY

sōl, sólis, *m.,* sun (*solar, solarium*)

ácer, ácris, ácre, sharp, keen, eager; severe, fierce (*acrid, acrimony, acrimonious, eager;* cp. **acerbus**)

fácilis, -e, easy, agreeable (*facile, facility, facilitate, difficult;* cp. **faciō**)

prímus, -a, -um, first, foremost, chief, principal (*primary, primate, prime, primeval, primer, premier, primitive, prim, primo-geniture, prima facie*)

púlcher, -chra, -chrum, beautiful, handsome; fine (*pulchritude*)

sápiēns, *gen.* **-éntis,** *as adj.,* wise, judicious; *as noun,* a wise man, philosopher (*homo sapiens, sapience, insipience, sapid, insipid, verbum sapienti*)

símilis, -e, similar, like, resembling (*similarly, simile, assimilate, dissimilar, dissimilarity, simulate, dissimulate, verisimilitude;* cp. *same*) + dat., p. 358.

All the irregular adjectival forms given above in this lesson.

appéllō (1), call, name (*appellation, appellative, appeal, appellant, appellate*)

RECOGNITION VOCABULARY

ma'ior [nātū], *adj.,* greater (*in birth*), older

maiórēs, -rum, *m.,* those greater (*in years*), ancestors

félix, *gen.* **fēlícis,** *adj. of 1 ending,* lucky, fortunate, happy (*felicitate, felicitation, felicitous, infelicitous, felicity, infelicity, Felix*)

PRACTICE AND REVIEW

1. Quisque cupit quam pulcherrima dōna accipere.
2. Quīdam habent plūrima sed plūra petunt.
3. Ille ōrātor, ab tyrannō acerbō expulsus, ducem iūcundiōrem quaesīvit.
4. Summum imperium optimīs virīs petendum est.
5. Maiōrem partem hostium hīc (*adv.*) vītābimus.
6. Ostendit hostēs signum lūce clārissimā dedisse.
7. Negāvit sē virōs līberōs umquam oppressisse.
8. Fidēlissimus servus plūs accipiēbat quam pessimus.
9. Aiunt hunc auctōrem vītam turpiōrem agere.
10. Cūr dī potentēs et immortālēs oculōs ā rēbus hūmānīs āvertērunt?
11. The very beautiful girl was more beautiful than her beautiful mother.
12. Some believe that the largest cities are worse than the smallest.
13. In return for very small gifts he sought more and greater ones.
14. Something better than the worst is not very good.

SENTENTIAE ANTĪQUAE

1. Videō meliōra probōque; peiōra faciō. (Ovid. — probō (1), *approve*.)
2. Quaedam carmina sunt bona; plūra sunt mala. (Martial. — carmen, -minis. n., *poem*.)
3. Hunc maiōrem fīlium amīcī meī adoptāvī et eum amāvī prō meō. (Terence. — adoptō (1).)

4. Optimum est. Nihil melius, nihil pulchrius vīdī. (Terence.)
5. Spērō tē et hunc nātālem et plūrimōs aliōs quam fēlīcissimōs āctūrum esse. (Pliny. — nātālis (diēs), *birthday*.)
6. Rōmānī prīmum diem ā sōle appellāvērunt, quī prīmus est omnium stēllārum. (Isidore, *Orīginēs*. — **sōle**, cp. Eng. *Sunday*. — stēlla, -ae, *star*.)
7. Quoniam cōnsilium et ratiō sunt in senibus, maiōrēs nostrī summum concilium appellāvērunt senātum. (Cicero. — concilium, -iī, *council*.)
8. Plūs operae studiīque in rēbus domesticīs pōnendum est etiam quam in rēbus mīlitāribus. (Cicero. — opera, -ae, *work, pains*. — domesticus, -a, -um. — pōnō, -ere, posuī, positum, *put*. — mīlitāris, -e.)
9. Neque enim perīculum in rē pūblicā fuit gravius umquam neque ōtium maius. (Cicero.)
10. Sumus sapientiōrēs quam illī quod nōs nātūram esse optimam ducem scīmus. (Cicero.)
11. Nātūra minimum petit; nātūrae autem sē sapiēns accommodat. (*Seneca. — accommodō (1), *adapt*.)
12. Maximum remedium īrae mora est. (*Seneca.)
13. Quī animum vincit et īram continet, eum cum summīs virīs nōn comparō sed eum esse simillimum deō dīcō. (Cicero. — comparō (1), *compare*.)
14. Dionȳsius, tyrannus urbis pulcherrimae, erat vir summae in vīctū temperantiae et in omnibus rēbus dīligentissimus et ācerrimus. Īdem tamen erat iniūstus. Quā ex rē, sī vērum dīcimus, vidēbātur miserrimus. (Cicero. — vīctus, -ūs, *mode of life*. — temperantia, -ae. - dīligēns, -ntis. — tamen, *nevertheless*. — in-iūstus, -a, -um, *unjust*.)

ETYMOLOGY

In many instances the irregular comparison of a Latin adjective can easily be remembered by English derivatives:

bonus
  melior: ameliorate
  optimus: optimist, optimum, optimal
magnus
  maior: major, majority, mayor
  maximus: maximum
malus
  peior: pejorative
  pessimus: pessimist
multus — plūs: plus, plural, plurality, nonplus
parvus
  minor: minor, minority, minus, minute, minuet, minister, minstrel
  minimus: minimum, minimize

      (prō)
          prior: prior, priority
          prīmus: prime, primacy, primary, primeval, primitive
      superus
          superior: superior, superiority
          summus: summit, sum, consummate
          suprēmus: supreme, supremacy

In the sentences 1. probe, probation, probable, probity, prove, approve, disprove, improve, reprove, reprobate. 6. stellar, interstellar, Stella. 8. opera, operetta.

Latin **plūs** is the parent of French *plus* and Italian *più*, words which are placed before adjectives to form the comparative degree in those Romance languages. If the definite article is then added to these comparatives, it converts them into superlatives.

Latin	French	Italian
longior	plus long	più lungo
longissimus	le plus long	il più lungo
cārior	plus cher	più caro
cārissimus	le plus cher	il più caro

Footnotes

[1]The ones important for this book are given in the paradigm; the others are **dissimilis, gracilis** (*slender*), and **humilis** (*low, humble*). Other adjs. in **-lis** are regular; e.g., **ūtilis, ūtilissimus.**

[2]Others less important for this book are:

exterus, -a, -um (*foreign*) exterior, -ius (*outer*) extrēmus, -a, -um (*outermost*)

īnferus, -a, -um (*that below*) īnferior, -ius (*lower*) īnfimus, -a, -um (*lowest*)

(prope, *near*) propior, -ius (*nearer*) proximus, -a, -um (*nearest*)

28

Subjunctive: Present Active and Passive; Jussive; Purpose

*A*lthough the subjunctive in English is moribund, it was very much alive among the Romans, and it appears on every page of a normal Latin text. Accordingly, both the forms and the common uses of the Latin subjunctive must be learned — thoroughly.

PRESENT SUBJUNCTIVE ACTIVE

1. la′udem	móneam	dúcam	a′udiam	cápiam
2. la′udēs	móneās	dúcās	a′udiās	cápiās
3. la′udet	móneat	dúcat	a′udiat	cápiat
1. laudḗmus	moneámus	dūcámus	audiámus	capiámus
2. laudḗtis	moneátis	dūcátis	audiátis	capiátis
3. la′udent	móneant	dúcant	a′udiant	cápiant

CONJUGATION OF PRESENT SUBJUNCTIVE ACTIVE AND PASSIVE

Note that in the first conjugation the characteristic -ā- of the present indicative becomes -ē- in the present subjunctive. In the other conjugations -ā- is consistently the sign of the present subjunctive.

The present passive subjunctive naturally follows the pattern of the active except that passive endings are used.

la'uder, laudḗris,[1] laudḗtur; laudḗmur, laudḗminī, laudḗntur
mónear, moneḗris, moneḗtur; moneḗmur, moneḗminī, moneántur
dúcar, dūcḗris, dūcḗtur; dūcḗmur, dūcḗminī, dūcántur
a'udiar, audiḗris, audiḗtur; audiḗmur, audiḗminī, audiántur
cápiar, capiḗris, capiḗtur; capiḗmur, capiḗminī, capiántur

TRANSLATION OF THE SUBJUNCTIVE

No translation has been given above because there is no one general rendering for all Latin subjunctives. In Latin the subjunctive can express the ideas of *command, purpose, result, characteristic, indirect question,* and the like; and the English translation must be fashioned to reproduce these ideas according to the context.

JUSSIVE SUBJUNCTIVE (= A COMMAND)

The subjunctive can be used both in main, or independent, verbs and in subordinate,[2] or dependent, verbs.

The jussive is among the most important of the independent uses of the subjunctive. The fact that "jussive" derives from **iussus (iubeō)** shows that this subjunctive indicates a command. The negative is **nē**.

Normally in prose the independent jussive is used only in the first[3] and the third persons singular and plural; the imperative is used for the second person singular and plural.

Servus id faciat, *let the slave do it.*
Servī id faciant, *let the slaves do it.*

Id faciāmus, *let us do it.*
Id fac *or* facite, *(you) do it.*

Nē stultōs laudet, *let him not praise fools.*
Nē nōs laudēmus, *let us not praise ourselves.*

PURPOSE Ut OR Nē + SUBJUNCTIVE)

The Romans did not express purpose by the infinitive,[4] as we so commonly do. Instead, they used **ut** (*in order that, so that, to*) or **nē** (*in order that...not, so that...not, not to*) with the subjunctive.

Hoc dīcit **ut** eōs **iuvet**

he says this $\begin{cases} \text{in order that he may help them.} \\ \text{to help them.} \end{cases}$

Hoc dīcit **nē** eōs **offendat**,

he says this $\begin{cases} \text{so that he may not offend them.} \\ \text{to offend them.} \end{cases}$

Hoc facit **ut** urbem **capiat**,
he does this in order to capture the city.

Hoc facit **nē capiātur.**
he does this in order not to be captured.

Librōs legimus **ut** multa **discāmus,**
we read books to learn many things.

Bonōs librōs nōbīs dent **nē** malōs **legāmus,**
let them give us good books so that we may not read bad ones.

VOCABULARY

árma, -órum, *n.,* arms, weapons (*armor, army, armament, armada, armistice, armadillo, alarm*)

occāsiō, -ōnis, *f.,* occasion, opportunity

vérbum, -ī, *n.,* word (*verb, adverb, verbal, verbiage, proverb*)

ut, *conj. introducing purpose,* in order that, so that, that, in order to, so as to, to

nē, *adv. and conj. with subjunctives of command and purpose,* not; in order that...not, that...not, in order not to

cédō, -ere, céssī, céssum, (go), withdraw; yield to, grant, submit (*accede, access, accession, antecedent, ancestor, cede, concede, deceased, exceed, intercede, precede, proceed, recede, secede, succeed*)

discédō, -ere, -céssī, -céssum, go away, depart

pra'estō, -áre, pra'estitī, pra'estitum, excel; exhibit, show, offer, supply, furnish

RECOGNITION VOCABULARY

benefícium, -iī, *n.,* benefit, kindness; favor (*benefice, beneficience, beneficiary*)

PRACTICE AND REVIEW

1. Auctor sapiēns turpia vītet.
2. Prō patriā etiam maiōra meliōraque faciāmus.
3. Adulēscēns discēdat nē haec verba acerba audiat.
4. Nē Croesus crēdat sē esse fēlīciōrem quam tē.
5. Quisque petit quam fēlīcissimum modum vītae.
6. Quīdam beneficia aliīs praestant ut beneficia similia recipiant.
7. Multī lūcem sōlis fuisse prīmum remedium putant.
8. Imperium ducī potentiōrī dabunt ut hostēs ācerrimōs āvertat.
9. Hīs verbīs nūntiātīs, pars hostium ducēs suōs relīquit.
10. Graecī putābant deōs immortālēs habēre corpora hūmāna et pulcherrima.
11. Let him not think that we are worse than they.
12. They will send him to do this very easy thing.
13. They said: "Let us call the tyrant a most illustrious man in order not to be expelled from the country."
14. Let them not order this very wise and very good man to depart.

SENTENTIAE ANTĪQUAE

1. Ratiō dūcat, nōn fortūna. (*Livy.)
2. Arma togae cēdant. (Cicero. — toga, -ae, the garment of peace and civil, in contrast to military, activity.)
3. Ex urbe discēde nē metū et armīs opprimar. (Cicero.)
4. Nunc ūna rēs mihi est facienda ut maximum ōtium habeam. (Terence.)
5. Rapiāmus, amīcī, occāsiōnem dē diē. (*Horace.)
6. Corpus enim multīs rēbus eget ut valeat; animus sē ipse alit. (Seneca. — egeō, -ēre, eguī, + abl., *need.*)
7. Quī beneficium dedit, taceat, narret quī accēpit. (*Seneca. — taceō, -ēre, tacuī, tacitum, *be silent.*)
8. Dē mortuīs nihil nisi bonum dīcāmus. (Diogenes Laertius. — mortuus, -ī, *a dead man.* — nisi, *except.*)
9. Parēns ipse nec habeat vitia nec toleret. (Quintilian. — parēns, parentis, *parent.*)
10. In hāc rē ratiō habenda est ut monitiō acerbitāte careat. (Cicero. — monitiō, -ōnis, *admonition.* — acerbitās, -tātis, noun of acerbus.)
11. Fēminae ad lūdōs veniunt ut videant — et ut ipsae videantur. (Ovid.)

CŪR?

Cūr nōn mitto meōs tibi, Pontiliāne, libellōs?
Nē mihi tū mittās, Pontilliāne, tuōs.
(*Martial 7.3. — Pontiliānus, -ī. — libellus, -ī, diminutive of liber.)

TO HAVE FRIENDS ONE MUST BE FRIENDLY

Ut praestem Pyladēn, aliquis mihi praestet Orestēn.
Hoc nōn fit verbīs. Mārce; ut amēris, amā.

(*Martial 6.11.9-10; Orestes and Pylades were a classic pair of very devoted friends. Martial cannot play the role of Pylades unless someone proves a real Orestes to him. — **Pyladēn** and **Orestēn** are Greek acc. sing. forms. — fit, *is accomplished*.)

ETYMOLOGY

Alarm derives ultimately from Italian *all' arme* (to arms), which stands for **ad illa arma.**

From **cessō** (1), an intensive form of **cēdō,** come *cease, cessation, incessant.*

In the sentences   6. indigent. 7. tacit, taciturn, reticent.

The **-a-** which is consistently found in the present subjunctive of all conjugations except the first in Latin is similarly found in the present subjunctive of all conjugations except the first in both Italian and Spanish. And Spanish even has the characteristic **-e-** of the Latin in the present subjunctive of the first conjugation.

Footnotes

[1] On the alternate ending in -re see Ch. 18, n. 2.
[2] I.e., verbs which are introduced by subordinating conjunctions (**ut, nē, cum,** etc.)
[3] This subjunctive when used in the first person is often labeled "hortatory"; but since no basic difference exists between this subjunctive as used in the first and the third persons, nothing is gained by the multiplication of terms.
[4] This point can hardly be overstressed, especially in translating from English to Latin. To be sure, the infinitive was sometimes employed to express purpose in poetry, but that special usage is none of our present concern.

29

Imperfect Subjunctive; Present and Imperfect Subjunctive of Sum; Result

*T*he imperfect subjunctive is perhaps the easiest of all subjunctives to recognize or to form. In effect it is the present **active** infinitive plus the active or the passive personal endings. Sample forms are given in the following paradigms.

IMPERFECT SUBJUNCTIVE ACTIVE AND PASSIVE

1.	laudáre-m	laudáre-r	dúcerer	audírem	cáperem
2.	laudáré-s	laudáré-ris	dūceréris	audírēs	cáperēs
3.	laudáre-t	laudáré-tur	dūcerétur	audíret	cáperet
1.	laudáré-mus	laudáré-mur	dūcerémur	audírémus	caperémus
2.	laudáré-tis	laudáré-minī	dūcereminī	audírétis	caperétis
3.	laudáre-nt	laudáré-ntur	dūceréntur	audírent	caperent

PRESENT AND IMPERFECT SUBJUNCTIVE OF *Sum* AND *Possum*

The present subjunctive of **sum** and **possum** is irregular and must be memorized. The imperfect subjunctive, however, follows the rule given above.

Present Subjunctive		Imperfect Subjunctive	
1. sim	póssim	éssem	póssem
2. sīs	póssīs	éssēs	póssēs
3. sit	póssit	ésset	pósset
1. sīmus	possímus	essḗmus	possḗmus
2. sītis	possítis	essḗtis	possḗtis
3. sint	póssint	éssent	póssent

Particular care must be taken to distinguish between the forms of the present and the imperfect subjunctive of **possum**.

USE OF THE IMPERFECT SUBJUNCTIVE

The imperfect subjunctive is used in purpose clauses and result clauses (see next paragraph) when the main verb is in a past tense.

Hoc dīxit (dīcēbat) ut eōs iuvāret,
he said (kept saying) this in order that he might help them or *to help them.*

Hoc fēcit (faciēbat) nē caperētur,
he did (kept doing) this that he might not be captured.

RESULT (*Ut* or *Ut Nōn* + SUBJUNCTIVE)

To express the idea of result, Latin employs the subjunctive introduced by **ut** (*so that*). If the clause is a negative one, the **ut** is followed by such negatives as **nōn, nēmō,** and **nihil.**

Often in the clause preceding a result clause there is a sign word which indicates that a result clause is to follow. Such sign words are **tam** (*so*), **ita** (*so*), **tantus, -a, -um** (*so great*).

Result clauses can readily be distinguished from purpose clauses (1) when they are negative (cp. **ut nōn** and **nē**) and (2) when the sign words appear in the preceding clause. Otherwise, one must rely on the meaning of the sentence.

Tanta fēcit ut urbem servāret, *he did* **such** *great things that he* **saved** *the city.* (Result)

Haec fēcit ut urbem servāret, *he did these things that he* **might save** *the city.* (Purpose)

Tam strēnuē labōrat ut multa perficiat, *he works* **so** *energetically that he* **may accomplish** *many things.* (Result)

Strēnuē labōrat ut multa perficiat, *he works energetically so that he* **may accomplish** *many things.* (Purpose)

Hoc **tantā** benevolentiā dīxit ut eōs nōn offenderet, *he said this with* **such great kindness that he** **did not offend** *them.* (Result)

Hoc dīxit **nē** eōs offenderet, *he said this* **in order that he** **might not** **offend** *them.* (Purpose)

Saltus erat angustus, ut paucī Graecī multōs Mēdōs prohibēre possent; *the pass was narrow, so that a few Greeks* **were able** *to stop many Persians.* (Result)

VOCABULARY

mēns, méntis, *f.,* mind, thought, intention (*mental, mention; Minerva* (?); cp. *mind*)

míles, mílitis, *m.,* soldier (*military, militaristic, militate, militant, militia*)

dúrus, -a, -um, hard, harsh, rough, stern, unfeeling (*dour, duration, during, duress, endure, obdurate*)

tántus, -a, -um, so large, so great, of such a size (*tantamount*)

íta, *adv. used with adjs., vbs., and advs.,* so, thus

sīc, *adv. most commonly with verbs,* so, thus

tam, *adv. with adjs. and advs.,* so, to such a degree

ut, *conj.* + *subj. of result,* so that; *cp.* **ut,** *purpose, Ch. 28*

quídem, *postpositive adv.,* indeed, certainly, at least, even; **nē . . . quidem,** not . . . even

díscō, -ere, dídicī, learn (*See* **discipulus** *below.*)

RECOGNITION VOCABULARY

discípulus, -ī, *m.,* learner, pupil (*disciple, discipline, disciplinary;* cp. **discō**)

PRACTICE AND REVIEW

1. Arma meliōra mīlitibus suīs dedit ut hostēs terrērent.
2. Hostēs quidem negāvērunt sē arma similia habēre.
3. Pars mīlitum lūcem vītāvit nē hīc (adv.) vidērentur.
4. Sōlem prīmam lūcem caelī appellābant.
5. Adulēscentēs sapientiae cēdant ut fēlīciōrēs sint.
6. Sapientēs putant beneficia esse potentiōra quam verba acerba et turpia.

7. Quīdam autem sapiēns verba tam acerba et dūra discipulīs dīxit ut discēderent.
8. Nūntiāvērunt auctōrem hōrum remediōrum esse virum potentissimum.
9. Nihil tam facile est ut sine labōre id facere possīmus.
10. Prō labōre studiōque patria nostra nōbīs plūrimās occāsiōnēs bonās praestat.
11. The words of the philosopher were very difficult, so that the pupils were unable to learn them.
12. They wished to understand these things so that they might not live base lives.
13. Those soldiers were so harsh that they received no kindnesses.
14. He announced that the crimes were so great that they terrified the minds of all citizens.

SENTENTIAE ANTĪQUAE

1. Vīvāmus, mea Lesbia, atque amēmus. (*Catullus. — Lesbia was Catullus' sweetheart.)
2. Tum ita perturbātus sum ut omnia timērem. (Cicero. — perturbō (1), *disturb, trouble.*)
3. Ita dūrus erās ut neque amōre neque precibus mollīrī possēs. (Terence. — prex, precis, f., *prayer.* — molliō (4), *soften.*)
4. Nēmō quidem tam ferus est ut nōn mītēscere possit, cultūrā datā. (Horace. — ferus, -a, -um, *wild.* — mītēscō, -ere, *become mild.* — cultūra, -ae.)
5. Difficile est saturam nōn scrībere; nam quis est tam patiēns malae urbis ut sē teneat? (Juvenal. — satura, -ae, *satire.* — patiēns, -ntis, *tolerant of.*)
6. Fuit quondam in hāc rē pūblica tanta virtūs ut virī fortēs cīvem perniciōsum ācriōribus suppliciīs quam acerbissimum hostem reprimerent. (Cicero. — perniciōsus, -a, -um, *pernicious.* — supplicium, -iī, *punishment.* — re-primō, cp. opprimō.)
7. Ita praeclāra est recuperātiō lībertātis ut nē mors quidem in hāc rē sit fugienda. (Cicero. — recuperātiō, -ōnis, *recovery.*)
8. Nē ratiōnēs meōrum perīculōrum ūtilitātem reī pūblicae vincant. (Cicero. — ūtilitās, -tātis, *advantage.*)
9. Eō tempore Athēniēnsēs tantam virtūtem praestitērunt ut decemplicem numerum hostium superārent, et hōs sīc perterruērunt ut in Asiam refugerent. (Nepos. — Athēniēnsēs, -ium, *Athenians.* — decemplex, -icis, *tenfold.* — per-terreō.)
10. Ōrātor exemplum petat ab illō Dēmosthene, in quō tantum studium tantusque labor fuisse dīcuntur ut impedīmenta nātūrae dīligentiā industriāque superāret. (Cicero. — exemplum, -ī, *example.* — impedīmentum, -ī. — dīligentia, -ae. — industria, -ae.)

11. Praecepta tua sint brevia ut cito mentēs discipulōrum ea discant teneantque memoriā fidēlī. (Horace. — praeceptum, -ī, *precept.* — cito, adv., *quickly.*)
12. Nihil tam difficile est ut nōn possit studiō investīgārī. (Terence. — investīgō (1), *track down, investigate.*)
13. Bellum autem ita suscipiātur ut nihil nisi pāx quaesīta esse videātur. (Cicero. — suscipiō, -ere, -cēpī, -ceptum, *undertake.* — nisi, *except.*)
14. Tanta est vīs probitātis ut eam in hoste dīligāmus. (Cicero. — probitās, -tātis, *uprightness, honesty.*)

ETYMOLOGY

In the sentences   2. perturb, perturbation. 3. precatory, precarious, pray, prayer. — mollify, v. Ch. 22, Sent. Ant. 6. 4. feral, ferocity, fierce. 5. patient. 6. supplicium, lit. *a kneeling;* hence suppliant, supplication. 10. exemplar, exemplary, exemplify. 12. vestige, vestigial. 14. probity.

The adverbial ending -*mente* or -*ment* which is so characteristic of Romance languages derives from Latin **mente** (abl. of **mēns**) used originally as an ablative of manner but now reduced to an adverbial suffix. The following examples are based on Latin adjectives which have already appeared in the vocabularies.

Latin Words	It. Adverb	Sp. Adverb	Fr. Adverb
dūrā mente	duramente	duramente	durement
clārā mente	chiaramente	claramente	clairement
sōlā mente	solamente	solamente	seulement
certā mente	certamente	certamente	certainement
dulcī mente	dolcemente	dulcemente	doucement
brevī mente	brevemente	brevemente	brièvement
facilī mente	facilmente	fácilmente	facilement

Latin **sīc** is the parent of It. *sì,* Sp. *sí,* and Fr. *si* meaning *yes.*

30

Perfect and Pluperfect Subjunctive Active and Passive; Indirect Questions; Sequence of Tenses

In the perfect system of the subjunctive, as in the perfect system of the indicative, all verbs follow the same basic rules of formation regardless of the conjugation to which they belong.

PERFECT SUBJUNCTIVE ACT.: or ACTIVE

perf. stem + **eri** + personal endings[1]
    Sing. laudā́v-erim, -erī́s, -erit
    Plu. laudāv-erí̄mus, -erí̄tis, -erint

PLUPERFECT SUBJUNCTIVE ACT.: or ACTIVE

perf. stem + **issē** + personal endings[2]
    Sing. laudāv-íssem, -íssēs, -ísset
    Plu. laudāv-issḗmus, -issḗtis, -íssent

PERFECT SUBJUNCTIVE PASSIVE

perf. pass. part. + pres. subj. of **sum**
    Sing. laudā́tus, -a, -um sim, sīs, sit
    Plu. laudā́tī, -ae, -a sí̄mus, sí̄tis, sint

PLUPERFECT SUBJUNCTIVE PASSIVE

perf. pass. part. + imperf. subj. of **sum**
Sing. laudátus, -a, -um éssem, éssēs, ésset
Plu. laudā́tī, -ae, -a essḗmus, essḗtis, éssent

Dūcō IN THE PERFECT SYSTEM OF THE SUBJUNCTIVE

Perf. Active.	Pluperf. Active	Perf. Pass.	Pluperf. Pass.
dū́xerim	dūxíssem	dúctus, -a, -um sim	dúctus, -a, -um éssem
dū́xerīs	dūxíssēs	dúctus, -a, -um sī́s	dúctus, -a, -um éssēs
dū́xerit	dūxísset	dúctus, -a, -um sit	dúctus, -a, -um ésset
dūxérimus	dūxissḗmus	dúctī, -ae, -a sī́mus	dúctī, -ae, -a essḗmus
dūxéritis	dūxissḗtis	dúctī, -ae, -a sī́tis	dúctī, -ae, -a essḗtis
dū́xerint	dūxíssent	dúctī, -ae, -a sint	dúctī, -ae, -a éssent

INDIRECT QUESTIONS

The three following sentences are direct questions.

Quid[3] Gāius facit?	*What is Gaius doing?*
Quid Gāius fēcit?	*What did Gaius do?*
Quid Gāius faciet?	*What will Gaius do?*

After verbs of *asking* and other appropriate verbs such as *saying, knowing,* and *perceiving,* these direct questions can be quoted indirectly in Latin by putting the verb in the subjunctive.

Rogant quid[3] Gāius faciat,	*they ask what Gaius is doing.*
Rogant quid Gāius fēcerit,	*they ask what Gaius did.*
Rogant quid Gāius factūrus sit,	*they ask what Gaius will do.*

SEQUENCE OF TENSES

There still remains the problem as to which of the four subjunctive tenses to use in a subordinate subjunctive clause after a given tense of the main verb.

For convenience tenses are divided into two groups, "primary" and "historical," as indicated in the following table.

Group	Main Verb	Subordinate Subjunctive
Primary[4]	Pres. or Fut.	Present (= action *at same time* or *after*)[6] Perfect (= action *before*)[7]
Historical[5]	Past Tenses	Imperfect (= action *at same time* or *after*)[6] Pluperfect (= action *before*)[7]

A primary tense of the main verb is followed by a primary tense of the subordinate subjunctive; a historical tense of the main verb is followed by a historical tense of the subordinate subjunctive.

After a primary main verb the *present* subjunctive indicates action occurring *at the same time* as that of the main verb or *after* that of the main verb. The *perfect* subjunctive indicates action which occurred *before* that of the main verb.

Similarly after a historical main verb the *imperfect* subjunctive indicates action occurring *at the same time* as that of the main verb or *after* that of the main verb. The *pluperfect* subjunctive indicates action which occurred *before* that of the main verb.

The rule for the sequence of tenses operates in purpose clauses, result clauses,[8] indirect questions, and similar constructions which you will learn.

Rogant, rogābunt - *They ask, will ask*
> quid faciat, *what he is doing* or *will do.*
> quid fēcerit, *what he did.*
> quid factūrus sit,[9] *what he will do.*

Rogāvērunt, rogābant - *They asked, kept asking*
> quid faceret, *what he was doing* or *would do.*
> quid fēcisset, *what he had done.*
> quid factūrus esset,[9] *what he would do.*

> Id facit (faciet) ut mē iuvet, *he does (will do) it to help me.*
> Id facit (faciēbat) ut mē iuvāret, *he did (kept doing) it to help me.*

> Tam dūrus est ut eum vītem, *he is so harsh that I avoid him.*
> Tam dūrus fuit (erat) ut eum vītārem, *he was so harsh that I avoided him.*

VOCABULARY

> **férrum, -ī,** *n.,* iron; sword (*ferric, ferrite, ferro-*)
> **málum, -ī,** *neut. of* **malus,** evil, misfortune, hurt, injury
> **céterī, -ae, -a,** the remaining, the rest, the other, all the others; *cp.* **alius,** another, other (*etc.*)
> **quántus, -a, -um,** how large, how great, how much; *cp.* **tantus** (*quantity, quantitative, quantum*)

dénique, *adv.*, at last, finally; lastly

iam, *adv.*, now, already, soon

cognóscō, -ere, cognóvī, cógnitum, become acquainted with, learn, recognize; *in perfect tenses*, know (*cognizance, cognizant, cognition, connoisseur, incognito, reconnaissance, reconnoiter); see also* **nōscō, -ere, nōvī,** nōtum (*noble, notice, notify, notion, notorious*)

comprehéndō, -ere, -héndī, -hénsum, grasp, seize, arrest; comprehend, understand (*comprehensive, comprehensible, incomprehensible*)

pónō, -ere, pósuī, pósitum, put, place, set (*See Etymology at end of chapter.*)

rógō, áre, -ávī, -átum, *ask* (*interrogate, abrogate, derogatory, prerogative, surrogate*)

RECOGNITION VOCABULARY

prímō, *adv.*, at first, at the beginning

únde, *adv.*, whence, from what *or* which place, from which

expónō, ex + pōnō, set forth, explain, expose

PRACTICE AND REVIEW

1. Rogāvit ubi discipulus haec didicisset.
2. Vidēbit quanta fuerit vīs illōrum verbōrum fēlīcium.
3. Hās īnsidiās exposuit nē rēs pūblica opprimerētur.
4. Cēterī expellantur nē occāsiōnem similem habeant.
5. Ita dūrus erat ut beneficia tua comprehendere nōn posset.
6. Cēterī quidem nesciēbant quam ācris esset mēns Caesaris.
7. Dēnique cognōscet cūr potentior pars mīlitum nōs vītet.
8. Iam cognōvī cūr clāra facta nōn sint facillima. (Remember that cognōvī means *I have learned, I know.*)
9. Quīdam auctōrēs appellābant arma optimum remedium malōrum.
10. Tell me in what lands liberty is found.
11. We did not know where the sword had been put.
12. He does not understand the first words of the letter which they wrote.
13. They asked why you could not learn what the rest had done.
14. Let all men now seek better things than money or supreme power so that their souls may be happier.

SENTENTIAE ANTĪQUAE

1. Vidētis quantum scelus contrā rem pūblicam vōbīs nūntiātum sit. (Cicero.)
2. Quam dulcis sit lībertās vōbīs dīcam. (Phaedrus.)
3. Rogābat dēnique cūr umquam fūgissent. (Horace.)
4. Nunc sciō quid sit amor. (*Virgil.)
5. Quaeris, Lesbia, quot bāsia tua mihi satis sint. (Catullus. — quot. indecl., *how many.* — bāsium, -iī, *kiss.*)

6. Videāmus uter plūs scrībere possit. (*Horace. — uter, utra, utrum, *which of two*.)

7. Multī dubitābant quid optimum esset. (*Cicero. — dubitō (1), *doubt, be uncertain*.)

8. Incipiam expōnere unde nātūra omnēs rēs creet alatque. (Lucretius. — creō (1), *create*.)

9. Dulce est vidēre quibus malīs ipse careās. (Lucretius.)

10. Auctōrem Troiānī bellī relēgī, quī dīcit quid sit pulchrum, quid turpe, quid ūtile, quid nōn. (Horace, — Troiānus, -a, -um, *Trojan*. — ūtilis, -e, *useful*.)

11. Doctōs rogābis quā ratiōne bene agere vītam possīs, utrum virtūtem doctrīna paret an nātūra det, quid minuat cūrās, quid tē amīcum tibi faciat. (Horace, — doctī, -ōrum, *the learned*. — utrum . . . an, *whether . . . or*. — doctrīna, -ae, *teaching*. — minuō, -ere, minuī, minūtum, *lessen*.)

12. Istī autem rogant tantum quid habeās, nōn cūr et unde. (Seneca. — tantum, adv., *only*.)

13. (Socrates' parting words to the jury which had condemned him to death.) Sed tempus est iam mē discēdere ut cicūtam bibam, et vōs discēdere ut vītam agātis. Utrum autem sit melius, dī immortālēs sciunt; hominem quidem nēminem scīre crēdō. (Cicero. — cicūta, -ae, *hemlock*. — bibō, -ere, bibī, *drink*. — nēmō homō, *no human being*.)

EVIDENCE AND CONFESSION

(In 63 B.C. Catiline, a bankrupt aristocrat, conspired to recoup his losses by a bloody revolution and confiscations in Rome. Cicero, the leading consul, by his oratory succeeded in forcing Catiline to flee from the city; but Catiline's lieutenants still remained in Rome, and Cicero lacked tangible evidence with which to convict them in court. In the following passage, however, he shows how he finally got the evidence and the confession that he needed.)

Sit dēnique scrīptum in fronte ūnīus cuiusque quid dē rē pūblicā sentiat; nam rem pūblicam labōribus cōnsiliīsque meīs ex igne atque ferrō ēreptam vidētis. Haec iam expōnam breviter ut scīre possītis quā ratiōne comprehēnsa sint. Semper prōvīdī quō modō in tantīs īnsidiīs salvī esse possēmus. Omnēs diēs cōnsūmpsī ut vidērem quid coniūrātī agerent. Dēnique litterās intercipere potuī quae ad Catilīnam ā Lentulō aliīsque coniūrātīs missae erant. Tum, coniūrātīs comprehēnsīs et senātū convocātō, ostendī litterās Lentulō et quaesīvī cognōsceretne signum. Dīxit sē cognōscere; sed prīmō negāvit sē dē hīs rēbus dictūrum esse. Mox autem ostendit quanta esset vīs cōnscientiae; nam repente omnem rem narrāvit. Tum cēterī coniūrātī sīc fūrtim inter sē aspiciēbant ut nōn ab aliīs indicārī sed indicāre sē ipsī vidērentur.

(Cicero, excerpts from *Cat. I* and *III.* — frōns, -ntis, f., *forehead.* — breviter, adv. of brevis. — prō-videō, *fore-see, give attention to.*— salvus, -a, -um, *safe.* — cōnsūmō, -ere, -sūmpsī, -sūmptum. — coniūrātus, -ī, *conspirator.* — intercipiō, -ere, -cēpī, interceptum. — mox, *soon.* — cōnscientia, -ae, *conscience.* — repente, adv., *suddenly.* — fūrtim, adv., *stealthily.*— inter sē aspiciō, -ere, -spexī, -spectum, *glance at each other.* — indicō (1), *accuse.*)

ETYMOLOGY

Further derivatives from the basic **prehendō,** *seize,* are: apprehend, apprentice, apprise, imprison, prehensile, prison, prize, reprehend, reprisal, surprise.

From **pōnō** come innumerable derivatives: apposite, apposition, component, composite, compost, compound, deponent, deposit, deposition, depot, exponent, exposition, expound, imposition, impost, impostor, juxtaposition, opponent, opposite, positive, post, postpone, preposition, proposition, propound, repository, supposition, transposition.

However, note that *pose* and its compounds derive, not from **pōnō** as one would think, but from the late Latin **pausāre,** which stems from Greek **pausis,** *a pause,* and **pauein,** *to stop.* In French this **pausāre** became *poser,* which took the place of **pōnō** in compounds. Consequently, the forms given above under **pōnō** are not etymologically related to the following words despite their appearance: compose, depose, expose, impose, oppose, propose, repose, suppose, transpose.

In the sentences   5. quotient, quota, quote. 7. indubitable. 8. creature, creative, creation, recreation, procreate. 11. doctor, doctrine. — diminish, diminution. 13. bibulous, bib, wine-bibber, beverage, imbibe. In the reading passage: front, frontal, affront, confront, effrontery, frontier, frontispiece. — provide, providence, provision, improvident, improvise, improvisation.

Footnotes

[1] Note the similarity of spelling in this and in the future perfect indicative.

[2] This amounts to the perf. act. inf. + endings: **laudāvisse-m.** Cp. the imperfect subjunctive.

[3] Naturally, the Romans used the interrogative and not the relative pronoun in both direct and indirect questions. See Ch. 19.

[4] Also called "principal." Neither term is particularly satisfactory. Note, however, that the present and the future indicative have this in common: they both indicate *incomplete* action (the present, action going

on; the future, action not yet started). They might well be labeled "incomplete."

[5] Well so called because they refer to past events; also called "secondary."

[6] Or call it *time contemporaneous* or *subsequent.*

[7] Or call it *time prior.*

[8] Sometimes the perfect subjunctive is used as a historical tense in result clauses.

[9] The future active participle + the subjunctive of **sum** constitute the relatively uncommon future subjunctive; the **sit** and **esset** above are used according to the sequence of tenses.

31

Cum with the Subjunctive; Ferō

CUM + SUBJUNCTIVE = WHEN, SINCE, ALTHOUGH

Cum is a subordinating conjunction as well as a preposition. **Cum**, the conjunction, usually takes the subjunctive, and such a clause states the circumstances under which the action of the main verb occurs.[1] In such instances **cum** is to be translated *when* or *since* or *although* according to the context.[2]

Cum hoc fēcisset, ad tē fūgit.
when he had done this, he fled to you.

Cum hoc scīret, potuit eōs iuvāre.
since he knew this, he was able to help them.

Cum hoc scīret, tamen nihil fēcit.
although he knew this, nevertheless he did nothing.

Cum Gāium dīligerēmus, nōn poterāmus eum iuvāre.
although we loved Gaius, we could not help him.

IRREGULAR Ferō, ferre, tuli lātum, bear, carry

Although **ferō** is surprisingly irregular in its principal parts, it follows the rules for the third conjugation as exemplified in **dūcō** with certain exceptions.

1. The present infinitive, fer-re, lacks the connecting vowel **e**; cp. **dūc-e-re**.
2. This same lack of connecting vowel is observable in certain forms of the present indicative and the imperative.

Present Indicative

Active	Passive
1. férō	féror
2. fers (cp. dúcis)	férris (dúceris)
3. fert (cp. dúcit)	fértur (dúcitur)
1. férimus	férimur
2. fértis	feríminī
(cp. dúcitis)	
3. férunt	ferúntur

Present Imperative

Active	
2. fer (dūc)[3]	2. férte (dúcite)

Infinitives

Active	Passive
Pres. férre (dúcere)	férrī (dúci)
Perf. tulísse	látum esse
Fut. látúrum esse	[látum írī]

If you have any doubt about the remaining forms of **ferō**, consult the paradigm in the Appendix.

VOCABULARY

ánnus, -ī, *m.,* year (*annals, anniversary, annuity, annual, biennial, perennial, centennial, millennium, superannuated*)

auxílium, -iī, *n.,* aid, help (*auxiliary*)

návis, -is, *f.,* ship, boat (*navy, navigable, navigate, nave*)

a´equus, -a, -um, level, even; calm; equal, just; favorable (*equable, equanimity, equation, equator, equilateral, equilibrium, equinox, equity, equivalent, equivocal, inequity, iniquity, adequate, coequal*)

ápud, *prep. + acc.,* among, in the presence of, at the house of

cum, *conj. + subj.,* when, since, although

támen, *adv.,* nevertheless, still

férō, férre, túlī, lātum, bear, carry, bring; suffer, endure, tolerate (*fertile, circumference, confer, defer, differ, infer, offer, prefer, proffer, refer, suffer, transfer;* cp. *bear*)

cónferō, férre, cóntuli, colátum, bring together, compare; **sē cōnferre,** betake oneself, go (*confer, cf., collate*)

ófferō, férre, óbtuli, oblátum, offer

respóndeō, -ēre, -spóndī, -spónsum, answer (*respond, response, responsive, responsibility, correspond*)

RECOGNITION VOCABULARY

exsílium, -iī, *n.,* exile, banishment

vīnum, -ī, *n.,* wine (*vine, vinegar, viniculture, viniferous, vintage, vinyl*)

medíocris, -e, ordinary, moderate, mediocre

PRACTICE AND REVIEW

1. Iam cognōvimus istās mentēs dūrās ferrum prō pāce offerre.
2. Nē adulēscentēs discant verba tam acerba et tam dūra.
3. Cum hī discessissent, alia occāsiō pācis numquam oblāta est.
4. Tantum auxilium nōbīs feret ut nē ācerrimī quidem mīlitēs hīc remanēre possint.
5. Rogābat cūr cēterī tantam fidem et spem apud nōs praestārent.
6. Cum patria nostra tanta beneficia offerat, quīdam tamen sē in īnsidiās cōnferunt.
7. Dēnique audiāmus quantae sint hae īnsidiae.
8. Haec scelera exposuī nē alia et similia ferrētis.
9. Respondērunt multa arma prīmā nāve lāta esse.
10. Cum bonī essent, fēlīcēs erant.
11. When the soldiers had been arrested, they offered us money.
12. Although life brings very difficult things, let us endure them all.
13. Since you know what help is being brought by our friends, these evils can be endured with courage.
14. Although his eyes could not see the light of the sun, nevertheless he used to do very many and very difficult things.

SENTENTIAE ANTĪQUAE

1. Potestne haec lūx esse tibi iūcunda cum sciās hōs omnēs cōnsilia tua cognōvisse? (Cicero.)
2. Themistoclēs, cum Graeciam servitūte Persicā līberāvisset et propter invidiam in exsilium expulsus esset, ingrātae patriae iniūriam nōn tulit quam ferre dēbuit. (Cicero. — Persicus, -a, um, —invidia, -ae, *jealousy, hatred.* —ingrātus, -a, um, *ungrateful.* — iniūria, -ae, *injury.* — dēbuit, *he ought to have.*)

3. Quae cum ita sint, Catilīna, cōnfer tē in exsilium. (Cicero. — quae cum = et cum haec.)

4. Ō nāvis, novī flūctūs bellī tē in mare referent! Ō quid agis? (Horace. — nāvis, *ship* (*of state*). — flūctus, -ūs, *billow*.)

5. Cum rēs pūblica immortālis esse dēbeat, doleō eam in vītā ūnīus mortālis cōnsistere. (Cicero. — doleō, -ēre, -uī, *grieve*. — cōnsisto, -ere, -stitī, + in, *depend on*.)

6. Cum illum hominem esse servum cognōvisset, eum comprehendit. (Cicero.)

7. Ille comprehēnsus, cum prīmō impudenter respondēre coepisset, dēnique tamen nihil negāvit. (Cicero. — impudenter, adv.)

8. Milō dīcitur per stadium vēnisse cum bovem umerīs ferret. (Cicero. — Milō, -ōnis, famous Greek athlete. — stadium, -iī. — bōs, bovis, *ox*. — umerus, -ī, *shoulder*.)

9. Quid vesper ferat, incertum est. (Livy. — vesper, -eris, m., *evening*.)

10. Ferte miserō auxilium. (Terence.)

11. Hoc ūnum sciō: quod fortūna fert, id ferēmus aequō animō (Terence.)

FACĒTIAE (WITTICISMS)

Cum Cicerō apud Damasippum cēnāret et ille, mediocrī vīnō positō, dīceret: "Bibe hoc Falernum; hoc est vīnum quadrāgintā annōrum," Cicerō respondit: "Bene aetātem fert!"

(Macrobius, *Sāturnālia* 2.3. — cēnō (1), *dine*. — positō, *served*. — bibe: v. Ch. XXX, Sent. Ant. 13. — Falernum, -ī, *Falernian wine*, actually a very famous wine, not a "mediocre" one. — quadrāgintā, indecl., *forty*.)

Augustus, cum quīdam eī libellum trepidē offerret, et modo prōferret manum et modo retraheret, "Putās," inquit, "tē assem elephantō dare?"

(Macrobius, *Sāturnālia* 2.4. — trepidē, adv., *in confusion*. — modo ...modo, *now...now*. — re-trahō. — as, assis, m., *a penny*, as children now offer peanuts. — elephantus, —ī.)

ETYMOLOGY

In the sentences 2. invidious, envious, envy. — ingrate, ingratitude. — injurious. 4. fluctuate. 5. condole, doleful, indolence. — consist, consistent. 8. bovine. — humerus, humeral. 9. vespers.

Footnotes

[1] The Romans did use **cum** with the indicative when they wished to emphasize the *time* or the *date* rather than the circumstances. This usage was relatively infrequent with past tenses; but **cum** with the indicative was the rule with the present and the future tenses.

[2] When **tamen**, *nevertheless*, appears after a **cum** clause, it is a good sign that **cum** means *although*.

[3] For **dīc, dūc, fac,** and **fer** see Ch. 8. The rules for present passive imperative will be learned later.

32

Adverbs: Formation and Comparison; Volō

*M*any adverbs are easily derived from adjectives, and many, like adjectives, are compared.

FORMATION OF ADVERBS IN THE POSITIVE DEGREE

From adjectives of the first and the second declensions adverbs can be made by adding -ē to the base.

long-ē	(*far;* longus, -a, -um)
līber-ē	(*freely;* līber, lībera, līberum)
pulchr-ē	(*beautifully;* pulcher, -chra, -chrum)

From adjectives of the third declension adverbs are normally made by adding **-iter** to the base; but if the base ends in **-nt-** only **-er** is added.

fort-iter	(*bravely;* fortis, -e)
ācr-iter	(*keenly;* ācer, ācris, ācre)
fēlīc-iter	(*happily;* fēlīx, gen. fēlīcis)
sapient-er	(*wisely;* sapiēns, gen. sapientis)

Other endings and peculiar forms are found, but they had best be learned as vocabulary items: **autem, etiam, ita, sīc, tam, tamen, diū, semper, facile,** etc.

COMPARATIVE OF ADVERBS

The comparative degree of adverbs is with few exceptions the **-ius** form which you have already learned as the neuter of the comparative degree of the adjective.

SUPERLATIVE OF ADVERBS

The superlative degree of adverbs, being normally derived from the superlative degree of adjectives, regularly ends in -ē according to the rule given above for converting adjectives of the first and the second declensions into adverbs.

COMPARISON OF IRREGULAR ADVERBS

When the comparison of an adjective is irregular (see Ch. 27), the comparison of the adverb derived therefrom normally follows the basic irregularities of the adjective but, of course, has adverbial endings.

Positive	Comparative[1]	Superlative[1]
lóngē (*far*)	lóngius (*farther, too f.*)	longíssimē (*farthest, very f.*)
līberē (*freely*)	līberius (*more f.*)	lībérrimē (*most, very f.*)
púlchrē (*beautifully*)	púlchrius (*more b.*)	pulchérrimē (*most b.*)
fórtiter (*bravely*)	fórtius (*more b.*)	fortíssimē (*most b.*)
ácriter (*keenly*)	ácrius (*more k.*)	ācérrimē (*most k.*)
fēlíciter (*happily*)	fēlícius (*more h.*)	fēlīcíssimē (*most h.*)
sapiénter (*wisely*)	sapiéntius (*more w.*)	sapientíssimē (*most w.*)
fácile (*easily*)	facílius (*more e.*)	facíllimē (*most e.*)
bénĕ (*well*)	mélius (*better*)	óptimē (*best*)
málĕ (*badly*)	pe'ius (*worse*)	péssimē (*worst*)
múltum (*much*)	plūs (*more*, quantity)	plūrimum (*most, very much*)
magnópere (*greatly*)	mágis (*more*, quality)	máximē (*most, especially*)
párum (*little, not very [much]*)	mínus (*less*)	mínimē (*least*)
(prō)	príus (*before, earlier*)	prímō (*first, at first*)[2] / prímum (*in the first place*)[3]
díū (*a long time*)	diútius (*longer*)	diūtíssimē (*very long*)

IRREGULAR Volō, velle, voluī, *wish*

Like **ferō**, **volō** is another verb of the third conjugation which, though regularly formed in most parts, is irregular at certain important points.

The perfect systems of the indicative and the subjunctive are formed in the regular way from **voluī** and should never trouble you.

In the present systems you should note that **vol-** is the stem of the indicative[4] and **vel-** is the stem of the subjunctive. Otherwise, the only irregularities are in the present tenses. However, the imperfect subjunctive is given in full here because of its easy confusion with the present subjunctive.

There is only one participle; there is no imperative; and there is no passive voice.

Pres. Ind.	Pres. Subj.	Impf. Subj.	Infinitives
1. vólō	vélim[5]	véllem	*Pres.* vélle
2. vīs	vélīs	véllēs	*Perf.* voluísse
3. vult	vélit	véllet	*Fut.* ——
1. vólumus	velímus	vellémus	**Participle**
2. vúltis	velítis	vellétis	*Pres.* vólēns
3. vólunt	vélint	véllent	

Nōlō, nōlle, nōlui (**ne-volo**), *not to wish, to be unwilling,* and **mālō, mālle, māluī,** (**magis-volo**), *wish rather, prefer,* follow **volō** closely. Only a few forms of these verbs appear in this book and they can easily be identified by referring to **nōlō** and **mālō** in the Appendix.

VOCABULARY

dīvítiae, -árum, *f.,* riches, wealth (*cp.* dīves *below*)

exércitus, -ūs, *m.,* army (*exercise*)

hónor, -óris, *m.,* honor, esteem; public office (*honorable, honorary, honorific, dishonor*)

All adverbs given in the list above.

āmíttō, -ere, -mísī, -míssum, lose, let go

vólō, vélle, vóluī,, wish, want, be willing, will (*volition, voluntary, involuntary, volunteer, volitive, voluptuous; nolens, volens*)

nólō, nólle, nóluī, not . . . wish, be unwilling (*nol-pros*)

RECOGNITION VOCABULARY

custódia, -ae, *f.,* custody; *in plu.,* guards (*custodian, custodial*)

lēx, légis, *f.,* law, statute; *cp.* iūs, *which emphasizes* right, justice (*legal, legislator, legitimate, loyal*)

sciéntia, -ae, *f.,* knowledge (*science, scientific; cp.* sciō, *Ch. 21*)

dīves, *gen.* dīvitis *or* dītis (*cons. stem adj. of 1 ending; see Ch. 16 n. 4*), rich (*Dives*)

pa'uper, *gen.* pa'uperis, of small means, poor

pār, *gen.* páris (*adj. of 1 ending + dat.*), equal, like (*par, pair, parity, peer, peerless, disparage, disparity, umpire, nonpareil*)

celériter, *adv. of* celer (*Ch. 16*), swiftly, quickly

páteō, -ére, pátuī lie open, be accessible, be evident (*pătent, pātent, patency*)

prohíbeō, -ére, -híbuī, -híbitum, keep (back), prevent,[6] hinder, restrain, prohibit (*prohibitive, prohibition, prohibitory*)

PRACTICE AND REVIEW

1. Prīmō nē mediocria quidem perīcula fortiter ferre poterant.
2. Maximē rogāvimus quantum auxilium nāvis ferret.
3. Dēnique armīs collātīs, dux respondit mīlitēs celerrimē discessūrōs esse.
4. Paria beneficia in omnēs cōnferre vultis.
5. Haec mala melius expōnant nē dīvitiās et honōrēs suōs āmittant.
6. At volumus cognōscere cūr verba eius tam dūra fuerint.
7. Cum cēterī hās īnsidiās cognōverint, vult in exsilium sē cōnferre.
8. Multīne discipulī tantum studium praestant ut hās sententiās facillimē ūnō annō legere possint?
9. Cum dīvitiās āmīsisset, tamen omnēs cīvēs mentem mōrēsque eius maximē laudābant.
10. Plūra meliōraque lēgibus aequīs quam ferrō faciēmus.
11. Do you (plu.) wish to live longer and better?
12. He wishes to speak very wisely so that they may yield to him very quickly.
13. When these plans had been learned, we asked why he had been unwilling to prepare the army with greatest care.
14. That wretched man so keenly wishes to have wealth that he is willing to lose his best friends.

SENTENTIAE ANTĪQUAE

1. Occāsiō nōn facile offertur sed facile āmittitur. (Publilius Syrus.)
2. Nōbīscum vīvere iam diūtius nōn potes; id nōn ferēmus. (Cicero.)
3. Vīs rēctē vīvere? Quis nōn? (*Horace. — rēctus, -a, -um, *straight, right*.)
4. Plūs scīs quid faciendum sit. (Terence.)
5. Mihi vērē dīxit quid vellet. (Terence.)
6. Parēs cum paribus facillimē congregantur. (*Cicero. — congregō (1), *gather into a flock*.)
7. Tē magis quam oculōs meōs amō. (Terence.)
8. Hominēs libenter id crēdunt quod volunt. (Caesar. libēns, -ntis, *willing*.)
9. Multa ēveniunt hominī quae vult et quae nōn vult. (Plautus. — ē-veniō, *happen*.)
10. Cōnsiliō melius vincere possumus quam īrā. (Publilius Syrus.)
11. Optimus quisque facere māvult quam dīcere. (Sallust. — māvult quam = magis vult quam.)
12. Omnēs sapientēs fēlīciter, perfectē, fortūnātē vīvunt. (Cicero. — perfectus, -a, -um, *complete*. — fortūnātus, -a, -um.)
13. Maximē eum laudant quī pecūniā nōn movētur. (Cicero.)

14. Sī vīs scīre quam nihil malī in paupertāte sit, cōnfer pauperem et dīvitem: pauper saepius et fidēlius rīdet. (Seneca. — nihil malī, *no evil.* — paupertās, -tātis, *small means.*)

15. Magistrī puerīs crustula dant ut prīma elementa discere velint. (Horace. — crustulum, -ī, *cookie.* — elementum, -ī.)

CIMŌNIS MŌRĒS

Cimōn celeriter ad summōs honōrēs pervēnit. Habēbat enim satis ēloquentiae, summam līberālitātem, magnam scientiam lēgum et reī mīlitāris, quod cum patre ā puerō in exercitibus fuerat. Itaque hic populum urbānum in suā potestāte facillimē tenuit et apud exercitum plūrimum valuit auctōritāte.

Post huius mortem Athēniēnsēs nōn sōlum in bellō sed etiam in pāce eum diū graviterque dēsīderāvērunt. Fuit enim vir tantae līberālitātis ut, cum multōs hortōs habēret, numquam in hīs custōdiās pōneret; nam hortōs līberrimē patēre voluit nē populus ab hīs frūctibus prohibērētur. Saepe autem, cum aliquem minus bene vestītum vidēret, suum amiculum dedit. Multōs locuplētāvit; multōs pauperēs mortuōs suō sūmptū extulit. Sīc minimē mīrum est sī propter mōrēs Cimōnis vita eius fuit sēcūra et mors eius fuit omnibus acerba.

(Nepos, *Cimōn.* — per-veniō. — ēloquentiae, gen. of ēloquentia. — līberālitās, -tātis. — mīlitāris, -e. potestās, -tātis, *power.* — plūrimum: treat as an adv. — auctōritās, -tātis, *authority;* the abl. tells in what respect. — dēsīderō (1), *long for, miss.* — hortus, -ī, garden, — vestītus, -a, um, *clothed.* — amiculum, -ī, *cloak.* — locuplētō (1), *enrich.* — mortuus, -a, -um, *dead.* — sūmptus, -ūs, *expense.*— extulit: ef-ferō, *bury.* — mīrus, -a, -um, *surprising.* — sē-cūrus, -a, -um: sē- means *without.*)

ETYMOLOGY

In the sentences   3. rectitude, rectify, direct, erect, correct; cp. right. 6. congregate, segregate, gregarious, aggregate. 9. event (=out-come), eventual. 12. perfect (= made or done thoroughly). *Cimōnis Mōrēs:* desire, desideratum. — vest, vestment, invest, divest. — sumptuous, sumptuary. — miraculous, admire.

Footnotes

[1] In advs., as in adjs., the *comparative* may have the force of *too* or *rather;* and the *superlative,* the force of *very.*

[2] In point of time.

[3] In the enumeration of items; but **quam prīmum,** *as soon as possible.*

[4] Pres. **vól-ō;** impf. **vol-ébam, vol-ébās,** etc.; fut. **vól-am, vól-ēs,** etc.

[5] Cp. **sim, sīs, sit,** etc.

[6] **prohibeō** + *acc.* + *infin.,* prevent (someone) from (doing).

33

Conditions

*T*wo basic clauses in a conditional sentence are (1) the conditional clause, introduced by **sī**, *if*, and (2) the conclusion.

A thorough knowledge of the following table of conditions and the memorization of the illustrative Latin examples and their English equivalents will make you master of any ordinary conditional sentence.

TABLE OF CONDITIONS

I. Simple Fact Present or Past.

    A. Present: present indicative in both clauses.[1]

    Sī id facit, prūdēns est; *if he is doing it, he is wise.*

    B. Past: past indicative (imperf. or perf.) in both clauses.

    Sī id fēcit, prūdēns fuit; *if he did it, he was wise.*

II. Future More or Less Vivid.

    A. More Vivid: future indicative in both clauses.

    Sī id faciet, prūdēns erit; *if he does (shall do) it, he will be wise.*

    Sī id fēcerit,[2] prūdēns erit;
    if he does (shall have done) it, he will be wise.

    B. Less Vivid[3]: present subjunctive in both clauses.

    Sī id faciat, prūdēns sit; *if he should do it,[4] he would be wise.*

III. Contrary to Fact Present or Past.

    A. Present: imperfect subjunctive in both clauses.

    Sī id faceret, prūdēns esset; *if he were doing it, he would be wise.*

    B. Past: pluperfect subjunctive in both clauses.

    Sī id fēcisset, prūdēns fuisset; *if he had done it, he would have been wise.*

OBSERVATIONS ON CONDITIONS

The simple present and past conditions will never trouble you; they are exactly like the English.

In the future conditions the distinction depends on the essential difference between the indicative and the subjunctive. The indicative, which indicates a fact, is naturally more certain and more vivid; the subjunctive, which basically expresses other ideas than facts, is less certain and less vivid.

In contrary to fact conditions the key is the conditional clause, which has the same tense in both English and Latin: sī id **faceret,** *if he were doing it;* sī id **fēcisset,** *if he had done it.*

There are occasional admixtures or variants of the regular conditions given above, but they are based on common sense and offer little difficulty.

The negative of **sī** is regularly **nisi** (*if...not, unless*): nisi id faciet, *if he does not do it* or *unless he does it.*

FURTHER EXAMPLES

Classify each of the following conditions.

1. Sī hoc dīcet, errābit; *if he says this, he will be wrong.*
2. Sī hoc dīcit, errat; *if he says this, he is wrong.*
3. Sī hoc dīxisset, errāvisset; *if he had said this, he would have been wrong.*
4. Sī hoc dīcat, erret; *if he should say this, he would be wrong.*
5. Sī hoc dīxit, errāvit; *if he said this, he was wrong.*
6. Sī hoc dīceret, errāret; *if he should say this, he would be wrong.*
7. Sī veniat, hoc videat; *if he should come, he would see this.*
8. Sī vēnit, hoc vīdit; *if he came, he saw this.*
9. Sī venīret, hoc vidēret; *if he were coming, he would see this.*
10. Sī veniet, hoc vidēbit; *if he comes, he will see this.*
11. Sī vēnisset, hoc vīdisset; *if he had come, he would have seen this.*

VOCABULARY

nox, nóctis, *f.,* night (*nocturnal, nocturne, equinox, noctiluca, noctuid*)

ops, ópis, *f.,* help, aid; **ópēs, ópum** (*plu.*), power, resources, wealth (*opulent, opulence*)

sálūs, salútis, *f.,* health, safety; greeting (*salubrious, salutary, salute, salutatory;* cp. **salveō, salvus**)

quis, quid, *after* **sī, nísi, nē, num,**[5] *indef. pron.,* anyone, anything, someone, something (*cp.* **quis? quid?**)

úllus, -a, -um, any; *for declension see Ch. 9.*

sī, *conj.,* if, in case

nísi, *conj.,* if...not, unless; except (*nisi prius*)

suscípiō, -cípere, -cḗpī, -céptum [sub-capiō], undertake (*susceptible, susceptibility*)

trắdō, -ere, trắdidī, trắditum [trāns-dō], give over, surrender; hand down, transmit, teach (*tradition, traditional, traitor*)

RECOGNITION VOCABULARY

cḗna, -ae, *f.,* dinner

plḗnus, -a, -um, full (*plenary, plenitude, plenty, replenish, plenipotentiary*)

cértē, *adv. of* **certus,** certainly

PRACTICE AND REVIEW

1. Sī exercitus auxilium et opem ferat, nāvēs cōnservāre possīmus.
2. Cum cōnsilia hostium eādem nocte cognōvissēs, prīmō tamen mīlitēs mittere nōluistī.
3. Sī dīvitiae nōs ab amōre et honōre prohibent, dīvitēsne sumus?
4. Pauper quidem nōn erit pār cēterīs nisi scientiam habēbit.
5. Sī īnsidiae eius patērent, ferrum eius nōn timērēmus.
6. Sī quis rogābit quid discās, dīc tē artem difficilem discere.
7. Lēgēs ita scrībantur ut pauper et dīves sint parēs.
8. Sī custōdiae dūriōrēs fortiōrēsque fuissent, numquam tanta scelera suscēpissēs.
9. Cum id cognōvisset, omnēs opēs suās celerrimē contulit.
10. Dūrum exsilium tantam mentem ūnō annō dēlēre nōn poterit.
11. If they should come, you would be happier.
12. If you had not answered very wisely, they would not have offered us peace.
13. If anyone does these things well, he will live better.
14. If you were willing to read better books, you would learn more.

SENTENTIAE ANTĪQUAE

1. Sī vīs pācem, parā bellum. (*Flavius Vegetius. — parā, *prepare for.*)
2. Arma sunt parvī pretiī nisi cōnsilium est in patriā. (Cicero. — pretium, -iī, *value.*)
3. Salūs omnium ūnā nocte āmissa esset nisi illa sevēritas contrā istōs suscepta esset. (Cicero. — sevēritās, -tātis.)
4. Sī quid dē mē posse agī putābis, id agēs — sī tū ipse ab istō perīculō eris līber. (Cicero.)
5. Sī essem mihi cōnscius ūllīus culpae, aequō animō hoc malum ferrem. (Phaedrus. — cōnscius, -a, -um, *conscious.*)

6. Laudās fortūnam et mōrēs antīquae plēbis; sed sī quis ad illa subitō tē agat, illum modum vītae recūsēs. (Horace. — plēbs, plēbis, f., *the common people.* — subitō, adv., *suddenly.* — recūsō (1), *refuse.*)
7. Minus saepe errēs sī sciās quid nesciās. (Publilius Syrus.)
8. Dīcēs "heu" sī tē in speculō vīderis. (Horace. — heu, interjection, Roman spelling of a sigh. — speculum, -ī, *mirror.*)

BRING YOUR OWN

Cēnābis bene, mī amīce, apud mē paucīs diēbus sī tēcum attuleris bonam atque magnam cēnam, nōn sine bellā puellā et vīnō et sale. Haec sī attuleris, inquam, cēnābis bene, nam sacculus tuī Catullī plēnus est arāneārum.

(Catullus 13, excerpt recast as prose. — cēnō (1), *dine.* — attuleris, ad-ferō. — sāl, salis, m., *salt, wit.* — inquam, *I say.* — sacculus, -ī, *purse.* — arānea, -ae, *spider's web.*)

TO THOSE WHO HAVE

Semper pauper eris sī pauper es, Aemiliāne:
dantur opēs nūllī nunc nisi dīvitibus.
(*Martial 5.81.; meter, elegiac couplet. — Aemiliānus, -ī.)

ARISTOTLE, TUTOR OF ALEXANDER

An Philippus, rēx Macedonum, voluisset Alexandrō, fīliō suō, prīma elementa litterārum trādī ab Aristotele, summō eius aetātis philosophō, aut hic suscēpisset hoc officium, nisi initia studiōrum pertinēre ad summam crēdidisset?

(Quintilian 1.1.23. — an, interrog. conj., *or, can it be that.* — Macedonēs, -um, *Macedonians.* — Aristotelēs, -is. — philosophus, -ī. — initium, -iī, *beginning.* — per-tineō ad, *relate to, affect.* — summa, -ae, f., *highest part, whole.*)

TARENTUM LOST AND REGAINED

Cum Quīntus Fabius Maximus magnō cōnsiliō Tarentum recēpisset et Salīnātor (quī in arce fuerat, urbe āmissā) dīxisset, "Meā operā, Quīnte Fabī, Tarentum recēpistī," Fabius, mē audiente, "Certē," inquit rīdēns, "nam nisi tū urbem āmīsissēs, numquam eam recēpissem."

(Cicero, *Dē Senectūte* 4.11. — Tarentum -ī, famous city in Magna Graecia. During the second Punic War, Tarentum revolted from the Romans to Hannibal, though the Romans under Marcus Livius, here called Salinator, continued to hold the citadel throughout this period. In 209 B.C. the city was recaptured by Fabius. — Salīnātor, -ōris. — arx, arcis, f., *citadel.* — meā operā, *thanks to me.*)

ETYMOLOGY

In the sentences 2. price, precious, prize, praise, appraise, appreciate, depreciate. 3. severe, persevere, perseverance, asseverate. 5. conscious, unconscious, conscience.

In the readings *Bring Your Own:* salary, salad, saline, salami, saltpeter. — sack. — *Aristotle:* initial, initiative. — pertain, pertinent, pertinacity, purtenance, appertain, appurtenance, impertinent, impertinence.

Footnotes

[1] In the conclusion the imperative or the jussive subjunctive may be used instead of the present indicative, just as in English.

Sī mē amās, id fac; *if you love me, do it.*

Sī mē amat, id faciat; *if he loves me, let him do it.*

[2] The Romans were also fond of using the *future perfect* in the conditional clause, but the idiomatic English translation rarely indicates that fact. The psychology of the future perfect is this: the action of the conditional clause is viewed as having been completed (= a past tense) before that of the conclusion; and, since the whole condition is projected into the future, the past future, or future perfect, tense is used.

[3] Also called "should-would" condition.

[4] Or *should he do it* or *were he to do it.*

34

Deponent Verbs; Ablative with Special Deponents

*T*he peculiarity of deponent verbs is that they have passive forms but active meanings.[1]

PRINCIPAL PARTS AND CONJUGATION

There are in effect no new forms to be learned. With a knowledge of the principal parts (1. *pres. ind.;* 2. *pres. inf.;* 3. *perf. ind.*) you can conjugate these verbs in the indicative and the subjunctive according to the rules for the passive, which you have already learned.

PRINCIPAL PARTS OF DEPONENTS

Pres. Ind.	Pres. Inf.	Perf. Ind.
hórtor, *I urge*	hortárī, *to urge*	hortátus (-a, -um) sum, *I urged*
fáteor, *I confess*	fatérī, *to confess*	fássus (-a, -um) sum, *I confessed*
séquor, *I follow*	séquī, *to follow*	secútus (-a, -um) sum, *I followed*
expérior, *I try*	experírī, *to try*	expértus (-a, -um) sum, *I tried*
pátior, *I suffer*	pátī, *to suffer*	pássus (-a, -um) sum, *I suffered*

SAMPLE FORMS OF HORTOR AND SEQUOR

Indicative

PRESENT

1. hórtor, *I urge*   séquor, *I follow*
2. hortáris,[2] *you urge*   séqueris,[2] *you follow*
3. hortátur, *he urges*   séquitur, *he follows*

1. hortámur, *we urge*   séquimur, *we follow*
2. hortáminī, *you urge*   sequíminī, *you follow*
3. hortántur, *they urge*   sequúntur, *they follow*

IMPERFECT

1. hortábar, *I was urging*   sequébar, *I was following*
2. hortābáris, *you were urging*   sequēbáris, *you were following,*
etc.   etc.

FUTURE

1. hortábor, *I shall urge*   séquar, *I shall follow*
2. hortáberis, *you will urge*   sequéris, *you will follow*
3. hortábitur, *he will urge*   sequétur, *he will follow*
etc.   etc.

PERFECT

hortátus, -a, -um sum, *I urged*   secútus, -a, -um sum, *I followed*
etc.   etc.

PLUPERFECT

hortátus, -a, -um éram, *I had urged*   secútus, -a, -um éram, *I had followed*
etc.   etc.

FUTURE PERFECT

hortátus, -a, -um érō, *I shall have urged*   secútus, -a, -um érō, *I shall have followed*
etc.   etc.

Subjunctive

PRESENT

hórter, hortéris, hortétur   séquar, sequáris, sequátur
etc.   etc.

IMPERFECT

hortárer, hortāréris, hortārétur   séquerer, sequeréris, sequerétur
etc.   etc.

PERFECT

hortā́tus, -a, -um sim, sīs, etc.   secū́tus, -a, -um sim, sīs, etc.

PLUPERFECT

hortā́tus, -a, -um éssem, etc.   secū́tus, -a, -um éssem, etc.

PARTICIPLES AND INFINITIVES

The participles and infinitives of typical deponent verbs are here given in full not because of any actually new forms but because of certain discrepancies in the general rule of passive forms with active meanings.

Participles

Pres. hórtāns, *urging*	séquēns, *following*
Perf. hortā́tus, -a, -um,	secū́tus, -a, -um,
having urged	*having followed*
Fut. hortātū́rus, -a, -um,	secūtū́rus, -a, -um,
about to urge	*about to follow*
Ger. hortándus, -a, -um,	sequéndus, -a, -um,
to be urged	*to be followed*

Infinitives

Pres. hortā́rī, *to urge*	séquī, *to follow*
Perf. hortā́tum, -am, -um esse	secū́tum, -am, -um esse,
to have urged	*to have followed*
Fut. hortātū́rum, -am, -um esse	secūtū́rum, -am, -um esse,
to be about to urge	*to be about to follow*

Deponents have all the participial forms that any verb has; but note the following points:

1. Present and future participles: active forms with active meanings.
2. Perfect participle: passive form with active meaning.
3. Gerundive: passive form with passive meaning.

Deponents have an infinitive for each tense; but note the following points:
1. Present and perfect infinitives: passive forms with active meanings.
2. Future infinitive: active form with active meaning.

Imperative

The present imperative of deponent verbs would naturally have the forms of the present "passive" imperative. These forms have not been given heretofore because they are found only in deponent verbs,[3] but they are easy to learn.

1. The second person singular has the same spelling as that of a present *active* infinitive. Thus, if there were a present active infinitive of **sequī,** it would be **sequere,** and this is the form of the imperative under discussion.[4]

2. The second person plural has the same spelling as that of the second person plural of the present indicative.

PRESENT IMPERATIVE OF DEPONENTS

2. hortắre, *urge*   fatére, *confess*   séquere   experíre   pátere
2. hortắminī, *urge* fatéminī, *confess* sequíminī experíminī patíminī

SEMI-DEPONENT VERBS

Semi-deponent ("half-deponent") is the name given to a few verbs which are normal in the present system but are deponent in the perfect system, as is clearly demonstrated by the principal parts. For example:

    aúdeō, *I dare*   audére, *to dare*   aúsus sum, *I dared*

ABLATIVE WITH SPECIAL DEPONENTS

The ablative of means is used idiomatically with a few deponent verbs, of which **ūtor** is by far the most common.[5] **Ūtor** is really a reflexive verb and means *to benefit oneself* by means of something.[6]

Ūtitur stilō,
    he is benefiting himself by means of a pencil.
    he is using a pencil.
Nōn audent ūtī nāvibus, *they do not dare to use the ships.*
Nōn ausī sunt ūtī nāvibus, *they did not dare to use the ships.*

FURTHER EXAMPLES OF DEPONENT FORMS IN SENTENCES

1. Eum patientem haec mala hortātī sunt,
    they encouraged him suffering[7] these evils.
2. Eum passūrum haec mala hortātī sunt,
    they encouraged him about to suffer these evils.
3. Is, haec mala passus, hortandus est;
    he, having suffered these evils, ought to be encouraged.
4. Is haec mala fortier patiētur,
    he will suffer these evils bravely.
5. Eum sequere et haec experíre,
    follow him and try these things.
6. Eum sequī et haec experīrī nōn ausus es,
    you did not dare to follow him and try these things.
7. Eum sequĕris/sequēris,
    you are following/ will follow him.
8. Eum hortēmur et sequāmur,
    let us encourage and follow him.

9. Cicerō Graecīs litterīs ūtēbātur,
   Cicero used to enjoy Greek literature.

VOCABULARY

áqua, -ae, *f.,* water (*aquatic, aquarium, Aquarius, aqueduct, suba-
   queous, ewer*)

árbitror, -árī, arbitrátus sum, judge, think (*arbiter, arbitration,
   arbitrator, arbitrary*)

aúdeō, -ére, aúsus sum, dare (*audacious, audacity*)

lóquor, lóquī, locútus sum, say, speak, tell (*loquacious, circumlocu-
   tion, eloquent, obloquy, soliloquy, ventriloquist*)

mórior, mórī, mórtuus sum, die (*moribund, mortuary;* cp. **mors**)

náscor, náscī, nátus sum, be born; spring forth (*agnate, cognate,
   innate, nascent, natal, nation, nature, naive;* cp. **nātūra**)

pátior, pátī, pássus sum, suffer, endure, permit (*passion, passive,
   patient, compassion, compatible, incompatibility, impatient, impas-
   sioned, impassive, dispassionate*)

proficíscor, proficíscī, proféctus sum, set out, start

séquor, séquī, secútus sum, follow (*consequent, consecutive, sequence, sequel, subsequent;* v. also Etymology at end of chapter.)

útor, útī, úsus sum, + abl.; use; enjoy, experience (*abuse, disuse,
   peruse, usual, usurp, usury, utensil, utilize, utility, utilitarian*) + abl.

RECOGNITION VOCABULARY

ínsula, -ae, *f.,* island (*insular, insularity, insulate, isolate, isolation*)

cónor, -árī, -átus sum, try, attempt (*conation, conative*)

ēgrédior, égredī, ēgréssus sum, go out (*aggression, congress,
   degrade, digress, egress, grade, gradient, gradual, graduate,
   ingredient, ingress, progress, regress, retrogress, transgress*)

PRACTICE AND REVIEW

1. Nisi quis eīs opem auxiliumque celeriter feret, morientur.
2. Cum urbs plēna custōdiārum esset, haec scelera suscipere nōn ausī estis.
3. Dīc cūr velīs tē ad istum dīvitem cōnferre. Vērē ac līberē loquere.
4. Dēnique, dīvitiīs trāditīs, eādem nocte in excilium profectī sumus.
5. Nē patiāmur hanc scientiam āmittī.
6. Arbitrātur mē meliōre vīnō apud mē ūsūrum esse.
7. Prīmō nōn comprehendistī quantus exercitus nōs sequerētur.
8. Respondit sē nōlle sequī ducem mediocris virtūtis.
9. Ex urbe ēgressus ferrō suō morī cōnātus est.
10. Aristotelēs arbitrābātur virtūtem in hominibus nōn nāscī.
11. They did not permit me to speak with him.

12. We kept thinking (**arbitror**) that he would use the office (**honor**) more wisely.
13. If any one should use this water, he would die.
14. If they had followed us, we should not have dared to put the iron on the ships.

SENTENTIAE ANTĪQUAE

1. Cēdāmus Phoebō et, monitī, meliōra sequāmur. (*Virgil. — Phoebus, -ī, *Apollo*, god of prophecy.)
2. Nam nēmō sine vitiīs nāscitur; optimus ille est quī minima habet. (Horace.)
3. Mundus est commūnis urbs deōrum atque hominum; hī enim sōlī ratiōne ūtentēs, iūre ac lēge[8] vīvunt. (Cicero.)
4. Tardē sed graviter vir sapiēns īrāscitur. (*Publilius Syrus. — tardus, -a, -um, *slow, late*. — īrāscor, -ī, īrātus sum, *become angry*.)
5. Quae cum ita sint, Catilīna, ēgredere ex urbe; patent portae; proficīscere; nōbīscum versārī iam diūtius nōn potes; id nōn feram, nōn patiar. (Cicero. — porta, -ae, *gate*. — versor, -ārī, versātus sum, *stay*.)
6. Cūra pecūniam crēscentem sequitur. (Horace. — crēscō, -ere, crēvī, crētum, *increase*.)
7. Sī in Britanniam profectus essēs, nēmō in illā tantā īnsulā iūre perītior fuisset. (Cicero. — perītus, -a, -um, + abl. *skilled in*.)
8. Nisi laus nova oritur, etiam vetus laus āmittitur. (Publilius Syrus. — orior (oreris, oritur: *3rd conj. forms in pres. ind.*), orīrī, ortus sum, *arise, begin*. — vetus, -eris, adj., *old*.)
9. Spērō autem mē secūtum esse in libellīs meīs tālem temperantiam ut nēmō bonus dē illīs querī possit. (Martial. — tālis, -e, *such*. — temperantia, -ae. — queror, querī, questus sum, *complain*.)
10. Lābuntur annī; dum loquimur, fūgerit aetās. (Horace. — lābor, , -ī, lāpsus sum, *slip, glide by*. — fūgerit, fut. perf.)
11. Hōrae quidem et diēs et annī discēdunt; nec praeteritum tempus umquam revertitur, nec quid sequātur, potest scīrī. (Cicero. — praeteritus, -a, -um, *past*. — revertor, -vertī, -vertī [perf. is active], -versum [dep. perf. partic.], *return*.)
12. Nōvistī mōrēs mulierum: dum mōliuntur, dum cōnantur, annus lābitur. (Terence. — mulier, -eris, woman. — mōlior, -īrī, -ītus sum, *plan*.)
13. Amīcitia rēs plūrimās continet; nōn aquā, nōn igne in pluribus locīs ūtimur quam amīcitiā. (Cicero.)
14. Homō stultus! Postquam dīvitiās habēre coepit, mortuus est! (Cicero. — postquam, conj., *after*.)
15. Ō passī graviōra, dabit deus hīs quoque fīnem. (*Virgil. — Ō passī, voc. plu., *O you...* — hīs = hīs rēbus gravibus. — quoque, adv., also.)

ETYMOLOGY

Sympathy derives from Greek **syn** (*with*) + **pathos** (*suffering*). What Latin-rooted word is the exact equivalent of *sympathy?*

Further words associated with **sequor:** execute, executive, executor, obsequious, prosecute, persecute, pursue, ensue, sue, suit, suite, sect, second. Related to **sequor** is **socius** (*a follower, ally*), whence social, society, associate, dissociate.

In the sentences   4. irate, irascible, irascibility. 5. portal, portcullis, porter (gate-keeper), portico, porch. — **Versārī** literally means *turn (oneself) around;* hence versatile, converse, conversant, conversation. 6. crescent, decrease, excrescence, increase, increment, accretion, accrue, crew, recruit, concrete. 8. veteran, inveterate. 9. intemperance. — querulous, quarrel. 10. lapse, collapse, elapse, relapse. 11. preterit. — revert, reverse, reversible, reversion.

Footnotes

[1]"Deponent" derives from **dē-pōnō**, *lay aside.* Though passive in form, these verbs have "laid aside" their passive meaning and taken an active one. In origin these were probably reflexive verbs.

[2]Also **hortā-re** and **seque-re**; v. Ch. 18, n. 2. This alternate ending, **-re**, holds for the 2nd per. sing. throughout the pres. system of the ind. and the subj.

[3]Professor Ralph L. Ward points out that "Latin verbs which have any active forms do not possess an imperative passive."

[4]Its spelling is also the same as that of the **-re** form of the 2nd per. sing. of the pres. ind.: **sequere** (v. n. 2 above).

[5]The others (**fruor, fungor, potior, vēscor**) are not important for this book.

[6]Cf. Fr. *se servir de,* "to use," orig. "to serve oneself with."

[7]A literal, rather than a literary, translation of the participles in this and the following sentences is given for illustrative purposes.

[8]The abl. here expresses the idea "in accordance with."

35

Dative with Special Verbs; Dative with Compounds

DATIVE WITH SPECIAL VERBS

In Latin certain verbs, usually intransitive, take the dative of indirect object, whereas, on the basis of their ordinary English equivalents, we should expect them to take the accusative.[1]

Crēdō **tibi,** *I believe you.*

Ignōscō **tibi,** *I forgive you.*

Since no simple or completely satisfactory rule can be given to cover this situation,[2] some of the more common of these verbs are listed with two suggestions:

(1) that you note carefully the English translation which does indicate the Latin dative by the preposition *to.*

(2) that you *memorize the brief Latin example* given with each verb, much as you memorize the gender of a noun.

crēdō + dat., *trust to, trust, believe* (**crēdō tibi,** *I believe you*)

ignōscō + dat., *grant pardon to, pardon, forgive* (**ignōscō tibi,** *I forgive you*)

imperō + dat., *give orders to, command* (**imperō tibi,** *I command you*)

noceō + dat., *do harm to, harm* (**noceō tibi,** *I harm you*)

parcō + dat., *be lenient to, spare* (**parcō tibi,** *I spare you*)

pāreō + dat., *be obedient to, obey* (**pāreō** tibi, *I obey you*)

persuādeō + dat., *make sweet to, persuade* (**persuādeō tibi,** *I persuade you*)

placeō + dat., *be pleasing to, please* (**placeō tibi,** *I please you*)

serviō + dat., *be a slave to, serve* (**serviō tibi,** *I serve you*)

studeō + dat., *direct one's zeal to, study* (**studeō litterīs,** *I study literature*)

Crēde mihi, *believe me.*
Ignōsce mihi, *pardon me, forgive me.*
Magister discipulīs nōn parcit, *the teacher does not spare the pupils.*
Hoc eīs nōn placet, *this does not please them.*
Nōn possum eī persuādēre, *I cannot persuade him.*
Variae rēs hominibus nocent, *various things harm men.*
Cicerō philosophiae studēbat, *Cicero used to study philosophy.*
Philosophiae servire est lībertās, *to serve philosophy is liberty.*

DATIVE WITH COMPOUND VERBS

Certain verbs in their simple form did not take the dative, but, when compounded with certain prepositions or prefixes,[3] they often acquired a *new* meaning[4] which made an indirect object possible — at least to the Roman mind. However, since many other verbs compounded with these prepositions or prefixes did not take the dative and since Roman usage often varied even for the same verb, no easy rule can be composed.[5] In the following list of sentences some without a dative have been included for illustrative purposes.

Sum amīcus, *I am a friend.*
Adsum amīcō, *I support my friend.*
Apposuit pānem amīcīs, *he served his friends bread.*
Advēnit ad nōs, *he reached us.*
Sequor eum, *I follow him.*
Obsequor eī, *I obey him.*
Erat dux, *he was a general.*
Praeerat exercituī, *he was in command of the army.*
Praeposuī *or* praefēcī eum exercituī, *I put him in command of the army.*
Praeposuī pecūniam amīcitiae, *I preferred money to friendship.*
Reposuī pecūniam in thēsaurum, *I put money back into the treasury.*
Reposuī spem in virtūte, *I put my hope in courage.*
Repugnāvī fratrī tuō, *I opposed your brother.*
Convocāvit amicīcōs, *he called his friends together.*
Composuit sē mihi, *he compared himself with me.*
Composuit verba cum factīs, *he compared words with deeds.*

VOCABULARY

advérsus, -a, -um, opposite, adverse (*adversary, adversative, adversity*)
ímperō (1), give orders to, command (*imperative, emperor;* cp. **imperium**)

míror, -árī, -átus sum, marvel at, admire, wonder (*admire, marvel, miracle, mirage, mirror*)

nóceō, -ére, nócuī, nócitum, do harm to, harm, injure (*innocent, innocuous, noxious, nuisance, obnoxious*)

párcō, -ere, pepércī, parsúrus, be lenient to, spare (*parsimonious, parsimony*)

páreō, -ére, párui, be obedient to, obey

persuádeō, -ére, -suásī, -suásum, make sweet to, persuade (*assuage, dissuade, suasion, suave;* cp. *sweet*)

pláceō, -ére, plácuī, plácitum, be pleasing to, please (*complacent, placable, implacable, placate, placid, plea, plead, please, pleasure, displease*)

sérviō, -íre, -ívī, -ítum, be a slave to, serve (*service, disservice, subserve, subservient, deserve, desert = reward, dessert;* cp. **servus, servitūs;** distinguish from **servāre**)

stúdeō, -ére, stúduī, direct one's zeal to, be eager for, study (*student;* cp. **studium**)

RECOGNITION VOCABULARY

praémium, -iī, *n.,* reward, prize (*premium*)

prae-, *as prefix,* before, in front of, forth; very; *see compounds under* **prae-** *in general vocabulary* (*pre-*)

antepónō, -ere, -pósuī, -pósitum, put before, prefer

ignóscō, -ere, ignóvī, ignótum, grant pardon to, forgive

PRACTICE AND REVIEW

1. Minerva nāta est plēna scientiae.
2. Custōdiae sī cum duce nostrō līberē loquantur et huic tyrannum trādere cōnentur, sine perīculō ex urbe ēgredī possint.
3. Pārēre lēgibus aequīs melius est quam tyrannō servīre.
4. Cum optimē honōribus ūsus esset, etiam pauperēs cīvēs eī crēdēbant.
5. Diū passus, fēlīciter apud amīcōs mortuus est.
6. Respondērunt sē hanc rem suscipere nōlle.
7. Cum dīves sīs, tamen opibus tuīs parcere vīs.
8. Ab illā īnsulā celeriter profectus, eādem nocte ad patriam nāve advēnit.
9. Cum hic mīles ducī vestrō nōn placēret, illa tanta praemia āmīsit.
10. Nisi mōrēs parēs scientiae sunt, scientia nōbīs nocēre potest.
11. Why does he wish to hurt his friend?
12. If he does not spare them, we shall not trust him.
13. Since you are studying Roman literature, you are serving a very difficult but a very great master.
14. If they were willing to please us, they would not be using their wealth thus against the state.

SENTENTIAE ANTĪQUAE

1. Nēmō līber est quī corporī servit. (Seneca.)
2. Imperium habēre vīs magnum? Imperā tibi. (Publil. Syri.)
3. Bonīs nocet quisquis pepercit malīs. (*Id. — quisquis, quid-quid, *whoever, whatever*.)
4. Cum tū omnia pecūniae postpōnās, mīrāris sī nēmō tibi amōrem praestat? (Horace. — post-pōnō.)
5. Frūstrā aut pecūniae aut imperiīs aut opibus aut glōriae student; potius studeant virtūtī et dignitātī et scientiae et alicui artī. (Cicero. — frūstrā, adv., *in vain*. — potius, adv., *rather*.)
6. Virtūtī melius quam Fortūnae crēdāmus; virtūs nōn nōvit calamitātī cēdere. (Publilius Syrus. — calamitās, -tātis.)
7. Et Deus ait: "Faciāmus hominem ad imāginem nostram et praesit piscibus maris bēstiīsque terrae." (Genesis. — imāgō, -inis, f. — prae-sum. — piscis, -is, m., *fish*. — bēstia, -ae, *beast*.)
8. Omnēs arbitrātī sunt tē dēbēre mihi parcere. (Cicero.)
9. Quid facere vellet, ostendit et illī servō spē lībertātis magnīsque praemiīs persuāsit. (Caesar.)
10. Sī cui librī Cicerōnis placent, ille sciat sē prōfēcisse. (Quintilian. — prōficiō, *progress*.)
11. In urbe nostrā mihi contigit docērī quantum īrātus Achillēs Graecīs nocuisset. (Horace. — con-tingō, -ere, con-tigī, -tāctum, *touch closely, fall to the lot of.* — quantum, adv. —īrātus, -a, -um, *angry*.)
12. Alicui rogantī melius quam iubentī pārēmus. (Publilius Syrus.)
13. Vīvite fortiter fortiaque pectora rēbus adversīs oppōnite. (Horace. — pectus, pectoris, n., *breast, heart*. — oppōnō, ob-pōnō, *set against*.)
14. Nōn ignāra malī miserīs succurrere discō. (*Virgil. — ignārus, -a, -um, *ignorant;* ignāră is fem. because it agrees with Dido, exiled queen, who speaks these words to shipwrecked Aeneas. — succurrō, sub-currō, *help*.)
15. Ignōsce saepe alterī, numquam tibi. (Publilius Syrus.)
16. Amīcitiam omnibus rēbus hūmānīs antepōnō. (Cicero.)

ETYMOLOGY

In the sentences   5. frustrate, frustration. 7. Pisces, piscatory, piscatology, piscary. — bestial, bestiality, bestialize, beast, beastly. 10. proficient, proficiency. 11. contingent, contingency, contiguous, contiguity, contact, contagion, contagious. 13. pectoral. — opposite, opposition. 14. succor.

Footnotes

[1]It may not help too much to learn that in Anglo-Saxon also many of these verbs took the dative and that in German they still do (e.g., *ich glaube, traue, verzeihe Ihnen*). Cp. French *croire à, se fier à, résister à, pardonner à.*

[2]A common rule lists verbs meaning *favor, help, harm, please, displease, trust, distrust, believe, persuade, command, obey, serve, resist, envy, threaten, pardon, spare.* But note such exceptions as **iuvō**, *help;* **laedō**, *injure;* **iubeō**, *order.*

[3]Among which are **ad, ante, con-** (=**cum**), **in, inter, ob, post, prae, prō, sub, super, re-** (in the sense of *against*).

[4]In the following examples, for instance, the preposition has not essentially altered the *basic* meaning of the verb, and so the dative is not used: **convocāvit senātum,** *he called the senate together;* **complēvit saccum,** *he filled the sack up;* **advēnit ad nōs,** *he came to us.*

[5]A helpful, though not infallible, criterion is this: if the simple verb can be put in the place of the compound one, the dative is not likely to be used. Cp. the examples in the preceding note.

36

Jussive Noun Clauses; Fīō

JUSSIVE NOUN CLAUSES
(Ut OR Nē + SUBJUNCTIVE)

*M*any *Latin verbs whose meaning contains some connotation of command or request may be followed by* **ut** *(negative,* **nē***) and a subordinate jussive subjunctive.*[1]

1. Hoc facite, *do this* (imperative). Direct command.
2. Hoc faciant, *let them do this* (jussive subj.). Direct command.
3. Imperāvit vōbīs ut hoc facerētis, *he commanded you to do this.*
4. Imperāvit eīs ut hoc facerent, *he commanded them to do this.*
5. Persuāsit eīs ut hoc facerent, *he persuaded them to do this.*
6. Petīvit ab[1] eīs nē hoc facerent, *he begged (from) them not to do this.*
7. Monuit eōs nē hoc facerent, *he warned them not to do this.*
8. Hortātus est eōs ut hoc facerent, *he urged them to do this.*

These clauses are commonly called "purpose" clauses because in appearance they are identical with purpose clauses, but a study of the examples given above reveals their essentially jussive nature.[2] In contrast to ordinary purpose clauses, which are of *adverbial* nature, the jussive clauses under discussion are called *noun* clauses because they are used as objects of the verbs on which they depend.

IRREGULAR Fīō

Fīō, fierī, factus sum, *be made, be done, become,* was used by the Romans as the passive of the simple verb **faciō.**[3] From the principal parts it is obvious that the perfect system is quite regular as the normal passive of facio; factus, -a, -um est, factus erat, factus sit, factus esset, factus esse, etc. Therefore, only the present need be learned as new. These forms follow.[4]

Indicative			Subjunctive	
Pres.	**Impf.**	**Fut.**	**Pres.**	**Impf.**
1. fīō	fīēbam	fīam	fīam	fīerem
2. fīs	fīēbās	fīes	fīas	fīerēs
3. fit	fīēbat	fīet	fīat	fīeret
1. fīmus	fīēbámus	fīēmus	fīāmus	fierémus
2. fītis	fīēbátis	fīētis	fīátis	fierétis
3. fīunt	fīēbant	fīent	fīant	fīerent

Infinitives		Participles	
Pres.	fīerī		
Perf.	fáctum, -am, -um esse	**Perf.**	fáctus, -a, -um
Fut.	fáctum īrī	**Fut.**	faciéndus, -a, -um

Be careful to observe the passive force of **fīō.**

Hoc facit (faciet), *he is doing* or *making this* (*will do* or *make*).

Hoc fit (fīet), *this is done* or *made* (*will be done* or *made*).

Hoc faciat, *let him do* or *make this*.

Hoc fīat, *let this be done* or *made*.

Dīcunt eum hoc facere, *they say that he is doing this.*

Dīcunt hoc fīerī, *they say that this is being done.*

Perīculum fit gravius, *the danger is becoming graver.*

VOCABULARY

tímor, -óris, *m.*, fear (*timorous;* cp. **timeō**)

lévis, -e, light, slight, easy, trivial (*levity, lever, levy, levee, Levant, leaven, legerdemain, alleviate, elevate, relevant, irrelevant, relieve, relief*)

accédō, -ere, -céssī, céssum, come (to), approach (*accede, access, accessible;* cp. **cēdō, discēdō**)

cógō, -ere, coégī, coáctum (**cum-ago**), drive *or* bring together, force, compel (*cogent, coaction, coactive, coagulate*)

cúrō (1), care for, attend to; take care (*cure, curator, procure, proctor, accurate;* cp. **cūra**)

fáteor, -érī, fássus sum, confess, admit (*confess, confession, profess, profession, professor*)

fíō, fíerī, fáctus sum, be made, be done, become, come about, happen, take place (*fiat*)

hórtor, -árī, hortátus sum, encourage, urge (*hortatory, exhort, exhortation*)

órō (1), speak, plead; beg, beseech, entreat (*orator, oration, oracle, orison, adore, inexorable, peroration*)

PRACTICE AND REVIEW

1. Poterāsne multīs persuādēre ut viam virtūtis sine praemiīs sequerentur?
2. Hic vult ad illam īnsulam proficīscī ut sine timōre vītam agat.
3. Petēbant ā nōbīs ut etiam in adversīs rēbus huic ducī pārērēmus et servīrēmus.
4. Haec ab eō facta sunt nē tantam occāsiōnem āmitteret.
5. Rogāmus tē ut honōre et opibus sapientius ūtāris.
6. Nisi quis hoc suscipere audēbit, nōlent nōbīs crēdere.
7. Rogāvit nōs cūr neque dīvitibus neque pauperibus placēre cōnātī essēmus.
8. Arbitrābātur fēlīcem vītam nōn ex dīvitiīs sed ex animō plēnō virtūtis nāscī.
9. Magnam scientiam et sapientiam magis quam magnās dīvitiās mīrēmur.
10. Senātus ducī imperāvit nē hostibus victīs nocēret.
11. That night they urged that this be done better.
12. If this is done, they will beg us not to spare him.
13. He wants to persuade more pupils to study good literature.
14. Since his hope is becoming very small, let him confess that he commanded (use **imperō**) them to do it.

SENTENTIAE ANTĪQUAE

1. Dīxitque Deus: "Fīat lūx." Et facta est lūx. (*Genesis.)
2. Fatendum est nihil dē nihilō posse fierī. (Lucretius. — nihilō, abl. of nihilum, -ī, = nihil.)
3. Magnae rēs nōn fīunt sine perīculō. (Terence.)
4. Hīs rēbus cognitīs, ille suōs hortātus est nē timērent. (Caesar.)
5. Omnia fīent quae fierī aequum est. (Terence.)
6. "Pater, ōrō tē ut mihi ignōscās." "Fīat." (Terence.)
7. Carpāmus dulcia; post enim mortem cinis et fābula fīēs. (Persius. — carpō, -ere, -psī, -ptum, *pluck, gather.* — cinis, -eris, m., *ashes.* — fābula, -ae, *story, tale.*)
8. Ante senectūtem cūrāvī ut bene vīverem; in senectūte cūrō ut bene moriar. (Seneca.)
9. Solōn dīxit sē senem fierī cotīdiē, aliquid addiscentem. (Cicero. — Solōn, -ōnis. —cotīdiē, adv., *daily.* — ad-discō.)
10. Caret pectus tuum inānī ambitiōne? Caret īrā et timōre mortis? Ignōscis amīcīs? Fīs lēnior et melior, accēdente senectūte? (Horace. — inānis, -e, *empty, vain.* — ambitiō, -ōnis, f. — lēnis, -e, *gentle, kind.*)
11. Hoc dūrum est; sed levius fit patientiā quidquid corrigere est nefās. (Horace. — patientia, -ae, — corrigō, -ere, -rēxī, -rēctum. — est nefās, *it is wrong, contrary to divine law.*)
12. Cēdāmus! Leve fit onus quod bene fertur. (Ovid. — onus, -eris, n., *burden.*)

13. Ego vōs hortor ut amīcitiam omnibus rēbus hūmānīs antepōnātis. (Cicero.)

14. Petō ā vōbīs ut patiāminī mē dē studiīs hūmānitātis ac litterārum loquī. (Cicero. — hūmānitās, -tātis, *culture*.)

MARTIAL'S BOOK

Sunt bona, sunt quaedam mediocria, sunt mala plūra
quae legis hīc; aliter nōn fit, Avīte, liber.
(*Martial 1.16. — meter, elegiac couplet. — sunt, *there are*. — hīc, adv. — aliter, *otherwise*. — Avītus, -ī, a friend of M.)

TESTIMONY AGAINST THE CONSPIRATORS

Senātum coēgī. Intrōdūxī Volturcium sine Gallīs. Fidem pūblicam eī dedī. Hortātus sum ut ea quae scīret sine timōre nūntiāret. Tum ille, cum sē ex magnō timōre recreāvisset, dīxit sē ab Lentulō habēre ad Catilīnam mandāta ut auxiliō servōrum ūterētur et ad urbem quam prīmum cum exercitū accēderet. Intrōductī autem Gallī dīxērunt sibi litterās ad suam gentem ab Lentulō datās esse et hunc imperāvisse ut equitātum in Italiam quam prīmum mitterent. Dēnique, omnibus rēbus expositīs, senātus dēcrēvit ut coniūrātī in custōdiam trāderentur.

(From Cicero, *Cat.* 3. — intrō-dūcō. — Volturcius, -iī, a conspirator of Catiline's band. — Gallus, -ī, *a Gaul;* Lentulus had been seeking to stir into rebellion against the Roman state the Gallic Allobroges, who had a delegation at Rome. — sē recreāre (1), *to recover*. — Lentulus, -ī, the leading conspirator at Rome in Catiline's absence. — mandātum, -ī, *order*. — quam prīmum, see Ch. 32, n. 3. — equitātus, -ūs, *cavalry*. — dēcernō, -ere, -crēvī, crētum, *decree*. — coniūrātus, -ī, *conspirator*.)

ETYMOLOGY

In the sentences   7. carp at, excerpt. — cinerary, incinerator, incinerate. 10. inane, inanity. — ambition; **ambitiō** literally meant *a going around* by a candidate to individual citizens in quest of political support. — lenient, leniency, lenity. 11. correct, incorrigible. *Testimony:* recreate, recreation. — mandate, mandatory, command, countermand, demand, remand. — equitation. — decree, decretal.

Footnotes

[1]The following list contains some of the more common of these verbs with an indication also of the case construction which follows each.

imperō eī ut	petō ab eō ut	hortor eum ut	ōrō eum ut
persuādeō eī ut	quaerō ab eō ut	moneō eum ut	rogō eum ut

[2]As a matter of fact, Latin purpose clauses were probably jussive in origin.

[3]However, when **faciō** was compounded with a preposition or a prefix, the passive was formed regularly; e.g., **per-ficiō** (-ere, -fēcī, -fectum) has **perficitur, perficiēbātur, perficiētur, perficī,** etc.

[4]All the infinitives and the participles have been given for the sake of completeness in these important items. The present imperative (**fī, fīte**) need not be learned now.

37

Conjugation of Eō; Constructions of Place and Time

IRREGULAR Eō

*T*he irregular verb *eō, īre, iī, itum,* go, is conjugated as follows.

INDICATIVE

Pres.	Impf.	Fut.	Perf.	Plupf.	Futpf.
1. eō	íbam	íbō	íī	íeram	íerō
2. īs	íbās	íbis	īstī	íerās	íeris
3. it	íbat	íbit	íit	íerat	íerit
1. ímus	ībámus	íbimus	íimus	ierámus	iérimus
2. ítis	ībátis	íbitis	ístis	ierátis	iéritis
3. éunt	íbant	íbunt	iérunt	íerant	íerint

SUBJUNCTIVE

Pres.	Impf.	Perf.	Plupf.
1. éam	írem	íerim	íssem
2. éās	írēs	íeris	íssēs
3. éat	íret	íerit	ísset
1. eámus	īrémus	ierímus	īssémus
2. eátis	īrétis	ierítis	īssétis
3. éant	írent	íerint	íssent

Imperative: 2. ī 2. íte

PARTICIPLES (in common use)

    Pres. íēns (gen. eúntis)   **Fut.** itúrus, -a, -um

INFINITIVES

    Pres. íre   **Perf.** ísse
    Fut. itúrum esse
    Gerund: eúndī[1]

OBSERVATIONS ON Eō

In the present system of ēo there are two major difficulties:

(1) The normal stem, **i**, as derived from the present infinitive, becomes **e** before **a, o,** and **u**; e.g., **eam, eō, eunt.** Give particular attention to the present indicative and the present subjunctive above. A similar change from **i** to **e** is seen in all forms of the present participle except the nominative singular and in the gerund.

(2) The future of this fourth conjugation verb has the endings of a first conjugation verb.

The perfect system is formed regularly except that **ii** before **s** usually contracts to **ī**; e.g., **īstī, īsse.**

Only the active forms are here presented; the rare impersonal passive does not appear in this book.

PLACE CONSTRUCTIONS

You have already learned how to use the proper prepositions and cases in the regular place constructions, but they are repeated here for review and for contrast with the special rules for the *names* of cities and towns and for **domus**.

I. Regular constructions: prepositions + proper case.
    (1) Place *where:* **in** + ablative.
        In illā urbe vīsus est, *he was seen in that city.*
    (2) Place *to which:* **in** or **ad** + accusative.
        In illam urbem ībit, *he will go into that city.*
    (3) Place *from which:* **ab, dē,** or **ex** + ablative.
        Ex illā urbe iit, *he went out of that city.*

II. Special constructions for names of cities and towns and for **domus**: no prepositions.

    (1) Place *where:* locative case.[2]

        Vīsus est Rōmae, Corinthī, Athēnīs, Delphīs, Carthāgine.[3]
        He was seen at Rome, Corinth, Athens, Delphi, Carthage.

(2) Place *to which:* accusative without a preposition.
>   Ībit Rōmam, Corinthum, Athēnās, Delphōs, Carthāginem.
>   *He will go to Rome, Corinth, Athens, Delphi, Carthage.*

(3) Place *from which:* ablative without a preposition.
>   Iit Rōmā, Corinthō, Athēnīs, Delphīs, Carthāgine.
>   *He went from Rome, Corinth, Athens, Delphi, Carthage.*

Concerning **domus** the best procedure is to learn the three forms practically as if they were adverbs:

domī (locative), *at home.*   Domī vīsus est, *he was seen at home.*
domum (acc.), *home* (= *to home*).   Domum ībit, *he will go home.*
domō (abl.), *from home.*   Domō iit, *he went from home.*

TIME CONSTRUCTIONS

Ablative or accusative without a preposition.

(1) Ablative: time *when* or *within which.* (See Ch. 15.)
>   Eōdem diē iit, *he went on the same day.*
>   Paucīs hōrīs domum ībit, *he will go home in a few hours.*

(2) Accusative: time *how long* (duration of time).
>   Multōs annōs vīxit, *he lived (for) many years.*
>   Paucās hōrās domī manēbit, *he will stay at home (for) a few hours.*

VOCABULARY

Athḗnae, -ā́rum, *f.,* Athens (cp. *athenaeum*)

dómus. -ūs(-ī), *f.,* house, home; **dómī,** at home; **dómum,** (to) home; **dómō,** from home (*domicile, domestic, domesticate, dome, major-domo*)

frā́ter, frā́tris, *m.,* brother (*fraternal, fraternity, fraternize, fratricide*)

Rōma, -ae, *f.,* Rome

grā́tus, -a, -um, pleasing, agreeable; grateful (*grace, grateful, gratitude, gratify, gratis, gratuitous, gratuity, ingrate, ingratiate, agree, congratulate;* cp. **grātiās agō**)

de'inde, *adv.,* thereupon, next, then

ut + *indicative,* as, when

éō, íre, íī, ítum, go (*ambition, circuit, concomitant, exit, initial, initiate, initiative, obituary, perish, preterit, sedition, transient, transit, transition, transitive, transitory*)

ábeō, -íre, -iī, -itum, go away, depart (**ab** + **eō**)

péreō, -íre, -iī, -itum, pass away, be destroyed, perish

rédeō, -íre, iī, -itum, go back, return (**red** + **eō**) interfícĭō, -ere, -fḗcĭ, -féctum, kill, murder

lícet, licḗre, lícuit, *impersonal,*[4] it is permitted, one may; *commonly with an infinitive as subject and with a dative of indirect object (license, licentious, illicit, leisure, viz. = vidḗlicet, sc. = scílicet)*

sóleō, -ḗre, sólitus sum, be accustomed

RECOGNITION VOCABULARY

Syrācúsae, -árum, *f.*, Syracuse

PRACTICE AND REVIEW

1. Petet ā frātre meō ut in urbem redeat.
2. Nisi domum eō diē redĭssēs, Athēnās profectī essēmus.
3. Nē levēs quidem timōrēs ferre poterātis.
4. Haec locūtī mihi nōn persuādēbunt ut opēs praemiīs bonae vītae antepōnam.
5. Multōs annōs eōs cīvitātī servīre coēgit.
6. At nōs, ipsī multa mala passī, cōnātī sumus cīs persuādēre nē cui nocērent.
7. Sī quis vult aliōs iuvāre, cūret ut ad eōs accēdat plēnus sapientiae.
8. Stōicī dīcēbant sē nātūrae pārēre. (Stōicī, -ōrum, *the Stoics.*)
9. Fateāmur haec difficillima Rōmae suscipienda esse.
10. Omnēs solent mīrārī ea pulcherrima quae Athēnīs vident.
11. Nisi vīs morī, ēgredere Syrācūsīs et sequere alium ducem Athēnās.
12. They commanded that this be done in Rome for many days.
13. Unless he goes to Syracuse in a few days, his father's fear will become greater.
14. He thought that his brother would not return home on that day.
15. Nobody may speak freely in that country, as we all know.

SENTENTIAE ANTĪQUAE

1. Mortālia facta perībunt. (*Horace. — mortālis, -e.)
2. Noctēs atque diēs patet iānua Plūtōnis. (Virgil. — iānua, -ae, *door.* Plūtō, -ōnis, the god of the dead.)
3. Annī eunt mōre modōque fluentis aquae. Numquam hōra quae praeteriit potest redīre; ūtāmur aetāte. (Ovid. — fluō, -ere, flūxī, flūxum, *flow.* — praeter-eō, *go by, pass.*)
4. Periī! Quid ego egī! Fīlius nōn rediit ā cēnā hāc nocte. (Terence.)
5. Frāter meus ōrat nē abeās domō. (Terence.)
6. Dīcit patrem ab urbe abīsse sed frātrem esse domī. (Terence.)
7. Tertiā hōrā ībam Sacrā Viā, ut meus mōs est. (Horace. — tertius, -a, -um, *third.* — Sacrā Viā, abl. of means or way by which; the Sacred Way was the main street through the Roman Forum.)
8. Dēnique Dāmoclēs, eum sic beātus esse nōn posset, ōrāvit Dionȳsium tyrannum ut abīre ā cēnā licēret. (Cicero.)

9. Eō tempore, Syrācūsīs captīs, Mārcellus multa Rōmam mīsit; Syrācūsīs autem multa atque pulcherrima relīquit. (Cicero.)
10. Diēs multōs in eā nāve fuī; ita adversā tempestāte ūsī sumus. (Terence. — tempestās, -tātis, *weather*.)
11. Īram populī ferre nōn poterō sī in exsilium ieris. (Cicero.)
12. Caesare interfectō, Brūtus Rōmā Athēnās fūgit. (Cicero.)
13. Ipse Rōmam redīrem sī satis cōnsilium dē hāc rē habērem. (Cicero.)
14. Nēmō est tam senex ut nōn putet sē ūnum annum posse vīvere. (Cicero.)

MĀRCUS QUĪNTŌ FRĀTRĪS

Licinius, servus Aesōpī nostrī, Rōmā Athēnās fūgit. Is Athēnīs apud Patrōnem prō liberō virō fuit. Deinde in Asiam abiit. Posteā Platō, quīdam, quī Athēnīs solet esse multum et quī tum Athēnīs fuerat cum Licinius Athēnās vēnisset, litterīs Aesōpī dē Liciniō acceptīs, hunc Ephesī comprehendit et in custōdiam trādidit. Petō ā tē, frāter, ut Ephesō rediēns servum Rōmam tēcum redūcās. Aesōpus enim ita īrāscitur propter servī scelus ut nihil eī grātius possit esse quam recuperātiō fugitīvī. Valē.

(Cicero, *Epistolae ad Qu. Frātrem* 1.2.14; Marcus Cicero wrote this letter to his brother Quintus, who was at the time the governor of Asia. — S. = salūtem dīcit, *says greetings*. — Aesōpus, -ī, the leading tragic actor of Rome. — Patrōn, -ōnis. — pro *as a*. — posteā, adv., *afterwards*. Plato, an Epicurean from Sardis. — multum, adv. — Ephesus, -ī, a city in Asia Minor. —īrāscor, -ī, īrātus sum, *be angry;* cp. **īra**. — recuperātiō, -ōnis, *recovery*.)

ETYMOLOGY

Vidēlicet, *namely,* derives from **vidēre licet.** In the medieval manuscripts this long word was often contracted to **vi-et,** and one abbreviation for **et** resembled a *z*; hence our abbreviation *viz.*

In the sentences   2. janitor, Janus, January. 7. tertiary, tertian. — Another famous street in Rome was **Via Lāta.** On the analogy of **Sacra Via** how is **Via Lāta (lātus, -a, -um,** *broad*) to be translated? 10. tempest, tempestuous. In the letter: *recuperate* and *recover* are etymological relatives: both derive from **recuperō** (1), *regain.*

Footnotes

[1]To be used later in Ch. 39.

[2]The locative case has the form of the genitive in the singular of the 1st and the 2nd declensions; but in the plural of the 1st and the 2nd declensions and throughout the 3d declension the locative has the form of the ablative (though a form ending in Ī is also found in the singular of the 3d declension: **Carthāgine** or **Carthāginī,** *at Carthage*).

[3]These locatives derive from the following nouns respectively: Rōma, -ae, f.; Corinthus, -ī, f.; Athēnae, -ārum, f.; Delphī, -ōrum, m.; Carthāgō, -inis, f.

[4]Impersonal verbs do not have a person as subject, but they can have an infinitive, a clause, or a neuter pronoun. Consequently, of the finite forms they have only the 3d person singular.

38

Relative Clauses of Characteristic; Dative of Reference

RELATIVE CLAUSES WITH THE INDICATIVE: FACT

Ever since Ch. 17, relative clauses with the indicative have been familiar to you. The indicative is used in a relative clause to state a fact about the antecedent.

RELATIVE CLAUSES WITH THE SUBJUNCTIVE: CHARACTERISTIC

The subjunctive is used in a relative clause to state a *characteristic* of the antecedent. The characteristic clauses have antecedents which are general, indefinite, interrogative, or negative,[1] and these clauses describe the antecedents as being *of such a sort as to..., of such a sort that..., the kind of person who..., the kind of thing which....*

Quis est quī hoc crēdat, *who is there who believes this (of such a sort that he would believe this)*?

Nēmō erat quī hoc crēderet, *there was no one who believed this.*

Sunt quī hoc faciant, *there are some who do this (of such a sort as to do this).*

Id nōn est quī hoc faciat, *he is not a person who does (would do) this.*

Hic est liber quem omnēs legant, *this is the kind of book which all read (a book which all would read).*

Hic est liber quem omnēs legunt, *this is the book which all are reading (= a fact).*

DATIVE OF REFERENCE OR INTEREST

The familiar dative of indirect object is very closely connected with the verb on which it depends. In fact, it is usually so essential to the verb that it might be called the complementary, or completing, dative.

The dative of reference, on the other hand, can be used in almost any circumstance[2] to designate a person[3] who is interested in, or concerned about, the situation. As a rule, the sentence is syntactically complete without the dative of reference, but the dative provides an emotional effect which the sentence would otherwise lack. The study of a few striking examples will give you the sense of this dative.[4]

Sī quis metuēns vīvet, līber **mihi** nōn erit umquam.
If anyone lives in fear, he will not ever be free — as I see it (**mihi**) *or to my way of thinking.*

Caret **tibi** pectus inānī ambitiōne?
Is your breast free from vain ambition — are you sure (**tibi**)?

Nūllīus culpae **mihi** cōnscius sum.
In my own heart (**mihi**), *I am conscious of no fault.*

VOCABULARY

cónsul, -ulis, *m.,* consul (*consular, consulate*)

dólor, -óris, *m.,* pain, grief (*doleful, dolorous, condole, condolences, indolent, indolence*)

ódium, -iī, *n.,* hatred (*odium, odious, annoy, ennui, noisome*)

ópus, óperis, *n.,* a work, task; deed, accomplishment (*opus, opera, operate, operative, inoperative, operand, operose, co-operate, uncooperative, inure*)

quárē, *adv., lit.* because of which thing (**quā rē**), wherefore; why

cōnsúmō, -ere, súmpsī, -súmptum (**sūmō,** take), consume, use up (*consumer, consumption, assume, assumption, presume, presumable, presumption, presumptive, presumptuous, resume, resumption*) dēféndō, -ere, -féndī, -fénsum, ward off; defend, protect (*defense, defensive, fence, fencing, fend, fender, offend*)

dúbitō (1), doubt, hesitate (*dubious, dubitable, dubitative, doubtful, doubtless, indubitable, undoubtedly*)

métuō , -ere, métuī, fear, dread (*cp.* **metus**)

RECOGNITION VOCABULARY

fātum, -ī, *n.*, fate (*fatal, fatalism, fatality, fateful*)

pēs, pédis, *m.*, foot (*pedal, pedate, pedestal, pedestrian, pedicel, pedigree, piedmont, pawn, peon, pioneer, biped, quadruped, impede, impediment, expedite, expedition, expeditious*)

PRACTICE AND REVIEW

1. Rēgī persuāsī ut frātrī tuō grātiōra praemia daret.
2. Deinde, ab eā īnsulā nāve profectus, Athēnās rediit et mortuus est.
3. Eum hortātī sumus ut ad Cacsarem sine timōre accēdere cōnārētur.
4. Solitī sunt eī crēdere quī philosophiae servīret et virtūtem sequerētur.
5. Sapiēns nōs ōrat nē virīs sententiārum adversārum noceāmus.
6. In illīs terrīs nōn licet litterīs bonīs vērīsque studēre, ut sub tyrannō saepe fit.
7. Cūrēmus nē cīvitātem eīs trādāmus quī sē patriae antepōnant.
8. Sunt quī levia opera mīrentur et semper sibi ignōscant.
9. Tam stultīs cōnsiliīs cīvitātī ūtēbātur ut multī cīvēs adversa patī cōgerentur.
10. Haec locūtus, fassus est illōs Rōmae interfectōs esse.
11. Cicero, who was the greatest Roman orator, was a consul who would obey the senate.
12. I shall persuade him to become better and to return to Rome, I assure you.
13. We begged them not to trust a man whom a tyrant pleased.
14. Wherefore, let that man who hesitates to defend our country depart to another land.

SENTENTIAE ANTĪQUAE

1. Sē ad pedēs Caesarī prōiēcērunt. (Caesar. — prō-iaciō.)
2. Hīc in nostrō numerō sunt quī dē exitiō huis urbis cōgitent. (Cicero. — exitium, -iī, *destruction*.)
3. Quis est cui haec rēs pūblica atque possessiō lībertātis nōn sint cārae et dulcēs? (Id. — possessiō, -ōnis.)
4. Quae domus tam stabilis est, quae cīvitās tam fīrma est quae nōn odiīs atque īnsidiīs possit dēlērī? (Id. — stabilis, -e. — fīrmus, -a,

-um. — quae...dēlērī, here the characteristic clause has the force of result.)

5. Quārē, quid est quod tibi iam in hāc urbe placēre possit, in quā nēmō est quī tē nōn metuat? (Id.)

6. Quis enim aut eum dīligere potest quem metuat aut eum ā quō sē metuī putet? (Id.)

7. Tibi sōlī necēs multōrum cīvium impūnītae ac līberae fuērunt. (Id. — nex, necis, f., *murder.* — impūnītus, -a, -um, *unpunished.*)

8. Habētis autem eum cōnsulem quī pārēre vestrīs dēcrētīs nōn dubitet et vōs dēfendere possit. (Id. — dēcrētum, -ī, *decree.*)

9. Ille mihi semper deus erit. (Virgil.)

10. Nūllus dolor est quem nōn longinquitās temporis minuat ac molliat. (*Cicero. — longinquitās, -tātis, *length.* — minuō, -ere, -uī, -ūtum, *diminish.* — molliō (4), *soften*)

11. Parāvisse dīvitiās fuit multīs hominibus nōn fīnis sed mūtātiō malōrum. (Epicurus quoted by Seneca. — mūtātiō, -ōnis, *change.*)

12. Nihil est opere et manū factum quod tempus nōn cōnsūmat. (Cicero.)

13. Vīribus corporis dēficientibus, vigor tamen animī dūrāvit illī ad vītae fīnem. (Pliny. — dēficiō, *fail.* — vigor, -ōris. — dūrō (1), *last.*)

14. Parce metuī, Venus: fāta tuōrum manent immōta tibi. Carthāgō nōn poterit rēgnum gentibus esse; Rōmānīs imperium sine fīne dedī. (Virgil. — Jupiter tells anxious Venus not to worry about her people, for he has decreed that the Romans, not the Carthaginians, shall be the lords of the world. — im-mōtus, -a, -um, *unchanged.* — rēgnum, -ī, *seat of empire.*)

ETYMOLOGY

The use of **opus** in the titles of musical works is well known; e.g., Beethoven's "Symphony No. 5 in C Minor, Opus 67." *Opera,* on the other hand, comes to us through Italian from **opera, -ae,** *effort, pains, work,* which clearly has the same root as **opus.** Finally, we have the term *magnum opus,* which is most commonly used in the literary field.

The *dubitative* (or *deliberative*) subjunctive is another of the independent subjunctives. On the basis of **dubitō** you should have a good sense of the idea conveyed by this subjunctive; e.g., Quid faciat? *What is he to do* (*I wonder*)? See pp. 209 fn. 16*a.* 247 fn. 13.

In the sentences   1. project, projection. 4. stable (adj.) — affirm, reaffirm, confirm, infirm, firmament, farm. 7. internecine — punitive. 10. **minuō,** cp. **minor** (Ch. 27): diminish, diminutive, diminuendo, diminution. 13. deficient, deficiency, defect, defective, defection. 14. reign, regnant, interregnum.

A few Romance derivatives follow:

Latin	Italian	Spanish	French
dolor	dolore	dolor	douleur
odium	odio	odio	odieux (odiōsus)
cōnsūmere	consumare[5]	consumir	consumer
dēfendere	difendere	defender	défendre
dubitāre	dubitare	dudar	douter
pēs, pedis	piede	pie	pied
fātum	fato	hado	(cp. fatal)

Footnotes

[1] Typical examples are: **sunt quī**, *there are people who;* **sunt quae**, *there are things which;* **quis est quī?** *who is there who?* **quid est quod?** *what is there which?* **nēmō est quī**, *there is no one who;* **nihil est quod**, *there is nothing which;* **sōlus est quī**, *he is the only one who.*

[2] That is, it need not be immediately associated with the verb. It may go with an adjective, for example, or it may modify the clause as a whole.

[3] Less frequently a thing.

[4] Not all datives of reference are so striking as these. Sometimes they are rendered by simple *to* or *for;* sometimes they are unimaginatively translated by a simple possessive, as would be possible in the 2nd example (**tibi**), though with considerable loss of force.

[5] In the meaning *to consummate* and in its form, the Italian verb is from Lat. **cōnsummāre**.

39

Gerund and Gerundive

THE GERUNDIVE

*T*he gerundive is already familiar to you as the verbal adjective ending in *-ndus, -nda, -ndum*.[1]

THE GERUND

The gerund is a verbal noun[2] declined in the four oblique cases[3] of the neuter singular. These forms are identical in spelling with the corresponding forms of the gerundive but are *active in meaning*.

DECLENSION OF THE GERUND

Gen. laudándī   dūcéndī   sequéndī   audiéndī
      (*of praising, leading, following, hearing*)
Dat. laudándō   dūcéndō   sequéndō   audiéndō
      (*to/for praising*, etc.)
Acc. laudándum dūcéndum sequéndum audiéndum
      (*praising*, etc.)
Abl. laudándō   dūcéndō   sequéndō   audiéndō
      (*by praising*, etc.)

Since the gerund is a verbal noun, it can be modified as a verb and used as a noun in the various cases.

studium **vīvendī** cum amīcīs, *fondness of (for) living with friends*
Operam dat **vīvendō** bene, *he gives attention to living well.*
Athēnās iit ad **vīvendum** bene, *he went to Athens to live well.*
Fēlīciōrēs fīmus **vivendō** bene, *we become happier by living well.*

GERUND IN PLACE OF THE GERUND WITH AN OBJECT

As a verbal word, the gerund may take the case construction required by its verb.

studium legendī librōs, *fondness of reading books.*
Discimus legendō librōs, *we learn by reading books.*

In practice, however, when the gerund would be followed by a noun in the accusative as a direct object, the Romans preferred to put this noun in the case in which the gerund would appear and to use the gerundive in agreement with the noun. The translation is the same no matter which construction is used.

In the examples which follow those marked A are what we should expect on the basis of the English expression; those marked B are the regular gerundive phrases which the Romans preferred.

A. studium legendī librōs
B. studium librōrum legendōrum
fondness of reading books

A. Operam dat legendō librōs.
B. Operam dat librīs legendīs.
He gives attention to reading books.

A. Vēnit ad legendum librōs.
B. Vēnit ad librōs legendōs.[4]
He came to read books.

A. Otium petit legendī librōs causā.
B. Otium petit librōrum legendōrum causā.[4]
He seeks leisure for the sake of reading books.

A. Discimus legendō librōs.
B. Discimus librīs legendīs.
We learn by reading books.

A. Hoc locūtus est dē legendō librōs.
B. Hoc locūtus est dē librīs legendīs.
He said this about reading books.

VOCABULARY

aedifícium, -iī, *n.,* building, structure (*edifice, edify, edile*)

iniúria, -ae, *f.,* injustice, injury, wrong (*injurious;* cp. **iūs**)

vōx, vócis, *f.,* voice, word (*vocal, vocalic, vocalize, vociferous, vowel; vox pop.;* cp. **vocō**)

cúpidus, -a, -um, desirous, eager, fond; + *gen.,* desirous of, eager for (*cp.* **cupiō, cupiditās**)

necésse, *indecl. adj. used as nom. or acc.,* necessary (*necessitate, necessitous, unnecessary*)

vétus, *gen.* **véteris** (*single-ending adj. of cons. decl., v. Ch. 16 n. 4*), old (*veteran, inveterate*)

étsī, *conj. with ind. or subj. according to rules for* **sī,** even if (**et-sī**), although

quási, *adv. or conj.,* as if, as it were (*quasi*)

expérior, -írī, -pértus sum, try test, experience (*experiment, expert, inexpert, inexperience;* cp. **periculum**)

oppúgnō (1), attack, assault, assail (*oppugn*)

PRACTICE AND REVIEW

1. Caesar eōs ōrābat nē fāta adversa metuerent.
2. Sī hoc fīat, omnēs ad tuum opus mīrandum accēdant.
3. Sī licēbit, paucīs diēbus domum ībimus ad nostrōs amīcōs videndōs.
4. Fassus est sē frātrem propter odium et timōrem interfēcisse.
5. Cōnsul ōtium suum cōnsūmpsit in magnīs operibus scrībendīs.
6. Sunt autem quī dolōrum vītandōrum causā, ut aiunt, semper levia opera faciant.
7. In rē pūblica gerendā multī nōn dubitant praemia grāta sibi quaerere.
8. Illī solent cōgere aliōs patriam trādere.
9. Nēmō est cui iniūria placeat.
10. Nisi sub pedibus tyrannōrum perīre volumus, lībertātī semper studeāmus.
11. They are going to Rome to talk about conquering the Greeks.
12. By remaining at Rome he persuaded them to become braver.
13. Who is there who has hope of doing great works without pain?
14. We urged the consul to serve the interest (**ūtilitās, -tātis**) of the state by attacking these injustices.

SENTENTIAE ANTĪQUAE

1. Coniūrātiōnem nāscentem nōn crēdendō corrōborāvērunt. (*Cicero. — coniūrātiō, -ōnis, conspiracy. — corrōborō* (1), *strengthen.*)
2. Malī dēsinant īnsidiās reī pūblicae cōnsulīque parāre et ignēs ad īnflammandam urbem. (*Cicero. — dēsinō, -ere, dēsiī, dēsitum, cease. — īnflammō* (1), *set on fire.*)

3. Multī autem propter glōriae cupiditātem sunt cupidī bellōrum gerendōrum. (Cicero.)

4. Veterem iniūriam ferendō invītāmus novam. (Publilius Syrus. — invītō (1).)

5. Cūrēmus nē poena maior sit quam culpa; prohibenda autem maximē est īra in pūniendō. (Cicero. — pūniō, -īre, -īvī, -ītum, *punish*.)

6. Syrācūsīs captīs, Mārcellus aedificiīs omnibus sīc pepercit quasi ad ea dēfendenda, nōn oppugnanda vēnisset. (Cicero.)

7. Rēgulus laudandus est in cōnservandō iūre iūrandō. (*Cicero. — Regulus, prisoner of the Carthaginians, swore to them that he would return to Carthage after a mission to Rome. — iūs iūrandum, iūris iūrandī, n., *oath*.)

8. Ego dīcam dē mōribus Sēstiī et dē studiō cōnservandae salūtis commūnis. (Cicero. — Sēstius, -iī.)

9. Senectūs nōs āvocat ā rēbus gerendīs et corpus facit infīrmius. (*Cicero. — infīrmus, -a, -um, *weak*.)

10. Cum recreandae vōcis infīrmae causā necesse esset mihi ambulāre, hās litterās dictāvī ambulāns. (Cicero. — recreō (1), *restore*. — ambulō (1), *walk*. — dictō (1), *dictate*.)

11. Semper metuendō sapiēns vītat malum. (Publilius Syrus.)

12. aec virtūs ex prōvidendō est appellāta prūdentia. (Cicero. — prō-videō. — prūdentia = prō-videntia.)

13. Fāma vīrēs acquīrit eundō. (Virgil. — fāma here = *gossip*. — acquīrō, ad -quaerō, *acquire*.)

14. Hae vicissitūdinēs fortūnae, etsī nōbīs iūcundae in experiendō nōn fuērunt, in legendō tamen erunt iūcundae. Recordātiō enim praeteritī dolōris dēlectātiōnem nōbīs habet. (Cicero. — vicissitūdō, -inis. — recordātiō, -ōnis, *recollection*. — praeteritus, -a, -um, *past*. — dēlectātiō, -ōnis, *delight*.)

ETYMOLOGY

The terms *gerund* and *gerundive* derive ultimately from the stem **gerund-** (= **gerend-**) of **gerō**. The gerund indicates a *doing* (action); the gerundive indicates what is *to be done*.

In late Latin the ablative of the gerund was used with increasing frequency as the equivalent of a present participle. From this usage derive the Italian and the Spanish present participles, which end in *-ndo* and are invariable.

Latin Gerund	It. Participle	Sp. Participle
dandō	dando	dando
faciendō	facendo	haciendo
dīcendō	dicendo	diciendo
pōnendō	ponendo	poniendo
cribendō	scrivendo	escribiendo

In the sentences   2. inflammation, inflammatory. 10. recreation. — amble, ambulatory, ambulance, preamble. — dictator. 14. delectable, delectation, delight; cp. delicious. — In **re-cord-ātiō** you see the stem of **cor, cordis,** *heart.* This shows that formerly the heart was regarded not only as the seat of the emotions but also as the mind and the seat of the memory, a belief reflected in our own phrase "learn by heart." Cp. also record, accord, concord, discord, cordial, cordate, courage. Incidentally, English *heart* is cognate with Latin **cord-.**

Footnotes

[1] Also called the *future passive* participle. See Ch. 24.

[2] Compare the English verbal noun in *-ing:* the art of *living* well; by *living* well. For the derivation of the terms *gerund* and *gerundive* see under Etymology on p. 191.

[3] I.e., all cases except the nominative. The missing nominative is supplied by the infinitive (e.g., **errāre est humānum**).

[4] Note two new ways of expressing purpose: **ad** and **causā** with the gerund or the gerundive.

40

Numerals; Genitive of the Whole

CARDINAL NUMERALS

In Latin most cardinal[1] numerals through 100 are indeclinable adjectives; the one form is used for all cases and genders. The following, however, are declined as indicated.

únus, úna, únum, *one* (See Ch. 9.)

| | duo, *two* | | trēs, *three* | | mille, *thousand* milia, *thousands* | |
	M.	F.	N.	M. & F.	N.	M.F.N.	N.
N.	dúo	dúae	dúo	trēs	tría	mílle	mília
G.	duórum	duárum	duórum	tríum	tríum	mílle	mílium
D.	duóbus	duábus	duóbus	tríbus	tríbus	mílle	mílibus
A.	dúōs	dúās	dúo	trēs	tría	mílle	mília
A.	duóbus	duábus	duóbus	tríbus	tríbus	mílle	mílibus

The cardinals indicating the hundreds from 200 through 900 are declined like adjectives of the first and second declensions; e.g., **ducentī, -ae, -a,** *two hundred.*

Mīlle, 1000, is an indeclinable *adjective* in the singular, but in the plural it becomes a neuter **i**-stem *noun* of the third declension.

The cardinals from **ūnus** through **vīgintī quīnque** should be memorized (see the list in the Appendix) and with them **centum** (100) and **mīlle.**

Trēs puerī rosās dedērunt duābus puellīs, *three boys gave roses to two girls.*
Octō puerī rosās dedērunt decem puellīs, *eight boys gave roses to ten girls.*

Ūnus vir vēnit cum quattuor servīs, *one man came with four slaves.*
Cōnsul vēnit cum centum virīs, *the consul came with 100 men.*
Cōnsul vēnit cum ducentīs virīs, *the consul came with 200 men.*
Cōnsul vēnit cum mille virīs, *the consul came with 1000 men.*
Cōnsul vēnit cum sex mīlibus virōrum, *the consul came with six thousand(s) (of) men.*

ORDINAL NUMERALS

The ordinal numerals, which indicate the order of sequence, are adjectives of the first and the second declensions (**prīmus, -a, -um; secundus, -a, -um;** etc.). The ordinals from **prīmus** through **duodecimus** should be learned.

GENITIVE OF THE WHOLE

The genitive of a word indicating the whole is used after a word designating a part of that whole.

pars urbis, *part of the city* (city = the whole)
fortissimus hōrum virōrum, *the bravest of these men*
nēmō amīcōrum meōrum, *no one of my friends*

This genitive of the whole can also be used after the neuter nominative and accusative of certain pronouns and adjectives such as **aliquid, quid, multum, plūs, minus, satis, nihil, tantum, quantum.**

aliquid salūtis, *some safety (something of safety)*
nihil temporis, *no time (nothing of time)*
quid cōnsiliī, *what plan?*
satis ēloquentiae, *sufficient eloquence*
plūs artis, *more art*

The genitive of the whole may itself be the neuter singular of a *second* declension adjective.

multum bonī, *much good* (lit. *of good*)
minus malī, *less evil (of evil)*
aliquid novī, *something new* (aliquid facile, *something easy*)
nihil certī, *nothing certain*

GENITIVE AND ABLATIVE WITH CARDINAL NUMERALS

With **mīlia** the genitive of the whole is used.

decem mīlia virōrum, *10,000 men* (but mīlle virī, *1000 men*)

With other cardinal numerals and with **quidam** the idea of the whole is regularly expressed by **ex** or **dē** and the ablative. This construction is sometimes found after other words.

trēs ex amīcīs meīs, *three of my friends* (*but* trēs amīcī = *three friends*)
quīnque ex eīs, *five of them*
centum ex virīs, *100 of the men*
quīdam ex eīs, *a certain one of them*

VOCABULARY

cáput, cápitis, *n.,* head (*cape* = *headland, capital, capitol, capitulate, captain, chief, chieftain, chef, chef-d' œuvre, chapter, cattle, chattels, cadet, cad, achieve, decapitate, recapitulate, precipice, occiput, sinciput, kerchief*)

dóminus, -ī, *m.,* master, lord (*dominate, dominant, domineer, dominion, domain, domino, domine, don, dungeon*)

sénsus, -ūs, *m.,* feeling, sense (*sensation, sensual, sensuous, senseless, insensate;* cp. **sentio**)

Cardinal numerals from **únus** to **vigíntī quínque**

Ordinal numerals from **prímus** to **duodécimus**

centum, *indecl. adj.,* a hundred (*cent, centenary, centennial, centi-, centigrade, centimeter, centipede, centurion, century, bicentenary, bicentennial, sesquicentennial, tercentenary*)

mílle, *indecl. adj. in sing.,* thousand; **mília, -ium,** *n. plu.,* thousands (*millennium, millennial, millepede, mile, milli-, milligram, millimeter, million, mill* (= 1/10 *cent*), *bimillennium, millefiori*)

iústus, -a, -um, just, right (*justice, justify, justification, adjust, adjustment, readjust, injustice, unjust;* cp. **iūs**)

tot, *indecl. adj.,* so many

omnínō, *adv.,* wholly, entirely, altogether

mísceō, -ére, míscuī, míxtum, mix (*miscellanea, miscellaneous, miscible, meddle, medley, melee, admixture, intermixture, promiscuous*)

repériō, -íre, répperī, repertum, find, discover, learn, get (*repertoire, repertory*)

PRACTICE AND REVIEW

1. Propter veterēs iniūriās frāter meus odium tuum expertus est.
2. Nōn necesse est ad cōnsulem accēdere quasi ad eum oppugnandum.
3. Magnīs vōcibus cōnsulem hortātī sumus nē eam pācem acciperet.
4. Quārē octāva nox cōnsūmenda erat in aedificiīs urbis nostrae dēfendendīs.
5. Etsī septem fīliī eius sunt cupidī magnōrum operum faciendōrum, eīs nōn licet domō abīre.
6. Multī eōrum solitī sunt fāta metuere.

7. Omnēs dubitāmus levēs timōrēs nostrōs fatērī.
8. Possumusne cōgere nōs dolōribus ferendīs fierī fortēs?
9. Novem ex mīlitibus, pedibus cūrātīs, ōrāvērunt ut domum redīrent.
10. Something good ought to be done by us.
11. By trying we can overcome the larger part of our ills.
12. Two thousand of the enemy and a hundred of your men went to Rome on the fifth day to seek peace. (Do not use *ut* to express purpose here.)
13. Wherefore, as you see, seven of the eleven just men will perish in three days unless you bring help.

SENTENTIAE ANTĪQUAE

1. Quattuor causās reperiō cūr senectūs misera videātur. Videāmus quam iūsta quaeque eārum sit. (Cicero.)
2. Nōn omnis moriar multaque pars meī vītābit sepulchrum. (Horace. — sepulchrum, -ī, *tomb*.)
3. Necesse est enim sit alterum dē duōbus: aut mors sēnsūs omnīnō aufert aut animus in alium locum morte abit. Sī mors somnō similis est sēnsūsque exstinguuntur, dī bonī, quid lucrī est morī! (Cicero. — **necesse est** may be followed by the subjunctive. — aufert = ab-fert. — somnus, -ī, *sleep*. — exstinguō, -ere, -stīnxī, -stinctum. — lucrum, -ī, *gain*.)
4. Aetās semper aliquid novī adfert. (Terence.)
5. Ūnum exemplum luxuriae aut cupiditātis multum malī facit. (Seneca. — luxuria, -ae.)
6. Mīror tot mīlia virōrum tam puerīliter identidem cupere currentēs equōs vidēre. (Pliny. — puerīliter, adv., based on puer, *childishly*. — identidem, adv., *again and again*. — currentēs, in the races.)
7. Nihil vacuī temporis ad litterās scrībendās habeō. (Cicero. — vacuus, -a, -um, *empty, free*.)
8. Quem nostrum[2] nescīre arbitrāris quōs convocāverīs et quid cōnsiliī cēperīs? (Cicero.)
9. Antōnius, ūnus ex inimīcīs, iussit Cicerōnem interficī et caput eius inter duās manūs in rōstrīs pōnī. (Livy. — inimīcus, -ī (in-amīcus), *personal enemy*. — rōstra, -ōrum, *rostra*.)
10. Omnēs quī habent aliquid nōn sōlum sapientiae sed etiam sānitātis volunt hanc rem pūblicam salvam esse. (*Cicero. — sānitās, -tātis. — salvus, -a, -um, *safe*.)
11. Dā mihi bāsia mīlle, deinde centum, deinde multa mīlia bāsiōrum. (Catullus.)
12. Homō sum; nihil hūmānī aliēnum ā mē putō. (Terence. — aliēnus, -a, -um ab = *foreign to*.)
13. Amīcus animum amīcī ita cum suō miscet ut faciat ūnum ex duōbus. (Cicero.)

14. Sex diēbus fēcit Dominus caelum et terram et mare et omnia quae in eīs sunt, et requiēvit diē septimō. (Exodus. — requiēscō, -ere, quiēvī, -quiētum, *rest.*)

ETYMOLOGY

The following are some of the English derivatives from the Latin cardinals and ordinals 2–12: (2) dual, duel, duet, double (cp. doubt, dubious), duplicity; second; (3) trio, triple, trivial; (4) quart, quarter, quartet, quatrain; (5) quinquennium, quintet, quintuplets, quincunx; (6) sextet, sextant; (7) September; (8) October, octave, octavo; (9) November, noon; (10) December, decimal, decimate, dime, dean; (12) duodecimal, dozen.

In the sentences   2. sepuchral. 3. somniferous, somnolent, somnambulate, somnambulism, somniloquist, insomnia. — extinguish, extinct. — lucre, lucrative. 6. puerile, puerility. 7. vacuum, vacuous. 9. inimical, enemy. 12. **Aliēnus** literally means *belonging to another* (**alius**); hence alien, alienate, alienation, inalienable.

The following table lists some Romance cardinal numbers derived from Latin.

Latin	Italian	Spanish	French
ūnus	un(o)	un(o)	un
duo	due	dos	deux
trēs	tre	tres	trois
quattuor	quattro	cuatro	quatre
quīnque	cinque	cinco	cinq
sex	sei	seis	six
septem	sette	siete	sept
octō	otto	ocho	huit
novem	nove	nueve	neuf
decem	dieci	diez	dix
ūndecim	undici	once	onze
duodecim	dodici	doce	douze
centum	cento	ciento	cent
mīlle	mille	mil	mille

Footnotes

[1] **Cardō, cardinis,** m., *hinge* (pivot and socket); hence *cardinal* means the hinge, pivotal, or principal numbers used in counting. They indicate "how many."

[2] **Nostrum** and **vestrum,** gen. plu. of the personal pronouns, are the forms used in the construction of the gen. of the whole. V. Ch. 11, n. 4.

Locī Antīquī

Although these passages chosen from ancient authors have been adapted to meet the linguistic experience of first-year students, they have been edited as little as possible; the language and the thoughts are those of the ancient writers. An asterisk before an author's name still means that the passage is here presented without change. In the case of poetry the lack of an asterisk regularly means that one or more verses have been omitted but that the presented verses have not been altered. In the case of a prose passage the lack of an asterisk indicates that words or sentences may have been omitted or that the wording has been somewhat simplified at one point or another.

Students should find the perusal of these varied passages interesting per se and should also find satisfaction and a sense of accomplishment in being able to translate passages of such maturity at their stage of Latin study.

1. CATULLUS' INFATUATION

Vīvāmus, mea Lesbia, atque amēmus!
Sōlēs occidere[1] et redīre possunt;
nōbīs cum[2] semel[3] occidit brevis lūx
nox est perpetua ūna dormienda.[4]
5 Dā mī[5] bāsia mīlle, deinde centum.
Dein, cum mīlia multa fēcerīmus,[6]
conturbābimus[7] illa, nē sciāmus,
aut nē quis malus invidēre[8] possit,
cum tantum sciat esse bāsiōrum. (**Catullus** 5)

2. DISILLUSIONMENT

Miser Catulle, dēsinās[1] ineptīre,[2]
et quod vidēs perīsse perditum[3] dūcās[4].
Fulsēre[5] quondam candidī[6] tibī sōlēs.
cum ventitābās[7] quō[8] puella dūcēbat,
5 amāta nōbīs quantum amābitur nūlla.
Fulsēre vērē[9] candidī tivī sōlēs.
Nunc iam illa nōn vult; tū quoque, impotēns,[10] nōlī[11];

nec quae fugit sectāre[12] nec miser vīve,
sed obstinātā[13] mente perfer,[14] obdūrā.[15]

10   Valē, puella, iam Catullus obdūrat,
nec tē requīret[16] nec rogābit invītam[17]; at tū dolēbis,[18]
cum rogāberis nūlla.
[19]Scelesta, vae tē! Quae tibī manet vīta!
Quis nunc tē adībit? Cui vidēberis bella?

15   Quem nunc amābis? Cuius esse dīcēris?
At tū, Catulle, dēstinātus obdūrā. (**Catullus** 8)

3. I HATE AND I LOVE

Ōdī[1] et amō! Quārē id faciam fortasse[2] requīris.
    Nescio, sed fierī[3] sentiō et excrucior.[4] (***Catullus** 85)

4. HOW DEMOSTHENES OVERCAME HIS HANDICAPS

Ōrātor imitētur[1] illum cui summa vīs dīcendī concēditur,[2] Dēmos-
thenem, in quō tantum studium fuisse dīcitur ut impedīmenta[3] nātūrae
dīligentiā[4] industriāque[5] superāret. Nam cum ita balbus[6] esset ut illīus ipsīus
artis[7] cui studēret prīmam litteram nōn posset dīcere, perfēcit[8] meditandō[9]
ut nēmō plānius[10] loquerētur. Deinde, cum spīritus[11] eius esset angustior,[12]
spīritū continendō multum perfēcit in dīcendō; et coniectīs[13] in ōs[14] cal-
culīs,[15] summā vōce versūs multōs ūnō spīritū prōnūntiāre[16] cōnsuēscēbat[17];
neque id faciēbat stāns[18] ūnō in locō sed ambulāns.[19] (**Cicero,** *Dē Ōrātōre*
1.61.260-1)

5. THE NERVOUSNESS OF EVEN A GREAT ORATOR

Ego tum ad respondendum surrēxī.[1] Quā sollicitūdine[2] animī surrēxī —
di[3] immortālēs! — et quō timōre! Semper equidem[4] magnō cum metū incipiō
dīcere. Quotiēnscumque[5] dīcō, mihi videor in iūdicium venīre nōn sōlum
ingeniī[6] sed etiam virtūtis atque officiī. Tum vērō[7] ita sum perturbātus[8] ut omnia
timērem. Tandem[9] mē collēgī[10] et sīc pugnāvī,[11] sīc omnī ratiōne contendī[12] ut
nēmō neglēxisse illam causam arbitrārētur. (**Cicero,** *Prō Cluentiō* 51)

6. THE TYRANT CAN TRUST NO ONE

Multōs annōs tyrannus Syrācūsānōrum[1] fuit Dionȳsius. Pulcherrimam
urbem servitūte oppressam tenuit. At ā bonīs auctōribus cognōvimus eum
fuisse hominem summae temperantiae[2] in vīctū[3] et in rēbus gerendīs ācrem
et industrium,[4] eundem tamen malum et iniūstum.[5] Quārē, omnibus virīs
bene vēritātem quaerentibus hunc vidērī miserrimum necesse est, nam
nēminī crēdere audēbat. Itaque propter iniūstam cupiditātem dominātūs[6]
quasi in carcerem[7] ipse sē inclūserat.[8] Quīn etiam,[9] nē tōnsōrī[10] collum[11]
committeret, fīliās suās artem tōnsōriam docuit.[12] Ita hae virginēs
tondēbant[13] barbam[14] et capillum[15] patris. Et tamen ab hīs ipsīs, cum iam

essent adultae,[16] ferrum remōvit, eīsque imperāvit ut carbōnibus[17] barbam et capillum sibi adūrerent.[18] (**Cicero**, *Tusculānae Disputātiōnēs* 5.20.57-58)

7. THE SWORD OF DAMOCLES

Hic quidem tyrannus ipse dēmōnstrāvit[1] quam beātus esset. Nam cum quīdam ex eius assentātōribus,[2] Dāmoclēs,[3] commemorāret[4] cōpiās eius, maiestātem[5] dominātūs, rērum abundantiam,[6] negāretque quemquam[7] umquam beātiōrem fuisse, Dionȳsius "Vīsne igitur," inquit, " Ō Dāmocle, ipse hanc vītam dēgustāre[8] et fortūnam meam experīrī?" Cum ille sē cupere dīxisset, hominem in aureō[9] lectō[10] collocārī[11] iussit mēnsāsque[12] ōrnāvit[13] argentō[14] aurōque.[15] Tum puerōs bellōs iussit cēnam exquīsītissimam[16] īnferre. Fortūnātus[17] sibi Dāmoclēs vidēbātur. Eōdem autem tempore Dionȳsius gladium[18] suprā[19] caput eius saetā equīna[20] dēmittī[21] iussit. Dāmoclēs, cum gladium vīdisset, timēns ōrāvit tyrannum ut abīre licēret, quod iam "beātus" nōllet esse. Satisne Dionȳsius vidētur dēmonstrāvisse nihil esse eī beātum cui semper aliquī[22] metus impendeat?[23] (*Ibid.* 61-62)

8. DERIVATION OF "PHILOSOPHUS" AND SUBJECTS OF PHILOSOPHY

Eī quī studia in contemplātiōne[1] rērum pōnēbant "sapientēs" appellābantur, et id nōmen ūsque[2] ad Pȳthagorae[3] aetātem mānāvit.[4] Hunc aiunt doctē[5] et cōpiōsē[6] quaedam cum Leonte[7] disputāvisse[8]; et Leōn, cum illīus ingenium et ēloquentiam[9] admīrātus esset,[10] quaesīvit ex eō quā arte maximē ūterētur. At ille dīxit sē artem nūllam scīre sed esse philosophum.[11] Tum Leōn, admīrātus novum nōmen, quaesīvit quī essent philosophī. Pȳthagorās respondit multōs hominēs glōriae aut pecūniae servīre sed paucōs quōsdam esse quī cētera prō nihilō[12] habērent sed nātūram rērum cognōscere cuperent; hōs sē appellāre "studiōsōs[13] sapientiae," id est enim "philosophōs."[14] Sīc Pȳthagorās huius nōminis inventor[15] fuit.

Ab antīquā philosophiā ūsque ad Sōcratem[16] philosophī numerōs et sīdera[17] tractābant[18] et unde omnia orīrentur[19] et quō discēderent. Sōcratēs autem prīmus philosophiam dēvocāvit ē caelō et in urbibus hominibusque collocāvit et coēgit eam dē vītā et mōribus rēbusque bonīs et malīs quaerere. (*Ibid.* 5.3.8-9; 5.4.10)

9. CICERO ON THE VALUE AND THE NATURE OF FRIENDSHIP

Ego vōs hortor ut amīcitiam omnibus rēbus hūmānīs antepōnātis. Sentiō equidem,[1] exceptā[2] sapientiā, nihil melius hominī ā deīs immortālibus datum esse. Dīvitiās aliī[3] antepōnunt; aliī, salūtem; aliī, potestātem[4]; aliī, honōrēs; multī, etiam voluptātēs.[5] Illa autem incerta sunt, posita nōn tam[6] in cōnsillīs nostrīs quam[6] in fortūnae vicissitūdinibus.[7] Quī autem in virtūte summum bonum pōnunt, bene illī quidem faciunt; sed ex ipsā virtūte amīcitia nāscitur nec sine virtūte amīcitia esse potest.

Dēnique cēterae rēs, quae petuntur, opportūnae[8] sunt rēbus singulīs[9]: dīvitae, ut eīs ūtaris; honōrēs, ut laudēris; salūs, ut dolōre careās et rēbus corporis ūtāris. Amīcitia rēs plūrimās continet; nūllō locō exclūditur[10]; numquam intempestīva,[11] numquam molesta[12] est. Itaque nōn aquā, nōn igne in locīs plūribus ūtimur quam amīcitiā; nam amīcitia secundās[13] rēs clāriōrēs facit et adversās rēs leviōrēs.

Quis est quī velit in omnium rērum abundantiā ita vīvere ut neque dīligat quemquam[14] neque ipse ab ūllō dīligātur? Haec enim est tyrannōrum vīta, in quā nūlla fidēs, nūlla cāritās,[15] nūlla benevolentia[16] potest esse; omnia semper metuuntur, nūllus locus est amīcitiae. Quis enim aut eum dīligat[16a] quem metuat aut eum ā quō sē metuī putet? Multī autem sī cecidērunt,[17] ut saepe fit, tum intellegunt quam inopēs[18] amīcōrum fuerint. Quid vērō stultius quam cētera parāre quae parantur pecūniā sed amīcōs nōn parāre, optimam et pulcherrimam quasi supellectilem[19] vitae?

Quisque ipse sē dīligit nōn ut aliam mercēdem[20] ā sē ipse petat sed quod per sē quisque sibi cārus est. Nisi idem[21] in amīcitiam trānsferētur,[22] vērus amīcus numquam reperiētur. Amīcus enim est is quī est tamquam[23] alter īdem.[24] Ipse sē dīligit et alterum quaerit cuius animum ita cum suō misceat ut faciat ūnum ex duōbus. Quid enim dulcius quam habēre quīcum[25] audeās sīc loquī ut[26] tēcum? (**Cicero**, *Dē Amīcitiā*, excerpts from Chs. 5, 6, 15, 21)

10. CICERO ON WAR

Quaedam officia sunt servanda etiam adversus[1] eōs ā quibus iniūriam accēpimus. Atque in rē pūblicā maximē cōnservanda sunt iūra bellī. Nam sunt duo genera dēcertandī[2]: ūnum per dispatātiōnem,[3] alterum per vim. Illud est proprium[4] hominis, hoc bēluārum[5]; sed bellum vī gerendum est sī disputātiōne ūtī nōn licet. Quārē suscipienda quidem bella sunt ut sine iniūriā in pāce vīvāmus; post autem victōriam[6] eī cōnservandī sunt quī nōn crūdēlēs,[7] nōn dūrī in bellō fuērunt, ut maiōrēs nostrī Sabīnōs[8] in cīvitātem etiam accēpērunt. At Carthāginem omnīnō sustulērunt; etiam Corinthum sustulērunt—quod nōn approbō[9]; sed crēdō eōs hoc fēcisse nē locus ipse ad bellum faciendum hortārī posset. Meā quidem sententiā,[10] pāx quae nihil īnsidiārum habeat semper quaerenda est. Ac aequitās[11] bellī fētiālī[12] iūre populī Rōmānī perscrīpta est.[13] Quārē potest intellegī nūllum bellum esse iūstum nisi quod aut rēbus repetītīs[14] gerātur aut ante dēnūntiātum sit.[15]

Nūllum bellum dēbet suscipī ā cīvitāte optimā nisi aut prō fidē aut prō salūte. Illa bella sunt iniūsta quae sine causā sunt suscepta. Nam extrā[16] ulcīscendī[17] aut prōpulsandōrum[18] hostium causam nūllum bellum cum aequitāte[19] gerī potest. Noster autem populus sociīs[20] dēfendendīs terrārum[21] omnium potītus est.[22] (**Cicero**, *Dē Officiīs* 1.11.34-36 and *Dē Rē Pūblicā* 3.23.34-35)

11. ROMAN WITTICISMS CITED BY CICERO

Nobody Home[1]

Nāsīca[1] ad poētam Ennium[2] vēnit. Cum ab ōstiō[3] Ennium quaesīvisset et ancilla[4] dīxisset eum domī nōn esse, sēnsit illam dominī iussū[5] id dīxisse et Ennium intus[6] esse. Post paucōs diēs cum Ennius ad Nāsīcam vēnisset et eum ab ōstiō quaereret, Nāsīca ipse exclāmāvit[7] sē domī nōn esse. Tum Ennius "Quid?" inquit, "Ego nōn cognōscō vōcem tuam?" Nāsīca respondit: "Homō es impudēns.[8] Ego cum tē quaererem, ancillae tuae crēdidī tē domī nōn esse; tū mihi ipsi nōn crēdēs?"

Hang Her!

Cum quidam querēns[9] dīxisset uxōrem[10] suam suspendisse[11] sē dē fīcū,[12] amīcus illīus "Amābō tē," inquit, "dā mihi ex istā arbore[13] surculōs[14] quōs[15] seram.[16]"

Certainly He Aroused Pity!

In eōdem genere est quod Catulus[17] dīxit cuidam ōrātōrī malō. Cum hic sē misericordiam[18] ōrātiōne[19] mōvisse putāret, rogāvit Catulum vidērēturne misericordiam mōvisse. "Ac magnam quidem," inquit, "nēminem enim putō esse tam dūrum cui ōrātiō tua nōn vīsa sit digna[20] misericordiā." (**Cicero,** *Dē Ōratōre* 2.276 and 278)

12. POMPEY, CAESAR, AND CICERO

(Pompey and Caesar both bid for Cicero's support in the civil war that followed Caesar's crossing of the Rubicon in 49 B.C.)

Gn. Magnus[1] Prōcōnsul[2] Salūtem Dīcit Cicerōnī Imperātōrī[3]

Sī valēs, bene est. Tuās litterās libenter[4] lēgī; recognōvī[5] enim tuam prīstinam[6] virtūtem etiam in salūte commūnī. Cōnsulēs ad eum exercitum vēnērunt quem in Āpūliā[7] habuī. Magnopere tē hortor ut tē ad nōs cōnferās, ut commūnī cōnsiliō reī pūblicae miserae opem atque auxilium ferāmus. Moneō ut viā[8] Appiā iter[9] faciās et cclcriter Brundisium[10] veniās.

Caesar Imperātor Salūtem Dīcit Cicerōnī Imperātōrī

Cum Brundisium festīnem[11] atque sim in itinere, exercitū iam praemissō,[12] dēbeō tamen ad tē scrībere et grātiās tibi agere, etsī hoc fēcī saepe et saepius factūrus videor; ita dignus[13] es. Imprīmīs,[14] quoniam cōnfīdō[15] mē celeriter ad urbem ventūrum esse, ā tē petō ut tē ibi videam ut tuō cōnsiliō, dignitāte,[16] ope ūtī possim. Festīnātiōnī[17] meae brevitātīque[18] litterārum ignōscēs; cētera ex Furniō[19] cognōscēs. (**Cicero,** *Epistulae ad Atticum* 8.11; 9.6.)

13. HANNIBAL; THE SECOND PUNIC WAR

Hannibal,[1] fīlius Hamilcaris,[2] Carthāgine nātus est. Odium patris ergā[3] Rōmānōs sīc cōnservāvit ut numquam id dēpōneret.[4] Nam post bellum Pūnicum,[5] cum ex patriā in excilium expulsus esset, nōn relīquit studium bellī Rōmānīs īnferendī.[6] Quārē, cum in Syriam[7] vēnisset, Antiochō[8] rēgī haec locūtus est ut hunc quoque[9] ad bellum cum Rōmānīs indūcere[10] posset:

"Mē novem annōs nātō, pater meus Hamilcar, in Hispāniam[11] imperātor proficīscēns Carthāgine, sacrificium[12] dīs fēcit. Eōdem tempore quaesīvit ā mē vellemne sēcum proficīscī. Cum id libenter[13] audīvissem et ab eō petere coepissem nē dubitāret mē dūcere, tum ille 'Faciam,' inquit, 'sī mihi fidem quam quaerō dederis.' Tum mē ad āram[14] dūxit et mē iūrāre[15] iussit mē numquam in amīcitiā cum Rōmānīs futūrum esse. Id iūs iūrandum[16] patrī datum ūsque[17] ad hanc aetātem ita cōnservāvī ut nēmō sit quī plūs odiī ergā Rōmānōs habeat."

Hāc igitur aetāte Hannibal cum patre in Hispāniam profectus est. Post multōs annōs, Hamilcare et Hasdrubale[18] interfectīs, exercitus eī imperium trādidit. Sīc Hannibal, quīnque et vīgintī annōs nātus, imperātor[19] factus est. Tribus annīs omnēs gentēs Hispāniae superāvit et trēs exercitūs maximōs parāvit. Ex hīs ūnum in Āfricam[20] mīsit, alterum cum frātre in Hispāniā relīquit, tertium in Italiam sēcum dūxit.

Ad Alpēs[21] vēnit, quās nēmō umquam ante eum cum exercitū trānsierat.[22] Alpicōs[23] cōnantēs prohibēre eum trānsitū [24] occīdit[25]; loca patefēcit[26]; itinera[27] mūnīvit[28]; effēcit[29] ut[30] elephantus[31] īre posset quā[32] anteā[33] ūnus homō vix[34] poterat rēpere.[35] Sīc in Italiam pervēnit et, Scīpiōne[36] superātō, Etrūriam[37] petīvit. Hōc in itinere tam gravī morbō[38] oculōrum adfectus est[39] ut posteā[40] numquam dextrō[41] oculō bene ūterētur.

Multōs ducēs exercitūsque Rōmānōs superāvit; longum est omnia proelia[42] ēnumerāre.[43] Post Cannēnsem[44] autem pugnam nēmō eī in aciē[45] in Italiā restitit.[46] Cum autem P. Scīpiō tandem[47] in Āfricam invāsisset,[48] Hannibal, ad patriam dēfendendam revocātus, Zamae[49] victus est. Sīc post tot annōs Rōmānī sē perīculō Pūnicō līberāvērunt. (**Nepos**, *Hannibal*, excerpts)

14. AUTOBIOGRAPHICAL NOTES BY HORACE

Nūlla fors[1] mihi tē, Maecēnās,[2] obtulit: optimus Vergilius et post hunc Varius[3] dīxērunt quid essem. Ut ad tē vēnī, singultim[4] pauca locūtus (nam pudor[5] prohibēbat plūra profārī[6]), ego nōn dīxī mē clārō patre nātum esse sed narrāvī quod eram. Respondēs,[7] ut tuus mōs est, pauca. Abeō et post nōnum mēnsem[8] mē revocās iubēsque esse in amīcōrum numerō. Hoc magnum esse dūcō, quod[9] placuī tibi, quī bonōs ā turpibus sēcernis[10] nōn patre clārō sed vītā et pectore[11] pūrō.[12]

Atquī[13] sī mea nātūra est mendōsa[14] vitiīs mediocribus ac paucīs sed aliōquī[15] rēcta,[16] sī neque avāritiam neque sordēs[17] quisquam[18] mihi obiciet,[19] sī pūrus sum et īnsōns[20] (ut mē laudem!) et vīvō cārus amīcīs, causa fuit pater meus. Hic enim, cum pauper in parvō agrō[21] esset, tamen nōluit mē puerum in lūdum Flāviī[22] mittere sed ausus est mē Rōmam ferre ad artēs discendās quās senātōrēs[23] suōs fīliōs docent. Ipse mihi paedagōgus[24] incorruptissimus[25] erat. Mē līberum servāvit nōn sōlum ab omnī factō sed etiam ab turpī opprobriō.[26] Quārē laus illī ā mē dēbētur et grātia[27] magna.

Sic Rōmae nūtrītus sum[28] atque doctus sum quantum[29] īrātus Achillēs Graecīs nocuisset. Deinde bonae Athēnae mihi[29] plūs artis adiēcērunt,[30] scīlicet[31] ut vellem rēctum ā curvō[32] distinguere[33] atque inter silvās Acadēmī[34] quaerere vēritātem. Sed dūra tempora mē illō locō grātō ēmōvērunt et aestus[35] cīvīlis[37] bellī mē tulit in arma Brūtī.[38] Tum post bellum Philippēnse[39] dīmissus sum[40] et audāx[41] paupertās[42] mē humilem[43] et pauperem coēgit versūs facere. (**Horace**, *Saturae* 1.6 and *Epistulae* 2.2, excerpts in prose form)

15. HORACE LONGS FOR THE SIMPLE, PEACEFUL COUNTRY LIFE ON HIS SABINE FARM

Ō Rūs,[1] quandō[2] tē aspiciam?[3] Quandō mihi licēbit nunc librīs veterum auctōrum, nunc somnō[4] et ōtiō ūtī sine cūrīs sollicitae[5] vītae? Ō noctēs cēnaeque deōrum! Sermō[6] oritur[7] nōn dē vīllīs[8] et domibus aliēnīs[9]; sed id quaerimus quod magis ad nōs pertinet[10] et nescīre malum est: utrum[11] dīvitiīs an virtūte hominēs fīant beātī; quid nōs ad amīcitiam trahat, ūsus[12] an rēctum[13]; et quae sit nātūra bonī[14] et quid sit summum bonum.

Inter haec Cervius[15] fābulam[16] narrat. Mūs[17] rūsticus,[18] impulsus[19] ab urbānō[20] mūre, domō rūsticā ad urbem abiit ut, dūrā vītā relictā, in rēbus iūcundīs cum illō vīveret beātus. Mox,[21] autem, multa perīcula urbāna expertus, rūsticus "Haec vīta," inquit, "nōn est mihi necessāria.[22] Valē; mihi silva[23] cavusque[24] tūtus[25] ab īnsidiīs placēbit." (**Horace**, *Saturae* 2.6, excerpts in prose form)

16. WHO IS FREE?

Quis igitur līber est? Sapiēns—quī sibi imperat, quem neque fortūna adversa neque paupertās[1] neque mors neque vincula[2] terrent, quī potest cupīdinibus[3] fortiter respondēre honōrēsque contemnere,[4] quī in sē ipsō tōtus[5] est. (**Horace**. *Saturae* 2.7.83 ff. in prose form)

17. WHY NO LETTERS?
C.[1] Plīnius Fabiō[2] Suō S.[3]

Mihi nūllās epistulās[4] mittis. "Nihil est," inquis, "quod scrībam." At hoc ipsum scrībe; nihil esse quod scrībās; vel[5] illa verba sōla ā quibus maiōrēs nostrī incipere solēbant: "Sī valēs, bene est; ego valeō." Hoc mihi sufficit[6]; est enim maximum. Mē lūdere[7] putās? Sēriō[8] petō. Fac ut sciam quid agās. Valē. (**Pliny** 1.11)

18. WHAT PLINY THINKS OF THE RACES
C. Plīnius Calvisiō[1] Suō S.

Hoc omne tempus inter tabellās[2] ac libellōs iūcundissimā quiēte[3] cōnsūmpsī. "Quemadmodum,[4]" inquis, "in urbe potuisti?" Circēnsēs[5] erant quō genere spectāculī[6] nē levissimē quidem teneor. Nihil novum, nihil varium,[7] nihil quod semel[8] spectāvisse[9] nōn sufficiat.[10] Quārē mīror tot mīlia virōrum tam puerīliter[11] identidem[12] cupere currentēs equōs vidēre. Valē. (**Pliny** 9.6)

19. PLINY ENDOWS A SCHOOL

Nūper[1] cum[2] Cōmī[3] fuī, vēnit ad mē salūtandum[4] fīlius amīcī cuiusdam. Huic ego "Studēs?" inquam. Respondit: "Etiam." "Ubi?" "Mediolānī.[5]" "Cūr nōn hīc[6]?" Et pater eius, quī ipse puerum ad mē addūxerat, respondit: "Quod nūllōs magistrōs hīc habēmus." Huic aliīsque patribus quī audiēbant ego: "Quārē nūllōs?" inquam. "Nam ubi iūcundius līberī[7] vestrī discere possunt quam hīc in urbe vestrā et sub oculīs patrum? Atque ego, quī nōndum[8] līberōs habeō, prō rē pūblicā nostrā quasi prō parente[9] tertiam partem eius pecūniae dabō quam cōnferre vōbīs placēbit. Nihil enim melius praestāre līberīs vestrīs, nihil grātius patriae potestis." (**Pliny** 4.13)

20. PRETTY IS AS PRETTY DOES

Bella es, nōvimus[1]; et puella,[2] vērum est;
et dīves, quis enim potest negāre?
Sed cum[3] tē nimium, Fabulla,[4] laudās,
nec dīves neque bella nec puella es. (***Martial** 1.64)

21. DOCTOR DIAULUS

Nūper[1] erat medicus,[2] nunc est vespillo[3] Diaulus.[4]
Quod vespillō facit, fēcerat et[5] medicus. (******Id.*, 1.47)

22. AUTHORS' READINGS

Ut recitem[1] tibi nostra rogās epigrammata.[2] Nōlō.
Nōn audīre, Celer,[3] sed recitāre cupis. (******Id.*, 1.63)

23. LARGE GIFTS—YES, BUT ONLY BAIT

"Mūnera[1] magna tamen mīsit." Sed mīsit in hāmō[2];
et piscātōrem[3] piscis[4] amāre potest? (*Id.*, 6.63.5-6)

24. SCHOOLMASTER

Lūdī magister, parce simplicī turbae.[2]
Aestāte[3] puerī sī valent, satis discunt. (*Id.*, 10.62.1 & 12)

25. THE LORD'S PRAYER

Et cum ōrātis nōn eritis sīcut[1] hypocritae,[2] quī amant in synagōgīs[3] et in angulīs[4] plateārum[5] stantēs[6] ōrāre ut videantur ab hominibus: āmēn[7] dīcō vōbīs, recēpērunt mercēdem[8] suam. Tū autem cum ōrābis, intrā[9] in cubiculum[10] tuum et, clausō[11] ōstiō[12] tuō, ōrā Patrem tuum in abscondito[13]; et Pater tuus quī videt in abscondito reddet[14] tibi....Sic ergō[15] vōs ōrābitis: Pater noster qui es in caelīs, sānctificētur[16] nōmen tuum; adveniat rēgnum[17] tuum; fīat voluntās[18] tua sīcut in caelō et[19] in terrā. Pānem[20] nostrum supersubstantiālem[21] dā nōbīs hodiē,[22] et dīmitte[23] nōbīs[24] dēbita[25] nostra, sīcut et nōs dīmittimus dēbitōribus[26] nostrīs; et nē[27] indūcās nōs in temptātiōnem[28]: sed līberā nos ā malō. (*Vulgate,* *Matthew 6.5-6, 9-13)

26. THE DAYS OF THE WEEK

Diēs dictī sunt ā deīs quōrum nōmina Rōmānī quibusdam stēllīs[1] dēdicāvērunt.[2] Primum enim diem ā Sōle appellāvērunt, quī prīnceps[3] est omnium stēllārum ut īdem diēs caput est omnium diērum. Secundum diem ā Lūnā[4] appellāvērunt, quae ex Sōle lūcem accēpit. Tertium ab stēllā Mārtis,[5] quae vesper[6] appellātur. Quārtum ab stēllā Mercuriī.[7] Quīntum ab stēllā Iovis.[8] Sextum ā Veneris[9] stēllā, quam Lūciferum[10] appellāvērunt, quae inter omnēs stēllās plūrimum lūcis habet. Septimus ab stēllā Sāturnī,[11] quae dīcitur cursum[12] suum trīgintā[13] annīs explēre.[14] Apud Hebraeōs[15] autem diēs prīmus dīcitur ūnus diēs sabbatī[16], quī apud nōs diēs dominicus[17] est, quem pāgānī[18] Sōlī dēdicāvērunt. Sabbatum autem septimus diēs ā dominicō est, quem pāgānī Sāturnō dēdicāvērunt. (**Isidore Of Seville,** *Orīgine* 5.30; 7th cen.)

27. CAEDMON'S ANGLO-SAXON VERSES AND THE DIFFICULTIES OF TRANSLATION

Cum Caedmon[1] corpus somnō[2] dedisset, angelus[3] Dominī eī dormientī[4] "Caedmon," inquit, "cantā[5] mihi prīncipium[6] creātūrārum.[7]" Et statim[8] coepit cantāre in laudem Deī creātōris[9] versus quōs numquam audīverat, quōrum hic est sēnsus: "Nunc laudāre dēbēmus auctōrem rēgnī[10] caelestis,[11] potestātem[12] creātōris et cōnsilium illīus, facta Patris glōriae, quī, omnipotēns[13] custōs[14] hūmānī generis, filiīs hominum caelum et terram creāvit.[15]" Hic est sēnsus, nōn autem ōrdō[16] ipse verbōrum quae dormiēns ille cantāvit; neque enim possunt carmina,[17] quamvīs[18] optimē composita,[19] ex aliā[20] in aliam linguam[21] ad verbum[22] sine dētrīmentō[23] suī decōris[24] ac dignitātis[25] trānsferrī.[26] (**Bede,** *Historia Ecclēsiastica Gentis Anglōrum* 4.24; 8th cen.)

28. WHO WILL PUT THE BELL ON THE CAT'S NECK?

Mūrēs[1] iniērunt[2] cōnsilium quō modō sē ā cattō[3] dēfendere possent et quaedam sapientior quam cēterae ait: "Ligētur[4] campāna[5] in collō[6] cattī. Sīc poterimus eum eiusque īnsidiās vītāre." Placuit omnibus hoc cōnsilium, sed alia mūs "Quis igitur," inquit, "est inter nōs tam audāx[7] ut campānam in collō cattī ligāre audeat?" Respondit ūna mūs: "Certē nōn ego." Respondit alia: "Certē nōn ego audeō prō tōtō mundō cattō ipsī appropinquāre.[8]" Et idem cēterae dīxērunt.

Sic saepe hominēs, cum quendam āmovendum esse arbitrantur et contrā eum īnsurgere[9] volunt, inter sē dīcunt: "Quis appōnet sē contrā eum? Quis accūsābit[10] eum?" Tum omnēs, sibi timentēs, dīcunt: "Nōn ego certē! Nec ego!" Sīc illum vīvere patiuntur. (**Odo De Cerinton**, *Narrātiōnēs*, 12th cen.)

29. THE DEVIL AND A THIRTEENTH-CENTURY SCHOOLBOY

In illā ecclēsiā[1] erat scholāris[2] parvus. Cum hic diē quādam[3] versūs compōnere ex eā māteriā[4] ā magistrō datā nōn posset et trīstis[5] sedēret,[6] diabolus[7] in fōrmā hominis vēnit. Cum dīxisset: "Quid est, puer? Cūr sīc trīstis sedēs?" respondit puer: "Magistrum meum timeō quod versūs compōnere nōn possum dē themate[8] quod ab eō recēpī." Et ille: "Visne mihi servīre sī ego versūs tibi compōnam?" Puer, nōn intellegēns quod[9] ille esset diabolus, respondit: "Etiam, domine, parātus sum facere quidquid[10] iusseris—dummodo[11] versūs habeam et verbera[12] vītem." Tum, versibus statim[13] dictātīs,[14] diabolus abiit. Cum puer autem hōs versūs magistrō suō dedisset, hic, excellentiam[15] versuum mīrātus, timuit, dūcēns scientiam in illīs dīvīnam,[16] nōn hūmānam. Et ait: "Dīc mihi, quis tibi hōs versūs dictāvit?" Prīmum puer respondit: "Ego, magister!" Magistrō autem nōn crēdente et verbum interrogātiōnis[17] sacpius repetente, puer omnia tandem[18] cōnfessus est.[19] Tum magister "Fīlī," inquit, "ille versificātor[20] fuit diabolus. Cārissime, semper illum sēductōrem[21] et eius opera cavē.[22]" Et puer diabolum eiusque opera relīquit. (**Caesar Of Heisterbach**, *Mīrācula* 2.14; 13th cen.)

Footnotes

1

METER: Phalaecean, or hendecasyllabic.

[1]**occidō (ob-cadō), -ere, occidī, occāsum,** fall down, set

[2]**cum** *with ind.: v. Ch. 31 n.1*

[3]**semel,** *adv.,* once

[4]**dormiō, -īre, -īvī, -ītum,** sleep

[5]**mī = mihi**

[6]Because **conturbābimus** is future, **fecerīmus** is fut. perf. ind., despite the **ī,** which the meter requires to be long.

[7]**con-turbō** (1), throw into confusion

[8]**in-videō,** look upon with the evil eye, be envious

2

METER: choliambic.

[1]**dēsinō, -ere, -siī, -situm,** cease (**dēsinās** = *juss. subj.* for **dēsine**)

[2]**ineptiō** (4), play the fool

[3]**perdō, -ere, perdidī, perditum,** destroy, lose

[4]**dūcō,** consider

[5]**fulgeō, -ēre, fulsī,** shine (**fulsēre = fulsērunt**)

[6]**candidus, -a, -um,** bright

[7]**ventitō** (1), *frequentative form of* **veniō,** come often

[8]**quō,** *adv.,* whither, where

[9]**vērē,** *adv. of* **vērus**

[10]**im-potēns,** weak, hopelessly in love

[11]**nōlī,** *imperative of* **nōlō**

[12]**sectāre,** *impv. of* **sector, -ārī, sectātus sum,** follow eagerly, pursue; *word order:* **sectāre (eam) quae fugit**

[13]**obstinātus, -a, -um,** firm

[14]**per-ferō**

[15]**obdūrō** (1), *vb. of adj.* **dūrus**

[16]**re-quaerō**

[17]**invītus, -a, -um,** unwilling

[18]**doleō, -ēre, -uī, -itūrus,** grieve, suffer

[19]*V. notes on lines 13-15 in Ch. 19*

VOCABULARY: **perdō, quō, vērē, requīrō, invītus, doleō.**

3

METER: elegiac couplet.

[1]**ōdī,** *defective vb.,* I hate

[2]**fortasse,** *adv.,* perhaps

[3]**fierī,** *sc.* **hoc** *as subj.*

[4]**excruciō** (1), torment, *lit.* crucify

4

[1]imitor, -ārī, -ātus sum
[2]con-cēdō
[3]impedīmentum, -ī
[4]dīligentia, -ae
[5]industria, -ae
[6]balbus, -a, -um, stuttering
[7]artis, *sc.* rhētoricae, rhetorical
[8]perficiō, do thoroughly, bring about, accomplish
[9]meditor, -ārī, -ātus sum, practice
[10]plānius, *compar. of adv.* plānē
[11]spīritus, -ūs, breathing, breath
[12]angustus, -a, -um, narrow, short
[13]con-iciō (iaciō)
[14]ōs, ōris, *n.*, mouth
[15]calculus, -ī, pebble
[16]prōnūntiō (1)
[17]cōnsuēscō, -ere, -suēvī, -suētum, become accustomed
[18]stō, stāre, stetī, statum, stand
[19]ambulō (1), walk
VOCABULARY: concēdō, perficiō, angustus, coniciō, ōs, cōnsuēscō, stō.

5

[1]surgō, -ere, surrēxī, surrēctum, get up, arise
[2]sollicitūdō, -inis, f., anxiety
[3]dī = deī
[4]equidem = quidem, *used with the 1st person*
[5]quotiēnscumque, whenever
[6]ingenium, -iī, innate ability, talent
[7]vērō, in truth, indeed
[8]perturbō (1), perturb
[9]tandem, *adv.*, finally, at last
[10]colligō, -ere, -lēgī, -lēctum, gather together
[11]pugnō (1), fight
[12]contendō, -ere, -tendī -tendum, strive
VOCABULARY: equidem, ingenium, vērō, tandem, colligō, pugnō, contendō.

6

[1]Syrācūsānī, -ōrum, Syracusans
[2]temperantia, -ae
[3]vīctus, -ūs, mode of life
[4]industrius, -a, -um
[5]in-iūstus, -a, -um
[6]dominātus, -ūs, absolute rule or power
[7]carcer, -eris, m., prison
[8]inclūdō, -ere, -clūsī, -clūsum, shut in
[9]quīn etiam, moreover
[10]tōnsor, -ōris, barber
[11]collum, -ī, neck
[12]doceō may take two objects.
[13]tondeō, -ēre, totondī, tōnsum, shear, clip
[14]barba, -ae, beard
[15]capillus, -ī, hair
[16]adultus, -a, -um
[17]carbō, -ōnis, m., glowing coal

[18]adūrō, -ere, -ussī, -ustum, singe
VOCABULARY: temperantia, iniūstus, inclūdō, removeō.

7

[1]dēmōnstrō (1), point out, show
[2]assentātor, -ōris, flatterer "yes-man"
[3]Dāmoclēs, -is
[4]commemorō (1), mention, recount
[5]maiestās, -tātis, greatness
[6]abundantia, -ae
[7]quisquam, quidquam, anyone, anything
[8]dēgustō (1), taste, try
[9]aureus, -a, -um, golden
[10]lectus, -ī, couch
[11]col-locō, place
[12]mēnsa, -ae, table
[13]ōrnō (1), adorn
[14]argentum, -ī, silver
[15]aurum, -ī, silver
[16]exquīsītus, -a, -um: ex-quaesītus
[17]fortūnātus, -a, -um
[18]gladius, -iī, sword
[19]suprā, *adv. and prep.* + *acc.*, above
[20]saetā, equīnā, by a horsehair
[21]dēmittō, let down
[22]aliquī, -qua, -quod, *adj. of* aliquis
[23]impendeō, -ēre, hang over, threaten
VOCABULARY: dēmōnstrō, quisquam, collocō, aurum, gladius, suprā.

8

[1]contemplātiō, -ōnīs
[2]ūsque, *adv.*, all the way, even to
[3]Pȳthagorās, -ae, *m.*
[4]mānō (1), flow, extend
[5]doctē, learnedly
[6]copiōsē, fully
[7]Leōn, -ontis, ruler of Phlius
[8]disputō (1), discuss
[9]ēloquentia, -ae
[10]admīror (1), wonder at, admire
[11]philosophus, -ī
[12]nihilum, -ī, = nihil
[13]studiōsus, -a, -um, fond of
[14]philosophus: *Greek philos*, fond of, + *sophia*, wisdom
15inventor, -ōris, *cp.* inveniō
[16]Sōcratēs, -is
[17]sīdus, -eris, *n.*, constellation
[18]tractō (1), handle, investigate, treat
[19]orior, -īrī, ortus sum, arise, proceed, originate
VOCABULARY: ūsque, admīror, orior, quō, collocō.

9

[1]equidem, *v. Loc. Atiq. 5*
[2]excipiō, -ere, -cēpī, -ceptum, except
[3]aliī...aliī some...others

[4]potestās, -tātis, power
[5]voluptās, -tātis, pleasure
[6]tam...quam, so much...as
[7]vicissitūdō, -inis
[8]opportūnus, -a, -um, suitable
[9]singulus, -a, -um, single, separate
[10]exclūdō, -ere, -clūsī, -clūsum
[11]intempestīvus, -a, -um, unseasonable
[12]molestus, -a, -um, troublesome
[13]secundus, -a, -um, favorable
[14]quemquam, v. L.A. 7
[15]cāritās, -tātis, affection
[16]bene-volentia, -ae, goodwill
[16a]deliberative subjunctive; v. pp. 185, 236 fn. 13.
[17]cadō, -ere, cecidī, cāsum, fall
[18]inops, -opis, adj., bereft of
[19]supellex, -lectilis, f., furniture
[20]mercēs, -ēdis, f., pay, reward
[21]idem, neut.
[22]trāns-ferō, transfer, direct
[23]tamquam, as it were, so to speak
[24]idem, masc.
[25]habēre quīcum = habēre eum cum quō
[26]ut, as
VOCABULARY: equidem, potestās, secundus, quisquam, cadō, trānsferō.

10

[1]adversus, prep. + acc., toward
[2]dēcertō (1), fight (to a decision)
[3]disputātiō, -ōnis, discussion
[4]proprius, -a, -um, characteristic of
[5]bēlua, -ae, wild beast
[6]victōria, -ae
[7]crūdēlis, -e, cruel
[8]Sabīnī, -ōrum
[9]approbō (1), approve
[10]sententiā: abl. here expressing accordance
[11]aequitās, -tātis, fairness, justice
[12]fētiālis, -e, fetial, referring to a college of priests who were concerned with treaties and the ritual of declaring war
[13]per-scrībō, write out, place on record
[14]re-petō, seek again
[15]dēnūntiō (1), declare officially
[16]extrā, prep. + acc., beyond
[17]ulcīsor, -ī, ultus sum, avenge, punish
[18]prōpulsō (1), repel
[19]aequitās, -tātis, fairness
[20]socius, -iī, ally
[21]terrārum: depends on potītus est
[22]potior, -irī, potītus sum, + gen. (or abl.), get possession of
VOCABULARY: dēcertō, proprius, crūdēlis, iniūstus, potior.

11

[1]P. Cornēlius Scipiō Nāsīca, celebrated jurist
[2]Ennius, early Roman poet

[3]ōstium, -iī, door
[4]ancilla, -ae, maid
[5]iussū, at the command of
[6]intus, adv., inside
[7]exclāmō (1)
[8]impudēns, -ntis
[9]queror, -ī, questus sum, complain
[10]uxor, -ōris, wife
[11]suspendō, -ere, -pendī, -pēnsum, hang
[12]fīcus, -ūs, f., fig tree
[13]arbor, -oris, f., tree
[14]surculus, -ī, shoot
[15]quōs = ut eōs, rel. clause of purpose
[16]serō, -ere, sēvī, satum, plant
[17]Catulus, -ī, distinguished contemporary of Cicero
[18]misericordia, -ae, pity
[19]ōrātiō, -ōnis
[20]dignus, -a, -um, + abl., worthy of
VOCABULARY: queror, arbor, misericordia, ōrātiō, dignus + abl.

12

[1]Gnaeus Pompeius Magnus
[2]prō-cōnsul
[3]imperātor, -ōris, general
[4]libenter, with pleasure
[5]re-cognōscō, recognize
[6]prīstinus, -a, -um, former
[7]Apūlia, -ae, district in S. Italy
[8]viā, abl. of way by which, means; the Via Appia, first of the great Roman roads, was built in the 4th century B.C. under the supervision of Appius Claudius.
[9]iter, itineris, n., road, journey
[10]Brundisium, -iī, in S. Italy, port of departure for Greece
[11]festīnō (1), hurry
[12]praemittō, send ahead
[13]dignus, -a, -um, worthy
[14]imprīmīs, especially
[15]cōnfīdō, -ere, -fīsus sum, be confident
[16]dignitās, -tātis
[17]festīnātiō, -ōnis, noun of festīnō
[18]brevitās, -tātis
[19]Furnius, -iī, name of a friend
VOCABULARY: imperātor, libenter, iter, dignus, cōnfīdō.

13

[1]Hannibal, -alis, illustrious general who led the Carthaginian forces against the Romans in the Second Punic (= Carthaginian) War, 218-202 B.C.
[2]Hamilcar, -aris
[3]ergā + acc., toward
[4]dē-pōnō
[5]Pūnicus, -a, -um
[6]bellum īn-ferō, make war on
[7]Syria, -ae
[8]Antiochus, -ī

[9] quoque, too, also

[10] in-dūcō

[11] Hispānia, -ae, Spain

[12] sacrificium, -iī

[13] libenter, with pleasure

[14] āra, -ae, altar

[15] iūrō (1), swear

[16] iūs iūrandum, iūris iūrandī, n., oath

[17] ūsque, adv., even (to)

[18] Hasdrubal, -alis, *next in command after Hamilcar*

[19] imperātor, -ōris, commander-in-chief

[20] Āfrica, -ae

[21] Alpēs, -ium, f., the Alps

[22] trāns-eō

[23] Alpicī, -ōrum, men of the Alps

[24] trānsitus, -ūs, crossing; *cp.* trāns-eō

[25] occīdō, -ere, occīdī, occīsum, cut down

[26] pate-faciō, make open, open up

[27] iter, itineris, n., road

[28] mūniō (4), fortify, build

[29] efficiō, bring it about, cause

[30] ut...posset: *noun cl. of result, obj. of* effēcit

[31] elephantus, -ī

[32] quā, adv., where

[33] anteā, adv., before, formerly

[34] vix, adv., scarcely

[35] rēpō, -ere, rēpsī, rēptum, crawl

[36] Scīpiō, -ōnis, *father of the Scipio mentioned below*

[37] Etrūria, -ae, *district N. of Rome, Tuscany*

[38] morbus, -ī, disease

[39] adficiō, afflict

[40] posteā, adv., afterwards

[41] dexter, -tra, -trum, right

[42] proelium, -iī, battle

[43] ēnumerō (1)

[44] Cannēnsis pugna, battle at Cannae, *where in 216 B.C. Hannibal cut the Roman army to shreds*

[45] aciēs, -ēī, f., battle line

[46] resistō, -ere, restitī, + *dat.*, resist

[47] tandem, adv., at last, finally

[48] invādō, -ere, -vāsī, -vāsum, go into, invade

[49] Zama, -ae, *city S. of Carthage in N. Africa*

VOCABULARY: quoque, libenter, ūsque, imperātor, occīdō, iter, efficiō, quā, anteā, vix, posteā, proelium, tandem.

14

[1] fors, fortis, f., chance, accident

[2] Maecēnās, -ātis, *Augustus' unofficial prime minister and Horace's patron*

[3] Varius, -iī, *an epic poet*

[4] singultim, adv., stammeringly

[5] pudor, -ōris, m., bashfulness, modesty

[6] profor, - ārī, -ātus sum, speak out

[7] respondēs, abeō, revocās, iubēs: *in vivid narration the present tense was often used by the Romans with*

the force of the perfect. This is called the historical present.

[8] mēnsis, -is, m., mouth

[9] quod, the fact that

[10] sēcernō, -ere, -crēvī, -crētum, separate

[11] pectus, -oris, n., breast, heart

[12] pūrus, -a, -um

[13] atquī, *conj.*, and yet

[14] mendōsus, -a, -um, faulty

[15] aliōquī, adv., otherwise

[16] rēctus, -a, -um, straight, right

[17] sordē, -ium, f., filth

[18] quisquam, v. L.A. 7

[19] ob-iciō, cast in one's teeth

[20] īnsōns, -ntis, guiltless

[21] ager, agrī, m., field

[22] Flāvius, -iī, *teacher in Horace's small home town of Venusia*

[23] senātor, -ōris

[24] paedagōgus, -ī, slave who attended a boy at school

[25] in-corruptus, -a, -um, uncorrupted

[26] opprobrium, -iī, reproach

[27] grātia, -ae, gratitude

[28] nūtriō (4), nourish, bring up

[29] quantum, *acc. as adv.*

[30] ad-iciō, add

[31] scīlicet (scīre-licet), naturally, of course, clearly, namely

[32] curvus, -a, -um, curved, wrong

[33] distinguō, -ere, -stīnxī, -stīnctum, distinguish

[34] silva, -ae, wood, forest

[35] Acadēmus, -ī; *Plato used to teach in the grove of Academus.*

[36] aestus, -ūs, tide

[37] cīvīlis, -e; *after the assassination of Julius Caesar on the Ides of March, 44 B.C., civil war ensued between the Caesarians, led by Antony and Octavian, and the "Republicans," led by Brutus and Cassius.*

[38] Brūtus, -ī

[39] Philippēnsis, -e, *adj.*, at Philippi, *where in 42 B.C. Brutus was defeated*

[40] dī-mittō, discharge

[41] audāx, -ācis, daring, bold

[42] paupertās, -tātis, poverty

[43] humilis, -e, humble

VOCABULARY: sēcernō, quisquam, ager, grātia, silva, audāx, humilis.

15

[1] rūs, rūris, n., country

[2] quandō, when?

[3] aspiciō, -ere, -spexī, -spectum, look at, see

[4] somnus, -ī, sleep

[5] sollicitus, -a, -um, troubled, anxious

[6] sermō, -ōnis, m., conversation

[7] orior, v. L.A. 8 and p. 167 S.A. 8

[8] vīlla, -ae

⁹**aliēnus, -a, -um**, belonging to another
¹⁰**per-tineō**, pertain
¹¹**utrum...an**, whether...or
¹²**ūsus, -ūs**, advantage
¹³**rēctum, -ī**, the right
¹⁴**bonum, -ī**, the good
¹⁵**Cervius, -iī**, *a rustic friend*
¹⁶**fābula, -ae**, story
¹⁷**mūs, mūris**, *m/f.*, mouse
¹⁸**rūsticus, -a, -um**, rustic, country
¹⁹**im-pellō**, urge, persuade
²⁰**urbānus, -a, -um**, city
²¹**mox**, *adv.*, soon
²²**necessārius, -a, -um**
²³**silva, -ae**, *v. L.A. 14*
²⁴**cavus, -ī**, hole
²⁵**tūtus, -a, -um**, safe
VOCABULARY: **quandō, aspicio, somnus, orior, utrum...an, silva, tūtus.**

16
¹**paupertās, -tātis**, poverty
²**vinculum, -ī**, fetter
³**cupīdō, -inis**, *f.*, desire
⁴**contemnō, -ere, -tempsī, -temptum**, contemn, despise
⁵**tōtus, -a, -um**, whole, entire; *for decl. v. Ch. 9*
VOCABULARY: **tōtus.**

17
¹**C. = Gāius**
²**Fabius, -iī**
³**S. = salūtem (dīcit)**
⁴**epistula, -ae**, letter
⁵**vel**, or, *an optional alternative;* **aut** *means* or *without any option*
⁶**sufficiō**, be sufficient
⁷**lūdō, -ere, lūsī, lūsum**, play, jest
⁸**sēriō**, *adv.*, seriously
VOCABULARY: **vel.**

18
¹**Calvisius, -ī**
²**tabella, -ae**, writing pad
³**quiēs, -ētis**, *f.*, quiet
⁴**quem-ad-modum**, *adv.*, how
⁵**Circēnsēs (lūdī)**, games, *races in the Circus Maximus*
⁶**spectāculum, -ī**
⁷**varius, -a, -um**, different
⁸**semel**, *adv.*, once
⁹**spectō (1)**, look at, see
¹⁰**sufficiō**, *v. L. A. 17*
¹¹**puerīliter**, *adv., based on* **puer**
¹²**identidem**, repeatedly
VOCABULARY: **quiēs, quemadmodum, varius.**

19
¹**nūper**, *adv.*, recently
²**cum + *ind.*, *v. Ch. 31 n. 1***
³**Cōmum, -ī**, Como, *Pliny's birthplace in N. Italy*

⁴**salūtō (1)**, greet
⁵**Mediolānum, -ī**, Milan
⁶**hīc**, *adv.*
⁷**līberī, -ōrum**, children
⁸**nōndum**, *adv.*, not yet
⁹**parēns, -ntis**, parent
VOCABULARY: **cum + ind., nūper, līberī, nōndum, parēns.**

20
METER: Phalaecean.
¹**nōvimus: nōscō = cognōscō**
²**puella (es)**
³**cum + *ind.*, *v. Ch. 31 n. 1***
⁴**Fabulla, -ae**

21
METER: elegiac couplet.
¹**nūper**, *v. L.A. 19*
²**medicus, -ī**, doctor
³**vespillō, -ōnis**, undertaker; *the* **o** *shortened for the meter.*
⁴**Diaulus, -ī**
⁵**et**, also

22
METER: elegiac couplet.
¹**recitō (1)**, read aloud
²**epigramma, -atis**, *n.*
³**Celer, -eris**

23
METER: elegiac couplet.
¹**mūnus, mūneris**, n., gift
²**hāmus, -ī**, hook
³**piscātor, -ris**, fisherman
⁴**piscis, -ōis**, *m.*, fish
VOCABULARY: **mūnus.**

24
METER: choliambic.
¹**simplex, -plicis**, simple, unaffected
²**turba, -ae**, throng
³**aestās, -tātis**, *f.*, summer
VOCABULARY: **aestās.**

25
¹**sīcut**, just as
²**hypocrita, -ae**, *m.*, hypocrite
³**synagōga, -ae**, synagogue
⁴**angulus, -ī**, corner
⁵**platea, -ae**, street
⁶**stō, stāre, stetī, statum**, stand
⁷**āmēn**, *adv.*, truly, verily
⁸**mercēs, -ēdis**, *f.*, wages, reward
⁹**intrō (1)**, enter
¹⁰**cubiculum, -ī**, bedroom, room
¹¹**claudō, -ere, clausī, clausum**, close
¹²**ōstium, -iī**, door
¹³**in abscondītō**, in (a) secret (place)
¹⁴**red-dō, -dere, -didī, -ditum**, give back, answer, requite

[15]ergō, *adv.*, therefore
[16]sānctificiō (1), treat as holy
[17]rēgnum, -ī, kingdom
[18]voluntās, -tātis, will, wish
[19]et, also
[20]pānis, -is, *m.*, bread
[21]supersubstantiālis, -e, necessary to the support of life
[22]hodiē (hōc diē), *adv.*, today
[23]dī-mittō, send away, dismiss
[24]nōbīs, *dat. of ref.*
[25]dēbitum, -ī, n., that which is owing, debt (*figuratively*) = sin
[26]dēbitor, -ōris, one who lit. or fig. owes something, and so one who has not yet fulfilled his duty
[27]nē indūcās, *neg. juss. subj.; the regular class, prose construction is* nōlī indūcere.
[28]temptātiō, -ōnis
VOCABULARY: sīcut, stō, claudō, reddō, ergō, rēgnum, voluntās, hodiē.

26
[1]stella, -ae, star
[2]dēdicō (1)
[3]prīnceps, -cipis, chief
[4]luna, -ae, moon
[5]Mārs, Mārtis
[6]vesper, -eris, *m.*, evening star
[7]Mercurius, -iī
[8]Iuppiter, Iovis, Iovī, Iovem, Iove, Jupiter
[9]Venus, Veneris
[10]Iuppiter, Iovis, Iovī, Iovem, Iove, Jupiter
[11]Venus, Veneris
[12]Lūci-fer, -ferī
[13]Saturnus, -ī
[14]cursus, -ūs, course
[15]trīgintā, thirty
[16]ex-pleō, -ēre, -plēvī, -plētum, fill out
[17]Hebraeī, -ōrum, the Hebrews
[18]sabbatum, -ī, the Sabbath
[19]dominicus, -a, -um, belonging to the Lord, Lord's
[20]pāgānus, -ī, a country man, peasant, pagan
VOCABULARY: stēlla, prīnceps, lūna, vesper, Iuppiter, cursus, expleō.

27
[1]Caedmon, *Anglo-Saxon poet of the 7th cen.*
[2]somnus, -ī, sleep
[3]angelus, -ī, angel
[4]dormiō (4), sleep
[5]cantō (1), sing
[6]prīncipium, -iī, beginning
[7]creātūra, -ae, creature
[8]statim, immediately
[9]creātor, -ōris
[10]rēgnum, -ī, kingdom
[11]caelestis, -e, *adj. of* caelum
[12]potestās, -tātis, power

[13]omni-potēns
[14]custōs, -tōdis, guardian
[15]creō (1), create
[16]ōrdō, -inis, *m.*, order
[17]carmen, -minis, *n.*, song, poem
[18]quamvīs, although
[19]com-pōnō, put together, compose
[20]aliā...aliam, one...another
[21]lingua, -ae, tongue, language
[22]ad verbum, to a word, literally
[23]dētrīmentum, -ī, loss
[24]decor, -ōris, *m.*, beauty
[25]dignitās, -tātis
[26]trāns-ferō
VOCABULARY: somnus, statim, rēgnum, potestās, custōs, creō, ōrdō, compōnō.

28
[1]mūs, mūris, *m./f.*, mouse
[2]in-eō, enter on, form
[3]cattus, -ī (*late Lat. for* fēles, -is), cat
[4]ligō (1), bind
[5]campāna, -ae (*late Lat. for* tintinnābulum), bell
[6]collum, -ī, neck
[7]audāx, -ācis, *adj.* of audeō
[8]appropinquō (1), + *dat.*, approach
[9]īnsurgō, -ere, -surrēxī, -surrēctum, rise up
[10]accūsō (1)
VOCABULARY: audāx, appropinquō.

29
[1]ecclēsia, -ae, church
[2]scholāris, -is, scholar
[3]diē quādam: diēs *is sometimes f.*
[4]māteria, -ae, material
[5]trīstis, -e, sad
[6]sedeō, -ēre, sēdī, sessum, sit
[7]diabolus, -ī, devil
[8]thema, -atis, *n.*, theme, subject
[9]quod, that, *introducing an indirect statement, common in Medieval Lat.*
[10]quidquid, whatever
[11]dummodo + *subj.*, provided
[12]verbera, -um, *n.*, blows, a beating
[13]statim, immediately
[14]dictō (1), dictate
[15]excellentia, -ae
[16]dīvīnus, -a, -um; dīvīnam *is pred. acc.*
[17]interrogātiō, -ōnis, *f.*
[18]tandem, at last
[19]cōnfiteor, -ērī, -fessus sum
[20]versificātor, -ōris, versifier
[21]sēductor, -ōris, seducer
[22]caveō, -ēre, cāvī, cautum, beware, avoid
VOCABULARY: trīstis, sedeō, quisquis, statim, tandem, cōnfiteor, caveō.

Loci Immūtātī

*T*he *Locī Immūtātī* are offered for those who may finish all the *Locī Antīquī* before the end of the first year, and for self-tutoring students who wish to try their wits on some unaltered classical Latin.

These passages are straight Latin, unchanged except for omissions, which have been regularly indicated by three dots. Naturally this genuinely literary material had to be rather heavily annotated, but more in the matter of vocabulary than in other respects. All new words outside the vocabularies of the forty regular chapters have been explained at the bottom of the pages either by vocabulary entries or by cross reference to some prior occurrence of the word. These cross references have been used deliberately to advise the student of the repetition of a word and to encourage him to review for a moment a passage formerly read. New grammatical principles have been treated as they occur, either by a brief statement in the notes or by reference to the Appendix.

Among the most common abbreviations used in the notes are:

App., Appendix
Ch., Chapter
cp., compare
Gk., Greek
id. (*idem*), the same
L.A., *Locī Antīqui*
L.I., *Locī Immūtātī*
lit., literally
sc. (*scīlicet*), namely, supply
s.v. (*sub verbō*), under the word
v. (*vidē*), see

1. A DEDICATION

Cui dōnō[1] lepidum[2] novum libellum[3]
āridō[4] modo[5] pūmice[6] expolītum[7]?
Cornēlī,[8] tibi, namque[9] tū solēbās
meās esse aliquid putāre nūgās,[10]

5   iam tum cum ausus es ūnus Italōrum[11]
omne aevum[12] tribus explicāre[13] chartīs,[14]
doctīs,[15] Iuppiter, et labōriōsīs.[16]
Quārē habē tibi quidquid hoc libellī[17]
quālecumque,[17] quod, O patrōna[18] virgō,

10   plūs[19] ūnō maneat[20] perenne[21] saeclō.[22] (**Catullus** 1)

2. LESBIA[1]

Ille[2] mī[3] pār esse deō[4] vidētur,
ille, sī fās est,[5] superāre dīvōs[6]
quī sedēns[7] adversus[8] identidem[9] tē[10]
spectat[11] et audit

5   dulce[12] rīdentem, miserō quod[13] omnīs[14]
ēripit sēnsūs mihi[15]: nam simul[16] tē
Lesbia, adspexī,[17] nihil est super[18] mī[19]
...(**Catullus** 51. 1-7)

3. HOW MANY KISSES[1]

Quaeris quot[2] mihi bāsiātiōnēs[3]
tuae, Lesbia, sint satis superque.[4]
Quam magnus numerus Libyssae[5] harēnae[6]
laserpīciferīs[7] iacet[8] Cyrēnīs,[9]
...

5   aut quam sīdera[10] multa, cum tacet[11] nox,
fūrtīvōs[12] hominum vident amōrēs,
tam tē[13] bāsia[14] multa bāsiāre[15]
vēsānō[16] satis et super Catullō est. (**Catullus** 7.1-4, 7-10)

4. DEATH OF A PET SPARROW

Lūgēte,[1] Ō Venerēs[2] Cupīdinēsque[3]
et quantum est hominum[4] venustiōrum[5]!
Passer[6] mortuus est meae puellae,
passer, dēliciae[7] meae puellae,

5   quem plūs illa oculīs suīs amābat.
Nam mellītus[8] erat, suamque nōrat[9]
ipsam[10] tam bene quam[11] puella mātrem;
nec sēsē[12] ā gremiō[12] illius movēbat,
sed circumsiliēns[13] modo hūc[14] modo illūc[15]

10   ad sōlam dominam[16] ūsque[17] pīpiābat.[18]
      Quī[19] nunc it per iter[20] tenebricōsum[21]
      illūc unde negant redīre quemquam.[22]
      At vōbīs male sit,[23] malae tenebrae[24]
      Orcī,[25] quae omnia bella dēvorātis[26];
15   tam bellum mihi[27] passerem abstulistis.[28]
      Ō factum male! Iō[29] miselle[30] passer!
      Tuā nunc operā[31] meae puellae
      flendō[32] turgidulī[33] rubent[34] ocellī.[35] (**Catullus** 3)

5. FRĀTER AVĒ, ATQUE VALĒ[1]

      Multās per gentēs et multa per aequora[2] vectus[3]
      adveniō hās miserās, frāter, ad īnferiās,[4]
      ut tē postrēmō[5] dōnārem[6] mūnere[7] mortis
      et mūtam[8] nēquīquam[9] adloquerer[10] cinerem,[11]
5   quandoquidem[12] fortūna mihi[13] tētē[14] abstulit[14] ipsum,
      heu[16] miser indignē[17] frāter adempte[18] mihī.[19]
      Nunc tamen intereā[20] haec,[21] prīscō[22] quae mōre[23] parentum[24]
      trādita sunt trīstī[25] mūnere ad īnferiās,[26]
      accipe frāternō[27] multum[28] mānantia[29] flētū,[30]
10   atque in perpetuum,[31] frāter, avē[32] atque valē. (**Catullus** 101)

6. VITRIOLIC DENUNCIATION[1] OF THE LEADER OF A CONSPIRACY AGAINST THE ROMAN STATE

Quō ūsque[2] tandem[3] abūtēre,[4] Catilīna, patientiā nostrā? Quam diū etiam furor[5] iste tuus nōs ēlūdet[6]? Quem ad fīnem sēsē[7] effrēnāta[8]. iactābit[9] audācia[10]? Nihilne[11] tē nocturnum[12] praesidium[13] Palātī,[14] nihil[11] urbis vigiliae,[15] nihil timor populī, nihil concursus[16] bonōrum omnium, nihil hic mūnītissimus[17] habendī senātūs locus, nihil hōrum ōra[18] vultūsque[19] mōvērunt? Patēre tua cōnsilia nōn sentīs? Cōnstrictam[20] iam omnium hōrum scientiā tenērī coniūrātiōnem[21] tuam nōn vidēs? Quid proxima,[24] quid superiōre[23] nocte ēgerīs, ubi fuerīs, quōs convocāverīs,[24] quid consilī[25] cēperīs, quem nostrum[26] ignōrāre[27] arbitrāris?

Ō tempora[28]! Ō mōrēs! Senātus haec intellegit, cōnsul videt; hic tamen vīvit. Vīvit? Immō[29] vērō[30] etiam in senātum venit, fit pūblicī cōnsilī particeps,[31] notat[32] et dēsignat[33] oculīs ad caedem[34] ūnum quemque nostrum.[26] Nōs autem, fortēs virī, satis facere reī pūblicae vidēmur sī istīus furōrem ac tēla[35] vītāmus. Ad mortem tē, Catilīna, dūcī iussū[36] cōnsulis iam prīdem[37] oportēbat[38]; in tē cōnferrī pestem[39] quam tū in nōs māchināris[40]...

Habēmus senātūs cōnsultum[41] in tē, Catilīna, vehemēns[42] et grave. Nōn deest[43] reī pūblicae cōnsilium, neque auctōritās[44] huius ōrdinis[45]; nōs, nōs, dīcō apertē,[46] cōnsulēs dēsumus... At nōs vīcēsimum[47] iam diem patimur hebēscere[48] aciem[49] hōrum auctōritātis. Habēmus enim eius modī[50] senātūs cōnsultum,... quō ex[51] senātūs cōnsultō cōnfestim[52] tē interfectum esse, Catilīna, convēnit.[53] Vīvis, et vīvis nōn ad dēpōncndam,[54] sed ad cōnfirmandam[55] audāciam. Cupiō, patrēs cōnscrīptī,[56] mē esse clēmentem[57]; cupiō in tantīs reī pūblicae perīculīs mē nōn dissolūtum[58] vidērī, sed iam mē ipse inertiae[59] nēquitiaeque[60] condemnō.[61]

Castra[62] sunt in Italiā contrā populum Rōmānum in Etrūriae[63] faucibus[64] collocāta[65]; crēscit[66] in diēs singulōs[67] hostium numerus; eōrum autem castrōrum imperātōrem[68] ducemque hoistium intrā[69] moenia[70] atque adeō[71] in senātū vidēmus, intestīnam[72] aliquam cotīdiē[73] perniciem[74] reī pūblicae mōlientem[75]...

Quae[76] cum ita sint, Catilīna, perge[77] quō[78] coepistī. Ēgredere[79] aliquandō[80] ex urbe; patent portae[81]; proficīscere. Nimium diū tē imperātōrem tua illa Mānliāna[82] castra dēsīderant.[83] Ēdūc[84] tēcum etiam omnēs tuōs; sī minus,[85] quam plūrimōs; pūrgā[86] urbem. Magnō mē metū līberāveris dum modo[87] inter mē atque tē mūrus[88] intersit.[89] Nōbīscum versārī[90] iam diūtius nōn potes; nōn feram, nōn patiar, nōn sinam[91]...

Quamquam[92] nōn nūllī[93] sunt in hōc ōrdine quī aut ea quae imminent[94] nōn videant, aut ea quae vident dissimulent[95] quī[96] spem Catilīnae mollibus[97] sententiīs aluērunt coniūrātiōnemque nāscentem nōn crēdendō corrōborāvērunt[98]; quōrum[99] auctōritātem secūtī,[100] multī nōn sōlum improbī,[101] vērum[102] etiam imperītī,[103] sī in hunc animadvertissem,[104] crūdēliter[105] et rēgiē[106] factum esse[107] dīcerent. Nunc intellegō, sī iste, quo intendit,[108] in Mānliāna castra pervēnerit,[109] nēminem tam stultum fore[110] quī nōn videat coniūrātiōnem esse factam, nēminem tam improbum[111] quī nōn fateātur.

Hōc autem ūnō interfectō, intellegō hanc reī pūblicae pestem[112] paulisper[113] reprimī,[114] nōn in perpetuum[115] comprimī[116] posse. Quod sī[117] sē ēiēcerit,[118] sēcumque suōs[119] ēdūxerit, et eōdem[120] cēterōs undique[121] collēctōs[122] naufragōs[123] adgregārit,[124] existinguētur[125] atque dēlēbitur nōn modo haec tam adulta[126] reī pūblicae pestis, vērum etiam stirps[127] ac sēmen[128] malōrum omnium... Quod sī[117] ex tantō latrōciniō[129] iste ūnus tollētur, vidēbimur fortasse[130] ad[131] breve quoddam tempus cūrā et metū esse relevāti,[132] autem residēbit[133]...

Quārē sēcēdant[134] improbī[101]; sēcernant[135] sē ā bonīs; ūnum in locum congregentur[136]; mūrō dēnique (id quod saepe iam dīxī) sēcernantur ā nōbīs; dēsinant[137] īnsidiārī[138] domī suae[139] cōnsulī, circumstāre[140] tribūnal[141] praetōris urbānī,[142] obsidēre[143] cum gladiīs cūriam,[144] malleolōs[145] et facēs[146] ad īnflammandam[147] urbem comparāre[148]; sit dēnique īnscrīptum[149] in fronte[150] ūnīus cuiusque quid dē rē pūblicā sentiat. Polliceor[151] hoc vōbīs, patrēs cōnscrīptī,[56] tantam in nōbīs cōnsulibus fore[110] dīligentiam,[152] tantam in- vōbīs auctōritātem,[44] tantam in equitibus[153] Rōmānīs virtūtem, tantam in omnibus

Itaque hesternō[74] diē L. Flaccum et C. Pomptīnum praetōrēs,[75] fortissimōs atque amantissimōs[76] reī pūblicae[77] virōs, ad mē vocāvī, rem exposuī,
quid fierī[78] placēret ostendī. Illī autem, quī omnia dē rē pūblicā praeclāra[79]
atque ēgregia[80] sentīrent,[81] sine recūsātiōne[82] ac sine ūllā morā negōtium[81]
suscēpērunt et, cum advesperāsceret,[84] occultē[85] ad pontem[86] Mulvium
pervēnērunt atque ibi in proximīs vīllīs[87] ita bipertītō[88] fuērunt ut
Tiberis[89] inter eōs et pōns interesset.[90] Eōdem[91] autem et ipsī sine
cuiusquam suspīciōne[92] multōs fortēs virōs ēdūxerant, et ego[90] ex
praefectūrā[93] Reātīnā[94] complūrēs[95] dēlēctōs[96] adulēscentēs, quōrum
operā[97] ūtor assiduē[98] in rē pūblicā , praesidiō[88] cum gladiīs[100] mīseram.
Interim,[101] tertiā ferē [102] vigiliā[102] exāctā,[104] cum iam pontem Mulvium
magnō comitātū[105] lēgātī Allobrogum ingredī[106] inciperent ūnāque[107] Volturcius, fit in eōs impetus[108]; ēdūcuntur[109] et ab illīs gladiī et ā nostrīs.[110]
Rēs praetōribus erat nōta[111] sōlīs, ignōrābātur[24] ā cēterīs. Tum interventū[112]
Pomptīnī atque Flaccī pugna[113] sēdātur.[114] Litterae, quaecumque[115] erant in
eō comitātū, integrīs[116] signīs praetōribus trāduntur; ipsī, comprehēnsī, ad
mē, cum iam dīlūcēsceret,[117] dēdūcuntur. Atque hōrum omnium scelerum
improbissimum[118] māchinātōrem,[119] Cimbrum Gabīnium,[120] statim[121] ad mē
nihildum[122] suspicantem,[123] vocāvī. Deinde item[124] arcessītus est[125] L.
Statilius, et post eum C. Cethēgus. Tardissimē[126] autem Lentulus vēnit...

Senātum frequentem[127] celeriter, ut vīdistis, coēgī. Atque intereā [128]
statim admonitū[129] Allobrogum C. Sulpicium praetōrem, fortem virum,
mīsī quī ex aedibus[130] Cethēgī, sī quid tēlōrum[131] esset, efferret[132]; ex
quibus[133] ille maximum sīcārum[134] numerum et gladiōrum extulit.[135]

Introdūxī[136] Volturcium sine Gallīs; fidem pūblicam[157] iussū[138] senātūs
dedī; hortātus sum ut ea quae scīret sine timōre indicāret.[139] Tum ille dīxit,
cum vix[840] sē ex magnō timōre recreāsset,[141] ā P. Lentulō sē habēre ad
Catilīnam mandāta[65] et litterās ut servōrum praesidiō[142] ūterētur,[143] ut ad
urbem quam prīmum[144] cum exercitū accēderet; id[145] autem eō cōnsiliō ut,[146]
cum urbem ex[147] omnibus partibus, quem ad modum[148] discrīptum dis-
tribūtumque erat,[149] incendissent[150] caedemque[151] īnfīnītam[152] cīvium fēcissent, praestō[153] esset ille[154] quī et fugientēs exciperet[155] et sē cum hīs
urbānīs[158] ducibus coniungeret.[157]

Introductī[136] autem Gallī iūs iūrandum[158] sibi et litterās ab Lentulō,
Cethēgō, Statiliō ad suam gentem datās esse dīxērunt atque ita sibi ab hīs
et a L. Cassiō esse praescrīptum[159] ut equitātum[160] in Italiam quam prīmum
mitterent[161]...

Ac nē longum sit,[162] Quirītēs, tabellās[163] prōferrī[164] iussimus quae ā
quōque[165] dīcēbantur datae.[166] Prīmum[167] ostendimus Cethēgō signum;
cognōvit. Nōs līnum[168] incīdimus[169]; lēgimus. Erat scrīptum ipsīus[170] manū
Allobrogum senātuī et populō sēsē[171] quae eōrum lēgātīs cōnfirmāsset[172]
factūrum esse; ōrāre ut item[124] illī facerent quae sibi eōrum lēgātī recēpis-
sent. Tum Cethēgus (quī paulō[173] ante aliquid tamen dē gladiīs[100] ac sīcīs,[134]

bonīs cōnsēnsiōnem,[154] ut Catilīnae profectiōne[155] omnia patefacta, illūstrāta,[157] oppressa, vindicāta[158] esse videātis.

Hīsce[159] ōminibus,[160] Catilīna, cum summā reī pūblicae salūte,[161] cu tuā peste[39] ac perniciē,[162] cumque eōrum exitiō[163] quī sē tēcum omnī scele parricīdiōque[164] iūnxērunt, proficīscere ad impium[165] bellum ac nefārium.[1 Tū, Iuppiter, quī eīsdem[167] quibus haec urbs auspiciīs ā Rōmulō[168] c cōnstitūtus,[169] quem Statōrem[170] huius urbis atque imperī[171] vērē[1 nōmināmus,[173] hunc et huius sociōs ā tuīs cēterīsque templīs,[174] ā tēctīs[17 urbis ac moenibus,[70] ā vītā fortūnīsque cīvium arcēbis[176]; et hominēs bonōrum inimīcōs,[177] hostēs patriae, latrōnēs[178] Italiae, scelerum foedere[179 inter sē ac nefāriā societāte[180] coniūnctōs,[181] aeternīs[182] suppliciīs[183] vīvōs[184] mortuōsque mactābis.[185] (**Cicero**, *In Catilinam Ōrātiō I*, excerpts)

7. THE ARREST AND TRIAL OF THE CONSPIRATORS[1]

Rem pūblicam, Quirītēs,[2] vitamque[3] omnium vestrum, bona,[4] fortūnās, coniugēs[5] līberōsque[6] vestrōs, atque hoc domicilium[7] clārissimī imperī, fortūnātissimam[8] pulcherrimamque urbem, hodiernō[9] diē deōrum immortālium summō ergā[10] vōs amōre, labōribus, cōnsiliīs, perīculīs meīs, ē flammā[11] atque ferrō ac paene[12] ex faucibus[13] fātī ēreptam et vōbīs cōnservātam ac restitūtam[14] vidētis[15]... Quae[16] quoniam in senātū illūstrāta,[17] patefacta,[18] comperta[19] sunt per mē, vōbīs iam expōnam breviter, Quirītēs, ut[20] et[21] quanta[22] et quā ratiōne investīgāta[23] et comprehēnsa sint, vōs, quī ignōrātis[24] et exspectātis, scīre possītis.

Prīncipiō,[25] ut[26] Catilīna paucīs ante diēbus[27] ērūpit ex urbe, cum sceleris suī sociōs, huiusce[29] nefāriī[30] bellī ācerrimōs ducēs, Rōmae relīquisset, semper vigilāvī[31] et prōvīdī,[32] Quirītēs, quem ad modum[33] in tantīs et tam absconditīs[34] īnsidiīs salvī[35] esse possēmus. Nam tum cum ex urbe Castilīnam ēiciēbam[36] (nōn enim iam vereor[37] huius verbī invidiam,[38] cum illa[39] magis[40] sit timenda, quod[41] vīvus exierit) —sed tum cum[42] illum extermināri[43] volēbam, aut[44] reliquam[45] coniūrātōrum[46] manum simul[47] exitūram[48] aut eōs quī restitissent[49] īnfirmōs[50] sine illō ac dēbilēs[51] fore[52] putābam. Atque ego, ut vīdī, quōs maximō furōre[53] et scelere esse īnflammātōs[54] sciēbam, eōs nōbīscum esse et Rōmae remānsisse, in eō[55] omnēs diēs noctēsque cōnsūmpsī ut quid agerent, quid mōlīrentur, sentīrem ac vidērem...Itaque, ut comperī[19] lēgātōs[56] Allobrogum[57] bellī Trānsalpīnī[58] et tumultūs[58] Gallicī[60] excitandī[61] causā, ā P. Lentulō[62] esse sollicitātōs,[63] eōsque in Galliam[64] ad suōs cīvēs eōdemque itinere cum litterīs mandātīsque[65] ad Catilīnam esse missōs, comitemque[66] eīs adiūnctum esse[67] T. Volturcium,[68] atque huic esse ad Catilīnam datās litterās, facultātem[69] mihi oblātam putāvī ut—quod[70] erat difficillimum quodque ego semper optābam[71] ab dīs immortālibus—tōta rēs nōn sōlum ā mē sed etiam ā senātū et ā vōbis manifestō[72] dēprehenderētur.[73]

quae apud ipsum erant dēprehēnsa,174 respondisset dīxissetque[175] sē
semper bonōrum ferrāmentōrum[176] studiōsum[177] fuisse) recitātīs[178] litterīs
dēbilitātus[179] atque abiectus[180] cōnscientiā,[181] repente[182] conticuit.[183]

Intrōductus est Statilius; cognōvit et signum et manum suam. Recitātae
sunt tabellae in[184] eandem ferē sententiam; cōnfessus est.[185]

Tum ostendī tabellās Lentulō, et quaesīvī cognōsceretne[186] signum.
Adnuit[187]... Leguntur eādem ratiōne ad senātum Allobrogum populumque
litterae.[188] Sī quid[189] dē hīs rēbus dīcere vellet,[190] fēcī potestātem.[191] Atque
ille prīmō quidem negāvit. Post[192] autem aliquantō,[193] tōtō iam indiciō[194]
expositō atque ēditō,[195] surrēxit[196]; quaesīvit ā Gallīs quid sibi esset cum eīs,
quam ob rem[197] domum[198] suam vēnissent, itemque[124] ā Volturciō. Quī cum
illī[199] breviter cōnstanterque[20] respondissent per quem ad eum quotiēnsque[201]
vēnissent, quaesīssentque[202] ab eō nihilne[186] sēcum[203] esset dē fātīs
Sibyllīnīs[204] locūtus, tum ille subitō,[205] scelere dēmēns,[206] quanta cōnscientiae vīs esset ostendit. Nam cum id posset īnfitiārī,[207] repente[205] praeter[208]
opīniōnem[209] omnium cōnfessus est[185]...

Gabīnius deinde intrōductus, cum prīmō impudenter[210] respondēre
coepisset, ad extrēmum[211] nihil ex eīs[212] quae Gallī īnsimulābant[213] negāvit.

Ac mihi[214] quidem, Quirītēs, cum[215] illa[216] certissima vīsa sunt
argūmenta[217] atque indicia[194] sceleris, tabellae, signa, manūs, dēnique ūnīus
cuiusque cōnfessiō,[218] tum[215] multō[219] certiōra illa, color,[220] oculī, vultūs,[221]
taciturnitās.[222] Sīc enim obstupuerant,[223] sīc terram intuēbantur,[224] sīc
fūrtim[225] nōn numquam inter sēsē aspiciēbant[226] ut nōn iam ab aliīs indicārī[227]
sed indicāre sē ipsī vidērentur.

Indiciīs expositīs atque ēditīs,[195] Quirītēs, senātum cōnsuluī[228] dē
summā rē pūblicā[229] quid fierī placēret. Dictae sunt ā prīncipibus ācerrimae
ac fortissimae sententiae, quās senātus sine ūllā varietāte[230] est secūtus...

Quibus prō tantīs rēbus, Quirītēs, nūllum ego ā vōbīs praemium virtūtis,
nūllum īnsigne[231] honōris, nūllum monumentum[232] laudis postulō[233] praeter-
quam[234] huius diēī memoriam sempiternam[235]...

Vōs, Quirītēs, quoniam iam est nox, venerātī[236] Iovem illum
custōdem[237] huius urbis ac vestrum, in vestra tēcta[238] discēdite; et ea,
quamquam[239] iam est perīculum dēpulsum,[240] tamen aequē ac[241] priōre
nocte[242] custōdiīs vigiliīsque dēfendite. Id nē vōbīs diūtius faciendum sit
atque ut in perpetuā pāce esse possītis prōvidēbō. (**Cicero**, *In Catilīnam
Ōrātiō III*, excerpts)

DE VĪTĀ ET MORTE 8-10

8. A. SOCRATES' "EITHER-OR" BELIEF[1]

Quae est igitur eius ōrātiō[2] quā[3] facit eum Platō ūsum apud iūdicēs[4] iam
morte multātum[5]?

"Magna mē," inquit "spēs tenet iūdicēs, bene mihi ēvenīre[6] quod mittar[7] ad mortem. Necesse[8] est enim sit[9] alterum dē duōbus, ut aut[10] sēnsūs omnīnō omnēs mors auferat[11] aut in alium quendam locum ex hīs locīs morte migrētur.[12] Quam ob rem,[13] sīve[14] sensus exstinguitur[15] morsque eī somnō[16] similis est quī nōn numquam etiam sine vīsīs[17] somniōrum[18] plācātissimam[19] quiētem[20] adfert,[21] dī[22] bonī, quid lucrī[23] est ēmorī[24]! aut quam multī diēs reperīrī possunt quī tālī noctī antepōnantur? Cui sī similis futūra est[25] perpetuitās[26] omnis cōnsequentis[27] temporis, quis[28] mē[29] beātior?

"Sin[30] vēra[31] sunt quae dīcuntur, migrātiōnem[32] esse mortem in eās ōrās[33] quās quī[34] ē vītā excessērunt[35] incolunt,[36] id multō[37] iam beātius est... Haec peregrīnātiō[38] mediocris vōbīs vidērī potest? Ut vērō[39] colloquī[40] cum Orpheō, Mūsaeō,[41] Homērō, Hēsiodō[42] liceat, quantī[43] tandem aestimātis[44]?... Nec enim cuiquam[45] bonō malī[46] quicquam ēvenīre potest nec vīvō nec mortuō[47]...

"Sed tempus est iam hinc[48] abīre mē, ut moriar, vōs, ut vītam agātis. Utrum[49] autem sit melius, dī immortālēs sciunt; hominem quidem scīre arbitror nēminem,"[50] (**Cicero**, *Tusculānae Disputātiōnēs*, 1.40.97-1-41-99, excerpts)

9. B. A MORE POSITIVE VIEW ABOUT IMMORTALITY[1]

Artior[2] quam solēbāt[3] somnus[4] (mē) complexus est[5]... (et) Āfricānus sē ostendit eā fōrmā[6] quae mihi ex imāgine[7] eius quam ex ipsō erat nōtior.[8] Quem ubi agnōvī,[9] equidem[10] cohorruī[11];... quaesīvī tamen vīveretne[12] ipse et Paulus[13] pater et aliī quōs nōs exstīnctōs[14] arbitrārēmur.

"Immō[15] vērō," inquit, "hī vīvunt quī ē corporum vinclīs[16] tamquam ē carcere[17] ēvolāvērunt[18]; vestra vērō quae dīcitur vīta mors est. Quīn[19] tū aspicis ad tē venientem Paulum patrem?"

Quem ut vīdī, equidem vim[20] lacrimārum[21] prōfūdī. Ille autem mē complexus[5] atque ōsculāns[22] flēre[23] prohibēbat.[24] Atque ego ut prīmum[25] flētū[26] repressō[27] loquī posse coepī, "Quaesō,[28]" inquam, "pater sānctissime[29] atque optime, quoniam haec est vīta, ut Africānum audiō dīcere, quid moror[30] in terrīs? Quīn[31] hūc[32] ad vōs venīre properō[33]?"

"Nōn est ita,[34]" inquit ille. "Nisi enim deus is,[35] cuius hoc templum[36] est omne quod cōnspicis,[37] istīs tē corporis custōdiīs līberāverit, hūc[32] tibi aditus[38] patēre non potest. Hominēs enim sunt hāc lēge[39] generātī,[40] quī tuērentur[41] illum globum[42] quem in hōc templō medium vidēs, quae terra dīcitur, iīsque[43] animus datus est ex illīs sempiternīs[44] ignibus quae sīdera[45] et stēllās vocātis... Quārē et tibi, Pūblī,[46] et piīs[47] omnibus retinendus[48] est animus in custōdiā corporis, nec iniussū[49] eius ā quō ille[50] est vōbīs datus ex hominum vītā migrandum est,[51] nē mūnus[52] hūmānum adsignātum[53] ā deō dēfūgisse[54] videāminī... Iūstitiam[55] cole[56] et pietātem,[57] quae cum sit magna[58] in[59] parentibus[60] et propinquīs,[61] tum[62] in[59] patriā maxima est. Ea vīta via est in caelum et in hunc coetum[63] eōrum quī iam vīxērunt et corpore laxātī[64] illum incolunt[65] locum... quem vōs, ut ā Graīs accēpistis, orbem lacteum,[66] nuncupātis[67]" ...

Et ille, "Tū vērō... sīc habētō[68] nōn esse tē mortālem, sed corpus hoc[69]; nec enim tuīs[70] es quem fōrma ista dēclārat,[71] sed mēns cuiusque is est quisque, nōn ea figūra [= fōrma] quae digitō[72] dēmōnstrārī[73] potest. Deum tē igitur scītō[74] esse, sīquidem[75] deus est quī viget,[76] quī sentit, quī meminit,[77] quī prōvidet,[78] quī tam regit[79] et moderātur[80] et movet id corpus cui[81] praepositus est[82] quam[83] hunc mundum ille prīnceps[84] deus.[85] (**Cicero**, excerpts from *Somninum Scīpiōnis*, 2ff. = *Dē Rē Pūblicā*, 6.10 ff.)

10. C. ON CONTEMPT OF DEATH[1]

Sed quid[2] ducēs et prīncipēs[3] nōminem[4] cum legiōnēs[5] scrībat Catō[6] saepe alacrēs[7] in eum locum profectās[8] unde reditūrās[8] sē nōn arbitrārentur? Parī animō Lacedaemoniī[9] in Thermopylīs[10] occidērunt,[11] in quōs[12] Simōnidēs:

Dīc, hospes,[13] Spartae[14] nōs tē[15] hīc[16] vīdisse iacentīs,[17]
Dum sānctīs[18] patriae lēgibus obsequimur.[19]

Virōs commemorō.[20] Quālis[21] tandem Lacaena? Quae, cum fīlium in proelium[22] mīsisset et interfectum[23] audīsset, "Idcircō,[24]" inquit, "genueram[25] ut esset quī[26] prō patriā mortem nōn dubitāret occumbere.[27]"

...Admoneor[28] ut aliquid etiam dē humātiōne[29] et sepultūrā[30] dīcendum[31] exīstimem[32]... Sōcratēs, rogātus ā Critōne[33] quem ad modum[34] sepelīrī[35] vellet, "Multam vērō," inquit, "operam,[36] amīcī, frūstrā[37] cōnsūmpsī. Critōnī enim nostrō nōn persuāsī mē hinc[38] āvolātūrum,[39] neque meī[40] quicquam relictūrum[41] ... Sed, mihi crēde, (Critō), nēmō mē vestrum,[42] cum hinc excesserō,[43] cōnsequētur.[43a]" ...

Dūrior Diogenēs[44] Cynicus prōicī[45] sē iussit inhumātum.[46] Tum amīcī, "Volucribusne[47] et ferīs[48]?" "Minimē[49] vērō," inquit; "sed bacillum[50] propter[51] mē, quō abigam,[52] pōnitōte.[53]" "Quī[54] poteris?" illī; "nōn enim sentiēs." "Quid igitur mihi ferārum laniātus[55] oberit[56] nihil sentientī[57]?" (**Cicero**, *Tusculānae Disputātiōnēs*, 1.42.101-43.104, excerpts)

11. LITERATURE: ITS VALUE AND DELIGHT[1]

Quaerēs ā nōbīs, Grattī, cūr tantō opere[2] hōc homine dēlectēmur.[3] Quia[3a] suppeditat[4] nōbīs ubi[5] et animus ex hōc forēnsī[6] strepitū[7] reficiātur[8] et aurēs[9] convīciō[10] dēfessae[11] conquiēscant[12]... Quārē quis tandem mē reprehendat,[13] aut quis mihi iūre[14] suscēnseat,[15] sī[16] quantum[17] cēterīs ad suās rēs obeundās[18] quantum ad fēstōs[19] diēs lūdōrum celebrandōs,[20] quantum ad aliās voluptātēs[21] et ad ipsam requiem[22] animī et corporis concēditur[23] temporum, quantum aliī tribuunt[24] tempestīvīs[25] convīviīs,[26] quantum dēnique alveolō,[27] quantum pilae,[28] tantum[29] mihi egomet[30] ad haec studia recolenda[31] sūmpserō[32]? Atque hoc ideō[33] mihi concēdendum est magis quod ex hīs studiīs haec quoque[34] crēscit[35] ōrātiō[36] et facultās,[37] quae, quantacumque[38] est in mē, numquam amīcōrum perīculīs dēfuit[39]...

Plēnī omnēs sunt librī, plēnae sapientium vōcēs, plēna exemplōrum[40] vetustās[41]; quae iacērent[42] in tenebrīs[43] omnia, nisi litterārum lūmen[44] accēderet. Quam multās nōbīs imāginēs[45] — nōn sōlum ad intuendum,[46] vērum[47] etiam ad imitandum[48] — fortissimōrum virōrum expressās[49] scrīptōrēs[50] et Graecī et Latīnī reliquērunt! Quās ego mihi semper in administrandā[51] rē pūblicā prōpōnēns[52] animum et mentem meam ipsā cōgitātiōne[53] hominum excellentium[54] cōnfōrmābam.[55]

Quaeret quispiam,[56] "Quid? illī ipsī summī virī quōrum virtūtēs litterīs prōditae sunt,[57] istāne doctrīnā[58] quam tū effers[59] laudibus ērudītī fuērunt[60]?" Difficile est hoc dē omnibus cōnfīrmāre,[61] sed tamen est certum quid respondeam...: saepius ad laudem atque virtūtem nātūram sine doctrīnā quam sine nātūrā valuisse[62] doctrīnam. Atque īdem[63] ego contendō,[64] cum ad nātūram eximiam[65] et illūstrem[66] accesserit[67] ratiō quaedam cōnfōrmātiōque[68] doctrīnae, tum illud nesciō quid[69] praeclārum[70] ac singulāre[71] solēre exsistere[72]...

Quod sī[73] nōn hic tantus frūctus ostenderētur, et sī ex hīs studiīs dēlectātiō[74] sōla peterētur, tamen, ut opīnor,[75] hanc animī remissiōnem[76] hūmānissimam ac līberālissimam[77] iūdicārētis. Nam cēterae[78] neque temporum[79] sunt neque aetātum[79] omnium neque locōrum[79]; at haec studia adulēscentiam[80] alunt, senectūtem oblectant,[81] rēs secundās[82] ōrnant,[83] adversīs[84] perfugium[85] ac sōlācium[86] praebent,[87] dēlectant domī, nōn impediunt[88] forīs,[89] pernoctant[90] nōbīscum, peregrīnantur,[91] rūsticantur.[92] (**Cicero,** *Prō Archiā,* 6.12-7.16, excerpts).

ANECDOTES FROM CICERO 12-16

12. A DEATH OF A PUPPY (EXAMPLE OF AN OMEN)

L. Paulus[1] cōnsul iterum,[2] cum eī[3] bellum[4] ut cum rēge Perse[5] gereret[6] obtigisset,[7] ut[8] eā ipsā diē domum ad vesperum[9] rediit, filiolam[10] suam Tertiam,[11] quae tum erat admodum[12] parva, ōsculāns[13] animadvertit[14] trīsticulam.[15] "Quid est,[16]" inquit, "mea Tertia? Quid[17] trīstis[18] es?" "Mī[19] pater," inquit, "Persa[20] periit." Tum ille artius[21] puellam complexus,[22] "Accipiō," inquit, "mea filia, ōmen.[23]" Erat autem mortuus catellus[24] eō nōmine. (**Cicero,** *Dē Dīvīnātiōne,* 1.46.103)

13. B. TOO CONSCIENTIOUS (AN EXAMPLE OF IRONY)

Est huic fīnitimum[1] dissimulātiōnī[2] cum honestō[3] verbō vītiōsa[4] rēs appellātur: ut cum Āfricānus cēnsor[5] tribū[6] movēbat eum centuriōnem[7] quī in Paulī pugnā[8] nōn adfuerat,[9] cum ille sē custōdiae causā dīceret in castrīs[10] remānsisse quaereretque cūr ab eō notārētur[11]: "Nōn amō," inquit, "nimium dīligentēs.[12]" (**Cicero,** *Dē Ōrātōre,* 2.67.272)

14. C. QUAM MULTA NŌN DĒSĪDERŌ!

Sōcratēs, in pompā[1] cum magna vīs[2] aurī[3] argentīque[4] ferrētur, "Quam multa nōn dēsīderō[5]!" inquit.

Xenocratēs,[6] cum lēgātī[7] ab Alexandrō[8] quīnquāgintā[9] eī talenta[10] attulissent[11] (quae erat pecūnia temporibus illīs, Athēnīs praesertim,[12] maxima), abdūxit[13] lēgātōs ad cēnam in Acadēmīam[14]; iīs apposuit[15] tantum quod satis esset, nūllō apparātū.[16] Cum postrīdiē[17] rogārent eum cui numerārī[18] iubēret, "Quid? Vōs hesternā,[19]" inquit, "cēnulā[20] nōn intellēxistis mē pecūniā nōn egēre[21]?" Quōs cum trīstiōrēs[22] vīdisset, trīgintā[23] minās[24] accēpit nē aspernārī[25] rēgis līberālitātem[26] vidērētur.

At vērō[27] Diogenēs[28] līberius,[29] ut[30] Cynicus, Alexandrō rogantī ut dīceret sī quid opus[31] esset: "Nunc quidem paululum,[32]" inquit, "ā sōle.[33]" Offēcerat[34] vidēlicet[35] aprīcantī.[36] (**Cicero**, *Tusculānae Disputātiōnēs*, 5.32.91-92)

15. D. WHAT MAKES A GOOD APPETITE

Dārēus[1] in fugā[2] cum aquam turbidam[3] et cadāveribus[4] inquinatam[5] bibisset,[6] negāvit umquam sē bibisse iūcundius.[7] Numquam vidēlicet[8] sitiēns[9] biberat. Nec ēsuriēns[10] Ptolemaeus[11] ēderat,[12] cui cum peragrantī[13] Aegyptum,[14] comitibus[15] nōn cōnsecūtīs[16] cibārius[17] in casā[18] pānis datus esset, nihil vīsum est illō pāne[19] iūcundius. Sōcratem ferunt,[20] cum ūsque[21] ad vesperum[22] contentius[23] ambulāret[24] quaesītumque esset[25] ex eō quārē id faceret, respondisse sē, quō[26] melius cēnāret,[27] obsōnāre[28] ambulandō famem.[29]

Quid? Vīctum[30] Lacedaemoniōrum[31] in philitiīs[32] nōnne[33] vidēmus? Ubi[34] cum tyrannus cēnāvisset Dionȳsius, negāvit sē iūre[35] illō nigrō quod cēnae[36] caput erat dēlectātum.[37] Tum is quī illa coxerat,[38] "Minimē mirum[39]; condīmenta[40] enim dēfuērunt.[41] "Quae tandem?" inquit ille. "Labor in vēnātū,[42] sūdor,[43] cursus[44] ad Eurōtam,[45] famēs[29] sitis.[46] Hīs enim rēbus Lacedaemoniōrum epulae[47] condiuntur.[48]

Cōnfer sūdantēs,[49] ructantēs[50] refertōs[51] epulīs[47] tamquam[52] opīmōs bovēs.[53] Tum intellegēs quī voluptātem[54] maximē sequantur, eōs minimē cōnsequī[55]; iūcunditātemque[56] vīctūs[57] esse in dēsideriō,[58] nōn in satietāte.[59] (*Ibid.*, 5.34.97-98 and 100, excerpts)

16. E. THEMISTOCLES; FAME AND EXPEDIENCY

Themistoclēs fertur[1] Serīphiō cuidam in iūrgiō[3] respondisse, cum ille dīxisset nōn eum suā sed patriae glōriā splendōrem[4] assecūtum[5]: "Nec hercule,[6] inquit, "sī ego Serīphius essem, nec tū, sī Athēniēnsis[7] essēs, clārus umquam fuissēs." (**Cicero**, *Dē Senectūte*, 3.8)

Themistoclēs, post victōriam[8] eius bellī quod cum Persīs[9] fuit, dīxit in cōntiōne[10] sē habēre cōnsilium reī pūblicae salūtāre,[11] sed id scīrī nōn opus esse.[12] Postulāvit[13] ut aliquem populus daret quīcum[14] commūnicāret.[15] Datus est Aristīdēs. Huic[16] ille (dixit) classem[17] Lacedaemoniōrum, quae subducta esset[18] ad Gythēum,[19] clam[20] incendī[21] posse, quō factō frangī[22] Lacedaemoniōrum opēs necesse esset.[23] Quod Aristīdēs cum audīsset, in cōntiōnem[10] magnā exspectātiōne[24] vēnit dīxitque perūtile[25] esse cōnsilium quod Themistoclēs adferret, sed minimē honestum.[26] Itaque Athēniēnsēs, quod honestum nōn esset, id nē ūtile quidem putāvērunt, tōtamque eam rem, quam nē audierant quidem, auctōre Aristīde[27] repudiāvērunt.[28] (**Cicero**, *De Officiīs* 3.11.48-49)

17. GET THE TUSCULAN COUNTRY HOUSE READY[1]

Tullius[2] S.D.[3] Terentiae[4] Suae

In Tusculānum[5] nōs ventūrōs[6] putāmus aut Nōnīs[7] aut postrīdiē.[8] Ibi ut[9] sint omnia parāta. Plūrēs[10] enim fortasse[11] nōbīscum erunt et, ut arbitror, diūtius ibi commorābimur.[12] Lābrum[13] sī in balneō[14] nōn est, ut[15] sit; item[16] cētera quae sunt ad vīctum[17] et ad valētūdinem[18] necessāria.[19] Valē. Kal. Oct.[20] dē Venusīnō.[21] (**Cicero**, *Epistulae ad Familiārēs*,14.20)

18. LIVY ON THE DEATH OF CICERO[1]

M. Cicerō sub adventum[2] triumvirōrum[3] cesserat urbe... Prīmō in Tusculānum[4] fūgit; inde trānsversīs[5] itineribus[6] in Formiānum,[7] ut ab Caiētā[8] nāvem cōnscēnsūrus,[9] proficīscitur. Unde aliquotiēns[10] in altum[11] provectum,[12] cum modo ventī[13] adversī[14] rettulissent,[15] modo ipse iactātiōnem[16] nāvis... patī nōn posset, taedium[17] tandem eum et fugae[18] et vītae cēpit, regressusque[19] ad superiōrem vīllam[20]... "Moriar," inquit, "in patriā saepe servātā." Satis cōnstat[21] servōs fortiter fidēliterque parātōs fuisse ad dīmicandum,[22] ipsum dēpōnī[23] lectīcam[24] et quiētōs[25] patī quod sors[26] inīqua[27] cōgeret iussisse. Prōminentī[28] ex lectīcā praebentīque[29] immōtam[30] cervīcem[31] caput praecīsum est.[32]

Manūs quoque[33] scrīpsisse in[34] Antōnium aliquid exprobrantēs[35] praecīdērunt. Ita relātum[36] caput ad Antōnium, iussūque[37] eius inter duās manūs in Rōstrīs[38] positum,[39] ubi ille cōnsul, ubi saepe cōnsulāris,[40] ubi eō ipsō annō adversus[41] Antōnium...(quanta nūlla umquam hūmāna vōx[42]!) cum admīrātiōne[43] ēloquentiae[44] audītus fuerat. Vix[45] attollentēs[46] prae[47] lacrimīs[48] oculōs, hominēs intuērī[49] trucīdāta[50] membra[51] eius poterant. Vīxit trēs et sexāgintā[52] annōs... Vir magnus, ācer, memorābilis[53] fuit, et in cuius laudēs persequendās[54] Cicerōne laudātōre opus[55] fuerit.[56] (**Livy**, 120.50)

19. MILTIADES AND THE BATTLE OF MARATHON[1]

Eīsdem temporibus Persārum[2] rēx Dārēus,[3] ex Asiā in Eurōpam[4] exercitū trāiectō,[5] Scythīs[6] bellum īnferre[7] dēcrēvit.[8] Pontem[9] fēcit in Histrō[10] flūmine,[11] quā[12] cōpiās trādūceret.[13] Eius pontis, dum ipse abesset,[14] custōdēs[15] relīquit prīncipēs[16] quōs sēcum ex Iōniā et Aeolide[17] dūxerat; quibus singulārum[18] urbium perpetua dederat imperia. Sīc enim facillimē putāvit sē[19] Graecā linguā[20] loquentēs[21] qui Asiam incolerent[22] sub suā retentūrum[23] potestāte, sī amīcīs suīs oppida[24] tuenda[25] trādidisset.[26] In hōc[27] fuit tum numcrō Miltiadēs.[28] Hic, cum crēbrī[29] adferrent[30] nūntiī[29] male rem gerere Dārēum premīque ā Scythīs, hortātus est pontis custōdēs nē ā Fortūnā[31] datam occāsiōnem[32] līberandae Graeciae dīmitterent.[33]

Nam sī cum eīs cōpiīs, quās sēcum trānsportārat,[34] interīsset[35] Dārēus, nōn sōlum Eurōpam fore[35] tūtam,[36] sed etiam eōs quī Asiam incolerent[22] Graecī genere[37] līberōs ā Persārum futūrōs dominātiōne[38] et perīculō. Id facile efficī[39] posse[40]; ponte enim rescissō[41] rēgem vel[42] hostium ferrō vel inopiā[43] paucīs diēbus interitūrum.[35] Ad hoc cōnsilium cum plērīque[44] accēderent,[45] Histiaeus[46] Mīlēsius...[dīxit] adeō[47] sē abhorrēre[48] ā cēterōrum cōnsiliō ut nihil putet ipsīs ūtilius quam cōnfirmārī[49] rēgnum[50] Persārum. Huius cum sententiam plūrimī essent secūtī, Miltiadēs... Chersonēsum[28] relīquit ac rūrsus[51] Athēnās dēmigrāvit.[52] Cuius[53] ratiō etsī nōn valuit, tamen magnopere est laudanda cum amīcior[54] omnium libertātī quam suae fuerit dominātiōnī.[38]

Dārēus autem, cum ex Eurōpā in Asiam redīsset, hortantibus amicīs ut Graeciam redigeret[53] in suam potestātem,[56] classem[57] quīngentārum[58] nāvium comparāvit[59] eīque[60] Dātim praefēcit[61] et Artaphernem,[62] eīsque ducenta[63] (mīlia) peditum,[64] decem equitum[65] milia dedit—causam interserēns[66] sē hostem esse Athēniēnsibus[67] quod eōrum auxiliō Iōnes[68] Sardīs[69] expugnāssent[70] suaque[71] praesidia[72] interfēcissent. Illī praefectī[74] rēgiī,[74] classe ad Eubocam[75] appulsā[76] celeriter Eretriam[77] cēpērunt, omnēsque eius gentis cīvēs abreptōs[78] in Asiam ad rēgem mīsērunt. Inde[79] ad Atticam[80] accessērunt ac suās cōpiās in campum[81] Marathōna[82] dēdūxērunt. Is abest ab oppidō circiter[83] mīlia passuum[84] decem.

Hōc tumultū[85] Athēniēnsēs tam propinquō[86] tamque magnō permōtī[87] auxilium nūsquam[88] nisi ā Lacedaemoniīs petīvērunt Phīdippumque,[89] cursōrem eius generis quī hēmerodromoe[90] vocantur, Lacedaemonem[91] mīsērunt ut nūntiāret quam celerrimō opus esse[92] auxiliō. Domī autem creant[93] decem praetōrēs,[94] quī exercituī praeessent,[95] in eīs Miltiadem; inter quōs magna fuit contentiō[96] utrum[97] moenibus[98] sē dēfenderent an obviam[99] īrent hostibus aciēque[100] dēcernerent.[101] Ūnus[102] Miltiadēs maximē nītēbātur[103] ut prīmō tempore castra fieren[t104]...

Hōc tempore nūlla cīvitās Athēniēnsibus auxiliō[105] fuit praeter[106] Plataeēnsēs[107]; ea mīlle mīsit mīlitum.[108] Itaque hōrum adventū[109] decem mīlia armātōrum[110] complēta sunt,[111] quae manus mīrābilī[112] flagrābat[113] pugnandī[114] cupiditāte; quō[115] factum est[116] ut plūs quam collēgae[117] Miltiadēs valēret.[118]

Eius ergō[119] auctōritāte[120] impulsī[121] Athēniēnsēs cōpiās ex urbe ēdūxērunt locōque[122] idōneō[123] castra fēcērunt. Dein[124] posterō[125] diē sub montis rādīcibus[126] aciē[100] regiōne[127] īnstrūctā[128] nōn apertissimā[129] —namque[130] arborēs[131] multīs locīs erant rārae[132]—proelium commīsērunt[133] hōc cōnsiliō ut et montium altitūdine[134] tegerentur[135] et arborum tractū[136] equitaātus[137] hostium impedīrētur,[138] nē multitūdine[139] clauderentur.[140] Dātis,[62] etsī nōn aequum locum[141] vidēbat suīs, tamen frētus[142] numerō cōpiārum suārum cōnflīgere[143] cupiēbat, eōque[144] magis quod, priusquam[145] Lacedaemoniī subsidiō[146] venīrent, dīmicāre[147] ūtile[148] arbitrābātur.

Itaque in aciem peditum[64] centum (mīlia), equitum[65] decem mīlia prōdūxit[149] proeliumque commīsit. In quō[150] tantō[151] plūs[152] virtūte valuērunt Athēniēnsēs ut decemplicem[153] numerum hostium prōflīgārint,[154] adeōque[47] eōs perterruērunt ut Persae nōn castra sed nāvēs petierint. Quā pugnā[155] nihil adhūc[156] existit[157] nōbilius[158]; nūlla enim umquam tam exigua[159] manus tantās opēs prōstrāvit. (**Nepos**, *Miltiadēs*, 3-5, excerpts)

20. THEMISTOCLES AND THE BATTLE OF SALAMIS[1]

Themistoclēs[2] ad (bellum Corcȳraeum[3]) gerendum praetor[4] ā populō factus, nōn sōlum praesentī[5] bellō sed etiam reliquō6 tempore ferōciōrem[7] reddidit[8] cīvitātem. Nam cum pecūnia pūblica, quae ex metallīs[9] redībat, largītiōne[10] magistrātuum[11] quotannīs[12] interīret,[13] ille persuāsit populō ut eā pecūniā classis[14] centum nāvium aedificārētur.[15] Quā[16] celeriter effectā,[17] prīmum Corcȳraeōs frēgit,[18] deinde maritimōs praedōnēs[19] cōnsectandō[20] mare tūtum[21] reddidit.[8] In quō[22] ...perītissimōs[23] bellī nāvālis[24] fēcit Athēniēsēs. Id quantae salūtī[25] fuerit[26] ūniversae[27] Graeciae, bellō cognitum est Persicō.[28] Nam cum Xerxēs[29] et marī et terrā[30] bellum ūniversae īnferret Eurōpae, cum tantīs cōpiīs eam invāsit[31] quantās neque ante nec posteā habuit quisquam.[32] Huius enim classis mīlle et ducentārum nāvium longārum[33] fuit, quam duo mīlia onerāriārum[34] sequēbantur. Terrestris[35] autem exercitus septingenta (mīlia) peditum,[37] equitum[38] quadringenta[39] mīlia fuērunt.[40]

Cuius dē adventū[41] cum fāma in Graeciam esset perlāta[42] et maximē Athēniēnsēs petī dīcerentur propter pugnam[43] Marathōniam, misērunt Delphōs[44] cōnsultum[45] quidnam[46] facerent[47] dē rēbus suīs. Dēliberantibus[48] Pȳthia[49] respondit ut[50] moenibus[51] līgneīs[52] sē mūnīrent.[53] Id respōnsum[54] quō[55] valēret cum intellegeret nēmō. Themistoclēs persuāsit cōnsilium esse[56] Apollinis ut in nāvēs sē suaque[57] cō ferrent: eum[58] enim ā deō significārī[59] mūrum ligneum. Tālī[60] cōnsiliō probātō,[61] addunt[62] ad superiōrēs (nāvēs) totidem[63] nāvēs trirēmēs,[64] suaque omnia quae movērī poterant partim[65] Salamina,[66] partim Troezēna[67] dēportant.[68] Arcem[69] sacerdōtibus[70] paucīsque maiōribus nātū[71] ad sacra[72] prōcūranda[73] trādunt; reliquum[6] oppidum relinquunt.

Huius[74] cōnsīlium plērīsque cīvitātibus[75] displicēbat[76] et in terrā dīmicārī[77] magis placēbat. Itaque missī sunt dēlēctī[78] cum Leōnidā,[79] Lacedaemoniōrum rēge, quī Thermopylās[80] occupārent[81] longiusque barbarōs[82] prōgredī nōn paterentur. Iī vim hostium nōn sustinuērunt,[83] eōque locō omnēs interiērunt.[13]

At classis commūnis Graeciae trecentārum[84] nāvium, in quā ducentae[84] erant Athēniēnsium,[85] prīmum apud Artemīsium[86] inter Euboeam continentemque[87] terram cum classiāriīs[88] rēgiīs[89] cōnflīxit.[90] Angustiās[91] enim Themistoclēs quaerēbat, nē multitūdine[92] circumīrētur.[93] Hinc[94] etsī parī proeliō[95] discesserant, tamen eōdem locō nōn sunt ausī manēre, quod erat perīculum nē,[96] sī pars nāvium adversāriōrum[97] Euboeam superāsset,[98] ancipitī[99] premerentur perīculō. Quō[100] factum est ut[101] ab Artemīsiō discēderent et exadversum[102] Athēnās apud Salamīna classem suam cōnstituerent.[103]

At Xerxēs, Thermopylīs expugnātīs,[104] prōtinus[105] accessit astū,[106] idque, nūllīs dēfendentibus, interfectīs sacerdōtibus[70] quōs in arce[69] invēnerat, incendiō[107] dēlēvit. Cuius flammā perterritī[108] classiāriī cum manēre nōn audērent et plūrimī hortārentur ut domōs[109] suās discēderent moenibusque sē dēfenderent, Themistoclēs ūnus restitit[110] et ūniversōs[111] parēs esse posse aiēbat,[112] dispersōs[113] testābātur[114] peritūrōs; idque Eurybiadī,[115] rēgī Lacedaemoniōrum, quī tum summae[116] imperiī praeerat,[117] fore[118] adfīrmābat.[119]

Quem cum minus quam vellet movēret, noctū[120] dē servīs suīs[121] quem habuit[122] fidēlissimum ad rēgem mīsit ut eī nūntiāret suīs verbīs[123] adversāriōs eius[124] in fugā[125] esse; quī[126] sī discessissent,[127] maiōre cum labōre... (eum) bellum cōnfectūrum,[127] cum singulōs[128] cōsectāri[20] cōgerētur; quōs sī statim aggrederētur,[129] brevī (tempore) ūniversōs oppressūrum... Hāc rē audītā barbarus, nihil dolī[130] subesse[131] crēdēns, postrīdiē[132] aliēnissimō[133] sibi locō, contrā[134] opportūnissimō[135] hostibus, adeō[136] angustō[137] marī[138] cōnflīxit[139] ut eius multitūdō[92] nāvium explicārī[140] nōn potuerit[141]... Victus ergō est magis etiam cōnsiliō Themistoclī quam armīs Graeciae... Sīc ūnīus virī prūdentiā[142] Graecia līberāta est Eurōpaeque succubuit[143] Asia.

Haec (est) altera victōria quae cum Marathōniō possit comparārī[144] tropaeō.[145] Nam parī modō apud Salamīna parvō numerō nāvium maxima post hominum memoriam classis est dēvicta. (**Nepos**, *Themistoclēs*, 2-4, excerpts)

21. ARISTIDES THE JUST

Aristīdēs,[1] Lȳsimachī[2] fīlius, Athēniēnsis, aequālis[3] ferē[4] fuit Themistoclī[5] atque cum eō dē prīncipātū[6] contendit[7]... In hīs autem cognitum est quantō[8] antistāret[9] ēloquentia[10] innocentiae.[11] Quamquam enim adeō[12] excellēbat13 Aristīdēs abstinentiā[14] ut ūnus[15] post hominum memoriam... cognōmine[16] "Iūstus" sit appellātus, tamen ā Themistocle collabefactus[17] testulā[18] illā[19] exsiliō[20] decem annōrum[21] multātus est.[22]

Quī quidem cum intellegeret reprimī[23] concitātam[24] multitūdinem[25] nōn posse, cēdēnsque animadvertisset[26] quendam scrībentem ut patriā pellerētur,[27] quaesīsse ab eō[28] dīcitur quārē id faceret aut quid Aristīdēs commīsisset cūr[29] tantā poenā dignus[30] dūcerētur. Cui ille respondit sē ignōrāre[31] Aristīdēn, sed sibi nōn placēre[32] quod tam cupidē labōrāsset[33] ut praeter[34] cēterōs "Iūstus" appellārētur. Hic decem annōrum lēgitimam[35] poenam nōn pertulit. Nam postquam[36] Xerxēs in Graeciam dēscendit,[37] sextō ferē annō quam[38] erat expulsus, populī scītō[39] in patriam restitūtus est.[40]

Interfuit[41] autem pugnae[42] nāvālī[43] apud Salamīna quae facta est priusquam[44] poenā līberārētur. Īdem[45] praetor[46] fuit Athēniēnsium apud Plataeās[47] in proeliō[48] quō fūsus[49] (est) barbarōrum exercitus Mardoniusque[50] interfectus est... Huius aequitāte[51] factum est,[52] cum in commūnī classe[53] esset Graeciae simul[54] cum Pausaniā[55] (quō duce[56] Mardonius erat fugātus[57]), ut summa imperiī[58] maritimī[59] ab Lacedaemoniīs trānsferrētur[60] ad Athēniēnsēs; namque[61] ante id tempus et marī et terrā ducēs erant Lacedaemoniī. Tum autem et[62] intemperantiā[63] Pausaniae et iūstitiā[64] factum est[51] Aristīdis ut omnēs ferē[4] cīvitātēs Graeciae ad Athēniēnsium societātem[65] sē applicārent[66] et adversus barbarōs hōs ducēs[67] dēligerent[68] sibi.

Quōs[69] quō[70] facilius repellerent,[71] sī forte[72] bellum renovāre[73] cōnārentur, ad classēs aedificandās[74] exercitūsque comparandōs[75] quantum pecūniae[76] quaeque[77] cīvitās daret, Aristīdēs dēlēctus est[68] quī cōnstitueret,[78] eiusque arbitriō[79] quadringēna[80] et sexāgēna talenta quotannīs Dēlum[81] sunt conlāta; id enim commūne aerārium[82] esse voluērunt. Quae omnis pecūnia posterō[83] tempore Athēnās trānslāta est.[84] Hic quā[85] fuerit[86] abstinentiā, nūllum est certius indicium[87] quam quod,[88] cum tantīs rēbus praefuisset,[89] in tantā paupertāte[90] dēcessit,[91] ut quī[92] efferrētur vix[93] relīquerit. Quō[94] factum est ut[51] fīliae eius pūblicē[95] alerentur et dē commūnī aerāriō[82] dōtibus[96] datīs collocārentur.[97] (**Nepos**, *Aristīdēs*, excerpts)

22. TIMOLEON[1]

Diōne[2] Syrācūsīs interfectō, Dionȳsius[3] rūrsus[4] Syrācūsārum potītus est.[5] Cuius adversāriī[6] opem ā Corinthiīs[7] petiērunt ducemque, quō[8] in bellō ūterentur, postulārunt.[9] Hūc[10] Tīmoleōn[11] missus incrēdibilī[12] fēlīcitāte[13] Dionȳsium tōtā Siciliā[14] dēpulit.[15] Cum (eum) interficere posset, nōluit, tūtōque[16] ut Corinthum[17] pervenīret[18] effēcit,[19] quod utrōrumque[20] Dionȳsiōrum opibus Corinthiī saepe adiūtī fuerant...eamque praeclārum[21] victōriam dūcēbat[22] in quā plūs esset clēmentiae[23] quam crūdēlitātis[24]...

Quibus rēbus cōnfectīs,[25] cum propter diūturnitātem[26] bellī nōn sōlum regiōnēs[27] sed etiam urbēs dēsertās[28] vidēret, conquīsīvit[29]... colōnōs.[30] Cīvibus veteribus sua[31] restituit,[32] novīs[33] bellō vacuēfactās[34] possessiōnēs[35] dīvīsit[36]; urbium moenia[37] disiecta[38] fānaque[39] dētēcta[40] refēcit[41]; cīvitātibus lēgēs lībertātemque reddidit[42] ... Cum tantīs esset opibus[43] ut etiam invītīs[44] imperāre posset, tantum[45] autem amōem haberoman e back 50 up 45 size 8 -ret omnium Siculōrum[46] ut nūllō recūsante[47] rēgnum[48] obtinēre[49] licēret, māluit[50] sē dīligī quam metuī. Itaque, cum prīmum[51] potuit, imperium dēposuit[52] ac prīvātus[53] Syrācūsīs...vīxit. Neque vērō[56] id imperītē[55] fēcit, nam quod cēterī rēgēs imperiō potuērunt, hic benevolentiā[56] tenuit...

Hic cum aetāte iam prōvectus esset,[57] sine ūllō morbō[58] lūmina[59] oculōrum āmīsit. Quam calamitātem[60] ita moderātē[61] tulit ut... (nēmō) eum querentem[62] audierit[63]... Nihil umquam neque însolēns[64] neque glōriōsum[65] ex ōre[66] eius exiit.[67] Quī quidem, cum suās laudēs audīret praedicārī,[68] numquam aliud dīxit quam[69] sē in eā rē maximē dīs[70] agerc grātiās... quod, cum Siciliam recreāre[71] cōnstituissent,[72] tum sē potissimum[73] ducem esse voluissent. Nihil enim rērum hūmānārum sine deōrum nūmine[74] gerī putābat...

Proelia[75] maxima nātālī[76] suō diē fēcit omnia; quō factum est ut[77] eius diem nātālem fēstum[78] habēret ūniversa Sicilia...

Cum quīdam Dēmaenetus[79] in cōntiōne[80] populī dē rēbus gestīs[81] eius dētrahere[82] coepisset ac nōnnūlla inveherētur[83] in Tīmoleonta, dīxit nunc dēmum[84] sē vōtī esse damnātum[85]; namque hoc ā dīs immortālibus semper precātum[86] ut tālem lībertātem restitueret[87] Syrācūsānīs in quā cuivīs[88] licēret dē quō vellet impūne[89] dīcere.[90]

Hic cum diem suprēmum obīsset,[91] pūblicē[92] ā Syrācūsānīs in gymnasiō,[93] quod Tīmoleontēum[94] appellātur, tōtā celebrante[95] Siciliā, sepultus est.[96] (**Nepos**, *Tīmoleōn*, 2-5, excerpts)

23. HORACE'S "CARPE DIEM"

Tū nē quaesierīs[1] — scīre nefās[2] — quem[3] mihi, quem[3] tibi
fīnem dī[4] dederint,[5] Leuconoē,[6] nec Babylōniōs
temptārīs[7] numerōs.[8] Ut melius,[9] quidquid erit, patī.
...

Spem longam[10] resecēs[·11] Dum loquimur fūgerit[12] invida[13]
5   aetās. Carpe diem,[14] quam minimum[15] crēdula[16] posterō.[17]
                    (**Horace**, *Odes*, 1.11, excerpts)

24. INTEGER VITAE

Integer[1] vītae scelerisque pūrus[2]
nōn eget[3] Maurīs[4] iaculīs[5] neque arcū[6]
nec venēnātīs[7] gravidā[8] sagittīs[9]
      Fusce,[10] pharetrā.[11]
...

5   Namque[12] mē silvā[13] lupus[14] in Sabīnā[15]
dum meam cantō[16] Lalagēn[17] et ultrā[18]
terminum[19] cūrīs vagor[20] expedītīs[21]
      fūgit[22] inermem.[23]
...

Pōne mē pigrīs[24] ubi nūlla campīs[24]
10   arbor[25] aestīvā[26] recreātur[27] aurā,[28]
quod[29] latus mundī nebulae[30] malusque[31]
      Iuppiter urget[32];
pōne sub currū[33] nimium propinquī[34]
sōlis in terrā domibus negāta:
15   dulce[35] rīdentem Lalagēn amābō
dulce loquentem.
                    (*Id., Odes*, 1.22.1-4, 9-12, 17-24)

25. AUREA MEDIOCRITĀS — THE GOLDEN MEAN

Rēctius[1] vīvēs, Licinī,[2] neque altum[3]
semper urgendō[4] neque, dum procellās[5]
cautus[6] horrēscis,[7] nimium premendō
    lītus[8] inīquum.[9]
5   Auream[10] quisquis[11] mediocritātem[12]
dīligit, tūtus[13] caret obsolētī[14]
sordibus[15] tēctī,[16] caret invidendā[17]
    sōbrius[18] aulā.[19]
Saepius ventīs[20] agitātur[21] ingēns[22]
10   pīnus[23] et celsae[24] graviōre cāsū[25]
dēcidunt[26] turrēs[27] feriuntque[28] summōs
    fulgura[29] montēs.[30]
Spērat[31] īnfestīs,[32] metuit secundīs[33]
alteram[34] sortem[35] bene praeparātum[36]
15   pectus.[37] Īnfōrmēs[38] hiemēs[39] redūcit[40]
    Iuppiter[41]; īdem[42]
summovet.[43] Nōn[44] sī male[45] nunc, et ōlim[46]
sīc erit: quondam[47] citharā[48] tacentem[49]
suscitat[50] Mūsam,[51] neque semper arcum[52]
20   tendit[53] Apollō.[54]
Rēbus angustīs[55] animōsus[56] atque
fortis appārē[57]; sapienter[58] īdem[59]
contrahēs[60] ventō[20] nimium secundō[33]
    turgida[61] vēla.[62]
             (*Id., Odes*, 2.10)

26. LĀBUNTUR ANNĪ

Eheu![1] fugācēs,[2] Postume, Postume,
lābuntur[3] annī; nec pietās[4] moram
    rūgīs[5] et īnstantī[6] senectae[7]
    adferet indomitaeque[8] mortī.

    ...

5   Frūstrā[9] cruentō[10] Mārte[11] carēbimus
frāctīsque[12] raucī[13] flūctibus[14] Hadriae[15];
    frūstrā[9] per autumnōs[16] nocentem
    corporibus[17] metuēmus Austrum.[18]
Vīsendus[19] āter[20] flūmine[21] languidō
10   Cōcȳtos[22] errāns et Danaī genus[23]
    īnfāme[24] damnātusque[25] longī
    Sīsyphus[26] Aeolidēs[27] labōris.[28]
Linquenda[29] tellūs[30] et domus et placēns
uxor,[31] neque hārum,[32] quās colis,[33] arborum

15   tē praeter[34] invīsās[35] cupressōs[36]
         ūlla[37] brevcm dominum sequētur.
                 (*Id.*, *Odes*, (II.14. 1-4, 13-24)

27. A SENSE OF BALANCE IN LIFE

     Vīvitur[1] parvō bene cui[2] paternum[3]
     splendet[4] in mēnsā[5] tenuī[6] salīnum,
     nec levēs[7] somnōs[8] timor aut cupīdō
         sordidus[9] aufert.[10]
5   Quid[11] brevī fortēs[12] iaculāmur[13] aevō
     multa? Quid[14] terrās aliō calentēs
     sōle mūtāmus Patriae quis exsul[15]
         sē quoque[16] fūgit?[17]
     Scandit[18] aerātās[19] vitiōsa[20] nāvēs
10   cūra nec turmās[21] equitum relinquit,
     ōcior[22] cervīs[23] et agente nimbōs[24]
         ōcior Eurō.[25]
     Laetus[26] in praesēns[27] animus quod ultrā est
     ōderit[28] cūrāre et amāra[29] lentō[30]
15   temperet[31] rīsū[32]: nihil est ab omnī
         parte[33] beātum.
              (*Id.*, *Odes*, 2.16. 13-28)

28. DIĒS FĒSTUS

     Hic diēs[1] vērē mihi fēstus[2] ātrās[3]
     eximet[4] c*u*p!45 –rās: ego nec tumultum[5]
     nec morī per vim metuam tenente
         Caesare[6] terrās.
5   Ī,[7] pete unguentum,[8] puer,[9] et corōnās,[10]
     et cadum[11] Marsī[12] memorem[13] duellī,
     Spartacum[14] sī quā[15] potuit vagantem[16]
         fallere[17] testa.[18]
             (*Id.*, *Odes*, 3.14. 13-20)

29. A MONUMENT MORE LASTING THAN BRONZE

     Exēgī[1] monumentum[2] aere[3] perennius[4]
     rēgālīque[5] sitū[6] pȳramidum[7] altius,[8]
     quod nōn imber[9] edāx,[10] nōn Aquilō[11] impotēns[12]
     possit dīruere[13] aut innumerābilis[14]
5   annōrum seriēs[15] et fuga[16] temporum.
     Nōn omnis moriar, multaque pars meī
     vītābit Libitīnam[17]...
             (*Id.*, *Odes*, 3.30. 1-7)

30. THE OTHER PERSON'S FAULTS AND OUR OWN

Pērās[1] imposuit[2] Iuppiter nōbīs duās:
propriīs[3] replētam[4] vitiīs post tergum[5] dedit,[6]
aliēnīs[7] ante pectus[8] suspendit[9] gravem.
Hāc rē vidēre nostra mala nōn possumus;
5   aliī simul[10] dēlinquunt,[11] censōrēs[12] sumus.
(Phaedrus, Fābulae, 4.10)

31. SOUR GRAPES

Famē[1] coācta vulpēs[2] altā[3] in vīneā[4]
ūvam[5] appetēbat,[6] summīs saliēns[7] vīribus.
Quam[6] tangere ut nōn potuit, discēdēns ait:
"Nōndum[9] mātūra[10] est; nōlō acerbam sūmere.[11]"
5   Quī facere[12] quae nōn possunt verbīs ēlevant,[13]
adscrībere[14] hoc dēbēbunt exemplum[15] sibī.
(Phaedrus, Fābulae, 4.3)

32. THE FOX AND THE TRAGIC MASK

Persōnam[1] tragicam[2] forte[3] vulpēs[4] vīderat.
"Ō quanta speciēs,[5]" inquit, "cerebrum[6] nōn habet!"
Hoc illīs dictum est quibus honōrem et glōriam
Fortūna tribuit,[7] sēnsum commūnem abstulit.[8]
(Phaedrus, Fābulae, 1.7)

33. THE STAG AT THE SPRING

Ad[1] fontem[2] cervus,[3] cum bibisset,[4] restitit,[5]
et in liquōre[6] vīdit effigiem[7] suam.
Ibi dum rāmōsa[8] mīrāns[9] laudat cornua,[10]
crūrumque[11] nimiam[11] a tenuitātem[12] vituperat,[13]
5   vēnantum[14] subitō[15] vōcibus conterritus,[16]
per campum[17] fugere coepit, et cursū[18] levī
canēs[19] ēlūsit.[20] Silva[21] tum excēpit[22] ferum,[23]
in quā retentīs[24] impedītus[25] cornibus,[10]
lacerārī[26] coepit morsibus[27] saevīs[28] canum.[19]
10   Tunc moriēns vōcem hanc ēdidisse[29] dīcitur:
"Ō mē infēlīcem![30] quī nunc dēmum[31] intellegō
ūtilia[32] mihi quam[33] fuerint quae[34] dēspexeram,[35]
et quae[34] laudāram,[36] quantum lūctūs[27] habuerint."
(Phaedrus, Fābulae, 1.12)

34. THE FOX GETS THE RAVEN'S CHEESE

Quī sē laudārī gaudet[1] verbīs subdolīs,[2]
ferē[3] dat poenās turpī paenitentiā.[4]

Cum dē fenestrā[5] corvus[6] raptum cāseum[7]
comēsse[8] vellet, celsā[9] rcsidēns[10] arbore,[11]
5 hunc vīdit vulpēs[12]; deinde sīc coepit loquī:
"Ō quī tuārum, corve, pennārum[13] est nitor[14]!
Quantum decōris[15] corpore et vultū geris![16]
Sī vōcem habērēs, nūlla prior[17] āles[18] foret."[19]
At ille stultus, dum vult vōcem ostendere,
10 ēmīsit[20] ōre[21] cāseum,[7] quem celeriter
dolōsa[22] vulpēs avidīs[23] rapuit dentibus.[24]

(Phaedrus, Fābulae, 1.13. 1-10)

35. THE ASS AND THE OLD SHEPHERD

In prīncipātū[1] commūtandō[2] cīvium
nīl[3] praeter[4] dominī nōmen mūtant pauperēs.
Id esse vērum parva haec fābella[5] indicat.[6]
Asellum[7] in prātō[8] timidus[9] pāscēbat[10] senex.
5 Is, hostium clamōre[11] subitō[12] territus,
suādēbat[13] asinō[7] fugere nē possent capī.
At ille lentus:[14] "Quaesō,[15] num[16] bīnās[17] mihī
clītellās[18] impositūrum[19] victōrem[20] putās?"
Senex negāvit. "Ergō[21] quid rēfert meā[22]
10 cui serviam clītellās dum[23] portem[24] meās?"

(Phaedrus, Fābulae, 1.15)

36. THE TWO MULES AND THE ROBBERS

Mūlī[1] gravātī[2] sarcinīs[3] ībant duō.
Ūnus ferēbat fiscōs[4] cum pecūniā;
alter tumentēs[5] multō saccōs[6] hordeō.[7]
Ille onere[8] dīves, celsā[9] cervīce[10] ēminēns[11]
5 clārumque collō[12] iactāns[13] tintinnābulum[14];
comes[15] quiētō[16] sequitur et placidō[17] gradū.[18]
Subitō[19] latrōnēs[20] ex īnsidiīs advolant,[21]
interque caedem[22] ferrō mūlum lancinant[23];
dīripiunt[24] nummōs,[25] neglegunt vīle[26] hordeum.[7]
10 Spoliātus[27] igitur cāsūs[28] cum flēret[29] suōs,
"Equidem,[30]" inquit alter, "mē contemptum[31] gaudeō.[32]
Nam nihil āmīsī, nec sum laesus[33] vulnere."[34]
Hōc argūmentō[35] tūta[36] est hominum tenuitās[37];
magnae perīclō[38] sunt opēs obnoxiae.[39]

(Phaedrus, Fābulae, 2.7)

37. DELIGHTS OF THE COUNTRY

C.[1] PLĪNIUS CALPURNIŌ MACRŌ[2] SUŌ S.[1]

Bene est[3] mihi quia[4] tibi est bene. Habēs uxōrem[5] tēcum, habēs fīlium; frueris[6] marī,[7] fontibus,[8] viridibus,[9] agrō, vīllā[10] amoenissimā.[11] Neque enim dubitō esse amoenissimam,[12] in quā sē composuerat[13] homō[14] fēlīcior antequam[15] "fēlīcissimus" fieret. Ego in Tuscīs[16] et vēnor[17] et studeō, quae[18] interdum[19] alternīs,[20] interdum simul[21] faciō; nec tamen adhuc[22] possum prōnūntiāre[23] utrum[24] sit difficilius capere aliquid an scrībere. Valē. (**Pliny,** 5.18)

38. C. PLĪNIUS CANĪNIŌ[1] SUŌ S.

Studēs an[2] piscāris[3] an vēnāris[4] an simul[5] omnia? Possunt enim omnia simul fierī ad Lārium[6] nostrum.[7] Nam lacus[8] piscem,[9] ferās[10] silvae[11] quibus lacus cingitur,[12] studia altissimus[13] iste sēcessus[14] adfatim[15] suggerunt.[16] Sed sīve[17] omnia simul sīve aliquid facis, nōn possum dīcere "invideō"[18]; angor[19] tamen... Numquamne hōs artissimōs laqueōs[20] ...abrumpam?[21] Numquam, putō. Nam veteribus negōtiīs[22] nova accrēscunt,[23] nec tamen priōra peraguntur[24]; tot nexibus,[25] tot quasi catēnīs[26] maius in diēs[27] occupātiōnum[28] agmen[29] extenditur.[30] Valē. (*Id.* 2.8, excerpts)

39. HAPPY MARRIED LIFE

C. PLĪNIUS GEMINŌ SUŌ S.

Grave vulnus[1] Macrinus noster accēpit: āmīsit[2] uxōrem[3] singulāris[4] exemplī[5]... Vīxit cum hāc trīgintā[6] novem annīs[7] sine iurgiō,[8] sine offēnsā.[9] Quam illa reverentiam[10] marītō[11] suō praestitit, cum ipsa summam merērētur![12] Quot[13] quantāsque virtūtēs ex dīversīs[14] aetātibus sūmptās[15] collēgit[16] et miscuit! Habet quidem Macrinus grande[17] sōlācium,[18] quod tantum bonum tam diū tenuit; sed hinc[19] magis exacerbātur[20] quod āmīsit. Nam fruendīs[21] voluptātibus[22] crēscit[23] carendī dolor. Erō ergō[24] suspēnsus[25] prō homine amīcissimō[26] dum[27] admittere[28] āvocāmenta[29] et cicātrīcem[30] patī possit, quam nihil aequē ac[31] necessitās[32] ipsa et diēs[33] longa et satietās[34] dolōris indūcit.[35] Valē. (*Id.,* 8.5, excerpts)

40. FAITHFUL IN SICKNESS AND IN DEATH

C. PLINIUS NEPOTĪ SUŌ S.

(...Fannia[1]) neptis[2] Arriae[3] illīus[4] quae marītō[5] et sōlācium[6] mortis et exemplum[7] fuit. Multa[8] referēbat[9] aviae[10] suae nōn minōra hōc,[11] sed obscūriōra,[12] quae tibi exīstimō tam[13] mīrābilia[14] legentī[15] fore[16] quam mihi audientī fuērunt.

Aegrōtābat[17] Caecīna Paetus, marītus eius, aegrōtābat et fīlius, uterque[18] mortiferē,[19] ut vidēbātur. Fīlius dēcessit[20] eximiā[21] pulchritūdine,[22] parī verēcundiā,[23] et parentibus[24] nōn minus ob[25] alia cārus quam quod fīlius erat. Huic illa ita fūnus[26] parāvit...ut ignōrāret[27] marītus. Quīn immō,[28] quotiēns[29] cubiculum[30] eius intrāret,[31] vīvere fīlium atque etiam commodiōrem[32] esse simulābat[33]; ac persaepe[34] interrogantī[35] quid ageret puer respondēbat, "Bene quiēvit,[36] libenter[37] cibum[38] sūmpsit."[39] Deinde, cum diū cohibitae[40] lacrimae[41] vincerent prōrumperentque,[42] ēgrediēbātur[43]; tunc sē dolōrī dabat. Satiāta,[44] siccīs[45] oculīs, compositō[46] vultū[47] redībat, tamquam[48] orbitātem[49] forīs[50] relīquisset.[51] Praeclārum[52] quidem illud[53] eiusdem: ferrum stringere,[54] perfodere[55] pectus,[56] extrahere[57] pugiōnem,[58] porrigere[59] marītō, addere[60] vōcem immortālem ac paene[61] dīvīnam,[62] "Paete, nōn dolet."[63] ... Valē. *(Id.,* 3.16, excerpts)

41. A SWEET, BRAVE GIRL

C. PLĪNIUS MARCELLĪNŌ SUŌ S.

Trīstissimus[1] haec tibi scrībō, Fundānī nostrī fīliā minōre defūnctā,[2] quā puellā[3] nihil umquam fēstīvius,[4] amābilius, nec longiōre vītā... dignius[6] vīdī. Nōndum[7] annōs trēdecim implēverat,[8] et iam illī[9] anīlis[10] prūdentia,[11] mātrōnālis[12] gravitās[13] erat, et tamen suāvitās[14] puellāris[15]...Ut[16] illa patris cervīcibus[17] inhaerēbat[18]! Ut nōs, amīcōs paternōs,[19] et amanter[20] et modestē[21] complectēbātur[22]! Ut nūtrīcēs,[23] ut paedagōgōs,[24] ut praeceptōrēs[25] prō suō quemque officiō dīligēbat! Quam studiōsē,[26] quam intelligenter[27] lēctitābat[28]!...

Quā illa[29] temperantiā,[30] quā patientiā,[31] quā etiam cōnstantiā[32] novissimam valētūdinem[33] tulit! Medicīs[34] obsequēbātur[35]; sorōrem,[36] patrem adhortābātur[37]; ipsamque sē dēstitūtam[38] corporis vīribus vigōre[39] animī sustinēbat.[40] Dūrāvit[41] hic[42] illī ūsque[43] ad extrēmum,[44] nec aut spatiō[45] valētūdinis aut metū mortis īnfrāctus est[46] ... Ō trīste plānē[47] acerbumque fūnus[48] ...Iam dēstināta erat[49] ēgregiō[50] iuvenī,[51] iam ēlēctus[52] nūptiārum[53] diēs, iam nōs vocātī. Quod gaudium[54] quō maerōre[55] mūtātum est!

Nōn possum exprimere[56] verbīs quantum animō vulnus[57] accēperim cum audīvī Fundānum ipsum praecipientem,[58] quod[59] in vestēs[60] margarīta,[61] gemmās[62] fuerat ērogātūrus,[63] hoc in tūs[64] et unguenta[65] et odōrēs[66] impenderētur[67] ... Sī quās[68] ad eum dē dolōre tam iūstō litterās mittēs, mementō[69] adhibēre[70] sōlācium[71] ...mollem[72] et hūmānum. *(Id.,* 5.16, excerpts)

42. PLINY'S CONCERN ABOUT A SICK FREEDMAN

C. PLĪNIUS VALERIŌ PAULĪNŌ SUŌ S.

Videō quam molliter[1] tuōs[2] habeās[3]; quō simplicius[4] tibī cōnfitēbor[5] quā indulgentiā[6] meōs[2] tractem.[7] Quod sī[8] essem nātūrā asperior et dūrior, frangeret[9] mē tamen īnfirmitās[10] lībertī[11] meī Zōsimī,[12] cui tantō[13] maior hūmānitās[14] exhibenda[15] est, quantō[13] nunc illā[16] magis eget.[17] Homō probus,[18] officiōsus,[19] litterātus[20]; et ars quidem eius et quasi īnscrīptiō[21] —

cōmoedus[21] ...Ūtitur et citharā[22] perītē.[23] ūtitur et citharā Īdem tam commodē[24] ōrātiōnēs[25] et historiās[26] et carmina[27] legit ut hoc sōlum didicisse videātur.

Haec tibi sēdulō[28] exposuī quō[29] magis scīrēs quam multa ūnus mihi et quam iūcunda ministeria[30] praestāret. Accēdit[31] longa iam cāritās[32] hominis, quam ipsa perīcula auxērunt[33] ... Ante aliquot[34] annōs,[35] dum intentē instanterque[36] prōnūntiat,[37] sanguinem[38] reiēcit[39]; atque ob[40] hoc in Aegyptum[41] missus ā mē, post longam peregrīnātiōnem[42] cōnfīrmātus[43] rediit nūper.[44] Deinde...veteris īnfīrmitātis[45] tussiculā[46] admonitus,[47] rūrsus[48] sanguinem reddidit.[49]

Quā ex causā dēstināvī[50] eum mittere in praedia[51] tua quae Forō Iūliī[52] possidēs.[53] Audīvī enim tē referentem[54] esse ibi āera[55] salūbrem[56] et lac[57] eius modī cūrātiōnibus[58] accommodātissimum.[59] Rogō ergō[60] scrībās[61] tuīs[62] ut illī vīlla, ut domus[63] pateat... Valē. (*Id.*, 5.19, excerpts)

ON BEHALF OF A PENITENT FREEDMAN 43-44

43. C. PLĪNIUS SABĪNIĀNŌ SUŌ S.

Libertus[1] tuus, cui suscēnsēre[2] tē dīxerās, vēnit ad mē...Flēvit[3] multum, multum rogāvit, multum etiam tacuit[4]; in summā,[5] fēcit mihi fidem paenitentiae.[6] Vērē[7] crēdō ēmendātu,[8] quia[9] dēlīquisse[10] sē sentit. Īrāsceris,[11] sciō; et īrāsceris meritō,[12] id quoque[13] sciō; sed tunc praecipua[14] mānsuētūdinis[15] laus cum[16] īrae causa iūstissima est. Amāstī[17] hominem et, spērō, amābis; interim[18] sufficit[19] ut exōrārī[20] tē sinās[21] ...Nē torserīs[22] illum, nē torserīs etiam tē; torquēris[23] enim, cum tam lēnis[24] īrāsceris. Vereor[25] nē videar nōn rogāre sed cōgere, sī precibus[26] eius meās iūnxerō. Iungam tamen tantō plēnius[27] et effūsius,[28] quantō[29] ipsum[30] ācrius[31] sevēriusque[32] corripuī[33] ...Valē. (*Id.* 9.21, excerpts)

44. C. PLĪNIUS SABĪNIĀNŌ SUŌ S.

Bene fēcistī[1] quod lībertum[2] aliquandō[3] tibi cārum redūcentibus[4] epistulīs[5] meīs in domum,[6] in animum recēpistī. Iuvābit hoc tē, mē certē iuvat; prīmum,[7] quod tē tam tractābilem[8] videō ut in īrā regī possīs; deinde, quod tantum mihi tribuis[9] ut vel[10] auctōritātī[11] meae pāreās vel precibus[12] indulgeās.[13] Igitur laudō et grātiās agō... Valē. (*Id.*, 9.24, excerpts)

45. SELECTION OF A TEACHER

C. PLĪNIUS MAURICŌ SUŌ S.

Quid ā tē mihi iūcundius potuit iniungī[1] quam ut praeceptōrem[2] frātris tuī līberīs[3] quaererem? Nam beneficiō[4] tuō in scholam[5] redeō et illam dulcissimam aetātem quasi resūmō.[6] Sedeō[7] inter iuvenēs,[8] ut solēbam, atque etiam experior quantum apud illōs auctōritātis[9] ex studiīs habeam. Nam proximē[10] frequentī[11] audītōriō[12] inter sē cōram[13] multīs ōrdinis[14] nostrī clārē[15] loquēbantur: intrāvī,[16] conticuērunt[17]; quod[18] nōn referrem,[19] nisi ad illōrum magis laudem quam ad meam pertinēret[20]... Cum omnēs quī profitentur[21] audierō, quid dē quōque sentiam scrībam efficiamque,[22] quantum tamen epistulā cōnsequī[23] poterō, ut ipse omnēs audisse videāris. Dēbeō enim tibi, dēbeō memoriae frātris tuī hanc fidem, hoc studium, praesertim[24] super[25] tantā rē. Nam quid magis interest vestrā[26] quam ut līberī... dignī[27] illō patre, tē patruō[28] reperiantur?...Valē. *(Id.,* 2.8 excerpts)

46. MARONILLA HAS T.B.

Petit Gemellus[1] nūptiās[2] Marōnillae[3]
et cupit et īnstat[4] et precātur[5] et dōnat.[6]
Adeōne[7] pulchra est? Immō[8] foedius[9] nīl[10] est.
Quid ergō[11] in illā petitur et placet? Tussit.[12] (**Martial,** 1.10)

47. WAS PAULA ONE OF THE DEMIMONDE?

Nūbere[1] vīs Prīscō[2]: nōn mīror,[3] Paula[4]; sapīstī.[5]
Dūcere6 tē nōn vult Prīscus: et ille sapit. *(Id.,* 9.10)

48. THE OLD BOY DYED HIS HAR

Mentīris1 iuvenem[2] tīnctīs,[3] Laetīne,[4] capillīs,[5]
    tam subitō[6] corvus[7] quī modo[8] cycnus[9] erās.
Nōn omnēs fallis[10]; scit tē Prōserpina[11] cānum[12]:
    persōnam[13] capitī[14] dētrahet[15] illa[16] tuō. *(Id.,* 3.43)

49. WHAT'S IN A NAME?

Cinnam,[1] Cinname,[2] tē iubēs vocārī.
Nōn est hic, rogo, Cinna, barbarismus[3]?
Tū sī Fūrius[4] ante dictus essēs,
Fūr[5] istā ratiōne dīcerēris. *(Id.,* 6.17)

50. FAKE TEARS

Āmissum[1] nōn flet[2] cum sōla est Gellia[3] patrem;
    Sī quis adest,[4] iussae[5] prōsiliunt[6] lacrimae.[7]
Nōn lūget[8] quisquis[9] laudārī, Gellia, quaerit;
    Ille dolet[10] vērē[11] quī sine teste[12] dolet. *(Id.,* 1.33)

51. EVEN THOUGH YOU DO INVITE ME — I'LL COME!

Quod convīvāris[1] sine mē tam saepe, Luperce,[2]
    invēnī noceam quā ratiōne tibi.
Īrārāscor[3]: licet[4] ūsque vocēs mittāsque[5] rogēsque —
    "Quid faciēs?" inquis. Quid faciam? Veniam! *(Id.,* 6.51)

---

52. THE PIG!

Nōn cēnat[1] sine aprō[2] noster, Tite,[3] Caeciliānus.
 Bellum[4] convīvam[5] Caeciliānus habet. (*Id.* 7.59)

53. GOOD RIDDANCE

Quid mihi reddat ager[1] quaeris, Line, Nōmentānus?
 Hoc mihi reddit ager: tē, Line, nōn videō. (*Id.* 2.38)

54. PRO-*CRAS*-TINATION

Crās[1] tē vīctūrum, crās dīcis, Postume,[2] semper.
 Dīc[1] mihi, crās istud,[4] Postume, quando[4a] venit?
Quam longēst[5] crās istud? ubi est? aut unde petendum[6]?
 Numquid[7] apud Parthōs Armeniōsque[8] latet[9]?
5 Iam crās istud habet Priamī[10] vel Nestoris[11] annōs.
 Crās istud quantī[12] dīc mihi possit emī[13]?
Crās vīvēs? Hodiē[14] iam vīvere, Postume, sērum[15] est.
 Ille sapit[16] quisquis,[17] Postume, vīvit herī.[18] (*Id.*, 5.58)

55. ISSA

Issa[1] est passere[2] nēquior[3] Catullī:
Issa est pūrior[4] ōsculō[5] columbae;[6]
Issa est blandior[7] omnibus puellīs;
Issa est cārior Indicīs[8] lapillīs[9];
5 Issa est dēliciae[10] catella[11] Pūblī.[12]

Hanc tū, sī queritur,[13] loquī putābis.
Sentit trīstitiamque[14] gaudiumque.[15]
...
 Hanc nē lūx rapiat suprēma[16] tōtam,
pictā[17] Pūblius exprimit[18] tabellā
10 in quā tam similem vidēbis Issam[19]
ut sit tam similis sibi nec[20] ipsa.
Issam dēnique pōne cum[18] tabellā:
aut utramque[21] putābis esse vēram[22]
aut utramque putābis esse pictam.[17] (*Id.*, 1.109)

56. ARRIA: "PAETE, NŌN DOLET."

Casta[1] suō gladium[2] cum trāderet Arria[3] Paetō,
 quem dē vīsceribus[4] strīnxerat[5] ipsa suīs,
"Sī qua fidēs,[6] vulnus[7] quod fēcī nōn dolet,[8]" inquit,
"sed quod tū faciēs, hoc mihi, Paete, dolet." (*Id.* 1.13)

Footnotes

1

METER: Phalaecean, or hendecasyllabic.

[1] **dōnō** (1), (=**dō**), present, dedicate

[2] **lepidus, -a, -um**, pleasant, neat

[3] **libellus, -ī**, *m.*, little book

[4] **āridus, -a, -um**, dry, arid

[5] **modo**, *adv.*, just now

[6] **pūmex, -icis**, *m.*, pumice stone. *The ends of a volume were smoothed with pumice.*

[7] **expoliō** (4), smooth, polish

[8] *voc.; Cornelius Nepos, biographer and historian; v.p. xx.*

[9] *strong form of* **nam** = for (indeed, surely)

[10] **nūgae, -ārum**, trifles, nonsense

[11] **Italī, -ōrum**, the Italians; *initial i long here for meter. This work, now lost, was apparently less annalistic than most histories by Romans.*

[12] **aevum, -ī**, time

[13] **explicō** (1), unfold, explain

[14] **charta, -ae**, leaf of (papyrus) paper; *here* = volume

[15] **doctus, -a, -um**, learned

[16] **labōriōsus, -a, -um**, laborious

[17] *gen. of whole; lit.* whatever of book this is of whatsoever sort; *i.e.,* this book such as it is. **quāliscumque, quālecumque**, of whatever sort *or* kind

[18] **patrōna, -ae**, protectress; protectress maiden (**virgō**) = Muse

[19] *adv., comp. of* **multum**

[20] let *or* may it remain

[21] **perennis, -e**, lasting, perennial

[22] **saeclum**, *syncopated form of* **saeculum, -ī**, age, century; **saeclō** *here is abl. of comparison,* App. *p. 359.*

2

METER: Sapphic stanza.

[1] *V. p. xix,* **Catullus**. *This selection is part of Catullus' free adaption of a famous ode by the Greek poetess Sappho.*

[2] that man

[3] = **mini**; *L.A. 1 n. 5*

[4] *dat. with* **pār**

[5] **fās est**, it is right

[6] = **deōs**

[7] *L.A. 29 n. 6.*

[8] **adversus, -a, -um**, facing, opposite (you)

[9] **identidem**, *adv.*, again and again

[10] *object of* **spectat** *and* **audit**

[11] **spectō** (1), look at

[12] *adv. of* **dulcis**

[13] which thing, *nom.*

[14] = **omnēs**, *modifying* **sēnsūs**

[15] *dat. of separation (= reference) instead of abl. of separation with compounds of* **ab, dē, ex** *and sometimes* **ad**

[16] = **simul ac (atque)**, as soon as

[17] = **aspexit**; *L. A. 15 n. 3*

[18] = **superest**, is left, remains

[19] *The rest of this sentence (i.e., verse 8) is lost from the manuscripts.*

3

METER: Phalaecean.

[1] *This poem is obviously a companion piece to L.A. I.*

[2] how many, *indeclinable adj. modifying* **bāsiātiōnēs**

[3] **bāsiātiō, -ōnis**, *f.*, kiss

[4] and to spare, and more

[5] **Libyssus, -a, -um**, Libyan

[6] **harēna, -ae**, sand (*cp.* **arena**)

[7] **laserpīcī-fer, -a, -um**, bearing laserpicium, *a medicinal plant*

[8] **iaceō, -ēre, iacuī**, lie; *not to be confused with* **iaciō**

[9] **Cȳrēnae, -ārum**, Cyrene, *city of North Africa; short* **y** *here for meter.*

[10] **sīdus, -eris**, *n.*, star, constellation

[11] **taceō, -ēre, uī, -itum**, be silent

[12] **fūrtīvus, -a, -um**, stealthy, furtive (**fūr**, thief)

[13] *subject of* **bāsiāre**

[14] **bāsium, -iī**, kiss

[15] **bāsiō** (1), to kiss kisses = to give kisses; **basiāre** *is subject of* **est satis.**

[16] **vēsānus, -a, -um**, mad, insane

4

METER: Phalaecean.

[1] **lūgeō, -ēre, lūxī, lūctum**, mourn, grieve

[2] **Venus, -eris**, *f.*, Venus; *here plu. as* **Cupīdinēs** *is.*

[3] **Cupīdō, -inis**, *m.*, Cupid, *often in the plu. as is Greek Eros and as we see in art.*

[4] *gen. of whole with* **quantum** (*cp.* L.I. *1 n. 17*): how much of people there is = all the people there are

[5] **venustus, -a, -um**, charming, graceful; **venustiōrum** = more charming than ordinary men

[6] **passer, -eris**, *m.*, sparrow (*a bird which, incidentally, was sacred to Venus*)

[7] **dēliciae, -ārum**, *f. plu.*, delight, darling, pet

[8] **mellītus, -a, -um**, sweet as honey

[9] *contracted form* = **nōverat** (*from* **nōscō**)

[10] **suam ipsam**, its very own (mistress)

[11] **tam...quam**, as...as

[12] **sēsē** = **sē** (*acc.*); **gremium, -iī**, lap

[13] **circumsiliō** (4), jump around

[14] **hūc**, *adv.*, hither, to this place

[15] **illūc**, *adv.*, thither, to that place

[16] **domina, -ae**, mistress (*cp.* dominus)

[17] *adv.*, continuously, constantly (*v. L.A. 8 n. 2; 13 n. 17*)

[18] **pīpiō** (1), chirp

[19] **quī** = **et hic**, *conjunctive use of the relative at the beginning of a sentence*

[20] *L.A. 12 n. 9; 13 n. 27*

[21] **tenebricōsus, -a, -um**, dark, gloomy

[22] *L.A. 7 n. 7; 14 n. 18*

[23]may it be bad (*lit.* badly). *The subjunctive expresses a wish.*

[24]tenebrae, -ārum, *f.,* darkness

[25]Orcus, -ī, *m.,* Orcus, the underworld

[26]dēvorō (1), devour, consume

[27]*dative of separation; v. L.I. 2 n. 15*

[28]auferō, auferre, abstulī, ablātum, take away

[29]iō, *exclamation of pain, oh!, or of joy,* hurrah!

[30]misellus, -a, -um, *diminutive of* miser, wretched, poor, unhappy; *a colloquial word*

[31]tuā operā, thanks to you: opera, -ae, work, pains, effort

[32]fleō, -ēre, flēvī, flētum, weep

[33]turgidulus, -a, -um, (somewhat) swollen

[34]rubeō, -ēre, be red

[35]ocellus, -ī, *diminutive* of oculus, poor little eye

5

METER: elegiac couplet.

[1]*Catullus journeyed to Bithynia on the staff of Memmius, the governor, apparently for two prime reasons. He undoubtedly wanted to get away from Rome in order to regain his equilibrium and fortitude after his final break with the notorious Lesbia. The present poem shows that he also deeply desired to carry out the final funeral rites for his dearly beloved brother, who had died in a foreign land far from his loved ones.*

[2]aequor, -oris, *n.,* flat surface, the sea

[3]vehō, -ere, vexī, vectum, carry

[4]inferiae, -ārum, *f.,* offerings in honor of the dead

[5]postrēmus, -a, -um, last

[6]dōnō (1), present you with; *cp. the idiom in L.I. 1 line 1.*

[7]mūnus, -eris, *n.,* service, gift; *L.A. 23n. 1.*

[8]mūtus, -a, -um, mute, silent

[9]*adv.,* in vain

[10]ad-loquor, address

[11]cinis, cineris, *m. but occasionally f. as here,* ashes (*cp.* incinerator)

[12]*conj.,* since

[13]*L.I. 2 n. 15.* Final ī *is long here because of meter.*

[14]= tē

[15]*L.I. 4 n. 28.*

[16]*interjection, Latin spelling for a sigh*

[17]*adv.,* undeservedly

[18]adimō, -ere, adēmī, adēmptum, take away; adēmpte, *voc. agreeing with* frāter

[19]*Parallels* mihī *in preceding line.*

[20]*adv.,* meanwhile

[21]*neut. acc. plu., obj. of* accipe

[22]prīscus, -a, -um, ancient

[23]*Ch. 34 n. 6*

[24]*L.A. 19 n. 9*

[25]*L.A. 29 n. 5*

[26]ad īnferiās, as offerings (*to the dead*), īnferiae, -ārum

[27]frāternus, -a, -um, fraternal, of a brother, a brother's

[28]*adv. with* mānantia

[29]mānō (1), flow, drip with; mānantia *modifies* haec *in line 7.*

[30]flētus, -ūs, *m.,* weeping, tears

[31]forever

[32]avē = salvē

6

[1]*For the general situation of this speech see the introductory note to the reading passage in Ch. 30. Since Cicero as yet lacked evidence that would stand in court, this speech is a magnificent example of bluff; but it worked to the extent of forcing Catiline (though not the other leaders of the conspiracy) to leave Rome for his army encamped at Fiesole near Florence.*

[2]clear up to what point = how far

[3]*L.A. 13 n. 47*

[4]= abūtēris; ab-ūtor, abuse

[5]furor, -ōris, *m.,* madness

[6]ēlūdō, -ere, ēlūsī, ēlūsum, mock, elude

[7]= sē

[8]effrēnātus, -a, -um, unbridled; *cp.* frēnum, bridle, *and the frenum of the upper lip*

[9]iactō (1), *frequentative form of* iaciō, toss about, vaunt

[10]audācia, -ae, boldness, audacity

[11]nihil = strong nōn; not at all

[12]nocturnus, -a, -um, *adj. of* nox

[13]praesidium, -iī, *n.,* guard

[14]Palātium, -ī, *n.,* the Palatine hill. *From the sumptuous dwellings on the Palatine comes our word "palace."*

[15]vigilia, -ae, *f.,* watch; *plu.,* watchmen, sentinels

[16]concursus, -ūs, *m.,* gathering

[17]mūnītus, -a, -um, fortified

[18]*L.A. 4 n. 14; here* = expression

[19]vultus, -ūs, face

[20]cōnstringō, -ere, -strīnxī, -strictum, bind, curb

[21]coniūrātiō, -ōnis, *f.,* conspiracy (a swearing together)

[22]proximus, -a, -um, nearest, last (*sc.* nocte)

[23]the night before (that)

[24]con-vocō

[25]*What kind of gen.? (Ch. 40 p. 194)*

[26]*gen. of* nōs (*Ch. 11 n. 4*)

[27]ignōrō (1), be ignorant, not know

[28]*The accus. was used in exclamatory expressions.*

[29]*adv.,* on the contrary; nay more

[30]*L.A. 5 n. 7*

[31]particeps, -cipis, *m.,* participant

[32]notō (1), mark out, note

[33]dēsignō (1), mark out, designate, choose

[34]caedēs, -is, *f.,* slaughter

[35]tēlum, -ī, weapon

[36]iussū, *chiefly in abl.,* by *or* at the command of

[37]long ago

[38]oportet, -ēre, oportuit, *impersonal,* it is necessary; dūcī *is its subj.*

[39]pestis, -is, *f.,* plague, destruction

[40]**māchinor** (1), contrive (*cp. "machine"*); **in nōs, in** + *acc. sometimes means* against (**contrā**)

[41]**cōnsultum, -ī,** decree

[42]**vehemēns,** *gen.* **-entis,** emphatic, vehement

[43]**dē + sum,** be wanting, fail + *dat.*

[44]**auctōritās, -tātis,** *f.,* authority

[45]*L.A. 27 n. 16*

[46]*adv.,* openly

[47]**vīcēsimus, -a, -um,** twentieth

[48]**hebēscō, -ere,** grow dull

[49]**aciēs, -ēī,** *f.* sharp edge

[50]**eius modī,** of this sort; *modifies* **cōnsultum**

[51]*here* = in accordance with

[52]*adv.,* at once

[53]**convenit, -īre, convēnit,** *impers.,* it is fitting

[54]**dē + pōnō,** put aside

[55]**cōnfirmō** (1), strengthen

[56]**patrēs cōnscrīptī,** senators

[57]**clēmēns,** *gen.* **-entis,** merciful, gentle

[58]**dissolūtus, -a, -um,** lax

[59]**intertia, -ae,** inactivity; *example of genitive of thing charged:* "I condemn myself *on charge of inactivity,* find myself guilty of inactivity."

[60]**nēquitia, -ae,** worthlessness; *gen. of charge*

[61]**condemnō** (1), find guilty, condemn

[62]**castra, -ōrum,** *n.,* a camp (*n. plu. form but sing. meaning*)

[63]**Etrūria, -ae,** Etruria

[64]**faucēs, -ium,** *f.* (*plu.*), jaws, narrow pass

[65]*L.A. 7 n. 11*

[66]**crēscō, -ere, crēvī, crētum,** increase

[67]from day to day

[68]*L.A. 12 n. 3*

[69]**intrā,** *prep.* + *acc.,* within

[70]**moenia, -ium,** *n. plu.,* walls, fortifications

[71]*adv.,* so even

[72]**intestīnus, -a, -um, internal**

[73]*adv.,* daily

[74]**perniciēs, -ēī,** *f.,* slaughter, destruction

[75]**molior, -īrī, -ītus sum,** build, plan; **mōlientem** *goes with* **ducem** *and has* **perniciem** *as its object.*

[76]= **et haec,** *conjunctive use of the relative; L.I. 4 n. 19.*

[77]**pergō, -ere, perrēxī, perrēctum,** proceed, continue

[78]**quō,** *L.A. 2 n. 8. A few lines before these words Cicero said:* **cōnfirmāstī,** (you asserted) **tē ipsum iam esse exitūrum** (*from* **ex-eō**).

[79]**ēgredior, -ī, ēgressus sum,** go out, depart. *What is the form of* **ēgredere**? (*p. 164, imperative*)

[80]*adv.,* at some time, at last

[81]**porta, -ae,** gate

[82]*Manlius was in charge of Catiline's army at Fiesole.*

[83]**dēsīderō** (1) desire, miss

[84]**ē-dūcō, -ere,** *etc.*

[85]**minus = nōn omnēs**

[86]**pūrgō** (1), cleanse

[87]**dum modo** + *subjunctive* = *a proviso,* provided only; *cp. L.A. 29 n. 11.*

[88]**mūrus, -ī,** wall

[89]**inter-sum**

[90]**versor, -ārī, versātus sum,** dwell, remain

[91]**sinō, -ere, sīvī, situm,** allow

[92]**quamquam,** and yet

[93]**nōn nūllī,** not none = some, several

[94]**immineō, -ēre,** overhang, threaten

[95]**dissimulō** (1), conceal

[96]**quī = et hī**

[97]**mollis, -e,** soft, weak

[98]**corrōborō** (1), strengthen; *cp.* corroborate

[99]**quōrum = et eōrum**

[100]**secūtī,** *participle going with* **multī**

[101]**improbus, -a, -um,** wicked, depraved

[102]**vērum etiam = sed etiam**

[103]**imperītus, -a, -um,** inexperienced

[104]**animadvertō, -ere, -vertī, -versum,** notice; *with* **in** + *acc.* = inflict punishment on. *This is a mixed condition of what general category?* (*Ch. 33 p. 157–158*)

[105]*adv. of* **crūdēlis**

[106]**rēgiē,** *adv.,* (in the fashion of a king), tyrannically

[107]*Supply* **id** *as subject.*

[108]**intendō, -ere, -tendī, -tēnsum,** intend; *parenthetical clause*

[109]**per-veniō ad** *or* **in** + *acc.,* arrive at, reach; **pervēnerit** = *perf. subjunctive for a future perfect indicative in a more vivid condition. For the subjunctive in subordinate clauses in indirect statement, see App., p. 360*

[110]**fore,** *an uninflected form of* **futūrus, -a, -um, esse**

[111]*V. n. 101 above.*

[112]*V. n. 39 above.*

[113]*adv.,* for a little while

[114]**re-primō,** press back, check

[115]*L.I. 5 n. 31*

[116]**comprimō, -ere, -pressī, -pressum,** suppress

[117]**quod sī,** but if

[118]*fut. perf. ind. What kind of condition?*

[119]**suōs (virōs)**

[120]*adv.,* to the same place

[121]**undique,** from all sides

[122]**colligō,** *L.A. 5 n. 10*

[123]**naufragus, -ī,** (shipwrecked) ruined man

[124]**adgregō** (1), gather

[125]**exstinguō, -ere, -stīnxī, -stīnctum,** extinguish

[126]**adultus, -a, -um,** mature

[127]**stirps, stirpis,** *f.,* stem, stock

[128]**sēmen, -inis,** *n.,* seed

[129]**latrōcinium, -ī,** brigandage; band of brigands

[130]*adv.,* perhaps

[131]*here* = for

[132]**relevō** (1), relieve

[133]**re-sideō** (= **sedeō**), **-ēre, -sēdī, -sessum,** (sit down), remain

[134]**sē-cēdō** (**sē** = apart, away). *Why subjunctive?* (*p. 132*)

[135]*L.A. 14 n. 10*
[136]congregō (1), gather together
[137]dēsinō, -ere, -sīvī, -situm, cease
[138]īnsidior, -ārī, -ātus sum, plot against + *dat.*
[139]domī suae, *locative, p. 179. Catiline had tried to have Cicero assassinated.*
[140]circum-stō, -āre, -stetī, stand around, surround
[141]tribūnal, -ālis, *n.*
[142]praetor urbānus, *judicial magistrate who had charge of civil cases between Roman citizens*
[143]obsideō, -ere, -sēdī, -sessum, besiege, beset
[144]cūria, -ae, senate house
[145]malleolus, -ī, firebrand
[146]fax, facis, *f.,* torch
[147]īnflammō (1), set on fire
[148]= parāre
[149]īn-scrībō
[150]frōns, frontis, *f.,* forehead
[151]polliceor, -ērī, pollicitus sum, promise
[152]dīligentia, -ae
[153]eques, equitis, *m.,* horseman, knight. *Here the* equitēs *are the wealthy business class in Rome.*
[154]cōnsēnsiō, -ōnis, *f.,* agreement, harmony
[155]profectiō, -ōnis, *f.,* departure; *cp.* profiscīscor
[156]patefaciō, -ere, -fēcī, -factum, make open, disclose; *cp.* pateō
[157]illūstrō (1), bring to light
[158]vindicō (1), avenge, punish
[159]hīs-ce = hīs + *intensive enclitic* -ce; *abl. case with* omnibus
[160]ōmen, ōminis, *n.,* omen: "with these omens" or "with these words which I have uttered as omens," *abl. of attendant circumstance without* cum (*Ch. 24 n.1*)
[161]cum...salūte (peste, exitiō) *abl. of attendant circumstance* (*Ch. 24 n. 1*) *with* cum, *here indicating the result:* "to the safety of state, to your own destruction,..."
[162]perniciēs, -ēī, *f.,* disaster, calamity
[163]exitium, -iī, ruin
[164]parricīdium, -iī, murder
[165]impius, -a, -um, wicked, disloyal
[166]nefārius, -a, -um, infamous, nefarious
[167]eīsdem auspiciīs quibus haec urbs (cōnstitūta est); auspicia, -ōrum, auspices
[168]Rōmulus, -ī, *the founder of Rome*
[169]cōnstituō, -ere, -stituī, -stitūtum, establish
[170]Stator, -ōris, *m.,* the Stayer (of flight), the Supporter, Jupitor Stator
[171]imperī = imperiī, *gen. sing.* (*Ch. 4 n. 1*)
[172]*L.A. 2 n. 9*
[173]nōminō (1), name, call (*cp.* nōmen)
[174]templum, -ī, temple
[175]tēctum, -ī, roof, house
[176]arceō, -ēre, -uī, ward off
[177]inimīcus, -ī, personal enemy; inimīcōs, hostēs, *etc. are in apposition with* hominēs.

[178]latrō, -ōnis, *m.,* robber, bandit
[179]foedus, -eris, *n.,* treaty, bond
[180]societās, -tātis, *f.,* fellowship, alliance (*cp.* socius)
[181]con (together) + iungō: coniūnctōs *modifies* latrōnēs, *etc.*
[182]aeternus, -a, -um, eternal
[183]supplicium, -iī, punishment
[184]vīvus, -a, -um, living, alive
[185]mactō (1), punish, pursue. *The skeleton outline of the sentence is this:* Tū (quī... es cōnstitūtus, quem... nōmināmus) hunc et sociōs ā templīs...fortūnīsque cīvium arcēbis; et hominēs (inimīcōs...coniūnctōs) suppliciīs vīvōs mortuōsque mactābis.

7

[1]*Cicero here tells how, shortly after his first speech against Catiline, he secured the written evidence necessary for the trial and conviction of the conspirators.*
[2]fellow-citizens, *an old word of uncertain origin*
[3]*The Romans regularly used the singular even when referring to a number of people; we use the plural, "lives."*
[4]*neut. plu.,* good things = goods
[5]coniūnx, -iugis, *f.,* wife (*cp.* coniungō)
[6]*L.A. 19 n. 7*
[7]domicilium, -iī, home (*cp.* domus)
[8]fortūnātus, -a, -um (*cp.* fortūna)
[9]hodiernus diēs, this day, today (*cp.* hodiē)
[10]ergā, *prep.* + *acc.* toward
[11]flamma, -ae, flame
[12]*adv.,* almost
[13]*L.I. 6 n. 64*
[14]restituō, -ere, -stituī, -stitūtum, restore
[15]*The skeleton of the sentence is this:* Rem pūblicam (...urbem) amōre deōrum(...perīculīs meīs) ē flammā (...faucibus fātī) ēreptam (...restitūtam) vidētis.
[16]*conjunctive use of the relative; neut. nom. plu.*
[17]*L.I. 6 n. 157*
[18]*L.I. 6 n. 156*
[19]comperiō, -īre, -perī, compertum, find out
[20]*introduces* possītis
[21]et...et
[22]*nom. neut. plu., subj. of* comprehēnsa sint
[23]investīgō (1), track out, investigate
[24]*L.I. 6 n. 27*
[25]*adv.,* in the first place
[26]*ut* + *ind. here* = ever since
[27]before by a few days (*abl. of degree of difference, p. 281*) = a few days ago; *actually some three weeks before*
[28]ērumpō, -ere, -rūpī, -ruptum, burst forth
[29]huius + ce, *L.I. 6 n. 159*
[30]*L.I. 6 n. 166*
[31]vigilō (1), watch, be vigilant
[32]prō-videō, foresee, make provision
[33]quem ad modum, how

[34]absconditus, -a, -um, hidden

[35]salvus, -a, -um, safe

[36]*When* cum *was felt to be strictly temporal (as when preceded by such words as* tum *or* eō tempore) *rather than circumstantial, it was used with the indicative; v. Ch. 31 n. 1.*

[37]vereor, -ērī, veritus sum, fear

[38]invidia, -ae, hatred, unpopularity

[39]illa (invidia)

[40]*comparative of* magnopere

[41]*This clause is a noun clause in apposition with* illa (invidia). *The perfect subjunctive* (exierit) *is used in informal indirect discourse indicating what people may say:* "he went out alive (vīvus)."

[42]tum cum, *mere repetition of* tum cum *above as Cicero starts the sentence over again.*

[43]exterminō (1), banish (ex + terminus, boundary)

[44]aut...exitūram (esse) aut...fore putābam

[45]reliquus, -a, -um, remaining, the rest of

[46]coniūrātus, -ī, conspirator

[47]*adv.,* at the same time

[48]ex-eō; exitūram (esse)

[49]restō, -āre, -stitī, stay behind, remain

[50]infirmus, -a, -um, weak

[51]dēbilis, -e, helpless, weak

[52]*L.I. 6 n. 110*

[53]*L.I. 6 n. 5*

[54]*L.I. 6 n. 147*

[55]in eō ut sentīrem et vidērem quid...mōlīrentur: in this -that I might see...; *the* ut-*clause of purpose is in apposition with* eō.

[56]lēgātus, -ī, ambassador

[57]Allogrogēs, -um, *m.,* the Allobroges, *a Gallic tribe whose ambassadors had come to Rome to make complaints about certain Roman magistrates.*

[58]Trānsalpīnus, -a, -um, Transalpine

[59]tumultus, - us, *m.,* uprising

[60]Gallicus, -a, -um, Gallic

[61]excitō (1), excite, arouse

[62]*Publius Lentulus after having been consul in 71 B.C. was removed from the Senate on grounds of moral turpitude. He was now one of the leading conspirators and at the same time he was holding the office of praetor.*

[63]sollicitō (1), stir up

[64]Gallia, -ae, Gaul

[65]mandātum, -ī, order, instruction

[66]comes, -itis, *m.,* companion

[67]ad-iungō

[68]Titus Volturcius, *an errand-boy for Lentulus*

[69]falcultās, -tātis, *f.,* opportunity

[70]quod, a thing which. *The antecedent of* quod *is the general idea in the* ut-*clause.*

[71]optō (1), desire

[72]*adv.,* clearly

[73]dēprehendō (cp. comprehendō), detect, comprehend

[74]hesternō dīē, yesterday

[75]*Though praetors were judicial magistrates, they did possess the imperium by which they could command troops.*

[76]most loving of the state = very patriotic

[77]*objective genitives; App. p. 357*

[78]fierī, *subject of* placēret (it was pleasing) *used impersonally*

[79]praeclārus, -a, -um, noble

[80]ēgregius, -a, -um, excellent, distinguished

[81]*subjunctive in a characteristic clause*

[82]recūsātiō, -ōnis, *f.,* refusal

[83]negōtium, -iī, business, matter

[84]advesperāscit, -ere, -perāvit, *impersonal inceptive,* it is approaching evening (*cp.* vespers)

[85]*adv.,* secretly

[86]pōns, pontis, *m.,* bridge; *the Mulvian bridge across the Tiber near Rome.*

[87]vīlla, -ae, country house

[88]*adv.,* in two divisions

[89]Tiberis, -is, *m.,* the Tiber

[90]inter-sum, be between

[91]*adv.,* to the same place

[92]suspīciō, -ōnis, *f.,* suspicion

[93]praefectūra, -ae, prefecture, *a city of the Roman allies governed by a Roman prefect*

[94]Reātinus, -a, -um, of Reate, *A Sabine town about forty miles from Rome.*

[95]complūrēs, -a, *plural adj.,* very many

[96]dēligō, -ere, -lēgī, -lēctum, choose, select

[97]opera, -ae, help; *why abl.?*

[98]*adv.,* constantly

[99]*L.I. 6 n. 13*

[100]gladius, -iī, sword

[101]*adv.,* meanwhile

[102]ferē, *adv.,* about, almost; *usually follows the word it modifies*

[103]vigilia, -ae, watch. *The night was divided into four watches.*

[104]exigō, -ere, -ēgī, -āctum, finish

[105]comitātus, -ūs, company, retinue. *The ablative of accompaniment may be used without cum in military expressions.*

[106]ingredior, -gredī, -gressus sum, enter on

[107]and together with (them)

[108]impetus, -ūs, attack

[109]ēducuntur...gladiī, swords were drawn

[110]nostrīs (virīs)

[111]nōscō = cognōscō

[112]interventus, -ūs, intervention

[113]pugna, -ae, fight

[114]sēdō (1), settle, stop (*not to be confused with* sedeō, sit)

[115]quīcumque, quaecumque, quodcumque, whoever, whatever

[116]integer, -gra, -grum, untouched, whole

[117]dīlūcēscit, -ere, -lūxit, it grows light, dawn comes

[118]*L.I. 6 n. 101*
[119]**māchinātor, -ōris,** *m.,* contriver, plotter
[120]**Cimber Gabīnius**
[121]*L.A. 27 n. 8*
[122]**nihil-dum,** nothing yet
[123]**suspicor, -ārī, -ātus sum,** suspect
[124]*adv.,* likewise
[125]**arcessō, -ere, -īvī, -ītum,** summon
[126]**tardē,** *adv.,* slowly
[127]**frequēns,** *gen.* **-entis,** *adj.,* crowded, full
[128]*adv.,* meanwhile
[129]**admonitus, -ūs,** warning, suggestion
[130]**aedēs, -ium,** *f.,* house
[131]**tēlum, -ī,** weapon; **tēlōrum** is *gen. of whole with* **quid:** anything of weapons = any weapons
[132]*relative clause of purpose:* **quī** = **ut** is; *cp. L.A. 11 n. 15*
[133]*Antecedent* is **aedibus.**
[134]**sīca, -ae,** dagger
[135]**efferō; ex-ferō**
[136]**intrō-dūcō** = *Eng.* introduce
[137]promise of protection in the name of the state
[138]*L.I. 6 n. 36*
[139]**indicō** (1), indicate, make known
[140]*L.A. 13 n. 34*
[141]*The perfect endings in* -āvi-, -ēvi-, -ōvi- *often contract to* ā, ē, ō, *respectively. So here* **recreāvisset** *has contracted to* **recreāsset.** *Perfects in* -īvi- *may lose the* v *but the two resultant vowels rarely contract to* ī *except before* ss *and* st: **audīverat, audierat; audīvisse, audīsse; quaesīssent**
[142]*L.I. 6 n. 13. Why abl.?*
[143]*indirect command with* **mandāta et litterās**
[144]**quam prīmum,** as soon as possible
[145](that he should do) this (**id**) with this plan (in mind) that...
[146]*The rest of the sentence can be outlined thus:* **ut** (*cum...partibus* [quem ad modum...distributum erat] *incendissent et...fēcissent*) **praestō esset ille** (*quī et...exciperet et...coniungeret*)
[147]in
[148]**quem ad modum,** as
[149]*impersonal passive verbs:* as had been marked out and assigned
[150]**incendō, -ere, -cendī, -cēnsum,** set fire to
[151]**caedēs, -is,** *f.,* slaughter
[152]**infīnītus, -a, -um,** unlimited
[153]*adv.,* on hand, ready
[154]**ille** = Catiline
[155]**ex-cipiō,** pick up, capture
[156]**urbānus, -a, -um,** of the city, urban
[157]**con + iungō.** *Why are* **exciperet** *and* **coniungeret** *in the subjunctive?* (*L.A. 11 n. 15*)
[158]**iūs, iūrandum, iūris iūrandī,** *n.,* oath
[159]**prae-scīrbō,** order, direct; **esse praescrīptum,** *impersonal passive* (it had been commanded to them-

selves, **sibi**) *but translate as personal:* they had been directed.
[160]**equitātus, -ūs,** cavalry
[161]*jussive noun clause depending on* **esse praescrīptum.**
[162]to be brief
[163]**tabella, -ae,** tablet: *very shallow trays, not unlike the modern slate, filled with wax on which writing was done with a sharp-pointed stilus. Two of these closed face to face, tied together with a string, and sealed with wax and the impression of a signet ring, were the equivalent of a modern letter in an envelope.*
[164]**prō-ferō**
[165]*from* **quisque**
[166]**datae (esse); datae** *is nom. fem. plu. to agree with* **quae (tabellae),** *the subject of* **dīcēbantur.**
[167]*p. 153, comparison of adverbs*
[168]**līnum, -ī,** string
[169]**incīdō, -ere, -cīdī, -cīsum,** cut
[170](**Cethēgī**) **ipsīus:** *emphatic because letters were often written by an amanuensis, a slave to whom the letter was dictated.*
[171]**sēsē** = **sē** (*i.e., Cethegus*), *subject of* **facturum esse** *and also of* **ōrāre**
[172]**cōnfirmō** (1), assert, declare; *subjunctive in indirect discourse* (*v. p. 360*)
[173]a little before (before by a little), *abl. of degree of difference, App. p. 359*
[174]**dēprehendō, -ere, -hendī, -hēnsum,** seize
[175]**respondisset dīxissetque,** *subjunctives in relative clauses of characteristic, which have the force of concessive clauses* (= *although*)
[176]**ferrāmentum, -ī,** *n.,* weapon
[177]**studiōsus, -a, -um,** fond of (*i.e., he was a collector.*)
[178]**recitō** (1), read aloud
[179]**dēbilitō** (1), weaken
[180]**abiectus, -a, -um,** downcast
[181]**cōnscientia, -ae,** knowledge, conscience
[182]*adv.,* suddenly
[183]**conticēscō, -ticēscere, -ticuī,** become silent
[184]to
[185]*L.A. 29 n. 19*
[186]*Here* -ne *is used to introduce an indirect question.*
[187]**adnuō, -ere, -nuī,** nod assent
[188]*nom. case*
[189]*What does* **quis, quid** *mean after* **sī, nisi, nē, num?**
[190]**vellet,** *subjunctive because it is a subordinate clause in an implied indirect statement for Cicero's original words:* "**sī quid...dīcere vīs**"
[191]**potestās, -tātis,** *f.,* power, opportunity
[192]*an adv.* here
[193]**aliquantō,** *abl. of degree of difference* (by somewhat) *equivalent to an adverb:* somewhat, a little
[194]**indicium, -ī,** evidence, information
[195]**ē-dō, -ere, ēdidī, ēditum,** give forth, publish
[196]**surgō, -ere, surrēxī, surrēctum,** get up, arise

[197]**quam ob rem** = **quāre**
[198]*What is the construction? (Ch. 37 Vocab., s.v.* **domus**)
[199]*dat. case*
[200]**constanter,** *adv.,* consistently, steadily
[201]**quotiēns,** *adv.,* how often
[202]*contracted form, n. 141 above*
[203]**sēcum:** *an indirect reflexive referring to the subject of* **quaesīssent;** *translate* to them.
[204]**fāta Sibyllīna,** *a collection of ancient prophecies for which the Romans had very high respect. By these Lentulus had sought to prove to the Allobroges that he was destined to hold the regnum and imperium at Rome.*
[205]*adv.,* suddenly; *synonym* = **repente** *(n. 182)*
[206]**dē-mēns,** *gen.* **-mentis,** out of one's mind
[207]**īnfitior, -tiārī, -tiātus sum,** deny
[208]**praeter,** *prep. + acc.,* contrary to
[209]**opīniō, -ōnis,** *f.,* expectation
[210]*adv.,* impudently
[211]**ad extrēmum,** at the last, finally
[212]**eīs** = *neut. plu.,* those things
[213]**īnsimulō** (1), charge
[214]*depends on* **vīsa sunt**
[215]**cum...tum,** not only...but also *(cp.* **nōn sōlum...sed etiam)**
[216]**illa argūmenta atque indicia** *(viz.,* **tabellae...confessiō) certissima vīs sunt**
[217]**argūmentum, -ī,** proof
[218]**cōnfessiō, -ōnis,** *f.* = *Eng.*
[219]*lit.* more certain by much. *What kind of abl. is* **multō?** *(App. p. 359)*
[220]**color...taciturnitās,** *in apposition with* **illa,** *which is nom. neut. plu.* **color, -ōris,** *m.,* = *Eng.*
[221]*L.I. 6 n. 19*
[222]**taciturnitās, -tātis,** *f.,* silence *(cp.* taciturn)
[223]**obstupēscō, -ere, -stupuī,** become stupefied, be thunderstruck
[224]**intueor, - erī, -tuitus sum,** look at
[225]*adv.,* stealthily, furtively *(in the fashion of a* **fūr,** thief)
[226]*L.A. 15 n. 3*
[227]**indicō** (1), accuse *(cp.* **indicium,** *n. 194 above)*
[228]**cōnsulō, -ere, -suluī, -sultum,** consult, ask advice of
[229]highest interest of the state
[230]**varietās, -tātis,** *f.,* variation
[231]**īnsigne, -is,** *n.,* sign, symbol
[232]**monumentum, -ī** = *Eng.*
[233]**postulō** (1), request, demand
[234]except
[235]**sempiternus, -a, -um,** eternal
[236]**veneror, -ārī, -ātus sum,** worship
[237]*L.A. 27 n. 14*
[238]*L.I. 6 n. 175*
[239]**quamquam,** *conj.,* although
[240]**dēpellō,** drive off, avert
[241]**equally as** = just as

[242]last night
8
[1]*As part of his demonstration that death is not an evil, Cicero cites Socrates' views as given in Plato's "Apology," Socrates defense of his life before the jury that finally condemned him to death.*
[2]*L.A. 11 n. 19*
[3]**quā... ūsum,** which Plato represents him as using; **quā,** *abl. with the participle* **ūsum**
[4]**iūdex, -dicis,** *m.,* juror
[5]**multō,** (1), punish, sentence
[6]**ē-veniō,** turn out; *impersonal inf. in indirect statement*
[7]*subordinate clause in indirect statement*
[8]**necesse,** *indecl. adj.,* (it is) necessary
[9]*Supply* **ut** *before* **sit:** that there be one of two possibilities, *with the* **ut...migrētur** *clause in apposition with* **duōbus**
[10]**aut...aut**
[11]*L.I. 4 n. 28*
[12]**migrō** (1), depart, migrate; **migrātur** *as impersonal passive,* one departs
[13]= **quāre**
[14]= **sī**
[15]*L.I. 6 n. 125*
[16]*L.A. 15 n. 4*
[17]**vīsum, -ī,** vision
[18]**somnium, -iī,** dream
[19]**plācātus, -a, -um,** peaceful
[20]*L.A. 18 n. 3*
[21]**ad-ferō -ferre, attulī, allātum,** bring
[22]**dī** = **deī** *voc. plu.*
[23]*what kind of gen.? (Ch. 40 p. 194)*
[24]**ē-morior,** die (off)
[25]**futūra est,** is going to be
[26]**perpetuitās, -tātis,** *f.,* perpetuity
[27]**cōn-sequor**
[28]**quis (est)**
[29]**mē,** *abl. of comparison, v. App. p. 359*
[30]**sīn,** *conj.,* but if
[31]**vērus, -a, -um,** true: **(ea) sunt vēra**
[32]**migrātiō, -ōnis,** *f.,* the noun of **migrō,** *n. 12 above*
[33]**ōra, -ae,** shore, region
[34]**(eī) quī**
[35]**ex-cēdō** = **discēdō**
[36]**incolō, -ere, -uī,** inhabit
[37]*abl. of degree of difference, App. p. 359*
[38]**peregrīnātiō, -ōnis,** *f.,* travel abroad
[39]**vērō,** *L.A. 5 n. 7; cp.,* **vērus,** *n. 31 above*
[40]**col-loquor,** talk with, converse *(cp.* colloquial)
[41]*Orpheus and Musaeus were famous poets and musicians before the time of Homer*
[42]*Hesiod, a Greek epic poet chronologically next after Homer.*
[43]**quantī (pretiī),** of how much (value), *gen. of indefinite value.* **quantī...aestimātis,** how valuable, pray, do you estimate this is?

[44]**aestimō** (1), estimate, value

[45]**quisquam, quidquam (quicquam)**, anyone, anything (*L.A. 7 n. 7*); **cuiquam** *modified by* **bonō**: to any good man

[46]**malī** (*gen.*) *depends on* **quicquam**: anything of evil = any evil

[47]**vīvō** *and* **mortuō** *modify* **cuiquam bonō. vīvus, -a, -um,** *adj. of the verb* **morior**

[48]*adv.*, from this place

[49]**uter, utra, utrum,** which (of two)

[50]**hominem...nēminem,** no man

9

[1]*In these excerpts Scipio Africanus Minor (the Younger, hero of the Third Punic War in 146 B.C.) tells how the deceased Scipio Africanus Maior (the Elder, hero of the Second Punic War who defeated Hannibal in 202 B.C.) appeared to him in a dream and discoursed on the nature of life here and hereafter.*

[2]**artus, -a, -um,** deep (sleep); narrow

[3]**solēbat (esse)**

[4]*L.I. 8 n. 16*

[5]**complector, -ī, -plexus sum,** embrace

[6]*abl. of description, App. p. 360*

[7]**imāgō, -inis,** *f.,* image; *here* = portrait mask of an ancestor. *The* **imāginēs** *of a Roman patrician's ancestors were displayed in the atrium of the house.*

[8]**nōtus, -a, -um,** known, familiar

[9]**agnōscō** (*cp.* **cognōscō**), recognize

[10]*L.A. 5 n. 4*

[11]**cohorrēscō, -ere, -horruī,** shudder

[12]**-ne** *here introducing an indirect question,* whether

[13]**L. Aemilius Paulus,** *father of Africanus Minor*

[14]**exstīnctōs (esse): exstinguō,** *L.I. 6 n. 125*

[15]*L.I. 6 n. 29*

[16]= **vinculīs: vinculum, -ī** bond, fetter

[17]**carcer, -eris,** *n.,* prison

[18]**ē-volō** (1), fly away; *not to be confused with* **volō, velle**

[19]**quīn aspicis:** why, don't you see?

[20]**vim** = **cōpiam**

[21]**lacrima, -ae,** tear

[22]**ōsculor, -ārī, -ātus sum,** kiss

[23]**fleō, -ēre, flēvī, flētum,** weep

[24]**prohibeō,** forbid

[25]**ut prīmum,** as soon as

[26]**flētus, -ūs,** *noun of* **fleō,** *n. 23 above*

[27]**re-primō (premō)**

[28]**quaesō, -ere,** *commonly exclamatory:* I beg you!, pray tell!, please

[29]**sānctus, -a, -um,** holy

[30]**moror, -ārī, -ātus sum,** delay, wait

[31]why not?

[32]**hūc,** *adv.,* to this place, here

[33]**properō** (1), hasten

[34]= that is not the way

[35]order = **is deus**

[36]**templum, -ī,** sacred area, temple

[37]**cuius...cōnspicis:** whose this temple is **or** to whom belongs this temple — everything which you behold. *Apparently, as he says* "hoc templum," *he makes a sweeping gesture with his arm to indicate the universe and then adds* "omne quod cōnspicis" *to make this even clearer.* **cōnspiciō** = **aspiciō**

[38]**aditus, -ūs,** approach, entrance

[39]*abl. of accordance:* in accordance with this law, on this condition

[40]**generō** (1), create

[41]**tueor, -ērī, tūtus sum,** watch, protect. *Why subjunctive? (L.A. 11 n. 15)*

[42]**globus, -ī,** sphere, globe

[43]*i.e.,* **hominibus**

[44]*L.I. 7 n. 235*

[45]**sīdus, -eris,** *n.,* constellation; **stēlla, -ae,** star

[46]**Pūblius,** praenomen *(first name) of Africanus Minor*

[47]**pius, -a, -um,** loyal, devout

[48]**re-tineō,** retain, preserve

[49]**iniussū,** *abl. as adverb,* without the command (of); *cp.* **iussū**

[50]**ille (animus)**

[51]*L.I. 8 n. 12*

[52]**mūnus, mūneris,** *n.,* duty, service

[53]**adsignō** (1), assign

[54]**dē-fugiō,** flee from, avoid

[55]**iūstitia, -ae,** justice (*cp.* **iūstus**)

[56]**colō, -ere, -uī, cultum,** cultivate, cherish

[57]**pietās, -tātis,** *f.,* loyalty, devotion (*cp.* **pius,** *n. 47 above*)

[58]important

[59]in the case of

[60]*L.A. 19 n. 9*

[61]**propinquus, -ī,** relative

[62]surely

[63]**coetus, -ūs,** gathering, company

[64]**laxō** (1), set free

[65]*L.I. 8 n. 36*

[66]**orbis (-is) lacteus (-ī),** *m.,* the Milky Way (orb), *which Cicero here says is a term received from the Greeks* (ut ā Graīs, *i.e.* Graecīs, acceptistis), *who called it* galaxias kyklos (= lacteus orbis); *cp. our word* galaxy.

[67]**nuncupō** (1) = **appellō**

[68]**habētō,** *future imperative,* you shall consider; consider

[69]*sc.* **esse mortāle**

[70]**tuīs,** to your (friends), *dat. depending on* **dēclārat**

[71]**dēclārō** (1) = *Eng.*

[72]**digitus, -ī,** finger (*cp.* **digit**)

[73]*L.A. 7 n. 1*

[74]**sciō** *another future imperative,* you shall know; know

[75]*conj.,* since

[76]**vigeō -ēe, viguī** be strong, be active

[77]**meminī meminisse,** *defective found only in perf. system,* remember

[78]**prō-videō**, see ahead, foresee
[79]**regō, -ere, rēxī, rēctum**, rule
[80]**moderor, -ārī, -ātus sum**, control
[81]*Why dat? (Ch. 35 p. 170)*
[82]**prae-pōnō**, put in charge of
[83]*as*
[84]**prīnceps, -cipis**, *here an adj.*, chief, foremost
[85]*From the preceding clause supply* **regit**, *etc. as verbs.*

10

[1]*If death is such a great evil, how can the following attitudes be explained?*
[2]**quid**, *as adv.*, why? (= **cūr**?)
[3]**prīnceps, -cipis**, *m.*, chief (*cp. L.I. 9 n. 84*)
[4]**nōminō** (1), name, mention (*cp.* **nōmen**)
[5]**legiō, -ōnis**, *f.*, legion
[6]**Catō, -ōnis**, *m.*, Cato, *the famous censor, who wrote a now-lost history of Rome called the Origines.*
[7]**alacer, -cris, -cre**, eager, happy. *We should use an adverb instead of a predicate adj.*: eagerly
[8]**profectās (esse); reditūrās (esse)**
[9]**Lacedaemoniī, -ōrum**, *m.*, Spartans
[10]**Thermopylae, -ārum**; *480 B.C. Leonidas the leader*
[11]**occīdō, -ere, occīdī, occāsum**, fall, perish; *to be carefully distinguished from* **occīdō** (long-ī-), cut down, kill
[12]*on whom Simonides (wrote); Simonides a sixth-century Greek poet famous especially for his poems and epigrams in the elegiac couplet.*
[13]**hospes, -itis**, *m.*, stranger
[14]**Sparta, -ae**, *f.*, Spartae, *dat. depending on* **dīc**
[15]**tē vīdisse nōs**
[16]*adv.*
[17]= **iacentēs: iaceō, -ēre, iacuī**, lie; *not to be confused with* **iaciō**
[18]**sānctus, -a, -um**, sacred (*cp.* saint)
[19]**ob-sequor** + *dat.*, obey
[20]**commemorō** (1), call to mind mention (*cp.* **memoria**)
[21]What kind of person, then, was the Spartan woman? **quālis, -e**, what kind of
[22]*L.A. 13 n. 42*
[23]**(eum) interfectum (esse)**
[24]*adv.*, for that reason
[25]**gignō -ere, genuī genitum**, beget (*cp.* generate), bear
[26](the kind of person) who
[27]**occumbō -ere, -cubuī -cubitum**, meet
[28]**ad-moneō= moneō**, remind
[29]**humātiō, -ōnis**, *f.* burial (*cp* .humus, earth)
[30]**sepultūra, -ae**, funeral (*cp.* sepulchre)
[31]**dīcendum (esse)**
[32]**exīstimō** (1), think
[33]**Critō, -ōnis**, *m.*, Crito, *a friend of Socrates*
[34]*L.I. 7 n. 33*
[35]**sepeliō, -īre, -īvī, -pultum**, bury
[36]**opera, -ae**, effort, pains
[37]**frūstrā**, *adv.*, in vain (*cp.* frustrate)
[38]**hinc**, *L.I. 8 n. 48*

[39]**ā-volō** (1), *cp.* **ē-volō** *L.I. 9 n. 18;* **avolātūrum (esse)**, *inf. in indirect statement with* **persuāsī**
[40]**meī**, *gen. of* **ego**, *depending on* **quicquam** (**quidquam**, *L.A. 7 n. 7*). *What kind of gen.? (Ch. 40 p. 194)*
[41]**relictūrum (esse)**
[42]*gen. of* **vōs**
[43]*Note* **cum** *with this indicative; v. Ch. 31 n. 1;* **excēdō**, *cp.* **discēdō**
[43a]**cōnsequor, -ī, -secūtus sum**, overtake, catch
[44]*Diogenes, the Cynic philosopher, famed for his asceticism and independence*
[45]**prō-iciō** (**iaciō**), throw out
[46]**inhumātus, -a, -um**, unburied
[47]**volucris, -is**, *f.*, bird
[48]**fera, -ae**, *f.*, wild beast; *dat. with* **prōicī** *understood*
[49]**minimē**, no, not at all
[50]**bacillum, -ī**, staff (*cp.* **bacillus**, *a New Latin form*)
[51]*here* = near
[52]**abigō, -ere, -ēgī, -āctum**, drive away; *sc.* **volucrēs et ferās**. *Why subjunctive? (L.a. 11 n. 15)*
[53]*fut. imperative* = you shall put
[54]**quī**, *adv.*, how?
[55]**laniātus, -ūs**, lacerating
[56]**obsum, -esse, -fuī, -futūrus**, be against, hurt. *Why does oberit have the dative* **mihi**? *(Ch. 35 p. 170)*
[57]**sentientī** *modifies* **mihi** *and has* **nihil** *as its object.*

11

[1]*In the course of a speech defending the citizenship of the poet Archias against the charges of a certain Grattius, Cicero pronounced one of the world's finest encomiums on the inestimable value and delight of literature.*
[2]**tantō opere**, so greatly (*cp.* **magnopere**)
[3]**dēlectō** (1), delight, charm. *The* **homine** *is the poet Archias.*
[3]**aquia**, because
[4]**suppeditō** (1), supply
[5]the means by which
[6]**forēnsis, -e**, *adj.*, of the forum. *By Cicero's time the Forum was primarily the political and legal center of Rome.*
[7]**strepitus, -ūs**, din
[8]**re-ficiō**, refresh, revive
[9]**auris, -is**, *f.*, ear
[10]**convīcium, -iī**, wrangling
[11]**dēfessus, -a, -um**, exhausted
[12]**conquiēscō, -ere, -quiēvī, -quiētum**, find rest
[13]**reprehendō, -ere, -hendī, -hēnsum**, censure; reprehendat, *deliberative, or dubitative, subjunctive. The deliberative subjunctive is used in questions implying doubt, indignation, or impossibility.* **Quis mē reprehendat**: who is to blame me (I wonder)? *See p. 186. Etymology.*
[14]**iūre** = **cum iūre**, *abl. of manner that has virtually become an adverb:* rightly

[15]**suscēnseō, -ēre, -uī**, be incensed, + *dat.*
[16]**sī** *introduces* **sūmpserō**. *The only real difficulty with this complex clause is the involvement of the* **quantum** *clauses. Although these clauses should be read and understood in the order in which they stand, the following outline may prove a welcome guide.* Quis mē reprehendat...sī ego tantum temporum ad haec studia sūmpserō quantum temporum cēterīs ad suās rēs (fēstōs diēs, voluptātēs, *etc.*) concēditur, quantum temporum aliī tribuunt convīviīs (alveolō, pilae)?
[17]**quantum (temporum)**
[18]**ob-eō**, attend to
[19]**fēstus, -a, -um**, festive
[20]**celebrō** (1), celebrate
[21]**voluptās, -tātis**, *f.*, pleasure
[22]**requiēs, -ētis**, *acc.* **requiētem** *or* **requiem**, rest
[23]**concēdō**, grant, concede
[24]**tribuō, -ere, -uī, -ūtum**, allot
[25st]**empestīvus, -a, -um**, timely; here = early, *beginning in the afternoon so as to be conveniently prolonged.*
[26]**convīvium, -iī**, banquet
[27]**alveolus, -ī**, gaming board
[28]**pila, -ae**, ball (*cp.* pill)
[29]**tantum (temporum)...quantum**, as much...as
[30]**ego-met**, *an emphatic form of* **ego**
[31]**re-colō, -ere, -uī, -cultum**, renew
[32]**sūmō, -ere, sūmpsī, sūmptum**, take
[33]*adv.*, for this reason, therefore
[34]**quoque**, *adv., L.A. 13 n. 9*
[35]**crēscō, -ere, crēvī, crētum**, increase
[36]**ōrātiō, -ōnis**, *f.*, eloquence
[37]**facultās, -tātis**, *f.*, skill. *Combine with* **ōrātiō** *and translate:* this oratorical skill.
[38]**quantuscumque, -acumque, -umcumque**, however great
[39]**dē-sum**, be lacking
[40]**exemplum, -ī**, example; **exemplōrum** *also goes with* **plēnī** *and* **plēnae**.
[41]**vetustās, -tātis**, *f.*, antiquity
[42]**iaceō**, *L.I. 3 n. 8, what kind of condition?*
[43]**tenebrae, -ārum**, darkness
[44]**lūmen, -inis**, *n.*, light
[45]**imāgō, -ginis**, *f.*, portrait, picture
[46]**intueor**, gaze on, contemplate, *L.I. 7 n. 224*
[47]but
[48]**imitor, -ārī, -ātus sum**, imitate
[49]**ex-primō (premō)**, describe, portray
[50]**scrīptor, -ōris**, writer
[51]**administrō** (1), manage
[52]**prō-pōnō**, put forward, set before; **prōpōnēns** *has* **quās** *as direct obj. and* **mihi** *as indirect obj.*
[53]**cōgitātiō, -ōnis**, *f.*, thought; *cp.* **cōgitō**
[54]**excellēns**, *gen.* **-ntis**, superior, remarkable
[55]**cōnfōrmō** (1), mold
[56]**quispiam, quae-, quid-**, someone

[57]**prōdō, -ere, -didī, -ditum**, transmit, reveal
[58]**doctrīna, -ae**, instruction
[59]**efferō, -ferre, extulī, ēlātum**, lift up, extol
[60]**ērudiō** (4), educate, train
[61]**cōnfirmō** (1), assert
[62]**valuisse ad laudem**, to be powerful toward praise = to have led to praise; *inf. in indirect discourse*
[63]**idem ego**, I the same person = I also
[64]maintain
[65]**eximius, -a, -um**, extraordinary
[66]**illustris, -e**, noble, brilliant
[67]**accēdō** *here* = be added
[68]**cōnfōrmātiō, -ōnis**, *f.*, molding, shaping
[69]**nesciō quis, nesciō quid**, *indef. prn., lit.* I know not who/what = some (uncertain) person *or* thing; *the* **nesciō** *remains unchanged in this phrase.*
[70]**praeclārus, -a, -um**, magnificent, splendid
[71]**singulāris, -e**, unique, extraordinary
[72]**exsistō, -ere, exstitī**, arise, appear, exist
[73]**quod sī**, *L. I. 6 n. 117*
[74]**dēlectātiō, -ōnis**, *f.*, delight, enjoyment
[75]**opīnor, -ārī, -ātus sum**, think
[76]**remissiō, -ōnis**, *f.*, relaxation
[77]**liberālis, -e**, liberal, noble
[78]**cēterae (remissiōnēs** or **dēlectātiōnēs)**
[79]*gen. of possession used in predicate = predicate genitive; supply* **omnium** *with each gen.:* the other delights do not belong to all times...
[80]**adulēscentia, -ae**, youth
[81]**oblectō** (1), give pleasure to, delight (= **dēlectō**)
[82]*L.A. 9 n. 13*
[83]**ōrnō** (1), adorn
[84]**adversus, -a, -um**, adverse; **adversīs (rēbus)**
[85]**perfugium, -iī**, refuge
[86]**sōlācium, -iī**, solace, comfort
[87]**praebeō, -ēre, -uī, -itum**, offer, furnish
[88]**impediō** (4), hinder, impede
[89]**forīs**, *adv.*, outdoors, abroad
[90]**pernostō** (1), spend the night
[91]**peregrīnor, -ārī, -ātus sum**, travel abroad
[92]**rūsticor, -ārī, -ātus sum**, go to the country

12
[1]*L. Aemelius Paulus Macedonicus was the father of Scipio Africanus Minor (v. L.I. 9 n. 13). As consul in 168 B.C. he brought the war with Macedonia to a successful conclusion by the defeat of the Macedonian King, Perseus. This explains why, before setting out against Perseus, he interpreted the chance words "Persa periit" as a favorable omen. The Romans believed seriously in the importance of omens.*
[2]*adv.*, a second time
[3]*ind. obj. of* **obtigisset**
[4]*obj. of* **gereret**
[5]**Perseus, -eī; Perse** *abl.*
[6]**ut...gereret**, *noun clause subject of* **obtigisset**

[7]**obtingō, -ere, obtigī,** touch, fall to one's lot
[8]**ut** *here with indicative*
[9]**vesper, -erī,** *m.,* evening (*cp.* vespers)
[10]**fīli (a)** *with the diminutive ending* -ola, *little daughter*
[11]*Tertia, a name meaning* third. *The Romans often used ordinal numerals as names, though commonly without strict regard to the number of children they had; e.g.,* Secundus, Quintus, Sextus, Decimus.
[12]*adv.,* very
[13]**ōsculor, -ārī, -ātus sum,** kiss
[14]**anim-ad-vertō,** turn the mind to, notice, observe
[15]**trīsticulus, -a, -um,** rather sad, *diminutive of* **tristis**
[16]What is it? What is the matter?
[17]**quid = cūr**
[18]*L.A. 29 n. 5*
[19]**mī,** *voc. of* **meus,** *Ch. 3*
[20]**Persa,** *the name of her pet*
[21]*adv.,* closely
[22]**complector, -ī, -plexus sum,** embrace
[23]**ōmen, īnis,** *n.* omen, sign; *i.e., the omen of his victory over Perseus*
[24]**catellus, -ī,** puppy

13

[1]**fīnitimus, -a, -um,** neighboring; akin to: **est fīnitinum,** it is akin to
[2]**dissimulātiō, -ōnis,** *f.,* irony
[3]**honestus, -a, -um,** honorable, fine
[4]**vitiōsus, -a, -um,** faulty, bad
[5]**cēnsor, -ōris,** *m.,* censor, *Roman magistrate among whose duties was the assigning of citizens to their proper rank according to their property and service and the removal of names from the census rolls when citizens proved unworthy of citizenship.*
[6]**tribus, -ūs,** *f.,* tribe, *a political division of the Roman people*
[7]**centuriō, -ōnis,** *m.,* centurion
[8]**pugna, -ae,** battle
[9]**ad-sum,** be present
[10]**castra, -ōrum,** *n. pl.,* camp
[11]**notō** (1), mark, *here with the* **nota cēnsōria** *placed opposite a citizen's name to indicate his removal from the citizen list in disgrace.*
[12]**dīligēns,** gen. **-ntis,** diligent, conscientious

14

[1]**pompa, -ae,** parade
[2]**vīs** here = quantity (*cp.* **cōpia**)
[3]*L.A. 7 n. 15*
[4]**argentum, -ī,** silver
[5]*L.I. 6 n. 83*
[6]**Xenocratēs, -is,** *pupil of Plato and later head of the Academy*
[7]*L.I. 7 n. 56*
[8]**Alexander, -drī**
[9]*indecl. adj.,* fifty
[10]**talentum, -ī,** a talent, a large sum of money
[11]**ad-ferō**

[12]*adv.,* especially
[13]**ab-dūcō**
[14]**Acadēmīa, -ae,** *f.,* the Academy, *a gymnasium in a grove just outside of Athens. Here Plato established his school, which might be called the first European university.*
[15]**ap-pōnō,** place near, serve
[16]**apparātus, -ūs,** equipment, splendor
[17]*adv.,* on the next day
[18]**numerō** (1), count, pay out; *sc.* **pecūniam** *as subject of* **numerārī**
[19]**hesternus, -a, -um,** of yesterday
[20]**cēnula, -ae,** diminutive of **cēna**
[21]**egeō, -ēre, eguī,** need, *with abl.; cp.* **careō** + *abl.,* Ch. 20, p. 94
[22]**trīstis, -e,** *L.A. 29 n. 5*
[23]*indecl. adj.,* thirty
[24]**mina, -ae,** a Greek coin = $16.00(?)
[25]**aspernor, -ārī, -ātus sum,** spurn, despise
[26]**liberālitās, -tātis,** *f.,* generosity
[27]*L.A. 5 n. 7*
[28]*L.I. 10 n. 44*
[29]*adv.,* freely, boldly
[30]as a Cynic, being a Cynic
[31]**opus** (*indecl.*) **est,** is necessary: if he needed anything
[32]*adv.* a little
[33]*i.e.,* you are blocking my sunlight
[34]**officiō, -ere, -fēcī, -fectum** + *dat.,* be in the way, obstruct
[35]**vidē-licet,** *adv.* (you may see), clearly, evidently
[36]**aprīcor, -ārī, -ātus sum,** sun oneself

15

[1]*Darius III, defeated by Alexander the Great in 331* B.C. *The spelling* **Dārīus** *reflects later Greek pronunciation.*
[2]**fuga, -ae,** flight
[3]**turbidus, -a, -um,** turbid, roiled
[4]**cadāver, -eris,** *n.,* corpse (*cp.* cadaverous)
[5]**inquinātus, -a, -um,** polluted
[6]**bibō, -ere, bibī,** drink
[7]*adv.,* pleasantly
[8]*L.I. 14 n. 35*
[9]**sitiō** (4), be thirsty
[10]**ēsuriō** (4), be hungry
[11]*Which Egyptian king of this name is unknown?*
[12]**edō, -ere, ēdī, esum,** eat (*cp.* edible)
[13]**per-agrō** (1), wander through
[14]**Aegyptus, -ī,** *f.,* Egypt
[15]**comes, -itis,** *m.,* companion
[16]**cōn-sequor**
[17]**cibārius...pānis,** ordinary (coarse) bread; **pānis, -is,** *m.*
[18]**casa, -ae,** cottage, hut
[19]*Note that this ablative depends on a comparative.. p.282*
[20]**ferō** *here* = report, say
[21]*L.I. 8 n. 2*

[22]*L.I. 12 n. 9*

[23]**contentē**, strenuously, *adv. from* **contendō**, struggle

[24]**ambulō** (1), walk

[25]it had been asked of him, he had been asked

[26]**quō**, *regularly used instead of* **ut** *to introduce a purpose containing a comparative*

[27]**cēnō** (1), dine

[28]**obsōnō** (1), buy provisions, *here* = provide (an appetite)

[29]**famēs, -is,** *f.,* hunger

[30]**vīctus, -ūs,** living, mode of living, food

[31]*L.I. 10 n. 9*

[32]**philitia, -ōrum,** *n.,* public meals *(for Spartan citizens of military age)*

[33]**nōnne,** *App. p. 361*

[34]**ubi** = among the Lacedamonians

[35]**iūs, iūris,** *n.,* soup

[36]*dat. of purpose, App. p. 358*

[37]**dēlectātum (esse)**

[38]**coquō, -ere, coxī, coctum,** cook *(cp.* concoct)

[39]**mirus, -a, -um,** wonderful, surprising

[40]**condīmentum, -ī,** *n.,* seasoning, condiment

[41]**dē-sum,** be lacking

[42]**vēnātus, -ūs,** *m.,* hunting

[43]**sūdor, -ōris,** *m.,* sweat

[44]**cursus, -ūs,** running

[45]at the Eurotas (**Eurōtās, -ae,** *m., river on which Sparta was located*)

[46]**sitis, -is,** *f.,* thirst

[47]**epulae, -ārum,** *f. pl.,* banquet

[48]**condiō** (4), season, spice

[49]**sūdō** (1), sweat

[50]**ructō** (1), belch

[51]**refertus, -a, -um,** stuffed, crammed, + *abl.*

[52]*adv.,* as if, so to speak

[53]**opīmus, -a, -um,** fertile, fat; **bōs, bovis,** *m.,* ox

[54]**voluptās, -tātis,** *f.,* pleasure

[55]**cōn-sequor,** follow up, gain

[56]**iūncunditās, -tātis,** *f.,* pleasure, charm

[57]*n. 30 above; here* = food

[58]**dēsīderium, -ī,** desire

[59]**satietās, -tātis,** *f.,* abundance, satisfy

16

(For more about Themistocles and Aristides see selections 20 and 21 below.)

[1]*L.I. 15 n. 20*

[2]**Serīphius, -ī,** *inhabitant of Seriphus, a small island in the Aegean Sea.*

[3]**iūrgium, -ī,** quarrel

[4]**splendor, -ōris,** *m.,* distinction, honor

[5]**as-sequor = ad-sequor,** gain, attain

[6]**hercule,** *a mild oath,* by Hercules

[7]**Athēniēnsis, -e,** Athenian

[8]**victōria, -ae** = *Eng.*

[9]**Persae, -ārum,** *m.,* the Persians

[10]**cōntiō, -ōnis,** *f.,* assembly

[11]**salūtāris, -e,** salutary, advantageous; *modifies* **cōnsilium**

[12]**opus est,** it is necessary

[13]**postulō** (1), demand, request

[14]**quīcum, quī** = *old abl. form* + **cum,** with whom

[15]**commūnicō** (1), communicate, share

[16]**huic** = *the last mentioned,* Aristides

[17]**classis, -is,** *f.,* fleet

[18]**sub-dūcō,** beach; *subj. because subord. clause in indirect discourse (App. p. 360). Because of their shallow draft and small size, ancient ships were more often beached than anchored.*

[19]**Gythēum, -ī,** *the port of Sparta*

[20]*adv.,* secretly

[21]**incendō, -ere, -cendī, -cēnsum,** set on fire, burn

[22]**frangō, -ere, -frēgī, -frāctum,** break, crush

[23]**necesse (***indecl. adj.***) est,** it is necessary

[24]**exspectātiō, -ōnis,** *f.,* expectation, *abl. of attendant circumstance*

[25]**per-ūtilis, -e,** very useful, advantageous

[26]*L.I. 13 n. 3*

[27]**auctōre Aristīde,** *abl. abs.*

[28]**repudiō** (1), reject

17

[1]*A homely little letter which serves as an antidote to Cicero's usually lofty concerns.*

[2]**(Marcus) Tullius (Cicerō)**

[3]**salūtem dīcit**

[4]**Terentia, -ae,** wife of Cicero

[5]**Tusculānum, -ī,** *n.,* Tusculan estate (**praedium**) *southeast of Rome in Latium*

[6]**ventūrōs (esse)**

[7]**Nōnae, -ārum,** the Nones *were the seventh day in March, May, July, October; the fifth day in other months.*

[8]*adv.* the day after

[9]**(cūrā) ut,** take care that

[10]**plūrēs,** several people

[11]*adv.,* perhaps

[12]**com-moror, -ārī, -ātus sum,** remain

[13]**lābrum, -ī,** a wash basin or a bath

[14]**balneum, -ī,** bathroom

[15]**(cūrā) ut**

[16]*adv.,* likewise

[17]*L.I. 15 n. 30*

[18]**valētūdō, -inis,** f., health

[19]**necessārius, -a, -um** = *Eng.*

[20]**Kalendīs Octōbribus,** on the Kalends of October = October 1st

[21]*sent from his estate at Venusia, in Apulia. The year is said to be 47* B.C.

18

[1]in 43 B.C.

[2]**adventus, -ūs,** arrival

[3]triumvirī, -ōrum, *m.*, commission of three men, *the second triumvirate composed of Antony, Octavian, and Lepidus*

[4]*L.I. 7 n. 5*

[5]trānsversus, -a, -um, transverse, crosswise

[6]*L.I. 12 n. 9*

[7]Formiānum, -ī, *n.*, estate near Formiae, *which was nearly 100 miles south of Rome on the Appian Way near the sea*

[8]Caiēta, -ae, *f., a sea-coast town not far from Formiae*

[9]as he was going to board ship (cōnscendō, -ere, -scendī, -scēnsum, ascend)

[10]*adv.*, several times

[11]altum, -ī, *n.*, the deep, the sea

[12]prō-vehō, -ere, -vexī, -vectum, carry forward; provectum (having sailed out) *goes with* eum *below*

[13]ventus, -ī, wind

[14]adversus, -a, -um = *Eng.*

[15]re-ferō, -ferre, rettulī, relātum, carry back

[16]iactātiō, -ōnis, *f.*, tossing

[17]taedium, -ī, weariness, disgust

[18]fuga, -ae, flight; fugae *depends on* taedium

[19]regredior, -ī, -gressus sum, go back

[20]villa, -ae = *Eng.*

[21]cōnstat, it is agreed

[22]dīmicō (1), fight (to the finish)

[23]dē-pōnō, put down

[24]lectīca, -ae, litter

[25](eōs) quiētōs, them quiet, *subj. of* patī; *but we say:* them quietly. (quiētus, -a, -um)

[26]sors, sortis, *f.*, lot

[27]inīquus, -a, -um, unfavorable, unjust (in-aequus)

[28]prōmineō, -ēre, -uī, jut out, step forth: (eī) prōminentī, for him stepping forth = as he stepped forth, *dat. of reference or interest, which is far more eloquent than the English version* (Ch. 38 pp. 183-184)

[29]praebeō, -ēre, -buī, -bitum (prae-habeō), hold out, offer

[30]immōtus, -a, -um, unmoved, unflinching

[31]cervīx, -vīcis, *f.*, neck

[32]praecīdō, -ere, -cīdī, cīsum (prae-caedō, cut), cut off — by the soldiers whom Antony had sent to execute Cicero in reprisal for Cicero's "Philippics" denouncing Antony. Such were the horrors of the proscriptions.

[33]*L.A. 13 n. 9*

[34]against

[35]exprobrō (1), reproach, charge: (milites), exprobrantēs (manūs) scrīpsisse aliquid, manūs praecīdērunt

[36]re-ferō; relātum (est)

[37]iussū, *L.I. 6 n. 36*

[38]rōstra, -ōrum, *n.*, speaker's platform, rostra; *here the famous Rostra in the Roman Forum*

[39]positum est

[40]cōnsulāris, -is, *m.*, ex-consul

[41]adversus, *prep. + acc.*, against

[42]quanta...vōx (fuerat), how great no voice had been = greater than any voice had been

[43]admīrātiō, -ōnis, *f.* = *Eng.*

[44]ēloquentia, -ae, *f.*; ēloquentiae. *obj. gen., App. p. 357*

[45]*L.A. 13 n. 34*

[46]attollō, -ere, raise, lift

[47]prae, *prep. + abl.*, because of

[48]lacrima, -ae, tear

[49]intueor, -ērī, -tuitus sum, look at

[50]trucīdō (1), cut to pieces, butcher

[51]membrum, -ī, member (of the body)

[52]*indecl. adj.*, sixty

[53]memorābilis, -e, remarkable, memorable

[54]per-sequor, follow up, set forth

[55]opus est + *abl.* = there is need of (Cicero)

[56]fuerit, *perf. subj. potential subj.*, there would be need of

19

[1]*490 B.C., the first major battle of the Persian wars and one of the most illustrious victories in the apparently unending conflict between democracies and autocracies (despotisms): the relatively few Athenians, practically alone, against the hordes of the Persian autocracy.*

[2]*L.I. 16 n.9*

[3]*Darius I. Persian king 421-486 B.C.*

[4]*Europa, -ae, Europe*

[5]trāiciō, -ere, -iēcī, -iectus, transfer

[6]Scythae, -ārum, *m.*, the Schthians, *a nomadic people of southeastern Europe;* Scythīs, *dat. with compound verbs* (Ch. 35 p. 170)

[7]bellum in -ferō (-ferre, -tulī, -lātus), make war upon, + *dat.*

[8]dēcernō, -ere, -crēvī, -crētum, decree, decide

[9]*L.I. 7 n. 86*

[10]Hister, -trī, *m.*, the Danube

[11]flūmen, -minis, *n.*, river

[12]quā, *rel. adv. instead of rel. prn.*, where, by which, *referring to* pontem

[13]trā (= trāns)-dūcō. *Why the subj. in the rel. clause?* (*L.A. 11 n. 15*)

[14]ab-sum, be away, be absent; abesset, *subj. of implied indirect discourse, the thought in his mind being:* "while I shall be away"

[15]as guards, *L.A. 27 n. 14*

[16]prīnceps, -cipis, *m.*, chief

[17]Ionia and Aeolis, *Greek sections of Asia Minor*

[18]singulī, -ae, -a (*plu.*), separate, one each

[19]sē, *acc., subj. of* retentūrum (*esse*)

[20]lingua, -ae, tongue, language

[21]the Greek-speaking peoples, *obj. of* retentūrum

[22]incolō, -ere, -uī, inhabit

[23]retentūrum (esse); re-tineō

[24]oppidum, -ī, town; *occasionally* city

[25]tuenda, (the towns) to be protected = the protection of the towns (tueor, -ērī, tūtus sum, look at, protect)

[26]future more vivid condition in indirect statement: eōs retinēbō sī amīcīs oppida trādiderō.

[27]hōc modifies numerō. Note carefully that a characteristic of Nepos' style is the fondness for separating modifiers from the words which they modify. Be sure to match up such separated words accurately according to the canons of agreement.

[28]Miltiadēs, -is, m., Miltiades, Athenian general, hero of Marathon, who many years before the Battle of Marathon had been sent by the Athenians to rule over the Thracian Chersonesus, a peninsula west of the Hellespont.

[29]crēber, -bra, -brum, numerous; nūntius, -iī, messenger

[30]ad-ferō, report

[31]Fortūna is here regarded as a person (deity). Why is ā used?

[32]occāsiō, -ōnis, f., opportunity

[33]dī-mittō, let go, lose

[34]trānsportō (1), transport, take across; trānsportārat = trānsportāverat

[35i]indirect statement depending on the idea of saying in hortātus est of the preceding sentence; direct form: sī Dārēus interierit, Eurōpa erit tūta. inter-eō, perish

[36]tūtus, -a, -um, L.A. 15 n. 25

[37]abl. of specification (App. p. 358), Greek in respect to race or by race

[38]dominātiō, ōnis, f. = Eng.

[39]ef-ficiō, accomplish

[40]still indirect statement

[41]rescindō, -ere, rescidī, rescissum, cut down

[42]vel...vel, either...or

[43]inopia, -ae, need, privation

[44]plērīque, -ōrumque, m., most people, very many (plērusque, -aque, -umque, the greater part, very many)

[45]What does "accede" mean in English?

[46]Histiaeus, -ī, m., tyrant of Miletus in Asia Minor

[47]adv., so, to such a degree

[48]ab-horreō, -ēre, -uī, shrink from, be averse to

[49]cōnfirmō (1), strengthen

[50]L.A. 25 n. 17; subj. of cōnfirmārī

[51]adv., again

[52]dēmigrō (1), depart (cp. migrate)

[53]conjunctive use of relative

[54]amīcus, -a, -um, adj., friendly, favorable

[55]redigō, -ere, -ēgī, -āctum, reduce

[56]L.A. 9 n. 4

[57]L.I. 16 n. 17

[58]quīngentī, -ae, -a, 500

[59]comparāvit here = strong form of parāvit

[60]eī (= classī), dat. with compounds

[61]prae-ficiō, + dat., put in charge or command of

[62]Dātis, -tidis, acc. —Datim, Datis, a general; Artaphernēs, -is, Artaphernes, nephew of Darius

[63]ducentī, -ae, -a, 200

[64]pedes, -itis, m., foot-soldier

[65]eques, equitis, m., horseman

[66i]interserō, -ere, allege

[67]L.I. 16 n. 7

[68]Iōnēs, -um, m., the Ionians, A Greek people inhabiting the central western coast of Asia Minor; -ēs, Greek ending

[69]Sardēs, -ium, acc. Sardis, Sardis, capital of the Persian province of Lydia in western Asia Minor

[70]expugnō (1), take by storm

[71]sua, refers to Sardis

[72]L.I. 6 n. 13

[73]praefectus, -ī, commander, deputy

[74]rēgius, -a, -um, royal

[75]Euboea, -ae, Euboea, a large island off the eastern shore of central Greece

[76]appellō, -ere, -pulī, -pulsum, drive, bring to land

[77]Eretria, -ae, Eretria, a city of the western central coast of Euboea

[78]ab-ripiō = ēripiō; abreptōs...misērunt, they carried away and sent to

[79]inde, adv., from that place

[80]Attica, -ae, Attica, district in central Greece of which the capital was Athens (somewhat unusually called an oppidum in the next sentence; v. n. 25 above.)

[81]campus, -ī, field, plain

[82]Marathōn, -ōnis, acc. -ōna, f., Marathon

[83]adv., about

[84]passus, -ūs, pace (ca. 5'); mīlia passuum, thousands of paces = miles

[85]tumultus, -ūs, disturbance, uprising

[86]propinquus, -a, -um, near, neighboring

[87]per-moveō, move thoroughly, trouble

[88]adv., nowhere

[89]Phīdippus, -ī, m., Phidippus, an Athenian courier (cursor, -ōris, m., runner)

[90]hēmerodromus, -ī, m. (-dromoe, Gk. nom. plu.), day runner (Gk. word), professional runner. Herodotus says that Phidippus (or Phidippides) covered the 140 miles between Athens and Sparta in two days. Quī agrees with hēmerodromoe rather than generis since a rel. prn. agrees with a pred. noun rather than with the antecedent.

[91]Lacedaemōn, -onis, f., Lacedaemon, Sparta

[92]opus est + abl. (of means), there is need of, an impersonal construction in which opus remains indeclinable; opus esse, inf. in ind. statement with auxiliō in abl.

[93]creō (1), create, elect; creant, historical present (L.A. 14 n. 7)

[94]praetor, -ōris, called stratēgoi, generals, by the Athenians

[95]prae-sum + *dat.*, be in charge of; *why subj.? (L.A. 11 n. 15)*

[96]contentiō, -ōnis, *f.*, controversy

[97]utrum...an, *L.A. 15 n. 11*

[98]moenia, -ium, *n. pl.*, walls (of a city or a camp)

[99]obviam (*adv.*) īre + *dat.*, go to meet

[100]aciēs, -ēī, *f.*, line of battle

[101]decernō, -ere, -crēvī, -crētum, decide

[102]*alone, i.e., of the ten generals*

[103]nītor, nīsī, nīxus sum, strive labor

[104]castra, *L.I. 6 n. 62;* that a camp should be made = to take the field

[105]*dat.; why? (App. p. 358)*

[106]praeter, *prep.* + *acc.*, beyond except

[107]Plataeēnsēs, -ium, *m.*, the men of Plataea, *a city in Boeotia just over the border from Attica*

[108]mille here = *a noun with gen. of whole* mīlitum. *This is regular with* mīlia *but uncommon with* mīlle *(Ch. 40, p. 193)*

[109]adventus, -ūs, approach

[110]armātī, -ōrum, armed men

[111]compleō, -ēre, -plēvī, -plētum, fill out, complete

[112]mīrābilis, -e, wonderful, extraordinary; *modifies* cupiditāte

[113]flagrō (1), burn, be excited

[114]*L.A. 5 n. 11*

[115]because of which = and because of this

[116]it was made that = it happened that

[117]collēga, -ae, *m.*, colleague

[118]piūs...valēret, he had power more than = he had more power or influence than, he prevailed over, valēret, *why subj.? Result.*

[119]*L.A. 25 n. 15*

[120]*L.I. 6 n. 44*

[121]impellō, -ere, -pulī, -pulsum, impel

[122]locō, *place where, no prep. necessary with* locō

[123]idoneus, -a, -um, suitable

[124]dein - deinde

[125]posterus, -a, -um, next following

[126]rādīx, -īcis, *f.*, root, base; mōns, montis, *m.*, mountain

[127]regiō, -ōnis, *f.*, region

[128]instruō, -ere, -strūxī, -strūctum, draw up (battle line)

[129]*interlocked word order:* aciē īnstrūcta (in) regiōne nōn apertissimā; apertus, -a, -um, open

[130]namque, *conj.*, more emphatic form of nam

[131]*L.A. 11 n. 13*

[132]rārus, -a, -um, scattered: there were scattered trees...

[133]proelium, *L.A. 13 n. 42;* proelium committere, join battle

[134]altitūdō, -inis, *f.*, height

[135]tegō, -ere, tēxī, tēctum, cover, protect

[136]tractus, -ūs, dragging

[137]equitātus, -ūs, cavalry

[138]impediō (4), hinder, impede

[139]multitūdō-inis, *f.*, large number

[140]claudō *L.A. 25 n. 11; here* enclose, surround

[141]locum (esse) nōn aequum suīs

[142]frētus, -a, -um, + *abl.*, relying on

[143]cōnflīgō, -ere, -flīxī, -flīctum, fight (*cp.* conflict)

[144]eō, *adv.*, on that account

[145]priusquam *and* antequam, before, + *indicative denote an actual fact;* + *subjunctive denote anticipation as here:* before they could come

[146]*dat.*

[147]dīmicō, *L.I. 18 n. 22*

[148]ūtilis, -e, useful, advantageous

[149]prō-dūcō

[150]in quō (proeliō)

[151]*abl. of degree of difference (App. p. 359)*

[152]they were strong by so much more (strength) in respect to courage = they were so much more powerful in the matter of courage

[153]decemplex, *gen.* -plicis, *adj.*, tenfold

[154]prōflīgō (1), overthrow; prōflīgārint = gāverint. *Why subj.?*

[155]*abl. of comparison (App. p. 359)*

[156]ad-hūc, *adv.*, thus far, hitherto

[157]existō, -ere, existitī, arise, exist, be

[158]nōbilis, -e, famous

[159]exiguus, -a, -um, small, scanty. "Never did so many owe so much to so few."

[160]prōsternō, -ere, -strāvī, -strātum, overthrow, throw down

20

[1]*480 B.C. The Battle of Salamis was the naval counterpart of Marathon except that this time Athens had the help of Sparta.*

[2]Themistoclēs, -is, *or* -ī, Themistocles, *a talented Athenian.*

[3]Corcȳraeus, -a, -um, Corcyraen; *Corcyra, a large island off the northwest coast of Greece. Actually Nepos is in error about Themistocles' command in the Corcyraean affair but he is correct about the tremendous importance of Themistocles' big-navy policy.*

[4]*L.I. 19 n. 94*

[5]praesēns, *gen.* -ntis, *adj.*, present

[6]reliquus, -a, -um, remaining, rest of

[7]ferōx, *gen.* -ōcis, *adj.*, fierce, bold, confident

[8]reddō here = render

[9]metallum, -ī, a mine, *silver mines at Laurium in Attica south of Athens*

[10]largītiō, -ōnis, *f.*, generosity, liberality

[11]magistrātus, -ūs, civil office; civil officer, magistrate

[12]*adv.*, annually

[13]inter-eō, be lost, perish (*cp.* pereō): interīret, *subjunctive introduced by* cum; the subject is pecūnia.

[14]*L.I. 16 n. 17*

[15]aedificō (1), build (*cp.* edifice)

[16]quā (classe)

[17]efficiō, *L.I. 19 n. 39*

[18]frangō, -ere, frēgī frāctum, break, overcome

[19]maritimus (-a, -um = *Eng.; cp.* mare) praedō (-ōnis, *m.,* robber) = pirate; *obj. of* cōnsectandō

[20]cōnsector, -āris, -ātus sum, pursue, hound (*cp.* cōnsequor)

[21]tūtus, *L.A. 15 n. 25*

[22]in (doing) which

[23]perītus, -a, -um, + *gen.,* skilled in; *pred. acc.* (Ch. 14 n. 6)

[24]nāvālis, -e, *adj.; cp.* nāvis

[25]quantae salūtī, *dat. of purpose with a dat. of reference,* Graeciae (*App. p. 358*)

[26]*Why subj.?*

[27]ūniversus, -a, -um, entire, whole, as a whole

[28]Persicus, -a, -um, Persian; *the Second Persian War*

[29]Xerxēs, -is or -ī, *m.,* Xerxes, *son of Darius and king of the Persians, 485-465* B.C.

[30]mari et terrā (*or* terrā marīque) *abl. of place where, without a prep., regular in this formula*

[31]invādō, -ere, -vāsī, -vāsum, move against, invade

[32]*L.A. 7 n. 7*

[33]nāvium longārum, of 1,200 men-of-war, *gen. of description* (*App. p. 357*); his fleet was of 1,200 ships = his fleet consisted of...

[34]onerāria, -ae (nāvis), transport

[35]terrestris exercitus, land army

[36]septingentī, -ae, -a, seven hundred

[37]*L.I. 19 n. 64*

[38]*L.I. 19 n. 65*

[39]quadringentī, -ae, -a, four hundred

[40]*Though the subject,* exercitus, *is singular,* fuērunt *is plural according to the idea of plurality which precedes it.*

[41]adventus, -ūs, approach, arrival

[42]per-ferō

[43]*L.I. 13 n. 8*

[44]*acc. of place to which. At Delphi was the famous oracle of Apollo.*

[45]*accusative case of the supine of* cōnsulō *used to express purpose* = to consult

[46]quisnam, quidnam, who *or* what in the world

[47]*both indirect question and deliberative subjunctive; v. L.I. 11 n. 13*

[48]dēlīberō (1), deliberate; (eīs) dēlīberantibus, *dat.*

[49]Pȳthia, -ae, the Pythian priestess, *who gave the response of Apollo*

[50]ut = *indirect command:* that they should; *not indirect statement*

[51]*L.I. 6 n. 70*

[52]ligneus, -a, -um, wooden

[53]mūniō (4), fortify, defend

[54]respōnsum, -ī, *n., the noun of* respondeō, *subject of* valēret

[55]quō (*adv.*) valēret, *lit.* in what direction this was strong or valid = in what way this applied *or* what this meant

[56]esse. *The inf. shows that this is indirect statement with* persuādeō *and not the more common indirect command introduced by* ut: he persuaded (them) that it was the advice of Apollo that they should betake...

[57]sua, their things = their possessions

[58]eum mūrum ligneum, that wooden wall (= the ships)

[59]significō (1), signify, mean; significārī, *indirect statement depending on a verb of saying understood*

[60]tālis, -e, such

[61]probō (1), approve

[62]ad-dō, -dere, -didī, -ditum, add

[63]totidem, *indecl. adj.,* just as many

[64]trirēmis, -e, having three banks of oars

[65]partim, *adv.,* partly

[66]Salamīs, -īnis, *acc.* Salamīna, *f.,* Salamis, *island on west coast of Attica; acc. of place to which (islands as well as cities and towns)*

[67]Troezēn, -ēnis, *f.,* Troezēna = *Gk. acc. form,* Troezen, *southeastern part of Argolis, across the Saronic Gulf from Athens.*

[68]dēportō (1), carry off

[69]arx, arcis, *f.,* citadel, acropolis (*of the city of Athens, which at the end of the sentence is again referred to as* oppidum; *v. L.I. 19 n. 24 and 80.*)

[70]sacerdōs, -dōtis, *m.,* priest

[71]maiōrēs nātū, those greater in respect to birth = old men, elders

[72]sacer, sacra, sacrum, sacred; sacra, *n. plu.* sacred vessels, *or* rites

[73]prōcūrō (1), take care of

[74]*i.e.,* Themistocles'

[75]plērīsque cīvitātibus, *i.e., the allies of the Athenians; dat. with* displicēbat (*Ch. 35 p. 169*); plērīsque, *L.I. 19 n. 44*

[76]dis-placeō

[77]*L.I. 18 n. 22;* dīmicārī, *impers. pass., lit.* that it be fought, *but translate* that the war be fought. *The infinitive* dīmicārī *is subject of* placēbat.

[78]dēlēctus, -a, -um, chosen, picked; chosen men

[79]Leōnidās, -ae, *m.,* Leonidas

[80]Thermopylae, -ārum, *f.,* Thermopylae, *a mountain pass near the southern border of Thessaly*

[81]occupō (1), seize

[82]barbarus, -a, -um, foreign, uncivilized, barbarian (*commonly applied by a kind of ethnocentrism to those not of the Greek and Roman civilization*)

[83]sustineō, -ēre, -tinuī, -tentum, sustain; *the subject is* iī (= eī)

[84]*See appendix under Numerals (cardinals 200 and 300);* ducentae (nāvēs)

[85]*predicate gen. of possession:* were of the Athenians = belonged to the Athenians

[86]apud Artemīsium, near Artemisium, *promontory at northern tip of Euboea*

[87]continēns terra, continentis terrae, the mainland

[88]classiārius, -iī, a marine (*lit.* a soldier of the fleet)

[89]**rēgius, -a, -um,** royal
[90]*L.I. 19 n. 143*
[91]**angustiae, -ārum,** *f. plu.,* narrow place
[92]**multitūdō, -inis,** *f.,* large number, multitude
[93]**circum-eō,** surround
[94]*L.I. 8 n. 48*
[95]**proelium,** *L.A. 13 n. 42;* **parī proeliō,** the battle was a draw
[96]**nē** = lest, *similar to the construction after verbs of fearing.* (App. p. 282)
[97]**adversārius, -a, -um,** hostile; **adversārius, -iī,** *m.,* opponent, enemy
[98]*a future more vivid condition in a* **nē-** *clause. The original thought was* **sī pars superāverit,...** **premēmur;** *the future perfect indicative* **superāverit** *becomes pluperfect subjunctive* **superāsset.**
[99]**anceps,** *gen.* **ancipitis,** *adj.,* two-headed, double
[100]**quō = quārē**
[101]*result clause, subject of* **factum est:** wherefore it was made that = the result was that
[102]**exadversum,** *prep. + acc.,* opposite
[103]**cōnstituō, -ere, -stituī, -stitūtum,** draw up, establish
[104]**expugnō,** *L.I. 19 n. 70*
[105]*adv.,* immediately
[106]**astū,** *n. indecl.,* the city (= Athens), *obj. of* **accessit**
[107]**incendium, -iī,** burning, fire. *The marks of this fire can still be seen on some of the marble pieces later built into the wall of the Acropolis.*
[108]**per-terreō**
[109]*place to which without a preposition as in the singular* **domum**
[110]**resistō, -ere, restitī,** make a stand, resist
[111]all together (united) they could be equal (to the Persians)
[112]*imperf. of* **ait**
[113]**di-spergō, -ere, -spersī, -spersus,** scatter
[114]**testor, -ārī, -ātus, sum,** testify, declare
[115]**Eurybiadēs, -is,** *m.,* Eurybiades; **Eurybiadī** *depends on* **adfirmābat.**
[116]**summa, -ae,** highest place
[117]**summae imperiī** *(gen. of whole)* **praeerat,** he was in charge of the highest part of the command = he was commander-in-chief
[118]*Subject of* **fore** (= **futūrum esse**) *is* **id.**
[119]**adfirmō** (1), assert, declare
[120]*adv.,* at night
[121](illum) **dē servīs suīs,** that one of his slaves
[122]consider
[123]in his (Themistocles') own words, *i.e.,* in his own name
[124]**adversāriōs** (= **hostēs**) **eius** (= **rēgis**)
[125]**fuga, -ae,** flight
[126]**quī = et eī**
[127]**sī discessissent...** (eum) **bellum cōnfectūrum** (esse), *another future more vivid condition in indirect statement:* **sī discesserint** *(fut. perf.),* **tū bellum**

cōnficiēs...; cōnficiō, -ere, -fēcī, -fectum, finish, accomplish
[128]one at a time
[129]**aggredior, -gredī, -gressus sum,** attack
[130]**dolus, -ī,** deceit, trick. *What kind of gen. is* **dolī**? (*Ch. 40 p. 194*)
[131]**sub-sum,** be under, be concealed
[132]*L.I. 17 n. 8*
[133]**aliēnus, -a, -um,** foreign, unfavorable
[134]*adv.,* on the contrary
[135]**opportūnus, -a, -um,** advantageous, *referring to* **locō**
[136]*L.I. 19 n. 47*
[137]*L.A. 4 n. 12*
[138]*abl. of place where without a preposition*
[139]*L.I. 19 n. 143*
[140]**explicō** (1), spread out, deploy
[141]*The perfect subjunctive is not uncommon in result clauses in historical sequence* (*Ch. 30 n. 8*)
[142]**prūdentia, -ae,** foresight, discretion
[143]**succumbō, -ere, -cubuī,** submit, succumb
[144]**comparō** (1), compare
[145]**Marathōniō tropaeō,** trophy or victory at Marathon
[146]**dē-vincō,** conquer completely

21

[1]**Aristīdēs, -is,** *m.,* Aristides, *Athenian statesman and general*
[2]**Lȳsimachus, -ī,** Lysimachus
[3]**aequālis, -is,** *m.,* an equal in age, a contemporary
[4]*L.I. 7 n. 102*
[5]**Themistoclī,** here gen. of possession; *v. L.I. 20 n. 2*
[6]**principātus, -ūs,** first place, leadership
[7]*L.A. 5 n. 12*
[8]*abl. of degree of difference* (*App. p. 359*) *depending on the idea of comparison in* **antistāret:** how much
[9]**anti-stō, -āre, -stetī,** stand before = excel
[10]*L.I. 18 n. 44; Themistocles was eloquent.*
[11]**innocentia, -ae,** harmlessness; integrity. *Why dative?* (*Ch. 35 p. 170*)
[12]*L.I. 19 n. 47*
[13]**excellō, -ere, -uī, -celsum,** excel; **excellēbat:** *note that* **quamquam** (although) *is used with the indicative.*
[14]**abstinentia, -ae,** self-restraint, *especially in matters involving public funds,* uprightness (*cp.* **innocentia** *in n. 11*); **abstinentiā,** *abl. of specification* (*App. p. 359*)
[15]**ūnus = sōlus**
[16]**cognōmen, -minis,** *n.,* here = epithet, apellative. *Of the three regular Roman names* (**praenōmen, nōmen, cognōmen**) *the* **cognōmen** (*cp.* **cognōscō**) *seems to have originated as a kind of nickname.*
[17]**collabefiō, fierī, -factus sum,** be overthrown, be ruined
[18]**testula, -ae,** (little potsherd), ostracism; **testulā** *abl. of accordance* (*Ch. 34 n. 6*) *or perhaps means. Look*

*up the interesting history of ostracism, a political
safety valve against tyranny.*

[19]**ille,** *in the unusual position of following its noun* = that
famous

[20]**exsiliō,** *abl. of penalty* (= *a form of abl. of means*)

[21]**decem annōrum,** *gen. of description* (*App. p. 357*)

[22]**multō** (1), punish

[23]**re-primō, -ere, -pressī, -pressum,** press back, check

[24]**concitō** (1), arouse, excite

[25]*L.I. 20 n. 92*

[26]**animadvertō, -ere, -ī, -versus,** notice

[27]*indirect command:* writing that he should be driven out

[28]**eō,** *i.e., the* **quendam** *above*

[29](what he had committed) that

[30]**poenā dignus,** *L.A. 11 n. 20*

[31]**ignōrō** (1), not know, be unacquainted with

[32]**sibi nōn placēre** (impersonal), it was not pleasing to
him = he was displeased (because...)

[33]**labōrō** (1), labor, work

[34]**praeter,** *prep.* + *acc.,* beyond

[35]**lēgitimus, -a, -um,** fixed by law, legal

[36]**postquam,** *conj.* + *perf. ind.,* after

[37]**dēscendō, -ere, -scendī, -scēnsum,** descend, march on

[38]**quam** = **postquam; post** *sometimes omitted after an
ordinal number in the ablative of time construction*

[39]**scītum, -ī,** decree (*cp.* plebiscite)

[40]**restituō, -ere, -stituī, -stitūtum,** restore

[41]**inter-sum** + *dat.,* be present at, take part in

[42]*L.I. 13 n. 8*

[43]**nāvālis, -e,** *adj. of* **nāvis**

[44]**priusquam** + *subj., L.I. 19 n. 145*

[45]the same man = he also

[46]*L.I. 19 n. 94*

[47]**Plataeae, -ārum,** Plataea; *v. L.I. 19 n. 107*

[48]*L.A. 13 n. 42*

[49]**fundō, -ere, fūdī, fūsum,** pour out, rout

[50]**Mardonius, -iī,** Mardonius, *Persian general under
Xerxes in command of the "barbarians"*

[51]**aequitās, -tātis,** *f.,* equity, fairness; **aequitāte,** *abl. of
cause* (*App. p. 359*)

[52]**factum est...ut summa imperiī trānsferrētur,** *it hap-
pend that the chief command was transferred;* **ut...
trānsferrētur,** *noun clause of result used as subject
of* **factum est;** *cp L.A. 13n. 30*

[53]*L.I. 16 n. 17*

[54]*adv.,* at the same time

[55]**Pausaniās, -ae,** *m.,* Pausanias, *a Spartan, victor over
the Persians at Plataea in 479 B.C. but a person
whose selfish ambition was too great to permit his
continuing long as commander-in-chief of the
united Greek forces.*

[56]*abl. abs.*

[57]**fugō** (1), put to flight, rout; *not to be confused with*
fugiō

[58]*L.I. 20 n. 117*

[59]**maritimus, -a, -um,** *adj. of* **mare**

[60]**trāns-ferō,** *L.A. 9 n. 22*

[61]*L.I. 19 n. 130*

[62]**et...et**

[63]**intemperantia, -ae,** intemperance, arrogance

[64]**iūstitia, -ae,** *noun of* **iūstus**

[65]**societās, -tātis,** *f.,* confederacy, alliance

[66]**applicō** (1), attach

[67]**hōs ducēs,** these (= the Athenians) as leaders (*pred.
acc., Ch. 14 n. 6*)

[68]**dēligō, -ere, dēlēgī, dēlēctum** = **legō**

[69]= **barbarōs**

[70]*L.I. 15 n. 26*

[71]**re-pellō**

[72]*adv.,* by chance

[73]*If* novus *is new, what must the verb* **re-novō** (1) mean?

[74]*L.I. 20 n. 15*

[75]**comparō** = **parō.** *Both gerundive phrases belong in
the* **quantum** *clause.*

[76]*What kind of gen.?* (*Ch. 40 p. 194*)

[77]**quaeque cīvitās: quaeque,** *fem. adjectival form of*
quisque

[78]**cōnstituō, -ere, -stituī, -stitūtum,** establish, decide;
quī cōnstitueret, *rel. cl. of purpose, which has as
its object the* **quantum...daret** *clause.*

[79]**arbitrium, -ī,** judgment, decision; **arbitriō,** *what kind
of abl.?* (*Ch. 34 n. 6*)

[80]**quadringēna et sexāgēna** (*distributive numerals*)
talenta quotannīs, 460 talents each year

[81]**Dēlos, -ī,** *f.,* Delos, *small island in the center of the
Cyclades in the Aegean*

[82]**aerārium, -iī,** treasury

[83]**posterus, -a, -um,** coming after (post), later

[84]**trāns-ferō,** *L.A. 13 n. 22*

[85]**quā abstinentiā,** *abl. of description* (*App. p. 360*): *of
what integrity he was = how great was his integrity*

[86]*perf. subj., indirect quest. depending on* **indicium**

[87]**indicium, -iī,** indication, proof

[88]the fact that

[89]**prae-sum** + *dat.,* be in charge of

[90]**paupertās, -tātis,** *f.,* poverty

[91]**dē-cēdō,** depart, die (*cp.* the deceased)

[92]**quī** = *old form of abl.:* by which he might be buried =
enough to bury him

[93]*L.A. 13 n. 34*

[94]*adv.,* wherefore

[95]*adv.,* at public expense

[96]**dōs, dōtis,** *f.,* dowry

[97]**collocō** (1), place, settle in marriage

22

[1]*Timoleon, who came from a noble family at Corinth,
was a great champion of liberty against tyranny. By
334 B.C. he was in Sicily fighting the Carthaginians,
expelling tyrants, and establishing democracies.*

[2]**Diōn, Diōnis,** *m.,* Dion, *relative and friend of the
tyrant Dionysius the Elder. With the aid of Plato he
tried — but in vain — to give a noble pattern to the*

*life of Dionysius the Younger, who followed his
father in tyranny. After finally exiling Dionysius the
Younger from Syracuse, he himself ruled tyranically
and was assassinated in 353 B.C.*
[3]**Dionȳsius, -iī,** Dionysius the Younger
[4]*L.I. 19 n. 51*
[5]**potior** + *gen. or abl., L.A. 10 n. 22*
[6]*L.I. 20 n. 97*
[7]**Corinthiī, -ōrum,** *m.,* Corinthians
[8]**quō,** *abl. depending on* **ūterentur** *(Ch. 34 p. 165)*
[9]**postulō** (1), request
[10]*adv.,* to this place, hither
[11]**Timoleōn, -ontis,** *m.,* Timoleon
[12]**incrēdibilis, -e,** incredible
[13]**fēlīcitās, -tātis,** *f.,* happiness, good fortune
[14]*abl. of separation*
[15]**dē-pellō**
[16]**tūtō,** *adv.,* safely
[17]**Corinthus, -ī,** *f.,* Corinth, *on the Isthmus of Corinth*
[18]*L.I. 6 n. 109*
[19]*L.A. 13 n. 29 and 30*
[20]**uterque, utraque, utrumque,** each; here = both
[21]**prae-clārus, -a, -um,** noble, famous
[22]**dūcō** *here* = consider
[23]**clēmentia, -ae,** mercy
[24]**crūdēlitās, -tātis,** *f.,* cruelty
[25]*L.I. 20 n. 127 These words refer not only to the expul-
sion of Dionysius, but also to a great victory over
the Carthaginians in Sicily as recounted in the
omitted passages.*
[26]**diūturnitās, -tātis,** *f.,* long duration
[27]**regiō, -ōnis,** *f.,* region; *here* = country districts
[28]**dēsertus, -a, -um,** deserted
[29]**con-quīrō, -ere, -quīsīvī, -quīsītum (quaerō),** seek
out, gather together
[30]**colōnus, -ī,** settler, colonist
[31]**sua,** *neuter plu.*
[32]*L.I. 21 n. 40*
[33]**novīs (colōnīs)**
[34]**vacuē-faciō,** make empty
[35]**possessiō, -ōnis,** *f.,* possession, property
[36]**dīvididō, -ere, dīvīsī, dīvīsum,** divide, distribute
[37]**moenia,** *L.I. 6 n. 70*
[38]**dis-iciō,** throw apart, scatter
[39]**fānum, -ī,** shrine, temple *(cp. profane, fanatic, fan =
devotee)*
[40]**dē-tegō, -ere, -tēxī, -tēctum,** unroof, uncover *(cp.
detect)*
[41]**re-ficiō**
[42]**red-dō,** *L.A. 25 n. 14*
[43]although he was **tantīs opibus:** *abl. of description*
(App. p. 360)
[44]**invītus, -a, -um,** *L.A. 2 n. 17.* (Siculīs) etiam invītīs,
(the Sicilians) even against their will; *case Ch. 34
p. 165*

[45]**tantum...licēret: cum,** although, *introduces this
clause as well as the preceding one.*
[46]**Siculī, -ōrum,** the Sicilians
[47]**recūsō** (1), make objection, refuse
[48]*L.I. 25 n. 17*
[49]**obtineō, -ēre, -tinuī, -tentum,** occupy, hold
[50]**mālō, mālle, māluī,** prefer; *conjugation App. Irregular Verbs. pp. 372 ff.*
[51]**cum prīmum,** as soon as
[52]**dē-pōnō,** *L.I. 6 n. 54*
[53]**prīvātus, -ī,** private citizen; as a private citizen he...
[54]*L.A. 5 n. 7*
[55]*adv.,* unskilfully, ignorantly
[56]**benevolentia, -ae,** good-will, kindness
[57]**prō-vehō, -ere, -vexī, -vectum,** carry forward
[58]**morbus, -ī,** disease, sickness
[59]**lūmen, -minis,** *n.,* light; sight
[60]**calamitās, -tātis,** *f.,* misfortune
[61]*adv.,* with moderation
[62]**queror,** *L.A. 11 n. 9*
[63]*perf. subj. in historical sequence, Ch. 30 n. 8*
[64]**insolēns, gen. -entis,** *adj.,* arrogant, insolent
[65]**gloriōsus, -a, -um** *here* = boastful
[66]*L.A. 4 n. 14*
[67]**ex-eō**
[68]**praedicō** (1), declare, relate
[69]**aliud quam,** other than
[70]**dīs = deīs**
[71]**re-creō** (1), recreate, restore, revive
[72]*L.I. 21 n. 78*
[73]*adv.,* especially, above all
[74]**nūmen, -minis,** *n.,* divine power, command
[75]*L.A. 13 n. 42*
[76]**nātālis diēs, nātālis diēī,** *m.,* birthday
[77]**quō..ut,** *L.I. 21 n. 52*
[78]**fēstus, -a, -um,** festive
[79]**Dēmaenetus, -ī,** *m.,* Demaenetus, *an enemy of
Timoleon*
[80]**cōntiō, -ōnis,** *f.,* assembly
[81]**rēs gestae, rērum gestārum,** *f. plu.* (*lit.* things done),
exploits, deeds
[82]**dē-trahō,** detract, disparage
[83]**nōnnūlla** (*L.I. 6 n. 93*) *is neut. acc. plu. —* **invehor,
-ī, invectus sum** (*deponent form of* **in-vehō**), + in +
acc., make an attack on, inveigh against: **nōnnūlla
inveherētur** in, he made some attacks on
[84]*adv.,* at last
[85]**damnō** (1) + *gen.,* condemn on the charge of; **vōtī
damnārī,** to be condemned to pay a vow = to have
a vow or prayer granted
[86]**precor, -ārī, -ātus sum,** beseech
[87]*L.I. 21 n. 40 Why subjunctive? (Ch. 36 p. 174).*
[88]*dat. case of* **quī-vīs, quae-vīs, quid-vīs (quod-vīs),**
indef., anyone at all, anything at all
[89]*adv.,* with impunity
[90]**dīcere,** *subject of* **licēret**

[91]ob-eō, meet

[92]pūblicē, *adv. of* pūblicus

[93]gymnasium, -iī, *n.*, gymnasium, *which in Greek had a much broader meaning than it does in English*

[94]Timoleonteum (gymnasium)

[95]celebrō (1), celebrate

[96]sepeliō, -īre, sepelīvī, sepultum, bury

23

METER: Greater Asclepiad.

[1]nē quaesierīs (= quaesīverīs): nē + *perf. subj. = a colloquial prohibition (negative command)*, do not seek

[2]nefās, *n., indecl.*, wrong, sin; nefās (est), it is wrong

[3]quem, *modifies* fīnem

[4]dī = deī

[5]*Why perf. subj. here? (Ch. 30 p. 142)*

[6]Leuconoē, -es, *f.*, Leuconoë, *a Greek name*

[7]temptō (1), try; temptārīs = temptāverīs, *another neg. command*

[8]numerōs, *calculations employed by astrologers in casting horoscopes; "Babylonian" because astrology was associated with the East. With the decay of belief in the old-time religion in Rome during the first century B.C., astrology and superstitions prospered. Apparently Leuconoë had visited a fortune teller.*

[9]ut melius (est), how (much) better it is

[10]*i.e., projected too far into the future*

[11]resecō, -āre, -secuī, -sectum, cut off, prune back; resecēs, *poetic use of the pres. subj. (jussive) for the pres. imperative*

[12]*fut. perf. ind. = will have become past tense before you know it*

[13]invidus, -a, -um, envious

[14]carpō, -ere, carpsī, carptum, pluck, seize

[15]minimum, *adv.* = minimē

[16]crēdulus, -a, -um, believing in, trusting + *dat.*; crēdula, *nom. fem. sing. agreeing with the subj. of carpe, i.e.* Leuconoë

[17]posterō (diēī), *L.I. 19 n. 125*

24

METER: Sapphic stanza.

[1]integer, -gra, -grum, untouched, blameless; (vir) integer vītae *(poetic gen. of specification)*, the person blameless in his life

[2]pūrus, -a, -um, pure, free from; sceleris, *poetic gen. of separation or specification*

[3]egeō, -ēre, eguī, need + *abl. (Ch. 20 p. 94)*

[4]Maurus, -a, -um, Moorish (= Mauritanian); *poets prefer specific words rather than general.*

[5]iaculum, -ī, missile, javelin (*cp.* iaciō)

[6]arcus, -ūs, bow

[7]venēnātus, -a, -um, poisonous, dipped in poison

[8]gravidus, -a, -um, laden (with); *cp.* gravis

[9]sagitta, -ae, arrow (*cp.* sagittate leaf)

[10]Fuscus, -ī, *m.*, Fuscus, *a literary man and a close, sometimes waggish, friend of Horace*

[11]pharetra, -ae, quiver

[12]*L.I. 19 n. 130*

[13]*L.A. 14 n. 34*

[14]lupus, -ī, wolf

[15]Sabīnus, -a, -um, Sabine; *cp. L.A. 15*

[16]cantō (1), sing about; dum + *historical present (L.A. 14 n. 7) to denote continued action in past time: while I was singing about*

[17]Lalagē, -ēs, *acc.* Lalagēn *(Greek noun), f.*, Lalage, *name of a girl — a most mellifluous name!*

[18]ultrā, *prep.* + *acc.*, beyond

[19]terminus, -ī, boundary (*cp.* terminus, term, terminate)

[20]vagor, - arī, -ātus sum, wander, ramble (*cp.* vagary, vagabond)

[21]expediō, -īre, -īvī, -ītum, disentangle, set free; cūrīs expedītīs, *abl. abs.*

[22]*Note the interlocked word order of this stanza, which is so characteristic of Latin poetry:* mē *(obj. of* fūgit) *at the beginning modified by* inermem *at the end;* silvā in Sabīnā, *place where phrase interrupted by* lupus *subj. of* fūgit; *all this separated from the main verb by a double* dum *clause.*

[23]inermis, -e, unarmed; *cp.* integer vitae...nōn eget iaculīs.

[24]piger, -gra, -grum, lazy, sluggish, torpid (*because frozen), modifying* campīs (campus, -ī, field) *in a place-where phrase without a preposition (the omission of a preposition is common in poetry). The order of the thought is:* pōne mē (in) pigrīs campīs ubi...

[25]*L.A. 11 n. 13*

[26]aestīvus, -a, -um, summer (*cp.* aestās)

[27]re-creō (1), *L.I. 22 n. 71*

[28]aura, -ae, breeze

[29]= (or put me) *in* eō latere mundī quod...; latus, -eris, *n.*, side, region

[30]nebula, -ae, mist, fog

[31]malus = inclement, *because Jupiter is here god of the weather*

[32]urgeō, -ēre, ursī, urge, press, oppress

[33]currus, -ūs, chariot

[34]propinquus, -a, -um, neighboring, near. *What zone is this?*

[35]dulce, *poetic for* dulciter. *These exquisitely mellifluous last lines somewhat onomatopoetically suggest the dulcet timbre of Lalage's voice and laugh.*

25

METER: Sapphic stanza.

[1]*adv.*, rightly, well, suitably

[2]Licinī, *voc. of* Licinius, *a person who seems to have been wanting in the virtue of moderation*

[3]*L.I. 18 n. 11*

[4]*L.I. 24 n. 32; i.e.*, heading out to the deep

[5]procella, -ae, storm, gale

[6] **cautus, -a, -um,** cautious, circumspect: while you in your caution

[7] **horrēscō, -ere, horruī,** begin to shudder at, begin to dread

[8] **lītus, -toris,** *n.,* seashore, coast; **altum** *and* **lītus** = *extremes*

[9] **inīquus, -a, -um,** unequal; *here* = treacherous

[10] **aureus, -a, -um,** golden

[11] **quisquis, quidquid,** whoever, whatever

[12] **mediocritās, -tātis,** *f.,* moderation, the mean between extremes. *Note that Horace does not say that "mediocrity" is golden! The idea of* (**aurea**) **mediocritās** *was common in Greek ethical thought, and Aristotle made it a cardinal virtue in his "Ethics."*

[13] **tūtus,** secure (in his philosophy of the "golden mean") he is free from...

[14] **obsolētus, -a, -um,** worn out, dilapidated

[15] **sordēs, -ium,** *f., plu.,* dirt, filth; **sordibus,** *what kind of abl.?* (*Ch. 20 p. 94*)

[16] *L.I. 6 n. 175*

[17] **invideō, -ēre, -vīdī, -vīsum,** envy; **invidendā,** sure to be envied

[18] **sōbrius, -a, -um,** sober-minded, moderate, in his sobriety

[19] **aula, -ae,** palace

[20] *L.I. 18 n. 13*

[21] **agitō** (1), agitate, toss

[22] **ingēns,** *gen.* **-entis,** huge

[23] **pīnus, -ī,** *f.,* pine

[24] **celsus, -a, -um,** high, lofty

[25] **cāsus, -ūs,** fall, destruction

[26] **dēcidō, -ere, -cidī,** fall down (*cp.* **cadō**)

[27] **turris, -is,** *f.,* tower

[28] **feriō** (4), strike

[29] **fulgur, -uris,** *n.,* lightning, thunderbolt

[30] *L.I. 19 n. 126*

[31] anticipate, expect

[32] **īnfestus, -a, -um,** unsafe, dangerous, adverse; **īnfestīs** (**rēbus**) *dative, lit.:* for his adverse circumstances (= in adversity) he anticipates the other (= the opposite) fortune (**sortem**)

[33] **secundus, -a, -um,** (*lit.* following) favorable; **secundīs** (**rēbus**) *balances* **īnfestīs:** for his favorable circumstances (= in prosperity) he apprehends the opposite fortune.

[34] **alter,** *the* other of two; *here* = the opposite

[35] **sors, sortis,** *f.,* lot fortune; **sortem,** *obj. of* **spērat** *and* **metuit**

[36] **prae-parō** (1), make ready in advance, prepare: well prepared (*by the philosophy of life which Horace is here enunciating*)

[37] **pectus, -toris,** *n.,* breast, heart; *subj. of* **spērat** *and* **metuit**

[38] **īnfōrmis, -e,** shapeless, hideous, horrid

[39] **hiems, hiemis,** *f.,* stormy weather, winter

[40] **re-dūcō**

[41] Jupiter *as god of sky and weather*

[42] **īdem,** the same god = he also

[43] **sum-moveō,** remove, drive away, *sc.* **hiemēs**

[44] **nōn,** *modifies* **sīc erit**

[45] **male (est),** it is bad, things are bad

[46] **et ōlim,** also in the future

[47] *adv. here* sometimes

[48] **cithara, -ae,** lyre

[49] **taceō,** *L.I. 3 n. 11*

[50] **suscitō** (1), arouse; **suscitat,** *subj. is* **Apollō**

[51] **Mūsa, -ae,** *f.,* a Muse

[52] *L.I. 24 n. 6*

[53] **tendō, -ere, tetendī, tēnsum,** stretch

[54] **Apollō, -inis,** *m.,* Apollo, *god of the sun, prophecy, poetry, and music; also god of archery, pestilence, and medicine. Apollo has two aspects: happy and constructive* (**Mūsam**); *unhappy and destructive* (**arcum**).

[55] **rēbus angustīs,** *abl. abs.,* when things are narrow (= difficult), *i.e.,* in adversity

[56] **anim-ōsus, -a, -um** (**-ōsus,** *suffix* = full of), spirited

[57] **appāreō, -ēre, -uī, -itum,** show one's self; **appārē,** *analyze the form carefully.*

[58] *adv.,* wisely = if you are wise

[59] *cp. n. 42 above*

[60] **con-trahō,** draw in, shorten

[61] **turgidus, -a, -um,** swollen

[62] **vēlum, -ī,** sail

26

METER: Alcaic stanza.

[1] **eheu,** *cp.* **heu** *L.I. 5 n. 16. This sigh is emphasized by the repetition of Postumus' name.*

[2] **fugāx,** *gen.* **-ācis,** *adj.,* fleeting

[3] **lābor, -ī, lāpsus sum,** slip, glide

[4] **pietās, -tātis,** *f.,* loyalty, devotion, piety

[5] **rūga, -ae,** wrinkle (*cp.* corrugated)

[6] **īnstāns,** *gen.* **-antis,** pressing, urgent

[7] **senecta, -ae** = **senectūs**

[8] **indomitus, -a, -um,** untamable, invincible

[9] *adv.,* in vain. *What is the significance of its emphatic position?*

[10] **cruentus, -a, -um,** bloody

[11] **Mārs, Mārtis,** *m.,* Mars, *god of war*; **Marte,** *what abl.?* (*Ch. 20 p. 94*)

[12] **frangō, -ere, frēgī, frāctum,** break

[13] **raucus, -a, -um,** hoarse

[14] **flūctus, -ūs,** *m.,* wave; **frāctīs flūctibus,** broken waves = breakers

[15] **Hadria, -ae,** *m.,* Adriatic Sea

[16] **autumnus, -ī,** autumn, *unhealthy part of the year because of the Sirocco*

[17] *depends on* **nocentem;** *what case?* (*Ch. 35 p. 169*)

[18] **auster, -trī,** *m.,* the south wind, *the Sirocco blowing from the Sahara*

[19] **vīsō, -ere, vīsī, vīsum,** visit; **vīsendus (est)**

[20]āter, ātra, ātrum, dark, *modifying* Cōcytos

[21]flūmen, *L.I. 19 n. 11;* languidus, -a, -um, sluggish, weak

[22]Cōcytos, -ī, *m.,* Cocytus, the river of wailing, *one of the rivers surrounding Hades;* Cōcytos, *Gk. nom.*

[23]Danaī genus (genus, -eris, *n.), the offspring of* Danaüs, *whose 49 daughters murdered their husbands and in Hades were punished by having to pour water eternally into a sieve*

[24]infāmis, -e, infamous

[25]damnō (10) condemn

[26]Sisyphus, -ī, *m.,* Sisyphus, *who was condemned eternally to roll up a hill a stone which rolled down again — an exquisite nightmare*

[27]Aeolidēs, -ae, *m.,* son of Aeolus

[28]*After verbs of accusing, condemning, and acquitting the genitive can be used to express the charge or the penalty involved; cp. L.I. 6 n. 59-60.*

[29]linquenda (est), *balancing* vīsendus *in contrast;* linquō = relinquō

[30]tellūs, -ūris, *f.,* earth, land

[31]uxor, -ōris, *f.,* wife

[32]hārum arborum; *L.A. 11 n. 13*

[33]colō, -ere, -uī, cultum, cultivate

[34]praeter, *prep. + acc.,* beyond, except

[35]invīsus, -a, -um, hated, hateful; invīsās, *agreeing with* cupressōs

[36]cupressus, -ī, *f.,* cypress (tree); invīsās cupressōs, invīsās *simply because they were used at funerals and were planted near tombs*

[37]neque ūlla hārum arborum, nor any = and none

[38]brevem dominum, *in appos. with* tē; brevem, *implying that life is brief*

27

METER: Sapphic stanza.

[1]vīvitur parvō bene (ab eō) cuī, it is lived on little well by him for whom: vīvitur, *impersonal passive* = he lives well on little (*i.e.,* not in abject poverty and not in the lap of luxury).

[2]cuī, *dat. of reference but most easily translated by* whose

[3]paternum salīnum (salīnum, -ī), paternal salt-cellar; *the long list of words derived from* sāl *provides some idea of the importance of salt and the salt-cellar.*

[4]splendeō, -ēre, shine

[5]mēnsa, -ae, table

[6]tenuis, -e, plain, simple

[7]levis, -e, *here* = gentle

[8]*L. A. 15 n. 4*

[9]sordidus, -a, -um, sordid (*cp.* sordēs *L.I. 25 n. 15*); cupīdō *is masculine in Horace.*

[10]auferō (ab-ferō), *L.I. 4 n. 28*

[11]*L.I. 12 n. 17*

[12]fortēs (virī) brevī aevō (aevum, -ī, time, life); *state case and syntax of* brevī aevō (*App. p. 360*)

[13]iaculor, -ārī, -ātus sum, aim at

[14]Quid...mūtāmus, *lit.* why do we exchange lands warmed by another sun? *The expression is poetic and in part illogical but the sense is clear:* why do we exchange our lands for those warmed by another sun? "The pasture is always greener..."

[15]exsul, exsulis, *m.,* exile: who an exile of (from) his native land

[16]*L.A. 13 n. 9*

[17]fūgit, *perf.,* has ever fled

[18]scandō, -ere, scandī, scānsum, climb up

[19]aerātus, -a, -um, fitted with bronze, *probably referring to the bronze beaks of the men-of-war* (longae nāvēs), *which were faster than the ordinary ships — though even these cannot outstrip anxiety.*

[20]vitiōsus, -a , -um, vicious, morbid

[21]turma, -ae, a troop of cavalry (equitum, *L.I. 19 n. 65*). *A person cannot ride fast enough to escape care.*

[22]ōcior, -ius, *adj. in comparative degree,* swifter, agreeing with cūra

[23]cervus, -ī, stag; cervīs, *abl. of comparison (App. p. 359)*

[24]nimbus, -ī, rain cloud

[25]Eurus, -ī wind (from the southeast)

[26]laetus, -a, -um, happy, joyful

[27]praesēns, *gen.* -entis, *adj.,* present; in praesēns (tempus) for the present (*cp. the* carpe diem *philosophy*)

[28]ōdī, ōdisse, ōsūrus, *defective verb in perf. system with meanings of present system:* ōdī (I hate), ōderam (I hated), *etc.,* ōderit, *perf. subj.,* jussive, let (the laetus animus) refuse to (hate to) be anxious about (cūrāre)

[29]amārus, -a, -um, bitter, disagreeable; amāra, *n. plu.*

[30]lentus, -a, -um, pliant, tenacious, slow, lingering; *here* = tolerant, quiet

[31]temperō (1), control, temper

[32]rīsus, -ūs, laughter (*cp.* rīdeō)

[33]ab omnī parte, from every part = in every respect, completely

28

METER: Sapphic stanza.

[1]Hic diēs, *referring to Augustus' return from the campaign of 27-25 B.C. in Spain*

[2]fēstus, -a, -um, festive

[3]*L.I. 26 n. 20*

[4]eximō, -ere, -ēmī, -ēmptum, take away

[5]*L.I. 19 n. 85*

[6]Caesar = Augustus. *When G. Octavius was adopted by his great-uncle, G. Iulius Caesar, his name became G. Iulius Caesar Octavianus, to which the senate added the title of Augustus in 27 B.C.*

[7]from eō

[8]unguentum, -ī, ointment, perfume

[9]puer = slave; *cp. French* garçon

[10]corōna, -ae, crown, wreath

[11]cadus, -ī, wine jar

[12]**Marsus, -a, -um,** Marsian; **duellum** = *old form of*
bellum: Marsī duellī, *of the Marsian, or Social,*
War of 91-88 B.C., by which the **sociī** *(allies) of*
Rome in Italy gained full citizenship; i.e., a 65-year-
old wine.
[13]**memor,** *gen.,* **-oris,** *adj.,* mindful
[14]**Spartacus, -ī,** Spartacus, *the gladiator who led the*
slaves in revolt against Rome, 73-71 B.C.
[15]anywhere or in any way
[16]*L.I. 24 n. 20*
[17]**fallō, -ere, fefellī, falsum,** deceive, escape the notice
of
[18]**testa, -ae,** jug
29
METER: Lesser Asclepiad.
[1]**exigō, -ere, -ēgī, -āctum,** complete, finish
[2]**monumentum, -ī** = *Eng.*
[3]**aes, aeris,** *n.,* bronze; **aere,** *App. p. 360*
[4]**perennis, -e,** lasting (throughout the year)
[5]**rēgālis, -e,** royal
[6]**situs, -ūs,** site, situation; *here* = structure
[7]**pȳramis, -idis,** *f.,* pyramid
[8]**altus, -a, -um,** high; **altius** *agrees with* **monumen-**
tum.
[9]**imber, -ris,** *m.,* storm
[10]**edāx,** *gen.* **edacis,** *adj.,* greedy, destructive
[11]**aquilō, -ōnis,** *m.,* north wind
[12]**impotēns,** *gen.* **-ntis,** *adj.,* powerless (to injure my
monument)
[13]**dīruō, -ere, -ruī, -rutum,** raze, destroy
[14]**in-numerābilis, -e** = *Eng.*
[15]**seriēs, -ēī,** *f.,* succession
[16]*L.I. 20 n. 125*
[17]**Libitīna, -ae,** Libitina, *goddess of funerals*; death
30
METER: Iambic trimeter.
Phaedrus: freedman of Augustus, who made extensive
use of Aesop's fables.
[1]**pēra, -ae,** wallet
[2]**im-pōnō,** + *dat.,* put on
[3]**proprius, -a, -um,** one's own, *here* = our own
[4]**repleō, -ēre, -plēvī, -plētum,** fill; **(pēram) replētam**
[5]**tergum, -ī,** back
[6]**dedit,** *here* = put
[7]**aliēnus, -a, -um,** belonging to another; **aliēnīs (vitiīs),**
abl. with **gravem**
[8]*L.I. 25 n. 37;* **pectus nostrum**
[9]**suspendō, -ere, -pendī, -pēnsum,** hang, suspend; **(al-**
terum pēram) gravem...suspendit
[10]**simul** = **simul ac,** as soon as
[11]**dēlinquō, -ere, -līquī, -lictum,** fail, commit a crime
[12]**cēnsor, -ōris,** *m.,* censor; censurer, severe judge
31
METER: Iambic trimeter.
[1]**famēs,** *L.I. 15 n. 29* (not **fāma**); *abl. sing. always has*
ē of 5th decl.

[2]**vulpēs, -is,** *f.,* fox
[3]*L.I. 29 n. 8*
[4]**vīnea, -ae,** vineyard
[5]**ūva, -ae,** bunch of grapes
[6]**ap-petō** (= **ad-petō**), reach toward, desire (*cp.* appetite); **appetēbat,** *bring out the force of the imper-*
fect ending.
[7]**saliō, -īre, -uī, saltum,** jump
[8]**quam** = **ūvam**
[9]*L.A. 19 n. 8*
[10]**mātūrus, -a, -um,** ripe
[11]**sūmō, -ere, sūmpsī, sūmptum,** take
[12]*compl. inf. with* **possunt**
[13]**ēlevō** (1), disparage, weaken
[14]**ad-scrībō,** assign
[15]*L.I. 11 n. 40*
32
METER: Iambic trimeter.
[1]**persōna, -ae,** mask *worn by actors*
[2]**tragicus, -a, -us,** tragic
[3]*adv.,* by chance
[4]*L.I. 31 n. 2*
[5]**speciēs, -ēī,** *f.,* appearance, form
[6]**cerebrum, -ī,** brain
[7]**tribuō, -ere, -uī, -ūtum,** allot, assign, give
[8]*L.I. 4 n. 28*
33
METER: Iambic trimeter.
[1]near
[2]**fōns, fontis,** *m.,* spring
[3]*L.I. 27 n. 23*
[4]*L.I. 15 n. 6*
[5]**restō, -āre, restitī,** remain (standing)
[6]**liquor, -ōris,** *m.,* liquid
[7]**effigiēs, -ēī,** image, likeness
[8]**rāmōsus, -a, -um,** branching
[9]**mīror, -ārī, -ātus sum,** marvel at, wonder
[10]*Ch. 20 p. 93*
[11]**crūs, crūris,** *n.,* leg
[11a]**nimius, -a, -um,** excessive
[12]**tenuitās, -tātis,** *f.,* thinness
[13]**vituperō** (1), blame, find fault with
[14]**vēnor, -ārī, -ātus sum,** hunt; **vēnantum,** *gen. plu. of*
pres. part.
[15]*L.I. 7 n. 205*
[16]**con-territus**
[17]*L.I. 19 n. 81*
[18]*L.I. 15 n. 44*
[19]**canis, -is,** *m./f.,* dog
[20]**ēlūdō, -ere, -lūsī, -lūsum,** evade
[21]*L.A. 14 n. 34*
[22]**ex-cipiō,** take capture
[23]**ferus, -ī,** wild animal
[24]**re-tentus, -a, -um,** held back, held fast
[25]*L.I. 19 n. 138*
[26]**lacerō** (1), tear to pieces (*cp.* lacerate)

[27]morsus, -ūs, bite
[28]saevus, -a, -um, fierce, savage
[29]ēdō, -ere, -didī, -ditum, give out, utter
[30]infēlix, gen. -fēlicis, adj., unhappy; mē infēlicem, acc. of exclamation, L.I. 6 n. 28
[31]dēmum, at last
[32]L.I. 19 n. 148
[33]quam ūtilia
[34](ea, those things) quae
[35]dēspiciō, -ere, -spexī, -spectum, look down on, despise
[36]= laudāveram
[37]lūctus, -ūs, m., grief, sorrow; lūctūs, gen. (Ch. 40 p. 194)

34

METER: Iambic trimeter.
[1]gaudeō, -ēre, gāvīsus sum, rejoice, be glad
[2]subdolus, -a, -um, deceitful
[3]adv., generally, usually
[4]paenitentia, -ae, repentance
[5]fenestra, -ae, window
[6]corvus, -ī, raven
[7]cāseus, -ī, cheese
[8]comedō, comedere or comēsse; - edī, -ēsum, eat up
[9]L.I. 25 n. 24
[10]resideō, -ēre, -sēdī, -sessum, sit, be sitting
[11]L.A. 11 n. 13
[12]L.I. 31 n. 2
[13]penna, -ae, feather
[14]nitor, -ōris, m., brightness, beauty; quī est nitor, what (= how great) is the beauty
[15]decor, decōris, m., grace, beauty
[16]you bear, i.e., have in your body and face (L.I. 6 n. 19); (in) corpore, prepositions often omitted in poetry
[17]prior, pred. adj. after foret, better, finer
[18]āles, ālitis, f., bird
[19]foret = esset
[20]ē-mittō
[21]L.A. 4 n. 14
[22]dolōsus, -a, -um, crafty, cunning
[23]avidus, -a, -um, greedy, eager
[24]dēns, dentis, m., tooth

35

METER: Iambic trimeter.
[1]prīncipātus, -ūs, rule, dominion
[2]com-mūtō (1), change
[3]nīl = nihil
[4]L.I. 26 n. 34
[5]fābella, -ae, fable
[6]L.I. 7 n. 139
[7]asellus, -ī, a little ass, diminutive of asinus, -ī, an ass (second line below)
[8]prātum, -ī, meadow
[9]timidus, -a, -um, timid
[10]pāscō, -ere, pāvī, pastum, pasture

[11]clāmor, -ōris, m., shouting
[12]subitus, -a, -um, sudden or subitō, adv., suddenly
[13]suādeō, -ēre, suāsī, suāsum, urge
[14]lentus, -a, -um, slow, motionless, apathetic
[15]quaesō, -ere, beg, beseech, = quaerō
[16]num, v. end vocabulary
[17]bīnās clītellās, two pairs of panniers (i.e., instead of the present single pair); bīnī, -ae, -a, distributive numeral used with a regularly plural noun
[18]clītellae, -ārum, a pair of panniers
[19]im-pōnō = in + pōnō
[20]victor, -ōris = Eng.
[21]L.A. 25 n. 15
[22]what difference does it make to me, highly idiomatic
[23]dum (modo) + subj. here = provided
[24]portō, (1), bear, carry

36

METER: Iambic trimeter.
[1]mūlus, -ī, mule
[2]gravō (1), load, burden
[3]sarcina, -ae, bundle, pack
[4]fiscus, -ī, basket
[5]tumeō, -ēre, swell, be swollen
[6]saccus, -ī, sack
[7]hordeum, -ī, barley
[8]onus, -eris, n., burden, load
[9]L.I. 25 n. 24
[10]cervīx, -vīcis, f., neck
[11]ēmineō, -ēre, -minuī, stand out, be conspicuous
[12]collum, -ī, neck
[13]iactō (1) toss
[14]tintinnābulum, -ī, bell, a delightfully onomatopoetic word
[15]comes, comitis, m/f., companion
[16]quiētus, -a, -um, quiet
[17]placidus, -a, -um, placid, gentle
[18]gradus, -ūs, step
[19]subitō, L.I. 7 n. 205
[20]latrō, -ōnis, m., bandit, robber
[21]advolō (1), fly, hasten
[22]L.I. 7 n. 151
[23]lancinō (1), mangle
[24]dīripiō, -ere, -ripuī, -reptum, plunder
[25]nummus, -ī, currency, money
[26]vīlis, -e, cheap
[27]spoliō (1), rob
[28]cāsus, -ūs, accident
[29]fleō, -ēre, flēvī, flētum, weep, bewail
[30]L.A. 5 n. 4
[31]contemnō, -ere, -tempsī, -temptum, despise; contemptum (esse)
[32]L.I. 34 n. 1
[33]laedō, -ere, laesī, laesum, injure
[34]vulnus, -neris, n., wound
[35]argūmentum, -ī, evidence, proof
[36]tūtus, -a, -um, L.A. 15 n. 25

[37]tenuitās, -tātis, *f.*, poverty

[38]perīclum, -ī, *Early Latin form, used instead of* perīculum *in Classical Latin poetry whenever it was metrically convenient*

[39]obnoxius, -a, -um, subject to, exposed to

37

[1]*L.A. 17 n. 1 and 3*

[2]*Calpurnius Macer*

[3]: it is

[4]quia, *conj.*, because

[5]*L.I. 26 n. 31*

[6]fruor, -ī, frūctus sum, + *abl.*, enjoy *(cp.* frūctus, -ūs*)*

[7]*What case? (Ch. 34 p. 165 and p. 168, n. 4)*

[8]*L.I. 33 n. 2*

[9]viridis, -e, green; viridia, *gen.* viridium, *n. plu. as a* noun, green things, greenery

[10]*L.I. 7 n. 87*

[11]amoenus, -a, -um, pleasant

[12]amoenissimam, *agreeing with* villam *understood as subj. of* esse

[13]com-pōnō, *here* = compose, quiet; sē compōnere, to compose oneself, to rest

[14]the man, *apparently referring to a former owner who had been* happier (fēlīcior) *on this estate as an ordinary person* (homō) *before he could realize his ambition of becoming* "most happy" (fēlīcissimus), *i.e., before he could achieve some very high position which did not give him supreme happiness after all.*

[15]antequam + *subjunctive, L.I. 19 n. 145*

[16]*lit.* in the Tuscans = on my Tuscan estate

[17]vēnor, -ārī, -ātus sum, hunt

[18]quae, *neuter plu. referring to* vēnor *and* studeō *as antecedents*

[19]*adv.*, sometimes, at times

[20]*adv.*, alternately, by turns

[21]*adv.*, at the same time, simultaneously. *In another letter (1.6), Pliny tells how he combined hunting and studying in one operation.*

[22]*adv.*, thus far, till now

[23]prōnūntiō (1), proclaim

[24]utrum...an, *L.A. 15 n. 11*

38

[1]*Pliny and Caninius were fellow townsmen from Comum (Como) at the south end of beautiful Lake Larius (Como) in northern Italy.*

[2]*an, in questions,* or

[3]piscor (1), to fish

[4]*L.I. 37 n. 17*

[5]*L.I. 37 n. 21*

[6]Lārius, -ī, *m.*, Lake Larius (now Lake Como)

[7]*Note 1 above shows why Pliny says* nostrum.

[8]lacus, -ūs, lake

[9]piscis, -is, *m.*, fish

[10]fera (*sc.* bēstia), -ae, *f.*, wild animal

[11]*L.A. 14 n. 34*

[12]cingō, -ere, cīnxī, cīnctum, surround, gird

[13]*L.I. 29 n. 8*

[14]sēcessus, -ūs, retreat, summer place

[15]*adv.*, sufficiently, abundantly

[16]sug-gerō, -ere, -gessī, -gestum, furnish, afford, supply

[17]sīve...sīve, (sī-ve), if...or if, whether...or

[18]*L.I. 25 n. 17*

[19]angō, -ere, torment

[20]artus, -a, -um, close, narrow; laqueus, -ī, noose, cord

[21]ab-rumpō, -ere, -rūpī, -ruptum, break off, sever. *Pliny is tied up in Rome.*

[22]negōtium, -iī, business; duty

[23]accrēscō, -ere, -crēvī, -crētum, increase; nova (negōtia) accrēscunt (veteribus negōtiīs) new duties increase by...*or* are added to...

[24]per-agō, complete

[25]nexus, -ūs, coils, obligations

[26]catēna, -ae, chain

[27]in diēs, from day to day

[28]occupātiō, -ōnis, *f.*, occupation, employment

[29]agmen, -minis, *n.*, line of march, column

[30]ex-tendō, -ere, -tendī, -tentum, extend, increase

39

[1]*L.I. 36 n. 34*

[2]he lost (*not* sent away)

[3]*L.I. 26 n. 31*

[4]singulāris, -e, extraordinary

[5]exemplum, -ī, example, nature, type

[6]*indecl.*, thirty

[7]*The abl. is sometimes used instead of the accusative to express the idea of extent of time.*

[8]iūrgium, -iī, quarrel

[9]offēnsa, -ae, hatred, affront

[10]reverentia, -ae, respect

[11]marītus, -ī, husband

[12]mereor, -ērī, meritus sum, deserve

[13]quot, *indecl. adj.*, how many (*cp.* tot)

[14]dīversus, -a, -um, diverse, different

[15]*L.I. 31 n. 11*

[16]*L.A. 5 n. 10*

[17]grandis, -e, great

[18]sōlācium, -iī, consolation, comfort

[19]hinc *here* = from this cause

[20]exacerbō (1), exasperate; embitter

[21]*L.I. 37 n. 6*

[22]voluptās, -tātis, *f.*, pleasure

[23]*L.I. 11 n. 35*

[24]*L.A. 25 n. 15*

[25]suspēnsus, -a, -um, in suspense, anxious

[26]amīcus, -a, -um, *adj.*, friendly

[27]dum, until, *used with the subjunctive to imply intention or expectancy*

[28]ad-mittō, admit, receive

[29]āvocāmentum, -ī, diversion

[30]cicātrix, -trīcis, *f.*, scar, *which implies healing*

[31]aequē ac, equally as, quite so well as

[32]necessitās (-tātis, *f.,*) ipsa, necessity itself, sheer necessity

[33]*here* = time

[34]satietās, -tātis, *f.,* satiety

[35]in-dūcō, bring on, induce

40

[1]Fannia (est)

[2]neptis, -is, granddaughter

[3]Arria, -ae, Arria (Maior), *brave wife of Caecina Poetus. When, because of his part in a conspiracy against the emperor Claudius, he had to commit suicide in 42* A.D., *Arria committed suicide with him, actually setting him an example as indicated at the end of the letter. (Cp. L.I. 56 below.)*

[4]ille, the famous *when immediately following its noun*

[5]*L.I. 39 n. 11;* marītō, *dat.*

[6]sōlācium, -iī, solace, comfort

[7]*L.I. 11 n. 40*

[8]*neut. acc. plu.*

[9]re-ferō, -ferre, rettulī, relātum, report, relate; referēbat, *subject = Fannia, who related these episodes during a conversation with Pliny on the preceding day.*

[10]avia, -ae, grandmother; aviae, *gen. case*

[11]hōc, *abl. of comparison, referring to the relative clause of the preceding sentence*

[12]obscūrus, -a, -um, obscure, unknown

[13]tam...quam, as...as

[14]mīrābilis, -e, wonderful, astonishing

[15]legentī, to be construed with tibi

[16]fore = futūra esse, *future inf. in indirect discourse depending on* exīstimō (1), think

[17]aegrōtō (1), be sick

[18]*L.I. 22 n. 20*

[19]mortiferē, *adv.* (mors-ferō), fatally

[20]dē-cēdō, go away, die (*cp.* deceased)

[21]eximius, -a, -um, extraordinary

[22]pulchritūdō, -dinis, *f.,* beauty; eximiā pulchritūdine, *abl. depending on* filius (*App. p. 359) but more easily translated if we supply a word like* puer: filius dēcessit — (puer) eximiā pulchritūdine, *etc.*

[23]verecūndia, -ae, modesty

[24]*L.A. 19 n. 9*

[25]ob, *prep. + acc.,* on account of; toward

[26]fūnus, -eris, *n.,* funeral

[27]*L.I. 21 n. 31*

[28]quīn immō, why, on the contrary

[29]*adv.,* as often as

[30]cubiculum, -ī, bedroom

[31]intrō (1), enter; intrāret: *in Silver Latin the imperfect subjunctive of customary action is often found in place of the indicative.*

[32]commodus, -a, -um, suitable, satisfactory; *here* = better

[33]simulō (1) pretend

[34]per-saepe, *adv.,* very often

[35]interrogō (1), ask, inquire (*cp.* rogō); (marītō) interrogantī

[36]quiēscō, -ere, quiēvī, quiētus, rest, be quiet

[37]*L.A. 12 n. 4*

[38]cibus, -ī, food

[39]*L.I. 31 n. 11*

[40]cohibeō, -ere, -uī, -itum, hold together, hold back, restrain

[41]lacrima, -ae, tear

[42]prōrumpō, -ere, -rūpī, -ruptum, burst forth

[43]*L.I. 6 n. 79*

[44]satiō (1), satisfy (*cp.* satis)

[45]siccus, -a, -um, dry; siccīs, oculīs, *abl. abs.*

[46]*L.I. 37 n. 13*

[47]*L.I. 6 n. 19*

[48]tamquam, as if

[49]orbitās, -tātis, *f.,* bereavement, loss

[50]*adv.,* out of doors, outside

[51]*What kind of condition in the* tamquam *clause? (Ch. 33 p. 157–158*

[52]*L.I. 22 n. 21*

[53]that deed

[54]stringō, -ere, -strīnxī, strictus, draw; stringere, *inf. in apposition with* illud

[55]perfodiō, -ere, -fōdī, -fossum, pierce (*lit.* dig through)

[56]pectus, *L.I. 25 n. 37*

[57]ex-trahō

[58]pugiō, -ōnis, *m.,* dagger

[59]porrigō, -ere, -rēxī, -rēctum, hold out, extend

[60]ad-dō, -ere, -didī, -ditum, add

[61]*adv.,* almost

[62]dīvīnus, -a, -um = *Eng.*

[63]doleō, - ere, -uī, -itūrus, suffer pain, grieve; cause pain; (pugiō) nōn dolet, does not cause pain, does not hurt

41

[1]*L.A. 29 n. 5*

[2]dēfungor, -ī, -fūnctus sum, finish *or* complete life, die. *Merrill cites the discovery of the family tomb near Rome in 1880 and in it a cinerary urn with the inscription:* Dīs mānibus Miniciae Mārcellae, Fundānī fīliae. Vīxit annīs XII, mēnsibus XI, diēbus VII: *To the divine shades of Minicia Marcella... (The abbreviations in the inscription have been expanded.)*

[3]puellā, *abl. of comparison (App. p. 359)*

[4]fēstīvus, -a, -um, pleasant, agreeable

[5]amābilis, -e, lovable, lovely

[6]dignus + *abl., L.A. 11 n. 20*

[7]*L.A. 19 n. 8*

[8]impleō, -ēre, -plēvī, -plētum, fill up, complete

[9]*dat. of possession (App. p. 358)*

[10]anīlis, -e, *adj.,* of an old woman

[11]prūdentia, -ae, foresight, wisdom

[12]mātrōnālis, -e, *adj.,* of a matron, matronly

[13]gravitās, -tātis, *f.,* seriousness, dignity

[14] suāvitās, -tātis, *f.*, sweetness
[15] puellāris, -e, *adj.*, girlish
[16] how
[17] cervīx, -īcis, *f., usu. plu.* (cervīcēs) *as here*, neck
[18] inhaereō, -ēre, -haesī, -haesum, cling
[19] paternus, -a, -um, paternal, of a father
[20] *adv. of* amāns
[21] *adv.*, modestly
[22] complector, -ī, -plexus sum, embrace
[23] nūtrīx, -īcis, *f.*, nurse
[24] paedagōgus, -ī, tutor, slave who escorted children
[25] praeceptor, -ōris, *m.*, teacher (in a school); *not a private tutor*
[26] *adv. of* studiōsus, full of studium
[27] *adv. of* intelligēns
[28] lēctitō (1), read (eagerly)
[29] *What case?*
[30] temperantia, -ae, self-control
[31] patientia, -ae, *Eng.*
[32] cōnstancia, -ae, firmness
[33] valētūdō, -dinis, *f., here* = bad health, illness
[34] medicus, -ī, doctor
[35] obsequor, + *dat.*, obey (*cp. obsequious*)
[36] soror, sorōris, sister
[37] adhortor = hortor
[38] dēstituō, -ere, -stituī, -stitūtum, desert, abandon
[39] vigor, -ōris, *m.*, vigor; vigōre, *abl. of means with* sustinēbat
[40] sustineō, *L.I. 20 n. 83:* (puella) sustinēbat sē ipsam
[41] dūrō (1), endure
[42] hic (vigor animī)
[43] *L.A. 8 n. 2*
[44] extrēmum, -ī, *n.*, = finis
[45] spatium, -iī, space, duration
[46] infringō, -ere, -frēgī, -frāctum, break
[47] *adv.*, clearly
[48] *L.I. 40 n. 26; here* = mors
[49] dēstinō (1), bind, engage
[50] ēgregius, -a, -um, excellent, distinguished
[51] iuvenis, -is, *m.*, young man
[52] ē-ligō = legō
[53] nūptiae, -ārum, *plu.*, wedding
[54] gaudium, -iī, joy
[55] maeror, -ōris, *m.*, grief
[56] ex-primō (= premō), express
[57] *L.I. 36 n. 34*
[58] praecipiō, -ere, -cēpī, -ceptum, direct
[59] *The antecedent is* hoc *in the following line.*
[60] vestis, -is, *f.*, garment, clothes
[61] margarītum, -ī, pearl
[62] gemma, -ae, jewel
[63] ērogō (1), *pay out, spend*; fuerat ērogātūrus (*active periphrastic*) he had been about to spend, had intended to spend (on clothes, jewels, *etc.*, for the wedding)
[64] tūs, tūris, *n.*, incense

[65] *L.I. 28 n. 8*
[66] odor, -ōris, *m.*, perfume
[67] impendō, -ere, -pendī, -pēnsum, expend; impenderētur, *subjunctive of indirect command depending on* praecipientem
[68] quās, *meaning after* sī, nisi, nē, num: *Ch. 33 vocab.*
[69] meminī, meminisse, *defective verb*, remember; mementō, (*fut.*) *imperative*, remember
[70] adhibeō, -ere, -hibuī, -hibitum, use, furnish
[71] sōlācium, -iī, comfort
[72] mollis, -e, soft, gentle

42
[1] molliter, *adv. of* mollis, *L.I. 41 n. 72*
[2] tuōs (servōs et lībertōs); *so* meōs *below*
[3] treat
[4] simpliciter, *adv.*, frankly, candidly; quō simplicius by which (*degree of difference*) more frankly = the more frankly (*in which expression "the" is not the definite article but an old Anglo-Saxon instrumental case of degree of difference of a demonstrative pronoun*)
[5] *L.A. 29 n. 19*
[6] indulgentia, -ae, kindness
[7] tractō (1), handle, treat
[8] *L.I. 6 n. 117*
[9] *L.I. 16 n. 22*
[10] infirmitās, -tātis, *f.*, illness, weakness
[11] lībertus, - i, freedman (*a slave who had somehow secured his freedom*) *in contrast to a* līber vir (*one who was born free*). *A freedman commonly remained closely attached to his former master.*
[12] Zōsimus, -ī, Zosimus, apparently a Greek.
[13] *abl., App. p. 359*
[14] hūmānitās, -tātis, *f.*, kindness
[15] ex-hibeō, show, exhibit
[16] *Why abl.?* (*Ch. 20 p. 94*)
[17] *L.A. 24 n. 3*
[18] probus, -a, -um, honorable, fine
[19] officiōsus, -a, -um, obliging, courteous
[20] litterātus, -a, -um, well-educated; *Greek slaves especially were often well educated.*
[21] inscrīptiō, -ōnis, *f., here* = label, *a placard hung around a slave's neck in the slave market to indicate his special abilities.* — cōmoedus, -ī, comic actor or a slave trained to read at dinners scenes from famous comedies. *Although this was Zosimus' specialty, we find him in the next two sentences surprisingly versatile and talented.*
[22] *L.I. 25 n. 48*
[23] *adv.*, skilfully (*cp.* perītus, *L.I. 20 n. 23*)
[24] commodē, fitly, satisfactorily (*cp.* commodus, *L.I. 40 n. 32*)
[25] *L.A. 11 n. 19*
[26] historia, -ae = *Eng.*
[27] carmen, -minis, *n.*, song, poem
[28] *adv.*, carefully

[29]L.I. 15 n. 26
[30]ministerium, -iī, service
[31]L.I. 11 n. 67
[32]cāritās, -tātis, f., dearness, affection (cp. cārus)
[33]augeō, -ēre, auxī, auctum, increase
[34]aliquot, indecl. adj., several, some
[35]ante...annōs, several years ago
[36]earnestly and emphatically
[37]prōnūntiō (1), declaim, recite
[38]sanguis, -inis, m., blood
[39]re-iciō, reject, spit out
[40]L.I. 40 n. 25
[41]Aegyptus, -ī, f., Egypt
[42]peregrīnātiō, -ōnis, f., travel or sojourn abroad
[43]cōnfīrmō (1), strengthen
[44]nūper, L.A. 19 n. 1
[45]infirmitās, -tātis, f., weakness, sickness
[46]tussicula, -ae, slight cough
[47]ad-monitus = monitus
[48]rūrsus, L.I. 19 n. 51
[49]reddidit = reiēcit
[50]dēstinō (1), intend, resolve
[51]praedium, -iī, country seat
[52]Forum Iūliī, Forī Iūliī, Forum of Julius, *modern Fréjus, a coastal town of southern France*: Forō, *place where*
[53]possideō, -ēre, possēdī, possessum, possess, own
[54]L.I. 40 n. 9
[55]āēr, āeris, m., air; āera = *Gk. acc. sing. form*
[56]salūbris, -e, healthful; *still so regarded*
[57]lac, lactis, n., milk; *i.e., for the milk cure*
[58]cūrātiō, -ōnis, f., cure
[59]accommodātus, -a, -um, suited
[60]ergō, L.A. 25 n. 15
[61](ut) scrībās: ut *is sometimes omitted in such clauses. What kind of subj.?*
[62]tuīs, your servants (cp. n. 2 above)
[63]ut vīlla (pateat), ut domus pateat: *i.e., he is to have access to the great house itself as well as to the estate.* vīlla, L.I. 7 n. 87

43
[1]L.I. 42 n. 11
[2]suscēnseō, -ere, -cēnsuī, -cēnsum, + dat., be angry with
[3]fleō, -ēre, flēvī, flētum, weep
[4]taceō, -ēre, -uī, -itum, be silent (cp. tacit)
[5]summa, -ae, f., sum
[6]paenitentia, -ae, repentance
[7]L.A. 2 n. 9
[8]ēmendō (1), correct; (eum) ēmendātum (esse)
[9]L.I. 37 n. 4
[10]dēlinquō, -ere, -līquī, -lictum, fail (in duty), commit a crime
[11]īrāscor, -ī, īrātus sum, be angry
[12]adv., rightly (with merit)
[13]L.A. 13 n. 9

[14]praecipuus, -a, -um, special
[15]mānsuētūdō, -inis, f., gentleness, mildness
[16]cum + ind., Ch. 31 n. 1
[17]contracted form, L.I. 7 n. 141
[18]adv., meanwhile (cp. intereā)
[19]sufficiō, -ere, -fēcī, -fectum, be sufficient, suffice; suffict, subject = ut-clause
[20]ex-ōrō, stronger form of ōrō
[21]sinō, -ere, sīvī, situm, permit, allow
[22]torqueō, -ēre, torsī, tortum, twist, torture; nē tor- serīs, L.I. 23 n. 1
[23]torquēris, you are tormented = you torment yourself (reflexive use of the passive)
[24]lēnis, -e, gentle, kind; agreeing with subj. of īrāsceris: you, such a gentle person
[25]vereor, -ērī, -ītus sum, fear; construction with verbs of fearing (App. p. 360)
[26]prex, precis, f., prayer
[27]plēnē, adv. of plēnus
[28]effūsē, adv., profusely, unrestrainedly
[29]tantō...quantō, the more...the more, abl. of degree of difference (App. p. 359)
[30](lībertum) ipsum
[31]ācriter, adv. of ācer
[32]sevērē, adv., seriously, severely
[33]cor-ripiō, -ere, -ripuī, -reptum, seize, accuse, blame

44
[1]you did well because = thank you for
[2]lībertum (v. preceding letter), in thought, the object of both redūcentibus and recēpistī
[3]adv., once
[4]re-dūcō
[5]epistulīs, here plu. of a single letter (the preceding one) on the analogy of litterae, -ārum
[6]Both prepositional phrases, connected by et under- stood, depend on recēpistī
[7]prīmum, adv., first
[8]tractābilis, -ē, tractable, compliant
[9]tribuō, -ere, tribuī, tribūtum, attribute, ascribe
[10]vel...vel, either...or; cp. L.A. 17 n. 5
[11]L.A. 6 n. 44
[12]L.A. 43 n. 26
[13]indulgeō, -ēre, -dulsī, -dultum, yield to, gratify

45
[1]in-iungō, enjoin, impose
[2]L.I. 41 n. 25
[3]L.A. 19 n. 7
[4]beneficiō tuō, thanks to you
[5]schola, -ae, school
[6]re-sūmō, -ere, -sūmpsī, -sūmptum, resume
[7]L.I. 29 n. 6
[8]iuvenis, -is, m./f., a young person, a youth
[9]gen. depending on quantum
[10]adv., very recently
[11]frequēns, gen. -entis, adj., crowded

[12]**audītōrium, -iī,** lecture room, school; **auditōriō,** *place where without a preposition*

[13]**cōram,** *prep. + abl.,* in the presence of

[14]*L.A. 27 n. 16; i.e., the senatorial order*

[15]**clārē** (*adv. of* **clārus**), *here* = loudly

[16]*L.I. 40 n. 31*

[17]**conticēscō, -ere, -ticuī,** become silent

[18]**quod,** *having as antecedent the whole preceding idea*

[19]*L.I. 40 n. 9*

[20]**pertineō, -ēre, -uī, -tentum,** pertain to

[21]**profiteor, -ērī, -fessus sum,** teach, *a late meaning of the word*

[22]**efficiō...ut,** *L.A. 13 n. 29 and 30*

[23]**cōn-sequor,** accomplish

[24]*adv.,* especially

[25]**super,** *prep. + abl.,* about

[26]**interest vestrā,** interests you *(highly idiomatic)*

[27]**dignus,** *L.A. 11 n. 20*

[28]**patruus, -ī,** (paternal) uncle; **tē patruō** *is in the same construction as* **illō patre.**

46

METER: Choliambus.

[1]**Gemellus, -ī,** *Gemellus, one of the legacy hunters of the imperial period, who sought to curry favor with the childless rich in the hope of being named for a substantial sum in the will*

[2]**nūptiae, -ārum,** *f. plu.,* marriage

[3]**Marōnilla, -ae; Marōnillae,** the marriage of M. — *to himself, of course;* marriage with M.

[4]**īnstō, -āre, -stitī,** press on, insist, persist

[5]**precor, -ārī, precātus sum,** beg, entreat (*cp.* **prex**)

[6]**dōnō** (1), give (*cp.* **dōnum**)

[7]**adeō-ne,** *adv., L.I. 19 n. 47*

[8]*L.I. 6 n. 29*

[9]**foedus, -a, -um,** foul, ugly, loathsome

[10]*L.I. 35 n. 3*

[11]*L.A. 25 n. 15*

[12]**tussiō** (4), have a cough

47

METER: Elegiac couplet.

[1]**nūbō, -ere, nūpsī, nūptum,** + *dat.,* put on the veil for someone = marry (*said of a woman marrying a man*)

[2]**Prīscus, -ī,** Priscus, *who apparently had everything*

[3]**mīror,** *L.I. 33 n. 9*

[4]**Paula, -ae,** Paula, *who in Martial's opinion was somehow no match for Priscus*

[5]**sapiō, -ere, -iī,** have taste, be sensible, be wise

[6]**dūcere,** *the masculine equivalent of* **nūbere** *above:* **dūcere tē (in mātrimōnium),** to marry you

48

METER: Elegiac couplet.

[1]**mentior, -īrī, -ītus sum,** lie, declare falsely, *here* = imitate

[2]*L.I. 45 n. 8*

[3]**tingō, -ere, -tinxī, tinctus,** wet, dye

[4]**Laetīnus, -ī,** Laetinus

[5]**capillī, -ōrum,** hair

[6]*L.I. 7 n. 205*

[7]*L.I. 34 n. 6*

[8]*L.I. 1 n. 5*

[9]**cycnus, -ī,** swan

[10]**fallō,** *L.I. 28 n. 17;* **nōn ōmnēs (fallis)** *seems to imply that the hair dyes were good enough to deceive at least some people.*

[11]**Prōserpina, -ae,** Proserpina, *goddess of the underworld, and so of death*

[12]**cānus, -a, -um,** gray; **tē (esse) cānum**

[13]*L.I. 32 n. 1*

[14]*L.I. 2 n. 15*

[15]**dē-trahō**

[16]**illa** = Proserpina

49

METER: Phalaecean, or hendecasyllabic.

[1]**Cinna, -ae,** *m.,* Cinna, *a Roman family name*

[2]**Cinnamus, -ī,** *m.,* Cinnamus, *a slave name meaning "cinnamon." The Romans often gave such names to slaves. Cinnamus, now a freedman, wanted to change his name to a Roman one for obvious reasons.*

[3]**barbarismus, -ī,** *m.,* a barbarism, an impropriety of speech

[4]**Fūrius, -ī,** *m.,* Furius, *an old Roman name*

[5]**Fūr,** *from* **fūr, fūris,** *m.,* thief; *cp.* **fūrtīvus,** *L.I. 3 n. 12*

50

METER: Elegiac couplet.

[1]**āmissum patrem**

[2]**fleō, -ēre, flēvī, flētum,** weep; weep for, lament

[3]**Gellia, -ae,** Gellia

[4]**ad-sum,** be present

[5]at her bidding; *how literally?*

[6]**prōsiliō** (4), leap forth

[7]*L.I. 40 n. 41*

[8]**lūgeō, -ēre, lūxī, lūctum,** mourn

[9]*L.I. 25 n. 11*

[10]*L.A. 2 n. 18*

[11]*L.A. 2 n. 9*

[12]**testis, -is,** *m.,* witness

51

METER: Elegiac couplet.

[1]**convīvor, -ārī, -ātus sum,** to feast

[2]**Lupercus, -ī,** *m.,* Lupercus

[3]*L.I. 43 n. 11*

[4]**licet ūsque (ut) vocēs** (it is even permitted that you call), you may even invite me, *or* even though you invite me

[5]send a slave as a special messenger

52

METER: Elegiac couplet.

[1]*L.I. 15 n. 27*

[2]**aper, aprī,** wild boar

[3]**Titus, -ī,** Titus

[4]**bellus, -a, -um**
[5]**convīva, -ae,** *m.,* guest; *Caecilianus' only guest is the*
aper!

53
METER: Elegiac couplet.
[1]**ager (agrī,** *m.,* farm) **Nōmentānus,** my farm at
Nomentum, *in the Sabine country of central Italy*

54
METER: Elegiac couplet.
[1]*adv.,* tomorrow
[2]*No doubt Martial intended to have us think of*
Horace's Postumus in L.I. 26 above.
[3]**dīc,** *imperative (Ch. 8, p. 36)*
[4]**crās istud,** that "tomorrow" of yours, *subj. of* **venit**
[4a]**quando,** when?
[5]**longē,** far *(space)*
[6]**petendum** (est)
[7]**numquid latet,** it does not lie hidden, does it?
[8]*among the Parthians and Armenians, i.e.,* at land's end
in the East
[9]**lateō, -ēre, -uī,** lie hidden
[10]**Priamus, -ī,** Priam, *aged king of Troy*
[11]**Nestōr, -oris,** Nestor, *Greek leader famed for his years*
and wisdom
[12]**quantī,** *gen. of indefinite value:* at what price, for how
much *(L.I. 8 n. 43)* can that tomorrow be bought
[13]**emō, -ere, ēmī, ēmptum,** buy
[14]*L.A. 25 n. 22*
[15]**sērus, -a, -um,** late; **sērum,** *pred. adj. in neut.* to agree
with **hodiē vīvere** *which is subj. of* **est**
[16]*L.I. 47 n. 5*
[17]*L.I. 25 n. 11*
[18]*adv.* yesterday

55
METER: Phalaecean or hendecasyllabic.
[1]**Issa,** *colloquial and affectionate form for* **Ipsa** *and*
here used as the name of a pet dog

[2]**passer,** *L.I. 4 n. 6;* **passere,** *abl. depending on*
nēquior *(App. p. 359);* **passer Catullī,** *another*
literary reference (L.I. 4).
[3]**nēquam,** *indecl. adj.;* **campar, nēquior, -ius,** worth-
less, good for nothing, mischievous
[4]*L.I. 24 n. 2*
[5]**ōsculum, -ī,** kiss
[6]**columba, -ae,** dove
[7]**blandus, -a, -um,** flattering, caressing, coaxing
[8]**Indicus, -a, -um,** of India
[9]**lapillus, -ī,** precious stone, gem
[10]*L.I. 4 n. 7*
[11]**catella, -ae,** little dog
[12]**Pūblī = Pūbliī,** *gen. sing. (Ch. 4 n. 1), of* **Pūblius**
[13]*L.A. 11 n. 9, here* = whimper
[14]**trīstitia, -ae,** sadness
[15]*L.I. 41 n. 54*
[16]**lūx (diēs) suprēma = mors**
[17]**pingō, -ere, pīnxī, pictum,** paint; **pictā tabellā,** by a
painted tablet = in a painting
[18]**exprimō, -ere, -pressī, pressum,** express, portray
[19]**tam similem...Issam:** an Issa (of the painting) so
similar (to the real Issa)
[20]**nec** *here* = not even
[21]**uterque,** *L.I. 22 n. 20*
[22]*L.I. 8 n. 31*

56
METER: Elegiac couplet.
[1]**castus, -a, -um,** pure, guiltless
[2]*L.I. 7 n. 100*
[3]**Arria, -ae, Paetus, -ī,** *L.I. 40*
[4]**vīscera, -um,** *n. plu.,* vitals
[5]**stringō, -ere, strīnxī, strictus,** draw
[6]*i.e., if you have any faith in me*
[7]*L.I. 36 n. 34*
[8]*L.I. 40 n. 63*

Optional Self-Tutorial Exercises

The optional exercises have been included in the hope of enriching the potential of this book for its various types of users.

1. "Repetītiō māter memoriae." In language study the value of repetition is indisputable. To the already large amount of repetition achieved in the regular chapters these exercises add even more of this practice. The phrases and sentences have deliberately been made simple so that the immediate points in forms and syntax may stand out strikingly. The words are purposely limited to those of the formal lesson vocabularies, which obviously should be memorized before turning to these tutorial exercises. As a result of their very nature and purpose, such sentences can make no claim to inspiration. Some hints of the worthwhile reading matter for which one studies Latin are to be found in the Sententiae Antiquae *and the reading passages from the ancient authors, which are the heart of this book; but if one wants additional repetitious drill by which to establish linguistic reflexes, one can find it here in these self-tutorial exercises. As has been suggested elsewhere, be sure always to read aloud every Latin word and sentence — carefully, for such a practice enables one to learn through the ear as well as the eye and can provide many of the benefits of a language laboratory.*

2. To students enrolled in a regular Latin course these exercises with their keys can prove valuable for review and self-testing and can be helpful in preparation for examinations.

3. Also to the private individual who wishes to learn or review Latin by himself these exercises are certain to be valuable, for by them he can give himself tests which can be corrected via the key. Also, doing these examples with benefit of key will give him greater confidence in tackling the regular exercises of the book.

4. All students can test themselves in simple Latin composition by translating the English sentences of the key back into Latin and checking this work via the corresponding Latin sentences of the exercises.

5. In the translations ordinarily only one of the various meanings of a word given in the vocabulary will be used in any specific instance. If at times the translations are somewhat formal, the reason is that they can in this way follow the Latin more closely; and certainly these particular sentences are intended to provide practice in understanding Latin rather than practice in literary expression. Polished literary expression in translation is most desirable and should be practiced in connection with the other exercises in this book.

6. The answer keys have been placed by themselves after the exercises in order that the testing of oneself may be fairer and also in order that the exercises may be used for practice in class when the instructor wishes. It hardly need be added that the surest way to test oneself is to write out the answers before *turning to the key.*

7. Finally, let it be emphasized once again that for maximum value you must say aloud all the Latin words, phrases, and sentences, and that you must have studied the text of each lesson carefully through the vocabulary before turning to these exercises.

EXERCISES FOR CHAPTER 1

1. Give the English pronouns equivalent to each of the following Latin personal endings: (1) -t, (2) -mus, (3) -ō, (4) -nt, (5) -s, (6) -tis.

2. Name the following forms and translate each: (1) monēre, (2) vidēre, (3) valēre, (4) dēbēre.

3. Name the following forms and translate each: (1) vocāre, (2) servāre, (3) dare, (4) cōgitāre, (5) laudāre, (6) amāre, (7) errāre.

4. Name the following forms and translate each: (1) vocā, (2) servā, (3) dā, (4) cōgitā, (5) laudā, (6) amā, (7) monē, (8) vidē, (9) valē.

5. Name the following forms and translate each: (1) vocāte, (2) servāte, (3) date, (4) cōgitāte, (5) laudāte, (6) amāte, (7) monēte, (8) vidēte, (9) valēte.

6. Translate the following words: (1) vocat, (2) cōgitāmus, (3) amant, (4) dēbēs, (5) videt, (6) vident, (7) dēbēmus, (8) valēs, (9) errātis, (10) vidēmus, (11) amat, (12) vidētis, (13) errās, (14) dant, (15) servāmus, (16) dat, (17) amant, (18) vidēs.

7. Monent mē sī errō. 8. Monet mē sī errant. 9. Monēte mē sī errat. 10. Dēbēs monēre mē. 11. Dēbētis servāre mē. 12. Nōn dēbent laudāre mē. 13. "Quid dat?" "Saepe nihil dat." 14. Mē saepe vocant et (*and*) monent. 15. Nihil videō. Quid vidēs? 16. Mē laudā sī nōn errō. 17. Sī valētis, valēmus. 18. Sī valet, valeō. 19. Sī mē amat, dēbet mē laudāre. 20. Cōnservāte mē. 21. Nōn dēbeō errāre. 22. Quid dēbēmus laudāre? 23. Videt; cōgitat; monet.

EXERCISES FOR CHAPTER 2

1. Give the Latin for the definite article "the" and the indefinite article "a."

2. Name the Latin case for each of the following constructions or ideas:
(1) direct object of a verb; (2) possession; (3) subject of a verb; (4) means; (5) direct address; (6) indirect object of a verb.

3. Name the case, number and syntactical usage indicated by each of the following endings of the first declension: (1) -ās; (2) -a; (3) -am; (4) -ae (plu.).

4. Name the case(s) and number indicated by the following endings, and wherever possible name the English preposition(s) which can be associated with them: (1) -ārum; (2) -ā; (3) -ae; (4) -īs.

5. Translate the following nouns and state the syntactical usage of each as indicated by its ending: (1) puellam; (2) puella; (3) puellās; (4) puellae (plural form); (5) patriās; (6) patriam; (7) patria; (8) patriae (plu.); (9) pecūniam; (10) pecūnia; (11) poenās; (12) poenam.

6. Translate the following nouns in accordance with their case endings:
(1) puellae (sing.); (2) puellārum; (3) Ō patria; (4) patriae (sing.); (5) pecūniā; (6) pecūniae (sing.); (7) poenīs; (8) poenā; (9) poenārum.

7. Given the following nominative singular forms, write the Latin forms requested in each instance: (1) *multa pecūni*a in the genitive and the

accusative singular; (2) *magna fāma* in dat. and abl. sing.; (3) *vīta mea* in gen. sing. and nom. plu.; (4) *fortūna tua* in acc. sing. and plu.; (5) *magna patria* in gen. sing. and plu.; (6) *fortūna mea* in abl. sing. and plu.; (7) *magna poena* in dat. sing. and plu.; (8) *multa philosophia* in dat. and abl. plu.

8. Translate each of the following phrases into Latin according to the case either named or indicated by the English preposition in each instance: (1) by much money; (2) of many girls; (3) to/for my country; (4) great life (as direct object of a verb); (5) by your penalties; (6) many countries (subject of a verb); (7) to/for many girls; (8) of my life; (9) O fortune; (10) girl's; (11) girls'; (12) girls (direct address); (13) the girls (direct object of a verb); (14) the girls (subject of a verb).

9. Valē, patria mea. 10. Fortūna puellae est magna. 11. Puella fortūnam patriae tuae laudat. 12. Ō puella, patriam tuam servā. 13. Multae puellae pecūniam amant. 14. Puellae nihil datis. 15. Pecūniam puellae videt. 16. Pecūniam puellārum nōn vidēs. 17. Monēre puellās dēbēmus. 18. Laudāre puellam dēbent. 19. Vīta multīs puellīs fortūnam dat. 20. Vītam meam pecūniā tuā cōnservās. 21. Fāma est nihil sine fortūnā. 22. Vitam sine pecūniā nōn amātis.

23. Sine fāma et fortūnā patria nōn valet. 24. Īram puellārum laudāre nōn dēbēs. 25. Vitam sine poenīs amāmus. 26. Sine philosophiā nōn valēmus. 27. Quid est vīta sine philosophiā?

EXERCISES FOR CHAPTER 3

1. Name the case, number, and syntactical usage indicated by each of the following endings of masculines of the 2nd declension: (1) -um; (2) -ī (plu.); (3) -us; (4) -ōs; (5) -e.
2. Name the case(s) and number of the following endings, and name the English preposition which can be associated with each: (1) -ō; (2) -ōrum; (3) -ī (sing.); (4) -īs.
3. Translate the following nouns and state the syntactical usage of each as indicated by its ending: (1) filiōs; (2) filiī (plu.); (3) filium; (4) populum; (5) popule; (6) populus; (7) vir; (8) virōs; (9) virī (plu.); (10) virum; (11) amīce; (12) amīcī (plu.); (13) amīcōs; (14) amīcum.
4. Translate the following in accordance with their case endings: (1) filiōrum meōrum; (2) filiō meō; (3) populī Rōmānī (sing.); (4) populō Rōmānō; (5) virīs; (6) virī (sing.); (7) virōrum; (8) amīcōrum paucōrum; (9) amīcīs paucīs; (10) amīcō meō; (11) amīcī meī (sing.); (12) multīs puerīs.
5. Given the following nom. sing. forms, write the Latin forms requested in each instance: (1) *populus Rōmānus* in gen. and abl. sing.; (2) *magnus vir* in acc. and abl. plu.; (3) *puer meus* in dat. and abl. plu.; (4) *magnus numerus* in dat. and abl. sing.; (5) *magnus vir* in voc. sing. and plu.; (6) *filius meus* in gen. sing. and plu.

6. Translate the following phrases into Latin according to the case named or indicated by the English preposition in each instance: (1) of many boys; (2) to/for the Roman people; (3) my sons (object of verb); (4) O my sons; (5) a great number (obj. of verb); (6) by the great number; (7) O great man; (8) to/for many boys; (9) the great man (subj. of verb); (10) of the Roman people.

7. Valē, mī amīce. 8. Populus Rōmānus sapientiam fīliī tuī laudat. 9. Ō vir magne, populum Rōmānum servā. 10. Numerus populī Rōmānī est magnus. 11. Multī puerī puellās amant. 12. Fīliō meō nihil datis. 13. Virōs in agrō videō. 14. Amīcum fīliī meī vidēs. 15. Amīcum fīliōrum tuōrum nōn videt. 16. Dēbēmus fīliōs meōs monēre. 17. Dēbent fīlium tuum laudāre. 18. Vīta paucīs virīs fāmam dat. 19. Mē in numerō amīcōrum tuōrum habēs. 20. Virī magnī paucōs amīcōs saepe habent.

21. Amīcus meus semper cōgitat. 22. Fīlius magnī virī nōn semper est magnus vir. 23. Sapientiam magnōrum virōrum nōn semper vidēmus. 24. Philosophiam, sapientiam magnōrum virōrum, laudāre dēbētis.

EXERCISES FOR CHAPTER 4

1. A 2nd-declension neuter has the same forms as the regular 2nd-declension masculine except in three instances. Name these three instances and give their neuter endings.
2. Name the case(s), number and syntactical usage indicated by each of the following endings of the 2nd- declension neuter nouns: (1) -a; (2) -nm.
3. Name the case(s) and number of the following 2nd- declension neuter endings and name the English preposition(s) which can be associated with each: (1) -ō; (2) -ōrum; (3) -ī; (4) -īs.
4. Translate the following neuter nouns and state the syntactical usage of each as indicated by its ending: (1) bella; (2) bellum; (3) officium; (4) officia; (5) perīcula.
5. Translate the following phrases in accordance with their case endings: (1) bellōrum malōrum; (2) bellō malō; (3) bellī malī; (4) bellīs malīs; (5) officiī magnī; (6) officiīs magnīs; (7) perīculō parvō.
6. Given the following nom. sing. forms, write the Latin forms requested in each instance: (1) *bellum parvum* in nom. and acc. plu.; (2) *ōtium bonum* in acc. sing. and plu.; (3) *perīculum magnum* in gen. sing. and plu.; (4) *officium vērum* in acc. and abl. sing.
7. Translate the following phrases into Latin in accordance with the case named or indicated by the English preposition in each instance: (1) O evil war; (2) to/for great duty; (3) by the great danger; (4) good leisure (object of verb); (5) by many wars; (6) of good leisure; (7) by the dangers of many wars; (8) small wars (subject of verb); (9) small wars (obj. of verb); (10) O foolish wars; (11) the small war (subj.)

8. Ōtium est bonum.

9. Multa bella ōtium nōn cōnservant. 10. Perīculum est magnum. 11. In magnō
perīculō sumus. 12. Et ōtium perīcula saepe habet. 13. Vīta nōn est sine
multī perīculīs. 14. Bonī virī ōtium amant. 15. Stultus vir perīcula bellī
laudat. 16. Ōtium bellō saepe nōn cōnservāmus. 17. Populus Rōmānus
ōtium bonum nōn semper habet. 18. Patriam et ōtium bellīs parvīs saepe
servant. 19. Multae puellae sunt bellae. 20. Vērī amīcī sunt paucī.
21. Amīcus meus est vir magnī officiī. 22. Officia magistrī sunt multa et
magna. 23. Vir párvī ōtiī es. 24. Virī magnae cūrae estis. 25. Sine morā
cūram officiō dare dēbēmus. 26. Sine oculīs vita est nihil.

EXERCISES FOR CHAPTER 5

1. Name the *personal* endings of the future tense of the first two conjugations.
2. Are these the same as the endings of the present tense? If not, point out the
   differences.
3. Name the future tense sign in the first two conjugations.
4. How, in effect, can the following verb endings be translated: (1) -bimus;
   (2) -bit; (3) -bitis; (4) -bō; (5) -bunt?
5. When an adjective of the 1st and 2nd declensions has the masculine ending
   in -*er*, how can you tell whether the *e* survives in the other forms or is lost?
6. How do English words like *liberty*, *pulchritude*, and *nostrum* help with the
   declension of Latin adjectives?
7. Translate the following forms: (1) manēbunt; (2) manēbit; (3) manēbimus;
   (4) dabō; (5) dabitis; (6) dabit; (7) vidēbis; (8) vidēbimus; (9) vocābunt;
   (10) vocābis; (11) habēbis; (12) habēbunt.
8. Translate into Latin: (1) we shall give; (2) you (sing.) will remain; (3) they
   will see; (4) we shall call; (5) he will call; (6) you (plu.) will see; (7) I shall
   see; (8) they will have; (9) we shall have; (10) we have; (11) he will have;
   (12) he has.

9. Magister noster mē laudat et tē laudābit. 10. Līberī virī perīcula nostra
superābunt. 11. Filiī nostrī puellās pulchrās amant. 12. Amīcus noster
in numerō stultōrum nōn remanēbit. 13. Culpās multās habēmus et
semper habēmus et semper habēbimus. 14. Perīcula magna animōs nostrōs
nōn superant. 15. Pulchra patria nostra est lībera. 16. Līberī virī estis;
patriam pulchram habēbitis. 17. Magistrī līberī officiō cūram dabunt.
18. Malōs igitur in patrā nostrā superābimus. 19. Sī īram tuam
superābis, tē superābis. 20. Propter nostrōs animōs multī sunt līberī.

21. Tē, Ō patria lībera, amāmus et semper amābimus. 22. Sapientiam
pecūniā nōn cōservābitis. 23. Habetne animus tuus satis sapientiae?

EXERCISES FOR CHAPTER 6

1. What connection can be traced between the spelling of *complementary* in the term *complementary infinitive* and the syntactical principle?

2. In the verb *sum* and its compounds what do the following personal endings mean: (1) -mus; (2) -nt; (3) -s; (4) -t; (5) -ō; (6) -m; (7) -tis?

3. If the verb *possum* is composed of *pot + sum*, where among the various forms is the *t* changed to *s* and where does it remain unchanged?

4. Translate the following random forms: (1) erat; (2) poterat; (3) erit; (4) poterit; (5) sumus; (6) possumus; (7) poterāmus; (8) poterimus; (9) poteram; (10) eram; (11) erō; (12) poterō; (13) erunt; (14) poterunt; (15) poterant; (16) esse; (17) posse.

5. Translate into Latin: (1) we are; (2) we were; (3) we shall be; (4) we shall be able; (5) he is able; (6) he will be able; (7) he was able; (8) to be able; (9) they were able; (10) they are able; (11) they will be able; (12) they are; (13) to be; (14) I was able.

6. Patria vestra erat lībera. 7. Poteram esse tyrannus. 8. Amīcus vester erit tyrannus. 9. Librum meum vocābō *Bellum Meum.* 10. Ubi tyrannus est, ibi virī nōn possunt esse līberī. 11. In patriā nostrā nōn poterat remanēre. 12. Tyrannī multa vitia semper habēbunt. 13. Tyrannōs superāre nōn poterāmus. 14. Tyrannum nostrum superāre dēbēmus. 15. Tyrannus bonōs superāre poterat; sed ibi remanēre nōn poterit. 16. Poteritis perīcula tyrranī vidēre. 17. Vitia tyrannōrum tolerāre nōn possumus. 18. Īnsidiās tyrannī nōn tolerābis. 19. Ōtium in patriā vestrā nōn potest esse perpetuum. 20. Dēbēs virōs līberōs dē tyrannīs monēre. 21. Magister vester librōs pulchrōs semper amat. 22. Librī bonī vērīque poterant patriam cōnservāre. 23. Librīs bonīs patriam vestram cōnservāre poteritis. 24. Tyrannī sapientiam bonōrum librōrum superāre nōn poterunt. 25. Malī librōs bonōs nōn possunt tolerāre.

EXERCISES FOR CHAPTER 7

1. In the 3rd declension do the case endings of feminine nouns differ from those of masculine nouns as they do in the 1st and 2nd declensions already learned?

2. Do neuter nouns of the 3rd declension have any case endings which are identical with those of neuter nouns of the 2nd declension? If so, name them.

3. Name the gender(s) and case(s) indicated by each of the following endings in the 3rd declension: (1) -ēs; (2) -a; (3) -em.

4. Name the case(s) and number of the following 3rd- declensional endings: (1) -ibus; (2) -ī; (3) -e; (4) -em; (5) -um; (6) -is; (7) -ēs.

5. To indicate the gender of the following nouns give the proper nominative singular form of *magnus, -a, -um* with each: (1) tempus; (2) virtūs; (3) labor; (4) cīvitās; (5) mōs; (6) pāx; (7) rēx; (8) corpus; (9) vēritās; (10) amor.

6. Translate the following phrases in accordance with their case endings wherever possible; where they are nominative or accusative so state: (1) labōre multō; (2) labōrī multō; (3) labōris multī; (4) labōrēs multī; (5) pācis perpetuae; (6) pāce perpetuā; (7) pācī perpetuae; (8) cīvitātum parvārum; (9) cīvitātem parvam; (10) cīvitātēs parvās; (11) cīvitātēs parvae; (12) cīvitāte parvā; (13) tempora mala; (14) tempus malum; (15) temporī malō; (16) temporum malōrum; (17) temporis malī; (18) mōrī tuō; (19) mōre tuō; (20) mōris tuī; (21) mōrēs tuī; (22) mōrēs tuōs; (23) mōrum tuōrum.

7. Translate the following phrases into Latin in accordance with the case named or indicated by the English preposition: (1) to/for great virtue; (2) great virtue (subject); (3) great virtues (object of verb); (4) of great virtues; (5) with great courage; (6) our time (obj. of verb); (7) our times (subj.); (8) our times (obj.); (9) to/for our times; (10) to/for our time; (11) of our time; (12) of our times; (13) my love (obj.); (14) my loves (obj.); (15) to/for my love; (16) by my love; (17) of my love; (18) of my loves.

8. Meum tempus ōtiō est parvum. 9. Virtūs tua est magna. 10. Pecūnia est nihil sine mōribus bonīs. 11. Virtūtēs hominum multōrum sunt magnae. 12. Mōrēs hominis bonī erunt bonī. 13. Hominī litterās dabunt. 14. Hominēs multōs in cīvitāte magnā vidēre poterāmus. 15. Magnum amōrem pecūniae in multīs hominibus vidēmus. 16. Paucī hominēs virtūtī cūram dant. 17. Cīvitās nostra pācem hominibus multīs dabit. 18. Pāx nōn potest esse perpetua. 19. Sine bonā pāce cīvitātēs temporum nostrōrum nōn valēbunt. 20. Post multa bella tempora sunt mala. 21. In multīs cīvitātibus terrīsque pāx nōn poterat valēre. 22. Sine magnō labōre homō nihil habēbit. 23. Virgō pulchra amīcōs mōrum bonōrum amat. 24. Hominēs magnae virtūtis tyrannōs superāre audēbunt. 26. Amor patriae in cīvitāte nostrā valet.

EXERCISES FOR CHAPTER 8

1. (1) In the 3d conjugation what tense is indicated by the stem vowel **e**? (2) Can you think of some mnemonic device to help you remember this important point?

2. (1) In the 3d conjugation what tense is indicated by the vowels **i, ō, u**? (2) What mnemonic device may help here?

3. State the person, number, and tense indicated by each of the following endings: (1) -imus; (2) -ēs; (3) -unt; (4) -et; (5) -itis; (6) -ēmus; (7) -ō; (8) -ent; (9) -it; (10) -ētis; (11) -is; (12) -am.

4. What form of the verb does each of the following endings indicate: (1) -e; (2) -ere; (3) -ite?

5. Given the verbs **mittō, mittere,** *send*; **agō, agere,** *do;* **scrībō, scrībere,** *write,* translate each of the following forms according to its ending: (1) mittent; (2) mittit; (3) mittunt; (4) mittam; (5) mitte; (6) mittimus; (7) mittētis; (8) mittis; (9) mittite; (10) mittitis; (11) mittet; (12) mittēmus; (13) **agit;**

(14) agent; (15) agunt; (16) agētis; (17) agimus; (18) agam; (19) agēmus; (20) agis; (21) agitis; (22) scrībet; (23) scrībunt; (24) scrībam; (25) scrībe; (26) scrībitis; (27) scribēmus; (28) scrībit; (29) scrībis; (30) scrībent.

6. Given **pōnō, pōnere,** *put*, translate the following phrases into Latin: (1) they are putting; (2) we shall put; (3) put (imperative sing.); (4) he puts; (5) they will put; (6) I shall put; (7) you (sing.) are putting; (8) you (plu.) will put; (9) put (imv. plu.); (10) we put; (11) you (plu.) are putting; (12) he will put.

7. Quid agunt? Quid agētis? 8. Hominem ad mē dūcunt. 9. Dūc hominem ad mē, et hominī grātiās agam. 10. Dum tyrannus cōpiās dūcit, possumus nihil agere. 11. Litterās ad virginem scrībit. 12. Librum magnum scrībis. 13. Librōs bonōs scrībēs. 14. Librōs dē pāce scribēmus. 15. Cōpiamne librōrum bonōrum habētis? 16. Magister multōs puerōs docet. 17. Pueri magistrō grātiās nōn agunt. 18. Paucī cīvitātī nostrae grātiās agent. 19. Tyrannus magnās cōpiās ex cīvitāte nostrā dūcet. 20. Magna cōpia pecūniae hominēs ad sapientiam nōn dūcit. 21. Librīne bonī multōs ad ratiōnem dūcent? 22. Dūcimusne saepe hominēs ad ratiōnem? 23. Ratiō hominēs ad bonam vitam dūcere potest. 24. Agitisne bonam vitam? 25. Amīcō bonō grātiās semper agite.

EXERCISES FOR CHAPTER 9

1. Explain the term *demonstrative* pronoun and adjective.
2. Translate each of the following according to case(s) and number, indicating also the gender(s) in each instance:

(1) illī	(10) illīs	(19) huius	(28) ūnā
(2) illa	(11) illō	(20) hunc	(29) tōtī
(3) illīus	(12) illārum	(21) hōs	(30) tōtīus
(4) ille	(13) hōc	(22) huic	(31) tōta
(5) illā	(14) hoc	(23) hōrum	(32) tōtum
(6) illud	(15) haec	(24) hās	(33) nūllīus
(7) illōrum	(16) hae	(25) hīs	(34) nūllī
(8) illae	(17) hāc	(26) ūnīus	(35) nūlla
(9) illōs	(18) hanc	(27) ūnī	(36) nūllōs

3. How can the presence of a noun be helpful in determining the form of a modifying demonstrative?

4. Translate the following phrases into Latin in the declensional forms indicated:

(1) this girl (nom.)	(18) of that girl alone
(2) these girls (nom.)	(19) of tyrants alone
(3) these times (acc. plu.)	(20) the whole state (acc.)
(4) to/for this time	(21) of the whole country
(5) to/for this boy	(22) to/for the whole country
(6) of this time	(23) of no reason
(7) of that time	(24) no reason (acc.)
(8) by this book	(25) no girls (nom.)
(9) by that book	(26) to/for no book
(10) that girl (nom.)	(27) no books (acc.)
(11) those times (nom.)	(28) to/for one state
(12) those times (acc.)	(29) to/for one girl
(13) that time (nom.)	(30) of one time
(14) to/for this state alone	(31) of one war
(15) of this state alone	(32) to/for the other book
(16) to/for that boy alone	(33) by another book
(17) to/for that girl alone	

5. Hī tōtam cīvitātem dūcent (dūcunt). 6. Ille haec in illā terrā vidēbit (videt). 7. In illō librō illa dē hōc homine scrībet (scrībam). 8. Ūnus vir istās cōpiās in hanc terram dūcit (dūcet). 9. Magister haec alterī puerō dat. 10. Hunc librum dē aliō bellō scrībimus (scrībēmus). 11. Tōta patria huic sōlī grātiās agit (aget). 12. Tōtam cūram illī cōnsiliō nunc dant. 13. Amīcus huius hanc cīvitātem illō cōnsiliō cōnservābit. 14. Alter amīcus tōtam vītam in aliā terrā aget. 15. Hic vir sōlus mē dē vitiīs huius tyrannī monēre poterat. 16. Nūllās cōpiās in alterā terrā habētis. 17. Illī sōlī nūlla perīcula in hōc cōnsiliō vident. 18. Nōn sōlum mōrēs sed etiam īnsidiās illīus laudāre audēs. 19. Propter īnsidiās enim unīus hominis haec cīvitās nōn valet.

EXERCISES FOR CHAPTER 10

1. Name the conjugation indicated by each of the following endings: (1) -ere; (2) -ēre; (3) -īre; (4) -āre.
2. State the person, number, and tense indicated by the following endings from the 4th conjugation and the **-iō** 3d: (1) -iunt; (2) - iēs; (3) -īs; (4) -iēmus; (5) -īmus; (6) -ī; (7) -iētis; (8) -īte; (9) -ītis; (10) -iō; (11) -it; (12) -e.
3. State three points at which **-iō** verbs of the 3d conjugation differ from verbs of the 4th conjugation.

4. Translate the following in accordance with their specific forms:

(1) veniet	(6) audiētis	(11) venīre	(16) faciunt
(2) venit	(7) audītis	(12) facit	(17) facis
(3) veniunt	(8) venīte	(13) faciet	(18) faciam
(4) venient	(9) veniēs	(14) faciēmus	(19) faciēs
(5) audīs	(10) venī	(15) facimus	(20) facere

5. Given **sentiō, sentīre,** *feel*, and **iaciō, iacere,** *throw*, translate the following phrases into Latin:

(1) I shall feel	(8) feel (imv. sing.)	(15) throw (imv. sing.)
(2) we shall feel	(9) he will feel	(16) you (plu.) are throwing
(3) he feels	(10) we feel	(17) we shall throw
(4) you (plu.) feel	(11) he is throwing	(18) throw (imv. plu.)
(5) they will feel	(12) he will throw	(19) to throw
(6) they do feel	(13) I shall throw	(20) you (sing.)are throwing
(7) to feel	(14) we are throwing	

6. Ex hāc terrā fugimus. 7. Cum fīliā tuā fuge. 8. In illum locum fugient. 9. Tempus fugit; hōrae fugiunt; senectūs venit. 10. Venīte cum amīcīs vestrīs.

11. In patriam vestram veniunt. 12. Ō vir magne, in cīvitātem nostram venī. 13. Fīliam tuam in illā cīvitāte veniēs. 14. Parvam pecūniam in viīs invenīre possunt. 15. Tyrannus viam in hanc cīvitātem invenit. 16. Illōs cum amīcīs ibi capiētis. 17. Ad tē cum magnīs cōpiīs venīmus. 18. Invenietne multam fāmam glōriamque ibi? 19. Iste bellum semper facit. 20. Istī hominēs pācem nō facient. 21. Multī hominēs illa faciunt sed haec nōn faciunt. 22. Officium nostrum facimus et faciēmus. 23. Magnam cōpiam librōrum faciam. 24. Puerī cum illō virō bonō vīvunt. 25. In librīs virōrum antīquōrum multam philosophiam et sapientiam veniētis.

EXERCISES FOR CHAPTER 11

1. Name the nominative singular and plural of the following:
   (1) 3d personal pronoun; (2) 1st per. prn.; (3) 2nd per. prn.
2. Translate the following pronouns in accordance with case(s) and number; where a form is nom. or acc. so specify.
   (1) vōbīs; (2) nōbīs; (3) nōs; (4) vōs; (5) tuī; (6) meī; (7) mihi; (8) tibi; (9) tē; (10) mē.
3. Translate the following third-personal pronouns in accordance with their gender(s), number(s), and case(s): (1) eōs; (2) eās; (3) eōrum; (4) eārum; (5) eius; (6) eā; (7) ea; (8) eō; (9) eī; (10) eīs; (11) eae; (12) id.

4. Give the Latin for the following:

(1) his	(10) to her	(19) it (neut. acc.)
(2) her (possess.)	(11) by/w./fr. hcr	(20) you (emphatic nom. plu.)
(3) their (masc.)	(12) by/w./fr. him	(21) you (emphatic nom. sing.)
(4) their (fem.)	(13) to/for you (plu.)	(22) you (acc. plu.)
(5) them (fem.)	(14) to/for you (sing.)	(23) us
(6) them (masc.)	(15) they (masc.)	(24) we
(7) them (neut.)	(16) they (neut.)	(25) to/for us
(8) its	(17) they (fem.)	(26) I (emphatic form)
(9) to him	(18) to/for it	(27) to/for you (sing.)

5. Hī tibi id dabunt. 6. Ego vōbīs id dabō. 7. Vōs eīs id dabitis. 8. Eī idem dabō. 9. Nōs ei ea dabimus. 10. Ille mihi id dabit. 11. Vōbīs librōs eius dabimus. 12. Nōbīs librōs eōrum dabis. 13. Pecūniam eōrum tibi dabimus. 14. Pecūniam eius mihi dabunt. 15. Librōs eius ad eam mittēmus. 16. Librum eius ad tē mittam. 17. Ille autem pecūniam eōrum ad nōs mittet. 18. Eās cum eā mittimus. 19. Eum cum eīs mittō. 20. Eōs cum amīcīs eius mittēmus. 21. Tū mē cum amīcō eōrum mittēs. 22. Vōs mēcum ad amīcum eius mittunt. 23. Nōs tēcum in terram eōrum mittit. 24. Eās nōbīscum ad amīcōs eōrum mittent. 25. Eum vōbīscum ad amīcōs eōrum mittam. 26. Tē cum eō ad mē mittent.

EXERCISES FOR CHAPTER 12

1. Name the principal parts of a Latin verb in their regular sequence.

2. Give the principal parts of **mittō**, labeling and translating each one.

3. You must know the principal parts and meaning of all the verbs in the list in Chap. 12 and of those given in the vocabularies of the remaining chapters. What is the best way to learn them?

4. Vice versa, you must also be able to tell from what verb any specific verb form comes. Practice on the following list by naming the first principal part of each of the verbs in the list.

(1) mīsērunt	(6) actum	(11) remānserant	(16) dīxērunt
(2) laudāveram	(7) est	(12) scrīpsimus	(17) erat
(3) vīcit	(8) dedimus	(13) fuit	(18) vīxī
(4) dictum	(9) futūrus	(14) fēcit	(19) facere
(5) fēcistī	(10) ēgimus	(15) fugere	(20) vīsum

5. Translate the following endings of the perfect system according to person, number, and tense in each instance, using these conventions: -ī = I (perfect) ...; -eram = I had ...; -erō = I shall have...; (1) -istis; (2) -it; (3) -ērunt; (4) -istī; (5) -imus; (6) -erat; (7) -erimus; (8) -erāmus; (9) -erās; (10) -erint; (11) -erant; (12) -erit; (13) -erātis.

6. Translate the following in accordance with the person, number, and tense of each:

(1) vīdērunt	(10) vīxistī	(19) fugit	(28) remānsimus
(2) viderant	(11) vīxērunt	(20) fūgit	(29) remmānserāmus
(3) vīdistī	(12) vincet	(21) fugiunt	(30) vēnit
(4) fēcit	(13) vīcit	(22) fūgērunt	(31) venit
(5) facit	(14) vīcimus	(23) servāvit	(32) venītis
(6) fēcerāmus	(15) vincimus	(24) servāvērunt	(33) vēnistis
(7) fēcimus	(16) dedistī	(25) servāvistis	(34) vēnērunt
(8) faciēmus	(17) dederātis	(26) servāverat	(35) veniunt
(9) fēcērunt	(18) dedimus	(27) servāverit	(36) vēnerant

7. Illī fūgerant (fugient; fugiunt; fūgērunt). 8. Hī remānsērunt (remanent; remanēbunt; remānserant). 9. Rēx Asiam vīcerat (vincit; vīcit; vincet). 10. Rēgēs Asiam vicērunt (vincent; vincunt; vīcerant). 11. Rēgēs Asiam habuērunt (habent; habēbunt; habuerant). 12. Caesar in eandem terram vēnerat (vēnit; venit; veniet). 13. Caesar eadem dīxit (dīcit; dixerat; dīcet). 14. Vōs nōbis pācem dedistis (dabitis; dederātis). 15. Tū litterās ad eam mīsistī (mittēs; mittis; mīserās). 16. Eōs in eādem viā vīdimus (vidēmus; vīderāmus). 17. Diū vīxerat (vīxit; vīvet). 18. Id bene fēcerās (faciēs; fēcistī; facis). 19. Cīvitātem eōrum (eius) servāvī (servābō; servāveram). 20. Eum in eōdem locō invēnērunt (invēnerant; invenient). 21. Deus hominibus lībertātem dederat (dedit; dat; dabit). 22. Mihi grātiās ēgērunt (agent; ēgerant; agunt). 23. Vōs fuistis (erātis; estis; eritis; fuerātis) virī līberī.

EXERCISES FOR CHAPTER 13

1. State the essential nature of reflexive pronouns, showing how, as a logical consequence, they differ from other pronouns.
2. Explain why the declension of reflexive pronouns begins with the genitive rather than with the nominative.
3. In what reflexive pronouns is the spelling the same as that of the corresponding simple pronoun?
4. Translate the following reflexive forms in accordance with their case(s) and number(s): (1) mihi; (2) tē; (3) nōbīs; (4) sibi; (5) vōs; (6) sē; (7) vōbīs.
5. Explain why the singular of *suus* can mean *their own* as well as *his own*, and the plural can mean *his own* as well as *their own*.
6. Explain why *eōrum* always means *their* and *eius* always means *his (her, its)* regardless of whether the nouns on which they depend are singular or plural.
7. Although *sē* and *ipse* can both be translated into English by *himself*, explain the basic difference between the Latin words.

8. Caesar *eōs* servāvit.
9. Caesar *eum* servāvit.
10. Caesar *sē* servāvit.
11. Rōmānī *sē* servāvērunt.
12. Rōmānī *eōs* servavērunt.
13. Rōmānī *eum* servāvērunt.
14. Caesar amīcum *suum* servāvit.
15. Caesar amīcōs *suōs* servāvit.
16. Caesar amīcum *eius* servāvit.
17. Caesar amīcōs *eius* servāvit.
18. Caesar amīcum *eōrum* servāvit.
19. Caesar amicōs *eōrum* servāvit.
20. Rōmānī amīcum *suum* servāvērunt.
21. Rōmānī amīcōs *suōs* servāvērunt.
22. Rōmānī amīcum *eōrum* servāvērunt.
23. Rōmānī amīcōs *eōrum* servāvērunt.
24. Rōmānī amīcum *eius* servāvērunt.
25. Rōmānī amīcōs *eius* servāvērunt.
26. Caesar *ipse eum* servāvit.
27. Caesar *ipse sē* servāvit.
28. Caesarem *ipsum* servāvērunt.
29. Amīcum Caesaris *ipsīus* servāvērunt.
30. Amīcum Rōmānōrum *ipsōrum* servāvērunt.
31. Amcus Caesaris *ipsīus* sē servāvit.
32. Amīcī Caesaris *ipsīus* sē servāvērunt.
33. Amīcus Caesaris *ipsīus eum* servāvit.
34. *Ipsī* amīcī Caesaris *eum* servāvērunt.
35. Nōs nōv servāvērunt.
36. Nōs servāvimus.
37. Rōmānōs *ipsōs* servāvimus
38. Rōmānī *ipsī tē* nōn servāvērunt.
39. Tū *tē* servāvistī.
40. Tū Rōmānōs *ipsōs* servāvistī.
41. *Mihi* nihil dedit.
42. *Mihi* nihil dedī.
43. *Sibi* nihil dedit.
44. *Sibi* nihil dedērunt.
45. *Eīs* nihil dedērunt.
46. *Eī* nihil dedērunt.
47. *Mē* vīcī.
48. *Mē* vīcērunt.
49. Īram *eōrum* vīcērunt.
50. Īram *suam* vīcērunt.
51. Īram *suam* vīcit.
52. Fīliōs *suōs* vīcit.
53. Fīliōs *suōs* vīcērunt.

EXERCISES FOR CHAPTER 14

1. In what specific case ending of all *i*-stem nouns does the characteristic *i* appear?
2. What are the future *i*-stem peculiarities of neuters in -*e*, -*al*, and -*ar*?
3. Translate each of the following according to its case(s) and number; when a form is nom. or acc. label it as such.

(1) arte   (9) corporum   (17) rēgum   (25) virōs
(2) artium   (10) partis   (18) rēgī   (26) virī
(3) artēs   (11) partibus (19) nōmina (27) vīrēs
(4) marī   (12) partium (20) animālia (28) virīs
(5) maribus (13) urbe   (21) animālī (29) vīs
(6) mare   (14) urbī   (22) animālis (30) vim
(7) maria   (15) urbium (23) animālium (31) vīribus
(8) corpora (16) urbēs   (24) vīrium   (32) vī

4. Of the forms in #3 above, list those which are **i**- stem forms.
5. Translate the following phrases into Latin:
(1) by/w./fr. great force   (9) by/w./fr. a great sea

(2) great man (acc.)   (10) a great sea (acc.)
(3) of great strength   (11) great force (acc.)
(4) to/for great force   (12) of many men (vir)
(5) of many citizens   (13) by/w./fr. great strength
(6) by/w./fr. a good citizen (14) by great force
(7) to/for many citizens   (15) great strength (acc.)
(8) many seas (nom.)

6. What kind of idea is expressed by each of the following ablatives? (1) cum rēge; (2) oculīs meīs; (3) cum cūrā; (4) labōre meō.

7. Translate each of the following verb forms and name the verb from which each comes: (1) cucurrērunt; (2) currimus; (3) cucurristī; (4) trāxerāmus; (5) trahet; (6) trahunt; (7) gessit; (8) gerit; (9) gerunt; (10) gerēmus; (11) tenent; (12) tenēbunt; (13) tenuērunt; (14) tenuimus.

8. Multa bella cum Rōmānīs gessit. 9) Cīvitātem magnā cum sapientiā gessērunt. 10. Ipse cīvitātem vī cōpiārum tenuit. 11. Illa animālia multōs hominēs in mare trāxērunt. 12. Hoc magnā cum arte dīxistī. 13. Cum cūrā trāns urbem cucurrimus. 14. Magnā cum parte cīvium ad nōs vēnit. 15. Iūra cīvium vī vincet. 16. Eum ad mortem trāns terram eius trāxistis. 17. Nōs cum cīvibus multārum urbium iungēmus. 18. Rēgī ipsī hās litterās cum virtūte scrīpsit. 19. Vīs illōrum marium erat magna. 20. Artem Graecōrum oculīs meīs vīdī. 21. Sententiās multās pulchrāsque ex virīs antīquīs trāximus.

22. Name the type of ablative found in each of the following sentences above: 8, 9, 10, 12, 13, 14, 15, 17, 18, 20.

EXERCISES FOR CHAPTER 15

1. (1) What is the tense sign of the Latin imperfect tense in each of the four conjugations?
   (2) Is this found consistently throughout all six persons or is it somewhat modified?
   (3) What is the tense sign of the future indicative in the *-āre* and the *-ēre* verbs (i.e., the first two conjugations)?
   (4) What is the tense sign of the future in the *-ere* and *-īre* verbs?

2. What is the basic force of the imperfect tense as compared with that of the perfect tense?

3. Translate the following forms in such a way as to make clear the difference between the imperfect and the perfect tenses.
   (1) veniēbat (3) faciēbam   (5) iaciēbat   (7) scrībēbāmus
   (2) vēnit   (4) fēcī   (6) iēcērunt   (8) scrīpsimus

4. When the Romans put a word of time in the ablative case without a preposition, what kind of ideas did they express?

5. Study the ablatives in the following sentences. Then translate the sentences and name the type of ablative found in each one.

(1) Cum amīcīs veniēbat.　(4) Paucīs hōrīs librum scrīpsit.
(2) Ūnā hōrā veniet.　(5) Illō tempore librum scrīpsit.
(3) Eōdem tempore vēnit.　(6) Cum cūrā librum scrībēbat.

6. Illō tempore sōlō perīcula timuit; sed mortem semper timēbat. 7. Multī rēgēs pecūniam inter miserōs cīvēs iaciēbant. 8. Iste tyrannus sē semper laudābat. 9. Cīvēs illārum urbium lībertātem exspectābant. 10. Urbem ūnā hōrā sapientiā suā cōnservāvērunt. 11. In urbem cum amīcō meō veniēbam. 12. Bella magna cum virtūte gerēbātis. 13. Itaque Rōmānī Graccōs vīcērunt. 14. Patrēs fīliōs suōs saepe timēbant — et nunc timent! 15. Vīdistīne patrem meum eō tempore? 16. Ubi hanc pecūniam invēnistis?

17. Vēnērunt, et idem nōbis dīcēbat. 18. Librōs eius numquam intellegēbam.

19. Vītam nostram numquam mutāvimus. 20. Cīvitās nostra lībertātem et iūra cīvium cōnservābat. 21. Rōmānī mōrēs temporum antīquōrum laudābant.

EXERCISES FOR CHAPTER 16

1. If one has carefully learned the declension of **cīvis** and **mare** one can easily decline the 3d-declension adjective **fortis, forte** with the exception of one form. What is that form?
2. (1) Adjectives of the 3d declension may be classified as adjectives of 3 endings, 2 endings, or 1 ending. Which type is by far the most common? (2) In what one case do adjectives of 1 and 3 endings differ from those of 2 endings?
3. Cite and label three endings in which adjectives of the 3d declension show themselves to be i-stems.
4. Of the endings of the 3d-declension adjectives none is likely to cause recognition difficulty except perhaps the ablative singular. What is the normal ending of the ablative singular in all genders?
5. Can 3d-declension adjectives be used with nouns of the 1st or the 2nd declension?
6. Translate the following phrases in accordance with their case(s) and number. When they are nom. or acc., so indicate.

(1) dulcī puellae	(8) omnia nōmina	(15) beātō hominī
(2) dulcī puellā	(9) omnia maria	(16) omnī marī
(3) dulcī mātre	(10) omnī parte	(17) omnī bonae artī
(4) dulcī mātrī	(11) omnium partium	(18) omnī bonā arte
(5) beātae mātrī	(12) omnium rēgum	(19) omnis bonae artis
(6) beātā mātre	(13) omnium bellōrum	(20) vī celerī
(7) omnia bella	(14) beātō homine	

7. Aetās longa saepe est difficilis. 8. Aetās difficilis potest esse beāta. 9. Quam brevis erat dulcis vīta eius! 10. Memoria dulcis aetātis omnēs hominēs adiuvat. 11. Librum brevem brevī tempore scrīpsistī. 12. In omnī marī hoc animal potēns inveniēbāmus. 13. In omnī terrā multōs virōs fortēs vidēbitis. 14. Celer rūmor (celeris fāma) per omnem terram cucurrit. 15. Illud bellum breve erat difficile. 16. Omnia perīcula paucīs hōris superāvimus. 17. Tyrannus potēns patriam eōrum vī celerī vincet. 18. Brevī tempore omnia iūra civium mūtābit. 19. Difficilem artem lībertātis dulcis nōn intellēxērunt. 20. Hominēs officia difficilia in omnibus terrīs timent.

EXERCISES FOR CHAPTER 17

1. Define the terms "antecedent" and "relative pronoun."
2. (1) What determines the *case* of the Latin relative pronoun?
   (2) What determines the *gender* and the *number* of the relative pronoun?
3. State in what ways a relative agrees with its antecedent.
4. Name (1) the English relative pronoun which refers to persons and (2) the one which refers to anything else. (3) Since in Latin the one relative pronoun serves both purposes, what two English meanings does it have?
5. Translate the following in accordance with their case(s) and number(s). When a form is nom. or acc., so indicate if the translation does not make the point clear.

(1) cui	(4) cuius	(7) quā	(10) quās
(2) quōs	(5) quibus	(8) quī	(11) quōrum
(3) quae	(6) quod	(9) quem	(12) quam

6. Cīvem laudāvērunt **quem** mīserātis. 7. Cīvēs laudāvērunt **quōs** mīserātis. 8. Cīvem laudāvērunt **quī** patriam servāverat. 9. Cīvēs laudāvērunt **quī** patriam servāverant. 10. Cīvem laudāvērunt **cuius** fīlius patriam servāverat. 11. Cīvēs laudāvērunt **quōrum** fīliī patriam servāverant. 12. Cīvem laudāvērunt **cui** patriam commīserant. 13. Cīvēs laudāvērunt **quibus** patriam commīserant. 14. Cīvem laudāvērunt **quōcum** (= cum quō, v. p. 52 n. 9) vēnerant. 15. Cīvēs laudāvērunt **quibuscum** (= **cum quibus**, p. 52. n. 9) vēnerant. 16. Cum cīve vēnit **cui** vītam suam commīserat. 17. Tyrannī iūra cīvium dēlent **quōs** capiunt. 18. Tyrannus urbem dēlēvit ex **quā** cīvēs fūgerant. 19. Tyrannus urbem dēlēvit in **quam** cīvēs fūgerant. 20. Tyrannus urbēs dēlēvit ex **quibus** cīvēs fūgerant. 21. Tyrannus urbēs dēlēvit in **quās** cīvēs fūgerant. 22. Perīculum superāvit **quod** timuimus. 23. Perīcula superāvit **quae** timuimus. 24. Puellīs **quās** laudābat librōs dedit. 25. Vir **cuius** fīliam amās in urbem veniēbat. 26. Virō **cuius** fīliam amās vītam suam commīsit. 27. Mātrem adiuvābat, **quae** multōs fīliōs habuit. 28. Mātribus **quae** multōs fīliōs habuērunt rēx pecūniam dabat.

EXERCISES FOR CHAPTER 18

1. Define the term "passive voice" by explaining the etymology of "passive."
2. What is the difference between the ablative of means and the ablative of agent in both meaning and construction?
3. (1) What one letter occurs in 5 of the 6 passive personal endings and can thus be regarded as the peculiar sign of the passive?
   (2) Does this characteristically passive letter occur in any of the corresponding active personal endings?
4. Give the English pronoun by which each of the following passive endings can be translated: (1) -mur; (2) -tur; (3) -r; (4) -ntur; (5) -ris; (6) -minī.
5. (1) Name the tense signs of the imperfect and the future in the passive voice of the 1st and 2nd conjugations.
   (2) Are these the same as the tense signs in the active voice?
6. If -**bar** can be translated "I was being..." and -**bor**, "I shall be...," translate each of the following: (1) -bimur; (2) -bāminī; (3) -bātur; (4) -beris; (5) -buntur; (6) -bāmur; (7) -bitur; (8) -bāris; (9) -biminī; (10) -bantur.
7. Mē terrent; ab eīs terreor; vī eōrum terreor. 8. (1) Tyrannus hanc urbem dēlēbat. (2) Haec urbs ā tyrannō dēlēbātur; īnsidiīs dēlēbitur. 9. Ab amīcīs movēbātur; cōnsiliīs eōrum movēbātur. 10. Vīribus hominum nōn dēlēmur, sed possumus īnsidiīs dēlērī. 11. Nōn bellō dēlēbiminī, sed amōre ōtiī et cōnsiliīs hominum malōrum. 12. Tū ipse nōn mūtāris, sed nōmen tuum mūtātur. 13. (1) Multī hominēs amōre pecūniae tenentur. (2) Aliī ab tyrannīs tenēbantur. (3) Paucī amōre vēritātis amīcitiaeque tenēbuntur. 14. Corpus puerī in mare ab istō homine trahēbātur, sed puer ab amīcīs cōnservābitur. 15. Librī huius generis puerīs a magistrō dabantur, sed paucī legēbantur. 16. Lībertās populō ab rēge brevī tempore dabitur. 17. Patria nostra ā cīvibus fortibus etiam nunc servārī potest. 18. Fortūnā aliōrum monērī dēbēmus. 19. Cōnsiliīs istīus tyrannī quī trāns mare vīvit terrēmur; sed lībertātem amāmus et bellum magnā cum virtūte gerēmus. 20. Ab amīcīs potentibus adiuvābimur. 21. Omnēs virōs nostrōs laudāmus, quī virtūte et vēritāte moventur, nōn amōre suī.

EXERCISES FOR CHAPTER 19

1. Name the two basic verbal elements (1) of which the perfect passive indicative of all verbs is composed, and (2) of which the pluperfect passive indicative is composed.
2. In translation how does (1) **vir missus est** differ from **vir mittitur**; and (2) **vir missus erat,** from **vir mittēbātur**?
3. What is the use of the interrogative pronoun?
4. In what forms does the interrogative pronoun differ conspicuously in spelling from the relative?
5. By what two syntactical criteria can the interrogative pronoun be distinguished from the relative even when both have the same spelling?

6. Translate the following in accordance with their forms.

(1) movētur	(6) dēlēbantur	(11) tenēbāmur
(2) mōtus est	(7) dēlētī sunt	(12) mōtātus erat
(3) mōtum erat	(8) tenēmur	(13) mūtātus est
(4) movēbātur	(9) tentī sumus	(14) mūtātur
(5) dēlētī erant	(10) tentī erāmus	(15) mūtēbātur

7. Translate the following forms of the interrogative pronoun:
(1) cuius?; (2) quem?; (3) quī?; (4) quid?; (5) quōrum?; (6) cui?; (7) quās?; (8) quis?; (9) quae?

8. **Ā quō** liber parātus est (parātus erat, parābātur)? 9. Magister **ā quō** liber parātus est labōre superātur. 10. **Cui** liber datus est (dabātur, datus erat)? 11. **Quid** puerō dictum est (dīcēbātur, dīcitur, dictum erat)? 12. **Quid** puerō dictum est **cui** liber datus est? 13. **Qui** puer servātus est? 14. Puerum **quī** servātus est ego ipse vīdī. 15. **Cuius** fīliī servātī sunt? 16. Senem **cuius** fīliī servātī sunt numquam vīdī. 17. **Quis** missus est? 18. Ā cīve **quī** missus erat pāx et lībertās laudātae sunt. 19. **Quī** missī sunt? 20. Ā cīvibus **quī** missī erant amīcitia laudāta est. 21. **Quōs** in urbe vīdistī? 22. Ubi sunt novī amīcī **quōs** in urbe vīdistī? 23. **Quae** ā tē ibi inventa sunt? 24. Ubi sunt corpora **quae** ā tē ibi inventa sunt? 25. **Ā quibus** hoc dictum est? 26. **Quibus** hoc dictum est? 27. Hominēs miserī **quibus** haec dicta sunt ex urbe fūgērunt. 28. **Quōrum** fīliī ab eō laudātī sunt? 29. Patrēs **quōrum** fīliī laudātī sunt eī grātiās agent. 30. **Quid** vōs terret? 31. **Quod** perīculum vōs terret? 32. At perīculum **quod** vōs terret ā cīvibus fortibus victum est.

EXERCISES FOR CHAPTER 20

1. Indicate the force of the following masculine and feminine endings of the 4th declension: (1) -um; (2) -uum; (3) -ū; (4) -us; (5) -ūs; (6) -uī.

2. Translate the following nouns in accordance with their case forms:

(1) manuī	(6) frūctibus	(11) senātūs (sing.)
(2) manus	(7) frūctum	(12) senātuī
(3) manuum	(8) frūctūs	(13) senātus
(4) manū	(9) frūctuum	(14) senātū
(5) manūs	(10) frūctū	

3. (1) What gender predominates in the 4th declension?
(2) Name the noun which is the most common exception to this rule.

4. (1) Explain the difference of idea between the ablative of place from which and the ablative of separation.
   (2) Which of the two is regular with verbs of freeing, lacking and depriving?
   (3) Which of the two is regular with verbs of motion?

5. State any differences of construction between them.

6. Quis ad nōs eō tempore vēnit? 7. Senex magnae fāmae ex patriā suā ad senātum nostrum fūgit. 8. Quid ab eō dictum est? 9. Hoc ab illō virō dictum est: "Libertāte carēmus." 10. "Nōs servitūte et gravī metū liberāte." 11. Cōpiae nostrae bellum longum contrā ācrēs manūs tyrannī gessērunt. 12. Illae manūs ācrēs quās tyrannus contrā nōs illā ex terrā mīsit ā nōbīs victae sunt. 13. Post haec cīvēs quī tyrannum timuērunt ex patriā suā in cīvitātem nostram ductī sunt. 14. Eōs sceleribus istīus tyrannī līberāvimus. 15. Nunc omnī metū carent. 16. Fīliī eōrum bonōs librōs in lūdīs nostrīs cum studiō legunt. 17. Itaque multōs versūs manibus suīs scrīpsērunt. 18. Hī versūs nōbīs grātiās magnās agunt. 19. In hīs versibus senātus populusque Rōmānus laudantur. 20. Nam illī miserī nunc frūctūs pācis lībertātisque sine metū habent. 21. Quoniam aliōs adiūvimus, etiam nōs ipsī frūctum magnum habēmus. 22. Virī bonī cōpiā hōrum frūctuum numquam carēbunt. 23. Aetāte nostrā multī hominēs vitam in metū et servitūte agunt. 24. Dēbēmus illōs miserōs metū līberāre. 25. Nam quis potest beātus esse sī aliī hominēs frūctibus pācis libertātisque carent?

26. What idea is expressed by each of the following ablatives respectively? tempore (6), patriā (7), eō (8), virō (9), metū (10), nōbīs (12), patriā (13), sceleribus (14), metū (15), studiō (16), manibus (17), cōpiā (22), aetāte (23), metū (24).

EXERCISES FOR CHAPTER 21

1. Give the passive personal endings of the present and future tenses.

2. Repeat *aloud* the present and future passive of the model verbs **dūcō, audiō,** and **capiō.**

3. How can the present passive infinitive be distinguished from the active in the 1st, 2nd, and 4th conjugations? Illustrate by changing the following active infinitives into passive ones: (1) sentīre; (2) movēre; (2) servāre; (4) scīre; (5) tenēre. Translate each.

4. What is exceptional about the form of the present passive infinitive of the 3d conjugation? Illustrate by changing the following active infinitives into passive ones: (1) mittere; (2) iacere; (3) tangere; (4) trahere. Translate each.

5. Translate each of the following in accordance with its form:

(1) mittar	(7) rapitur	(13) raperis	(19) tangēminī
(2) mitteris	(8) rapiētur	(14) rapiēris	(20) sciēris
(3) mittēris	(9) rapī	(15) tanguntur	(21) scīris
(4) mittī	(10) rapimur	(16) tanguntur	(22) sciētur
(5) mittuntur	(11) rapientur	(17) tangī	(23) scītur
(6) mittor	(12) rapiuntur	(18) tangeris	(24) scīrī

6. Quis mittitur (mittētur, mittēbātur, missus est)? 7. Ā quō haec litterae mittentur (missae sunt, mittuntur)? 8. Cuius manū illae litterae scrīptae sunt (scrībentur)? 9. Quid dictum est (dicēbātur, dīcētur, dīcitur)? 10. "Quis rapiētur?" "Tū rapiēris." 11. "Quī rapientur?" "Vōs rapiēminī." 12. Diū neglegēris/neglegēminī (neglēctus es/ neglēctī estis). 13. Post multās hōrās liberātī sumus (liberābimur). 14. Cīvitātis causā eum rapī iussērunt. 15. Lībertātis causā cīvitās nostra ab alterō virō gerī dēbet. 16. Animus eius pecūniā tangī nōn poterat. 17. Amor patriae in omnī animō sentiēbātur (sentiētur, sentītur, sēnsus est). 18. Amōre patriae cum aliīs cīvibus iungimur (iungēbāmur, iungēmur). 19. Amīcitia nōn semper intellegitur, sed sentitur. 20. Sapientia et vēritās in stultīs hominibus nōn invenientur (inveniuntur, inventae sunt). 21. Sapientia etiam multā pecūniā nōn parātur (parābitur, parāta est). 22. Vēritās saepe nōn scītur (sciētur, scita est), quod studium eius est difficile. 23. Nōn sine magnō labōre vēritās inveniētur (inventa est, potest invenīrī). 24. Aliī studiō pecūniae atque laudis trahuntur; nōs dēbēmus amōre vēritātis sapientiaeque trahī.

EXERCISES FOR CHAPTER 22

1. As **u** is characteristic of the 4th declension, what vowel is characteristic of the 5th declension?
2. List the case endings of the 5th declension which are enough like the corresponding endings of the 3rd declension so that they can be immediately recognized without difficulty.
3. (1) What is the gender of most nouns of the 5th declension?
   (2) Name the chief exception.
4. Translate each of the following in accordance with its case(s) and number(s). Where a form is nom. or acc., so state.

(1) speī	(6) fidē	(11) diēbus	(16) reī
(2) spērum	(7) fidem	(12) rem	(17) ignium
(3) spem	(8) fideī	(13) rērum	(18) ignem
(4) spēbus	(9) diērum	(14) rē	(19) ignibus
(5) spēs	(10) diēs	(15) rēbus	(20) ignēs

5. Name the type of adverbial idea in each of the following, and then translate the sentence.

(1) In urbe remānsit.	(4) Cum eīs vēnit	(7) Illud igne factum est.
(2) Ūnā hōrā veniet.	(5) Ex urbe vēnit.	(8) Id ab eīs factum est.
(3) Eō tempore vēnit.	(6) Igne carent.	(9) Id cum fidē factum est.

6. Concerning each of the following adverbial ideas state whether in Latin the ablative alone expresses the idea, or whether the Romans used a preposition with the ablative, or whether a preposition was sometimes used and sometimes not. Base your answers on the rules learned thus far.

(1) personal agent	(5) means
(2) accompaniment	(6) manner
(3) separation	(7) place from which
(4) place where	(8) time when or within when

7. Eō tempore lībertātem cīvium cum fidē cōnservāvit. 8. Rem pūblicam magnā cum cūrā gessit. 9. Rēs pūblica magnā cūrā ab eō gesta est. 10. Multae rēs bonae in mediā urbe vīsae sunt. 11. Eō diē multās rēs cum spē parāvērunt. 12. Ignem ex manibus puerī ēripuimus. 13. Paucīs diēbus Cicerō rem pūblicam ē perīculō ēripiet. 14. Omnēs rēs pūblicās metū līberāvistī. 15. Terra hominēs frūctibus bonīs alit. 16. Incertās spēs eōrum virtūte suā aluit. 17. Hāc aetāte spēs nostrae ā tyrannīs tolluntur. 18. Ex illā rē pūblicā cum magnō metū vēnērunt. 19. Tōta gēns in fīnēs huius reī pūblicae cum magnā manū amīcōrum ūnō diē vēnit. 20. Nōn omnēs virī līberī audent sē cum hāc rē pūblicā iungere. 21. Sī illī fidē carent, nūlla spēs est amīcitiae et pācis. 22. Bona fidēs et amor huius reī pūblicae possunt nōs cōnservāre. 23. Tōtam vitam huic reī pūblicae dedistī.

24. What idea is expressed by each of the following ablatives? (The numbers refer to the sentences.) (7) tempore, fidē; (8) cūrā; (9) cūrā; (10) urbe; (11) diē, spē; (13) diēbus, perīculō; (14) metū; (15) frūctibus; (16) virtūte; (17) aetāte, tyrannīs; (18) rē pūblicā, metū; (19) manū diē; (21) fidē.

EXERCISES FOR CHAPTER 23

1. State what Latin participle is indicated by each of the following endings and give the English suffix or phrase which can be used as an approximate equivalent in each instance: (1) -tus; (2) -ns; (3) -sūrus; (4) -ntem; (5) -tūrus; (6) -ndus; (7) -sus; (8) -ntēs; (9) -sī; (10) -tīs.

Such forms should be practiced aloud until you have an immediate linguistic reflex to each one. These reflexes can be tested in the following exercise.

2. Translate the following participles in accordance with their tense and voice.

(1) futūrus	(7) versus	(13) faciendus	(19) datī
(2) pressūrus	(8) versūrus	(14) rapientēs	(20) datūrōs
(3) premēns	(9) dictus	(15) raptūrōs	(21) dantem
(4) pressus	(10) dīcēns	(16) cupīta	(22) mōtus
(5) premendus	(11) dictūrus	(17) cupientēs	(23) moventem
(6) vertēns	(12) factus	(18) dandum	(24) mōtūrī

3. Translate the following participles or participial phrases into Latin in their nom. sing. masc. form.

(1) (having been) seen	(10) (having been) conquered
(2) seeing	(11) about to conquer
(3) about to see	(12) conquering
(4) to be written	(13) about to join
(5) about to write	(14) joining
(6) (having been) written	(15) (having been) dragged
(7) sending	(16) dragging
(8) (having been) sent	(17) about to throw
(9) about to send	(18) (having been) thrown

4. Captus nihil dīxit. 5. Servitūte līberātus vītam iūcundam aget. 6. Dōna dantibus grātiās ēgit. 7. Aliquem dōna petentem nōn amō. 8. Hominī multam pecūniam cupientī pauca dōna sōla dabat. 9. Ad lūdum tuum fīlium meum docendum mīsī. 10. Iste, aliam gentem victūrus, magistrōs librōsque dēlēre cupiēbat. 11. Hīs īnsidiīs territī vītam miseram vivēmus. 12. Diū oppressī sē contrā opprimentem tyrannum vertere coepērunt. 13. Illī virī miserī, ā tyrannō vīsī, trāns fīnem cucurrērunt. 14. Ōrātor, tyrannum timēns iūcunda semper dīcēbat. 15. Aliquem nōs timentem timēmus. 16. Hī vincentēs omnia iūra cīvium victōrum tollent. 17. Ille miser fugitūrus cōnsilium amīcōrum petēbat. 18. Senex, ab amīcīs monitus, ad nōs fūgit. 19. Ipse ā sene iūcundō adiūtus pecūniā carentibus multās rēs dabat. 20. Quis hīs perīculīs līberātus deīs grātiās nōn dabit? 21. Iūnctī vōbīscum rem pūblicam cōnservābimus. 22. Fidem habentibus nihil est incertum.

EXERCISES FOR CHAPTER 24

1. (1) What are the two essential parts of a regular ablative absolute in Latin? (2) Can the noun or pronoun of an ablative absolute also appear as the subject or the object of the verb?

2. (1) Explain the term "absolute." (2) Guided by the examples in Chapter 24, p. 111, tell what punctuation usually indicates an ablative absolute, and show how this harmonizes with the term "absolute."

3. Should the ablative absolute always be translated literally? Explain.
4. Name five subordinating conjunctions in English which may be used to translate the ablative absolute depending on the requirements of the context.
5. State whether the Romans would have regarded any or all of the following sentences as incorrect, and explain why. (Examples in Chapter 24 will help you.)

(1) Urbe captā, Caesar eam dēlēvit.

(2) Caesar, urbem captus, eam dēlēvit.

(3) Caesar urbem captam dēlēvit.

(4) Urbe captā, Caesar gentēs multās dēlēvit.

6. (1) What idea is expressed by the -ndus participle (gerundive) + **sum**?
(2) Explain the agreement of the **-ndus, -nda, -ndum** participle.
(3) What Latin verb + the infinitive expresses a similar idea?

7. (1) Explain the syntax of **mihi** in the following sentence: Cīvitās mihi cōnservanda est.
(2) Fill out the blank in the following sentence with the Latin for "by me" and explain the construction: Cīvitās — cōnservāta est.

8. Bonīs virīs imperium tenentibus, rēs pūblica valēbit. 9. Hāc fāmā narrātā, dux urbem sine morā relīquit. 10. Omnī cupiditāte pecūniae glōriaeque ex animō expulsā, ille dux sē vīcit. 11. Omnis cupiditās rērum malārum nōbīs vincenda est sī bonam vītam agere cupimus. 12. Cīvibus patriam amantibus, possumus habēre magnās spēs. 13. Omnēs cīvēs istum tyrannum timēbant, quī expellendus erat. 14. Tyrannō superātō, cīvēs libertātem et iūra recēpērunt. 15. At tyrannō expulsō, alius tyrannus imperium saepe accipit. 16. Quis imperium accipiēns adiuvāre cīvitātem sōlam, nōn sē, cupit? 17. Multīs gentibus victīs, tōtum mundum tenēre cupīvistī. 18. Servitūs omnis generis per tōtum mundum opprimenda est. 19. Sī rēs pūblica nostra valet, nihil tibi timendum est. 20. Patria nostra cuique adiuvanda est quī nostrum modum vītae amat. 21. Omnia igitur iūra cīvibus magnā cūrā cōnservanda sunt. 22. Officiīs ā cīvibus relictīs, rēs pūblica in magnō perīculō erit. 23. Hīs rēbus gravibus dictīs, ōrātor ā nōbīs laudātus est. 24. Vēritās et virtūs omnibus virīs semper quaerendae sunt. 25. Vēritāte et virtūte quaesītīs, rēs pūblica cōnservāta est.

26. From the above sentences list:
A. 10 instances of the ablative absolute.
B. 7 instances of the -**ndus sum** construction (passive periphrastic).
C. 5 instances of the dative of agent.
D. 2 instances of the ablative of agent.

EXERCISES FOR CHAPTER 25

1. Review the present active and passive infinitives of all four conjugations.
2. If -tūrus (-sūrus) marks the future active participle, what form logically is -tūrus (-sūrus) esse?
3. If -tus (-sus) marks the perfect passive participle, what form logically is -tus (-sus) esse?
4. With what do the participial elements of the above infinitives (the -tūrus, -tūra, -tūrum and the -tus, -a, -um) agree?
5. To what English verb phrase is the Latin ending -isse equivalent? Repeat this sufficiently so that when you see -isse your linguistic reflex automatically and instantly gives you the proper tense and voice of the infinitive.
6. Now try your reflexes by translating the following forms in accordance with their tense and voice.

(1) mōvisse	(11) sustulisse	(21) quaesītum esse
(2) mōtus esse	(12) trāxisse	(22) expulsum esse
(3) mōtūrus esse	(13) tetigisse	(23) relictōs esse
(4) movērī	(14) amāvisse	(24) data esse
(5) dīcī	(15) vīcisse	(25) datūra esse
(6) scīrī	(16) vixisse	(26) versūrum esse
(7) servārī	(17) trāctōs esse	(27) pressūrōs esse
(8) rapī	(18) vīsam esse	(28) raptūrōs esse
(9) mittī	(19) raptum esse	(29) iussūrum esse
(10) crēdidisse	(20) missōs esse	(30) tāctūrōs esse

7. Explain the difference between a direct and an indirect statement.
8. Indicate what verbs in the following list may introduce an indirect statement and give their meanings.

(1) mittō	(7) videō	(13) audiō	(19) ostendō
(2) nūntiō	(8) nesciō	(14) sentiō	(20) spērō
(3) rīdeō	(9) parō	(15) agō	(21) iungō
(4) intellegō	(10) crēdō	(16) scrībō	(22) putō
(5) accipiō	(11) terreō	(17) audeō	(23) amō
(6) cupiō	(12) neglegō	(18) gerō	(24) negō

9. In what four main categories can we list most verbs which introduce indirect statements?
10. In English the indirect statement most often appears as a "that" clause, though an infinitive with subject accusative is sometimes used ("I believe that he is brave;" "I believe him to be brave"). What is the form of the indirect statement in classical Latin?
11. In what case did the Romans put the subject of an infinitive?
12. In Latin indirect discourse does the tense of the infinitive depend on the tense of the verb of saying? In other words, must a present infinitive be used only with a present main verb, a perfect only with a perfect main verb, etc.?

13. What time relative to that of the main verb does each of the following infinitive tenses indicate: (1) perfect; (2) future; (3) present?

14. Sciō tē hoc fēcisse (factūrum esse, facere). 15. Scīvī tē hoc fēcisse (factūrum esse, facere). 16. Crēdidimus eōs ventūrōs esse (vēnisse, venīre). 17. Crēdimus eōs ventūrōs esse (vēnisse, venīre). 18. Crās (*tomorrow*) audiet (A) eōs venīre (i.e., crās); (B) eōs vēnisse (e.g., herī, *yesterday*); (C) eōs ventūrōs esse (e.g., paucīs diēbus). 19. Hodiē (*today*) audit (A) eōs venīre (hodiē); (B) eōs vēnisse (herī); (C) eōs ventūrōs esse (mox, *soon*). 20. Herī (*yesterday*) audīvit (A) eōs venīre (herī); (B) eōs vēnisse (e.g., prīdiē, *the day before yesterday*); (C) eō ventūrōs (paucīs diēbus). 21. Spērant vōs eum vīsūrōs esse. 22. Sciō hoc ā tē factum esse. 23. Nescīvī illa ab eō facta esse. 24. Negāvērunt urbem ab hostibus capī (captam esse). 25. Scītis illōs esse (futūrōs esse, fuisse) semper fidēlēs. 26. Scīvistis illōs esse (futūros esse, fuisse) semper fidēlēs. 27. Putābant tyrannum sibi expellendum esse. 28. Crēdimus pācem omnibus ducibus quaerendam esse. 29. Dīcit pācem ab omnibus ducibus quaerī (quaesītam esse). 30. Dīxit omnēs ducēs pācem quaesītūrōs esse (quaerere, quaesīvisse). 31. Hostēs nostrī crēdunt omnem rem pūblicam sibi vincendam esse. 32. Hostēs spērant sē omnēs rēs pūblicās victūrōs esse. 33. Bene sciō mē multa nescīre; nēmō enim potest omnia scīre.

34. All infinitives except one in the above sentences are infinitives in indirect statement. Name that one exception.

35. Explain the syntax of the following words by stating in each instance (A) the form and (B) the reason for the form: (14) tē; fēcisse; (16) eōs; (17) ventūrōs esse; (21) eum; (22) hoc; (23) eō; (24) hostibus; (25) fidēlēs; (27) sibi; (28) pācem; ducibus; (29) ducibus; (30) pācem; (31) rem pūblicam; sibi; (32) rēs pūblicās.

EXERCISES FOR CHAPTER 26

1. (1) In the comparison of adjectives to what English ending does the Latin -ior correspond?
   (2) What mnemonic aid can be found in their superficial similarity?

2. (1) To what English adjectival ending does -issimus correspond
   (2) Can any mnemonic device be found here?

3. (1) To what part of an adjective are -ior and -issimus normally added?
   (2) Illustrate by adding these endings to the following adjectives: turpis; vēlōx, gen. vēlōcis, *swift*; prūdēns, gen. prūdentis, *prudent*.

4. If acerbus means *harsh* give (1) three possible forces of the comparative acerbior and (2) two possible forces of the superlative acerbissimus.

5. Give the meaning of quam (1) with the comparative degree (e.g., hic erat acerbior quam ille) and (2) with the superlative (e.g., hic erat quam acerbissimus).

6. What case follows **quam**, *than*?

7. (1) Do most adjectives of the third declension have consonant stems or
i-stems?
(2) Do comparatives have consonant stems or i-stems?

8. Nūntiāvērunt ducem quam fortissimum vēnisse. 9. Lūce clārissimā ab
omnibus vīsā, cōpiae fortissimae contrā hostēs missae sunt. 10. Istō homine
turpissimō expulsō, senātus cīvibus fidēliōribus dōna dedit. 11. Beātiōrēs
cīvēs prō cīvibus miseriōribus haec dulcia faciēbant. 12. Hic auctor est
clārior quam ille. 13. Quīdam dīxērunt hunc auctōrem esse clāriōrem quam
illum. 14. Librōs sapientiōrum auctōrum legite sī vītam sapientissimam
agere cupitis. 15. Quīdam auctōrēs quōrum librōs lēgī sunt acerbiōrēs.
16. Quibusdam librīs sapientissimīs lēctīs, illa vitia turpiōra vītāvimus.
17. Hic vir, quī turpia vitia sua superāvit, fortior est quam dux fortissimus.
18. Quis est vir fēlīcissimus? Is quī vītam sapientissimam agit fēlīcior est
quam tyrannus potentissimus. 19. Remedium vitiōrum vestrōrum vidētur
difficilius. 20. Ille dux putāvit patriam esse sibi cāriōrem quam vītam.
21. Manus adulēscentium quam fidēlissimōrum senātuī quaerenda est.

EXERCISES FOR CHAPTER 27

1. (1) What is peculiar about the comparison of adjectives in which the
masculine of the positive degree ends in **-er**?
(2) Does this hold for adjectives of any declension or only for those of
the 1st and 2nd declension?
2. (1) What is peculiar about the comparison of **facilis**?
(2) Do all adjectives in **-lis** follow this rule? Be specific.
3. Some of the most common adjectives are the most irregular in their
comparison. To illustrate how helpful English can be in learning these
irregular forms, write each of the following Latin adjectives on a new line:

   parvus, malus, bonus (prō), magnus, superus, multus;

and then, choosing from the following list, write opposite each of the Latin
adjectives the English words which suggest the comparative and the superlative respectively:

   pessimist, prime, minus, ameliorate, summit, maximum, supreme,
   optimist, plus, superior, pejorative, prior, major, minimum.

4. Translate the following:

(1) bellum minus	(13) fidēs minima	(25) plūrēs labōrēs
(2) bellum pessimum	(14) mare minus	(26) ducēs optimī
(3) bellum maius	(15) in marī minōre	(27) ducēs maiōrēs
(4) bella priōra	(16) maria maiōra	(28) ducēs meliōrēs
(5) liber simillimus	(17) frūctūs optimī	(29) dōna minima
(6) liber difficilior	(18) frūctus peior	(30) dōna plūra
(7) puer minimus	(19) hominēs ācerrimī	(31) dōna prīma
(8) puer melior	(20) hominēs ācriōrēs	(32) plūs laudis
(9) puella pulcherrima	(21) hominēs plūrēs	(33) plūrēs laudēs
(10) puella pulchrior	(22) labor difficillimus	(34) cīvēs pessimī
(11) puellae plūrimae	(23) labor suprēmus	(35) cīvēs meliōrēs
(12) fidēs maior	(24) plūs labōris	(36) cīvēs līberrimī

5. Facillima saepe nōn sunt optima. 6. Difficilia saepe sunt maxima. 7. Meliōra studia sunt difficiliōra. 8. Pessimī auctōrēs librōs plūrimōs scrībunt. 9. Hī librī peiōrēs sunt quam librī auctōrum meliōrum. 10. Puer minor maius dōnum accēpit. 11. Illa rēs pūblica minima maximās spēs habuit. 12. Plūrēs rivī crēdunt hoc bellum esse peius quam prīmum bellum. 13. Dux melior cum cōpiīs maiōribus veniet. 14. Acrēs ducēs ācriōrēs cōpiās ācerrimōrum hostium saepe laudābant. 15. Tyrannō pessimō expulsō, cīvēs ducem meliōrem et sapientiōrem quaesivērunt. 16. Meliōrī ducī maius imperium et plūs pecūniae dedērunt. 17. Cīvēs urbium minōrum nōn sunt meliōrēs quam eī urbium maximārum. 18. Nōs nōn meliōrēs sumus quam plūrimī virī priōrum aetātum. 19. Maiōrēs nostrī Apollinem (Apollō, acc.) deum sōlis appellābant.

EXERCISES FOR CHAPTER 28

1. What does the subjunctive usually indicate in Latin — a fact or something other than a fact?
2. Is the subjunctive more or less common in Latin than it is in English?
3. What vowel is the sign of the present subjunctive (1) in the first conjugation and (2) in the other conjugations?
4. When the verb of the *main clause* is in the subjunctive, what is the force of this subjunctive?
5. What idea is expressed by the subjunctive in a *subordinate clause* introduced by **ut** or **nē**?
6. In this chapter when **nē** is used with a *main verb* in the subjunctive, what kind of subjunctive is it?
7. Did the Roman prose-writers of the classical period use the infinitive to express purpose as we do in English?

8. Whenever in the following list a form is subjunctive, so label it, indicating also its person and number. The indicative forms are to be translated in accordance with their person, number, and tense.

(1) mittet	(11) audiēmur	(21) līberēminī
(2) mittat	(12) audiāmur	(22) līberābiminī
(3) mittit	(13) audīmur	(23) dēlentur
(4) det	(14) ēripiās	(24) dēleantur
(5) dat	(15) ēripis	(25) vincēris
(6) crēdant	(16) ēripiēs	(26) vinceris
(7) crēdunt	(17) sciuntur	(27) vincāris
(8) crēdent	(18) scientur	(28) dīcimus
(9) movent	(19) sciantur	(29) dīcēmus
(10) moveant	(20) līberāminī	(30) dicāmus

9. Ille dux veniat. Eum exspectāmus. 10. Cīvēs turpēs ex rē pūblicā discēdant ut in pāce vīvāmus. 11. Sī illī amīcōs cupiunt, vēra beneficia faciant. 12. Beneficia aliīs praestat ut amētur. 13. Haec verba fēlīcia vōbīs dīcō nē discēdātis. 14. Patriae causā haec difficillima faciāmus. 15. Illīs miserīs plūs pecūniae date nē armīs contrā hostēs careant. 16. Putat eōs id factūrōs esse ut īram meam vītent. 17. Arma parēmus nē lībertās nostra tollātur. 18. Armīsne sōlīs lībertās nostra ē perīculō ēripiētur? 19. Nē sapientēs librōs difficiliōrēs scrībant. 20. Sapientiam enim ā librīs difficiliōribus nōn accipiēmus. 21. Meliōra et maiōra faciat nē vītam miserrimam agat. 22. Haec illī auctōrī clarissimō nārrā ut in librō eius scrībantur. 23. Vēritātem semper quaerāmus, sine quā maximī animī nōn possunt esse fēlīcēs.

24. Explain the syntax of the following words (i.e., copy the words each on a new line, state the form, and give the reason for that form): (9) veniat; (10) discēdant, vīvāmus; (11) faciant; (12) praestat, amētur; (13) discēdātis; (14) faciāmus; (15) date, armīs, careant; (16) eōs, factūrōs esse, vītent; (17) parēmus, tollātur; (18) armīs, ēripiētur; (19) scrībant; (20) accipiēmus; (21) faciat, agat; (22) nārrā, scrībantur; (23) quaerāmus.

EXERCISES FOR CHAPTER 29

1. What is the easy rule for the recognition and the formation of the imperfect subjunctive active and passive?
2. Does this rule apply to such irregular verbs as **sum** and **possum**?
3. The indicatives in the following list are to be translated according to their forms. The subjunctives are to be so labeled, with indication also of their tense, person, and number.

(1) vocāret	(11) dīcat	(21) possīmus
(2) invenīrent	(12) dīcet	(22) essent
(3) vidērēmus	(13) dīcit	(23) accipiās
(4) dicerem	(14) sint	(24) accipiēs
(5) ēriperēs	(15) posset	(25) acciperēs
(6) servet	(16) possit	(26) expellēminī
(7) servārētis	(17) discēderent	(27) expellerēminī
(8) videat	(18) discēdent	(28) expellāminī
(9) inveniēs	(19) discēdant	(29) movērentur
(10) inveniās	(20) dēmus	(30) moventur

4. How can the idea of result be expressed in Latin?

5. How can result clauses be distinguished from purpose clauses?

6. When and where is the imperfect subjunctive used?

7. Optimōs librōs tantā cum cūrā lēgērunt ut magnam sapientiam discerent. 8. Bonōs librōs cum cūrā legēbāmus ut sapientiam discerēmus. 9. Optimī librī discipulī legendī sunt ut vēritātem et mōrēs bonōs discant. 10. Sapientissimī auctōrēs plūrēs librōs scrībant ut omnēs gentēs adiuvāre possint. 11. Animī plūrimōrum hominum tam stultī sunt ut discere nōn cupiant. 12. At multae mentēs ita ācrēs sunt ut bene discere possint. 13. Quīdam magistrī discipulōs tantā cum arte docēbant ut ipsī discipulī quidem discere cuperent. 14. Imperium istīus tyrannī tantum erat ut senātus eum expellere nōn posset. 15. Omnēs cīvēs sē patriae dent nē hostēs lībertātem tollant. 16. Caesar tam ācer dux erat ut hostēs mīlitēs Rōmānōs nōn vincerent. 17. Dūcimusne aliās gentēs tantā cum sapientiā et virtūte ut lībertās cōnservētur? 18. Tanta beneficia faciēbātis ut omnēs vōs amārent. 19. Tam dūrus erat ut nēmō eum amāret. 20. Multī cīvēs ex eā terrā fugiēbant nē ā tyrannō opprimerentur. 21. Lībertātem sīc amāvērunt ut numquam ab hostibus vincerentur.

22. Explain the syntax of the following words: (7) discerent; (8) discerēmus; (9) discant; (10) scrībant, possint; (11) cupiant; (12) possint; (13) cuperent; (14) posset; (15) dent, tollant; (16) vincerent; (17) cōnservētur; (18) amārent; (19) amāret; (20) opprimerentur; (21) vincerentur.

EXERCISES FOR CHAPTER 30

1. As the form of the imperfect subjunctive active is the present active infinitive plus personal endings, how can the pluperfect subjunctive active be easily recognized?

2. As the pluperfect indicative passive is the perfect passive particle + **eram** (i.e., the imperfect indicative of **sum**), what parallel rule holds for the pluperfect subjunctive passive?

3. If **positus est** is the perfect indicative passive, what most naturally is **positus sit?**

4. What forms of the active indicative do the forms of the perfect subjunctive active resemble in most instances?

5. State the tense, voice, person, and number of each of the following subjunctives:

(1) ponerētur   (5) posuerint   (9) darent   (13) dedissēs

(2) posuissem   (6) ponerēmus   (10) datī essēmus   (14) darētur

(3) positī sint   (7) posuissētis   (11) det   (15) dederīmus

(4) ponāmur   (8) positus esset   (12) datus sīs   (16) dedissent

6. (1) Name the primary tenses of the indicative.
(2) Name the primary tenses of the subjunctive.
(3) Name the historical tenses of the indicative.
(4) Name the historical tenses of the subjunctive.

7. (1) What time does the present subjunctive indicate relative to that of a primary main verb?
(2) What time does the imperfect subjunctive indicate relative to that of a historical main verb?
(3) What time does the perfect subjunctive indicate relative to that of a primary main verb?
(4) What time does the pluperfect subjunctive indicate relative to that of a secondary main verb?

8. Ubi dux est (fuit)? 9. Rogant ubi dux sit (fuerit). 10. Rogābant ubi dux esset (fuisset). 11. Rogābunt ubi dux sit (fuerit). 12. Nesciō ubi pecūnia posita sit. 13. Scīsne ubi pecūnia ponātur? 14. Scīvērunt ubi pecūnia ponerētur. 15. Nescīvit ubi pecūnia posita esset. 16. Vōbīs dīcēmus cūr mīles hoc fēcerit (faciat). 17. Mihi dīxērunt cūr mīles hoc fēcisset (faceret). 18. Dīc mihi quis vēnerit (veniat). 19 Ōrātor rogāvit cūr cēterī cīvēs haec cōnsilia nōn cognōvissent. 20. Ducī nūntiāvimus cēterōs mīlitēs in illam terram fugere (fūgisse). 21. Ducī nūntiāvimus in quam terram cēterī mīlitēs fugerent (fūgissent). 22. Audīvimus cīvēs tam fidēlēs esse ut rem pūblicam cōnservārent. 23. Audīvimus quid cīvēs fēcissent ut rem pūblicam cōnservārent. 24. Quaerēbant quōrum in rē pūblicā pāx invenīrī posset. 25. Cognōvimus pācem in patriā eōrum nōn inventam esse. 26. Illī stultī semper rogant quid sit melius quam imperium aut pecūnia. 27. Nōs quidem putāmus pecūniam ipsam nōn esse malam; sed crēdimus vēritātem et lībertātem et amīcitiam esse meliōrēs et maiōrēs. 28. Haec cupimus ut vītam pulchriōrem agāmus; nam pecūnia sōla et imperium possunt hominēs dūrōs facere, ut fēlicēs nōn sint. 29. Dēnique omnia expōnat ut iam comprehendātis quanta scelera contrā rem pūblicam commissa sint.

30. Explain the syntax of the following: (15) posita esset; (16) fēcerit; (17) fēcisset; (18) vēnerit; (20) fugere; (21) fugerent; (22) esse, cōnservārent; (23) fēcissent, cōnservārent; (24) posset; (25) inventam esse; (26) sit; (27) esse; (28) agāmus, sint; (29) expōnat, comprehendātis, commissa sint.

EXERCISES FOR CHAPTER 31

1. Name the three possible meanings of **cum** + the subjunctive.
2. When **tamen** follows a **cum**-clause, what does **cum** regularly mean?
3. (1) To what conjugation does **ferō** belong?

   (2) State the irregularity which the following forms of **ferō** have in common: ferre, fers, fert, fertis, ferris, fertur.
4. In the following list label the subjunctives and translate the rest according to their forms.

(1) ferat	(6) ferunt	(11) fertis	(16) tulisse
(2) fert	(7) ferent	(12) ferēris	(17) **lātūrus esse**
(3) ferret	(8) ferant	(13) ferris	(18) feren**dus**
(4) feret	(9) fertur	(14) fer	(19) **lātus esse**
(5) ferre	(10) ferte	(15) ferrī	(20) tulisset

5. Cum hoc dīxissēmus, illī respondērunt sē pācem aequam oblātūrōs esse. 6. Cum sē in aliam terram contulisset, tamen amīcōs novōs invēnit. 7. Cum amīcitiam nōbīs offerant, eīs auxilium offerēmus. 8. Cum perīculum magnum esset, omnēs cōpiās et arma brevī tempore contulērunt. 9. Quid tū fers? Quid ille fert? Dīc mihi cūr haec dōna offerantur. 10. Cum exposuisset quid peteret, negāvistī tantum auxilium posse offerrī. 11. Cum dōna iūcunda tulissent, potuī tamen īnsidiās eōrum cognōscere. 12. Cum cōnsilia tua nunc comprehendāmus, īnsidiās tuās nōn feremus. 13. Tanta mala nōn ferenda sunt. Cōnfer tē in exsilium. 14. Dēnique hī omnēs cīvēs reī pūblicae auxilium ferant. 15. Putābam eōs vīnum nāvibus lātūrōs esse. 16. Cum militēs nostrī hostēs vīcissent, tamen eīs multa beneficia obtulērunt. 17. Cum cognōvisset quanta beneficia cēterī offerrent, ipse aequa beneficia obtulit. 18. Cīvibus miserīs gentium parvārum multum auxilium dēbēmus offerre. 19. Cum cōnsul (*the consul*) haec verba dīxisset, senātus respondit pecūniam ad hanc rem collātam esse. 20. Explain the syntax of the following words: (5) dīxissēmus, oblātūrōs esse; (6) contulisset; (7) offerant; (8) esset; (9) offerantur; (10) exposuisset, peteret; (11) tulissent; (12) comprehendāmus; (13) cōnfer; (14) ferant; (15) nāvibus lātūrōs esse; (16) vīcissent; (17) offerent; (19) dixisset.

EXERCISES FOR CHAPTER 32

1. What is the regular positive ending (1) of adverbs made from adjectives of the first and the second declensions and (2) of adverbs made from adjectives of the third declension?
2. In English what adverbial ending is equivalent to the Latin adverbial **-e** or **-iter**?
3. Do all Latin adverbs of the positive degree end in **-e** or **-iter**?
4. (1) What is the ending of the comparative degree of an adverb in Latin?
   (2) With what form of the adjective is this identical?
   (3) In English how is the comparative degree of the adverb usually formed?
5. How does the base of the superlative degree of a Latin adverb compare with that of the corresponding adjective?
6. Translate each of the following adverbs in two ways: (1) līberius; (2) līberrimē.
7. Translate each of the following adverbs in accordance with its form.

(1) iūcundē	(6) breviter	(11) minimē	(16) minus
(2) iūcundius	(7) celerrimē	(12) magis	(17) facile
(3) iūcundissimē	(8) peius	(13) diūtius	(18) maximē
(4) melius	(9) fidēlius	(14) male	(19) gravissimī
(5) fidēlissimē	(10) facilius	(15) miserius	(20) celerius

8. (1) What is the stem of **volō** in the indicative?
   (2) What is the stem of **volō** in the present and the imperfect subjunctive?
9. To what other irregular verb is **volō** similar in the present subjunctive?
10. Label the subjunctives in the following list and translate the other forms.

(1) volēs	(7) vellēmus	(13) voluisse	(19) voluistī
(2) velīs	(8) voluissēs	(14) volunt	(20) vellet
(3) vīs	(9) volam	(15) voluimus	(21) nōlunt
(4) vellēs	(10) volēbunt	(16) velle	(22) nōllet
(5) vult	(11) volet	(17) voluerat	(23) nōlit
(6) velīmus	(12) vultis	(18) voluērunt	(24) nōlet

11. Quīdam volunt crēdere omnēs esse pārēs. 12. Quīdam negant mentēs quidem omnium hominum esse pārēs. 13. Hī dīvitiās celerrimē invēnērunt; illī diūtissimē erunt pauperēs. 14. Hic plūrimōs honōrēs quam facillimē accipere vult. 15. Nōs maximē volumus scientiam quaerere. 16. Cīvēs ipsī rem publicam melius gessērunt quam ille dux. 17. Ibi terra est aequior et plūs patet. 18. Nōs ā scientiā prohibēre minimē volent virī līberī; sed tyrannī maximē sīc volunt. 19. Tyrannus cīvēs suōs ita male opprimēbat ut semper līberī esse vellent. 20. Plūrima dōna līberrimē offeret ut exercitus istum tyrannum adiuvāre velit. 21. Cum auxilium offerre minimē vellent, nōluimus eīs beneficia multa praestāre. 22. Cum hostēs contrā nōs celeriter veniant, volumus nostrōs ad arma quam celerrimē vocāre.

23. Cum lībertātem lēgēsque cōnservāre vērē vellent, tamen scelera tyrannī diūtissimē ferenda erant. 24. Vult haec sapientius facere nē hanc quidem occasiōnem āmittat.

EXERCISES FOR CHAPTER 33

1. (1) What form of the verb is found in both clauses of a future less vivid condition?

   (2) Explain why this construction is called "less vivid" as compared with the more vivid.

2. (1) Name the specific type of condition (A) that has the imperfect subjunctive in both clauses and (B) that has the pluperfect subjunctive in both clauses.

   (2) In each of these conditions which part of the sentence is essentially the same in both Latin and English?

3. What is the regular negative of the conditional clause in Latin?

4. What type of Latin condition is translated by "should . . . would" and hence can be called a should-would condition?

5. What is the meaning of **quis, quid** after **sī, nisi, nē** and **num**?

6. Sī ratiō dūcit, fēlīx es.

7. Sī ratiō dūcet, fēlīx eris.

8. Sī ratiō dūcet, fēlīx sis.

9. Sī ratiō dūceret, fēlīx essēs.

10. Sī ratiō dūxisset, fēlīx fuissēs.

11. Sī pecūniam amās, sapientiā carēs.

12. Sī pecūniam amābis, sapientiā carēbis.

13. Sī pecūniam amēs, sapientiā careās.

14. Sī pecūniam amārēs, sapientiā carērēs.

15. Sī pecūniam amāvissēs, sapientiā caruissēs.

16. Sī vēritātem quaerimus, scientiam invenīmus.

17. Sī vēritātem quaerēmus, scientiam inveniēmus.

18. Sī vēritātem quaerāmus, scientiam inveniāmus.

19. Sī vēritātem quaererēmus, scientiam invenīrēmus.

20. Sī vēritātem quaesīvissēmus, scientiam invēnissēmus.

21. Nisi īram vītābitis, multōs amīcōs āmittētis.

22. Nisi īram vītāvissētis, multōs amīcōs āmīsissētis.

23. Nisi īram vītētis, multōs amīcōs āmittātis.

24. Nisi īram vītārētis, multōs amīcōs āmitterētis.

25. Nisi īram vītātis, multōs amīcōs āmittitis.

26. Nisi īram vītāvistis, multōs amīcōs āmīsistis.

27. Sī quis bonōs mōrēs habet, eum laudāmus.

28. Sī quis bonōs mōrēs habuisset, eum laudāvissēmus.

29. Sī quis bonōs mōrēs habeat, eum laudēmus.
30. Sī quis bonōs mōrēs habuit, eum laudāvimus (laudābāmus).
31. Sī quis bonōs mōrēs habēret, eum laudārēmus.
32. Sī quis bonōs mōrēs habēbit, eum laudābimus.
33. Sī istī vincent, discēdēmus.
34. Sī istī vincant, discēdāmus.
35. Sī istī vīcissent, discessissēmus.
36. Sī librōs bene lēgissēs, melius scrīpsissēs.
37. Sī librōs bene legēs, melius scrībēs.
38. Sī librōs bene legās, melius scrībās.
39. Name in sequence the types of conditions found in sentences 6-10 and 21-26.

EXERCISES FOR CHAPTER 34

1. State the chief peculiarity of deponent verbs.
2. Write a synopsis of the following verbs in the 6 tenses of the indicative and the 4 tenses of the subjunctive as indicated:

   (1) **cōnor** in the 1st person plural.
   (2) **loquor** in the 3d person singular.

3. (1) Write, label, and translate all the participles of **patior**.
   (2) Write, label, and translate all the infinitives of **patior**.

4. Using the proper form of **illud cōnsilium** fill in the following blanks to complete the idea suggested by the English sentence in each instance.

   (1) He will not follow that plan: nōn sequētur ———.
   (2) He will not use that plan: nōn utētur ———.
   (3) He will not permit that plan: nōn patiētur ———.

5. Explain the proper form of **illud consilium** in #4 (2) above.
6. Name the *active forms* found in deponent verbs.
7. Give the imperative forms of (1) **cōnor** and (2) **loquor**, and translate each one.
8. Translate the following participles: (1) locūtus; (2) mortuus; (3) cōnātus; (4) passus; (5) secūtus; (6) ēgressus; (7) profectus.
9. In the following list label any subjunctive forms and translate the rest:

(1) ūtētur	(6) ūsus esset	(11) patī	(16) patitur
(2) ūtātur	(7) ūsūrum esse	(12) passī sunt	(17) patiēmur
(3) ūtitur	(8) patiēris	(13) passum esse	(18) arbitrētur
(4) ūterētur	(9) pateris	(14) patientēs	(19) arbitrārētur
(5) ūsus	(10) patere	(15) patiātur	(20) patiendum est

10. Arbitrātur haec mala patienda esse. 11. Cōnābimur haec mala patī. 12. Nisi morī vis, patere haec mala. 13. Maxima mala passus, homō miser mortuus

est. 14. Tyrannus arbitrātus est eōs haec mala diū passūrōs esse. 15. Cum multa bella passī essent, istum tyrannum in exsilium expellere ausī sunt. 16. Sī hunc ducem novum sequeminī, lībertāte et ōtiō ūtēminī. 17. Hīs verbīs dictīs, eum sequī ausī sumus. 18. Haec verba locūtī, profectī sumus nē in eō locō miserō morerēmur. 19. Cum vōs cōnsiliō malō ūsōs esse arbitrārētur, tamen vōbīscum līberē locūtus est. 20. Sī quis vīnō eius generis ūtī audeat, celeriter moriātur. 21. Eōdem diē fīlius eius nātus est et mortuus est. 22. Omnibus opibus nostrīs ūtāmur ut patria nostra servētur. 23. Cum in aliam terram proficīscī cōnārētur, ā mīlitibus captus est. 24. Arbitrābar eum ex urbe cum amīcīs ēgressūrum esse. 25. Eā nocte profectus, Caesar ad quandam īnsulam clārissimam vēnit. 26. Sī melioribus librīs ūsī essent, plūra didicissent.

27. Name the type of condition found above in each of the following sentences: 12, 16, 20, 26.

28. Explain the syntax of the following: (14) passūrōs esse; (17) verbīs; (18) locūtī, morerēmur; (19) cōnsiliō, arbitrārētur; (21) diē; (22) ūtāmur; (25) nocte; (26) lībrīs.

EXERCISES FOR CHAPTER 35

1. A certain number of verbs, which in English apparently take a direct object, in Latin take a dative of indirect object. In lieu of a good rule to cover such verbs what two procedures can prove helpful?

2. Some other verbs also, when compounded with certain prepositions, may become capable of taking a dative.

   (1) What is the type of thinking that underlines this?
   (2) Do all verbs so compounded take the dative?

3. Copy each of the following verbs on a new line; after it write that one of the three forms **eī, eum, eō** which is in the case required by the verb; and then translate the whole expression, using the pronoun to mean "him" generally and "it" where necessary.

(1) cognōscunt	(7) patiuntur	(13) superant	(19) persuādent
(2) ignōscunt	(8) invenient	(14) crēdunt	(20) ūtuntur
(3) serviunt	(9) nocent	(15) carent	(21) pellunt
(4) servant	(10) iuvant	(16) student	(22) parcunt
(5) parāvī	(11) placent	(17) hortantur	(23) imperant
(6) pāruī	(12) iaciunt	(18) sequuntur	(24) iubent

4. Ducem servāvit. 5. Ducī servīvit. 6. Servī aliīs hominibus serviunt. 7. Virī fortēs aliōs servant. 8. Ille servus fīliō meō servīvit et eum servāvit. 9. Sī quis sibi sōlī serviet, rem publicam numquam servābit. 10. Sī quis

hunc labōrem suscēpisset, multōs servāvisset. 11. Deī mihi ignōscent; vōs Ō cīvēs, tōtī exercituī ignōscere. 12. Sī Deum nōbīs ignōscere volumus, nōs dēbēmus aliīs hominibus ignōscere. 13. Mihi nunc nōn crēdunt, neque umquam filiō meō crēdere volent. 14. Sī nōbīs crēdētis, vōbīs crēdēmus. 15. Cum bonā fidē carērēs, tibi crēdere nōn poterant. 16. Huic ducī pāreāmus ut nōbīs parcat et urbem servet. 17. Nisi Caesar cīvibus placēbit, vītae eius nōn parcent. 18. Litterīs Latīnīs studeō, quae mihi placent etiam sī amīcīs meīs persuadēre nōn possum. 19. Vēritātī et sapientiae semper studeāmus et pāreāmus. 20. Optimīs rēbus semper studēte sī vērē esse fēlīcēs vultis. 21. Hīs rēbus studentēs, et librīs et vītā ūtāmur. 22. Vir bonus nēminī nocēre vult: omnibus parcit, omnēs iuvat. 23. Haec praemia mīrantur.

24. Explain the syntax of the following: (5) ducī; (8) eum; (9) sibi; (11) exercituī; (12) hominibus; (13) fīliō; (15) fidē; (16) ducī, pāreāmus, servet; (17) cīvibus, vītae; (18) litterīs, amīcīs; (21) rēbus, librīs, ūtāmur; (22) omnibus.

EXERCISES FOR CHAPTER 36

1. We have already learned how the Romans expressed indirect statements (Chapter 25) and indirect questions (Chapter 30). Now after a verb having the connotation of command how did the Romans express an indirect command?

2. List some common Latin verbs which can take an indirect command.

3. In the following list label the subjunctives and translate the other forms.

(1) fiet	(6) fiunt	(11) fīmus	(16) faci**endus**
(2) fit	(7) fiebant	(12) fient	(17) fi**ā**mus
(3) fiat	(8) fīēs	(13) fīs	
(4) fieret	(9) fac**tus esse**	(14) fierem	
(5) fierī	(10) fierent	(15) fīant	

4. Dīxit eōs litterīs Latīnīs studēre. 5. Dīxit cūr litterīs Latīnīs studērent. 6. Dīxit ut litterīs Latīnīs studērent. 7. Ab eīs quaesīvimus cūr philosophiae Graecae studērent. 8. Quaerisne ut nātūram omnium rērum cognōscāmus? 9. Tē moneō ut his sapientibus parcās. 10. Mīlitēs monuit nē eīs pācem petentibus nocērent. 11. Nōbīs imperābit nē hostibus crēdāmus. 12. Tibi imperāvit ut ducī pārērēs. 13. Tē rogō cūr hoc fēcerīs. 14. Tē rogō ut hoc faciās. 15. Ā tē petō ut pāx fīat. 16. Ā mē petēbant nē bellum facerem. 17. Eum ōrāvī nē rēgī turpī pārēret. 18. Vōs ōrāmus ut discipulī ācerrimī fīātis.

19. Cūrāte ut hoc faciātis. 20. Caesar cūrāvit ut imperium suum maximum in cīvitāte fieret. 21. Ōrātor nōs hortātus est ut līberae patriae nostrae cum studiō servīrēmus. 22. Nōbīs persuāsit ut aequīs lēgibus semper ūterēmur. 23. Cōnāmur ducī persuādēre nē artibus et lēgibus patriae noceat. 24. Tyrannus imperat ut pecūnia fīat; et pecūnia fit. At ille stultus nōn sentit hanc pecūniam sine bonā fidē futūram esse nihil. 25. Plūrēs quidem discipulōs hortēmur ut linguae Latīnae studeant.

26. Explain the syntax of the following: (4) studēre; (5) studērent; (6) studērent; (7) studērent; (8) cognōscāmus; (9) parcās; (10) eīs, pācem; (11) hostibus; (13) fēcerīs; (14) faciās; (16) facerem; (18) fīātis; (22) lēgibus; (23) lēgibus; (24) futūram esse; (25) hortēmur.

EXERCISES FOR CHAPTER 37

1. (1) Name the tenses and moods in which the stem of **īre** is changed to **e** before **a, o,** and **u.**

    (2) Otherwise, what is the stem of **eō** in the indicative, subjunctive, imperative, and infinitives?
2. State the nominative singular and the nominative plural of the present participle of **eō**.
3. Write a synopsis of **eō** in the 2nd singular and the 3d plural indicative and subjunctive active.
4. In the following list label the subjunctives and translate the other forms.

(1) iimus	(7) itūrus esse	(13) iī	(19) euntēs
(2) īmus	(8) euntem	(14) ībat	(20) ībō
(3) īrēmus	(9) iērunt	(15) ierant	(21) iit
(4) ībimus	(10) eunt	(16) ierim	(22) ībāmus
(5) īssēmus	(11) eant	(17) īret	(23) īsset
(6) eāmus	(12) ībunt	(18) īsse	(24) eat

5. State how the Romans regularly expressed the following place concepts and translate the English example into Latin:

    (1) place from which: from (out of) that land.
    (2) place where: in that land; on that island.
    (3) place to which: into (to) that land.
6. State the general rules for these place constructions when the name of a city is involved.
7. Define the locative case, and state the nature of the locative forms.
8. State how the Romans expressed each of the following time concepts and translate the English example:

    (1) time when: on the same day.
    (2) time how long: for many days.
    (3) time within which: in one day.

9. What is peculiar about the principal parts of **licet**? Explain. Translate into Latin "You may go."

10. Translate each of the following words or phrases in accordance with the principles of this chapter.

(1) ūnum diem	(7) paucīs diēbus	(13) domum
(2) ūnō diē	(8) eādem nocte	(14) Athēnīs
(3) illō diē	(9) multōs diēs	(15) domī
(4) Rōmā	(10) in nāvem	(16) Athēnās
(5) Rōmae	(11) in nāve	(17) domō
(6) Rōmam	(12) ex nāve	(18) paucās hōrās

11. Paucīs hōrīs Rōmam ībimus. 12. Nōs ad urbem īmus; illī domum eunt. 13. Ut saepe fassī sumus, tibi nōn licet Rōmā Athēnās īre. 14. Cūr domō tam celeriter abīstī? 15. Rōmam veniunt ut cum frātre meō Athēnās eant. 16. Ad mortem hāc ex urbe abī et perī nē ego peream. 17. Frātre tuō Rōmae interfectō, Athēnās rediērunt. 18. Sī in fīnēs hostium hōc tempore eat, paucīs hōrīs pereat. 19. Negāvit sē velle in istā terrā multōs diēs remanēre. 20. Dīxistī tē domum Athēnīs ūnā hōrā reditūrum esse. 21. Ā tē petō ut ex nāve ad īnsulam brevī tempore redeās. 22. Eīs diēbus solitī sumus Athēnīs esse. 23. Sī amīcīs eius Rōmae nocuissent, Rōmam brevissimō tempore redīsset. 24. Cum frāter meus domī remanēret, ego tamen in novās terrās domō abiī. 25. Rōmānī, sī quid malum loquī volēbant, saepe dīcēbant: "Abī in malam rem."

26. Explain the syntax of the following words: (11) hōris, Rōmam; (12) domum; (13) Rōmā, Athēnās, īre; (14) domō; (15) Rōmam; (17) frātre; (18) tempore, eat, hōrīs; (19) velle, diēs; (20) domum, Athēnīs, hōrā, reditūrum esse; (21) tempore, redeās; (22) diēbus, Athēnīs; (23) amīcīs, Rōmae, redīsset; (24) domī, terrās, domō.

EXERCISES FOR CHAPTER 38

1. What does a relative clause with the indicative tell about the antecedent?
2. What does a relative clause with the subjunctive tell about the antecedent?
3. What commonly is the nature of the antecedent of a relative clause of characteristic?
4. What is the basic difference between the dative of indirect object and the dative of reference?
5. Amīcus meus quī cōnsulem dēfendit ipse erat vir clārissimus. 6. At nēmō erat quī istum hominem turpem dēfenderet. 7. Quid est quod virī plūs metuant quam tyrannum? 8. Quis est quī inter lībertātem et imperium tyrannī dubitet? 9. Rōmae antīquae erant quī pecūniam plūs quam rem

pūblicam amārent. 10. Abeat ā patriā iste homō malus quī odium omnium
cīvium bonōrum passus est. 11. Catilīna (= Catiline), quī tantās īnsidiās
contrā rem pūblicam fēcerat, ex urbe ā Cicerōne expulsus est. 12. Istī ducī
in exsilium abeuntī quae vita potest esse iūcunda? 13. Quis est quī tantum
dolōrem ferre possit? 14. Nisi quis iūcundus bonusque erit, vītam vērē
fēlicem mihi nōn vīvet. 15. Cōnsulī nōn crēdent quī opera turpia faciat.
16. Illī cōnsulī clārissimō crēdidērunt quī rem pūblicam cōnservāverat.
17. Cicerō erat cōnsul quī rem pūblicam salūtī suae antepōneret.
18. Scīvērunt quārē cōnsulem tam fortem sequī vellēmus. 19. Nihil sciō
quod mihi facilius esse possit. 20. Ducem quaerō quem omnēs laudent.
21. Illum ducem magnum quaerō quem omnēs laudant. 22. Rōmānī, quī
rēs pūblicās Graecās exercitibus suīs cēperant, ipsī Graecīs artibus captī
sunt. 23. Virīs antīquīs nihil erat quod melius esset quam virtūs et sapientia.
24. Nihil metuendum est quod animō nocēre nōn possit.

25. Analyze the relative clauses in the following pairs of sentences showing how
they differ in their force: 5 and 6; 15 and 16; 20 and 21.

26. Explain the syntax of the following words: (7) metuant; (8) dubitet;
(9) Rōmae; amārent; (10) abeat; passus est; (11) fēcerat; (12) ducī; potest;
(13) possit; (14) erit; mihi; (15) cōnsulī; (17) salūtī; antepōneret; (18)
vellēmus; (19) mihi; possit; (22) cēperant; (23) virīs; (24) animō; possit.

EXERCISES FOR CHAPTER 39

1. (1) Define the term *gerund*.
   (2) What is the ending of the gerund in English?
   (3) How is the gerund declined in Latin?
   (4) As a noun what is the syntax of the gerund in Latin?
   (5) What serves as the nominative of the gerund in Latin?

2. (1) What part of speech is the Latin gerundive?
   (2) What mnemonic device may help you to remember this?
   (3) As an adjective what is the syntax of the gerundive?
   (4) How is the gerundive declined?
   (5) How can the gerundive be distinguished from the gerund in Latin
   usage (though not in English translation)?

3. (1) How is the Latin gerund to be translated?
   (2) How is the gerundive in agreement with its noun to be translated?
   (3) For example, translate:
   (A) Discimus legendō cum cūrā (gerund).
   (B) Discimus librīs legendīs cum cūrā (gerundive).

4. Experiendō discimus.

5. Ad discendum vēnērunt.

6. Sē discendō dedit.

7. Discendī causā ad lūdum tuum vēnērunt.

8. Puer cupidus discendī ad lūdum iit.

9. Metus moriendī eum terrēbat.

10. Spēs vīvendī post mortem multōs hortātur.

11. Cōgitandō eōs superāvit.

12. Sē dedit —

(1) glōriae quaerendae.

(2) bellō gerendō

(3) pecūniae faciendae.

(4) imperiō accipiendō.

(5) cīvitātibus delendīs.

(6) huic ducī sequendō.

(7) patriae servandae

(8) pācī petendae.

(9) iniūriīs oppugnandīs.

(10) librīs scribendīs.

(11) librīs legendīs.

(12) philosophiae discendae.

(13) litterīs Latīnīs discendīs.

(14) vēritātī intellegendae.

(15) sapientiae quaerendae.

(16) hominibus adiuvandīs.

13. Rōmam vēnit

(1) ad hoc opus suscipiendum.

(2) ad lūdōs Rōmānōs videndōs.

(3) ad aedificia vetera videnda.

(4) ad pācem petendam.

(5) huius operis suscipiendī causā.

(6) philosophiae discendae causā.

(7) novōrum librōrum legendōrum causā.

14. Librum scrīpsit —

(1) dē dolōre ferendō.

(2) dē metū superandō.

(3) dē bonā vītā vivendā.

(4) dē rē pūblicā gerendā.

(5) dē bellō gerendō.

(6) dē libertāte dēfendendā.

(7) dē hostibus vincendīs.

(8) dē dōnīs dandīs.

15. Sapientiōrēs fīmus —

(1) Latīnīs litterīs legendīs.

(2) philosophiā discendā.

(3) vītā experiendā.

(4) metū vincendō.

(5) vēritāte sequendā.

16. Nōs ipsōs adiuvāmus —

(1) bonīs librīs semper legendīs.

(2) virīs miserīs metū liberandīs.

(3) auxiliō offerendō.

(4) aliīs adiuvandīs.

17. Multum tempus cōnsūmpsit —

(1) in cōgitandō (loquendō, currendō).

(2) in hīs operibus faciendīs.

(3) in viā inveniendā.

(4) in exercitū parandō.

(5) in cōpiīs parandīs.

18. Tempus huic librō sōlī scrībendō habuit.

EXERCISES FOR CHAPTER 40

1. State the difference between cardinal and ordinal numerals.

2. What cardinals are declined?

3. What ordinals are declined?

4. State the form or possible forms of each of the following: (1) duōbus; (2) mīlle; (3) tria; (4) duo; (5) quīnque; (6) mīlia; (7) decem; (8) duābus; (9) centum; (10) trium; (11) vīgintī; (12) octō.

5. Why is the genitive of the whole so called?

6. What construction did the Romans use after cardinal numerals?

7. Translate each of the following phrases.

(1) ūnus cīvis	(10) mīlle cīvēs
(2) decem cīvēs	(11) tria mīlia cīvium
(3) pars cīvium	(12) quīdam ex cīvibus
(4) trēs cīvēs	(13) quid speī
(5) trēs ex sex cīvibus	(14) minus metūs
(6) quīnque ex cīvibus	(15) multum laudis
(7) quīnque cīvēs	(16) satis auxili
(8) centum cīvēs	(17) plūs fideī
(9) centum ex cīvibus	(18) nihil aquae

8. Mīsit — (1) duōs mīlitēs; (2) duōs ex mīlitibus; (3) centum mīlitēs; (4) centum ex mīlitibus; (5) mīlle mīlitēs; (6) duo mīlia mīlitum (7) vīgintī quīnque mīlitēs. 9. Duo cōnsulēs vēnērunt — (1) cum multīs cīvibus; (2) cum tribus cīvibus; (3) cum duōbus ex cīvibus; (4) cum ūnō cīve; (5) cum vīgintī cīvibus; (6) cum mīlle cīvibus; (7) cum tribus mīlibus cīvium; (8) cum quōdam ex cīvibus. 10. Salvē, mī amīce. Quid agis? Quid novī est? 11. Salvē et tū. Bene. Nihil novī. 12. Vīsne audīre aliquid bonī? Satis dīvitiārum dēnique accēpī! 13. At quid bonī est in dīvitiīs sōlīs? Satisne etiam sapientiae habēs? 14. Ego dīvitiās sapientiae antepōnō. Nōn enim arbitror hominēs vītam fēlīcem sine cōpiā pecūniae reperīre posse. 15. Plūrimī autem virī dīvitēs multum metūs sentiunt. 16. Pauperēs saepe sunt fēlīciōrēs et minus metūs habent. 17. Pecūnia ipsa nōn est mala: sed rēs mentis animīque plūs opis ad fēliciter vīvendum offerunt. 18. Novem ex ducibus nōs hortātī sunt ut plūs auxiliī praestārēmus. 19. Quīnque ex custōdiīs interfectīs, pater meus cum duōbus ex fīliīs et cum magnō numerō amīcōrum in illam terram līberam fūgit. 20. Numquam satis ōtiī habēbit; at aliquid ōtiī melius est quam nihil. 21. Nostrīs temporibus omnēs plūs metūs et minus speī habēmus. 22. Magna fidēs et virtūs omnibus virīs reperiendae sunt.

Key to Exercises

KEY FOR CHAPTER 1

1. (1) he, she, it; (2) we; (3) I; (4) they; (5) you (sing.), (thou); (6) you (plu.)
2. The forms are present active infinitives of the 2nd conjugation. (1) to advise/warn; (2) to see; (3) to be strong; (4) to owe.
3. The forms are present active infintives of the 1st conjugation. (1) to call; (2) to save; (3) to give; (4) to think; (5) to praise; (6) to love; (7) to err.
4. The forms are present active imperatives 2nd person singular of the 1st or the 2nd conjugations. (1) call; (2) save; (3) give; (4) think; (5) praise; (6) love; (7) advise/warn; (8) see; (9) be strong/good-bye.
5. The forms are present active imperatives 2nd person plural of the 1st or the 2nd conjugations. (1) call; (2) save; (3) give; (4) think; (5) praise; (6) love; (7) advise/warn; (8) see; (9) be strong/good-bye.
6. (1) he/she/it calls, is calling, does call; (2) we think; (3) they love; (4) you (sing.) owe/ought; (5) he sees; (6) they see; (7) we owe/ought; (8) you (sing.) are strong; (9) you (plu.) err/are mistaken; (10) we see; (11) he/she/it loves; (12) you (plu.) see; (13) you (sing.) err; (14) they give; (15) we save; (16) he gives; (17) they love; (18) you (sing.) see.
7. They warn me if I err. 8. He warns me if they err. 9. Warn me if he errs. 10. You (sing.) ought to warn me. 11. You (plu.) ought to save me. 12. They ought not to praise me. 13. "What does he give?" "He often gives nothing." 14. They often call me and advise me. 15. I see nothing. What do you see? 16. Praise me if I do not make a mistake. 17. If you (plu.) are well, we are well. 18. If he is well, I am well. 19. If he (she) loves me, he (she) ought to praise me. 20. Save me. 21. I ought not to err. 22. What ought we to praise? 23. He sees; he ponders; he advises.

KEY FOR CHAPTER 2

1. In classical Latin there was no regular definite or indefinite article. The words *the* and *a* have to be added in the English translation according to the sense of a Latin passage. Thus **puella** may mean *the girl* or *a girl*, and **puellae** may mean *the girls* or *girls* according to the Latin context. Often in an isolated sentence *the* and *a* can be used interchangeably, or perhaps no article at all need be used.

2. (1) accusative case; (2) gen. case; (3) nom. case; (4) abl.; (5) voc.; (6) dat.

3. (1) acc. plu. as direct object of a verb; (2) nom. sing. as subject of a verb or voc. sing. for direct address; (3) acc. sing. as direct object; (4) nom. plu. subject, or voc. for direct address.

4. (1) gen. plu., of; (2) abl. sing., by/with/from, etc.; (3) gen. sing., of; dat. sing., to/for; nom. plu.; voc. plu.; (4) dat. plu., to/for; abl. plu., by/with/from, etc.

5. (1) girl, direct obj. of verb; (2) girl, subject or vocative; (3) girls, object; (4) girls, subj. or voc.; (5) countries, obj.; (6) country, obj.; (7) country, subj. or voc.; (8) countries, subj. or voc.; (9) money, obj.; (10) money, subj. or voc.; (11) penalties, obj.; (12) penalty, obj.

6. (1) of the girl, girl's, or to/for the girl; (2) of the girls, girls'; (3) O fatherland; (4) of or to/for the fatherland; (5) by/with, etc. money; (6) of or to/for money; (7) to/for or by/with, etc. penalties; (8) by/with etc. a penalty; (9) of penalties.

7. (1) multae pecūniae, multam pecūniam; (2) magnae fāmae, magnā fāmā; (3) vītae meae, vītae meae; (4) fortūnam tuam, fortūnās tuās; (5) magnae patriae, magnārum patriārum; (6) fortūnā meā, fortūnis meīs; (7) magnae poenae, magnīs poenīs; (8) multīs philosophiīs, multīs philosophiīs.

8. (1) multā pecūniā; (2) multārum puellārum; (3) meae patriae; (4) magnam vītam; (5) tuīs poenīs; (6) multae patriae; (7) multīs puellīs; (8) meae vītae; (9) Ō fortūna; (10) puellae; (11) puellārum; (12) puellae; (13) puellās; (14) puellae.

9. Farewell (goodbye), my native land. 10. The fortune of the girl (the girl's fortune) is great. 11. The girl is praising the fortune of your (sing.) country. 12. O girl, save your country. 13. Many girls love money. 14. You (plu.) are giving nothing to the girl, *or* you give nothing to a girl. 15. He sees the money of the girl, *or* the girl's money. 16. You (sing.) do not see the girls' money. 17. We ought to warn the girls. 18. They ought to praise the girl. 19. Life gives (good) fortune to many girls. 20. You (sing.) are saving my life by *or* with your money. 21. Fame is nothing without fortune. 22. You (plu.) do not like life without money. 23. A country is not strong without fame and fortune. 24. You (sing.) ought not to praise the anger of the girls. 25. We like a life without punishments. 26. We are not strong without philosophy. 27. What is life without philosophy?

KEY FOR CHAPTER 3

1. (1) acc. sing., obj.; (2) nom. plu. as subj., voc. plu. for direct address; (3) nom. sing., subj.; (4) acc. plu., obj.; voc. sing., direct address.

2. (1) dat. sing., to/for; abl. sing., by/with, etc.; (2) gen. plu., of; (3) gen. sing., of; (4) dat. plu., to/for; abl. plu., by/with, etc.

3. (1) sons, obj.; (2) sons, subj. or direct address; (3) son, obj.; (4) people, obj.; (5) people, direct address; (6) people, subj.; (7) man, subj. or direct address; (8) men, obj.; (9) men, subj. or direct address; (10) man, obj.; (11) friend, direct address; (12) friends, subj. or direct address; (13) friends, obj.; (14) friend, obj.

4. (1) of my sons; (2) to/for my son, by/ with, etc. my son; (3) of the Roman people; (4) to/for the Roman people, by/with, etc. the Roman people; (5) to/for the men, by/with, etc. the men; (6) of the man; (7) of the men; (8) of a few friends; (9) to/for or by/with, etc. a few friends; (10) to/for or by/with, etc., my friend; (11) of my friend; (12) to/for or by/with, etc. many boys.

KEY FOR CHAPTER 5

1. -ō, -s, -t, -mus, -tis, -nt.
2. They are the same.
3. -bi- (-b- in 1st per. sing.; -bu- in 3d per. plu.).
4. (1) we shall; (2) he will; (3) you (plu.) will; (4) I shall; (5) they will.
5. By learning the vocabulary form of the adjective: līber, lībera, līberum, pulcher, pulchra, pulchrum; and often by learning English derivatives (see p. 23 n. 2).
6. They show whether the **e** of a masculine in -er survives throughout the rest of the paradigm; liberty, **līber**, **lībera**, **līberum**; pulchritude, **pulcher**, **pulchra**, **pulchrum**.
7. (1) they will remain; (2) he will remain; (3) we shall remain; (4) I shall give; (5) you (plu.) will give; (6) he will give; (7) you (sing.) will see; (8) we shall see; (9) they will call; (10) you (sing.) will call; (11) you (sing.) will have; (12) they will have.
8. (1) dabimus; (2) manēbis; (3) vidēbunt; (4) vocābimus; (5) vocābit; (6) vidēbitis; (7) vidēbō; (8) servābunt; (9) habēbimus; (10) habēmus; (11) habēbit; (12) habet.
9. Our teacher praises me and he will praise you (sing.). 10. Free men will overcome our dangers. 11. Our sons love pretty girls. 12. Our friend will not stay in the company (number) of fools (v. p. 22 n. 5). 13. We have many faults and always shall have. 14. Great dangers do not overcome our courage. 15. Our beautiful country is free. 16. You (plu.) are free men; you will have a beautiful country. 17. Free teachers will give attention to duty. 18. Therefore, we shall overcome evil men (v. p. 22. n. 5) in our country. 19. If you (sing.) overcome (literally, will overcome) your anger, you will overcome yourself. 20. Because of our courage many men are free. 21. Thee, free fatherland (apposition, v. p. 14), we love and always shall love. 22. You (plu.) will not preserve wisdom by means of money. 23. Does your (sing.) soul possess enough wisdom?

KEY FOR CHAPTER 6

1. See Ch. 6, p. 28, s.v. "Complementary Infinitive."
2. (1) we; (2) they; (3) you (sing.); (4) he, she, it; (5) I; (6) I; (7) you (plu.).
3. See p. 27 bottom and p. 28 top.
4. (1) he, she, it was; (2) he, etc., was able; (3) he will be; (4) he will be able; (5) we are; (6) we are able; (7) we were able; (8) we shall be able; (9) I was able; (10) I was; (11) I shall be; (12) I shall be able; (13) they will be; (14) they will be able; (15) they were able; (16) to be; (17) to be able.
5. (1) sumus; (2) eramus; (3) erimus; (4) poterimus; (5) potest; (6) poterit; (7) poterat; (8) posse; (9) poterant; (10) possunt; (11) poterunt; (12) sunt; (13) esse; (14) poteram.
6. Your (plu.) country was free. 7. I was able to be tyrant. 8. Your friend will be tyrant. 9. I shall call my book *Mein Kampf*. 10. Where (there) is a tyrant, there men cannot be free. 11. He could not remain in our country. 12. Tyrants will always have many faults. 13. We were not able to overcome the tyrants. 14. We ought to overcome our tyrant. 15. The tyrant was able to overcome (the) good men; but he will not be able to remain there. 16. You (plu.) will be able to see the dangers of a tyrant. 17. We cannot tolerate the faults of tyrants. 18. You (sing.) will not tolerate the treachery of the tyrant. 19. The peace in your (plu.) country cannot be perpetual. 20. You (sing.) ought to warn free men about

5. (1) populī Rōmānī, populō Rōmānō; (2) magnōs virōs, magnīs virīs; (3) puei
   meīs, puerīs meīs; (4) magnō numerō, magnō numerō; (5) magne vir, mag
   virī; (6) filiī meī, fīliōrum meōrum.
6. (1) multōrum puerōrum; (2) populō Rōmānō; (3) filiōs meōs; (4) Ō filiī meī; (!
   magnum numerum; (6) magnō numerō; (7) Ō vir magne; (8) multīs puerīs; (!
   vir magnus; (10) populī Rōmānī.
7. Good-bye, my friend. 8. The Roman people praise your (sing.) son's wisdon
   9. O great man, save the Roman people. 10. The number of the Roman peopl
   is great. 11. Many boys love girls. 12. You (plu.) are giving nothing to my sor
   13. I see men in the field. 14. You (sing.) see the friend of my son. 15. He doe
   not see your (sing.) sons' friend. 16. We ought to warn my sons. 17. They ough
   to praise your (sing.) son. 18. Life gives fame to few men. 19. You (sing.
   consider me in the number (circle) of your friends. 20. Great men often hav
   few friends. 21. My friend is always thinking. 22. The son of a great man is no
   always a great man. 23. We do not always see (understand) the wisdom of grea
   men. 24. You (plu.) ought to praise philosophy, the wisdom of great men.

KEY FOR CHAPTER 4

1. Nom. sing. in -**um**; nom. and acc. plu. in -**a**. Actually the vocative should also
   be added here; but henceforth, since aside from the singular of 2nd-declension
   masculines in -**us** the vocatives follow the rule of having the same form as the
   nominative, little specific mention is made of the vocative.
2. (1) nom. plu. as subject; acc. plu. as obj.; (2) nom. sing. as subj.; acc. sing. as obj.
3. (1) dat. sing., to/for; abl. sing., by/with, etc.; (2) gen. plu., of; (3) gen. sing., of;
   (4) dat. plu., to/for; abl. plu., by/with, etc.
4. (1) wars, subj. or obj.; (2) war, subj. or obj.; (3) duty, subj. or obj.; (4) duties,
   subj. or obj.; (5) dangers, subj. or obj. Of course any of these forms could also
   be vocative.
5. (1) of evil wars; (2) to/for evil war, by/with, etc., evil war; (3) of evil war; (4)
   to/for evil wars, by/with, etc., evil wars; (5) of great duty or service; (6) to/for
   great duties, by/with, etc., great duties; (7) to/for small danger, by/with, etc.,
   small danger.
6. (1) bella parva, bella parva; (2) ōtium bonum ōtia bona; (3) perīculī magnī,
   perīculōrum magnōrum; (4) officium vērum, officiō vērō.
7. (1) Ō bellum malum; (2) officiō magnō; (3) perīculō magnō; (4) ōtium bonum;
   (5) multīs bellīs; (6) ōtiī bonī; (7) perīculīs multōrum bellōrum; (8) bella parva;
   (9) bella parva; (10) Ō bella stulta; (11) bellum parvum.
8. Peace (leisure) is good. 9. Many wars do not preserve peace. 10. The danger is
   great. 11. We are in great danger. 12. And leisure often has dangers. 13. Life
   is not without many dangers. 14. Good men love peace. 15. The foolish man
   praises the dangers of war. 16. Often we do not preserve the peace by war. 17.
   The Roman people do not always have good peace. 18. They often save the
   fatherland and peace by small wars. 19. Many girls are pretty. 20. True friends
   are few. 21 My friend is a man of great service. 22. The duties of a teacher are
   many and great. 23. You (sing.) are a man of little leisure. 24. You (plu.) are
   men of great care. 25. We ought to give attention to duty without delay. 26.
   Life is nothing without eyes.

tyrants. 21. Your (plu.) teacher always likes fine books. 22. Good, true books were able to save the country. 23. You (plu.) will be able to save your country with good books. 24. Tyrants will not be able to overcome the wisdom of good books. 25. Bad men cannot tolerate good books.

KEY FOR CHAPTER 7

1. No.
2. Yes: nominative and accusative plural.
3. (1) nom. and acc. plu. of masc. and fem.; (2) nom. and acc. plu. neut.; (3) acc. sing. masc. and fem.
4. (1) dat. and abl. plu.; (2) dat. sing.; (3) abl. sing.; (4) acc. sing. masc. and fem.; (5) gen. plu.; (6) gen. sing.; (7) nom. and acc. plu. masc. and fem.
5. (1) magnum tempus; (2) magna virtūs; (3) magnus labor; (4) magna cīvitās; (5) magnus mōs; (6) magna pāx; (7) magnus rēx; (8) magnum corpus; (9) magna vēritās; (10) magnus amor.
6. (1) by/with much labor; (2) to/for much labor; (3) of much labor; (4) many labors (nom.); (5) of perpetual peace; (6) by/with perpetual peace; (7) to/for perpetual peace; (8) of small states; (9) a small state (acc.); (10) small states (acc.); (11) small states (nom.); (12) by a small state; (13) bad times (nom. or acc. plu.); (14) bad time (nom. or acc. sing.); (15) to/for a bad time; (16) of bad times; (17) of a bad time; (18) to/for your habit; (19) by your habit; (20) of your habit; (21) your character (nom.); (22) your character (acc.); (23) of your character.
7. (1) magnae virtūtī; (2) magna virtūs; (3) magnās virtūtēs; (4) magnārum virtūtum; (5) magnā virtūte; (6) tempus nostrum; (7) tempora nostra; (8) tempora nostra; (9) temporibus nostrīs; (10) temporī nostrō; (11) temporis nostrī; (12) temporum nostrōrum; (13) amōrem meum; (14) amōrēs meōs; (15) amōrī meō; (16) amōre meō; (17) amōris meī; (18) amōrum meōrum.
8. My time for leisure is small. 9. Your (sing.) courage is great. 10. Money is nothing without good character. 11. The virtues of many human beings are great. 12. The character of a good man will be good. 13. They will give a letter to the man. 14. We were able to see many men in the great state. 15. We see a great love of money in many men. 16. Few men give attention to excellence. 17. Our state will give peace to many men. 18. Peace cannot be perpetual. 19. Without good peace the states of our times will not be strong. 20. Times are bad after many wars. 21. In many states and lands peace could not be strong. 22. Without great labor the man will have nothing. 23. The beautiful maiden loves friends of good character. 24. Men of great courage will dare to overcome tyrants. 25. Love of country is strong in our state.

KEY FOR CHAPTER 8

1. (1) Future. (2) See Ch. 8. Perhaps a better device is found in the fact that our word "future" ends in e: futur/e. The **a** in **dūcam** is the only exception among six forms.
2. (1) Present. (2) See Ch. 8.
3. (1) 1st per. plu. pres.; (2) 2nd sing. fut.; (3) 3d plu. pres.; (4) 3d sing. fut.; (5) 2nd plu. pres.; (6) 1st plu. fut.; (7) 1st sing. pres.; (8) 3d plu. fut.; (9) 3d sing. pres.; (10) 2nd plu. fut.; (11) 2nd sing. pres.; (12) 1st sing. fut.

4. (1) imperative sing.; (2) pres. inf.; (3) imv. plu.

5. (1) they will send; (2) he is sending; (3) they are sending; (4) I shall send; (5) send (sing.); (6) we are sending; (7) you (plu.) will send; (8) you (sing.) are sending; (9) send (plu); (10) you (plu.) send; (11) he will send; (12) we shall send; (13) he does; (14) they will do; (15) they are doing; (16) you (plu.) will do; (17) we are doing; (18) I shall do; (19) we shall do; (20) you (sing.) are doing; (21) you (plu.) are doing; (22) he will write; (23) they are writing; (24) I shall write; (25) write (sing.); (26) you (plu.) are writing; (27) we shall write; (28) he is writing; (29) you (sing.) are writing; (30) they will write.

6. (1) pōnunt; (3) pōnēmus; (3) pōne; (4) pōnit; (5) pōnent; (6) pōnam; (7) pōnis; (8) pōnētis; (9) pōnite; (10) pōnimus; (11) pōnitis; (12) pōnet.

7. What are they doing? What will you (plu.) do? 8. They are leading the man to me. 9. Lead (sing.) the man to me, and I shall thank the man. 10. While the tyrant leads the troops, we can do nothing. 11. He is writing a letter to the maiden. 12. You (sing.) are writing a great book. 13. You (sing.) will write good books. 14. We shall write books about peace. 15. Do you (plu.) have an abundance of good books? (For the **-ne** added to **cōpiam** see p. 24, Vocabulary s. v. **-ne**. Note also that **habetis** is *present tense* of a 2nd conjugation verb.) 16. The teacher teaches many boys. (N.B. **docet**, pres. of 2nd conjugation verb.) 17. The boys do not thank the teacher. 18. Few men will thank our state. 19. The tyrant will lead great forces out of our state. 20. A great abundance of money does not lead men to wisdom. 21. Will good books lead many men to reason? 22. Do we often lead men to reason? 23. Reason can lead men to a good life. 24. Are you (plu.) leading a good life? 23. Always thank (plu.) a good friend.

KEY FOR CHAPTER 9

1. See p. 40 (top) and p. 39 s.v. "Demonstratives."

2. (1) to/for that (m., f., n.); those (nom. m.) (2) that (nom. f.); those (nom./acc. n.)
   (3) of that (m., f., n.)   (4) that (nom. m.)
   (5) by that (f.)   (6) that (nom./acc.n.)
   (7) of those (m., n.)   (8) those (nom. f.)
   (9) those (acc. m.)   (10) to/for those (m., f., n.)
   (11) by that (m., n.)   (12) of those (f.)
   (13) by this (m., n.)   (14) this (nom./acc. n.)
   (15) this (nom. f.): these (nom./acc. n.) (16) these (nom. f.)
   (17) by this (f.)   (18) this (acc. f.)
   (19) of this (m., f., n.)   (20) this (acc. m.)
   (21) these (acc. m.)   (22) to this (m., f., n.)
   (23) of these (m., n.)   (24) these (acc. f.)
   (25) to/for these; by these (m., f., n.) (26) of one (m., f., n.)
   (27) to/for one (m., f., n.)   (28) by one (f.)
   (29) to/for the whole (m., f., n.);   (30) of the whole (m., f., n.)
       whole (nom. plu. n.)   (31) the whole (nom. f.);
   (32) the whole (acc. m.; nom./acc. n.)   whole (nom./acc./plu. n.)
   (33) of no (sing. m., f., n.)   (34) to/for no (sing. m., f., n.)
   (35) no (nom. sing. f.; nom./acc. plu. n.) (36) no (acc. plu. m.)

3. See text and examples on p. 39–40.

4. (1) hacc puella
    (2) hae puellae
    (3) haec tempora
    (4) huic temporī
    (5) huic puerō
    (6) huius temporis
    (7) illīus temporis
    (8) hōc librō
    (9) illō librō
    (10) illa puella
    (11) illa tempora

    (12) illa tempora
    (13) illud tempus
    (14) huic cīvitātī sōlī
    (15) huius cīvitātis sōlīus
    (16) illī puerō sōlī
    (17) illī puellae sōlī
    (18) illīus puellae sōlīus
    (19) tyrannōrum sōlōrum
    (20) tōtam cīvitātem
    (21) tōtīus patriae
    (22) tōtī patriae

    (23) nūllīus ratiōnis
    (24) nūllam ratiōnem
    (25) nūllae puellae
    (26) nūllī librō
    (27) nūllōs librōs
    (28) ūnī cīvitātī
    (29) ūnī puellae
    (30) ūnīus temporis
    (31) ūnīus bellī
    (32) alterī librō
    (33) aliō librō

5. These men will lead (lead) the whole state. 6. That man will see (sees) these things in that land. 7. In that book he will write (I shall write) those things about this man. 8. One man is leading (will lead) those forces into this land. 9. The teacher gives these things to the other boy. 10. We are writing (shall write) this book about another war. 11. The whole country thanks (will thank) this man alone. 12. They are now giving their entire attention to that plan. 13. This man's friend will save this state by that plan. 14. The other friend will lead (his) entire life in another land. 15. This man alone was able to warn me about the faults of this tyrant. 16. You (plu.) have no forces in the other land. 17. Those men alone see no dangers in this plan. 18. You (sing.) dare to praise not only the character but also the treachery of that man. 19. In fact, on account of the treachery of one man this state is not strong.

KEY FOR CHAPTER 10

1. (1) 3d; (2) 2nd; (3) 4th; (4) 1st.
2. (1) 3d plu. pres; (2) 2nd sing. fut.; (3) 2nd sing. pres.; (4) 1st plu. fut.; (5) 1st plu. pres; (6) imv. sing.; (7) 2nd plu. fut.; (8) imv. plu.; (9) 2nd plu. pres.; (10) 1st sing. pres.; (11) 3d sing. pres.; (12) imv. sing. Note: nos. 3, 5, 6, 8, 9 are 4th only; 12 is 3d only. The chief difference is the i of the 4th and the ĭ of the 3d. See p. 46 mid.
3. (1) pres. inf.; (2) imv. sing.; (3) short stem vowels in 2nd sing. and 1st and 2nd plu. of pres. ind. and in the imv. plu.

4. (1) he will come
    (2) he is coming
    (3) they are coming
    (4) they will come
    (5) you (sing.) hear
    (6) you (plu.) will hear
    (7) you (plu.) hear
    (8) come (plu.)
    (9) you (sing.) will come
    (10) come (sing.)

    (11) to come
    (12) he makes/does
    (13) he will make/do
    (14) we shall make
    (15) we are making
    (16) they make
    (17) you (sing.) make
    (18) I shall make
    (19) you (sing.) will make
    (20) to make

5. (1) sentiam   (6) sentiunt   (11) iacit   (16) iacitis
   (2) sentiēmus   (7) sentīre   (12) iaciet   (17) iaciēmus
   (3) sentit   (8) sentī   (13) iaciam   (18) iacite
   (4) sentītis   (9) sentiet   (14) iacimus   (19) iacere
   (5) sentient   (10) sentīmus   (15) iace   (20) iacis

6. We are fleeing from this land. 7. Flee (sing.) with your daughter. 8. They will flee into that place. 9. Time flees; the hours flee; old age is coming. 10. Come (plu.) with your friends. 11. They are coming into your country. 12. O great man, come into our state. 13. You (sing.) will find your daughter in that state. 14. They can find little money in the streets. 15. The tyrant is finding a way into this state. 16. You (plu.) will capture those men there with (their) friends. 17. We are coming to you with great forces. 18. Will he find much fame and glory there? 19. That man is always making war. 20. Those men will not make peace. 21. Many men do those things but do not do these things. 22. We are doing and will do our duty. 23. I shall make a great supply of books. 24. The boys live with that good man. 25. In the books of ancient men you (plu.) will find much philosophy and wisdom.

KEY FOR CHAPTER 11

1. (1) is, ea, id and ēi, eae, ea; (2) ego and nōs; (3) tū and vōs:

2. (1) to/for you (plu.); by/w./fr. you; (2) to/for us; by/w/fr. us; (3) we (nom.); us (acc.); (4) you (nom. plu.); you (acc. plu.); (5) of you (sing.); (6) of me; (7) to/for me; (8) to/for you (sing.); (9) you (acc. sing.); by/w/fr. you; (10) me (acc.); by/w/fr. me.

3. (1) them (masc.); (2) them (fem.); (3) their (masc. neut.); (4) their (fem.); (5) his, her, its; (6) by/w./fr. her; (7) she (nom.); they (nom. and acc. plu. neut.); (8) by/w./fr. him, it; (9) to/for him, her, it; they (masc. nom.); (10) to/for them (masc., fem., neut.); by/w./fr. them; (11) they (nom. fem.); (12) it (nom. or acc. sing.). N.B. in the sing. any one of the three Latin genders of **is, ea, id** may be translated by *it* when the antecedent of the pronoun is a word which in English is neuter. For instance, suppose that in a preceding sentence the word **pāx** appears. Then we read: Sine eā nūlla cīvitās valet. The Latin feminine **eā** becomes English *it* because in English *peace* is regarded as neuter.

4. (1) eius   (8) eius   (15) eī   (22) vōs
   (2) eius   (9) eī   (16) ea   (23) nōs
   (3) eōrum   (10) eī   (17) eae   (24) nōs
   (4) eōrum   (11) eā   (18) eī   (25) nōbīs
   (5) eās   (12) eō   (19) id   (26) ego
   (6) eōs   (13) vōbīs   (20) vōs   (27) tibi
   (7) ea   (14) tibi   (21) tū

5. These men will give it to you (sing.). 6. *I* shall give it to you (plu.). 7. *You* (plu.) will give it to them. 8. I shall give the same thing to him (her, it). 9. *We* shall give them (= those things) to him (her). 10. That man will give it to me. 11. We shall give you (plu.) his books. 12. You will give us their (masc.) books. 13. We shall give their money to you (sing.). 14. They will give his (her) money

to me. 15. We shall send his (her) books to her. 16. I shall send his (her) book to you (sing.). 17. That man, however, will send their money to us. 18. We are sending them (fem.) with her. 19. I am sending him with them. 20. We shall send them with his (her) friends. 21. *You* (sing.) will send me with their friend. 22. They are sending you (plu.) with me to his friend. 23. He is sending us with you (sing.) into their land. 24. They will send them (fem.) with us to their friends. 25. I shall send him with you (plu.) to their friends. 26. They will send you (sing.) with him to me.

KEY FOR CHAPTER 12

1. (1) pres. act. ind.; (2) pres. act. inf.; (3) perf. act. ind.; (4) perf. pass. partic.
2. (1) mittō, pres. act. ind., *I send*
   (2) mittere, pres. act. inf., *to send*
   (3) mīsī, perf. act. ind., *I sent*
   (4) missum, perf. pass. partic., *having been sent, sent*
3. See p. 56 s.v. "Principal Parts."

4.
(1) mittō	(6) agō	(11) remaneō	(16) dicō
(2) laudō	(7) sum	(12) scrībō	(17) sum
(3) vincō	(8) dō	(13) sum	(18) vīvō
(4) dīcō	(9) sum	(14) faciō	(19) faciō
(5) faciō	(10) agō	(15) fugiō	(20) videō

5. (1) you (plu. perf.)...; (2) he (perf.)...; (3) they (perf.)...; (4) you (sing. perf.)...; (5) we (perf.)...; (6) he had...; (7) we shall have...; (8) we had...; (9) you (sing.) had...; (10) they will have...; (11) they had...; (12) he will have...; (13) you (plu.) had....

6.
(1) they saw	(19) he flees
(2) they had seen	(20) he fled
(3) you (sing.) saw	(21) they flee
(4) he did	(22) they fled
(5) he does	(23) he saved
(6) we had done	(24) they saved
(7) we did	(25) you (plu.) saved
(8) we shall do	(26) he had saved
(9) they did	(27) he will have saved
(10) you (sing.) lived	(28) we remained
(11) they lived	(29) we had remained
(12) he will conquer	(30) he came
(13) he conquered	(31) he comes
(14) we conquered	(32) you (plu.) come
(15) we conquer	(33) you (plu.) came
(16) you (sing.) gave	(34) they came
(17) you (plu.) had given	(35) they come
(18) we gave	(36) they had come

7. Those men had fled (will flee; are fleeing; fled). 8. These men remained (remain; will remain; had remained). 9. The king had conquered (is conquering; con-

quered; will conquer) Asia. 10 The kings conquered (will conquer; are conquering; had conquered) Asia. 11. Kings possessed (possess; will possess; had possessed) Asia. 12. Caesar had come (came; is coming; will come) into the same land. 13. Caesar said (says; had said; will say) the same things. 14. *You* (plu.) gave (will give; had given) us peace. 15. *You* (sing.) sent (will send; are sending; had sent) a letter to her. 16. We saw (see; had seen) them in the same street. 17. He had lived (lived; will live) a long time. 18. You (sing.) had done (will do; did; are doing) it well. 19. I saved (shall save; had saved) their (his) state. 20. They found (had found; will find) him in the same place. 21. God had given (gave; gives; will give) liberty to men. 22. They thanked (will thank; had thanked; thank) me. 23. *You* (plu.) were (were; are; will be; had been) free men.

KEY FOR CHAPTER 13

1. See p.60, s.v. "Reflexive Pronouns."
2. See p.60, s.v. "Declension of Reflexive Pronouns."
3. In pronouns of the first and the second persons.

4. (1) to/for myself.
   (2) yourself (sing. acc.); by/w./fr. yourself.
   (3) to/for ourselves; by/w./fr. ourselves.
   (4) to/for himself (herself, itself); to/for themselves.
   (5) yourselves (acc.).
   (6) himself (acc.); by/w./fr. himself; themselves (acc.); by/w./fr. themselves.
   (7) to/for yourselves; by/w./fr. yourselves.

5. Since **suus, -a, -um** is an adjective, it must agree in number with the noun which it modifies. Since **suus** is a reflexive, it means *his own* or *their own* according to whether the subject of the verb is singular or plural. See, for example, sentences 15 and 20 below.

6. **Eōrum** and **eius** are fixed genitives of possession; and therefore, they do not, like **suus**, agree with the nouns on which they depend. See, for example, sentences 16-19 below.

7. See p.62, s.v. "The Intensive Pronoun." **Sē**, being reflexive, is used in the predicate and refers to the subject. **Ipse** can be used to emphasize a noun or pronoun in any part of a sentence. See, for example, sentences 27, 28, and 31 below.

8. Caesar saved them. 9. Caesar saved him (= another person). 10. Caesar saved himself. 11. The Romans saved themselves. 12. The Romans saved them (= others). 13. The Romans saved him. 14. Caesar saved his own friend. 15. Caesar saved his own friends. 16. Caesar saved his (= another's) friend. 17. Caesar saved his (= another's) friends. 18. Caesar saved their friend. 19. Caesar saved their friends. 20. The Romans saved their (own) friend. 21. The Romans saved their (own) friends. 22. The Romans saved their (= others') friend. 23. The Romans saved their (= others') friends. 24. The Romans saved his friend. 25. The Romans saved his friends. 26. Caesar himself saved him. 27. Caesar himself saved himself. 28. They saved Caesar himself. 29. They saved the friend of Caesar himself. 30. They saved the friend of the Romans themselves. 31. The friend of Caesar himself saved himself. 32. The friends of Caesar himself saved

themselves. 33. The friend of Caesar himself saved him. 34. Caesar's friends themselves saved him. 35. They did not save us. 36. We saved ourselves. 37. We saved the Romans themselves. 38. The Romans themselves did not save you. 39. *You* (sing.) saved yourself. 40. *You* saved the Romans themselves. 41. He gave nothing to me. 42. I gave nothing to myself. 43. He gave nothing to himself. 44. They gave nothing to themselves. 45. They gave nothing to them (= others). 46. They gave nothing to him. 47. I conquered myself. 48. They conquered me. 49. They conquered their (= others') anger. 50. They conquered their own anger. 51. He conquered his own anger. 52. He conquered his own sons. 53. They conquered their own sons.

KEY FOR CHAPTER 14

1. In the gen. plu.
2. -ī in abl. sing.; **-ia** in nom. and acc. plu.
3.   (1) by/w./fr. art
     (2) of the arts
     (3) arts (nom. or acc.)
     (4) to/for the sea; by/w./fr. the sea
     (5) to/for the seas; by/w./fr. the seas
     (6) the sea (nom. or acc.)
     (7) the seas (nom. or acc.)
     (8) bodies (nom. or acc.)
     (9) of bodies
     (10) of a part
     (11) to/for parts; by/w./fr. parts
     (12) of parts
     (13) by/w./fr./the city
     (14) to/for the city
     (15) of cities
     (16) cities (nom. or acc.)

     (17) of the kings
     (18) to/for the king
     (19) names (nom. or acc.)
     (20) animals (nom. or acc.)
     (21) to/for an animal; by/w./fr. an animal
     (22) of an animal
     (23) of animals
     (24) of strength
     (25) men (acc.)
     (26) of the man; men (nom.)
     (27) strength (nom. or acc. plu.)
     (28) to/for men; by/w./fr. strength
     (29) force (nom.); of force
     (30) force (acc.)
     (31) to/for strength; by/w./fr. strength
     (32) to/for force; by/w./fr. force

4. (2); (4) as abl.; (7); (12); (15); (20); (21) as abl; (23); (24); (30); (32) as abl.

5.   (1) vī magnā
     (2) virum magnum
     (3) vīrium magnārum
     (4) vī magnae
     (5) cīvium multōrum
     (6) cīve bonō
     (7) cīvibus multīs
     (8) maria multa
     (9) marī magnō
     (10) mare magnum
     (11) vim magnam
     (12) virōrum multōrum
     (13) vīribus magnīs
     (14) vī magnā
     (15) vīrēs magnās

6. (1) accompaniment; (2) means; (3) manner; (4) means
7. (1) they ran (currō); (2) we run (currō); (3) you (sing.) ran (currō); (4) we had dragged (trahō); (5) he will drag (trahō); (6) they are dragging (trahō); (7) he managed (gerō); (8) he manages (gerō); (9) they manage (gerō); (10) we shall manage (gerō); (11) they hold (teneō); (12) they will hold (teneō); (13) they held (teneō); (14) we held (teneō).
8. He waged many wars with the Romans. 9. They managed the state with great wisdom. 10. He himself held the state by the power of troops. 11. Those animals dragged many men into the sea. 12. You (sing.) said this with great skill. 13. We ran with care (carefully) across the city. 14. He came to us with a large part of

the citizens. 15. He will conquer the rights of the citizens by force. 16. You (plu.) dragged him to death across his land. 17. We shall join ourselves with the citizens of many cities. 18. He wrote this letter to the king himself with courage (courageously). 19. The violence of those seas was great. 20. I have seen the art of the Greeks with my own eyes. 21. We have drawn many beautiful thoughts from the ancients.

22. 8, accompaniment; 9, manner; 10, means; 12, manner; 13, manner; 14, accompaniment; 15, means; 17, accompaniment,; 18, manner; 20, means.

KEY FOR CHAPTER 15

1. (1) **-ba-**.
   (2) It is found in all six persons.
   (3) **-bi-**.
   (4) **-e-** except for the **-a-** in the first person sing.

2. The imperfect refers to repeated or customary action in past time; the perfect refers to a single act in past time.

3. (1) he used to come, was coming   (5) he was throwing, used to throw
   (2) he came, has come   (6) they threw, have thrown
   (3) I was doing, used to do   (7) we were writing, used to write
   (4) I did, have done   (8) we wrote, have written

4. Time when, at which, within which.

5. (1) He used to come (was coming, kept coming) with his friends.
       Ablative of accompaniment.
   (2) He will come in one hour. Abl. of time within which.
   (3) He came at the same time. Abl. of time when.
   (4) He wrote the book in a few hours. Time within which.
   (5) At that time he wrote a book. Time when.
   (6) He was writing the book with care. Manner.

6. At that time alone he feared the dangers; but he always used to fear (was afraid of) death. 7. Many kings used to throw money among the wretched citizens. 8. That tyrant always used to praise himself. 9. The citizens of those cities kept expecting liberty. 10. They saved the city in one hour by their own wisdom. 11. I used to come into the city with my friend. 12. You (plu.) used to wage great wars with courage (= courageously). 13. Therefore the Romans conquered the Greeks. 14. Fathers often used to fear their own sons — and they do (fear them) now! 15. Did you (sing.) see my father at that time? 16. Where did you (plu.) find this money? 17. They came, and he kept saying the same thing to us. 18. I never used to understand his books. 19. We have never changed our (way of) life. 20. Our state used to preserve the liberty and the rights of the citizens. 21. The Romans used to praise the customs of the ancient times.

KEY FOR CHAPTER 16

1. Abl. sing. masc. and fem.: **fortī** as compared with **cīve**.
2. (1) The adjective of 2 endings.
   (2) Nom. sing. masc. and fem.: fortis, fortis; ācer, ācris; potēns, potēns.

3. **-i**, abl. sing. of all genders; **-ium**, gen. plu. of all genders; **-ia**, nom. and acc. neut. plu.; but see p. 78 n. 4.
4. **-i**; but see p. 78 n. 4.
5. Yes.

6.   (1) to/for a sweet girl   (11) of all parts
      (2) by/w./fr. a sweet girl   (12) of all kings
      (3) by/w./fr. a sweet mother   (13) of all wars
      (4) to/for a sweet mother   (14) by/w./fr. a happy man
      (5) to/for a happy mother   (15) to/for a happy man
      (6) by/w./fr. a happy mother   (16) to/for or by/w./fr. every sea
      (7) all wars, nom. or acc. plu.   (17) to/for every good art
      (8) all names, nom. or acc. plu.   (18) by/w./fr. every good art
      (9) all seas, nom. or acc. plu.   (19) of every good art
      (10) by/w./fr. every part   (20) to/for, by/w./fr. swift force

7. A long life is often difficult. 8. A difficult life can be happy. 9. How brief was his sweet life! 10. The memory of a sweet period of life helps all men. 11. You (sing.) wrote a short book in a short time. 12. In every sea we kept finding this powerful animal. 13. In every land you (plu.) will see many brave men. 14. Swift rumor ran through every land. 15. That short war was difficult. 16. We overcame all dangers in a few hours. 17. The powerful tyrant will conquer their country with swift violence. 18. In a short time he will change all the rights of the citizens. 19. They did not understand the difficult art of sweet liberty. 20. Men fear difficult duties in all lands.

KEY FOR CHAPTER 17

1. See Ch. 17, p. 79, s. v. "Use and Agreement of the Relative."
2. (1) Its use in its own clause. (2) The antecedent.
3. In gender and number.
4. (1) who. (2) which. (3) who, which.

5. (1) to/for whom or which, masc. sing.
    (2) whom or which, masc. plu.
    (3) who/which, nom. sing. fem.
       who/which, nom. plu. fem.
       which, nom. or acc. plu. neut.
    (4) of whom/ which, sing.
    (5) to/for or by/w./fr. whom/which, plu.
    (6) which, nom. or acc. neut. sing.
    (7) by/w./fr. whom/which, fem. sing.
    (8) who/which, masc. sing. and plu.
    (9) whom/which, masc. sing.
    (10) whom/which, fem. plu.
    (11) of whom/which, masc. plu.
    (12) whom/which, fem. sing.

6. They praised the citizen whom you (plu.) had sent. 7. They praise the citizens whom you (plu.) had sent. 8. They praised the citizen who had saved the country.

9. They praised the citizens who had saved the country. 10. They praised the citizen whose son had saved the country. 11. They praised the citizens whose sons had saved the country. 12. They praised the citizen to whom they had entrusted the country. 13. They praised the citizens to whom they had entrusted the country. 14. They praised the citizen with whom they had come. 15. They praised the citizens with whom they had come. 16. He came with the citizen to whom he had entrusted his own life. 17. Tyrants destroy the rights of the citizens whom they capture. 18. The tyrant destroyed the city from which the citizens had fled. 19. The tyrant destroyed the city into which the citizens had fled. 20. The tyrant destroyed the cities from which the citizens had fled. 21. The tyrant destroyed the cities into which the citizens had fled. 22. He overcame the danger which we feared. 23. He overcame the dangers which we feared. 24. He gave books to the girls whom he was praising. 25. The man whose daughter you (sing.) love kept coming into the city. 26. He entrusted his own life to the man whose daughter you (sing.) love. 27. He used to help the mother, who had many sons. 28. The king used to give money to the mothers who had many sons.

KEY FOR CHAPTER 18

1. See p. 87 s. v. "The Passive Voice" and n. 5.

2. See p. 85 s. v. "Ablative of Personal Agent." Note that "agent" is a person; "means" is something other than a person.

3. (1) The letter **r**.
   (2) No.

4. (1) we; (2) he; (3) I; (4) they; (5) you (sing.); (6) you (plu.).

5. (1) -**ba**, imperf.; -**bi**- (-**bo**-, -**be**-, -**bu**-), fut.
   (2) Yes, with the minor exception of -**be**- in the 2nd per. sing.

6. (1) we shall be...; (2) you (plu.) were being...; (3) he was being...; (4) you (sing.) will be...; (5) they will be...; (6) we were being...; (7) he will be...; (8) you (sing.) were being...; (9) you (plu.) will be...; (10) they were being....

7. They terrify me; I am terrified by them; I am terrified by their violence. 8. (1) The tyrant was destroying this city. (2) This city was being destroyed by the tyrant; it will be destroyed by a plot. 9. He used to be aroused (moved) by his friends; he used to be aroused by their plans. 10. We are not being destroyed by the strength of men, but we can be destroyed by a plot. 11. You (plu.) will be destroyed not by war but by love of leisure and by the plans of evil men. 12. You yourself (sing.) are not being changed, but your name is being changed. 13. (1) Many men are possessed by the love of money. (2) Others used to be held by tyrants. (3) A few will be possessed by love of truth and friendship. 14. The boy's body was being dragged into the sea by that man, but the boy will be saved by his friends. 15. Books of this sort used to be given to the boys by the teacher, but few (books) used to be read. 16. Liberty will be given to the people by the king in a short time. 17. Our country can even now be saved by brave citizens. 18. We ought to be warned by the fortune of other men (others). 19. We are terrified by the plans of that tyrant who lives across the sea; but we love liberty, and we shall wage war with great courage. 20. We shall be helped by powerful friends. 21. We praise all our men, who are moved by courage and truth, not by love of themselves.

KEY FOR CHAPTER 19

1. (1) The perfect passive participle plus the present of **sum**.
   (2) The perfect passive participle plus the imperfect of **sum**.
2. (1) Vir missus est = *a man was (has been) sent*; vir mittitur = *a man is (is being) sent*. (see p. 88 s. v. "Observations.")
   (2) Vir missus erat = *a man had been sent*; vir mittēbātur = *a man was being (used to be) sent*.
3. An interrogative pronoun introduces a question.
4. **quis** (nom. sing. m. and f.); **quid** (nom. and acc. sing. n.).
5. See p. 89 s. v. "Interrogative **Quis**...."

6. (1) he is (is being) moved
   (2) he was (has been) moved
   (3) it had been moved
   (4) he was being moved
   (5) they had been destroyed
   (6) they were being destroyed
   (7) they were destroyed
   (8) we are held
   (9) we were held
   (10) we had been held
   (11) we were being held
   (12) he had been changed
   (13) he was (has been) changed
   (14) he is (is being) changed
   (15) he was being changed

7. (1) whose (sing.)?
   (2) whom (sing.)?
   (3) who (plu.)?
   (4) what (nom. and acc. sing.)?
   (5) whose (plu.)?
   (6) to whom (sing.)?
   (7) whom (fem. plu.)?
   (8) who (sing.)?
   (9) who (fem. plu.)?; what (neut. nom. and acc. plu.)?

8. By whom was the book prepared (had been prepared; was being prepared)? 9. The teacher by whom the book was prepared is overcome with work. 10. To whom was the book given (was being given, had been given)? 11. What was said (was being said, is said, had been said) to the boy? 12. What was said to the boy to whom the book was given? 13. Who was saved? What boy was saved? 14. I myself saw the boy who was saved. 15. Whose (sing.) sons were saved? 16. I never saw the old man whose sons were saved. 17. Who (sing.) was sent? 18. Peace and liberty were praised by the citizen who had been sent. 19. Who (plu.) were sent? 20. Friendship was praised by the citizens who had been sent. 21. Whom (plu.) did you (sing.) see in the city? 22. Where are the new friends whom you (sing.) saw in the city? 23. What things were found by you (sing.) there? 24. Where are the bodies which were found there by you (sing.)? 25. By whom was this (thing) said? 26. To whom was this said? 27. The wretched men to whom these things were said fled from the city. 28. Whose sons were praised by him? 29. The fathers whose sons were praised will thank him. 30. What terrifies you? 31. What danger terrifies you? 32. But the danger which terrifies you has been conquered by brave citizens.

KEY FOR CHAPTER 20

1. (1) object, acc. sing.; (2) of, plu.; (3) by/w./fr., sing.; (4) subject, sing.; (5) of (sing.); subject or object (plu.); (6) to/for,sing.

2. (1) to/for a hand (band)
   (2) a hand (subj.)
   (3) of hands
   (4) by/w./fr. a hand
   (5) of a hand; hands (subj./obj.)
   (6) to/for or by/w./fr. fruits
   (7) fruit (obj.)
   (8) of fruit; fruits (subj./obj.)
   (9) of fruits
   (10) by/w./fr. fruit
   (11) of the senate
   (12) to/for the senate
   (13) the senate (subj.)
   (14) by/w./fr. the senate

3. (1) Masculine; (2) **manus**.

4. (1) The ablative of place from which = motion apart; the ablative of separation = distance apart.
   (2) The ablative of separation.
   (3) The ablative of place from which.

5. Place from which regularly has a preposition (**ab, dē, ex**); for separation, see p. 94, middle.

6. Who came to us at that time? 7. An old man of great fame fled from his country to our senate. 8. What was said by him? 9. This (thing) was said by that man: "We lack liberty." 10, "Free us from slavery and heavy fear." 11. Our forces waged long war against the tyrant's fierce bands. 12. Those fierce bands which the tyrant sent against us from that land were conquered by us. 13. After this (*lit.* these things) the citizens who feared the tyrant were led from their own country into our state. 14. We freed them from the crimes of that tyrant. 15. Now they lack (are free from) every fear (anxiety). 16. Their sons eagerly (with zeal) read good books in our schools. 17. And so they have written many verses with their own hands. 18. These verses give great thanks to us. 19. In these verses the senate and the Roman people are praised. 20. For those unfortunate men now have the fruits of peace and liberty without fear. 21. Since we have helped others, even we ourselves have great enjoyment. 22. Good men will never lack an abundance of these fruits. 23. In our age many human beings pass their life in fear and slavery. 24. We ought to free those unfortunate men from fear. 25. For who can be happy if other human beings lack the enjoyments of peace and liberty?

26. (6) time when; (7) place from which; (8) agent; (9) agent; (10) separation; (12) agent; (13) place from which; (14) separation; (15) separation; (16) manner; (17) means; (22) separation; (23) time when; (24) separation.

KEY FOR CHAPTER 21

1. See p. 83–84.

2. Check with paradigms on p. 97 and repeat them until you can say them without hesitation.

3. In the passive infinitive the final e of the active infinitive has been changed to i: (1) sentīrī, *to be felt*; (2) movērī, *to be moved*; (3) servārī, *to be saved*; (4) scīrī, *to be known*; (5) tenērī, *to be held*.

4. The whole active ending -ere is changed to to -ī: (1) mittī, *to be sent*; (2) iacī, *to be thrown*; (3) tangī; *to be touched*; trahī, *to be drawn*.

5. (1) I shall be sent
   (2) you (sing.) are sent
   (3) you (sing.) will be sent
   (13) you (sing.) are seized
   (14) you (sing.) will be seized
   (15) they are touched

(4) to be sent
(5) they are sent
(6) I am sent
(7) he is seized
(8) he will be seized
(9) to be seized
(10) we are seized
(11) they will be seized
(12) they are seized

(16) they will be touched
(17) to be touched
(18) you (sing.) are touched
(19) you (plu.) will be touched
(20) you (sing.) will be known
(21) you (sing.) are known
(22) he will be known
(23) he is known
(24) to be known

6. Who is being sent (will be sent, used to be sent, was sent)? 7. By whom will this letter be sent (was sent, is sent)? 8. By whose hand was that letter written (will be written)? 9. What was said (was being said, will be said, is said)? 10 "Who (sing.) will be seized?" "You (sing.) will be seized." 11. "Who (plu.) will be seized?" "You (plu.) will be seized." 12. For a long time you (sing./plu.) will be neglected (were neglected). 13. After many hours we were freed (shall be freed). 14. For the sake of the state they ordered him to be seized. 15. For the sake of liberty our state ought to be managed by the other man. 16. His soul could not be touched by money. 17. In every soul the love of country used to be felt (will be felt, is felt, was felt). 18. We are joined (used to be joined, will be joined) to (*lit.*, with) other citizens by love of country. 19. Friendship is not always understood, but it is felt. 20. Wisdom and truth will not be found (are not found, were not found) in foolish men. 21. Wisdom is not obtained (will not be obtained, was not obtained) by even a great deal of money. 22. Truth often is not known (will not be known, was not known), because the study of it is difficult. 23. Not without great labor will truth be found (was found, can be found). 24. Others are drawn by eagerness for (*lit.*, of) money and fame; we ought to be drawn by love of truth and wisdom.

KEY FOR CHAPTER 22

1. e.
2. **-em, -ē; -ēs, -ēbus, -ēs, -ēbus** (also **-eī,** dat., and **-ērum,** gen.)
3. (1) Feminine. (2) **Diēs.**

4. (1) of hope; to/for hope
   (2) of hopes
   (3) hope (acc.)
   (4) to/for or by/w./fr. hopes
   (5) hope (nom.); hopes (nom., acc.)
   (6) by/w./fr. faith
   (7) faith (acc.)
   (8) of or to/for faith
   (9) of days
   (10) day (nom.); days (nom., acc.)
   (11) to/for or by/w./fr. days
   (12) thing (acc.)
   (13) of things
   (14) by/w./fr. a thing
   (15) to/for or by/w./fr. things
   (16) of or to/for a thing
   (17) of fires
   (18) fire (acc.)
   (19) to/for or by/w./fr. fires
   (20) fires (nom., acc.)

5. (1) place where; he remained in the city.
   (2) time within which; he will come in one hour.
   (3) time when; he came at that time.
   (4) accompaniment; he came with them.

(5) place from which; he came from the city.

(6) separation; they lack fire.

(7) means; that was done by fire.

(8) agent; it was done by them.

(9) manner; it was done faithfully (with faith).

6.   (1) **ab** + abl.

(2) **cum** + abl.

(3) abl. alone after verbs of freeing, lacking, and depriving; with other verbs **ab**, **dē**, **ex** is often used.

(4) **in** + abl.

(5) abl. alone

(6) **cum** + abl.; **cum** may be omitted when the noun is modified by an adj.

(7) **ab, dē , ex** + abl.

(8) abl. alone.

7. At that time he faithfully preserved the liberty of the citizens. 8. He managed the state with great care (= very carefully). 9. The state was managed by him with great care. 10. Many good things were seen in the middle of the city. 11. On that day they prepared many things hopefully. 12. We snatched the fire from the hands of the boy. 13. In a few days Cicero will rescue the republic from danger. 14. You (sing.) freed all the republics from fear. 15. The earth nourishes human beings with good fruits. 16. He nourished their uncertain hopes by his own courage. 17. In this age our hopes are being destroyed by tyrants. 18. They came from that state with great fear. 19. The whole clan came into the territory of this state with a large band of friends in one day. 20. Not all free men dare to join themselves with this republic. 21. If those men lack faith, there is no hope of friendship and peace. 22. Good faith and the love of this republic can save us. 23. You (sing.) have given (your) whole life to this state.

24. (7) time when; manner (8) manner; (9) manner; (10) place where; (11) time when; manner; (13) time within which; separation; (14) separation; (15) means; (16) means; (17) time when; agent; (18) place from which; manner; (19) accompaniment; time within which; (21) separation.

KEY FOR CHAPTER 23

1.   (1) perf. pass = having been... or Eng. perf. partic.

(2) pres. act. = -ing

(3) fut. act. = about to...

(4) pres. act. = -ing

(5) fut. act. = about to...

(6) fut. pass. = to be...

(7) perf. pass. = having been...

(8) pres. act. = -ing

(9) perf. pass. = having been (e.g., nom. plu.)

(10) perf. pass. = having been (dat. or abl. plu.)

2. (1) about to be
    (2) about to press
    (3) pressing
    (4) (having been) pressed
    (5) to be pressed
    (6) turning
    (7) (having been) turned
    (8) about to turn
    (9) (having been) said
    (10) saying
    (11) about to say
    (12) (having been) done
    (13) to be done
    (14) seizing
    (15) about to seize
    (16) (having been) desired
    (17) desiring
    (18) to be given
    (19) (having been) given
    (20) about to give
    (21) giving
    (22) (having been) moved
    (23) moving
    (24) about to move

3. (1) vīsus
    (2) vidēns
    (3) vīsūrus
    (4) scrībendus
    (5) scrīptūrus
    (6) scrīptus
    (7) mittēns
    (8) missus
    (9) misūrus
    (10) victus
    (11) victūrus
    (12) vincēns
    (13) iūnctūrus
    (14) iungēns
    (15) trāctus
    (16) trahēns
    (17) iactūrus
    (18) iactus

4. When captured (*lit.*, having been captured) he said nothing. 5. Freed from slavery he will lead a pleasant life. 6. He thanked those giving the gifts. 7. I do not like someone seeking gifts. 8. To a man desiring much money he used to give only a few gifts. 9. I sent my son to your school to be taught. 10. That man, when about to conquer another people, kept wishing to destroy (their) teachers and books. 11. Terrified by this plot we shall live a wretched life. 12. Long oppressed, they began to turn themselves against the oppressing tyrant. 13. Those unfortunate men, when seen by the tyrant, ran across the border. 14. The orator, because he feared the tyrant, always used to say pleasing things. 15. We fear someone fearing us. (= who fears us). 16. These men, if they conquer, will take away all the rights of the conquered citizens. 17. That wretched man on the point of fleeing kept seeking the advice of his friends. 18. The old man, warned by his friends, fled to us. 19. Having himself been helped by the pleasant old man, he kept giving many things to those lacking money. 20. Who when freed from these dangers will not thank the gods? 21. Joined with you (plu.) we shall save the republic. 22. To those having faith nothing is uncertain.

KEY FOR CHAPTER 24

1. (1) A noun (pronoun) + participle in abl.
   (2) No. (V. p. 112 top.)
2. (1) V. p. 115 n. 1.
   (2) As a rule commas separate an abl. abs. from the rest of the sentence. This makes it appear somewhat apart from the rest of the sentence.
3. No. Since this "absolute" construction is not too commonly favored in English, the literal translation if regularly adhered to would make rather clumsy English.
4. When, since, after, although, if. (V. p. 111.)
5. (1) Incorrect because the noun (**urbe**) of the abl. abs. is used (through its pronoun **eam**) as the object.

(2) Incorrect because **captus** means *having been* captured, not *having* captured.

(3) Correct because **urbem captam** (*the captured city*) stands as the natural object of **dēlēvit**.

(4) Correct because **urbe captā** is a normal abl. abs., the noun of which is not used elsewhere as subject or object.

6. (1) Obligation or necessity.

(2) It is really a predicate adjective; and so it naturally agrees with the subject of **sum**.

(3) **Dēbeō** + inf., though **dēbeō** more often expresses the idea of moral obligation.

7. (1) **Mihi** is dative of agent.

(2) **Ā mē**; abl of agent.

8. If (since, etc.) good men hold the power, the republic will be strong. 9. When (since, etc.) this rumor had been reported, the leader left the city without delay. 10. When every desire for (*lit.*, of) money and glory had been banished from his soul, that leader conquered himself. 11. Every desire for evil things ought to be conquered by us (= we ought to conquer...) if we wish to lead a good life. 12. If (since, etc.) the citizens love (their) country, we can have great hopes. 13. All citizens kept fearing that tyrant, who had to be banished. 14. When the tyrant had been overcome, the citizens regained their liberty and rights. 15. But after a tyrant has been expelled, another tyrant often gets the power. 16. Who in taking the power desires to help the state alone, not himself? 17. When many peoples had been conquered, you (sing.) desired to possess the whole world. 18. Slavery of every sort must be checked throughout the whole world. 19. If our republic is strong, nothing is to be feared by you (sing.). 20. Our country ought to be helped by each one who likes our mode of life. 21. All rights, therefore, ought to be preserved by the citizens with great care. 22. When duties have been deserted by the citizens, the state will be in great danger. 23. When these important things had been said, the orator was praised by us. 24. Truth and virtue ought always to be sought by all men. 25. When (since) truth and virtue had been sought, the republic was saved.

26. A. (8) virīs tenetibus; (9) fāmā narrātā; (10) cupidatāte expulsā; (12) cīvibus amantibus; (14) tyrannō superātō; (15) tyrannō expulsō; (17) gentibus victīs; (22) officiīs relictīs; (23) rēbus dictīs; (25) vēritāte... quaesītīs.

B. (11) vincenda est; (13) expellendus erat; (18) opprimenda est; (19) timendum est; (20) adiuvanda est; (21) cōnservanda sunt; (24) quaerendae sunt.

C. (11) nōbīs; (19) tibi; (20) cuique; (21) cīvibus; (24) virīs.

D. (22) ā cīvibus; (23) ā nōbīs.

KEY FOR CHAPTER 25

1. See pp. 85, 97, 116.
2. Future active infinitive.
3. Perfect passive infinitive.
4. They agree with the subject of the infinitive. See p. 121 n. 3.
5. Since it is the ending of the perfect active infinitive, -**isse** in effect means "to have...."

6. (1) to have moved
    (2) to have been moved
    (3) to be about to[1] move
    (4) to be moved
    (5) to be said
    (6) to be known
    (7) to be saved
    (8) to be seized
    (9) to be sent
    (10) to have believed
    (11) to have destroyed
    (12) to have drawn
    (13) to have touched
    (14) to have loved
    (15) to have conquered

    (16) to have lived
    (17) to have been drawn
    (18) to have been seen
    (19) to have been seized
    (20) to have been sent
    (21) to have been sought
    (22) to have been expelled
    (23) to have been left
    (24) to have been given
    (25) to be about to give
    (26) to be about to turn
    (27) to be about to press
    (28) to be about to seize
    (29) to be about to order
    (30) to be about to touch

7. See p. 117.

8. (2) nūntiō, **I** announce
    (4) intellegō, **I** understand
    (7) videō, **I** see
    (8) nesciō, **I** do not know
    (10) crēdō, **I** believe
    (13) audiō, **I** hear

    (14) sentiō, **I** feel, think
    (16) scrībō, **I** write
    (19) ostendō, **I** show
    (20) spērō, **I** hope
    (22) putō, **I** think
    (24) negō, **I** say that... not, deny

9. Saying, knowing, thinking, perceiving. See p. 119, bottom.
10. The infinitive with subject accusative; not a "that" clause.
11. The accusative.
12. No.
13. (1) The perfect infinitive = time *before* that of the main verb.
    (2) The future infinitive = time *after* that of the main verb.
    (3) The present infinitive = the *same time* as that of the main verb. See p. 118.
14. I know that you did (will do, are doing) this (thing). 15. I knew that you had done (would do, were doing) this. 16. We believed that they would come (had come, were coming). 17. We believe that they will come (came, are coming). 18. Tomorrow he will hear (A) that they are coming (i.e., tomorrow); (B) that they came (e.g., yesterday) *or* that they have come; (C) that they will come (e.g., in a few days). 19. Today he hears (A) that they are coming (today); (B) that they came (yesterday); (C) that they will come (soon). 20. Yesterday he heard (A) that they were coming (yesterday); (B) that they had come (e.g., the day before yesterday); (C) that they would come (in a few days). 21. They hope that you (plu.) will see him. 22. I know that this was done by you. 23. I did not know that those things had been done by him. 24. They said that the city was not being captured by the enemy (had not been captured). 25. You (plu.) know that those men are (will be, were/have been) always faithful. 26. You (plu.) knew that those men were (would be, had been) always faithful. 27. They kept thinking that the tyrant ought to be driven out by them (by themselves). 28. We believe that peace ought to be sought by all leaders. 29. He says that peace is being sought (was sought) by all leaders. 30. He said that all leaders would seek

(were seeking, had sought) peace. 31. Our enemies believe that they should conquer every state (every state ought to be conquered by themselves). 32. The enemy hope that they will conquer all states. 33. I well know that I do not know many things for no one can know all things.

34. **Scīre** (sentence 33) is a complementary infinitive depending on **potest**.

35.

Word	Form	Reason
(14) tē	acc.	subj. of inf. (fēcisse)
(14) fēcisse	perf. act. inf.	indir. statement
(16) eōs	acc.	subj. of inf. (ventūrōs esse)
(17) ventūrōs esse	fut. act. inf.	indir. state
(21) eum	acc.	obj. of inf. (vīsūrōs esse)
(22) hoc	acc	subj. of inf. (factum esse)
(23) eō	abl.	agent
(24) hostibus	abl.	agent
(25) fidēlēs	acc.	pred. adj. agreeing with illōs
(27) sibi	dat.	agent w. pass. periphrastic
(28) pācem	acc.	subj. of inf. (quaerendam esse)
(28) ducibus	dat.	agent w. pass. periphr.
(29) ducibus	abl.	agent
(30) pācem	acc.	obj. of inf. (quaesitūrōs esse)
(31) rem pūblicam	acc.	subj. of inf. (vicendam esse)
(31) sibi	dat.	agent w. pass. periphr.
(32) rēs pūblicās	acc.	obj. of inf.

KEY FOR CHAPTER 26

1. (1) Latin **-ior** corresponds to English *-er*.
   (2) They have a slight similarity in sound and they both have a final **r** as a sign of the comparative.
2. (1) Latin **-issimus** corresponds to English *-est*.
   (2) The s's which they have in common suggest s as a sign of the superlative.
3. (1) They are added to the *base* of the adjective. (See p. 122, middle and n. 2.)
   (2) turpior, turpissimus; vēlōcior, vēlocissimus; prūdentior, prūdentissimus
4. (1) **Acerbior** = harsher, rather harsh, too harsh.
   (2) **Acerbissimus** = harshest, very harsh.
5. (1) **Quam** with the comparative = *than* (this man was harsher than that one).
   (2) **Quam** with the superlative = *as...as possible*, *-st possible* (this man was as harsh as possible, the harshest possible).
6. There is no fixed case after **quam**, which is an adverb or conjunction of comparison. The second word of a comparison, which comes after **quam**, is put in the same case as that of the first of the two words compared. (See p. 123, mid.)
7. (1) Most have **i**-stems.
   (2) Comparatives have consonant stems. (Note, incidentally, that *comparative* and *consonant* both begin with the same sound.)
8. They announced that the bravest possible leader had come. 9. After a very clear light had been seen by all, the bravest troops were sent against the enemy. 10. When that very base man had been banished, the senate gave gifts to the more faithful citizens. 11. The more fortunate citizens used to do these pleasant things

on behalf of the more unfortunate citizens. 12. This author is more famous than that one. 13. Certain men said that this author was more famous than that one. 14. Read the books of wiser authors if you wish to lead the wisest (a very wise) life. 15. Certain authors whose books I have read are too (rather) harsh. 16. After reading certain very wise books, we avoided those baser faults. 17. This man, who has overcome his base faults, is braver than the very brave leader. 18. Who is the happiest man? He who leads the wisest life is happier than the most powerful tyrant. 19. The cure of your vices seems rather (too) difficult. 20. That leader thought that his country was dearer to him than life. 21. A band of the most faithful young men possible ought to be sought by the senate.

KEY FOR CHAPTER 27

1. (1) and (2) — see p. 127 item II.
2. See p. 127 item I.
3.

Positive	Comparative	Superlative
parvus	minus (minor, minus)	minimum (minimus)
malus	pejorative (peior)	pessimist (pessimus)
bonus	ameliorate (melior)	optimist (optimus)
(prō)	prior (prior)	prime (prîmus)
magnus	major (maior)	maximum (maximus)
superus	superior (superior)	supreme (suprēmus)
multus	plus (plūs)	summit (summus)

4.
(1) a smaller war
(2) the worst (very bad) war
(3) a greater war
(4) former wars
(5) a very similar book
(6) a more difficult book
(7) the smallest boy
(8) the better boy
(9) a very (most) beautiful girl
(10) a more beautiful girl
(11) very many girls
(12) greater faith
(13) very small faith
(14) a smaller sea
(15) in a smaller sea
(16) larger seas
(17) the best fruits
(18) worse fruit
(19) the fiercest (very fierce) men
(20) fiercer men
(21) more men
(22) most (very) difficult labor
(23) the last (supreme) labor
(24) more labor
(25) more labors
(26) the best leaders
(27) greater leaders
(28) better leaders
(29) the smallest gifts
(30) more gifts
(31) the first gifts
(32) more praise
(33) more praises
(34) the worst citizens
(35) better citizens
(36) very free citizens

5. The easiest things often are not the best. 6. The difficult things are often the greatest. 7. The better pursuits are more (rather) difficult. 8. The worst authors write very many books. 9. These books are worse than the books of better authors. 10. The smaller boy received a larger gift. 11. That very small republic had the greatest hopes. 12. More men believe that this war is worse than the

first war. 13. A better leader will come with greater forces. 14. Fierce leaders often used to praise the fiercer forces of the fiercest enemy. 15. When the very evil tyrant had been banished, the citizens sought a better and a wiser leader. 16. They gave the better leader greater power and more money. 17. Citizens of the smaller cities are not better than those of the largest cities. 18. We are not better than very many men of former ages. 19. Our ancestors used to call Apollo the god of the sun.

KEY FOR CHAPTER 28

1. Something other than a fact; e.g., the command and purpose clauses learned in this chapter. See p. 133, bottom.
2. See p. 132, top.
3. (1) **e**; (2) **a** (except that in the 3rd and 4th conjugations the forms **dūcam** and **audiam** are identical in the future indicative and the present subjunctive).
4. Command, called "jussive."
5. Purpose.
6. Jussive.
7. No. (See p. 136, mid. and n. 4.)
8. (1) he will send
    (2) subj., 3rd sing.
    (3) he is sending
    (4) subj., 3rd sing.
    (5) he gives
    (6) subj. 3rd plu.
    (7) they believe
    (8) they will believe
    (9) they move
    (10) subj., 3rd plu.
    (11) we shall be heard
    (12) subj., 1st plu. pass.
    (13) we are heard
    (14) subj., 2nd sing.
    (15) you (sing.) are seizing
    (16) you (sing.) will seize
    (17) they are known
    (18) they will be known
    (19) subj., 3rd plu. pass.
    (20) you (plu.) are freed
    (21) subj., 2nd. plu. pass.
    (22) you (plu.) will be freed
    (23) they are destroyed
    (24) subj., 3rd plu. pass.
    (25) you (sing.) will be conquered
    (26) you (sing.) are conquered
    (27) subj., 2nd sing.
    (28) we say
    (29) we shall say
    (30) subj., 1st plu.

9. Let that leader come. We are awaiting him. 10. Let the base citizens depart from (our) republic so that we may live in peace. 11. If those men desire friends, let them do real kindnesses. 12. He shows kindnesses to others in order to be loved (so that he may be loved). 13. I say these happy words to you so that you may not depart. 14. Let us do these very difficult things for the sake of our country. 15. Give more money to those unfortunate people so that they may not lack arms against the enemy. 16. He thinks that they will do it to avoid my anger. 17. Let us prepare arms so that our liberty may not be taken away. 18. Will our freedom be rescued from danger by arms alone? 19. Let philosophers not write too difficult books. 20. For (= the truth is) we shall not get wisdom from too difficult books. 21. Let him do better and greater things so that he may not lead a most wretched life. 22. Tell these things to that very famous author so that they may be written in this book. 23. Let us always seek the truth, without which the greatest souls cannot be happy.

24. | *Word* | *Form* | *Reason* |
|---|---|---|
| (9) veniat | pres. subj. | command (jussive) |
| (10) discēdant | pres. subj. | command |
| vivāmus | pres. subj. | purpose |
| (11) faciant | pres. subj. | command |
| (12) praestat | pres. ind. | statement of fact |
| amētur | pres. subj. | purpose |
| (13) discēdātis | pres. subj. | purpose |
| (14) faciāmus | pres. subj. | command |
| (15) date | imv. (= imperative) | command in 2nd per. |
| armīs | abl. | separation |
| careant | pres. subj. | purpose |
| (16) eōs | acc. | subj. of inf. |
| factūrōs esse | fut. act. inf. | indirect statement |
| vītent | pres. subj. | purpose |
| (17) parēmus | pres. subj. | command |
| tollātur | pres. subj. | purpose |
| (18) armīs | abl. | means |
| ēripiētur | fut. ind. | fact |
| (19) scrībant | pres. subj. | command |
| (20) accipiēmus | fut. ind. | fact |
| (21) faciat | pres. subj. | command |
| agat | pres. subj. | purpose |
| (22) nārrā | imv. | command in 2nd per. |
| scrībantur | pres. subj. | purpose |
| (23) quaerāmus | pres. subj. | command |

KEY FOR CHAPTER 29

1. Present active infinitive + personal endings. See p. 137, top.
2. Yes.
3.
   (1) impf. subj., 3 sing.
   (2) impf. subj., 3 plu.
   (3) impf. subj., 1 plu.
   (4) impf. subj., 1 sing.
   (5) impf. subj., 2 sing.
   (6) pres. subj., 3 sing.
   (7) impf. subj., 2 plu.
   (8) pres. subj., 3 sing.
   (9) you (sing.) will find
   (10) pres. subj., 2 sing.
   (11) pres. subj., 3 sing.
   (12) he will say
   (13) he says
   (14) pres. subj., 3 plu.
   (15) impf. subj., 3 sing.
   (16) pres. subj., 3 sing.
   (17) impf. subj., 3 plu.
   (18) they will depart
   (19) pres. subj., 3 plu.
   (20) pres. subj., 1 plu.
   (21) pres. subj., 1 plu.
   (22) impf. subj., 3 plu.
   (23) pres. subj., 2 sing.
   (24) you will get
   (25) impf. subj., 2 sing.
   (26) you (plu.) will be banished
   (27) impf. subj., 2 plu.
   (28) pres. subj., 2 plu.
   (29) impf. subj., 3 plu.
   (30) they are moved

4. **Ut** or **ut nōn** + subjunctive.
5. See p. 138, mid.

6. See p. 137–138.

7. They read the best books with such great care that they learned great wisdom. 8. We used to read good books with care so that we might learn wisdom. 9. The best books ought to be read by students in order that they may learn the truth and good character. 10. Let the wisest authors write more books so that they may be able to help all peoples. 11. The souls of very many men are so foolish that they do not wish to learn. 12. But many minds are so keen that they can learn well. 13. Some teachers used to teach their pupils so skillfully (with such great skill) that even the pupils themselves wanted to learn. 14. The power of that tyrant was so great that the senate could not drive him out. 15. Let all citizens dedicate (give) themselves to the country so that the enemy may not take away their liberty. 16. Caesar was such a keen leader that the enemy did not conquer the Roman soldiers. 17. Are we leading other peoples with such great wisdom and courage that liberty is being preserved? 18. You (plu.) used to do such great kindnesses that all loved you. 19. He was so harsh that no one loved him. 20. Many citizens kept fleeing from that land in order not to be oppressed by the tyrant. 21. They so loved liberty that they were never conquered by the enemy.

22.

Word	Form	Reason
(7) discerent	impf. subj.	result
(8) discerēmus	impf. subj.	purpose
(9) discant	pres. subj.	purpose
(10) scrībant	pres. subj.	command
possint	pres. subj.	purpose
(11) cupiant	pres. subj.	result
(12) possint	pres. subj.	result
(13) cuperent	impf. subj.	result
(14) posset	impf. subj.	result
(15) dent	pres. subj.	command
tollant	pres. subj.	purpose
(16) vincerent	impf. subj.	result
(17) cōnservētur	pres. subj.	result
(18) amārent	impf. subj.	result
(19) amāret	impf. subj.	result
(20) opprimerentur	impf. subj.	purpose
(21) vincerentur	impf. subj.	result

KEY FOR CHAPTER 30

1. It is the perfect active infinitive (-**isse**) + personal endings; e.g., **ponere-m** and **posuisse-m**.

2. It is the perfect passive participle + **essem** (the imperfect subjunctive of **sum**); e.g., **positus eram** and **positus essem**.

3. **Positus sit** is perfect subjunctive passive.

4. The future perfect indicative.

5. (1) impf. pass., 3 sing.
   (2) plupf. act., 1 sing.
   (3) perf. pass., 3 plu.
   (4) pres. pass., 1 plu.
   (5) perf. act., 3 plu.
   (6) impf. act., 1 plu.
   (7) plupf. act., 2 plu.
   (8) plupf. pass., 3 sing.
   (9) impf. act., 3 plu.
   (10) plupf. pass., 1 plu.
   (11) pres. act., 3 sing.
   (12) perf. pass., 2 sing.
   (13) plupf. act., 2 sing.
   (14) impf. pass., 3 sing.
   (15) perf. act., 1 plu.
   (16) plupf. act., 3 plu.

6. (1) Present and future. See p. 142, mid.
   (2) Present and perfect.
   (3) The past tenses.
   (4) Imperfect and pluperfect.

7. (1) The same time or time after (contemporaneous or subsequent). See p. 147, mid. and n. 6 and 7.
   (2) The same time or time after.
   (3) Time before (prior).
   (4) Time before (prior).

8. Where is (was) the leader? 9. They ask where the leader is (was). 10. They kept asking where the leader was (had been). 11. They will ask where the leader is (was). 12. I do not know where the money was put. 13. Do you (sing.) know where the money is being put? 14. They knew where the money was being put. 15. He did not know where the money had been put. 16. We shall tell you (plu.) why the soldier did (does) this. 17. They told me why the soldier had done (was doing) this. 18. Tell me who came (is coming). 19. The orator asked why the other citizens had not learned these plans. 20. We announced to the leader that the other soldiers were fleeing (had fled) into that land. 21. We announced to the leader into what land the other soldiers were fleeing (had fled). 22. We heard that the citizens were so faithful that they preserved the state. 23. We heard what the citizens had done to preserve the state. 24. They kept inquiring in whose state peace could be found. 25. We learned that peace had not been found in their country. 26. Those foolish men always ask what is better than power or money. 27. We certainly think that money itself is not bad; but we believe that truth and liberty and friendship are better and greater. 28. These things we desire so that we may live a finer life; for money alone and power can make men harsh, so that they are not happy. 29. Finally, let him explain all things so that you (plu.) may now understand how great crimes have been committed against the republic.

30. *Word*	*Form*	*Reason*
(15) posita esset	plupf. subj.	indirect question
(16) fēcerit	perf. subj.	ind. quest.
(17) fēcisset	plupf. subj.	ind. quest.
(18) vēnerit	perf. subj.	ind. quest.
(20) fugere	pres. inf.	ind. statement
(21) fugerent	impf. subj.	ind. quest.
(22) esse	pres. inf.	ind. state.
cōnservārent	impf. subj.	result

(23) fēcissent	plupf. subj.	ind. quest.
cōnservārent	impf. subj.	purpose
(24) posset	impf. subj.	ind. quest.
(25) inventam esse	perf. inf.	ind. state.
(26) sit	pres. subj.	ind. quest.
(27) esse	pres. inf.	ind. state.
(28) agāmus	pres. subj.	purpose
sint	pres. subj.	result
(29) exponat	pres. subj.	jussive
comprehendātis	pres. subj.	purpose
commissa sint	pres. subj.	ind. quest.

KEY FOR CHAPTER 31

1. When (circumstantial, which is to be distinguished from **cum** temporal), since, although.
2. Although.
3. (1) The 3rd conjugation.
   (2) They lack the connecting vowel **e/i**, which is seen in the corresponding forms of **dūcō**. (See p. 149, end.)

4. (1) pres. subj. act., 3 sing.
   (2) he bears
   (3) impf. subj. act., 3 sing.
   (4) he will bear
   (5) to bear
   (6) they bear
   (7) they will bear
   (8) pres. subj. act., 3 plu.
   (9) he is borne
   (10) bear (2 plu.)
   (11) you (plu.) bear
   (12) you (sing.) will be borne
   (13) you (sing.) are borne
   (14) bear (2 sing.)
   (15) to be borne
   (16) to have borne
   (17) to be about to bear
   (18) to be borne (gerundive)
   (19) to have been borne
   (20) plupf. subj. act., 3 sing.

5. When we had said this, they (those men) replied that they would offer a just peace. 6. Although he had gone into another country, nevertheless he found new friends. 7. Since they offer us friendship, we shall offer them aid. 8. Since the danger was great, they brought all their troops and arms together in a short time. 9. What do *you* (sing.) bring? What does he bring? Tell me why these gifts are offered. 10. When he had explained what he was seeking, you (sing.) said that such great aid could not be offered. 11. Although they had brought pleasing gifts, I was able nevertheless to recognize their treachery. 12. Since we now understand your plans, we will not endure your treachery. 13. Such great evils are not to be endured. Go (betake yourself) into exile. 14. Finally, let all these citizens bear aid to the republic. 15. I kept thinking that they would bring the wine in ships (*lit.*, by ships). 16. Although our soldiers had conquered the enemy, nevertheless they offered them many kindnesses. 17. When he had learned what great benefits the others were offering, he himself offered equal benefits. 18. We ought to offer much aid to the unfortunate citizens of small nations. 19. When the consul had spoken these words, the senate replied that money had been brought together for this purpose.

20.

Word	Form	Reason
(5) dīxissēmus	plupf. subj.	**cum** circumstantial
oblātūrōs esse	fut. inf.	ind. state.
(6) contulisset	plupf. subj.	**cum** *although*
(7) offerant	pres. subj.	**cum** *since*
(8) esset	impf. subj.	**cum** *since*
(9) offerantur	pres. subj.	ind. quest.
(10) exposuisset	plupf. subj.	**cum** circumstantial
peteret	impf. subj.	ind. quest.
(11) tulissert	plupf. subj.	**cum** *although*
(12) comprehendāmus	pres. subj.	**cum** *since*
(13) cōnfer	imv. 2 sing.	command
(14) ferant	pres. subj.	jussive (command)
(15) nāvibus	abl. plu.	abl. abs.
lātūrōs esse	fut. inf.	ind. state.
(16) vīcissent	plupf. subj.	**cum** *although*
(17) offerrent	impf. subj.	ind. quest.
(19) dīxisset	plupf. subj.	**cum** circumstantial

KEY FOR CHAPTER 32

1. (1) -**e**; (2) -**iter** (e.g., līberē, celeriter).
2. The ending -*ly* (e.g., freely, quickly).
3. No. For example, see the list on p. 152, mid.
4. (1) -**ius** (e.g., līberius, celerius).
   (2) It is identical with the nom. and acc. neut. sing.
   (3) It is usually formed by using more (*too, rather*) with the positive degree of the adverb (e.g., more/too freely, more quickly).
5. The base is the same in both instances.
6. (1) **līberius** = more/too/rather freely.
   (2) **līberrimē** = most/very freely.
7. (1) pleasantly
   (2) more/too pleasantly
   (3) most/very pleasantly
   (4) better
   (5) very faithfully
   (6) briefly
   (7) very quickly
   (8) worse
   (9) more faithfully
   (10) more easily
   (11) very little, least of all
   (12) more, rather
   (13) longer
   (14) badly
   (15) more wretchedly
   (16) less
   (17) easily
   (18) especially, most of all
   (19) very seriously
   (20) more swiftly
8. (1) **vol-**; (2) **vel-**. See p. 153, end.
9. It is similar to **sum**. See p. 154 n. 5.

10. (1) you (sing.) will wish   (13) to have wished
     (2) pres. subj., 2 sing.   (14) they wish
     (3) you (sing.) wish   (15) we wished
     (4) impf. subj., 2 sing.   (16) to wish
     (5) he wishes   (17) he had wished
     (6) pres. subj., 1 plu.   (18) they wished
     (7) impf. subj., 1 plu.   (19) you (plu.) wished
     (8) plupf. subj., 2 sing.   (20) impf. subj., 3 sing.
     (9) I shall wish   (21) they do not wish
     (10) they kept wishing   (22) impf. subj., 3 sing.
     (11) he will wish   (23) pres. subj., 3 sing.
     (12) you (plu.) wish   (24) he will not wish

11. Certain men wish to believe that all men are equal. 12. Certain men say that all men's minds at least are not equal. 13. These men obtained wealth very quickly; those will be poor for a very long time. 14. This man wishes to get very many honors as easily as possible. 15. We especially wish to seek knowledge. 16. The citizens themselves managed the state better than the leader. 17. There the land is more level and is more open. 18. Free men will have very little wish to keep us from knowledge; but tyrants especially so wish. 19. The tyrant used to oppress his citizens so badly that they always wished to be free. 20. He will offer very many gifts very freely so that the army may be willing to help that tyrant. 21. Since they had very little wish to offer aid, we were unwilling to show them many favors. 22. Since the enemy are coming swiftly against us, we want to call our men to arms as quickly as possible. 23. Although they truly wanted to preserve their liberty and laws, nevertheless the crimes of the tyrant had to be endured very long. 24. He wants to do these things more wisely so that he may not lose this occasion at least.

KEY FOR CHAPTER 33

1. (1) The present subjunctive. (2) See p. 158 s. v. "Observations."
2. (1) (A) Present contrary to fact; (B) past contrary to fact.
   (2) The conditional clause. See p. 158
3. **Nisi.**
4. The future less vivid condition.
5. See vocabulary p. 159.
6. If reason leads, you (sing.) are happy. 7. If reason leads, you will be happy. 8. If reason should lead, you would be happy. 9. If reason were leading, you would be happy. 10. If reason had led, you would have been happy. 11. If you (sing.) love money, you lack wisdom. 12. If you love money, you will lack wisdom. 13. If you should love money, you would lack wisdom. 14. If you were in love with money, you would lack wisdom. 15. If you had loved money, you would have lacked wisdom. 16. If we seek the truth, we find knowledge. 17. If we seek the truth, we shall find knowledge. 18. If we should seek the truth, we should find knowledge. 19. If we were seeking the truth, we should find knowledge. 20. If we had sought the truth, we should have found knowledge. 21. If you do not avoid anger, you will lose many friends. 22. If you had not

avoided anger, you would have lost many friends. 23. If you should not avoid anger (if you should fail to avoid anger), you would lose many friends. 24. If you were not avoiding anger, you would be losing many friends. 25. If you do not avoid anger, you are losing many friends. 26. If you did not avoid anger, you lost many friends. 27. If anyone has a good character, we praise him. 28. If anyone had had a good character, we should have praised him. 29. If anyone should have (were to have) a good character, we should praise him. 30. If anyone had a good character, we praised (used to praise) him. 31. If anyone were in possession of a good character, we should praise him. 32. If anyone has a good character, we shall praise him. 33. If those men win, we shall depart. 34. If those men should win, we should depart. 35. If those men had won, we should have departed. 36. If you had read books well, you would have written better. 37. If you read books well, you will write better. 38. If you were to read books well, you would write better.

39.   (6) simple present
      (7) fut. more vivid
      (8) fut. less vivid
      (9) pres. contr. to fact
      (10) past contr. to fact

      (21) fut. more vivid
      (22) past contr. to fact
      (23) fut. less vivid
      (24) pres. contr. to fact
      (25) simple present
      (26) simple past

KEY FOR CHAPTER 34

1. See p. 162

2.
Indicative

Pres.	cōnāmur	loquitur
Impf.	cōnābāmur	loquēbātur
Fut.	cōnābimur	loquētur
Perf.	cōnātī sumus	locūtus est
Pluperf.	cōnātī erāmus	locūtus erat
Fut. Perf.	cōnātī erimus	locūtus erit

Subjunctive

Pres.	cōnēmur	loquātur
Impf.	cōnārēmur	loquerētur
Perf.	cōnātī sīmus	locūtus sit
Pluperf.	cōnātī essēmus	locūtus esset

3. (1) Participles

Pres.	patiēns, *suffering*
Perf.	passus, *having suffered*
Fut.	passūrus, *about to suffer*
Ger.	patiendus, *to be endured*

(2) Infinitives

Pres.	patī, *to suffer*
Perf.	passus esse, *to have suffered*
Fut.	passūrus esse, *to be about to suffer*

4. (1) illud cōnsilium; (2) illō cōnsiliō; (3) illud cōnsilium

5. Ablative (of means) with special deponent verbs. See p. 165.

6. Pres. partic.; fut. partic.; fut. inf.; e.g., patiēns, passūrus, passūrus, esse in 3 above.

7. (1) cōnor
      2 sing. cōnāre, *try*
      2 plu. cōnāminī, *try*

  (2) loquor
      loquere, *speak*
      loquiminī, *speak*

8. (1) locūtus, *having said*
   (2) mortuus, *having died*
   (3) cōnātus, *having tried*
   (4) passus, *having suffered*

  (5) secūtus, *having followed*
   (6) ēgressus, *having gone out*
   (7) profectus, *having set out*

9. (1) he will use
   (2) pres. subj., 3 sing.
   (3) he uses
   (4) impf. subj., 3 sing.
   (9) you (sing.) are enduring
   (10) endure (imv.)
   (11) to endure
   (12) they endured
   (13) to have endured
   (14) enduring

  (5) having used
   (6) plupf. subj., 3 sing.
   (7) to be about to use
   (8) you (sing.) will endure
   (15) pres. subj., 3 sing.
   (16) he endures
   (17) we shall endure
   (18) pres. subj., 3 sing.
   (19) impf. subj., 3 sing.
   (20) it must be endured

10. He thinks that these evils ought to be endured. 11. We shall try to endure these evils. 12. If you do not wish to die, endure these evils. 13. Having endured the greatest evils, the poor man died. 14. The tyrant thought that they would endure these evils a long time. 15. When they had endured many wars, they dared to force that tyrant into exile. 16. If you follow this new leader, you will enjoy liberty and leisure. 17. When these words have been said, we dared to follow him. 18. Having spoken these words, we set out so that we might not die in that miserable place. 19. Although he thought that you had used a bad plan, nevertheless he spoke with you freely. 20. If anyone should dare to use wine of that sort, he would quickly die. 21. His son was born and died on the same day. 22. Let us use all our resources so that our country may be saved. 23. When he tried to set out into another land, he was captured by soldiers. 24. I kept thinking that he would go out of the city with his friends. 25. Having set out that night, Caesar came to a certain very famous island. 26. If they had used better books, they would have learned more.

27. (12) simple present; (16) future more vivid; (20) future less vivid; (26) past contrary to fact.

28.

Word	Form	Reason
(14) passūrōs esse	fut. inf.	ind. state.
(17) verbîs	abl.	abl. abs.
(18) locūtî	nom. plu.of perf. partic.	agrees w. subject of verb
morerēmur	impf. subj.	purpose
(19) cōnsiliō	abl.	special deponents
arbitrārētur	impf. subj.	**cum** *although*
(21) diē	abl.	time when
(22) ūtāmur	pres. subj.	jussive
(25) nocte	abl.	time when
(26) librîs	abl.	spec. deponents

KEY FOR CHAPTER 35

1. See p. 169.
2. See p. 173, mid. and n. 4 and 5.

3.
(1) eum; they recognize him.
(2) eī; they forgive him.
(3) eī; they serve him.
(4) eum; they save him.
(5) eum; I prepared him.
(6) eī; I obeyed him.
(7) eum; they endure him.
(8) eum; they will find him.
(9) eī; they injure him.
(10) eum; they help him.
(11) eī; they please him.
(12) eum; they throw him.
(13) eum; they overcome him.
(14) eī; they trust him.
(15) eō; they lack it.
(16) eī; they study it.
(17) eum; they urge him.
(18) eum; they follow him.
(19) eī ; they persuade him.
(20) eō; they use it (him).
(21) eum; they strike him.
(22) eī; they spare him.
(23) eī; they command him.
(24) eum; they order him.

4. He saved the leader. 5. He served the leader. 6. Slaves serve other men. 7. Brave men save others. 8. That slave served my son and saved him. 9. If anyone serves himself alone, he will never save the republic. 10. If someone had undertaken this work, he would have saved many men. 11. The gods will pardon me; you, O citizens, pardon the whole army. 12. If we want God to forgive us, we ought to forgive other men. 13. They do not trust me now, and they will never be willing to trust my son. 14. If you trust us, we shall trust you. 15. Since you lacked good faith, they could not trust you. 16. Let us obey this leader so that he may spare us and save the city. 17. If Caesar does not please the citizens, they will not spare his life. 18. I am studying Latin literature, which I like (pleases me) even if I cannot persuade my friends. 19. Let us always study and obey truth and wisdom. 20. Always study the best subjects if you wish to be truly happy. 21. As we study these subjects, let us use both books and life. 22. A good man wishes to harm nobody; he spares all, he helps all. 23. They marvel at (admire) these rewards.

24.

Word	Form	Reason
(5) ducī	dat.	special verbs
(8) eum	acc.	obj. of **servāvit**
(9) sibi	dat.	spec. verbs
(11) exercituī	dat.	spec. verbs
(12) hominibus	dat.	spec. verbs
(13) filiō	dat.	spec. verbs
(15) fidē	abl.	separation
(16) ducī	dat.	spec. verbs
pāreāmus	pres. subj.	jussive
servet	pres. subj.	purpose
(17) cīvibus	dat.	spec. verbs
vītae	dat.	spec. verbs
(18) litterīs	dat.	spec. verbs
amīcīs	dat.	spec. verbs
(21) rēbus	dat.	spec. verbs
librīs	abl.	spec. depon. verbs
ūtāmur	pres. subj.	jussive
(22) omnibus	dat.	spec. verbs

KEY FOR CHAPTER 36

1. Indirect command = ut (nē) + subjunctive. See p. 174.
2. E.g., imperō, dīcō, cūrō, moneō, hortor, persuādeō, petō, quaerō, ōrō, rogō. See p. 177 n. 1.
3.
(1) it will be made/done, he will become
(2) it is made/done, he becomes
(3) pres. subj., 3 sing.
(4) impf. subj., 3 sing.
(5) to be made/done, to become
(6) they are made/done, they become
(7) they were being made/ done, they were becoming
(8) you (sing.) will be made, become
(9) to have been made/done, become
(10) impf. subj., 3 plu.
(11) we are made, become
(12) they will be made, become
(13) you (sing.) are made, become
(14) impf. subj., 1 sing.
(15) pres. subj., 3 plu.
(16) gerundive, to be made/done
(17) pres. subj., 1 plu.

4. He said that they were studying Latin literature. 5. He told why they were studying Latin literature. 6. He said that they should study Latin literature (he told them to study...). 7. We asked them why they were studying Greek philosophy. 8. Do you ask that we learn (= ask us to learn) the nature of all things? 9. I warn you to spare these wise men. 10. He warned the soldiers not to injure those seeking peace. 11. He will command us not to trust the enemy. 12. He commanded you to obey the leader. 13. I ask you why you did this. 14. I ask you to do this. 15. I beg of you that peace be made. 16. They kept begging me not to make war. 17. I besought him not to obey the disgraceful king. 18. I beg you to become very keen pupils. 19. Take care that you do this. 20. Caesar took care that his power be made greatest in the state. 21. The speaker urged us to serve our free country eagerly. 22. He persuaded us that we should always use just laws. 23. We are trying to persuade the leader not to harm the arts and

laws of the country. 24. A tyrant commands that money be made; and money is made. But that fool does not perceive that this money will be nothing without good faith. 25. Let us urge more students certainly to study the Latin language.

26.

Word	*Form*	*Reason*
(4) studēre	pres. inf.	ind. state.
(5) studērent	impf. subj.	ind. quest.
(6) studērent	impf. subj.	ind. com.
(7) studērent	impf. subj.	ind. quest.
(8) cognōscāmus	pres. subj.	ind. com.
(9) parcās	pres. subj.	ind. com.
(10) eīs	dat.	spec. vbs.
pācem	acc.	obj. petentibus
(11) hostibus	dat.	spec. vbs.
(13) fēcerīs	perf. subj.	ind. quest.
(14) faciās	pres. subj.	ind. com.
(16) facerem	impf. subj.	ind. com.
(18) fiātis	pres. subj.	ind. com.
(22) lēgibus	abl.	spec. dep. vbs.
(23) lēgibus	dat.	spec. vbs.
(24) futūram esse	fut. inf.	ind. state.
(25) hortēmur	pres. subj.	jussive

KEY FOR CHAPTER 37

1. (1) Present indicative and present subjunctive.
   (2) It is **i**.
2. Nom. sing. = **iēns**; nom. plu. = **euntēs**. (see p. 179.)
3. In writing the synopsis of a verb one should follow the sequence of tenses in the indicative and the subjunctive as given above in #2 of the Key of Chapter 34. If this is done there is no need to label the tenses.
   Eō 2nd sing.: Indicative —īs, ībās, ībis, īstī, ierās, ieris.
   Subjunctive — eās, īrēs, ierīs, īssēs.
   Eō 3d plu.: Indicative — eunt, ībant, ībunt, iērunt, ierant, ierint.
   Subjunctive — eant īrent, ierint, īssent.

4. (1) we went
   (2) we are going
   (3) impf. subj., 1 plu.
   (4) we shall go
   (5) plupf. subj., 1 plu.
   (6) pres. subj., 1 plu.
   (7) to be about to go
   (8) going (acc. sing.)
   (9) they went
   (10) they are going
   (11) pres. subj., 3 plu.
   (12) they will go
   (13) I went
   (14) he was going
   (15) they had gone
   (16) perf. subj., 1 sing.
   (17) impf. subj., 3 sing.
   (18) to have gone
   (19) going (nom./acc. plu.)
   (20) I shall go
   (21) he went
   (22) we were going
   (23) plupf. subj., 3 sing.
   (24) pres. subj., 3 sing.

5. (1) **ab, dē, ex** + abl.: ab (ex) eā terra. (See p. 179 I.)
   (2) **in** + abl.: in eā terrā; in eā īnsulā .
   (3) **in** or **ad** + acc.: in (ad) eam terram.
6. (1) Place from which = abl. without a preposition. (See p. 179 II.)
   (2) Place where = locative without a preposition.
   (3) Place to which = accusative without a preposition.
7. The locative is the case which expresses the idea of "place where" when **domus** or the name of a city is used. See p. 179 II(1) and p. 182 n. 2.
8. (1) Time when = abl. without a prep.: eōdem diē.
   (2) Time how long = acc. usually without a prep.: multōs diēs.
   (3) Time within which = abl. without a prep.: ūnō diē.
9. Since an impersonal verb lacks the 1st and the 2nd persons sing. and plu., the 1st and the 3rd principal parts are given in the 3rd per. sing. See p. 179. Vocabulary s. v. **licet** and n. 4. **Licet tibi ire.**
10. (1) (for) one day
    (2) in one day
    (3) on that day
    (4) from Rome
    (5) at Rome
    (6) to Rome
    (7) in a few days
    (8) on the same night
    (9) (for) many days
    (10) into the ship
    (11) in the ship
    (12) out of the ship
    (13) home (= to home)
    (14) at/from Athens
    (15) at home
    (16) to Athens
    (17) from home
    (18) (for) a few hours

11. In a few hours we shall go to Rome. 12. We are going to the city; they are going home. 13. As we have often admitted, you may not (are not permitted to) go from Rome to Athens (*lit.*, to go is not permitted to you). 14. Why did you leave home (go away from home) so quickly? 15. They are coming to Rome in order to go to Athens with my brother. 16. Depart from this city to (your) death and perish so that I may not perish. 17. When your brother had been killed at Rome, they returned to Athens. 18. If he should go into the territory of the enemy at this time, he would perish in a few hours. 19. He said that he did not want to stay in that country many days. 20. You said that you would return home from Athens in one hour. 21. I beg of you to return from the ship to the island in a short time. 22. In those days we were accustomed to be at Athens. 23. If they had injured his friends at Rome, he would have returned to Rome in a very short time. 24. Although my brother stayed at home, I nevertheless went away from home into new lands. 25. The Romans, if they wanted to say something bad, often used to say: "Go to the devil."

26. (11) **hōrīs** = abl.: time within which; **Rōmam** = acc.: place to which; (12) **domum** = acc.: place to which; (13) **Rōmā** = abl.: place from; **Athēnās** = acc.: place to; **īre** = pres. inf.: subject of **licet**; (14) **domō** = abl.: place from; (15) **Rōmam** = acc.: place to; (18) **frātre** = abl.: abl. abs.; (18) **tempore** = abl.: time when; **eat** = pres. subj.: fut less vivid; **hōrīs** = abl.: time within; (19) **velle** = pres. inf.: ind. state.; **diēs** = acc.: time how long; (20) **domum** = acc.: place to; **Athēnīs** = abl.: place from; **hōrā** = abl.: time within; **reditūrum esse** = fut. inf.: ind. state.; (21) **tempore** = abl. time within; **redeās** = pres. subj.: ind. command; (22) **diēbus** = abl.: time when; **Athēnīs** = locative: place where; (23) **amīcīs** = dat.: spec. verbs; **Rōmae** = locative: place where; **redīsset** = plupf. subj.: past contr. to fact condit.; (24) **domī** = locative: place where; **terrās** = acc.: place to; **domō** = abl.: place from.

KEY FOR CHAPTER 38

1. A relative clause with the indicative tells a *fact* about the antecedent.

2. A relative clause with the subjunctive tells a *characteristic* of the antecedent, indicates it to be a person or thing of such a sort. See p. 182, top.

3. See p. 183 s. v. "Relative Clauses — Characteristic" and n. 1.

4. See p. 184, bottom.

5. My friend who defended the consul was himself a very famous man. 6. But there was no one who would defend that base fellow. 7. What is there which men fear more than a tyrant? 8. Who is there who would hesitate between liberty and the command of a tyrant? 9. At ancient Rome there were those who loved money more than the state. 10. Let that evil man depart from his country — he who has endured the hatred of all good citizens. 11. Catiline, who had made such a great plot against the state, was driven from the city by Cicero. 12. What life can be pleasant for that leader as he goes off into exile? 13. Who is there who would be able to bear such pain? 14. If a person is not agreeable and good, he will not live a truly happy life, it seems to me (**mihi**). 15. They will not trust a consul who would do base deeds. 16. They trusted that very illustrious consul who had saved the state. 17. Cicero was a consul who would place the state before his own safety. 18. They knew why we wanted to follow such a brave consul. 19. I know nothing which could be easier for me. 20. I am seeking a leader whom all men would praise. 21. I am seeking that great leader whom all men praise. 22. The Romans, who had captured the Greek republics with their own armies, themselves were taken captive by the Greek arts. 23. For the ancient men there was nothing which was better than courage and wisdom. 24. Nothing is to be feared which cannot injure the soul.

25. Sentences 5 and 6: The **quī... dēfendit** states a fact about the **amīcus**; it does not describe his character. The subjunctive clause in #6 tells what kind of person the **nēmō** was.

    Sentences 15 and 16: The subjunctive clause tells something about the character of this kind of consul. In sentence 16 we feel that we know the consul, about whom the relative clause simply gives an interesting fact.

    Sentences 20 and 21: In 20 the subjunctive **laudent** indicates the kind of leader I am looking for, not a specific leader. In 21 the indicative **laudant** indicates that I am looking for a specific leader who, as an incidental fact, has received much praise.

26. Syntax: (7) **metuat** = pres. subjunctive: characteristic; (8) **dubitet** = pres. subjunctive: characteristic; (9) **Rōmae** = locative; place where; **amārent** = impf. subj.: characteristic; (10) **abeat** = pres. subj.: jussive; **passus est** = perf. indicative: rel. cl. of fact; (11) **fēcerat** = plupf. ind.: rel. cl. of fact; (12) **ducī** = dat.: reference; **potest** = pres. ind.: main verb in a direct question; (13) **possit** = pres. subj.: characteristic; (14) **erit** = fut. ind.: fut. more viv. condit.; **mihi** = dat.: ref.; (15) **consulī** = dat.: spec. vbs.; (17) **salūtī** = dat.: compound vb.; **antepōneret** = impf. subj.: characteristic; (18) **velēmus** = impf. subj.: ind. question; (19) **mihi** = dat.: ref.; **possit** = pres. subj.: characteristic; (22) **cēperant** = plupf. ind.: rel. cl. of fact; (23) **virīs** = dat.: ref.; (24) **animō** = dat.: spec. vbs.; **possit** = pres. subj.: characteristic.

KEY FOR CHAPTER 39

1. (1) See p. 188 s. v. "The Gerund."
   (2) See p. 192 n. 2.
   (3) See p. 18.
   (4) In its four cases it is used as a noun is used. See p. 187, mid.
   (5) The infinitive; see p. 187 n. 3.
2. (1) See p. 188 top s. v. "The Gerundive."
   (2) The gerund**ive** is an adject**ive**.
   (3) As an adjective it modifies a noun or pronoun and agrees with that noun or pronoun in gender, number, and case.
   (4) The gerundive (e.g., **laudandus, -a, -um**) is declined as **magnus, -a, -um** is. See p. 188.
   (5) Since the gerund has only the endings **-ī, -ō, -um, -ō**, any feminine or any plural ending on an **-nd-** base is bound to indicate a gerundive; and also, if an **-nd-** form agrees with a noun as an adjectival modifier, it must be a gerundive.
3. (1) The Latin gerund is normally translated by the English gerund in *-ing* with any attending noun constructions or adverbial modifiers.
   (2) The gerundive is to be translated by the English as if it were a gerund with an object and any adverbial modifiers. In other words, both the gerund and the gerundive are to be translated in the same way. See p. 188, top.
   (3) (A) We learn by reading with care.
   (B) We learn by reading books with care.
4. We learn by experiencing. 5. They came to learn (for learning). 6. He gave (devoted) himself to learning. 7. They came to your school to learn (for the sake of learning). 8. The boy went to the school desirous of learning (eager to learn). 9. The fear of dying kept terrifying him. 10. The hope of living after death encourages many people. 11. By thinking (= by using his head) he overcame them. 12. He devoted (gave) himself — (1) to seeking glory. (2) to waging war. (3) to making money. (4) to getting power. (5) to destroying states. (6) to following this leader. (7) to saving his country. (8) to seeking peace. (9) to attacking wrongs. (10) to writing books. (11) to reading books. (12) to learning philosophy. (13) to learning Latin literature. (14) to understanding the truth. (15) to seeking wisdom. (16) to helping human beings. 13. He came to Rome — (1) to undertake this work. (2) to see the Roman games. (3) to see the old buildings. (4) to seek peace. (5) for the sake of undertaking this work (to undertake...). (6) for the sake of learning philosophy (to learn...). (7) for the sake of reading new books (to read...). 14. He wrote a book — (1) about enduring pain. (2) about overcoming fear. (3) about living a good life. (4) about managing the state. (5) about waging war. (6) about defending liberty. (7) about conquering the enemy. (8) about giving gifts. 15. We become wiser — (1) by reading Latin literature. (2) by learning philosophy. (3) by experiencing life. (4) by conquering fear. (5) by following truth. 16. We help our very selves — (1) by always reading good books. (2) by freeing unfortunate men from fear. (3) by offering aid. (4) by helping others. 17. He consumed much time — (1) in thinking (speaking, running). (2) in doing these tasks. (3) in finding the way.

(4) in preparing an army. (5) in preparing supplies (troops). 18. He had time for writing this book only.

KEY FOR CHAPTER 40

1. See pp. 193–194, and p. 197 n. 1.
2. See p. 193, top.
3. See p. 194, top.
4. (1) dat./abl. plu. m. and n.; (2) indecl. adj. agreeing with noun in any case; (3) nom./acc. plu. n.; (4) nom. plu. m. and n., acc. plu. n.; (5) any form in plu.; (6) nom./acc. plu. n.; (7) any form in plu.; (8) dat./abl. plu. f.; (9) any form in plu.; (10) gen. plu. any gender; (11) any form in plu.; (12) any form in plu.
5. The word which indicates the whole number or amount out of which a part is taken is normally put in the genitive case. See p. 192 s. v. "Genitive of the Whole."
6. **Ex** or **dē** + abl.

7. (1) one citizen   (7) 5 citizens   (13) what hope?
   (2) ten citizens   (8) 100 citizens   (14) less fear
   (3) part of the citizens (9) 100 of the citizens (15) more praise
   (4) three citizens   (10) 1000 citizens   (16) enough aid
   (5) 3 of the 6 citizens (11) 3000 citizens   (17) more faith
   (6) 5 of the citizens   (12) a certain one   (18) no water
                                of the citizens

8. He sent — (1) two soldiers; (2) two of the soldiers; (3) 100 soldiers; (4) 100 of the soldiers; (5) 1000 soldiers; (6) 2000 soldiers; (7) 25 soldiers. 9. Two consuls came — (1) with many citizens; (2) with three citizens; (3) with two of the citizens; (4) with one citizen; (5) with 20 citizens; (6) with 1000 citizens; (7) with 3000 citizens; (8) with a certain one of the citizens. 10. Hello, my friend. How do you do? What's new (the news)? 11. Greetings to you, too. Fine. No news. 12. Do you want to hear something good? I've finally got enough wealth! 13. But what good is there in wealth alone? Do you also have enough wisdom? 14. For my part I place wealth ahead of wisdom. For I do not think that human beings can find a happy life without a great deal of money. 15. However, very many rich men experience much fear. 16. Poor men are often happier and have less fear. 17. Money itself is not bad; but the things of the mind and the soul offer more help for living happily. 18. Nine of the leaders urged us to supply more aid. 19. When five of the guards had been killed, my father fled into that free land with two of his sons and with a large number of friends. 20. Never will he have enough leisure; yet some leisure is better than nothing. 21. In our times we all have too much of fear and too little of hope. 22. Great faith and courage must be found by all men.

Appendix

SOME ETYMOLOGICAL AIDS

TWO RULES OF PHONETIC CHANGE

"Phonetic" derives from Greek **phōnḗ**, *sound*, *voice*, *speech* (cp. phonograph, phonology, symphony, telephone). Consequently, phonetic change means a change which occurs in original speech sounds for one reason or another. Of the many instances of this in Latin, the following two rules of phonetic change are probably the most important ones for the beginner.

A. *Vowel weakening* usually occurs in the medial syllables of compounds according to the following outline.
1. ă > ĭ before a single consonant and before **ng**.
ă > ĕ before two consonants.
căpiō, căptum: ac-cĭpiō, ac-cēptum

350

făciō, făctum: per-fĭciō, pcr-fĕctum
făcilis: dif-fĭcilis
cădō, cāsum: oc-cĭdō, oc-cāsum (Note that long ā does not change.)
tăngō, tāctum: con-tĭngō, con-tāctum

2. ĕ > ĭ before a single consonant.
   tĕneō: con-tĭneō (*but* contentum)
   prĕmō: com-pĭrmō (*but* compressum)

3. ae > ī.
   quaerō, quaesĭtum: re-quīrō, re-quīsītum
   laedō, laesum: col-līdō, col-līsum
   caedō, caesum: in-cīdō, in-cīsum; oc-cīdō, oc-cīsum
   aestimō: ex-īstimō

4. au > ū.
   claudō: in-clūdō, ex-clūdō
   causor: ex-cūsō

B. *Assimilation* of the final consonant of a prefix to the initial consonant of the base word commonly occurs.

ad-capiō > ac-cipiō   in-mortālis > im-mortālis
dis-facilis > dif-ficilis   in-ruō > ir-ruō

PREFIXES

Listed here are important prefixes helpful in the analysis of both Latin words and English derivatives. The Latin prefixes have passed over into English unchanged except where indicated. Incidentally, most Latin prefixes were also used by the Romans as prepositions; but the few labeled "inseparable" appear only as prefixes.

ā-, ab-, away, from.
   ā-vocō, call away (*avocation*)
   ā-vertō, turn away (*avert*)
   ā-mittō, send away, let go, lose
   ab-sum, be away (*absent*)
   ab-eō, go away
   ab-dūcō, lead away (*abduct*)
ad- (*by assimilation* **ac-, af-, ag-, al-, an-, ap-, ar-, as-, at-**), to , towards, in addition.
   ad-vocō, call to, call (*advocate*)
   ad-dūcō, lead to (*adduce*)
   ad-mittō, send to, admit
   ac-cēdō, go to, approach (*accede*)
   ac-cipiō (**ad-capiō**), get, accept
   ap-pōnō, put to (*apposition*)
   as-sentiō, feel towards, agree to, assent
ante-, before.
   ante-pōnō, put before, prefer
   ante-cēdō, go before, precede, excel (*antecedent*)
circum-, around.

circum-dūcō, lead around
circum-veniō, come around, surround (*circumvent*)
circum-stō, stand around (*circumstance*)
com- (**com = cum**; *also appears as* **con-, cor-, col-, co-**), with, together; *intensive force:* completely, very, greatly, deeply, forcibly.
　con-vocō, call together (*convoke*)
　con-dūcō, lead together (*conduct*)
　com-pōnō, put together, compose (*component*)
　com-mittō, send together, bring together, entrust (*commit*)
　cōn-sentiō, feel together, agree (*consent*)
　cō-gō (**co-agō**), drive together, force (*cogent*)
　com-pleō, fill completely, fill up (*complete*)
　cōn-servō, save completely, preserve (*conserve*)
　con-cēdō, go completely, go away, yield, grant (*concede*)
　con-tendō, stretch greatly, strive, hurry (*contend*)
　col-laudō, praise greatly *or* highly
　cor-rōborō, strengthen greatly (*corroborate*)
contrā-, against, opposite. (*Not common as a prefix in Latin but fairly common in English, especially in the form* counter-.)
　contrā-dīcō, speak against *or* opposite, oppose, rely (*contradict*)
　contrā-veniō (*late Latin*), come against, oppose (*contravene*)
dē-, down, away, aside, out, off; *intensive force:* utterly, completely
　dē-dūcō, lead down *or* away, draw down (*deduce, deduct*)
　dē-pōnō, put aside, lay aside, entrust (*deponent, deposit*)
　dē-mittō, send down, throw down, let fall (*demit*)
　dē-veniō, come from, arrive at, reach
　dē-vocō, call away *or* off
　dē-cēdō, go away (*decease*)
　dē-mēns, out of one's mind, demented
　dē-certō, fight it out, fight to the finish
dis- (**dif-, dī-;** *inseparable*), apart, away, not.
　dis-pōnō, put apart in different places, arrange (*disposition*)
　dis-cēdō, go away, depart
　di-mittō, send away in different directions, let go (*dismiss*)
　dif-ferō, di-lātus, bear apart, scatter, put off, differ (*different, dilate*)
　dis-similis, not similar, unlike, dissimilar
　dis-ficilis, not easy, difficult
e-, ex- (**ef-**), from out, forth; *intensive force:* exceedingly, up
　ē-dūcō, lead out (*educe*)
　ex-cēdō, go out, from, away; go beyond (*exceed*)
　ē-mittō, send out, forth (*emit*)
　ē-vocō, call out, forth (*evoke*)
　ex-pōnō, put out, set forth, explain (*exponent, exposition*)
　ē-veniō, come out, forth; turn out, happen (*event*)
　ef-ficiō (**ex-faciō**), produce, accomplish, perform (*efficient, effect*)
　ex-pleō, fill up, complete
　ex-asperō, roughen exceedingly, irritate (*exasperate*)

in- (**im-, il-, ir-**; *sometimes* en- or em- *in Eng.*), in, into, on , upon, against. (*Also see* **in-** *below.*)

    in-vocō, call in, call upon (*invoke*)

    in-dūcō, lead in *or* into, introduce, impel (*induce*)

    im-mittō, send into, send against, let loose against

    im-pōnō, put in, lay upon (*impose*)

    in-veniō, come upon , find (*invent*)

    in-clūdō, shut in, shut (*include, enclose*)

    in-vādō, go into, move against (*invade*)

    ir-ruō, rush into *or* upon

    il-līdō (**in-laedō**), strike *or* dash against

    in-genium (**in** + **gen-**, *from* **gignō**, beget, give birth to), inborn nature, natural capacity, talent, character (*engine, ingenious*)

in- (**im-, il-, ir-**; *inseparable prefix; cognate with Eng.* un-), not, un-.

    in-certus, not certain, uncertain

    in-iūstus, not just, unjust (cp. *injustice*)

    in-fīnītus, not limited, unlimited (*infinite*)

    in-fīrmus, not firm, weak (*infirm*)

    im-mortālis, not mortal, deathless (*immortal*)

    il-litterātus, unlearned, ignorant (*illiterate*)

    ir-revocābilis, not-call-back-able, unalterable (*irrevocable*)

inter-, between, among.

    inter-veniō, come between; interrupt (*intervene*)

    inter-cēdō, go between (*intercede*)

    inter-mittō, place between, leave off (*intermittent*)

    inter-pōnō, put between, bring forward (*interpose*)

    inter-rēgnum, period between two reigns (*interregnum*)

intrō-, within, in. (*Also used as adv.*)

    intrō-dūcō, lead in (*introduce*)

    intrō-mittō, send in

    intrō-spiciō, look within (*introspect*)

ob- (**oc-, of-, op-**), towards, to, opposite, against, over.

    ob-dūcō, lead toward *or* against

    ob-veniō, come opposite, meet

    oc-currō, run to meet, meet (*occur*)

    of-ferō, bear towards, furnish (*offer*)

    op-pōnō, put opposite, set against, oppose (*opposition*)

per-, through; *intensive force:* thoroughly, very, completely.

    per-dūcō, lead through *or* along

    per-veniō, come through to, arrive at, reach

    per-ferō, carry through, bear thoroughly, endure

    per-mittō, let go through, entrust, allow (*permit*)

    per-ficiō (**-faciō**), do thoroughly, accomplish, finish (*perfect*)

    per-facilis, very easy

    per-paucus, very small

    per-brevis, very short, very brief

post-, after.

    post-pōnō, put after, esteem less, disregard (*postpone*)

    post-ferō, put after, esteem less, disregard (*postpone*)

    post-scrībō, write after, add (*postscript*)

prae-, before, infront, forth; *intensive force:* very. (*In Eng. also spelled* pre-.)

    prae-moneō, warn before, forewarn (*premonition*)

    prae-cēdō, go before, excel (*precede*)

    prae-pōnō, put before, place in command of, prefer (*preposition*)

    prae-mittō, send before *or* forth, set before (*premise*)

    prae-scrībō, write before, order (*prescribe, prescription*)

    prae-ferō, bear before, set before, prefer

    prae-clārus, very noble, very famous, excellent

prō-, before, in front, forth, out, away, instead of, for. (*Sometimes* pur- *in Eng.*)

    prō-vocō, call forth *or* out, challenge, excite (*provoke*)

    prō-videō, see ahead, foresee, care for (*provide, provision, purvey*)

    prō-dūcō, lead before *or* out, bring forth, prolong (*produce*)

    prō-cēdō, go forward, advance (*proceed*)

    prō-pōnō, put in front, set forth, declare (*proponent, purpose*)

    prō-mittō, send forth, assure (*promise*)

    prō-cōnsul, one who served in place of a consul (*proconsul*)

re- (**red-**; *inseparable*), back again.

    re-vocō, call back, recall (*revoke*)

    re-dūcō, lead back (*reduce*)

    re-cēdō, go back, retire (*recede*)

    re-pōnō, put back, replace, restore (*repository*)

    re-mittō, send back, give up (*remit*)

    red-dō, give back, restore, return

    red-eō, go back, return

sē- (*inseparable*), apart, aside, without.

    sē-dūcō, lead aside, separate (*seduce*)

    sē-cēdō, go apart, withdraw, retire (*secede*)

    sē-pōnō, put aside, select

    sē-moveō, move aside, separate

    sē-cūrus, without care, untroubled, serene (*secure*)

sub- (**suc-, suf-, sug-, sup-, sur-, sus-**), under, up (from beneath); rather, somewhat, a little, secretly.

    sub-dūcō, draw from under, withdraw secretly

    suc-cēdō, go under, go up, approach, prosper (*succeed*)

    sup-pōnō, put under; substitute (*supposition, supposititious*)

    sub-veniō, come under, help (*subvene, subvention*)

    sus-tineō (**-teneō**), hold up, support, endure (*sustain*)

super- (*also* sur- *in Eng.*), over, above.

    super-pōnō, place over *or* upon, set over (*superposition*)

    super-sedeō, sit above *or* upon, be superior to, be above, refrain from, desist (*supersede*)

    super-sum, be over and above, be left, survive

    superō, be above, surpass, conquer (*insuperable*)

superbus, above others, haughty, proud (*superb*)
super-vīvō, survive
super-ficiēs, surface
trāns- (trā-), across, over.
trāns-mittō, send across, cross over (*transmit*)
trā-dūcō, lead across (*traduce*)
trāns-eō, go across (*transition*)
trā-dō, go over, surrender, hand down (*tradition*)

SUFFIXES

Of the very numerous Latin suffixes only a few of the more important ones are listed here with their English equivalents.

1. Suffix denoting the *agent*, the *doer*, the *one who* (**-tor** or **-sor**).
-tor *or* -sor (cp. *Eng.* -er)
victor (vincō, victum[1], conquer), conqueror, victor
scrīptor (scrībō, scrīptum, write), writer
lēctor (legō, lēctum, read), reader
ōrātor (ōrō, ōrātum, [speak], plead), speaker, orator
auctor (augeō, auctum, increase), increaser, author
līberātor (līberō, līberātum, free), liberator
tōnsor (tondeō, tōnsum, shave, clip), barber
amātor (amō, amātum, love), lover

2. Suffixes denoting *action* or *result of action* (-or, -ium, -tiō). -or (*Eng.* -or)
amor (amō, love), love, amour
timor (timeō, fear), fear
dolor (doleō, suffer pain), pain, suffering, grief
error (errō, go astray, err), error
terror (terreō, frighten, terrify), fright, terror
-ium (*Eng.* -y; -ce *when* -ium *is preceded by* c *or* t)
studium (studeō, be eager), eagerness, study
colloquium (colloquor, talk with), talk, conference, colloquy
imperium (imperō, command), command, power
odium (ōdī, hate), hate
aedificium (aedificō, build) building, edifice
silentium (silēns, silentis, silent), silence
-tiō, -tiōnis, *or* -siō, -siōnis (*Eng.* -tion *or* -sion)
admonitiō (admoneō, admonitum, admonish) admonition
ratiō (reor, ratum, reckon, think), reckoning, plan, reason (*ration*)
ōrātiō (ōrō, ōrātum, [speak], plead), oration
nātiō (nāscor, nātum, be born), birth, nation
occāsiō (occidō, occāsum, fall down) a befalling, occasion, opportunity

3. Suffixes denoting *quality*, *state*, or *condition* (-ia, -tia, -tās, -tūdō).
-ia (*Eng.* -y)
miseria (miser, miserable), misery
insānia (īnsānus, insane), insanity

victōria (vicor, victor), victory
invidia (invidus, envious), envy
iniūria (iniūrus, wrong, unjust), injustice, injury
-tia (*Eng.* -ce)
    amīcitia (amīcus, friendly), friendship
    sapientia (sapiēns, wise), wisdom, sapience
    scientia (sciēns, knowing), knowledge, science
    iūstitia (iūstus, just), justice
    dīligentia (dīligēns, diligent), diligence
-tās, -tātis (*Eng.* -ty)
    lībertās (līber, free), freedom, liberty
    vēritās (vērus, true), truth, verity
    paupertās (pauper, poor), poverty
    cupiditās (cupidus, desirous, greedy), greed, cupidity
    gravitās (gravis, heavy, grave), weight, seriousness, gravity
    celeritās (celer, swift), swiftness, celerity
-tūdō, -tūdinis (*Eng.* -tude)
    multitūdō (multus, much, many), multitude
    magnitūdō (magnus, large, great), magnitude
    pulchritūdō (pulcher, beautiful), beauty, pulchritude
    sōlitūdō (sōlus, alone), solitude
    sollicitūdō (sollicitus, agitated, solicitous), solicitude

4. Adjectival suffix meaning *full of* (-ōsus).
-ōsus, -ōsa, -ōsum (*Eng.* -ous *or* -ose)
    studiōsus (studium, zeal), full of zeal, eager (*studious*)
    imperiōsus (imperium, command), full of command, imperious
    perīculōsus (perīculum, danger), full of danger, dangerous
    vitiōsus (vitium, fault, vice), faulty, vicious
    verbōsus (verbum, word), wordy, verbose

5. Adjectival suffix meaning *able to be, worthy to be;* sometimes *able to* (-bilis).
-bilis, -bile (*Eng.* -able, ible, -ble)
    laudābilis (laudō, praise), worthy to be praised, laudable
    amābilis (amō, love), worthy to be loved, lovable, amiable
    incrēdibilis (crēdō, believe), not worthy to be believed, incredible
    mōbilis (moveō, move), able to be moved, movable, mobile
    inexpugnābilis (expugnō, conquer), unconquerable
    stabilis (stō, stand), able to stand, stable

6. Adjectival suffixes denoting *pertaining* to (-ālis or -āris, -ānus, -icus).
    -ālis, -āle, *or* -āris, -āre (*Eng.* -al *or* -ar)
    mortālis (mors, death), pertaining to death, mortal
    vitālis (vīta, life), pertaining to life, vital
    fātālis (fātum, fate), fatal
    populāris (populus, people), popular
    vulgāris (vulgus, the common people), common, vulgar
-ānus, -āna, -ānum (*Eng.* -an *or* -ane)
    Rōmānus (Rōma, Rome), pertaining to Rome, Roman

hūmānus (**homō**, man), pertaining to man, human, humane
urbānus (**urbs**, city), urban, urbane
mundānus (**mundus**, world), worldly, mundane
-icus, -ica, -icum (*Eng.* -ic)
domesticus (**domus**, house), pertaining to the house, domestic
pūblicus (**populus**, people), pertaining to the people, public
rūsticus (**rūs**, country), rustic
cīvicus (**cīvis**, citizen), civic
classicus (**classis**, class), pertaining to the classes, of the highest class;
classic

SUPPLEMENTARY SYNTAX

The following constructions are listed for the benefit of students who plan to continue their study of Latin beyond the introductory year. The additional knowledge of these constructions enables one to skip Caesar and go on directly to Cicero with considerable confidence. Actually, a number of these constructions have already been encountered here and there in the forty formal chapters of this book. However, although such can be easily translated without benefit of syntactical labels, it seems wise to catalog them here along with the more difficult items.

GENITIVE OF MATERIAL

The genitive may indicate the material of which a thing is made.
pōculum **aurī**, *a goblet of gold*
Numerus **hostium** crēscit, *the number of the enemy is increasing.*
Mōns **aquae** secūtus est et tempestās trēs nāvēs cinxit aggere **harēnae**, *a mountain of water followed and the storm surrounded three ships with a mound of sand.*

GENITIVE OF DESCRIPTION

The genitive, when modified by an adjective, may describe a noun by indicating its character, quality or size.
vir **parvae sapientiae**, *a man of small wisdom*
liber **magnī ponderis**, *a book of great weight*
pāx in hominibus **bonae voluntātis**, *peace among men of good will*
Erat puella **brevis aetātis**, *she was a girl of short life.*
Laudābat parvulam formīcam **magnī labōris**, *he used to praise the tiny ant, (a creature) of great toil.*
Cōnsilium **eius modī** mihi placet, *a plan of this sort pleases me.*

OBJECTIVE GENITIVE

The objective genitive depends on a noun of verbal meaning and is used as the object of the verbal idea. It is sometimes translated by *for*.
amor **laudis**, *love of praise* (= amat laudem, *he loves praise.*)

cupiditās **pecūniae**, *greed for money* (= cupit pecūniam, *he longs for money*.)

metus **mortis**, *fear of death* (= metuit mortem, *he fears death*.)

spēs **salūtis**, *hope for safety* (= spērat salūtem, *he hopes for safety*.)

Fēmina erat dux **factī**, *a woman was the leader of the enterprise* (=dūxit factum.)

laudātor **temporis** āctī, *a praiser of the past* (= laudat tempus āctum.)

DATIVE OF PURPOSE

The dative may express the purpose of which a person or thing serves. A dative of reference (v. Ch. 38) often appears in conjunction with the dative of purpose, and this combination is called the double dative construction.

Petītiō mea **tibi** (dat. of ref.) summae **cūrae** (dat. of purp.) est, *my candidacy is (for) the greatest concern to you.*

Ea rēs **mihi** (ref.) summae **voluptātī** (purp.) erat, *that matter was for the greatest pleasure to me = gave me the greatest pleasure.*

Illī **nōbīs** (ref.) **auxiliō** (purp.) vēnērunt, *they came as an aid to us.*

Hōs librōs **dōnō** (purp.) mīsit, *he sent these books as a gift.*

Hoc mē iuvat et **mihi** (ref.) **mellī** (purp.) est, *this gratifies me and is (as) honey to me.*

Optant locum **tēctō** (purp.), *they desire a place for a roof (building).*

DATIVE OF POSSESSION

The dative can be used with *sum* to express the idea of possession.

Liber est **mihi**, *a book is to me = I have a book.*

(Contrast: liber est **meus**, *the book is mine.*)

Illī maior turba clientium est, *that man has a greater throng of retainers.*

Sunt **tibi** animus et mōrēs, *you have a soul and character.*

Haec **eīs** semper erunt, *they will always have these things.*

Prūdentia est illī **puellae**, *that girl has prudence.*

Ō virgō, nōn **tibi** est vultus mortālis, *O maiden, you do not have the face of a mortal.*

Sī umquam **mihi** fīlius erit . . . , *if I ever have a son . . . .*

DATIVE WITH ADJECTIVES

The dative is used with many Latin adjectives to indicate the direction in which the adjective is applicable. These generally correspond to English adjectives which can be followed by *to* or *for* (*friendly to, hostile to, suitable to* or *for, useful to, similar to, equal to,* etc.).

Mors est **somnō** similis, *death is similar to sleep.*

Sciēbam tē **mihi** fidēlem esse, *I knew that you were faithful to me.*

Est homō amīcus **amīcō**, *he is a man friendly to a friend.*

Quisque **sibi** cārus est, *each one is dear to himself.*

Potestne haec urbs **tibi** esse iūcunda, *can this city be pleasing to you?*

Ille mihi vidētur pār esse **deō**, *that man seems to me to be equal to a god.*

Proximī **Germānis** sunt, *they are nearest to the Germans.*

ABLATIVE OF SPECIFICATION

The ablative may be used to tell in what specific respect a verb or an adjective holds
true.

Hī omnēs **linguā, īstitūtis, lēgibus** inter sē differunt, *these all differ from
one another in language, customs, and laws.*

Illī **virtūte** omnibus (dat.) praestābant, *those men used to excel all in courage.*

Id genus erat intractābile **bellō**, *that race was unmanageable in war.*

Quis est praestantior aut **nōbilitāte** aut **probitāte** aut **studiō** optimārum artium? *Who is more outstanding in nobility or integrity or the pursuit of
the finest arts?*

Ager bene cultus est ūber **ūsū** et ōrnātus **speciē**, *a field well cultivated is rich
in usefulness and beautiful in appearance.*

Asia omnibus terrīs (dat.) antecellit **ūbertāte** agrōrum et **varietāte** frūctuum et
multitūdine eārum quae exportantur, *Asia excels all lands in richness of
fields and variety of fruits and large number of those things which are exported.*

ABLATIVE OF CAUSE

The ablative can be used to indicate a cause or reason.

Miser **timōre** dēlīrat, *the wretched man is insane with fear.*

Corpora eōrum **metū** dēbilia sunt, *their bodies are weak from fear.*

Aper **dentibus** timētur, *the boar is feared because of his teeth.*

Nihil arduum mortālibus est; caelum ipsum **stultitiā** petimus, *nothing is
(too) arduous for mortals; we seek the sky itself in our folly.*

Odiō tyrannī in exsilium fūgit, *because of his hatred of the tyrant he fled
into exile.*

Bonī **amōre** virtūtis peccāre ōdērunt, *good men because of their love of virtue hate to sin.*

ABLATIVE OF DEGREE OF DIFFERENCE

With comparatives and adverbs suggesting comparison the ablative can be used to
indicate the degree of difference in the comparison.

Tantō melius, *the better by so much = so much the better.*

Senex nōn facit ea quae iuvenis, at **multō** maiōra et meliōra facit, *an old
man does not do the things which a young man does, but he does much
greater and better things (greater by much).*

Multō ācrius iam vigilābō, *I shall now watch much more keenly.*

Rōmam **paucis** post **diēbus** vēnistī, *you came to Rome a few days afterwards (afterwards by a few days).*

Aberat ab eā urbe **tribus mīlibus** passuum, *he was three miles from that city
(was away by three miles).*

Bonae Athēnae **paulō** plūs artis adiēcērunt, *good Athens added a little more
skill (more by a little).*

ABLATIVE OF COMPARISON

Instead of the **quam** construction after a comparative (v. Ch. 26), the ablative of
comparison is commonly used if the first of the two things compared is in the
nominative or the accusative case.

Tua cōnsilia sunt clāriōra **lūce**, *your plans are clearer than light.*

Quis in Graeciā erat clārior **Themistocle**? *Who in Greece was more illustrious than Themistocles?*

Quis est **mē** beātior? *Who is happier than I?*

Patria est mihi multō (degree of difference) cārior meā **vītā**, *my country is
much dearer to me than my own life.*

Homērus dīcit ōrātiōnem ex Nestoris linguā flūxisse dulciōrem **melle**,
Homer says that speech flowed from Nestor's tongue sweeter than honey.

Illa eum plūs **oculīs** suīs amābat, *she used to love him more than her own eyes.*

Ō Fortūna, quis est crūdēlior **tē**? *O Fortune, who is more cruel than you?*

Argentum est vīlius **aurō**; aurum, **virtūtibus.** *Silver is cheaper than gold;
gold, than virtues.*

Exēgī monumentum **aere** perennius, *I have erected a monument more lasting than bronze.*

ABLATIVE OF DESCRIPTION

A noun and an adjective in the ablative may be used to describe another noun.
Frequently there is no difference between the ablative of description and the
genitive of description, but commonly the ablative denotes a physical
characteristic.

mīles **sauciā manū**, *the soldier with the wounded hand*

Ad eum adducta est virgō **eximiā fōrmā**, *to him was led a maiden of
exceptional beauty.*

Vīdī hominem **antiquā virtūte** et **fidē**, *I have seen a man of old-time virtue
and fidelity.*

Ego nātus sum **animō lēni**, *I was born a gentle-souled person.*

Es **ingeniō dūrō** atque **inexōrābilī**, *you are a person of harsh and
inexorable nature.*

Tū mē hortāris ut sim **animō magnō** et spem salūtis habeam, *you exhort me
to be of great courage and to have hope of safety.*

SUBORDINATE CLAUSES IN INDIRECT DISCOURSE

In indirect discourse, subordinate clauses regularly have verbs in the subjunctive
mood, even though they had the indicative in the direct form.

Lēgit librōs quōs **mīserās**, *he read the books which you had sent.*

Dīxit sē lēgisse librōs quōs **mīsissēs**, *he said that he had read the books
which you had sent.*

Eī malī quī in urbe manent **īfirmī** erunt sine duce, *those evil men who remain
in the city will be weak without their leader.*

Putō eōs malōs quī in urbe **maneant** īnfīrmōs futūrōs esse sine duce, *I think
that those evil men who remain in the city will be weak without their leader.*

Sī id crēdet, errābit. *If he believes this, he will be wrong.*

Dīcō sī id **crēdat** eum errātūrum esse. *I say that if he believes this he will be wrong.*

VERBS OF FEARING

Verbs denoting fear take subjunctive noun clauses introduced by **nē** (affirmative,
lest, that) or **ut** (negative, *that not*).

Metuō nē id crēdant, *I am afraid that they will believe this.*
Metuō ut id crēdant, *I am afraid that they will not believe this.*
Vereor ut hoc intellig possit, *I am afraid that this cannot be understood.*
Verentur nē Rōmae magnī tumultūs sint, *they fear that there may be great disturbances at Rome.*
At vereor ut hoc eī placeat, *but I am afraid that this will not please him.*
Verēmur nē nimium indulgēns sīs, *we fear that you may be too indulgent.*

OBJECTIVE INFINITIVE

The complementary infinitive has no subject accusative (v. Ch. 6). However, when an infinitive with subject accusative is used as the object of a verb, it is called an objective infinitive.

Volunt venīre, *they wish to come.* (compl. inf.)
Iussit eōs venīre, *he ordered them to come.* (obj. inf.)
Nōn possum loquī, *I cannot speak.* (compl. inf.)
Nōn patitur mē loquī, *he does not permit me to speak.* (obj. inf.)
Nōn audet īre, *he does not dare to go.* (compl. inf.)
Coēgērunt eum īre, *they forced him to go.* (obj. inf.)

-Ne, Num, Nōnne IN DIRECT QUESTIONS

When a Roman asked a genuine question (i.e., one which did not imply that he expected the answer to be "yes" or that he expected it to be "no") he appended the enclitic -ne to the first word of the question (v. Ch. 5). However, if the Roman expected the answer to be "no," he introduced the question with **num**. If he expected the answer to be "yes," he used **nōnne**.

Veniuntne? *Are they coming?*
Num veniunt? *They are not coming, are they?* (Expected answer is "no.")
Nōnne veniunt? *They are coming, aren't they?* (Expected answer is "yes.")
Scrīpsistīne illās litterās? *Did you write that letter?*
Num illās litterās scrīpsistī? *You did not write that letter, did you?*
Nōnne illās litterās scrīpsistī? *You wrote that letter, didn't you?*
Nōnne arma togae cessērunt, mē cōnsule? *Did not arms yield to the toga when I was consul?*
Nōnne vidēs quantum sit perīculum? *You see how great the danger is, do you not?*
Num audēs hoc negāre? *You don't dare to deny this, do you?*
Num dubitās hoc dīcere? *You do not hesitate to say this, do you? or Surely you do not hesitate to say this.*

SUMMARY OF FORMS

NOUNS - DECLENSION

First		Second			Third	
porta, -ae	amīcus, -ī	puer, -ī	ager, -grī	dōnum, -ī	rēx, rēgis	corpus, -oris
f., *gate*	m., *friend*	m., *boy*	m., *field*	n., *gift*	m., *king*	n., *body*

Sing.

N. port-a	amīc-us[1]	puer	ager	dōn-um	rēx	corpus
G. port-ae	amīc-ī	puer-ī	agr-ī	dōn-ī	rēg-is	corpor-is
D. port-ae	amīc-ō	puer-ō	agr-ō	dōn-ō	rēg-ī	corpor-ī
A. port-am	amīc-um	puer-um	agr-um	dōn-um	rēg-em	corpus
Ab. port-ā	amīc-ō	puer-ō	agr-ō	dōn-ō	rēg-e	corpor-e

Plu.

N. port-ae	amīc-ī	puer-ī	agr-ī	dōn-a	rēg-ēs	corpor-a
G. port-ārum	amīc-ōrum	puer-ōrum	agr-ōrum	dōn-ōrum	rēg-um	corpor-um
D. port-īs	amīc-īs	puer-īs	agr-īs	dōn-īs	rēg-ibus	corpor-ibus
A. port-ās	amīc-ōs	puer-ōs	agr-ōs	dōn-a	rēg-ēs	corpor-a
Ab. port-īs	amīc-īs	puer-īs	agr-īs	dōn-īs	rēg-ibus	corpor-ibus

ADJECTIVES - DECLENSION

First and Second Declensions

	Adjs. in -us, -a, -um		Adjs. in -er,-era, -erum, -er, -ra, -rum		
Masc.	**Fem.**	**Neut.**	**Masc.**	**Fem.**	**Neut.**
	Singular			**Singular[2]**	
N. magnus	magna	magnum	līber	lībera	līberum
G. magnī	magnae	magnī	līberī	līberae	līberī
D. magnō	magnae	magnō	līberō	līberae	līberō
A. magnum	magnam	magnum	līberum	līberam	līberum
Ab. magnō	magnā	magnō	līberō	līberā	līberō
	Plural			**Singular[2]**	
N. magnī	magnae	magna	pulcher	pulchra	pulchrum
G. magnōrum	magnārum	magnōrum	pulchrī	pulchrae	pulchrī
D. magnīs	magnīs	magnīs	pulbhrō	pulchrae	pulchrō
A. magnōs	magnās	magna	pulchrum	pulchram	pulchrum
Ab. magnīs	magnīs	magnīs	pulchrō	pulchrā	pulchrō

NOUNS - DECLENSION

Third (I-Stems)			Fourth		Fifth
cīvis, -is	urbs, -is	mare, -is	frūctus, -ūs	cornū-ūs	diēs, -ēī
m., *citizen*	f., *city*	n., *sea*	m., *fruit*	n., *horn*	m., *day*
Sing.					
N. cīv-is	urb-s	mar-e	frūct-us	corn-ū	di-ēs
G. cīv-is	urb-is	mar-is	frūct-ūs	corn-ūs	di-ēī
D. cīv-ī	urb-ī	mar-ī	frūct-uī	corn-ū	di-ēī
A. cīv-em	urb-em	mar-e	frūct-um	corn-ū	di-em
Ab cīv-e	urb-e	mar-ī	frūct-ū	corn-ū	di-ē
Plu.					
N. cīv-ēs	urb-ēs	mar-ia	frūct-us	corn-us	di-ēs
G. cīv-ium	urb-ium	mar-ium	frūct-uum	corn-uum	di-ērum
D. cīv-ibus	urb-ibus	mar-ibus	frūct-ibus	corn-ibus	di-ēbus
A. cīv-ēs	urb-ēs	mar-ia	frūct-ūs	corn-um	di-ēs
Ab. cīv-ibus	urb-ibus	mar-ibus	frūct-ibus	corn-ibus	di-ēbus

Vis is irregular: Sing., N. vīs, G. (vīs), D. (vī), A. vim. Ab. vī; Plu., N. vīrēs, G. vīrium, D. vīribus, A. vīrēs, Ab. vīribus.

ADJECTIVES - DECLENSION
Third Declension

Two endings		Three endings		One Ending		Comparatives[4]	
fortis, forte		ācer, ācris, ācre		potēns[3]		fortior, fortius	
brave		*keen, severe*		*powerful*		*braver*	
M. & F.	**N.**	**M. & F.**	**N.**	**M. & F.**	**N.**	**M. & F.**	**N.**
Sing.							
N. fortis	forte	ācer, ācris, ācre		potēns	potēns	fortior	fortius
G.	fortis	ācris		potentis		fortiōris	
D.	fortī	ācrī		potentī		fortiōrī	
A. fortem	forte	ācrem	ācre	potentem	potēns	fortiōrem	fortius
Ab.	fortī	ācrī		potentī		fortiōre	
Plu.							
N. fortēs	fortia	ācrēs	ācria	potentēs	potentia	fortiōrēs	fortiōra
G.	fortium	ācrium		potentium		fortiōrum	
D.	fortibus	ācribus		potentibus		fortiōribus	
A. fortēs[3a]	fortia	ācres[3a]	ācria	potentēs[3a]	potentia	fortiōrēs	fortiōra
Ab.	fortibus	ācribus		potentibus		fortiōribus	

PRONOUNS
Demonstrative

hic, *this*			ille, *that*		
M.	**F.**	**N.**	**M.**	**F.**	**N.**
Sing.					
N. hic	haec	hoc	ille	illa	illud
G. huius	huius	huius	illīus	illīus	illīus
D huic	huic	huic	illī	illī	illī
A. hunc	hanc	hoc	illum	illam	illud
Ab. hōc	hāc	hōc	illō	illā	illō
Plu.					
N. hī	hae	haec	illī	illae	illa
G. hōrum	hārum	hōrum	illōrum	illārum	illōrum
D. hīs	hīs	hīs	illīs	illīs	illīs
A. hōs	hās	haec	illōs	illās	illa
Ab. hīs	hīs	hīs	illīs	illīs	illīs

Relative quī, *who, which*			**Interrogative**[5] quis, *who?*		**Intensive** ipse, *himself,* etc.		
M.	**F.**	**N.**	**M. & F.**	**N.**	**M.**	**F.**	**N.**
Sing.							
N. quī	quae	quod	quis	quid	ipse	ipsa	ipsam
G. cuius	cuius	cuius	cuius	cuius	ipsīus	ipsīus	ipsīus
D. cui	cui	cui	cui	cui	ipsī	ipsī	ipsī
A. quem	quam	quod	quem	quid	ipsum	ipsum	ipsum
Ab. quō	quā	quō	quō	quō	ipsō	ipsā	ipsō
Plu.							
N. quī	quae	quae	(Plural is same		ipsī	ipsae	ipsa
G. quōrum	quārum	quōrum	as that of		ipsōrum	ipsārum	ipsōrum
D. quibus	quibus	quibus	relative.)		ipsīs	ipsīs	ipsīs
A. quōs	quās	quae			ipsōs	ipsās	ipsa
Ab. quibus	quibus	quibus			ipsīs	ipsīs	ipsīs

PRONOUNS

Demonstrative

is, *this, that, he, she, it*			īdem, *the same*		
M.	**F.**	**N.**	**M.**	**F.**	**N.**
Sing.					
N. is	ea	id	īdem	eadem	ĭdem
G. eius	eius	eius	eiusdem	eiusdem	eiusdem
D. eī	eī	eī	eīdem	eīdem	eīdem
A. eum	eam	id	eundem	eandem	idem
Ab. eō	eā	eō	eōdem	eādem	eōdem
Plu.					
N. eī, iī	eae	ea	eīdem, īdem	eaedem	eadem
G. eōrum	eārum	eōrum	eōrundem	eārundem	eōrundem
D. eīs, iīs	eīs, iīs	eīs, iīs	eīsdem[5a]	eisdem	eīsdem
A. eōs	eās	ea	eōsdem	eāsdem	eadem
Ab. eīs	eīs	eīs	eīsdem	eīsdem	eīsdem

Irregular Adjectives[6] sōlus, *alone, only*			**Personal**[7]		**Reflexive**[7] suī, *himself,* *herself, itself__*
M.	**F.**	**N.**	ego, *I*	tū, *you*	
Sing.					
N. sōlus	sōla	sōlum	ego	tū	—
G. sōlīus	sōlīus	sōlīus	meī	tuī	suī[8]
D. sōlī	sōlī	sōlī	mihi	tibi	sibi
A. sōlum	sōlam	sōlum	mē	tē	sē[9]
Ab. sōlō	sōlā	sōlō	mē	tē	sē[9]
Plu.					
N. sōlī	sōlae	sōla	nōs	vōs	—
G. sōlōrum	sōlārum	sōlōrum	{nostrum {nostrī	{vestrum {vestrī	suī
D. sōlīs	sōlīs	sōlīs	nōbīs	vōbis	sibi
A. sōlōs	sōlās	sōla	nōs	vōs	sē[9]
Ab. sōlīs	sōlīs	sōlīs	nōbīs	vōbīs	sē[9]

COMPARISON OF ADJECTIVES

Positive	Comparative	Superlative
Regular		
longus, -a, -um (*long*)	longior, -ius	longissimus, -a, -um
fortis, -e (*brave*)	fortior, -ius	fortissimus, -a, -um
fēlīx, *gen.* fēlicis, (*happy*)	fēlīcior, -ius	fēlīcissimus, -a, -um
sapiēns, *gen.* sapientis (*wise*)	sapientior, -ius,	sapientissimus, -a, -um
facilis, -e (*easy*)	facilior, -ius	facilimus, -a, -um
līber, -era, -erum (*free*)	līberior, -ius	līberrimus, -a, -um
pulcher, -chra, -chrum (*beautiful*)	pulchior, -ius	pulcherrimus, -a, -um
ācer, ācris, ācre (*keen*)	ācrior, -ius	ācerrimus, -a, -um
Irregular		
bonus, -a, -um (*good*)	melior, -ius	optimus, -a, -um
magnus, -a, -um (*large*)	maior, -ius	maximus, -a, -um
malus, -a, -um (*bad*)	peior, -ius	pessimus, -a, -um
multus, -a, -um (*much*)	—, plūs	plūrimus, -a, -um
parvus, -a, -um (*small*)	minor, minus	minimus, -a, -um
(prae, prō)	prior, -ius (*former*)	prīmus, -a, -um
superus, -a, -um (*that above*)	superior, -ius	summus (suprēmus) -a, -um

COMPARISON OF ADVERBS

Positive	Comparative	Superlative
Regular		
longē (*far*)	longius	longissimē
fortiter (*bravely*)	fortius	fortissimē
fēlīciter (*happily*)	fēlīcius	fēlīcissimē
sapienter (*wisely*)	sapientius	sapientissimē
facile (*easily*)	facilius	facillimē
līberē (*freely*)	līberius	līberrimē
pulchrē (*beautifully*)	pulchrius	pulcherrimē
ācriter (*keenly*)	ācrius	ācerrimē
Irregular		
bene (*well*)	melius	optimē
magnopere (*greatly*)	magis	maximē
male (*badly*)	peius	pessimē
multum (*much*)	plūs	plūrimum
parum (*little*)	minus	minimē
(prae, prō)	prius (*before*)	prīmum; prīmō
diū (*a long time*)	diūtius	diūtissimē

NUMERALS

Cardinals	Ordinals	Roman Numerals
1. ūnus, -a, -um	prīmus, -a, -um	I
2. duo, duae, duo	secundus, alter	II
3. trēs, tria	tertius	III
4. quattuor	quārtus	IIII; IV
5. quīnque	quīntus	V
6. sex	sextus	VI
7. septem	septimus	VII
8. octō	octāvus	VIII
9. novem	nōnus	VIIII; IX
10. decem	decimus	X
11. ūndecim	ūndecimus	XI
12. duodecim	duodecimus	XII

13. tredecim	tertius decimus	XIII
14. quattuordecim	quārtus decimus	XIIII; XIV
15. quīndecim	quīntus decimus	XV
16. sēdecim	sextus decimus	XVI
17. septendecim	septimus decimus	XVII
18. duodēvīginti	doudēvīcēsimus	XVIII
19. ūndēvīginti	ūndēvīcēsimus	XVIIII; XIX
20. vīginti	vīcēsimus	XX
21. vīginti ūnus, ūnīs et vīginti	vīcēsimus prīmus	XXI
30. trīginta	trīcēsimus	XXX
40. quadrāgintā	quadrāgēsimus	XXXX, XL
50. quinquāgintā	quīnquāgēsimus	L
60. sexāgintā	sexāgēsimus	LX
70. septuāgintā	septuāgēsimus	LXX
80. octōgintā	octōgēsimus	LXXX
90. nōnāgintā	nōnāgēsimus	LXXXX; XC
100. centum	centēsimus	C
101. centum ūnus	centēsimus prīmus	CI
200. ducentī, -ae, -a	duocentēsimus	CC
300. trecentī	trecentēsimus	CCC
400. quadringentī	quadringentēsimus	CCCC
500. quīngentī	quīngentēsimus	D
600. sescentī	sescentēsimus	DC
700. septingentī	septingentēsimus	DCC
800. octingentī	octingentēsimus	DCCC
900. nōngentī	nōngentēsimus	DCCCC
1000. mīlle	mīllēsimus	M
2000. duo mīlia	bis mīllēsimus	MM

Declension of Numerals

For the declension of **ūnus** see Ch. 9 or **sōlus** above.
For **duo, trēs,** and **mīlle** see Ch. 40.
The forms from **trecentī** through **nōngentī** are declined in the plural like **ducentī, -ae, -a.**
The ordinals are declined like **prīmus, -a, -um.**
The other forms are indeclinable.

CONJUGATIONS 1-4

Principal Parts

1*st*: laudō	laudāre	laudāvī	laudātum
2*nd*: moneō	monēre	monuī	monitum
3*rd*: dūcō	dūcere	dūxī	ductum
4*th*: audiō	audīre	audīvī	audītum
3*rd* (-*iō*): capiō	capere	cēpī	captum

Indicative Active

Present

laudō	moneō	dūcō	audiō	capiō
laudās	monēs	dūcis	audis	capis
laudat	monet	dūcit	audit	capit
laudāmus	monēmus	dūcimus	audimus	capimus
laudātis	monētis	dūcitis	audītis	capitis
laudant	monent	dūcunt	audiunt	capiunt

Imperfect

laudābam	monēbam	dūcēbam	audiēbam	capiēbam
laudābās	monēbās	dūcēbās	audiēbās	capiēbās
laudābat	monēbat	dūcēbat	audiēbat	capiēbat
laudābāmus	monēbāmus	dūcēbāmus	audiēbāmus	capiēbāmus
laudābātis	monēbātis	dūcēbātis	audiēbātis	capiēbātis
laudābant	monēbant	dūcēbant	audiēbant	capiēbant

Future

laudābō	monēbō	dūcam	audiam	capiam
laudābis	monēbis	dūcēs	audiēs	capiēs
laudābit	monēbit	dūcet	audiet	capiet
laudābimus	monēbimus	dūcēmus	audiēmus	capiēmus
laudābitis	monēbitis	dūcētis	audiētis	capiētis
laudābunt	monēbunt	dūcent	audient	capient

Perfect

laudāvī	monuī	dūxī	audīvī	cēpī
laudāvistī	monuistī	dūxistī	audīvistī	cēpistī
laudāvit	monuit	dūxit	audīvit	cēpit
laudāvimus	monuimus	dūximus	audīvimus	cēpimus
laudāvistis	monuistis	dūxistis	audīvistis	cēpistis
laudāvērunt	monuērunt	dūxērunt	audīvērunt	cēpērunt

Pluperfect

laudāveram	monueram	dūxeram	audīveram	cēperam
laudāverās	monuerās	dūxerās	audīverās	cēperās
laudāverat	monuerat	dūxerat	audīverat	cēperat
laudāverāmus	monuerāmus	dūxerāmus	audīverāmus	cēperāmus
laudāverātis	monuerātis	dūxerātis	audīverātis	cēperātis
laudāverant	monuerant	dūxerant	audīverant	cēperant

Future Perfect

laudāverō	monuerō	dūxerō	audīverō	cēperō
laudāveris	monueris	dūxeris	audīveris	cēperis
laudāverit	monuerit	dūxerit	audīverit	cēperit
laudāverimus	monuerimus	dūxerimus	audīverimus	cēperimus
laudāveritis	monueritis	dūxeritis	audīveritis	cēperitis
laudāverint	monuerint	dūxerint	audīverint	cēperint

Subjunctive Active

Present

laudem	moneam	dūcam	audiam	capiam
laudēs	moneās	dūcās	audiās	capiās
laudet	moneat	dūcat	audiat	capiat
laudēmus	moneāmus	dūcāmus	audiāmus	capiāmus
laudētis	moneātis	dūcātis	audiātis	capiātis
laudent	moneant	dūcant	audiant	capiant

Imperfect

laudārem	monērem	dūcerem	audīrem	caperem
laudārēs	monērēs	dūcerēs	audīrēs	caperēs
laudāret	monēret	dūceret	audīret	caperet
laudārēmus	monērēmus	dūcerēmus	audīrēmus	caperēmus
laudārētis	monērētis	dūcerētis	audīrētis	caperētis
laudārent	monērent	dūcerent	audīrent	caperent

Perfect

laudāverim	monuerim	dūxerim	audīverim	cēperim
laudāverīs	monuerīs	dūxerīs	audīverīs	cēperīs
laudāverit	monuerit	dūxerit	audīverit	cēperit
laudāverīmus	monuerīmus	dūxerīmus	audīverīmus	cēperīmus
laudāverītis	monuerītis	dūxerītis	audīverītis	cēperītis
laudāverint	monuerint	dūxerint	audīverint	cēperint

Pluperfect

laudāvissem	monuissem	dūxissem	audīvissem	cēpissem
laudāvissēs	monuissēs	dūxissēs	audīvissēs	cēpissēs
laudāvisset	monuisset	dūxisset	audīvisset	cēpisset
laudāvissēmus	monuissēmus	dūxissēmus	audīvissēmus	cēpissēmus
laudāvissētis	monuissētis	dūxissētis	audīvissētis	cēpissētis
laudāvissent	monuissent	dūxissent	audīvissent	cēpissent

Present Imperative Active

laudā	monē	dūc[10]	audī	cape
laudāte	monēte	dūcite	audīte	capite

Indicative Passive

Present

laudor	moneor	dūcor	audior	capior
laudāris(-re)	monēris(-re)	dūceris(-re)	audīris(-re)	caperis(-re)
laudātur	monētur	dūcitur	audītur	capitur
laudāmur	monēmur	dūcimur	audīmur	capimur
laudāminī	monēminī	dūciminī	audīminī	capiminī
laudantur	monentur	dūcuntur	audiuntur	capiuntur

Imperfect

laudābar	monēbar	dūcēbar	audiēbar	capiēbar
laudābāris(-re)	monēbāris(-re)	dūcēbāris(-re)	audiēbāris(-re)	capiēbāris(-re)
laudābātur	monēbātur	dūcēbātur	audiēbātur	capiēbātur
laudābāmur	monēbāmur	dūcēbāmur	audiēbāmur	capiēbāmur
laudābāminī	monēbāminī	dūcēbāminī	audiēbāminī	capiēbāminī
laudābantur	monēbantur	dūcēbantur	audiēbantur	capiēbantur

Future

laudābor	monēbor	dūcar	audiar	capiar
laudāberis(-re)	monēberis(-re)	dūcēris(-re)	audiēris(-re)	capiēris(-re)
laudābitur	monēbitur	dūcētur	audiētur	capiētur
laudābimur	monēbimur	dūcēmur	audiēmur	capiēmur
laudābiminī	monēbiminī	dūcēminī	audiēminī	capiēminī
laudābuntur	monēbuntur	dūcentur	audientur	capientur

Perfect

laudātus[11] sum	monitus sum	ductus sum	audītus sum	captus sum
laudātus es	monitus es	ductus es	audītus es	captus es
laudātus est	monitus est	ductus est	audītus est	captus est
laudātī sumus	monitī sumus	ductī sumus	audītī sumus	captī sumus
laudātī estis	monitī estis	ductī estis	audītī estis	captī estis
laudātī sunt	monitī sunt	ductī sunt	audītī sunt	captī sunt

Pluperfect

laudātus eram	monitus eram	ductus eram	audītus eram	captus eram
laudātus erās	monitus erās	ductus erās	audītus erās	captus erās
laudātus erat	monitus erat	ductus erat	audītus erat	captus erat
laudātī erāmus	monitī erāmus	ductī erāmus	audītī erāmus	captī erāmus
laudātī erātis	monitī erātis	ductī erātis	audītī erātis	captī erātis
laudātī erant	monitī erant	ductī erant	audītī erant	captī erant

Future Perfect

laudātus erō	monitus erō	ductus erō	audītus erō	captus erō
laudātus eris	monitus eris	ductus eris	audītus eris	captus eris
laudātus erit	monitus erit	ductus erit	audītus erit	captus erit
laudātī erimus	monitī erimus	ductī erimus	audītī erimus	captī erimus
laudātī eritis	monitī eritis	ductī eritis	audītī eritis	captī eritis
laudātī erunt	monitī erunt	ductī erunt	audītī erunt	captī erunt

Subjunctive Passive

Present

lauder	monear	dūcar	audiar	capiar
laudēris(-re)	moneāris(-re)	dūcāris(-re)	audiāris(-re)	capiāris(-re)
laudētur	moneātur	dūcātur	audiātur	capiātur
laudēmur	moneāmur	dūcāmur	audiāmur	capiāmur
laudēminī	moneāminī	dūcāminī	audiāminī	capiāminī
laudentur	moneantur	dūcantur	audiantur	capiantur

Imperfect

laudārer	monērer	dūcerer	audīrer	caperer
laudārēris(-re)	monērēris(-re)	dūcerēris(-re)	audīrēris(-re)	caperēris(-re)
laudārētur	monērētur	dūcerētur	audīrētur	caperētur
laudārēmur	monērēmur	dūcerēmur	audīrēmur	caperēmur
laudārēminī	monērēminī	dūcerēminī	audīrēminī	caperemini
laudārentur	monērentur	dūcerentur	audīrentur	caperentur

Perfect

laudātus sim	monitus sim	ductus sim	audītus sim	captus sim
laudātus sīs	monitus sīs	ductus sīs	audītus sīs	captus sīs
laudātus sit	monitus sit	ductus sit	audītus sit	captus sit
laudātī sīmus	monitī sīmus	ductī sīmus	audītī sīmus	captī sīmus
laudātī sītis	monitī sītis	ductī sītis	audītī sītis	captī sītis
laudātī sint	monitī sint	ductī sint	audītī sint	captī sint

Pluperfect

laudātus essem	monitus essem	ductus essem	audītus essem	captus essem
laudātus essēs	monitus essēs	ductus essēs	audītus essēs	captus essēs
laudātus esset	monitus esset	ductus esset	audītus esset	captus esset
laudātī essēmus	monitī essēmus	ductī essēmus	audītī essēmus	captī essēmus
laudātī essētis	monitī essētis	ductī essētis	audītī essētis	captī essētis
laudātī essent	monitī essent	ductī essent	audītī essent	captī essent

Present Imperative Passive

In practice the passive forms are found only in deponent verbs. (See Ch. 34, n. 3.)

Participles
Active

Pres. laudāns	monēns	dūcēns	audiēns	capiēns
Fut. laudātūrus	monitūrus	ductūrus	audītūrus	captūrus

Passive

Pres. laudātus	monitus	ductus	audītus	captus
Fut. laudandus	monendus	dūcendus	audiendus	capiendus

Infinitives
Active

Pres. laudāre	monēre	dūcere	audīre	capere
Perf. laudāvisse	monuisse	dūxisse	audīvisse	cepisse
Fut. ladātūrum esse	monitūrum esse	ductūrum esse	audītūrum esse	captūrum esse

Passive

Pres. laudārī	monērī	dūcī	audīrī	capī
Perf. laudātum esse	monitum esse	ductum esse	audītum esse	captum esse
Fut. laudātum īrī	monitum īrī	ductum īrī	audītum īrī	captum īrī

DEPONENT VERBS

Principal Parts

1st Conj.:	hortor	hortārī	hortātus sum (*urge*)
2nd Conj.:	fateor	fatērī	fassus sum (*confess*)
3rd Conj.:	sequor	sequī	secūtus sum (*follow*)
4th Conj.:	mōlior	mōlīrī	mōlītus (*work at*)
3rd (-iō):	patior	patī	passus sum (*suffer*)

Indicative

Present

hortor	fateor	sequor	mōlior	patior
hortāris(-re)	fatēris(-re)	sequeris(-re)	mōlīris(-re)	pateris(-re)
hortātur	fatētur	sequitur	mōlītur	patitur
hortāmur	fatēmur	sequimur	mōlīmur	patimur
hortāminī	fatēminī	sequiminī	mōlīminī	patiminī
hortantur	fatentur	sequuntur	mōliuntur	patiuntur

Imperfect

hortābar	fatēbar	sequēbar	mōliēbar	patiēbar
hortābāris(-re)	fatēbāris(-re)	sequēbāris(-re)	mōliēbāris(-re)	patiēbāris(-re)
hortābātur	fatēbātur	sequēbātur	mōliēbātur	patiēbātur
hortābāmur	fatēbāmur	sequēbāmur	mōliēbāmur	patiēbāmur
hortābāminī	fatēbāminī	sequēbāminī	mōliēbāminī	patiēbāminī
hortābantur	fatēbantur	sequēbantur	mōliēbantur	patiēbantur

Future

hortābor	fatēbor	sequar	mōliar	patiar
hortāberis(-re)	fatēberis(-re)	sequēris(-re)	mōliēris(-re)	patiēris(-re)
hortābitur	fatēbitur	sequētur	mōliētur	patiētur
hortābimur	fatēbimur	sequēmur	mōliēmur	patiēmur
hortābiminī	fatēbiminī	sequēminī	mōliēminī	patiēminī
hortābuntur	fatēbuntur	sequentur	mōlientur	patientur

Perfect

hortātus sum	fassus sum	secūtus sum	mōlītus sum	passus sum
hortātus es	fassus es	secūtus es	mōlītus es	passus es
hortātus est	fassus est	secūtus est	mōlītus est	passus est
hortātī sumus	fassī sumus	secūtī sumus	mōlītī sumus	passī sumus
hortātī estis	fassī estis	secūtī estis	mōlītī estis	passī estis
hortātī sunt	fassī sunt	secūtī sunt	mōlītī sunt	passī sunt

Pluperfect

hortātus eram	fassus eram	secūtus eram	mōlītus eram	passus eram
hortātus erās	fassus erās	secūtus erās	mōlītus erās	passus erās
hortātus erat	fassus erat	secūtus erat	mōlītus erat	passus erat
hortātī erāmus	fassī erāmus	secūtī erāmus	mōlītī erāmus	passī erāmus
hortātī erātis	fassī erātis	secūtī erātis	mōlītī erātis	passī erātis
hortātī erant	fassī erant	secūtī erant	mōlītī erant	passī erant

Future Perfect

hortātus erō	fassus erō	secūtus erō	mōlitus erō	passus erō
hortātus eris	fassus eris	secūtus eris	mōlitus eris	passus eris
hortātus erit	fassus erit	secūtus erit	mōlitus erit	passus erit
hortātī erimus	fassī erimus	secūtī erimus	mōlitī erimus	passī erimus
hortātī eritis	fassī eritis	secūtī eritis	mōlitī eritis	passī eritis
hortātī erunt	fassī erunt	secūtī erunt	mōlitī erunt	passī erunt

Subjunctive

Present

horter	fatear	sequar	mōliar	patiar
hortēris(-re)	fateāris(-re)	sequāris(-re)	mōliāris(-re)	patiāris(-re)
hortētur	fateātur	sequātur	mōliātur	patiātur
hortēmur	fateāmur	sequāmur	mōliāmur	patiāmur
hortēminī	fateāminī	sequāminī	mōliāminī	patiāminī
hortentur	fateantur	sequantur	mōliantur	patiantur

Imperfect

hortārer	fatērer	sequerer	mōlirer	paterer
hortārēris(-re)	fatērēris(-re)	sequerēris(-re)	mōlirēris(-re)	paterēris(-re)
hortārētur	fatērētur	sequerētur	mōlirētur	paterētur
hortārēmur	fatērēmur	sequerēmur	mōlirēmur	paterēmur
hortārēminī	fatērēminī	sequerēminī	mōlirēminī	paterēminī
hortārentur	fatērentur	sequerentur	mōlirentur	paterentur

Perfect

hortātus sim	fassus sim	secūtus sim	mōlitus sim	passus sim
hortātus sīs	fassus sīs	secūtus sīs	mōlitus sīs	passus sīs
hortātus sit	fassus sit	secūtus sit	mōlitus sit	passus sit
hortātī sīmus	fassī sīmus	secūtī sīmus	mōlitī sīmus	passī simus
hortātī sītis	fassī sītis	secūtī sītis	mōlitī sītis	passī sītis
hortātī sint	fassī sint	secūtī sint	mōlitī sint	passī sint

Pluperfect

hortātus essem	fassus essem	secūtus essem	mōlitus essem	passus essem
hortātus essēs	fassus essēs	secūtus essēs	mōlitus essēs	passus essēs
hortātus esset	fassus esset	secūtus esset	mōlitus esset	passus csset
hortātī essēmus	fassī essēmus	secūtī essēmus	mōlitī essēmus	passī essēmus
hortātī essētis	fassī essētis	secūtī essētis	mōlitī essētis	passī essētis
hortātī essent	fassī essent	secūtī essent	mōlitī essent	passī essent

Present Imperative

hortāre	fatēre	sequere	mōlire	patere
hortāminī	fatēminī	sequiminī	mōliminī	patiminī

Participles

Pres. hortāns	fatēns	sequēns	mōliēns	patiēns
Perf. hortātus	fassus	secūtus	mōlitus	passus
Fut. hortātūrus	fassūrus	secūtūrus	mōlitūrus	passūrus
Ger. hortandus	fatendus	sequendus	mōliendus	patiendus

Infinitives

Pres. hortārī	fatērī	sequī	mōlirī	patī
Perf. hortātum esse	fassum esse	secūtum esse	mōlitum esse	passum esse
Fut. hortātūrum esse	fassūrum esse	secūtūrum esse	mōlitūrum esse	passūrum esse

IRREGULAR VERBS

Principal Parts

sum	esse	fuī	futūrus	(*be*)
possum	posse	potuī		(*be able, can*)
volō	velle	voluī		(*wish, be willing*)
nōlō	nōlle	nōluī		(*not to wish, be unwilling*)
mālō	mālle	māluī		(*prefer*)
eō	īre	iī	itum	(*go*)

Indicative[12]

Present

sum	possum	volō	nōlō	mālō	eō
es	potes	vīs	nōn vīs	māvis	īs
est	potest	vult	nōn vult	māvult	it
sumus	possumus	volumus	nōlumus	mālumus	īmus
estis	potestis	vultis	nōn vultis	māvultis	ītis
sunt	possunt	volunt	nōlunt	mālunt	eunt

Imperfect

eram	poteram	volēbam	nōlēbam	mālēbam	ībam
erās	poterās	volēbās	nōlēbās	mālēbās	ībās
erat	poterat	volēbat	nōlēbat	mālēbat	ībat
erāmus	poterāmus	volēbāmus	nōlēbāmus	mālēbāmus	ībāmus
erātis	poterātis	volēbātis	nōlēbātis	mālēbātis	ībātis
erant	poterant	volēbant	nōlēbant	mālēbant	ībant

Future

erō	poterō	volam	nōlam	mālam	ībō
eris	poteris	volēs	nōlēs	mālēs	ībis
erit	poterit	volet	nōlet	mālet	ībit
erimus	poterimus	volēmus	nōlēmus	mālēmus	ībimus
eritis	poteritis	volētis	nōlētis	mālētis	ībitis
erunt	poterunt	volent	nōlent	mālent	ībunt

Perfect

fuī	potuī	voluī	nōluī	māluī	iī
fuistī	potuistī	voluistī	nōluistī	māluistī	īstī
fuit	potuit	voluit	nōluit	māluit	it
fuimus	potuimus	voluimus	nōluimus	māluimus	iimus
fuistis	potuistis	voluistis	nōluistis	māluistis	īstis
fuērunt	potuērunt	voluērunt	nōluērunt	māluērunt	iērunt

Pluperfect

fueram	potueram	volueram	nōlueram	mālueram	ieram
fuerās	potuerās	voluerās	nōluerās	māluerās	ierās
etc.	etc.	etc.	etc.	etc.	etc.

Future Perfect

fuerō	potuerō	voluerō	nōluerō	māluerō	ierō
fueris	potueris	volueris	nōlueris	mālueris	ieris
etc.	etc.	etc.	etc.	etc.	etc.

Subjunctive

Present

sim	possim	velim	nōlim	mālim	eam
sīs	possīs	velīs	nōlīs	mālīs	eās
sit	possit	velit	nōlit	mālit	eat
sīmus	possīmus	velīmus	nōlīmus	mālīmus	eāmus
sītis	possītis	velītis	nōlītis	mālītis	eātis
sint	possint	velint	nōlint	mālint	eant

Imperfect

essem	possem	vellem	nōllem	māllem	īrem
essēs	possēs	vellēs	nōllēs	māllēs	īrēs
esset	posset	vellet	nōllet	māllet	īret
essēmus	possēmus	vellēmus	nōllēmus	māllēmus	īrēmus
essētis	possētis	vellētis	nōllētis	māllētis	īrētis
essent	possent	vellent	nōllent	māllent	īrent

Perfect

fuerim	potuerim	voluerim	nōluerim	māluerim	ierim
fuerīs	potuerīs	voluerīs	nōluerīs	māluerīs	ierīs
fuerit	potuerit	voluerit	nōluerit	māluerit	ierit
fuerīmus	potuerīmus	voluerīmus	nōluerīmus	māluerīmus	ierīmus
fuerītis	potuerītis	voluerītis	nōluerītis	māluerītis	ierītis
fuerint	potuerint	voluerint	nōluerint	māluerint	ierint

Pluperfect

fuissem	potuissem	voluissem	nōluissem	māluissem	īssem
fuissēs	potuissēs	voluissēs	nōluissēs	māluissēs	īssēs
fuisset	potuisset	voluisset	nōluisset	mālluisset	īsset
fuissēmus	potuissēmus	voluissēmus	nōluissēmus	māluissēmus	īssēmus
fuissētis	potuissētis	voluissētis	nōluissētis	māluissētis	īssētis
fuissent	potuissent	voluissent	nōluissent	mālluissent	īssent

Present Imperative

es	—	—	nōlī	—	ī
este	—	—	nōlīte	—	īte

Participles

Pres. -	potēns	volēns	nōlēns	—	iēns (*gen.* euntis)
Perf. -	—	—	—	—	itum
Fut. futūrus	—	—	—	—	itūrus
Ger. -	—	—	—	—	eundus

Infinitives

Pr. esse	posse	velle	nōlle	mālle	īre
Pf. fuisse	potuisse	voluisse	nōluisse	māluisse	īsse
Fu. futūrum esse *or* fore	—	—	—	—	itūrum esse

IRREGULAR: ferō, ferre, tulī, lātus, bear

Indicative

Present Act.	Pass.	Imperfect Act.	Pass.	Future Act.	Pass.
ferō	feror	ferēbam	ferēbar	feram	ferar
fers	ferris(-re)	ferēbās	ferēbāris(-re)	ferēs	ferēris(-re)
fert	fertur	ferēbat	ferēbātur	feret	ferētur
ferimus	ferimur	ferēbāmus	ferēbāmur	ferēmus	ferēmur
fertis	feriminī	ferēbātis	ferēbāminī	ferētis	ferēminī
ferunt	feruntur	ferēbant	ferēbantur	ferent	ferentur

Perfect Act.	Pass.	Pluperfect Act.	Pass.	Future Perfect Act.	Pass
tulī	lātus sum	tuleram	lātus eram	tulerō	lātus erō
tulistī	lātus es	tulerās	lātus erās	tuleris	lātus eris
tulit	lātus est	tulerat	lātus erat	tulerit	lātus erit
etc.	etc.	etc.	etc.	etc.	etc.

Subjunctive

Present Act.	Pass.	Imperfect Act.	Pass.	Perfect Act.	Pass
feram	ferar	ferrem	ferrer	tulerim	lātus sim
ferās	ferāris(-re)	ferrēs	ferrēris(-re)	tuleris	lātus sis
ferat	ferātur	ferret	ferrētur	tulerit	lātus sit
				etc.	etc.
				Pluperfect	
ferāmus	ferāmur	ferrēmus	ferrēmur	tulissem	lātus essem
ferātis	ferāminī	ferrētis	ferrēminī	tulissēs	lātus essēs
ferant	ferantur	ferrent	ferrentur	tulisset	lātus esset
				etc.	etc.

Pres. Impv. Act.	Pass.	Participles Act.	Pass.	Infinitives Act.	Pass.
fer	—	*Pres.* ferēns	—	ferre	ferrī
		Perf. —	lātus	tulisse	lātum esse
ferte	—	*Fut.* lātūrus	ferendus	lātūrum esse	lātum īrī

IRREGULAR: fīō, fierī, factus sum, bemade, bedone, become

Indicative

Pres.	Impf.	Fut.	Perf.	Pluperf.	Fut. Perf.
fīō	fiēbam	fiam	factus sum	factus eram	factus erō
fīs	fiēbās	fiēs	factus es	factus erās	factus erit
fit	fiēbat	fiet	factus est	factus erat	factus erit
fīmus	fiēbāmus	fiēmus	factī sumus	factī erāmus	factī erimus
fītis	fiēbātis	fiētis	factī estis	factī erātis	factī eritis
fiunt	fiēbant	fient	factī sunt	factī erant	factī erunt

Subjunctive

Pres.	Impf.	Perf.	Pluperf.
fiam	fierem	factus sim	factus essem
fiās	fierēs	factus sis	factus essēs
fiat	fieret	factus sit	factus esset
fiāmus	ferrēmus	factī sīmus	factī essēmus
fiātis	fierētis	factī sītis	factī essētis
fiant	fierent	factī sint	factī essent

Part.	Inf.
Pres. —	fierī
Perf. factus	factum esse
Fut. faciendus	factum īrī

Imperative: fī, fīte

Footnotes

[1]The vocative singular of nouns like **amīcus** and of masculine adjectives like **magnus** ends in -e. The vocative singular of **fīlius** and of names in -ius ends in a single -ī (**fīlī, Vergilī**); the vocative singular of masculine adjectives in -ius ends in -ie (**ēgregius; ēgregie**). Otherwise, the vocative has the same form as the nominative in all declensions.

[2]The plural follows the pattern of the singular except that it has the plural endings.

[3]Present participles follow the declension of **potēns** except that they have ē in the ablative singular when used as genuine participles.

[3a]For -īs (acc. plu.) see p. 78 n. 3.

[4]For irregular **plūs** see Ch. 9.

[5]The interrogative adjective **quī? quae? quod?** meaning *what? which? what kind of?* has the same declension as that of the relative pronoun.

[5a]Also īsdem.

[6]Similarly **ūnus, tōtus, ūllus, nūllus, alius, alter** (v. Ch. 9).

[7]All forms of the pronouns of the first and second persons except the nom. sing. and the nom. plu. may also be used as reflexive pronouns.

[8]These forms are reflexive only. The nonreflexive forms of the third person are supplied by **is, ea, id** (v. Ch. 13).

[9]The form **sēsē** is also frequently found.

[10]The singular of the present imperative in the third conjugation regularly ends in -e: **scrībe, mitte, crēde**.

[11]The participles **laudātus (-a, -um)**, **monitus (-a, -um)**, etc., are used as predicate adjectives, and so their endings vary to agree with the subject.

[12]Note that the verbs in this list have no passive voice (except for the idiomatic impersonal passive of **eō**, which is not used in this book).

English-Latin Vocabulary

*A*n Arabic (1) in parentheses after a verb shows that this is a regular verb of the first conjugation with a sequence of principal parts reading -**āre**, -**āvi**, -**ātum**.

For prefixes and suffixes see the lists in the Appendix.

A

able (be able), possum, posse, potuī
about (concerning), dē + *abl.*
absolute ruler, tyrannus, -ī, *m.*
advice, cōnsilium, -iī, *n.*
after, post + *acc.*
against, contrā + *acc.*
all, omnis, -e
alone, sōlus, -a, -um
although, cum + *subj.*
always, semper
among, inter + *acc.*
and, et, -que
anger, īra, -ae, *f.*
announce, nūntiō (1)
answer, respondeō, -ēre, -spondī, -spōnsum
any (anyone, anything, *after* sī, nisi, nē, num), quis, quid
army, exercitus, -ūs, *m.*
arrest, comprehendō, -ere, -hendī, -hēnsum
art, ars, artis, *f.*
as (*conj.*), ut + *ind.*
as...as possible, quam + *superlative*
Asia, Asia, -ae, *f.*

ask, rogō (1)
at (= time), *abl. of time;* (**= place**), *locative of names of cities*
attack, oppugnō (1)
author, auctor, -ōris, *m.*
avert, āvertō, -ere, āvertī, āversmu

B

bad, malus, -a, -um
band, manus, -ūs, *f.*
base, turpis, -e
be, sum, esse, fuī, futūrus
beard, barba, -ae, f.
beautiful, pulcher, -chra, -chrum
beauty, fōrma, -ae, *f.*
because, quod
become, fīō, fierī, factus sum
beg, ōrō (1)
began, cocpī, coepisse; coeptum (*pres. system supplied by* incipiō)
begin, incipiō, -ere, -cēpī, ceptum. See **began** *above.*
believe, crēdō, -ere, crēdidī, crēditum
book, liber, -brī, *m.*

boy, puer, puerī, *m.*
brave, fortis, -e
brief, brevis, e.
bring, ferō, ferre, tulī, lātum
brother, frāter, -tris, *m.*
bull, bōs, bovis, *m./f.*
by (= agent), ā or ab + *abl.*;
  (= means), *simple abl.*

C

Caesar, Caesar, -aris, *m.*
call, vocō (1), appellō (1)
can, possum, posse, potuī
capture, capiō , -ere, cēpī, captum
care, cūra, -ae. *f.*
certain (definite, sure), certus, -a, -um;
  (*indefinite*) quīdam, quaedam,
  quiddam (*prn.*) *or* quoddam (*adj.*)
character, mōrēs, mōrum, *m.*
Cicero, Cicerō, -ōnis, *m.*
citizen, cīvis, -is, *m./f.*
city, urbs, -is, *m.*
come, veniō, -īre, vēnī, ventum
command (*noun*), imperium, -iī, *n.*;
  (*vb.*), imperō (1)
common, commūnis, -e
commonwealth, rēs pūblica, reī pūblicae, *f.*
concerning, dē + *abl.*
confess, fateor, -ērī, fassus sum
conquer, superō (1); vincō, -ere, vīcī, victum
consul, cōnsul, -ulis, *m.*
country, patria, -ae, *f.*; terra, -ae, *f.*
courage, virtūs, -tūtis, *f.*
crime, scelus, -eris, *n.*

D

danger, perīculum, -ī, *n.*
dare, audeō, -ēre, ausus sum
day, diēs, -ēī, *m.*
dear, cārus, -a, -um
death, mors, mortis, *f.*
deed, factum, -ī, *n.*
defend, dēfendō, -ere, -fendī, -fēnsum
depart, discēdō, -ere, -cessī, -cessum
deprived of (be), careō, -ēre, caruī, caritūrus
desire, cupiō, -ere, -īvī, -ītum
destroy, dēleō, -ēre, -ēvī, -ētum
die, morior, -ī, mortuus sum
difficult, difficilis, -e

do, faciō, -ere, fēcī, factum
dread, metus, -ūs, *m.*
drive out, expellō, -ere, -pulī, -pulsum

E

eagerness, studium, -iī, *n.*
eleven, ūndecim
endure, ferō, ferre, tulī, lātum;
  patior, -ī, passus sum
enemy, hostis, -is, *m.* (*usu. plu.*)
entrust, committō, -ere, -mīsī, -missum
err, errō (1)
esteem, dīligō, -ere, dīlēxī, dīlēctum
even, etiam; not even, nē... quidem
evil (*adj.*), malus, -a, -um; (*noun*), malum, -ī, *n.*
expel, expellō, -ere, -pulī, -pulsum
eye, oculus, -ī, *m.*

F

faith, fidēs, -eī, *f.*
false, falsus, -a, -um
fame, fāma, -ae, *f.*
father, pater, -tris, *m.*
fault, culpa, -ae, f.; vitium, -iī, n.
fear (*vb.*), timeō, -ēre, -uī; (*n.*),
  metus, -ūs, *m.*; timor, -ōris, *m.*
feel, sentiō, -īre, sēnsī, sēsum
few, paucī, -ae, -a (*plu.*)
fidelity, fidēs, -eī, *f.*
fifth, quīntus, -a, -um
find, inveniō, -īre, -vēnī, -ventum
first, prīmus, -a, -um
follow, sequor, -ī, secūtus sum
foolish, stultus, -a, -um
for (*conj.*), nam
force, vis, vīs, *f.*
forces (troops), cōpiae, -ārum, *f.*
fortune, fortūna, -ae, *f.*
free (*vb.*), līberō (1); (*adj.*), līber, -era, -erum
friend, amīcus, -ī, *m.*
friendship, amīcitia, -ae, *f.*
frighten, terreō, -ēre, -uī, -itum
from, ab; ex; dē: *all with abl.*

G

game, lūdus, -ī, *m.*
gift, dōnum, -ī, *n.*
girl, puella, -ae, *f.*
give, dō, dare, dedī, datum

glory, glōria, -ae, f.
go, eō, īre, iī, itum
go astray, errō (1)
good, bonus, -a, -um
gratitude, grātia, -ae, f.
great, magnus, -a, -um
Greek, Graecus, -a, -um; **a Greek**,
    graecus, -ī, m.
ground, terra, -ae, f.

H

happy, beātus, -a, -um; fēlix, -īcis
harsh, dūrus, -a, -um; acerbus, -a, -um
have, habeō, -ēre, -uī, -itum
he, is; *often indicated only by*
    the personal ending of the verb
heavy, gravis, -e
help (*vb.*), adiuvō, -āre, -iūvī, -iūtum;
    (*n.*), auxilium, -iī, n.
hesitate, dubitō (1)
himself, suī (*reflexive*); ipse (*intensive*)
his, eius (*not reflexive*); suus, -a, -um (*reflexive*)
hold, teneō, -ēre, -uī, tentum
home, domus, -ūs, f.; **at home**, domi ;
    (**to**) **home**, domum; **from home**, domō
honor, honor, honōris, m.
hope (*noun*), spēs, -eī, f.; (*vb.*), spērō (1)
however, autem (*postpositive*)
human being, homō, hominis, m.
hundred, centum
hurt, noceō, -ēre, -uī, -itum

I

if, sī ; **if...not**, nisi
ill (*noun*), malum, -ī, n.
illustrious, clārus, -a, -um
in, in + *abl.*
infancy, infantia, -ae, f.
injustice, iniūria, -ae, f.
into, in + *acc.*
iron, ferrum, -ī, n.
it, is, ea, id; *often indicated only*
    by personal ending of verb

J

join, iungō, -ere, iūnxī, iūnctum
just, iūstus, -a, -um

K

keenly, ācriter
kindness, beneficium, -iū, n.
king, rēx, rēgis, m.
know, sciō, -īre, -īvī, -ītum

L

labor, labor, -ōris, m.
lack, careō, -ēre, -uī, -itūrus
land, patria, -ae, f.; terra, -ae, f.
Latin, Latīnus, -a, -um
lead, dūcō, -ere, dūxī, ductum
leader, dux, ducis, m.
learn (**in the academic sense**), discō, -ere, didicī;
    (**get information**), cognōscō, -ere, -nōvī, -nitum
letter (**epistle**), litterae, -ārum, f.
liberty, libertās, tātis, f.
life, vita, -ae, f.
light, lūx, lūcis, f.
literature, litterae, ārum, f.
live, vīvō, -ere, vīxī, vīctum
long (**for a long time**), diū
lose, āmittō, -ere, -mīsī, -missum
love (*vb.*), amō (1)
luck, fortūna, -ae, f.

M

make, faciō, -ere, fēcī, factum
man, vir, virī, m.; homō, hominis, m.;
    often expressed by masc. of an adj.
many, multī, -ae, -a
master, magister, -trī, m.; dominus, -ī, m.
method, modus, -ī, m.
mind, mēns, mentis, f.
money, pecūnia, -ae, f.
mother, māter, -tris, f.
move, moveō, -ēre, mōvī, mōtum
much, multus, -a, -um
my, meus, -a, -um
myself (*reflexive*), meī, mihi, *etc.*;
    (*intensive*) ipse, ipsa, ipsum

N

name, nōmen, nōminis, n.
narrate, narrō
nation, gēns, gentis, f.
nature, nātūra, -ae, f.
neglect, neglegō, -ere, negēxī, neglēctum

neither...nor, neque...neque
never, numquam
nevertheless, tamen
night, nox, noctis, *f.*
no, nūllus, -a, -um
nobody, nēmō, *m./f. (For declension see Latin-English Vocabulary.)*
not, nōn; nē *with jussive and purpose ideas*
nothing, nihil (*indecl.*), *n.*
now, nunc
number, numerus, -ī, *m.*

O

obey, pāreō, -ēre, -uī
offer, offerō, -ferre, obtulī, oblātum
often, saepe
old man, senex, senis, *m.*
on (= place), in + *abl.*; (= time), *simple abl.*
on account of, propter + *acc.*
one, ūnus, -a, -um
or, aut
orator, ōrātor, -ōris, *m.*
order, iubeō, -ēre, iussī, iussum; imperō (1)
other, another, alius, alia, aliud;
  the other (of two), alter, -era, -erum;
  all the other, cēterī, -ae, -a
ought, dēbeō, -ēre, -uī, -itum
our, noster, -tra, -trum
overcome, superō (1)
overpower, opprimō, -ere, -pressī, -pressum
own, his own, suus, -a, -um; **my own**, meus, -a, -um

P

pain, dolor, -ōris, *m.*
part, pars, partis, *f.*
passion, cupiditās, -tātis, *f.*
peace, pāx, pācis, *f.*
penalty, poena, -ae, f.
people, populus, -ī, *m.*
perceive, sentiō, -īre, sēnsī, sēnsum
perish, pereō, -īre, -iī, -itum
permit, patior, -ī, passus sum;
  it is permitted, licet, licēre, licuit (*impers.*)
perpetual, perpetuus, -a, -um
persuade, persuādeō, -ēre, -suāsī, -suāsum
philosopher, sapiēns, -entis, *m.*
philosophy, philosophia, -ae, *f.*
place, locus, -ī, *m.*; *plu.*, loca, -ōrum, *n.*
plan, cōnsilium, -iī, *n.*

pleasant, iūcundus, -a, -um
please, placeō, -ēre, -uī, -itum
power (command), imperium, -iī, *n.*
powerful, potēns, *gen.* potentis
praise (*vb.*), laudō (1); (*n.*) laus, laudis, *f.*
prepare, parō (1)
preserve, cōnservō (1)
pupil, discipulus, -ī, *m.*
pursuit, studium, -iī, *n.*
put, pōnō, -ere, posuī, positum

Q

quickly, celeriter

R

read, legō, -ere, lēgī, lēctum
real, vērus, -a, -um
reason, ratiō, -ōnis, *f.*
receive, accipiō, -ere, -cēpī, -ceptum
regain, recipiō, -ere, -cēpī, -ceptum
remain, remaneō, -ēre, -mānsī, -mānsum
report, nūntiō (1)
reputation, fāma, -ae, *f.*
rest, the rest, cēterī, -ae, -a
return (go back), redeō, -īre, -iī, -itum
return (in return for), prō + *abl.*
right, iūs, iūris, *n.*
road, via, -ae, *f.*
Roman, Rōmānus, -a, -um
Rome, Rōma, -ae, *f.*
rule, regnum, -ī, *n.*

S

sake (for the sake of), *gen.* + causā
same, īdem, eadem, idem
save, cōnservō (1)
say, dīcō, -ere, dīxī, dictum
see, videō, -ēre, vīdī, vīsum
seek, petō, -ere, -īvī, -itum
senate, senātus, -ūs, *m.*
send, mittō, -ere, mīsī, missum
serious, gravis, -e
serve, serviō, -īre, -īvī, -itum
seven, septem
she, ea; *often indicated only by the personal ending of verb*
ship, nāvis, - is, *f.*
show, ostendō, -ere, -tendī, -tentum
shun, vitō (1); fugiō, -ere, fūgī, fugitūrus

sign, signum, -ī, *n*.
since, cum + *subj.; abl. abs.*
sleep, somnus, -ī, *m*.
small, parvus, -a, -um
so, ita, sīc (*usu. with vbs.*), tam (*usu. with adjs. and advs.*); **so great**, tantus, -a, -um
soldier, miles, mīlitis, *m*.
some, a certain one (*indefinite*), quīdam, quaedam, quiddam; (*more emphatic prn.*), aliquis, aliquid
son, filius, -iī, *m*.
sort, genus, generis, *n*.
soul, animus, -ī, *m*.
spare, parcō, -ere, pepercī, parsūrus
speak, dīcō, -ere, dīxī, dictum; loquor, -ī, locūtus sum
state, cīvitās, -tātis, *f.*; rēs pūblica, reī pūblicae, *f*.
strong, fortis, -e; **be strong**, valeō, -ēre, -uī, -itūrus
study (*noun*), studium, -iī, *n.*; (*vb.*), studeō, -ēre, -uī
suddenly, subitō, *adv*.
sure, certus, -a, -um
sweet, dulcis, -e
swift, celer, -eris, -ere
sword, ferrum, -ī, *n,*; gladius, -iī, *m*.
Syracuse, Syrācūsae, -ārum, *f*.

T

teach, doceō, -ēre, -uī, doctum
tell, dīcō, -ere, dīxī, dictum
terrify, terreō, -ēre, -uī, -itum
than, quam
thank, grātiās agō, -ere, ēgī, āctum
that (*demonstrative*), ille, illa, illud; is, ea, id; **that of yours**, iste, ista, istud
that (*subord. conj.*), *not expressed in ind. statement;* ut (*purpose and result*); **that...not**, nē (*purp.*), ut . . . nōn (*result*)
their, suus, -a, -um (*reflexive*); eōrum, eārum (*not reflex.*)
there, ibi
therefore, igitur
thing, rēs, reī, *f.*; *often merely the neuter of an adj.*
think, putō (1); arbitror, -ārī, -ātus sum
this, hic, haec, hoc; is, ea, id
thousand, mille (*indecl. adj. sing.*), mīlia, -ium, *n.* (*noun in plu.*)
three, trēs, tria

through, per + *acc*.
throw, iaciō, -ere, iēcī, iactum
thus, sīc
time, tempus, -oris, *n*.
to (**place to which**), ad + *acc.*; (**ind. obj.**), dat.; (**purpose**), ut + *subj.*, ad + *ger*.
tolerate, tolerō (1)
troops, cōpiae, -ārum, *f*.
true, vērus, -a, -um
trust, crēdō, -ere, crēdidī, crēditum
truth, vēritās, -tātis, *f*.
try, experior -īrī, expertus sum
two, duo, duae, duo
tyrant, tyrannus, -ī, *m*.

U

unable (be) nōn possum
uncertain, incertus, -a, -um
under, sub + *abl.* (= **place where**), + *acc.* (= **place to which**)
understand, intellegō, -ere, -lēxī, -lēctum; comprehendō, -ere, -hendī, -hēnsum
unfortunate, miser, -era, -erum
unless, nisi
unwilling (be), nōlō, nōlle, nōluī
urban, urbane, urbānus, -a, -um
urge, hortor, -ārī, -ātus sum
use, ūtor, -ī, ūsus sum

V

very: *express this by the superlative.*
vice, vitium, -iī, *n*.
Virgil, Vergilius, -iī, m.
virtue, virtūs, -tūtis, *f*.

W

want, volō, velle, voluī
war, bellum, -ī, *n*.
warn, moneō, -ēre, -uī, -itum
water, aqua, -ae, *f*.
wealth, divitiae, -ārum, *f*.
well (*adv.*), bene
what (*prn.*), quid; (*adj.*) quī, quae, quod
when, *participle; abl. abs.*; cum + *subj.*; (*interrog.*) quandō
where, ubi
wherefore, quārē
which (*rel. prn.*), quī, quae, quod
while, dum

who (*rel.*), quī, quae, quod
 (*interrog.*), quis, quid
whole, tōtus, -a, -um
why, cūr
willing (be), volō, velle, voluī
wisdom, sapientia, -ae, *f.*
wise, sapiēns, *gen.* sapientis
wisely, sapienter
with, cum + *abl.; abl. of means*
without, sine + *abl.*
word, verbum, -ī, *n.*
work, opus, operis, *n.*

write, scrībō, -ere, scrīpsī, scrīptum

Y

year, annus, -ī, *m.*
yield, cēdō, -ere, cessī, cessum
you, tū, tuī, *often expressed*
 simply by the personal ending of verb
your (*sing.*), tuus, -a, -um; (*plu.*),
 vester, -tra, -trum
yourself, tuī, tibi, *etc.*
youth, iuvenis, -is

Latin-English Vocabulary

An Arabic numeral after a vocabulary entry indicates the chapter in which the word is first introduced as an item of required vocabulary. An R. after the Arabic numeral shows that the word belongs to the recognition vocabulary of the chapter. The letters L.A. refer to the vocabularies in the Locī Antīquī.

Arabic (1) in parentheses after a verb shows that this is a regular verb of the first conjugation with a sequence of principal parts reading -āre, -āvī, -ātum.

For prefixes and suffixes see the lists in the Appendix.

A

ā *or* **ab,** *prep.* + *abl.*, from, away from; by (*agent*). 18

abeō, -īre, -iī, -itum, go away, depart. 37

absconditus, -a, -um, hidden, secret

absēns, *gen.* **-sentis,** *adj.*, absent, away

absum, abesse, āfuī, āfutūrus, be away, be absent

abundantia, -ae, *f.*, abundance

ac. *See* **atque.**

accēdō, -ere, -cessī, -cessum, come near, approach. 36

accipiō, -ere, -cēpī, -ceptum, take, get, receive, accept. 24

accommodō (1), adjust, adapt

accūsātor, -ōris, *m.*, accuser

accūsō (1), accuse

ācer, ācris, ācre, sharp, keen, eager, severe, fierce; *superl.* **ācerrimus, -a, -um.** 27

acerbitās, -tātis, *f.*, harshness

acerbus, -a, -um, harsh, bitter, grievous. 26

Achillēs, -is, *m.*, Greek hero, chief character in the *Iliad*

aciēs, -ēī, *f.*, sharp edge, keenness, line of battle

acquīrō, -ere, -quīsīvī, -quīsītum, acquire, gain

ad, *prep.* + *acc.*, to, up to, near to. 8

addiscō, -ere, -didicī, learn in addition

addūcō, -ere, -dūxī, -ductum, lead to, induce

adeō, -īre, -iī, itum, go to, approach

adferō, -ferre, attulī, allātum, bring

adficiō, -ere, -fēcī, -fectum, affect, afflict, weaken

adiciō, -ere, iēcī, -iectum, add

adiuvō, -āre, -iūvī, -iūtum, help, aid. 16

admīror, -ārī, -ātus sum, wonder at, admire. L.A. 8

admittō, -ere, -mīsī, -missum, admit, receive

admoneō = moneō

adnuō, -ere, -nuī, nod assent

adoptō (1), wish for oneself, select, adopt

adsum, -esse, adfuī, -futūrus, be near, be present, assist

adūlātiō, -ōnis, *f.,* fawning, flattery

adulēscēns, -ntis, *m.,* young man. 25 R.

adulēscentia, -ae, *f.,* youth

adultus, -a, -um, grown up, mature, adult

adūrō, -ere, -ussī, -ustum, set fire to, burn, singe

adveniō, -īre, -vēnī, -ventum, come (to), arrive

adversus, -a, -um, facing, opposite, adverse

adversus, *prep.* + *acc.,* toward, facing; against

advesperāscit, -ere, -perāvit, *impers.,* evening is coming on, it is growing dark

aedificium, -iī, *n.,* building, structure

aegrē, *adv.,* with difficulty, hardly, scarcely

aequitās, -tātis, *f.,* justice, fairness, equity

aequus, -a, -um, level, even, calm, equal, just, favorable. 31

aestās, -tātis, *f.,* summer. L.A. 24

aestus, -ūs, *m.,* heat, tide

aetās, -tātis, *f.,* period of life, life, age, an age, time. 16

aeternus, -a, -um, eternal

Agamemnon, -onis, *m.,* commander-in-chief of the Greek forces at Troy

ager, agrī, *m.,* field, farm. L.A. 14

agō, -ere, ēgī, āctum, drive, lead, do, act; *of time or life,* pass, spend; **grātiās agere** + *dat.,* thank. 8

agrīcultūra, -ae, *f.,* agriculture

ait, aiunt, he says, they say, assert. 25

Alexander, -drī, *m.,* Alexander the Great, renowned Macedonian general and king, 4th cen., B.C.

aliēnus, -a, -um, belonging to another (*cp.* **alius**), foreign, strange, alien

aliōquī, *adv.,* otherwise

aliquī, aliqua, aliquod, *indef. pronominal adj.,* some

aliquis, aliquid (*gen.* **alicuius;** *dat.* **alicui**), *indef. pron.,* someone, somebody, something. 23

aliter, *adv.,* otherwise

alius, alia, aliud, other, another. 18; **aliī...aliī,** some...others

alō, -ere, aluī, altum, nourish, support, sustain, increase, cherish. 22 R.

alter, altera, alterum, the other (of two), second. 9

altus, -a, -um, high, deep

ambitiō, -ōnis, *f.,* a canvassing for votes; ambition; flattery

ambulō (1), walk

āmēn, *adv. from Hebrew,* truly, verily, so be it

amīcitia, -ae, *f.,* friendship. 17

amiculum, -ī, *n.,* cloak

amīcus, -ī, *m.,* friend. 3

āmittō, -ere, -mīsī, -missum, lose, let go. 32

amō (1), love, like. 1

amor, -ōris, *m.,* love. 7

āmoveō, -ēre, -mōvī, -mōtum, move away, remove

an, *adv. and conj. introducing the second part of a double question* (*see* **utrum**), or; *used alone,* or, can it be that. L.A. 15

ancilla, -ae, *f.,* maidservant

angelus, -ī, *m.,* angel

angulus, -ī, *m.,* corner

angustus, -a, -um, narrow, limited. L.A. 4

animal, -ālis, *n.,* animal

animus, -ī, *m.,* soul, spirit, mind; **animī, -ōrum,** high spirits, pride, courage. 5

annus, -ī, *m.,* year. 31

ante, *prep.* + *acc.,* before (*in place or time*), in front of; *as adv.,* before, previously. 13

anteā, *adv.,* before, formerly. L.A. 13

antepōnō, -ere, -posuī, -positum, put before, prefer (+ *dat.*). 35

antīquus, -a, -um, ancient, old-time. 2

Apollō, -inis, *m.,* Phoebus Apollo, god of sun, prophecy, poetry, etc.

apparātus, -ūs, *m.,* equipment, splendor

appellō (1), call, name. 27

approbō (1), approve

appropinquō (1) + *dat.,* approach, draw near to. L.A. 28

aptus, -a, -um, fit, suitable

apud, *prep.* + *acc.,* among, in the presence of, at the house of. 31

aqua, -ae, *f.,* water. 34

āra, -ae, *f.,* altar

arānea, -ae, *f.,* spider's web

arbitror, -ārī, -ātus sum, judge, think. 34

arbor, -oris, *f.,* tree. L.A. 11

arcus, -ūs, *m.,* bow

argentum, -ī, *n.,* silver, money

argūmentum, -ī, *n.,* proof, evidence

arma, -ōrum, *n.,* arms, weapons. 28

arō (1), plow

ars, artis, *f.,* art, skill. 14

arx, arcis, *f.,* citadel, stronghold

as, assis, *m.,* small copper coin roughly equivalent to a cent

Asia, -ae, *f.,* Asia, commonly the
Roman province in Asia Minor. 12
asper, -era, -erum, rough, harsh
aspiciō, -ere, -spexī, -spectum, look at, behold.
L.A. 15
assentātor, -ōris, *m.,* yes-man, flatterer
astrum, -ī, *n.,* star, constellation
at, *conj.,* but; but, mind you; but, you say;
a more emotional adversative than sed. 19
āter, ātra, -ātrum, dark
Athēnae, -ārum, *f.,* Athens. 37
Athēniēnsis, -e, Athenian;
Athēniēnsēs, -ium, the Athenians
atque *or* **ac,** *conj.,* and, and also, and even. 21
atquī, *conj.,* and yet, still
auctor, -ōris, *m.,* author, originator. 26
auctōritās, -tātis, *f.,* authority
audācia, -ae, *f.,* daring, boldness, audacity
audāx, -ācis, *adj. of 1 end.,* daring, bold
audeō, -ēre, ausus sum, dare. 7; 34
audiō, -īre, -īvī, -ītum, hear, listen to. 23
audītor, -ōris, *m.,* hearer
auferō, -ferre, abstulī, ablātum, bear away, carry off
Augustus, -ī, *m.,* first Roman emperor
aureus, -a, -um, golden
auris, -is, *f.,* ear
aurum, -ī, *n.,* gold. L.A. 7
aut, *conj.,* or; **aut...aut,** either...or. 17
autem, *postpositive conj.,* however, moreover. 11
auxilium, -iī, *n.,* aid, help. 31
avāritia, -ae, *f.,* greed, avarice
avārus, -a, -um, greedy, avaricious
āvehō, -ere, -vexī, -vectum, carry away
āvertō, -ere, -vertī, -versum, turn away, avert. 23
āvocō (1), call away, divert

B

balbus, -a, -um, stammering, stuttering
barba, -ae, *f.,* beard
bāsium, -iī, *n.,* kiss
beātus, -a, -um, happy, fortunate. 16
bellicus, -a, -um, relating to war, military
bellum, -ī, *n.,* war. 4
bellus, -a, -um, pretty, handsome, charming. 4
bene, *adv.,* well. 11 (*comp.* **melius;**
superl. **optimē.** 32)
beneficium, -iī, *n.,* benefit, kindness, favor. 28 R.
benevolentia, -ae, *f.,* good will, kindness
bēstia, -ae, *f.,* animal, beast
bibō, -ere, bibī, drink

bis, *adv.,* twice
bonus, -a, -um, good. 4 (*comp.* **melior;**
superl. **optimus.** 27)
bōs, bovis, *m./f.,* bull, ox, cow
brevis, -e, short, small, brief. 16
brevitās, -tātis, *f.,* shortness, brevity
breviter, briefly
Britannia, -ae, *f.,* Britain
Brundisium, -iī, *n.,* important seaport in S. Italy
Brūtus, -ī, *m.,* famous Roman name:
L. Junius Brutus, who helped establish the
Roman republic; M. Junius Brutus, one of the
conspirators against Julius Caesar

C

C., abbreviation for the common name of **Gāius**
cadō, -ere, cedidī, cāsum, fall. L. A. 9
caecus, -a, -um, blind
caelestis, -e, heavenly, celestial
caelum, -ī, *n.,* sky, heaven. 12
Caesar, -aris, *m.,* Caesar, especially
Gaius Julius Caesar. 12
calamitās, -tātis, *f.,* misfortune, disaster
calculus, -ī, *m.,* pebble
campana, -ae, *f.,* bell (*late Lat.*)
candidus, -a, -um, shining, bright, white
canis, -is (*gen. plu.* **canum**), *m./f.,* dog
cantō (1), sing
capillus, -ī, *m.,* hair (*of head or beard*)
capiō, -ere, cēpī, captum, take, capture, seize,
get. 10
captō (1), grab, seek to get, hunt for (legacies,
etc.)
caput, capitis, *n.,* head. 40
carbō, -ōnis, *m.,* coal, charcoal
careō, -ēre, caruī, caritūrus + *abl. of separ.,* be
without, be deprived of, want,
lack, be free from. 20
cāritās, -tātis, *f.,* dearness, affection
carmen, -minis, *n.,* song, poem
carpō, -ere, carpsī, carptum, pluck, seize
Carthāgō, -inis, *f.,* Carthage, city in N. Africa
cārus, -a, -um, dear. 11
cāsus, -ūs, *m.,* accident, chance
catēna, -ae, *f.,* chain
Catilīna, -ae, *m.,* L. Sergius Catiline, leader of
the conspiracy against the Roman state in 63 B.C.
Catullus, -ī, *m.,* lyric poet
cattus, -ī, *m.,* cat (*late word for class.* **fēlēs, -is**)

causa, -ae, *f.,* cause, reason; case, situation;
  causā *with a preceding genitive,* for the
  sake of, on account of. 21
caveō, -ēre, cāvī, cautum, beware, avoid. L.A. 29
cavus, -ī, *m.,* hole
cēdō, -ere, cessī, cessum, go, withdraw;
  yield to, submit, grant. 28
celer, celeris, celere, quick, swift, rapid. 16
celeritās, -tātis, *f.,* speed, swiftness
celeriter, swiftly, quickly. 32 R.
cēna, -ae, *f.,* dinner. 33 R.
cēnō (1), dine
centum, *indecl. adj.,* a hundred
cernō, -ere, crēvī, crētum, distinguish,
  discern, perceive
certē, *adv.,* certainly. 33 R.
certus, -a, -um, definite, sure, certain, reliable. 19
cervus, -ī, *m.,* stag, deer
cēterī, -ae, -a, the remaining, the rest, the other. 30
Cicerō, -ōnis, *m.,* Cicero. 13
cicūta, -ae, *f.,* hemlock (*poison*)
cinis, cineris, *m.,* ashes
circēnsēs, -ium, *m.* (*sc.* **lūdī**), games in the Circus
cito, *adv.,* quickly
cīvilis, -e, civil, civic
civis, -is, *m.,* citizen, 14
cīvitās, -tātis, *f.,* state, citizenship. 7
clārus, -a, -um, clear, bright; renowned,
  famous, illustrious. 26
claudō, -ere, clausī, clausum, shut, close. L.A. 25
clēmentia, -ae, *f.,* mildness, gentleness, mercy
coepī, coepisse, coeptum (*defective vb.; pres.
  system supplied by* **incipiō**), began. 17
coērceō, -ēre, -uī, -itum, curb, check, repress
cōgitō (1), think, ponder, consider, plan. 1
cognōscō, -ere, -nōvī, -nitum, become acquainted
  with, learn, recognize; *in perf. tenses,* know. 30
cōgō, -ere, coēgī, coāctum, drive *or* bring
  together, force, compel. 36
colligō, -ere, -lēgī, -lēctum, gather together,
  collect. L.A. 5
collocō (1), place, put, arrange. L.A. 7; 8
collum, -ī, *n.,* neck
colō, -ere, -uī, cultum, cultivate; cherish
color, -ōris, *m.,* color
commemorō (1), remind, relate, mention
commisceō, -ere, -miscuī, -mixtum,
  intermingle, join
committō, -ere, -mīsī, -missum, entrust,
  commit. 15
commūnis, -e, common, general. 20

comparō (1), compare
compōnō, -ere, -posuī, -positum, put together,
  compose. L.A. 27
comprehendō, -ere, -hendī, -hēnsum, grasp,
  seize, arrest; comprehend, understand. 30
concēdō, -ere, -cessī, -cessum, yield, grant,
  concede. L.A. 4
concilium, -iī, *n.,* council
cōnferō, -ferre, -tulī, collātum, bring together,
  compare; **sē conferre,** betake oneself, go. 31
cōnfidō, -ere, -fīsus sum, have confidence in,
  believe confidently, be confident. L.A. 12
cōnfiteor, -ēri, -fessus sum, confess. L.A. 29
congregō (1), gather together, assemble
coniciō, -ere, -iēci, -iectum, throw, hurl,
  put with force; put together, conjecture. L.A. 4
coniūrātiō, -ōnis, *f.,* conspiracy
coniūrātus, -ī, *m.,* conspirator
cōnor, -ārī, -ātus sum, try, attempt. 34 R.
cōnscientia, -ae, *f.,* consciousness,
  knowledge; conscience
cōnscius, -a, -um, conscious, aware of
cōnservō (1), presence, conserve, maintain. 1
cōnsilium, -iī, *n.,* counsel, advice,
  plan, purpose; judgment, wisdom. 18
cōnsistō, -ere, -stitī + in, depend on
cōnstō, -āre, -stitī, -stātūrus + ex, consist of
cōnsuēscō, -ere, -suēvī, -suētum,
  become accustomed. L.A. 4
cōnsul, -ulis, *m.,* consul. 38
cōnsulō, -ere, -suluī, -sultum, look out for,
  have regard for
cōnsultum, -ī, *n.,* decree
cōnsūmō, -ere, -sūmpsī, -sūmptum, use up, consume. 38
contemnō, -ere, -tempsī, -temptum,
  despise, condemn
contendō, -ere, -tendī, -tentum, strive,
  struggle, contend, hasten. L.A. 5
contineō, -ēre, -tinuī, -tentum, hold together,
  keep, enclose, restrain, contain. 21
contingō, -ere, -tigī, tāctum, touch closely,
  befall, fall to one's lot
contrā, *prep. + acc.,* against. 20
conturbō (1), throw into confusion
convertō, -ere, -vertī, -versum, turn
  around, cause to turn
convocō (1), call together, convene
cōpia, -ae, *f.,* abundance, supply;
  cōpiae, -ārum, supplies, troops, forces. 8
cōpiōsē, *adv.,* fully, at length, copiously

Corinthus, -ī, f., Corinth
cornū, -ūs, n., horn
corōna, -ae, f., crown
corpus, corporis, n., body. 13
corrigō, -ere, -rēxī, -rēctum, make right, correct
corrōborō (1), strengthen
corrumpō, -ere, -rūpī, -ruptum, ruin, corrupt
cotidiē, adv., daily, every day
crās, adv., tomorrow
creātor, -ōris, m., creator
creātūra, -ae, f., creature (late Lat.)
crēber, -bra, -brum, thick, frequent, numerous
crēdō, -ere, crēdidī, crēditum, believe, trust. 25; + dat. 35
creō (1), create. L.A. 27
crēscō, -ere, -crēvī, crētum, increase
crūdēlis, -e, cruel. L.A. 10
crustulum, ī, n., pastry, cookie
cubiculum, -ī, n., bedroom, room
culpa, -ae, f., fault, blame. 5
culpō (1), blame, censure
cultūra, -ae, f., cultivation
cum, conj., with subj., when, since, although; with ind., when. 31
cum, prep. + abl., with. 10
cunctātiō, -ōnis, f., delay
cūnctātor, -ōris, m., delayer
cūnctor (1), delay
cupiditās, -tātis, f., desire, longing, passion, cupidity, avarice. 24 R.
cupīdō, -inis, f., desire, passion
cupidus, -a, -um, desirous, eager, fond. 39
cupiō, -ere, -īvī, -ītum, desire, wish, long for. 23
cūr, adv., why. 24
cūra, -ae, f., care, attention, caution, anxiety. 4
cūrō (1), care for, attend to; heal, cure; take care. 36
currō, -ere, cucurrī, cursum, run. 14
cursus, -ūs, m., a running, race; course. L.A. 26
curvus, -a, -um, curved, crooked, wrong
custōdia, -ae, f., protection, custody; in plu., guards. 32 R.
custōs, -tōdis, m., guardian, guard. L.A. 27

D

damnō (1), condemn
Dāmoclēs, -is, m., an attendant of Dionysius
dē, prep. + abl., down from, from; concerning, about. 3
dēbeō, -ēre, -uī, -itum, owe, ought, must. 1

dēbilitō (1), weaken
dēcernō, -ere, -crēvī, -crētum, decree
dēcertō (1), fight it out, fight to the finish, contend. L.A. 10
decimus, -a, -um, tenth
dēcipiō, -ere, -cēpi, -ceptum, deceive
decor, -ōris, m., beauty, grace
dēcrētum, -ī, n., decree
dēdicō (1), dedicate
dēfendō, -ere, -fendī, -fēnsum, ward off, defend, protect. 38
dēficiō, -ere, -fēcī, -fectum, fail
dēgustō (1), taste
deinde, adv., thereupon, next, then. 37
dēlectātiō, -ōnis, f., delight, pleasure, enjoyment
dēlectō (1), delight, charm, please
dēleō, -ēre, dēlēvī, dēlētum, destroy, wipe out, erase. 17
dēliberō (1), consider, deliberate
dēmēns, gen. -mentis, adj., out of one's mind, insane, foolish
dēmittō, -ere, -mīsī, -missum, let down, lower
dēmōnstrō (1), point out, show, demonstrate. L.A. 7
Dēmosthenēs, -is, m., most famous Greek orator, 4th cen. B.C.
dēnique, adv., at last, finally. 30
dēns, dentis, m., tooth
dēpōnō, -ere, -posuī, -positum, put down, lay aside
dēportō (1), carry off
dēsiderō (1), desire, long for, miss
dēsidiōsus, -a, -um, lazy
dēsinō, -ere, -sīvī, -situm, cease, leave off
dēsipiō, -ere, act foolishly
dēstinātus, -a, -um, resolved, resolute, firm
dētrīmentum, -ī, n., loss, detriment
deus, -ī, m. (nom. plu. deī or dī) god. 12
dēvocō (1), call down or away
dexter, -tra, -trum, right (= on the right-hand side)
diabolus, -ī, m., devil
dīcō, -ere, dīxī, dictum, say, tell, speak; call, name. 12
dictāta, -ōrum, n., things dictated, lessons, precepts
dictātor, -ōris, m., dictator
dictō (1), say repeatedly, dictate
diēs, -ēī, m., day. 22
difficilis, -e, hard, difficult, troublesome. 16
dignitās, -tātis, f., merit, prestige, dignity

dignus, -a, -um + *abl.*, worthy, worthy of. L.A. 11
dīligēns, *gen.* **-entis,** *adj.*, diligent, careful
dīligenter, *adv.*, diligently
dīligentia, -ae, *f.*, diligence
dīligō, -ere, dīlēxi, dīlēctum, esteem, love. 13 R.
dīmidium, -iī, *n.*, half
dimittō, -ere, -mīsī, -missum, send away, dismiss
Dionȳsius, -iī, *m.*, tyrant of Syracuse
discēdō, -ere, -cessī, -cessum, go away, depart. 28
discipulus, -ī, *m.*, learner, pupil, disciple. 29 R.
discō, -ere, didicī, learn. 29
disputātiō, -ōnis, *f.*, discussion
disputō, (1), discuss
dissimilis, -e, unlike, different
dissimulō (1), conceal
distinguō, -ere, -stīnxī, -stīnctum, distinguish
diū, *adv.*, long, for a long time. 12
dīves, *gen.* **dīvitis, ditis,** *adj.*, rich. 32 R.
dīvīnus, -a, -um, divine, sacred
dīvitiae, -ārum, *f.*, riches, wealth. 32
dō, dăre, dedī, dătum, give, offer. 1
doceō, -ēre, docuī, doctum, teach. 8
doctrīna, -ae, *f.*, teaching, instruction, learning
doctus, -a, -um, taught, learned, skilled
doleō, -ēre, -uī, -itūrus, grieve, suffer. L.A. 2
dolor, -ōris, *m.*, pain, grief. 38
domesticus, -a, -um, domestic; civil
domina, -ae, *f.*, mistress
dominātus, -ūs, *m.*, rule, mastery, tyranny
dominicus, -a, -um, belonging to a master; the Lord's
dominus, -ī, *m.*, master, lord. 40
domus, -ūs (-ī), *f.*, house, home; **domī,** at home; **domum,** (to) home; **domō,** from home. 37
dōnum, -ī, *n.*, gift, present. 23 R.
dormiō, -īre, -īvī, -ītum, sleep
dubitō (1), doubt, hesitate. 38
dubium, -iī, *n.*, doubt
dūcō, -ere, dūxī, ductum, lead; consider, regard; prolong. 8
dulcis, -e, sweet, pleasant, agreeable. 16
dum, *conj.*, while, as long as, until. 8
dummodo, *conj.* + *subj.*, provided
duo, duae, duo, two. 40
dūrō (1), harden, last, endure
dūrus, -a, -um, hard, harsh, rough, stern, unfeeling. 29
dux, ducis, *m.*, leader, guide, commander, general. 24

E

ē. *See* **ex.**
ecclēsia, -ae, *f.*, church (*ecclesiastical Lat.*)
ēducō (1), bring up, educate
ēdūcō, -ere, -dūxī, -ductum, lead out
efferō, -ferre, extulī, ēlātum, carry out; bury; lift up, exalt
efficiō, -ere, -fēcī, -fectum, accomplish, perform, bring about, cause. L.A. 13
effugiō, -ere, -fūgī, -fugitūrus, flee from, flee away, escape
egeō, -ēre, eguī, need, lack, want
ego, meī, I, *etc.* 11
ēgredior, ēgredī, ēgressus sum, go out, depart
ēiciō, -ere, -iēcī, -iectum, throw out, drive out. 15
elementum, -ī, *n.*, element, first principle
elephantus, -ī, *m.*, elephant
ēloquēns, *gen.* **-entis,** *adj.*, eloquent
ēloquentia, -ae, *f.*, eloquence
ēmendō (1), correct, emend
emō, -ere, ēmī, ēmptum, buy
ēmoveō, -ēre, -mōvī, -mōtum, move away, remove
enim, *postpositive conj.*, for, in fact, truly. 9
Ennius, -iī, *m.*, early Roman writer
ēnumerō (1), count up, enumerate
eō, īre, iī (or īvī), itum, go. 37
epigramma, -atis, *n.*, inscription, epigram
epistula, -ae, *f.*, letter, epistle
eques, equitis, *m.*, horseman
equidem, *adv. espec. common with 1st per.*, indeed, truly, for my part. L.A. 5; 9
equitātus, -ūs, *m.*, cavalry
equus, -ī, *m.*, horse
ergā, *prep.* + *acc.*, toward
ergō, *adv.*, therefore. L.A. 25
ēripiō, -ere, -ripuī, -reptum, snatch away, take away, rescue. 22
errō (1), wander, err, go astray, be mistaken. 1 R.
error, -ōris, *m.*, a going astray, error, mistake
et, *conj.*, and, 2; even (= **etiam**); **et . . . et,** both . . . and
etiam, *adv.*, even, also. 18
etsī, *conj.*, even if (**et-sī**), although. 39
ēveniō, -īre, -vēnī, -ventum, come out, turn out, happen
ēventus, -ūs, *m.*, outcome, result
ex *or* **ē,** *prep.* + *abl.*, out of, from within, from; by reason of, on account of. **Ex** *can be used before cons. or vowels;* **ē,** *before cons. only.* 8

excellentia, -ae, f., excellence, merit

excipiō, -ere, -cēpī, -ceptum, take out, except;
  take, receive, capture

exclāmō (1), cry out, call out

exclūdō, -ere, -clūsī, -clūsum, shut out, exclude

excruciō (1), torture, torment

excūsātiō, -ōnis, f., excuse

exemplar, -āris, n., model, pattern, original

exemplum, -ī, n., example, model

exercitus, -ūs, m., army. 32

eximius, -a, -um, extraordinary, excellent

exitium, -iī, n., destruction, ruin

expellō, -ere, -pulī, -pulsum, expel, banish. 24

experior, -īrī, -pertus sum,
  try, test, experience. 39

expleō, -ēre, -plēvī, -plētum, fill,
  fill up, complete. L.A. 26

expōnō, -ere, -posuī, -positum, set forth,
  explain, expose. 30 R.

exquisitus, -a, -um, sought-out, exquisite,
  excellent

exsilium, -iī, n., exile, banishment. 31 R.

exspectō (1), look for, expect, await. 15

exstinguō, -ere, -stīnxī, -stīnctum, extinguish

externus, -a, -um, foreign

extorqueō, -ēre, -torsī, -tortum, twist away, extort

extrā, prep. + acc., beyond, outside

extrēmus, -a, -um, outermost, last, extreme

F

Fabius, -iī, m., Roman name; especially Quintus
  Fabius Maximus Cunctator (the Delayer),
  celebrated for his delaying tactics (Fabian
  tactics) against Hannibal

fābula, -ae, f., story, tale; play

facile, adv., easily. 32

facilis, -e, easy; agreeable, affable;
  superl. facillimus. 27

faciō, -ere, fēcī, factum, make, do, accomplish,
  10; passive: fīō, fierī, factus sum. 36

factum, -ī, n., deed, act, achievement. 17 R.

facultās, -tātis, f., ability, skill, opportunity,
  means

falsus, -a, -um, false, deceptive

fāma, -ae, f., rumor, report; fame, reputation. 2

familia, -ae, f., household, family

fās, indecl., n., right, sacred duty; fās est,
  it is right, fitting, lawful

fateor, -ērī, fassus sum, confess, admit. 36

fātum, -ī, n., fate. 38 R.

fēlīciter, adv., happily. 32

fēlīx, gen. fēlīcis, adj., lucky,
  fortunate, happy. 27 R.

fēmina, -ae, f., woman. 16 R.

fenestra, -ae, f., window

ferē, adv., almost, nearly, generally

ferō, ferre, tulī, lātum, bear, carry, bring;
  suffer, endure, tolerate; say, report. 31

ferrum, -ī, n., iron, sword. 30

ferus, -a, -um, wild, uncivilized, fierce

festīnātiō, -ōnis, f., haste

festīnō (1), hasten, hurry

fīcus, -ī and -ūs, f., fig tree

fidēlis, -e, faithful, loyal. 25 R.

fidēs, -eī, f., faith, trust, trustworthiness, fidelity;
  promise, guarantee. 22

fīlia, -ae, f., daughter. 10

fīlius, -iī, m., son. 3

fīnis, -is, m., end, limit,
  boundary, purpose; fīnēs, -ium,
  (boundaries) territory. 21

fīō, fierī, factus sum, be made, be done, become. 36

fīrmus, -a, -um, firm, strong, reliable

flamma, -ae, f., flame, fire

flūctus, -ūs, m., billow, wave

flūmen, -minis, n., river

fluō, -ere, flūxī, flūxum, flow

fōrma, -ae, f., form, shape, beauty. 2 R.

formīca, -ae, f., ant

fōrmō (1), form, shape, fashion

fors, fortis, f., chance, fortune

forsan, adv., perhaps

fortasse, adv., perhaps

fortis, -e, strong, brave. 16

fortiter, adv., bravely. 32

fortūna, -ae, f., fortune, luck. 2

fortūnātē, adv., fortunately

fortūnātus, -a, -um, lucky, fortunate, happy

forum, -ī, n., market place, forum

foveō, -ēre, fōvī, fōtum, cherish

frāter, -tris, m., brother. 37

frōns, frontis, f., forehead, brow, front

frūctus, -ūs, f., fruit, profit, enjoyment. 20

frūgālitās, -tātis, f., frugality

frūstrā, adv., in vain

fuga, -ae, f., flight

fugiō, -ere, fūgī, fugitūrus, flee; avoid, shun. 10

fugitivus, -ī, m., fugitive, deserter, runaway slave

fugō (1), put to flight, rout

fulgeō, -ēre, fulsī, flash, shine

furor, -ōris, m., rage, frenzy, madness

fūrtificus, -a, -um, thievish
fūrtim, a*dv.,* stealthily, secretly

G

Gāius, -iī, *m.,* common praenomen (first name); usually abbreviated to C. in writing
Gallus, -ī, *m.,* a Gaul. The Gauls were a Celtic people who inhabited the district which we know as France
gaudium, -iī, *n.,* joy, delight
gēns, gentis, *f.,* clan, race, nation, people. 21
genus, generis, *n.,* kind, sort, class. 18
gerō, -ere, gessī, gestum, carry, carry on, manage, conduct, accomplish, perform. 14
gladius, -iī, *m.,* sword
glōria, -ae, *f.,* glory, fame. 5
Graecia, -ae, *f.,* Greece. 20
Graecus, -a, -um, Greek; **Graecus, -ī,** *m.,* a Greek. 6
grātia, -ae, *f.,* gratitude, favor, L.A. 14; **grātiās agere** + *dat.,* to thank. 8
grātus, -a, -um, pleasing, agreeable; grateful. 37
gravis, -e, heavy, weighty, serious, important, severe, grievous. 20
gravitās, -tātis, *f.,* weight, seriousness importance, dignity
graviter, *adv.,* heavily, seriously
gustō (1), taste

H

habeō, -ēre, habuī, habitum, have, hold, possess; consider, regard. 3
hāmus, -ī, *m.,* hook
Hannibal, -alis, *m.,* celebrated Carthaginian general in the 2nd Punic War, 218-201 B.C.
haud, *adv.,* not, not at all (*strong negative*)
heu, *interjection,* ah! (*a sound of grief or pain*)
hic, haec, hoc, *demonstr. adj. and pron.,* this, the latter; *at times weakened to* he, she, it, they. 9
hic, *adv.,* here. 25 R.
hinc, *adv.,* from this place, hence
hodiē, *adv.,* today. L.A. 25
Homērus, -ī, *m.,* Homer
homō, hominis, *m.,* human being, man. 7
honor, -ōris, *m.,* honor, esteem; public office. 32
hōra, -ae, *f.,* hour, time. 10
horrendus, -a, -um, horrible, dreadful
hortor, -ārī, -tātus sum, urge, encourage. 36
hortus, -ī, *m.,* garden

hospes, -pitis, *m.,* stranger, guest; host
hostis, -is, *m.,* an enemy (of the state); **hostēs, -ium,** the enemy. 25
hui, *interjection,* sound of surprise or approbation not unlike our "whee"
hūmānitās, -tātis, *f.,* kindness, refinement
hūmānus, -a, -um, pertaining to man, human, humane, kind, refined, cultivated. 25
humilis, -e, lowly, humble. L.A. 14
hypocrita, -ae, *m.,* hypocrite (*eccles. Lat.*)

I

iaceō, -ēre, iacuī, lie, lie prostrate, lie dead
iaciō, -ere, iēcī, iactum, throw, hurl. 15
iaculum, -ī, *n.,* dart, javelin
iam, *adv.,* now, already, soon. 30
iānua, -ae, *f.,* door
ibi, *adv.,* there. 6
īdem, eadem, idem, the same. 11
identidem, *adv.,* repeatedly, again and again
igitur, *postpositive conj.,* therefore, consequently. 5
ignārus, -a, -um, not knowing, ignorant
ignis, -is, *m.,* fire. 22
ignōscō, -ere, -nōvī, -nōtum + *dat.,* grant pardon to, forgive, overlook. 35
illacrimō (1) + *dat.,* weep over
ille, illa, illud, *demonstr. adj. and pron.,* that, the former; the famous; *at times weakened to* he, she, it, they. 9
illūdō, -ere, lūsī, -lūsum, mock, ridicule
imāgō, -ginis, *m.,* image, likeness
imitor, -ārī, -ātus sum, imitate
immineō, -ēre, overhang, threaten
immodicus, -a, -um, beyond measure, moderate, excessive
immortālis, -e, not subject to death, immortal. 25
immōtus, -a, -um, unmoved
impedīmentum, -ī, *n.,* hindrance, impediment
impediō, -īre, -īvī, -ītum, impede, hinder, prevent
impellō, -ere, -pulī, -pulsum, urge on, impel
impendeō, -ēre, hang over, threaten, be imminent
imperātor, -ōris, *m.,* general, commander-in-chief. L.A. 12; 13
imperiōsus, -a, -um, powerful, domineering, imperious
imperium, -iī, *n.,* power to command, supreme power, authority, command, control. 24
imperō (1), give orders to, command, + *dat.,* 35; + *dat.* + ut. 36

impleō, -ēre, -ēvī, -ētum, fill up, complete

imprīmīs, *adv.,* especially, particularly

imprōvidus, -a, -um, improvident

impudēns, *gen.,* **-entis,** *adj.,* shameless, impudent

impudenter, *adv.,* shamelessly, impudently

impūnītus, -a, -um, unpunished, unrestrained, safe

in, *prep. + abl.,* in, 3; *+ acc.,* into, toward, against. 9

inānis, -e, empty, vain

incertus, -a, -um, uncertain, doubtful

incipiō, -ere, -cēpī, -ceptum, begin, commence. 17

inclūdō, -ere, -clūsī, -clūsum, shut in, inclose. L.A. 6

incorruptus, -a, -um, uncorrupted, genuine, pure

incrēdibilis, -e, incredible

indicō (1), indicate, expose, accuse

indignus, -a, -um, unworthy

indūcō, -ere, -dūxī, -ductum, lead in, introduce, induce

industria, -ae, *f.,* industry, diligence

industrius, -a, -um, industrious, diligent

ineptiō, -īre, play the fool, trifle

inexpugnābilis, -e, impregnable, unconquerable

īnfantia, -ae, *f.,* infancy

īnferī, -ōrum, *m.,* those below, the dead

īnferō, -ferre, intulī, illātum, bring in, bring upon, inflict

īnfīnitus, -a, -um, unlimited, infinite

īnfīrmus, -a, -um, not strong, weak, feeble

īnflammō (1), set on fire, inflame

īnfōrmis, -e, formless, deformed, hideous

īnfortūnātus, -a, -um, unfortunate

ingenium, -iī, *n.,* that which is born in one, nature, talent. L.A. 5

ingēns, *gen.* **-entis,** *adj.,* huge

ingrātus, -a, -um, unpleasant, ungrateful

iniciō, -ere, -iēcī, -iectum, throw on *or* into, put on; inspire

inimīcus, -ī, *m.,* personal enemy

inīquus, -a, -um, unequal, unfair, unjust

initium, -iī, *n.,* beginning, commencement

iniūria, -ae, *f.,* injustice, injury, wrong

iniūstus, -a, -um, unjust. L.A. 6; 10

inops, *gen.* **-opis,** *adj.,* poor, needy

inquam. *See* **inquit.**

inquit, *defective verb,* he says, *placed after one or more words of a direct quotation;* **inquam,** I say, *and* **inquis,** you say, *are other forms.* 22

īnsānia, -ae, *f.,* insanity, folly

īnsciēns, *gen.* **-entis,** unknowing, unaware

īnscrībō, -ere, -scrīpsī, -scrīptum, inscribe, entitle

īnsidiae, -ārum, *f.* ambush, plot, treachery. 6 R

īnsōns, *gen.* **-ontis,** guiltless, innocent

īnstituō, -ere, -stituī, -stitūtum, establish, institute

īnsula, -ae, *f.,* island. 34

īnsurgō, -ere, -surrēxī, -surrēctum, rise up

integer, -gra, -grum, untouched, whole, unhurt

intellegō, -ere, -lēxī, -lēctum, understand. 15

intempestīvus, -a, -um, untimely

inter, *prep. + acc.,* between, among. 15

intercipiō, -ere, -cēpī, -ceptum, intercept

interdum, *adv.,* at times, sometimes

intereā, *adv.,* meanwhile

interficiō, -ficere, -fēcī, -fectum, kill, murder. 37

interrogātiō, -ōnis, *f.* interrogation, inquiry

intrō (1), walk into, enter

intrōdūcō, -ere, -dūxī, -ductum, lead in, introduce

intus, *adv.,* within

invādō, -ere, -vāsī, -vāsum, enter on, move against, assail

inveniō, -īre, -vēnī, -ventum, come upon, find. 10

inventor, -ōris, *m.,* inventor

investigō (1), track out, investigate

invictus, -a, -um, unconquered; unconquerable

invideō, -ēre, -vīdī, -vīsum, look at with envy, envy, be jealous of

invidia, -ae, *f.,* envy, jealousy, hatred

invīsus, -a, -um, hated; hateful

invītō (1), invite, summon

invītus, -a, -um, unwilling, against one's will. L.A. 2

iocus, -ī, *m.,* joke jest

ipse, ipsa, ipsum, *intensive pron.,* himself, herself, itself, *etc.* 13

īra, -ae, *f.,* ire, anger. 2 R.

īrāscor, -ī, īrātus sum, be angry

īrātus, -a, -um, angered, angry

irrītō (1), excite, exasperate, irritate

is, ea, id, *demonstr. pron., and adj.,* this, that; he, she, it. 11

iste, ista, istud, *demonstr. pron., and adj.,* that of yours, that; *sometimes with contemptuous force.* 9

ita, *adv. used with adjs., vbs., and advs.,* so, thus. 29
Italia, -ae, *f.,* Italy. 15
itaque, *adv.,* and so, therefore. 15
iter, itineris, *n.,* road, route, journey. L.A. 12; 13
iterō (1), repeat
iterum, *adv.,* again, a second time
iubeō, -ēre, iussī, iussum, bid, order, command. 21
iūcunditās, -tātis, *f.,* pleasure, charm
iūcundus, -a, -um, agreeable, pleasant, gratifying. 23
iūdex, -dicis, *m.,* judge, juror
iūdicium, -iī, *n.,* judgment, decision, opinion; trial. 19 R.
iūdicō (1), judge, consider
iungō, -ere, iūnxī, iūnctum, join. 13
Iuppiter, Iovis, *m.,* Jupiter, Jove. L.A. 26
iūrō (1), swear
iūs, iūris, *n.,* right, justice, law. 14; **iūs iūrandum, iūris iūrandī,** *n.,* oath
iussū, *abl.,* at the command of
iūstus, -a, -um, just, right. 40
iuvenis, -is (*gen., plu.* **iuvenum**), *m.,* a youth, young person
iuvō, -āre, iūvī, iūtum, help, aid, assist; please. 16

L

lābor, -ī, lāpsus sum, slip, glide
labor, -ōris, *m.,* labor, work, toil. 7
labōrō (1), labor; be in distress
labrum, -ī, *n.,* lip
lacessō, -ere, -īvī, -ītum, harass, attack
lacūnar, -āris, *n.,* paneled ceiling
lāetans, *gen.* **-antis,** *adj.,* rejoicing
laetus, -a, -um, happy, joyful
Latinus, -a, -um, Latin
laudātor, -ōris, *m.,* praiser
laudō (1), praise. 1
laus, laudis, *f.,* praise, glory, fame. 21
lēctor, -ōris, *m.,* reader
lectus, -ī, *m.,* bed
lēgātus, -ī, *m.,* ambassador, deputy
legiō, -ōnis, *f.,* legion
legō, -ere, lēgī, lēctum, pick out, choose; read. 18
lēnis, -e, smooth, gentle, kind
lentē, *adv.,* slowly

Lentulus, -i, *m.,* P. Cornelius Lentulus Sura, chief conspirator under Catiline, left in charge of the conspiracy when Catiline was forced to flee from Rome
Lesbia, -ae, *f.,* the name which Catullus gave to his sweetheart
levis, -e, light, slight, trivial. 36
lēx, lēgis, *f.,* law, statute. 32 R.
libellus, -ī, *m.,* little book
libenter, *adv.,* with pleasure, gladly, L.A. 12; 13
līber, lībera, līberum, free. 23
liber, librī, *m.,* book. 6
līberālitās, -tātis, *f.,* generosity, liberality
līberātor, -ōris, *m.,* liberator
līberē, *adv.,* freely
līberī, -ōrum, *m.,* (one's) children. L.A. 19
līberō (1), free, liberate. 19
lībertās, -tātis, *f.,* liberty, freedom. 12
licet, licēre, licuit, *impers.* + *dat. and infin.,* it is permitted, one may. 37
ligō (1), bind, tie
līmen, līminis, *n.,* threshold
lingua, -ae, *f.,* tongue, language
linteum, -ī, *n.,* linen, napkin
littera, -ae, *f.,* a letter of the alphabet; **litterae, -ārum,** a letter (epistle); literature. 7
locō (1), place, put
locuplētō (1), enrich
locus, -ī, *m.* (*plu. usu.* **loca, -ōrum,** *n.,*) place, 9; *plu.* **locī, -ōrum,** *m.,* passages in literary works
longē, *adv.,* far
longinquitās, tātis, *f.,* distance, remoteness
longus, -a, -um, long. 16
loquāx, *gen.* **-ācis,** *adj.,* talkative, loquacious
loquor, -ī, locūtus sum, say, speak, tell. 34
lucrum, -ī, *n.,* gain, profit
lūdō, -ere, lūsī, lūsum, play
lūdus, -ī, *m.,* game, sport; school. 18 R.
lūna, -ae, *f.,* moon. L.A. 26
lupus, -ī, *m.,* wolf
lūx, lūcis, *f.,* light. 26
luxuria, -ae, *f.,* luxury, extravagance

M

Maecēnās, -ātis, *m.,* unofficial "prime minister" of Augustus, and patron and friend of Horace
magis, *adv.,* more, rather
magister, -trī, *m.,* master, schoolmaster, teacher. 4

magnopere, *adv.,* greatly, exceedingly
  (*comp.* **magis;** *superl.* **maximē**). 32
magnus, -a, -um, large, great, important. 2
  (*comp.* **maior;** *superl.* **maximus,** 27); **maiōrēs,**
  -um, *m. plu.,* ancestors. 27 R.
maiestās, -tātis, *f.,* greatness, dignity, majesty
maior. *See* **magnus.**
maiōrēs, -um, *m. plu.,* ancestors. 27 R
male, *adv.,* badly, ill, wrongly
  (*comp.* **peius;** *superl.* **pessimē**). 32
mālō, mālle, māluī, wish rather, prefer
malum, -ī, *n.,* evil, misfortune. 30
malus, -a, -um, bad, wicked, evil. 4
  (*comp.* **peior;** *superl.* **pessimus,** 27)
mandātum, -ī, *n.,* order, command, instruction
maneō, -ēre, mānsī, mānsum, remain,
  stay, abide, continue. 5
manus, -ūs, *f.,* hand; band; handwriting. 20
Mārcellus, -ī, *m.,* Roman general who
  captured Syracuse in 212 B.C.
Mārcus, -ī, *m.,* common Roman first name,
  usually abbreviated to **M.** in writing
mare, -is, *n.,* sea. 14
marītus, -ī, *m.,* husband
māter, -tris, *f.,* mother. 16 R.
māteria, -ae, *f.,* material, matter
mātrimōnium, -iī, *n.,* marriage
maximus. *See* **magnus.**
medicus, -ī, *m.,* doctor
mediocris, -e, ordinary, moderate, mediocre. 31 R.
meditor, -ārī, -ātus sum, reflect upon, practice
medius, -a, -um, middle; *used partitively,*
  the middle of. 22 R.
mel, mellis, *n.,* honey
melior. *See* **bonus.**
meminī, meminisse, *defective,* remember
memor, *gen.,* **-oris,** *adj.,* mindful
memoria, -ae, *f.,* memory, recollection. 16
mendōsus, -a, -um, full of faults, faulty
mēns, mentis, *f.,* mind, thought, intention. 29
mēnsa, -ae, *f.,* table
mēnsis, -is, *m.,* month
mercēs, -ēdis, *f.,* pay, reward, recompense
merīdiānus, -a, -um, of midday, noon; southern
metuō, -ere, metuī, fear, dread. 38
metus, -ūs, *m.,* fear, dread, anxiety. 20
meus, -a, -um, my. 2
mīles, mīlitis, *m.,* soldier. 29
militāris, -e, military
mīlle, *indecl. adj. in sing.,* thousand;
  mīlia, -ium, *n., plu. noun,* thousands. 40

minimus. *See* **parvus.**
minor. *See* **parvus.**
minuō, -ere, -uī, -ūtum, lessen, diminish
miror, -ārī, -ātus sum, marvel at,
  admire, wonder
mīrus, -a, -um, wonderful,
  surprising, extraordinary
misceō, -ēre, miscuī, mixtum, mix, mingle. 40
miser, -era, -erum, wretched,
  miserable, unfortunate. 15
miserē, *adv.,* wretchedly
misericordia, -ae, *f.,* pity, mercy. L.A. 11
mītēscō, -ere, become *or* grow mild
mītis, -e, mild, gentle; ripe
mittō, -ere, mīsī, missum, send, let go. 11
modo, *adv.,* now, just now, only
modus, -ī, *m.,* measure, bound, limit;
  manner, method, mode, way. 22
molestus, -a, -um, troublesome,
  disagreeble, annoying
mōlior, -īrī, -ītus sum, work at,
  build, undertake, plan
molliō, -īre, -īvī, -ītum, soften
mollis, -e, soft, mild, weak
moneō, -ēre, monuī, monitum, remind, warn,
  advise, 1; **moneō eum ut** + *subj.* 36
monitiō, -ōnis, *f.,* admonition, warning
mōns, montis, *m.,* mountain
mōnstrum, -ī, *n.,* portent; monster
mora, -ae, *f.,* delay. 4
morbus, -ī, *m.,* disease, sickness
morior, morī, mortuus sum, die. 34
mortālis, -e, mortal
mortuus, -a, -um, dead
mōs, mōris, *m.,* habit, custom, manner;
  mōrēs, mōrum, habits, character. 7
moveō, -ēre, mōvī, mōtum,
  move; arouse, affect. 18
mox, *adv.,* soon
mulier, -eris, *f.,* woman
multō (1), punish, fine
multum, *adv.,* much (*comp.*
  plūs; *superl.* **plūrimum**). 32
multus, -a, -um, much, many, 2 (*comp.* **plūs;**
  superl. **plūrimus.** 27)
mundus, -ī, *m.,* world, universe. 21 R.
mūnīmentum, -ī, *n.,* fortification, protection
mūniō, -īre, -īvī, -ītum, fortify,
  defend; build (a road)
mūnus, mūneris, *n.,* service, office,
  function, duty; gift. L.A. 23

mūs, mūris, *m./f.*, mouse

mūsa, -ae, *f.*, a muse (one of
the goddesses of poetry, music, etc.)

mūtātiō, -ōnis, *f.*, change

mūtō (1), change, alter; exchange. 15

N

nam, *conj.*, for. 13

narrō (1), narrate, tell. 24 R.

nāscor, nāscī, nātus sum,
be born, spring forth. 34

nātālis, -is (*sc.* diēs), *m.*, birthday

nātiō, -ōnis, *f.*, nation, people

nātūra, -ae, *f.*, nature. 10

nauta, -ae, *m.*, sailor

nāvigātiō, -ōnis, *f.*, voyage, navigation

nāvigō (1), sail, navigate

nāvis, -is, *f.*, ship. 31

nē, *conj. introducing subj.*, that...not,
in order that...not, in order not to, 28;
adv. in nē...quidem, not...even. 29

-ne, *enclitic added to the emphatic word at the
beginning of a question the answer to which
may be either "yes" or "no," 5. It can be
used in both direct and indirect questions.*

nec. *See* neque.

necessārius, -a, -um, necessary

necesse, *indecl. adj.*, necessary, inevitable

necō (1), murder, kill

nefās, *n.*, *indecl.*, wrong, sin

neglegō, -ere, -lēxi, -lēctum, neglect,
disregard. 17

negō (1), deny, say that...not. 25

nēmō, (nullius), nēminī, nēminem,
(nūllō, -ā), *m./f.*, no one, nobody. 11

nepōs, -ōtis, *m.*, grandson

neque *or* nec, *conj.*, and not, nor;
neque...neque, neither...nor. 20

nesciō, -īre, -īvī, -ītum, not to
know, be ignorant. 25 R.

nēve, and not, nor (*used to
continue* ut *or* nē + *subj.*)

niger, -gra, -grum, black

nihil, *n.*, *indecl.*, nothing. 1; 4

nihilum, -ī, *n.*, nothing

nimis *or* nimium, *adv.*, too,
too much, excessively. 17

nisi, if...not, unless, except. 33

niveus, -a, -um, snowy, white

noceō, -ēre, nocuī, nocitum + *dat.*,
do harm to, harm, injure. 35

nōlō, nōlle, nōluī, not...wish, be unwilling. 32

nōmen, nōminis, *n.*, name. 13

nōn, *adv.*, not. 1

nōndum, *adv.*, not yet. L.A. 19

nōnne, *interrog. adv. which introduces questions
expecting the answer "yes"; see Appendix.*

nōnnūllus, -a, -um, some, several

nōnnumquam, sometimes

nōnus, -a, -um, ninth

nōscō. *See* cognōscō.

noster, -tra, -trum, our, ours

notārius, -iī, *m.*, writer of
shorthand, stenographer

novem, *indecl. adj.*, nine

novus, -a, -um, new, strange. 19

nox, noctis, *f.*, night. 33

nūllus, -a, -um, not any, no, none. 9

num, *interrog. adv.*: (1) *introduces
direct questions which expect
the answer "no"*; (2) *introduces indirect
questions and means* whether.

numerus, -ī, *m.*, number. 3

numquam, *adv.*, never. 13

nunc, *adv.*, now, at present. 9

nūntiō (1), announce, report, relate. 25

nūntius, -iī, *m.*, messenger, message

nūper, *adv.*, recently. L.A. 19

nūtriō, -īre, -īvī, -ītum, nourish, rear

O

Ō, *interjection*, O!, oh! 2

obdūrō (1), be hard, persist, endure

obiciō, -ere, -iēcī, -iectum,
offer; throw in one's teeth

obruō, -ere, -ruī, -rutum, overwhelm, destroy

obsequium, -iī, *n.*, compliance

obstinātus, -a, -um, firm resolved

occāsiō, -ōnis, *f.*, occasion, opportunity. 28

occidō, -ere, -cidī, -cāsum (cadō, fall),
fall down; set (*of the sun*)

occidō, -ere, -cīdī, -cīsum (caedō, cut),
cut down, kill, slay

occultē, *adv.*, secretly

occupō (1), seize

oculus, -ī, *m.*, eye. 4

ōdī, ōdisse, ōsūrus (*defective vb.*), hate

odium, -ī, *n.*, hatred. 38

Oedipūs, -podis, *m.*, Greek mythical
   figure said to have murdered his
   father and married his mother
offerō, -ferre, obtulī, oblātum, offer. 31
officium, -iī, *n.*, duty, service. 4
ōlim, *adv.*, at that time, once, formerly; in the
   future
omittō, -ere, -mīsī, -missum, let go, omit
omnīnō, *adv.*, wholly, entirely, altogether. 40
omnipotēns, *gen.* **-entis**, *adj.*,
   all-powerful, omnipotent
omnis, -e, all, every. 16
onerō (1), burden, load
onus, -eris, *n.*, burden, load
opera, -ae, *f.*, work, pains, help
oportet, -ēre, oportuit (*impers.*),
   it is necessary, it behooves one
oppōnō, -ere, -posuī, -positum, set
   against, oppose
opportūnē, *adv.*, opportunely
opportūnus, -a, -um, fit, suitable,
   advantageous, opportune
opprimō, -ere, -pressī, -pressum,
   suppress, overwhelm, overpower, check. 23
opprobrium, -iī, *n.*, reproach, taunt, disgrace
oppugnō (1), fight against, attack,
   assault, assail. 39
ops, opis, *f.*, help, aid; **opēs, opum**, *plu.*,
   power, resources, wealth. 33
optimus. *See* **bonus.**
optō (1), wish for, desire
opus, operis, *n.*, a work, task; deed,
   accomplishment. 38
ōrātiō, -ōnis, *f.*, speech. L.A. 11
ōrātor, -ōris, *m.*, orator, speaker. 23 R.
orbis, -is, *m.*, circle, orb;
   orbis terrārum, the world, the earth
ōrdō, ōrdinis, *m.*, rank, class, order. L.A. 27
orior, - īrī, ortus sum, arise, begin, proceed,
   originate. L.A. 8; 15; 34 (see note p. 167,
   S.A. 8)
ōrnō (1), equip, furnish, adorn
ōrō (1), [speak], plead, beg,
   beseech, entreat. 36
ōs, ōris, *n.*, mouth, face. L.A. 4
ostendō, -ere, ostendī, ostentum,
   exhibit, show, display. 23
ōstium, -iī, *n.*, entrance, door
ōtium, -iī, *n.*, leisure, peace. 4
ovis, -is, *f.*, sheep

P

paedagōgus, -ī, *m.*, slave who attended
   children, particularly at school
pāgānus, -ī, *m.*, a countryman, peasant; pagan
palam, *adv.*, openly, plainly
palma, -ae, *f.*, palm
pānis, -is, *m.*, bread
pār, *gen.* **paris**, *adj.*, equal, like. 32 R.
parcō, -ere, pepercī, parsūrus + *dat.*,
   be lenient to, spare. 35
parēns, -entis, *m./f.*, parent. L.A. 19
pāreō, -ēre, -uī + *dat.*, be obedient to, obey. 35
pariēs, -ietis, *m.*, wall
pariō, -ere, peperī, partum, beget, produce
parmula, -ae, *f.*, little shield
parō (1), prepare, provide, get, obtain. 19
pars, partis, *f.*, part, share; direction. 14
parum, *adv.*, little, too little, not very
   (much) (*comp.* **minus;** *superl.* **minimē**)
parvus, -a, -um, small, little, 4
   (*comp.* **minor;** *superl.* **minimus,** 27)
passer, -eris, *m.*, sparrow
patefaciō, -ere, -fēcī, -factum,
   make open, open; disclose, expose
pateō, -ēre, patuī, lie open, be open,
   be accessible, be evident. 32 R.
pater, -tris, *m.*, father. 15
patiēns, *gen.* **-ntis**, *adj.*, patient;
   + *gen.*, capable of enduring
patientia, -ae, *f.*, suffering, patience, endurance
patior, patī, passus sum, suffer, endure,
   permit. 34
patria, -ae, *f.*, fatherland,
   native land, (one's) country. 2
patrōnus, -ī, *m.*, patron, protector
paucī, -ae, -a, *adj. usu. in plu.*, few, a few. 3
pauper, *gen.*, **pauperis**, *adj.*,
   of small means, poor. 32 R.
paupertās, -tātis, *f.*, poverty,
   humble circumstances
pāx, pācis, *f.*, peace. 7
peccō (1), sin, do wrong
pectus, -toris, *n.*, breast, heart. 35 (S.A. 13)
pecūnia, -ae, *f.*, money. 2
peior. *See* **malus.**
pellō, -ere, pepulī, pulsum, strike, push, drive
   out. 24
per, *prep.* + *acc.*, through. 13
percipiō, -ere, -cēpī, -ceptum, gain, learn,
   perceive

perdō, -ere, perdidī, perditum, destroy, ruin, lose. L.A. 2

pereō, -īre, -iī, -itum, pass away, be destroyed, perish. 37

perfectus, -a, -um, complete, perfect

perferō, -ferre, -tulī, -lātum, bear, endure, suffer

perficiō, -ere, -fēcī, -fectum, do thoroughly, accomplish, bring about. L.A. 4

perīculōsus, -a, -um, dangerous

perīculum, - ī, *n.,* danger, risk. 4

perimō, -ere, perēmī, -ēmptum, destroy

perītus, -a, -um, skilled, expert

permittō, -ere, -mīsī, -missum, permit, allow

perniciōsus, -a, -um, destructive, pernicious

perpetuus, -a, -um, perpetual, lasting, uninterrupted, continuous. 6

perscrībō, -ere, -scrīpsī, -scriptum, write out, place on record

persequor, -ī, -secūtus sum, follow up, pursue, take vengeance on

Persicus, -a, -um, Persian

persuādeō, -ēre, -suāsī, -suāsum + *dat.,* make sweet to, persuade, 35; *+ dat. + ut,* 36

perterreō, -ēre, -uī, -itum, frighten thoroughly, terrify

pertineō, -ēre, -uī, -tentum, pertain to, relate to, concern

perturbō (1), throw into confusion, trouble, disturb, perturb

perveniō, -īre, -vēnī, -ventum + *ad,* come through to, arrive at, reach

pēs, pedis, *m.,* foot. 38 R.

pessimus. *See* **malus.**

pestis, -is, *f.,* plague, pestilence, curse, destruction

petō, -ere, petīvī, petītum, seek, aim at, beg, beseech, 23; **petō ab eō ut +** *subj.* 36

philosophia, -ae, *f.,* philosophy, love of wisdom. 2 R.

philosophus, -ī, *m.,* philosopher

piger, -gra, -grum, lazy, slow, dull

pīpiō (1), chirp, pipe

piscātor, -ōris, *m.,* fisherman

piscis, -is, *m.,* fish

placeō, -ēre, placuī, placitum + *dat.,* be pleasing to, please. 35

plācō (1), placate, appease

plānē, *adv.,* plainly, clearly

platea, -ae, *f.,* broad way, street

Platō, -ōnis, *m.,* the renowned Greek philosopher

plēbs, plēbis, *f.,* the common people, populace, plebeians

plēnus, -a, -um, full. 33 R.

plūrimus. *See* **multus.**

plūs. *See* **multus.**

poēma, -atis, *n.,* poem

poena, -ae, *f.,* penalty, punishment, 2 R.; **poenās dare,** pay the penalty

poēta, -ae, *m.,* poet

pōmum, -ī, *n.,* fruit, apple

pōnō, -ere, posuī, positum, put, place, set. 30

pōns, pontis, *m.,* bridge

populus, -ī, *m.,* the people, a people, nation. 3

porta, -ae, *f.,* gate, entrance

possessiō, -ōnis, *f.,* possession, property

possum, posse, potuī, be able, can, have power

post, *prep. + acc.,* after, behind. 7

posteā, *adv.,* afterwards. L.A. 13

postpōnō, -ere, -posuī, -positum, put after, consider secondary

postquam, *conj.,* after

potēns, *gen.* **-entis,** *pres. part. of* **possum** *as adj.,* able, powerful, mighty, strong. 26

potestās, -tātis, *f.,* power, ability, opportunity. L.A. 9; 27

potior, -īrī, potītus sum + *gen. or abl.,* get possession of, possess, hold. L.A. 10

potius, *adv.,* rather, preferably

praeceptum, -ī, *n.,* precept

praeclārus, -a, -um, noble, distinguished, famous

praeferō, -ferre, -tulī, -lātum, bear before, display; place before, prefer

praeficiō, -ere, -fēcī, -fectum, put in charge of

praemittō, -ere, -mīsī, -missum, send ahead *or* forward

praemium, -iī, *n.,* reward, prize. 35 R.

praesidium, -iī, *n.,* guard, detachment, protection

praestō, -āre, -stitī, -stitum, excel *(+ dat.);* exhibit, show, offer, supply. 28

praesum, -esse, -fuī, be at the head of, be in charge of

praetereō, -īre, -iī, -itum, go by, pass, omit

praeteritus, -a, -um, *perf. part. of* **praetereō** *as adj.,* past

premō, -ere, pressī, pressum, press, press hard, pursue. 23

pretium, -iī, *n.,* price, value, reward

prex, precis, *f.,* prayer

prīmō, *adv.,* at first, first, at the beginning. 30 R.

prīmum, *adv.,* first, in the first place; **quam prīmum,** as soon as possible prīmus. *See* prior. 27

prīnceps, -cipis, *adj. or n.*, chief. L.A. 26

prīncipium, -iī, *n.*, beginning

prior, prius, *compar. adj.*, former, prior;
  prīmus, -a, -um, first, foremost, chief,
  principal. 27

prius, *adv.*, before, previously

prīvātus, -ī, *m.*, private citizen

prīvō (1), deprive

prō, *prep. + abl.*, in front of, before, on behalf
  of, in return for, instead of, for, as. 26

probitās, -tātis, *f.*, uprightness, honesty, probity

probō (1), test; approve, recommend

prōcōnsul, -ulis, *m.*, proconsul,
  governor of a province

prōditor, -ōris, *m.*, betrayer, traitor

proelium, -iī, *n.*, battle. L.A. 13

prōferō, -ferre, -tulī, -lātum, bring forward,
  produce, make known, extend

proficīscor, -ī, profectus sum, set out, start. 34

profor, -ārī, -ātus sum, speak out

prōfundō, -ere, -fūdī, -fūsum, pour forth

prohibeō, -ēre, -hibuī, -hibitum, prevent,
  hinder, restrain, prohibit. 32 R.

prōiciō, -ere, -iēcī, -iectum, throw forward
  or out

prōnūntiō (1), proclaim, announce; declaim

prōpōnō, -ere, -posuī, -positum,
  put forward, propose

proprius, -a, -um, one's own, peculiar, proper,
  personal, characteristic. L.A. 10

propter, *prep. + acc.*, on account of, because of. 5

prōvideō, -ēre, -vīdī, -vīsum,
  foresee, provide, make provision

proximus, -a, -um (*superl. of*
  propior), nearest, next

prūdēns, *gen.* -entis, *adj.*, wise, prudent

prūdenter, wisely, discreetly

prūdentia, -ae, *f.*, foresight, wisdom, discretion

pūblicus, -a, -um, of the people, public;
  rēs pūblica, reī pūblicae, *f.*, the state

pudīcus, -a, -um, modest, chaste

pudor, -ōris, *m.*, modesty, bashfulness

puella, -ae, *f.*, girl. 2

puer, puerī, *m.*, boy. 3

puerīliter, *adv.*, childishly, foolishly

pugna, -ae, *f.*, fight, battle

pugnō (1), fight. L.A. 5

pulcher, -chra, -chrum,
  beautiful, handsome; fine. 5; 27

pulchrē, *adv.*, beautifully, finely

pulchritūdō, -dinis, *f.*, beauty

pūniō, -īre, - īvī, -ītum, punish

pūrgō (1), cleanse

pūrus, -a, -um, pure, free from

putō (1), reckon, suppose, judge,
  think, imagine. 25

Pȳthagorās, -ae, *m.*, Greek philosopher and
  mathematician of 6th cen. B.C.

Q

quā, *adv.*, by which route, where. L.A. 13

quadrāgintā, *indecl. adj.*, forty

quaerō, -ere, quaesīvī, quaesītum, seek
  look for, strive for; ask, inquire. 24

quam, *adv. and conj.*, how, 16 R.; than, 26;
  as...as possible (*with superl.*), 26

quamvīs, *adv. and conj.*, however much,
  however; although

quandō, *interrog. and rel. adv. and conj.*,
  when; sī quandō, if ever

quantus, -a, -um, how large,
  how great, how much. 30

quārē, *adv.*, because of which
  thing, wherefore, why. 38

quārtus, -a, -um, fourth

quasi, *adv. and conj.*, as if, as it were. 39

quattuor, *indecl. adj.*, four

-que, *enclitic conj.*, and. *It is appended to
  the second of two words to be joined.* 6

quemadmodum, *adv.*, in what manner, how.
  L.A. 18

queror, -ī, questus sum, complain, lament.
  L.A. 11

quī, quae, quod, *rel. pron.*, who, which, what,
  that. 17

quī? quae? quod?, *interrog. adj.*, what?
  which? what kind of? 19

quid, what. *See* quis.

quīdam, quaedam, quiddam (*pron.*) *or*
  quoddam (*adj.*), *indef. pron. and adj.*:
  as pron., a certain one *or* thing, someone,
  something; *as adj.*, a certain. 26

quidem, *postpositive adv.*, indeed,
  certainly, at least, even;
  nē...quidem, not even. 29

quiēs, -ētis, *f.*, quiet, rest, peace. L.A. 18

quīn etiam, *adv.*, why even,
  in fact, moreover

Quīntus, -ī, *m.*, Roman praenomen,
  abbreviated to Q. in writing.

quis? quid?, *interrog. pron.,*
who? what? which? 19

quis, quid, *indef. pron., after* **sī, nisi, nē,** *and*
num, anyone, anything, someone,
something. 33

quisquam, quidquam (*or* **quicquam**),
indef. pron. and adj., anyone,
anything. L.A. 7; 14

quisque, quidque, *indef. pron.,* each one,
each person. 24

quisquis, quidquid, *indef. pron.,*
whoever, whatever. L.A. 29

quō, *adv.,* to which *or* what place,
whither, where. L.A. 2

quod, *conj.,* because. 21

quōmodo, *adv.,* in what way, how

quondam, *adv.,* formerly, once. 22 R.

quoniam, *conj.,* since. 15

quoque, *adv.,* also, too. L.A. 13

quot, *indecl. adj.,* how many, as many

quotiēnscumque, *adv.,* however often, whenever

R

rapiō, -ere, rapuī, raptum, seize,
snatch, carry away. 21

rārus, -a, -um, rare

ratiō, ōnis, *f.,* reckoning, account;
reason, judgment, consideration;
system, manner, method. 8

recēdō, -ere, -cessī, -cessum, go back, retire,
recede

recipiō, -ere, -cēpī, -ceptum, take back,
regain, admit, receive. 24

recitō (1), read aloud, recite

recognōscō, -ere, -nōvī, -nōtum, recognize,
recollect

recordātiō, -ōnis, *f.,* recollection

recreō (1), restore, revive

rēctus, -a, -um, straight, right; **rēctum, -ī,** *n.,*
the right, virtue

recuperātiō, -ōnis, *f.,* recovery

recuperō (1), regain

recūsō (1), refuse

reddō, -ere, -didī, -ditum, give back, return.
L.A. 25

redeō, -īre, -iī, -itum, go back, return. 37

redūcō, -ere, -dūxī, -ductum, lead back, bring
back

rēgius, -a, -um, royal

rēgnum, -ī, *n.,* rule, authority, kingdom. L.A. 25

regō, -ere, rēxī, rēctum, rule, guide, direct

relegō, -ere, -lēgī, lēctum, read again, reread

relevō, (1), relieve, alleviate, diminish

relinquō, -ere, -līquī, -lictum, leave
behind, leave, abandon. 24

remaneō, -ēre, -mānsī, -mānsum, remain,
stay behind, abide, continue. 5

remedium, -iī, *n.,* cure, remedy. 26 R.

removeō, -ēre, -mōvī, -mōtum, remove. L.A. 6

reperiō, -īre, repperī, repertum, find,
discover, learn, get. 40

repetītiō, -ōnis, *f.,* repetition

repetō, -ere, -īvī, -ītum, seek again, repeat

rēpō, -ere, rēpsī, rēptum, creep, crawl

repugnō (1) + *dat.,* fight against, be incompatible
with

requiēscō, -ere, -quiēvī, -quiētum, rest

requīrō, -ere, -quīsīvī, -sītum, seek, ask for,
miss, need, require. L.A. 2

rēs, reī, *f.,* thing, matter, business, affair; **rēs
pūblica, reī pūblicae,** state, commonwealth. 22

resistō, -ere, -stitī, make a
stand, resist, oppose

**respondeō, -ēre, -spondī,
-spōnsum,** answer. 31

restituō, -ere, -stituī, -stitūtum, restore

retrahō, -ere, -trāxī, -tractum,
drag *or* draw back

reveniō, -īre, -vēnī, -ventum,
come back, return

revertor, -ī, -vertī (*perf. is act.*),
-versus sum, return

revocō (1), call back, recall

rēx, rēgis, *m.* king. 12

rhētoricus, -a, -um, of rhetoric, rhetorical

rideō , -ēre, rīsī, rīsum, laugh, laugh at. 24 R.

rogō (1), ask, ask for, 30;
rogō eum ut + *subj.,* 36

Rōma, -ae, *f.,* Rome. 37

Rōmānus, -a, -um, Roman. 3

rōstrum, -ī, *n.,* beak of a ship;
rōstra, -ōrum, the rostra, speaker's platform

rota, -ae, *f.,* wheel

rotundus, -a, -um, wheel-shaped, round

rūmor, -ōris, *m.,* rumor, gossip

ruō, -ere, ruī, rutum, rush, fall, be ruined

rūs, rūris, *n.,* the country (opposite of city)

rūsticus, -a, -um, rustic, rural

S

sabbatum, -ī, *n.*, the Sabbath

sacculus, -ī, *n.*, little bag, purse

sacrificium, -iī, *n.*, sacrifice

sacrilegus, -a, -um, sacrilegious, impious

saepe, *adv.*, often. 1

saeta equīna, -ae -ae, *f.*, horse-hair

sagitta, -ae, *f.*, arrow

sāl, salis, *m.*, salt; wit

salsus, -a, -um, salty, witty

salūbris, -e, healthy, salubrious

salūs, salūtis, *f.*, health, safety;
    greeting. 33

salūtō (1), greet

salveō, -ēre, be well, be in good health

salvus, -a , -um, safe, sound

sānctificō (1), sanctify, treat as holy

sānctus, -a, -um, sacred, holy

sānitās, -tātis, *f.*, health,
    soundness of mind, sanity

sānō (1), heal

sānus, -a, -um, sound, healthy, sane

sapiēns, *gen.* -entis, *adj.*, wise, judicious;
    as a noun, a wise man, philosopher. 27

sapienter, *adv.*, wisely, sensibly. 32

sapientia, -ae, *f.*, wisdom. 3

satiō (1), satisfy, sate

satis, *indecl. noun, adj., and adv.*,
    enough, sufficient(ly). 5

satura, -ae, *f.*, satire

scabiēs, -ēī, *f.*, the itch, mange

scelerātus, -a, -um, criminal, wicked, accursed

scelestus, -a, -um, wicked, accursed, infamous

scelus, sceleris, *n.*, evil deed,
    crime, sin, wickedness. 20

schola, -ae, *f.*, school

scientia, -ae, *f.*, knowledge, science, skill. 32 R.

sciō, scīre, scīvī, scītum, know. 21

scrībō , -ere, scrīpsī, scrīptum, write, compose. 8

scriptor, -ōris, *m.*, writer, author

sēcernō, -ere, -crēvī, -crētum, separate. L.A. 14

secundus, -a , -um, second; favorable. L.A. 9

sēcūrus, -a, -um, free from care, untroubled, safe

sed, *conj.*, but. 6

sedeō, -ēre, sēdī, sessum, sit. L.A. 29

sēductor, -ōris, *m. (ecclesiastical Lat.)*, seducer

semel, *adv.*, once

semper, *adv.*, always. 3

senātor, -ōris, *m.*, senator

senātus, -ūs, *m.*, senate. 20

senectūs, -tūtis, *f.*, old age. 10 R.

senex, senis, *adj. and n.*, old, aged; old man. 19

sēnsus, -ūs, *m.*, feeling, sense. 40

sententia, -ae, *f.*, feeling, thought,
    opinion, vote, sentence. 14

sentiō, -īre, sēnsī, sēnsum, feel,
    perceive, think, experience. 11

septem, *indecl. adj.*, seven

sepulchrum, -ī, *n.*, grave, tomb

sequor, sequī, secūtus sum, follow. 34

sēriō, *adv.*, seriously

sērius, -a, -um, serious, grave

sermō, -ōnis, *m.*, conversation, talk

serō, -ere, sēvī, satum, sow

serviō, -īre, -īvī, -ītum + *dat.*,
    be a slave to, serve. 35

servitūs, -tūtis, *f.*, servitude, slavery. 20

servō (1), preserve, keep, save, guard. 1

servus, -ī, *m.*, slave. 24

sevēritās, -tātis, *f.*, severity, sternness, strictness

sī, *conj.*, if. 1; 33

sīc, *adv. (most commonly with verbs)*, so, thus. 29

sīcut, *adv. and conj.*, as, just as,
    as it were. L.A. 25

sīdus, -eris, *n.*, constellation, star

signum, -ī, *n.*, sign, signal, indication, seal. 23

silentium, -iī, *n.*, silence

silva, -ae, *f.*, forest, wood. L.A. 14; 15

similis, -e, similar, like, resembling. 27

simplex, *gen.* -plicis, *adj.*, simple, unaffected

simulātiō, -ōnis, *f.*, pretense

sine, *prep. + abl.*, without. 2

singulī, -ae, -a (*plu.*), one each, single, separate

singultim, *adv.*, stammeringly

sitiō, -īre, -īvī, be thirsty

socius, -iī, *m.*, companion, ally

Sōcratēs, -is, *m.*, Socrates

sōl, sōlis, *m.*, sun. 27

soleō, -ēre, solitus sum, be accustomed. 37

sōlitūdō, -inis, *f.*, solitude, loneliness

sollicitō (1), stir up, arouse, incite

sollicitūdō, -inis, *f.*, anxiety, concern, solicitude

sollicitus, -a, -um, troubled, anxious, disturbed

Solōn, -ōnis, *m.*, Athenian sage and
    statesman of the 7th-6th cen. B.C.

sōlum, *adv.*, only, merely; **nōn sōlum...sed etiam,**
    not only...but also. 9

sōlus, -a, -um, alone, only, the only. 9

somnus, -ī, *m.*, sleep. L.A. 15; 27

Sophoclēs, -is, *m.*, one of the three
    greatest writers of Greek tragedy

sopor, -ōris, *m.,* deep sleep

sordēs, -lum, *f. plu.,* filth; meanness, stinginess

spargō, -ere, sparsī, sparsum, scatter, spread, strew

spectāculum, -ī, *n.,* spectacle, show

spectō (1), look at, see

spernō, -ere, sprēvī, sprētum, scorn, despise, spurn

spērō (1), hope for, hope. 25

spēs, -eī, *f.,* hope. 22

spīritus, -ūs, *m.,* breath, breathing

stabilis, -e, stable, steadfast

stadium, -iī, *n.,* stadium

statim, *adv.,* immediately, at once. L.A. 27; 29

statua, -ae, *f.,* statue

stēlla, -ae, *f.,* star. L.A. 26

stilus, -ī, *m.,* stilus (for writing)

stō, stāre, stetī, statum, stand, stand still *or* firm. L.A. 4; 18

studeō, -ēre, studuī + *dat.,* direct one's zeal to, be eager for, study. 35

studiōsus, -a, -um, full of zeal, eager, fond of

studium, -iī, *n.,* eagerness, zeal, pursuit, study. 19

stultus, -a, -um, foolish; **stultus, -ī,** *m.,* a fool. 4

sub, *prep.* + *abl. with verbs of rest,* + *acc. with verbs of motion,* under, up under, close to. 7 R.

subitō, *adv.,* suddenly

subitus, -a, -um, sudden

subiungō, -ere, -iūnxī, -iūnctum, subject, subdue

succurrō, -ere, -currī, -cursum, run up under, help

sufficiō, -ere, -fēcī, -fectum, be sufficient, suffice

sui (sibi, sē, sē), *reflex. pron. of 3rd per.,* himself, herself, itself, themselves. 13

sum, esse, fuī, futūrus, be, exist. 4; **est, sunt** *may mean* there is, there are

summa, -ae, *f.,* highest part, sum, whole

summus, -a, -um. *See* **superus.**

sūmō, -ere, sūmpsī, sūmptum, take, take up, assume

sūmptus, -ūs, *m.,* expense, cost

supellex, supellectilis, *f.,* furniture, apparatus

superbus, -a, -um, overbearing, haughty, proud

superior. *See* **superus.**

superō (1), be above, have the upper hand, surpass, overcome, conquer. 5

superus, -a, -um, above, upper; *comp.* **superior, -ius,** higher; *superl.* **suprēmus, -a, -um,** last, *or* **summus, -a, -um,** highest. 27

supplicium, -iī, *n.,* punishment

suprā, *adv. and prep.* + *acc.,* above. L.A. 7

suprēmus. *See* **superus.**

surculus, -ī, *m.,* shoot, sprout

surgō, -ere, surrēxī, surrēctum, get up, arise

suscipiō, -ere, -cēpī, -ceptum, undertake. 33

suspendō, -ere, -pendī, pēnsum, hang up, suspend

sustineō, -ēre,- tinuī, -tentum, hold up, sustain, endure

suus, -a, -um, *reflex. poss. adj.,* his own, her own, its own, their own. 13

synagōga, -ae, *f.,* synagogue

Syrācūsae, -ārum, *f. plu.,* Syracuse. 37

T

tabella, -ae, *f.,* writing tablet; **tabellae, -ārum** (*plu.*), letter, document

taceō, -ēre, -uī, -itum, be silent, leave unmentioned

tālis, -e, such, of such a sort

tam, *adv. used with adjs. and advs.,* so, to such a degree. 29

tamen, *adv.,* nevertheless, still. 31

tamquam, *adv.,* as it were, as if, so to speak

tandem, *adv.,* at last, finally. L.A. 13

tangō, -ere, tetigī, tāctum, touch. 21 R.

tantum, *adv.,* only

tantus, -a, -um, so large, so great, of such size. 29

tardus, -a, -um, slow, tardy

tegō, -ere, tēxī, tēctum, cover, hide, protect

temeritās, -tātis, *f.,* rashness, temerity

temperantia, -ae, *f.,* moderation, temperance, self-control. L.A. 6

tempestās, -tātis, *f.,* weather, storm

templum, -ī, *n.,* sacred area, temple

temptātiō, -ōnis, *f.,* trial, temptation

tempus, -oris, *n.,* time. 7

tendō, -ere, tetendī, tentum, *or* **tēnsum,** stretch, extend; go

teneō, -ēre, tenuī, tentum, hold, keep, possess, restrain. 14

terō, -ere, trīvī, trītum, rub, wear out

terra, -ae, *f.,* earth, ground, land, country. 7

terreō, -ēre, -uī, -itum, frighten, terrify. 18

tertius, -a, -um, third

thema, -matis, *n.,* theme

Themistoclēs, -is, *m.,* Themistocles, celebrated Athenian statesman and military leader who advocated a powerful navy at the time of the Persian Wars

timeō, -ēre, timuī, fear, be afraid, be afraid of. 15

timor, -ōris, *m.*, fear. 36

titulus, -ī, *m.*, label, title; placard

toga, -ae, *f.*, toga, the garb of peace

tolerō (1), bear, endure, tolerate. 6 R.

tollō, -ere, sustulī, sublātum, raise, lift up, take away, remove, destroy. 22

tondeō, -ēre, totondī, tōnsum, shear; clip

tōnsor, -ōris, *m.*, barber

tōnsōrius, -a, -um, of *or* pertaining to a barber, barber's

tot, *indecl. adj.*, so many. 40

tōtus, -a, -um (*gen.* tōtius), whole, entire. 9

tractō (1), drag about; handle, treat, discuss

trādō, -ere, trādidī, trāditum, give over, surrender, hand down, transmit, teach. 33

tragoedia, -ae, *f.*, tragedy

trahō, -ere, trāxī, tractum, drag; derive, get. 14 R.

trāns, *prep.* + *acc.*, across. 14 R.

trānseō, -īre, -iī, -itum, go across, cross

trānsferō, -ferre, -tulī, -lātum, bear across, transfer, convey. L.A. 19

trēdecim, *indecl. adj.*, thirteen

tremō, -ere, -uī, tremble

trepidē, *adv.*, with trepidation, in confusion

trēs, tria, three

trigintā, *indecl. adj.*, thirty

trīstis, -e, sad. L.A. 29

triumphus, -ī, *m.*, triumphal procession, triumph

Troia, -ae, *f.*, Troy

Troiānus, -a, -um, Trojan

tū, tuī, you. 11

Tullius, -iī, *m.*, Cicero's *nomen*

tum, *adv.*, then, at that time; thereupon, in the next place. 5

tumultus, -ūs, *m.*, uprising, disturbance

tumulus, -ī, *m.*, mound, tomb

tunc, *adv.*, then, at that time

turba, -ae, *f.*, uproar, disturbance, mob, crowd, multitude

turpis, -e, ugly, shameful, base, disgraceful. 26

tūtus, -a, -um, protected, safe, secure. L.A. 15

tuus, -a, -um, your, yours (*sing.*). 2; 4

tyrannus, -ī, *m.*, absolute ruler, tyrant. 6

U

ubi, *rel. adv. and conj.*, where; when; *interrog.*, where? 6

ulcīscor, -ī, ultus sum, avenge, punish for wrong done

ūllus, -a, -um, any. 9; 33

ultrā, *adv. and prep.* + *acc.*, on the other side, beyond

umbra, -ae, *f.*, shade

umerus, -ī, *m.*, shoulder, upper arm

umquam, *adv.*, ever, at any time. 23

unde, *adv.*, whence, from what *or* which place; from which, from whom. 30 R.

ūnus, -a, -um (*gen.* ūnius), one, single, alone. 9

urbānus, -a, -um, of the city, urban, urbane

urbs, urbis, *f.*, city. 14

ūsque, *adv.*, all the way, up (to), even (to). L.A. 8; 13

ūsus, -ūs, *m.*, use, experience, skill, advantage

ut, *conj.; A. with subjunctive, introducing* (1) *purpose, in order that, that to* (28); (2) *result, so that, that* (29); (3) *jussive noun clauses, to, that* (36); *B. with indicative, when, as* (37)

uter, utra, utrum, which (of two)

ūtilis, -e, useful, advantageous

ūtilitās, -tātis, *f.*, usefulness, advantage

ūtor, ūtī, ūsus sum, + *abl.*, use; enjoy, experience. 34

utrum...an, *adv. and conj.*, whether...or. L.A. 15

uxor, -ōris, *f.*, wife

V

vacō (1), be free from, be unoccupied

vacuus, -a, -um, empty devoid (of), free (from)

vae, *interjection*, alas, woe to

valeō, -ēre, valuī, valitūrus, be strong, have power; be well, fare well; valē (valēte), good-bye. 1

valētūdō, -dinis, *f.*, health, good health, bad health

varius, -a, -um, various, varied, different. L.A. 18

vehemēns, *gen.* -entis, *adj.*, violent, vehement, emphatic, vigorous

vehō, -ere, vexī, vectum, carry, convey

vel, *conj.*, or (*an optional alternative*). L.A. 17

vēlōx, *gen.* -ōcis, *adj.*, swift

venia, -ae, *f.*, kindness, favor, pardon

veniō, -īre, vēnī, ventum, come. 10

ventitō (1), come often

ventus, -ī, *m.*, wind

Venus, -eris, *f.*, Venus, goddess of grace, charm, and love

verbera, -um, *n., plu.*, blows, a beating

verbum, -ī, *n.* word. 28

vērē, *adv.*, truly, really, actually, rightly. L.A. 3

Vergilius, -iī, *m.*, Virgil

vēritās, -tātis, *f.*, truth. 17
vērō, *adv.*, in truth, indeed,
  to be sure, however. L.A. 5
versus, -ūs, *m.*, line, verse. 20
vertō, -ere, vertī, versum, turn, change. 23
vērus, -a, -um, true, real, proper
vesper, -eris *or* -erī, *m.*, evening star,
  evening
vespillō, -ōnis, *m.*, undertaker
vester, vestra, vestrum, your, yours (*plu.*). 6
vestiō, -īre, -īvī, -ītum, clothe
vetus, *gen.* veteris, *adj.*, old. 39
via, -ae, *f.*, road, street, way. 10
vīcīnus, -ī, *m.*, neighbor
vicissitūdō, -dinis, *f.*, change, vicissitude
victor, -ōris, *m.*, victor
victōria, -ae, *f.*, victory
victus, -ūs, *m.*, living, mode of life
videō, -ēre, vīdī, vīsum, see, observe;
  understand, 1; videor, -ērī, vīsus sum, be seen,
  seem, 18
vigilō (1), be awake, watch, be vigilant
vigor, -ōris, *m.*, vigor, liveliness
villa, -ae, *f.*, villa, country house
vincō, -ere, vīcī, victum, conquer, overcome
vinculum, -ī, *n.*, bond, fetter
vinum, -ī, *n.*, wine. 31 R.

vir, virī, *m.*, man, hero, a person of courage,
  honor, and nobility. 3
virgō, -ginis, *f.*, maiden, virgin. 7
virtūs, virtūtis, *f.*, manliness, courage,
  excellence, virtue, character, worth. 7
vīs, vīs, *f.*, force, power, violence;
  plu. vīrēs, vīrium, strength. 14
vīta, -ae, *f.*, life, mode of life. 2
vitiōsus, -a, -um, full of vice, vicious
vitium, -iī, *n.*, fault, vice, crime. 6
vītō (1), avoid, shun. 26
vīvō, -ere, vīxī, vīctum, live. 10
vix, *adv.*, hardly, scarcely, with difficulty. L.A. 13
vocō (1), call, summon. 1
volō, velle, voluī, wish, be willing, will. 32
volō (1), fly
voluntārius, -a, -um, voluntary
voluntās, -tātis, *f.*, will, wish. L.A. 25
voluptās, -tātis, *f.*, pleasure
vōx, vōcis, *f.*, voice, word. 39
vulgus, -ī, *n.*, the common people, mob, rabble
vulnus, vulneris, *n.*, wound

X

Xenophōn, -ontis, *m.*, Xenophon,
  Greek general and author

Abbreviations of Authors and Works

Caes., Caesar
  B.C., Bellum Civile
  B.G., Bellum Gallicum
Catull., Catullus (Poems)
Cic., Cicero
  Am., De Amicitia
  Arch., Oratio pro Archia
  Att., Epistulae ad Atticum
  Cat., Orationes in Catilinam
  De Or., De Oratore
  Div., De Divinatione
  Fam., Epistulae ad Familiares
  Fin., De Finibus
  Inv., De Inventione Rhetorica
  Leg., De Legibus
  Marcell, Oratio pro Marcello
  Off., De Officiis
  Or., Orator
  Phil., Orationes Philippicae in M. Antonium
  Pis., Oratio in Pisonem
  Q. Fr., Epistulae ad Q. Fratrem
  Rep., De Re Publica
  Sen., De Senectute
  Sex. Rosc., Oratio pro Sex. Roscio
  Sull., Oratio pro Sulla
  Tusc., Tusculanae Disputationes
  Verr., Actio in Verrem
Enn., Ennius (poet)

Hor., Horace
  A.P., Ars Poetica (Ep. 2.3)
  Ep., Epistulae, Epistles
  Epod., Epodes
  Od., Odes (Carmina)
  Sat., Satires
Juv., Juvenal (Satires)
Liv., Livy (Ab Urbe Condita)
Lucr., Lucretius
  (De Natura Rerum)
Mart., Martial (Epigrams)
Macr., Macrobius (Saturnalia)
Nep., Nepos
  Att., Atticus
  Cim., Cimon
  Milt., Miltiades
Ov., Ovid
  A. A., Ars Amatoria
  Am., Amores
  Her., Heroides
  Met., Metamorphoses
Pers., Persius (Satires)
Phaedr., Phaedrus (Fables)
Plaut., Plautus
  Aul., Aulularia
  Mil., Miles Gloriosus
  Most., Mostellaria
  Stich., Stichus

Plin., Pliny the Elder
  H. N., Historia Naturalis
Plin., Pliny the Younger
  Ep., Epistulae, Letters
Publil. Syr., Publilius Syrus (*Sententia*)
Quint., Quintilian
  Inst., Institutiones Oratoriae
Sall., Sallust
  Cat., Catilina
Sen., Seneca (rhetorician)
  Contr., Controversiae
Sen., Seneca (philosopher)
  Brev. Vit., De Brevitate Vitae
  Clem., De Clementia
  Cons. Polyb., Ad Polybium De
  Consolatione
  Ep., Epistulae
Suet., Suetonius
  Aug., Octavius Augustus Caesar
  Caes., Julius Caesar
Tac., Tacitus

Ann., Annales
Dial., Dialogus de Oratoribus
Ter., Terence
  Ad., Adelphi
  And., Andria
  Heaut., Heauton Timorumenos
  Hec., Hecyra
  Phorm., Phormio
Veg., Vegetius Renatus
  Mil., De Re Militari
Vell., Velleius Paterculus (hist.)
Virg., Virgil
  Aen., Aeneid
  Ecl., Eclogues
  Geor., Georgics
Vulg., Vulgate
  Exod., Exodus
  Gen., Genesis
  Job, Job

Index

References are to pages, unless otherwise stated; n. = note(s). For summary of forms see Appendix, pp. 362–374.

A

Ablative
  with **ab** after **petō** and **quaerō**, 177 n. 1
  absolute, 111 and 115 n. 3, 112; various meanings of, 115 n. 2
  of accompaniment, 66, 102, 115 n. 1; without **cum**, 243 n. 105
  of accordance, 168 n. 6, 209 #10 n. 10, 240 #5 n. 23
  as adverbial case, 7 and 11 n. 3
  of agent, 85; agent and means contrasted, 85, 102
  of attendant circumstance, 115 n. 1, 242 n. 160–161
  of cause, 359
  of comparison, 359
  of degree of difference, 359
  with **dē** or **ex** after cardinal numerals, 192
  with deponent verbs (**ūtor**, etc.), 165
  of description or quality, 360
  forms of. *See* Declension.
  of manner, 66, 102
  meanings of, common, 7 and 11 n. 5, 16 n. 1
  of means or instrument, 66, 102, 115 n. 1
  of penalty, 256 n. 20
  of place from which, 94, 102, 180; for **domō**, 179; with names of cities or towns, 179
  of place where, 102, 179
  without a preposition, 65
  with prepositions, 7
  of separation, 94, 102
  of specification, 156 (notes on reading), 358
  table of constructions with, 102
  of time when or within which, 71, 102, 180
  of way by which (= means), 181 S.A. 7, 209 #12 n. 8
Accent, 5 n. 4
Accompaniment, ablative of, 66, 102, 115 n. 1; without **cum**, 243 n. 105

Accordance, ablative of, 168 n. 8
Accusative
  as direct object of verb, 7
  of duration of time, 180
  of exclamation, 240 #6 n. 28, 262 #33 n. 30
  forms of. *See* Declension.
  as object of certain prepositions, 7
  of place to which with **ad** or **in**, 179; for **domum**, 180; with names of cities and towns, 179
  predicate, 67 sent. 1 and 69 n. 6
  as subject of infinitive, 117
  two accusatives of person and thing (e.g., with **doceō**), 208 #6 n. 12
Active voice, 84. *See also* Voice.
Adjectives
  agreement of, with noun, 8, 18
  comparison of
    irregular, 127–128; English derivatives, 130
    with **-limus** or **-rimus** in superlative, 127 and 131 n. 1
    meaning of comparative, 123, 124
    meaning of superlative, 123, 124, 156 n. 1; with **quam**, 124 Vocab.
    regular, 122; with **magis** and **maximē**, 126 n. 1
  with dative, 358
  declension of
    1st, 8, 18, 24, 40–41
    2nd, 13, 18, 24, 40–41
    3rd, 75–76
    comparatives, 123 n. 3
    -er adjs. of 1st and 2nd decl., 24 and 26 n. 2
    with genitive in **-ius**, 40–41
    present participles (verbal adjectives), 107 n. 6, 110
  definition and attributive use of, 8
  with genitive (**plēnus**), 72 sent. 3
  numerals, 193–194

Verb (*cont'd*)
    expression, Semi-deponent verbs, Stems, Tense, Voice.
vereor nē or **ut** + subjunctive, 360–361
vestrī, vestrum, pronouns, use of, 52 n. 4
Virgil, xx, 203
vīs, irregular noun of 3rd declension, 64
vōbīscum = cum vōbīs, 52 n. 9
Vocative:
    forms of, 7; in 2nd declension, 13, 14 and 16 n. 3; in 3rd declension, 31
    meaning and use of, 7
    of **meus fīlius** and names in **-ius,** 14
    of neuters of 2nd declension, 18
Voice:
    active, 84

Voice (*cont'd*)
    defined, 5 n. 1, 84 and 87 n. 1
    in deponents, 162–165
    passive, 84 and 87 n. 5
volō, 153–154 and 156 n. 4, 5
Vowels
    list and pronunciation of, xxiv
    long, shortened before **-t** and **-nt**, 5 n. 5
Vulgar Latin, xxvi n. 28
Vulgate, xv, xxvi n. 14, 205

W

Word order, 5 n. 10, 14-15, 258 n. 22

Location of the
Sententiae Antiquae

1. (1) Pers., Sat. 6.27. (2) Plaut., Most. 1.3.30. (3) Suet., Aug. 25 (4) Hor., Sat. 1.2.11. (5) Sen., Clem. 1.2.2. (6) Cic., Sest. 67.141. (7) Cic., Cat. 4.3. (8) Virg., Aen. 3.121 and 4.173 and 184. (9) Ter., Heaut. 190 et passim. (10) Cic., Fam. 2.16.4. (11) Hor., Sat. 1.9.78. (12) Hor., Sat. 1.10.81–83. (13) Cic., Cat. 1.12.30. (14) Cic., Inv. 1.1.1. (15) Publil. Syr., Sent. 321.

2. (1) Plaut., Stich. 5.2.2. (2) *Virg., Aen. 3.121. (3) Ter., Ad. 5.8.937. (4) Cic., Marcell. 4.12. (5) Cic., Verr. 2.4.54. (6) Hor., Sat. 2.7.22–24. (7) Sen., Ep. 8.1. (8) Sen., Ep. 17.5. (9) Cic., Fin. 3.1.2. (10) Sen., Ep. 8.5. (11) Sen., Ep. 18.14, De Ira 1.1.2; cp. Ch. 16 S.A.8. (12) Sen., Ep. 18.15. (13) Sen., Ep. 115.16. (14) Hor., Od. 3.11.45. (15) Cic., Pis. 10.22. (Vale Puella) Catull. 8.12–13.

3. (1) Cic., Cat. 4.1. (2) Hor., Sat. 2.6.41. (3) Phaedr., Fab. I. Prologus 4. (4) Cic., Tusc. 5.3.9. (5) Hor., Sat. 2.7.84 and 88. (6) Nep., Cim. 4. (7) Hor., Ep. 1.2.56. (8) Sen., Ep. 94.43. (9) Publil. Syr., Sent. 56. (10) Publil. Syr., Sent. 697. (11) Sen., Clem.1.2.2.

4. (1) Cic., Am. 15.54. (2) Ter., Heaut. 2.3.295–296. (3) Ter. Ad. 5.9.961. (4) Hor., Sat. 1.4.114. (5) Proverbial; cp. Cic., Phil. 12.2.5. (6) Hor., Od. 2.16.27–28. (7) Sen., De Ira II 18ff. and III init.; cp. Ter., Phor. 1.4.185. (8) Virg., Ecl. 5.61. (9) Hor., Sat. 1.1.25. (10) Ter., Ad. 4.5.701–702. (11) Catull. 5.7. (12) Vulgate, Ecclesiastes 1.15. (13) Cic., Am. 21.79. (14) Pers., Sat. 6.27. (15) Cic., Cat. 1.4.9.

5. (1) Cic., Cat. 1.9.23. (2) Cic., Cat. 1.13.31. (3) Cic., Off. 1.20.68. (4) Ov., Her. 3.85. (5) Cic., Fam. 14.3.1. (6) Ter., Ad. 5.8.937. (7) Ter., Ad. 5.9.992–993. (8) Cic., Att. 2.2. (9) Sen., Cons. Polyb. 9.6. (10) Ter., Ad. 5.8.937. (11) Sen., Ep. 17.5. (12) Virg., Ecl. 5.78. (13) Hor., Ep. 2.3.445–446 (Ars Poetica).

6. (1) Cic., Tusc. 5.20.57. (2) Cic., Tusc. 5.21.61. (3) Cic., Cat. 3.1.3. (4) Cic., Cat. 3.12.29. (5) Cic., Cat. 1.6.13. (6) Liv. 21.1.2. (7) Cic., Arch. 3.5. (8) Sen., Ep. 73.16. (9) Cic., Rep. 6.14 (Somnium Scipionis, Rockwood 3.6). (10) Publil. Syr. 302. (11) Liv., Preafatio 9. (12) Publil. Syr. 282.

7. (1) Ter., Heaut. 1.1.77. (2) Vulgate, Ecclesiastes 1.10. (3) Hor., Od. 3.1.2–4. (4) Hor., Sat. 2.7.22–23. (5) Hor., Ep. 1.16.52. (6) Mart. 12.6.11–12. (7) Hor., Sat. 1.6.15–16. (8) Cic.; cp. graffiti. (9) *Sen., Ep. 82.2. (10) Hor., Od. 3.1.37–40. (11) Cic., Phil. 10.10.20 (12) Hor., Sat. 1.9.59–60. (13) Cic., Cat. 3.12.29. (14) Vulgate, Luke, 2.14.

8. (1) Ter., Ad. 5.4.863. (2) Ter., Heaut. 3.1.432. (3) Laberius; see Macrobius *Saturnalia* 2.7. (4) Cic., Cat. 3.1.3. (5) Publil. Syr. 507; also Macrobius 2.7. (6) Sen., Ep. 8.3. (7) Catull. 49. (8) Liv. 26.50.1. (9) Cic., Tusc. 1.42.98. (10) Cic., Arch. 11.26. (11) Cic., Marcell. 5.15. (12) Hor., Ep. 2.2.65–66. (13) Hor., Ep. 1.2.1–2. (14) Sen., Ep. 106.12. (15) Sen., Ep. 7.8. (16) Liv. 22.39.21.

9. (1) Ter., Phor. 4.5.727. (2) Ter., Phor. 4.3.670. (3) Ter., Heaut. 4.3.709. (4) Cic., Am. 27.102. (5) Ter., Phor. 3.3.539. (6) Cic., Cat. 1.13.31. (7) Cic., Cat. 1.4.9. (8) Mart. 10.72.4. (9) Liv., 22.39.10.

10. (1) Cic., Off. 1.20.68. (2) Ter., Ad. 4.3.593. (3) Ter., Ad. 3.2.340. (4) Mart. 6.70.15. (5) Cic., Clu. 18.51. (6) Lucr. 6.93–95. (7) Pers. 5.153. (8) Hor., Epod. 13.3–4. (9) Cic., Sen. 19.67. (10) Virg., Georg. 3.284. (11) Virg., Aen. 3.395 (12) Publil. Syr. 764. (13) Cic., Am. 27.103. (14) Cic., Am. 24.89.

11. (1) Hor., Sat. 2.5.33. (2) Ter., Ad. 1.1.49. (3) Plin., Ep. 1.11.1. (4) Plin., Ep. 5.18.1. (5) Ter., Hec. 1.2.197. (6) Cic., Cat. 1.8.20. (7) Cic., Marcell. 11.33. (8) Cic., Fam. 1.5.b.2. (9) Cic., Cat. 1.5.10, 1.4.9. (10) Cic., Cat. 1.5.10. (11) Liv. 120 (see p. 224) (12) Hor., Ep. 2.2.58. (13) Mart. 12.47. (14) Cic., Am. 21.80.

12. (1) Vulgate, Genesis 1.1 and 27. (2) Suet., Caes. 37. (3) Ter., Hec. 3.5.461. (4) Cic., Sen. 19.68. (5) Sen., Brev. Vit.; see Duff, Silver Age p. 216. (6) Ter., Phor. 2.1.302. (7) Cic., Sen. 7.22. (8) Cic., Off. 1.24.84. Liberty: Tac., Ann. 1.1.1.; Laber. in Macr. Sat. 2.7. Untimely Death: Plin., Ep. 5.16.1–6; v. pp. 275–276 below.

13. (1) Caes., B.G. 1.21. (2) Cic., Sull. 24.67. (3) Cic. Cat. 3.10. (4) Cic., Am. 21.80. (5) Publil. Syr. 206. (6) Sen., Ep. 7.8. (7) Sen., Ep. 80.3. (8) Phaedr. 4.21.1.

14. (1) Vulg., Gen. 1.10. (2) Lucr. 5.822–823. (3) Virg., Ecl. 2.33. (4) Hor., Sat. 1.1.33–34. (5) Ter., Phor. 3.2.506. (6) Hor., Od. 3.1.13. (7) Ennius in Cic's Rep. 3.3.6. (8) Sall., Cat. 3.4. (9) Hor., Od. 3.30.6–7. (10) Hor., Ep. 2.3.268–269. (11) Cic., Sen. 6.17. (12) Hor., Ep. 1.11.27. (13) Cic., Cat. 1.11.28. (14) Cic., Cat. 1.11.28. (15) Cic., Cat. 4.10.22.

15. (1) Ter., Hec. 3.4.421–422. (2) Cic., Fam. 16.9.2. (3) Cic., Arch. 3.5. (4) Tac., Ann. 12.32. (5) Cic., Cat. 3.2.3. (6) Cic., Verr. 2.5.62. (7) Catull. 3.5 and 10. (8) Ter., Ad. 5.4 passim.

16. (1) Phaedr., 3.7.1. (2) Virg., Geor. 1.145. (3) Ter., Phor. 1.4.203. (4) Cic., Or. 59.200. (5) Virg., Aen. 3.657–658. (6) Virg., Aen. 4.569–570. (7) Juv. 1.30. (8) Hor., Ep. 1.2.62; cp. Ch. 2 S.A.11. (9) Servius on Aen. 1.683. (10) Hor., Od. 2.16.27–28. (11) Phaedr., Fab. 1. Prologus 3–4. (12) Cic., Leg. 1.22.58. (13) Sen., Clem. 1.19.6. (14) Proverbial. (15) Cic., Sen. 19.70. (16) Vell., Historiae Romanae 2.66.3 (cp. Duff., Silver Age p. 91).

17. (1) Ter., Phor. 2.1.287–288. (2) Cic., N.D. 3.34.83. (3) Cic., Cat. 1.12.30. (4) Publil. Syr. 321. (5) Hor., Ep. 1.2.40–41. (6) Cic., Sen. 14.47. (7) Publil. Syr. 353. (8) Publil. Syr. 232. (9) Cic., Am. 15.54. (10) Publil. Syr. 86. (11) Cic., Am. 25.92. (12) Cic., Am. 27.102. (13) Sen., Ep. 7.1 and 8. (14) Mart. 1.38.

18. (1) Virg., 5.231. (2) Tac., Ann. 15.59. (3) Cic., Cat. 1.3.6. (4) Publil. Syr. 393. (5) Ov., Met. 4.428. (6) Plin., Ep. 9.6.1. (7) Cic., Fam. 9.20.3. (8) Lucr. 3.830–831. (9) Ov., Met. 15.165,178,215–216. (10) Publil. Syr. 37. (11) Cic., Marcell. 2.7. (12) Ennius (See Duff, Golden Age p. 148.) (13) Hor., Sat. 1.2.11. (14) Juv. 1.74.

19. (1) Catull., 1.1. (2) Lucr. 1.112. (3) Cic., Cat. 3.5.13. (4) Cic., Sest. 67–141. (5) Ter., Hec. 1.2.132. (6) Cic., Cat. 1.4.9. (7) Cic., Planc. 33.80. (8) Cic., Am. 15.55.

20. (1) Mart. 13.94.1. (2) Cic., Fin. 5.29.87. (3) Cic., Am. 12.42. (4) Cic., De Or. 1.61.261. (5) Hor., Od. 1.38.1. (6) Hor., Sat. 1.3.66. (7) Cic., Sen. 5.15 (8) Sen., Clem. 1.6.2–3. (9) Cic., Off. 1.2.4. (10) Quint., Inst. 8.3.41. (11) Hor., Od. 1.22.1–2. (12) Cic., Fam. 16.9.3. (13) Cic., Cat. 3.5.10. (14) Cic., Cat. 1.1.3. (15) Cic., Cat. 1.9.23. (16) Cic. 1.5.10.

21. (1) Publil. Syr. 507. (2) Mart. 1.86.1–2. (3) Cic., Cat. 1.11.27. (4) Virg., Ecl. 4.35–36. (5) Hor., Epod. 16.1–2. (6) Cic., Am. 6.22. (7) Cic., Sen. 19.69. (8) Cic., N.D. 2.62.154. (9) Cic., Sen.

17.59. (10) Phaedr., App. 27 (Cp. p. 154 inf. S.A.8). (11) Vulg., Job 28.12. (12) Liv., 22.39.19. Universality of Ancient Greek: Cic., Arch. 11.26 and 10.23.

22. (1) Cic., Att. 9.10.3. (2) Hor., Od. 2.3.1–2. (3) Cic., Rep. 3.31. (4) Cic., Cat. 1.1.3. (5) Cic., Marcell. 10.32. (6) Cic., Cat. 1.12.30. (7) Cic., 3.1.1. (8) Liv. 32.33.10. (9) Plaut., Aul. 4.10.772. (10) Cic., Am. 17.64. (11) Hor., Ep. 2.3.148–149. (12) Virg., Georg. 2.490 and 493. (13) Sen., Ep. 17.12. (14) Hor., Ep. 1.1.19. (15) Hor., Sat. 1.1.106–107.

23. (1) Virg., Aen. 2.49. (2) Cic., 1.2.6. (3) Liv. 44.42.4. (4) Hor., Sat. 1.1.68–69. (5) Cic., N.D 2.4.12. (6) Hor., Ep. 2.1.156. (7) Nep., Att. 4. (8) Quint., Inst. Praef. 5. (9) Hor., Sat. 1.10.72. (10) Quint., Inst. 11.3.157. (11) Cic., N.D. 3.33.82. (12) Cic., Sen. 3.9. (13) Hor., Ep. 1.16.66. (14) Sen., Ep. 61.3. (15) Hor., Ep. 1.18.71.

24. (1) Cp. Plutarch, Cato ad fin. (2) Plin. (Elder), H.N. or N.H. 33.148. (3) Caes., B.C. 2.43. (4) Hor., Sat. 1.1.69–70. (5) Cic., Sex. Rosc. 1.3. (6) Cic., Marcell. 8.24. (7) Hor., Od. 3.14.14–16. (8) Cic., Rep. 2.30. (9) Tac., Dial. 5.

25. (1) Ter., Heaut. Prolog. 18. (2) Cic., 1.11.27. (3) Cic., Cat. 1.11.27. (4) Cic., Cat. 3.2.4. (5) Cic., Cat. 4.10.22. (6) Cic., Off. 1.1.1. (7) Ter., Phor. 4.1.581–582. (8) Cic., Sen. 16.56. (9) Enn. in Cic., Div. 2.56.116. (10) Cic., Tusc. 1.42.101. (11) Cic., Tusc. 5.37.108. (12) Cic., quoted in Dumesnil's Lat. Synonyms s.v. abnuere. (13) Cic., Tusc. 5.40.118. (14) Cic., Sen. 21.77. (15) Cic., Sen. 19.68. (16) Plin., Ep. 7.9.15.

26. (1) Cic. Sen. 16.55. (2) Cic., Cat. 1.3.6. (3) Sen., Contr. 6.7.2; Publil. Syr. 253. (4) Cic., Cat. 3.1.5. (5) Sen., Ep. 61.3. (6) Mart. 10.47. (7) Ov., Her. 17.71–72. (8) Hor., Epod. 2.1,7,8. (9) Cic., Am. 26.99. (10) Cic., Sen. 19.68. (11) Mart. 1.107.1–2. (12) Mart. 14.208. (13) Cic., Off. 1.22.74. (14) Catull. 12.

27. (1) Ov., Met. 7.21–22. (2) Mart. 1.16.1. (3) Ter., Ad. 1.1.47–48. (4) Ter., Ad. 5.5.884, 5.7.922. (5) Plin., Ep. 10.88. (6) See Loci Antiqui #26, p. 206. (7) Cic., Sen. 6.19. (8) Cic., Off. 1.22.78. (9) Cic., Off. 1.22.77. (10) Cic., Sen. 2.5. (11) Sen., Ep. 17.9. (12) See Ch. 4 S.A.7. (13) Cic., Marcell. 3.8. (14) Cic., Tusc. 5.20.57–5.21.62.

28. (1) Liv. 22.39.21. (2) Cic., Off. 1.22.77. (3) Cic., Cat. 1.7.18. (4) Ter., Phor. 5.5.831. (5) Hor., Epod. 13.3–4. (6) Sen., Ep. 80.3. (7) Sen. (8) Diog. Laert.: a Latin translation from his Greek.

(9) Quint., Inst. 2.2.5. (10) Cic., Am. 24.89. (11) Ov., A.A.1.97.

29. (1) Catull. 5.1. (2) Cic., Clu. 18.51. (3) Ter., Phor. 3.2.497–498. (4) Hor., Sat. 1.30. (5) Juv., Sat. 1.30. (6) Cic., Cat. 1.1.3. (7) Cic., Phil. 10.10.20. (8) Cic., Phil. 4.5.9. (9) Nep., Milt. 5. (10) Cic., De Or. 1.61.260. (11) Hor., A.P. (Ep. 2.3) 335–336. (12) Ter., Heaut. 4.2.675. (13) Cic., Off. 1.23.80. (14) Cic., Am. 9.29.

30. (1) Cic., Cat. 4.3.6. (2) Phaedr. 3.7.1. (3) Hor., Sat. 1.5.67–68. (4) Virg., Ecl. 8.43. (5) Catull. 7.1–2. (6) Hor., Sat. 1.4.16. (7) Cic., Marcell. 10.30. (8) Lucr. 1.55–56. (9) Lucr. 2.4. (10) Hor., Ep. 1.2.1–4. (11) Hor., Ep. 1.18.96–97, 100–101. (12) Sen., Ep. 115.14. (13) Cic., Tusc. 1.41.99.

31. (1) Cic., Cat. 1.6.15. (2) Cic., Am. 12.42. (3) Cic., Cat. 1.5.10 and 1.9.23. (4) Hor., Od. 1.14.1–2. (5) Cic., Marcell. 7.22. (6) Cic., Q. Fr. 1.2.4.14. (7) Cic., Cat. 3.5.12. (8) Cic., Sen. 10.33. (9) Liv. 45.8. (10) Ter., Ad. 2.1.155. (11) Ter., Phor. 1.2.137–138.

32. (1) Publil. Syr. 512. (2) Cic., Cat. 1.5.10. (3) Hor., Ep. 1.6.29. (4) Ter., Ad. 5.9.996. (5) Ter., Heaut. 4.1.622. (6) Cic., Sen. 3.7. (7) Ter., Ad. 4.5.701. (8) Caes., B.G. 3.18. (9) Plaut., Trin. 2.2.361. (10) Publil. Syr. 129. (11) Sall., Cat. 8. (12) Cic., Fin. 3.7.26. (13) See Ch. 18 S.A.12. (14) Sen., Ep. 80.6. (15) Hor., Sat. 1.1.25–26.

33. (1) Veg., Mil. Prologium 3. (2) Cic., Off. 1.22.76. (3) Cic., Sull. 31.87. (4) Cic., Q. Fr. 1.3.5. (5) Phaedr. App. 18. (6) Hor., Sat. 2.7. 22–24. (7) Publil. Syr. 412. (8) Hor., Od. 4.10.6.

34. (1) Virg., Aen. 3.188. (2) Hor., Sat. 1.3.68–69. (3) Cic., N.D. 2.62.154. (4) Cp. Sen., De Ira 2.9.1 and Cic., Tusc. 3.9.19. (5) Cic., Cat. 1.5.10. (6) Hor., Od. 3.16.7. (7) Cic., Fam. 7.10.1. (8) Publil. Syr. 350. (9) Mart. Bk. I Praef. 1–2. (10) Hor., Od. 2.14.2 and 1.11.7–8. (11) Cic., Sen. 19.69. (12) Ter., Heaut. 1.2.239–240. (13) Cic., Am. 6.22. (14) Cic., De Or. 2.67.274. (15) Virg., Aen. 1.199.

35. (1) Sen., cp. Ep. 8.7; and Hor., Sat. 2.7.83 ff. and Ep. 1.16.66. (2) Publil. Syr. 290. (3) Publil. Syr. 99. (4) Hor., Sat. 1.1.86–87. (5) Cic., Fin.

1.18.60, 4.24.65. De. Or. 1.3.10 et passim. (6) Publil. Syr. 767 and 493. (7) Vulg., Gen. 1.26. (8) Cic., Rep. 2.24.59. (9) Caes., B.G. 4.23 and 5.45. (10) Quint., Inst. 10.1.112. (11) Hor., Ep. 2.2.41–42. (12) Publil. Syr. 687. (13) Hor., Sat. 2.2.135–136. (14) Virg., Aen. 1.630. (15) Publil. Syr. 288.

36. (1) Vulg., Gen. 1.3. (2) Lucr. 1.205. (3) Ter., Heaut. 2.3.314. (4) Caes., B.C. 2.43. (5) Ter., Ad. 3.4.505. (6) Ter., Heaut. 5.5.1049 and 1067. (7) Pers. 5.151–152. (8) Sen., Ep. 61.2. (9) Cic., Sen. 8.26. (10) Hor., Ep. 2.2.206–211. (11) Hor., Od. 1.24.19–20. (12) Ov., Am. 1.2.10. (13) Cic., Am. 5.7. (14) Cic., Arch. 2.3.

37. (1) Hor., Ep. 2.3.68. (2) Virg., Aen. 6.126. (3) Ov., A.A. 3.62–65. (4) Ter., Hec. 1.2.132; Ad. 1.1.26. (5) Ter., Ad. 5.5.882. (6) Ter., Ad. 4.1.517, 4.2.556. (7) Hor., Sat. 1.9.1. (8) Cic., Tusc. 5.21.62. (9) Cic., Verr. 2.4.54.120. (10) Ter., Hec. 3.4.421 and 423. (11) Cic., Cat. 1.9.23. (12) Nep., Att. 8; Cic., Phil. 2.12.28, T.D. 5.109 (names changed). (13) Cic., Att. 12.50. (14) Cic., Sen. 7.24.

38. (1) Caes., B.G., 1.31. (2) Cic., Cat. 1.4.9. (3) Cat., 4.7.16. (4) Cic., Am. 7.23. (5) Cic., Cat. 1.6.13. (6) Cic., Am. 15.53. (7) Cic., Cat. 1.7.18. (8) Cic., Cat. 4.11.24. (9) Virg., Ecl. 1.7. (10) Cic., Fam. 4.5.6. (11) Sen., Ep. 17.11. (12) Cic., Marcell. 4.11. (13) Plin., Ep. 5.16.4–5. (14) Virg., Aen. 1.257–258, 17, 280.

39. (1) Cic., Cat. 1.12.30. (2) Cic., 1.13.32. (3) Cic., Off. 1.22.74. (4) Publil. Syr. 762. (5) Cic., Off. 1.25.89. (6) Cic., Verr. 2.4.54. (7) Cic., Off. 3.32.113. (8) Cic., Sest. 2.5. (9) Cic., Sen. 5.15. (10) Cic., Att. 2.23.1. (11) Publil. Syr. 704. (12) Cic., Leg. 1.23.60. (13) Virg., Aen. 4.175. (14) Cic., Fam. 5.12.4.

40. (1) Cic., Sen. 5.15. (2) Hor., Od. 3.30.6–7. (3) Cic., Tusc. 1.41.97. (4) Ter., Ad. 5.4.856. (5) Sen., Ep. 7.7. (6) Plin., Ep. 9.6.2. (7) Cic., 2.23.1. (8) Cic., Cat. 1.1.1. (9) Liv.: see Loci Immutati #18 p. 224. (10) Cic., Marcell. 10.32. (11) Catull. 5.7–8. (12) Ter., Heaut. 1.1.77. (13) Cic., Am. 21.81. (14) Vulg., Exod. 20.11.